Street by Stre

CH00347720

LANCASHIRE

PLUS FORMBY, RAMSBOTTOM, SOUTHPORT

Enlarged Areas Blackburn, Blackpool, Burnley, Lancaster, Preston

2nd edition April 2002
lst edition May 2001

© Automobile Association Developments Limited 2002

Published by AA Publishing (a trading name of Automobile Association Developments Limited, whose registered office is Millstream, Maidenhead Road, Windsor, Berkshire SL4 5GD. Registered number 1878835).

The Post Office is a registered trademark of Post Office Ltd. in the UK and other countries.

Mapping produced by the Cartographic Department of The Automobile Association. A01226

A CIP Catalogue record for this book is available from the British Library.

Printed in Italy by Printer Trento srl

The contents of this atlas are believed to be correct at the time of the latest revision. However, the publishers cannot be held responsible for loss occasioned to any person acting or refraining from action as a result of any material in this atlas, nor for any errors, omissions or changes in such material. The publishers would welcome information to correct any errors or omissions and to keep this atlas up to date. Please write to Publishing, The Automobile Association, Fanum House (FH17), Basing View, Basingstoke, Hampshire, RG21 4EA.

Ref: MD077z

Key to map pages ii-iii

Key to map symbols iv-1

Enlarged scale pages 2-11

Street by Street 12-371

Index – towns & villages 372-374

Index – streets 375-465

Index – featured places 465-478

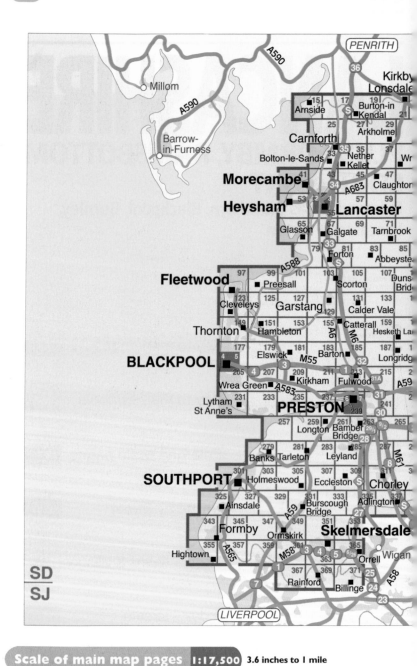

ii

PENRITH

Kirkby
Lonsdale

Millom

36

A590

A590

15　　17　　19
Arnside　　　Burton-in
Kendal　　　21

25　　27　　29
Arkholme

Carnforth

Barrow-
in-Furness

33　35　35　　37
Bolton-le-Sands　Nether　　Wr
Kellet

Morecambe

41　43　45　47
34　　　　Claughton
A683

Heysham

53　2　3　57　59
55
Lancaster

Glasson　65　67　69　71
Galgate　Tarnbrook

79　33　81　83　85
Forton　　　Abbeyste

A588

97　99　101　103　105　107
Preesall　　　Scorton　Duns
Brid

Fleetwood

123　125　127　131　133
Cleveleys　Garstang　Calder Vale
129

149　151　153　155　159
Thornton　Hambleton　Catterall　Hesketh La

A6
M6

177　179　181　183　185　187　1
Elswick　M55　Barton　Longridg

BLACKPOOL
4　5

32

265　4　207　209　211　1　213　215　2
3　Kirkham　Fulwood　31A　A59
Wrea Green　A583

231　233　235　237　6　7　241　2
Lytham　31
St Anne's　PRESTON　249　30

257　259　261　263　265
Longton　Bamber　29H
Bridge　28

279　281　283　285　287　2
Banks　Tarleton　Leyland

M61

301　303　305　307　309　8
SOUTHPORT　Holmeswood　Eccleston　11

Chorley

325　327　329　331　333　335　337
Ainsdale　Burscough　Adlington
A59　Bridge

343　345　347　349　351　353
Formby　Ormskirk　Skelmersdale
27

355　357　359　361　365
Hightown　3　4　5　26
A565　M58　363　Orrell　Wigan

367　369　371　25
Rainford　Billinge　24
23

SD
SJ

LIVERPOOL

Scale of main map pages　1:17,500　3.6 inches to 1 mile

0　　　　　1/2　　　miles　　　1
0　　　1/2　　　1　kilometres　1 1/2

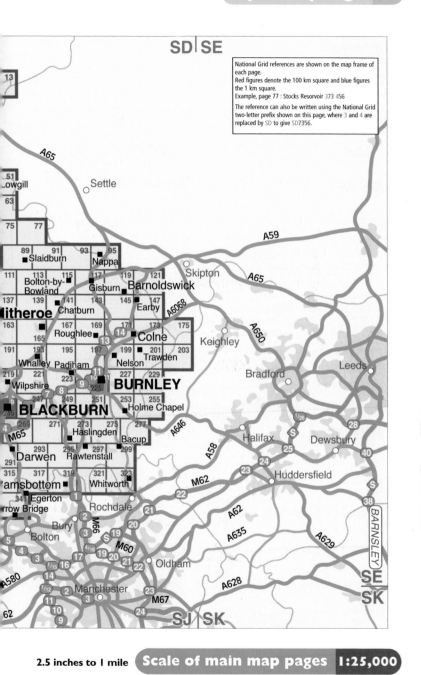

SD | SE

National Grid references are shown on the map frame of each page.
Red figures denote the 100 km square and blue figures the 1 km square.
Example, page 77 : Stocks Resorvoir 373 456

The reference can also be written using the National Grid two-letter prefix shown on this page, where 3 and 4 are replaced by SD to give SD7356.

A65

13

51
owgill   ● Settle
63

75   77

89   91   93   95
   ● Slaidburn   ■ Nappa

111   113   115   117   119   121
   Bolton-by-   Gisburn ■   Barnoldswick   ● Skipton
   Bowland

137   139   141   143   145   147
   litheroe   Chatburn   Earby

163   167   169   171   173   175
         Roughlee   13   14   ● Colne

191   193   195   197   199   201   203
   Whalley   Padiham   Nelson   Trawden

219   221   223   225   227   229
   ■ Wilpshire   11   BURNLEY

7   8   9
4
245   247   249   251   253   255
9
   BLACKBURN   ■ Holme Chapel

269   271   273   275   277
M65   Haslingden
293   295   297   299
   Darwen   Rawtenstall   Bacup
291

315   317   319   321   323
amsbottom ■   Whitworth

341   Egerton
rrow Bridge   ● Rochdale

   Bury

   Bolton   M66

   M60

A580   ● Oldham

62   Manchester

M67

SJ | SK

A59

A65

A6068

A650

● Keighley

Bradford   ● Leeds

A646

1/26   ● 28
Halifax   S   Dewsweden
25   Dewsbury   40
A58   24
23   ● Huddersfield
M62   S   38
A62
A635   BARNSLEY

A629

SE
SK

A628

2.5 inches to 1 mile   **Scale of main map pages   1:25,000**

0   1/2   miles   1   1 1/2

0   1/2   kilometres   1 1/2   2

iv

Junction 9	Motorway & junction	⊖	Underground station
Services	Motorway service area	⊖	Light Railway & station
	Primary road single/dual carriageway	+++++++++	Preserved private railway
Services	Primary road service area	*LC*	Level crossing
	A road single/dual carriageway	•—•—•—	Tramway
	B road single/dual carriageway	-----------	Ferry route
	Other road single/dual carriageway	··············	Airport runway
	Minor/private road, access may be restricted	─·─·─·─	Boundaries - borough/district
← ←	One-way street	▼▼▼▼▼▼	Mounds
	Pedestrian area	**93**	Page continuation 1:25,000
==========	Track or footpath	**7**	Page continuation to enlarged scale 1:17,500
	Road under construction		River/canal, lake, pier
╞ = = = ╡	Road tunnel		Aqueduct, lock, weir
AA	AA Service Centre	465 ▲ Winter Hill	Peak (with height in metres)
P	Parking		Beach
P+	Park & Ride		Coniferous woodland
	Bus/Coach station		Broadleaved woodland
	Railway & main railway station		Mixed woodland
	Railway & minor railway station		Park

Cemetery			Theme Park	
Built-up area			Abbey, cathedral or priory	
Featured building			Castle	
City wall			Historic house or building	
A&E	24-hour Accident & Emergency hospital		Wakehurst Place NT	National Trust property
PO	Post Office			Museum or art gallery
Public library			Roman antiquity	
Tourist Information Centre			Ancient site, battlefield or monument	
Petrol station (Major suppliers only)			Industrial interest	
Church/chapel			Garden	
Toilet			Arboretum	
Toilet with disabled facilities			Farm or animal centre	
PH	Public house (AA recommended)			Zoological or wildlife collection
Restaurant (AA inspected)			Bird collection	
Theatre or performing arts centre			Nature reserve	
Cinema			Visitor or heritage centre	
Golf course			Country park	
Camping (AA inspected)			Cave	
Caravan Site (AA inspected)			Windmill	
Camping & Caravan Site (AA inspected)			Distillery, brewery or vineyard	

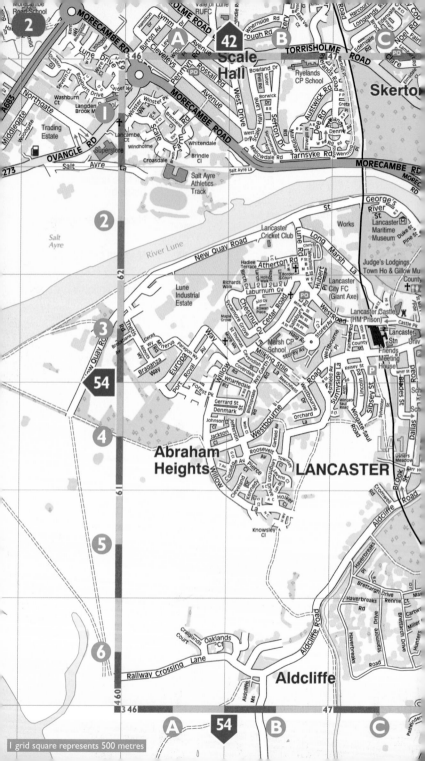

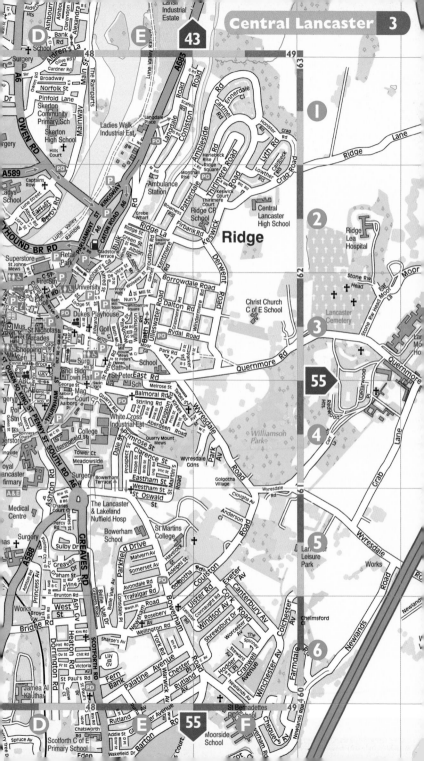

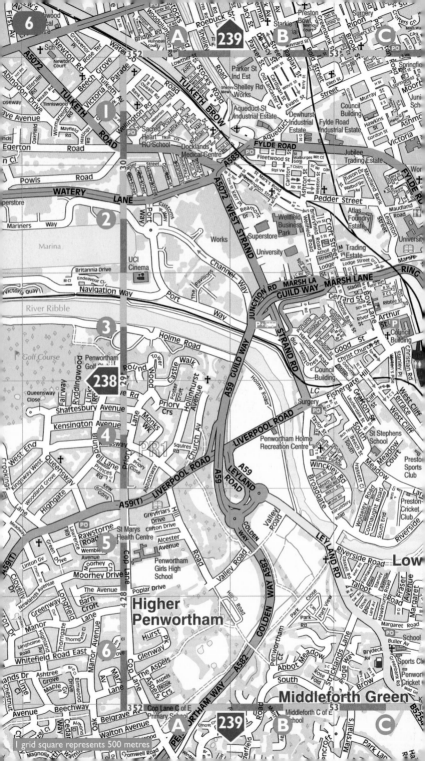

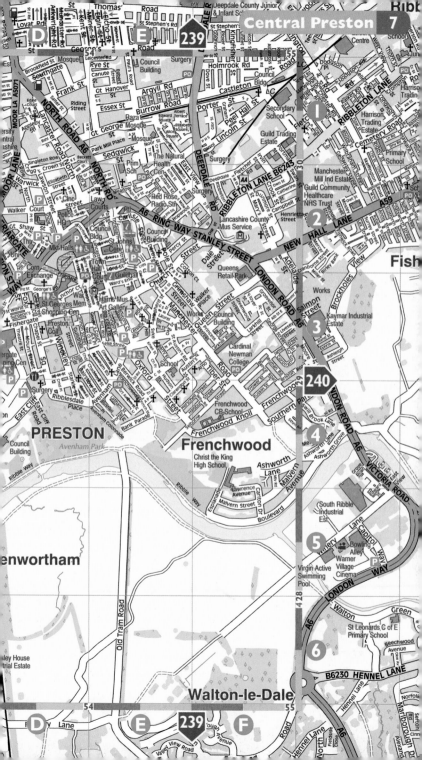

I grid square represents 500 metres

I grid square represents 500 metres

12

A   B   C   D   E

3 65   66   67

83

Barbondale

Barbon Beck

Fell Ho

1

2

82

3

Fell Road

Bullpot Farm

Casterton
Fell

4

81

Cow
Pot

Gale
Garth

5

Lancaster
Hole

6

80

Hellot Scales Barn

Ease
Gill
Kirk

Smithy
House

Whittle Hole

7

479

8

Leck
Fell

3 65   66   67

A   B   ▼23   C   D   E

Short
Drop

High

Lost
John's
Cave

1 grid square represents 500 metres

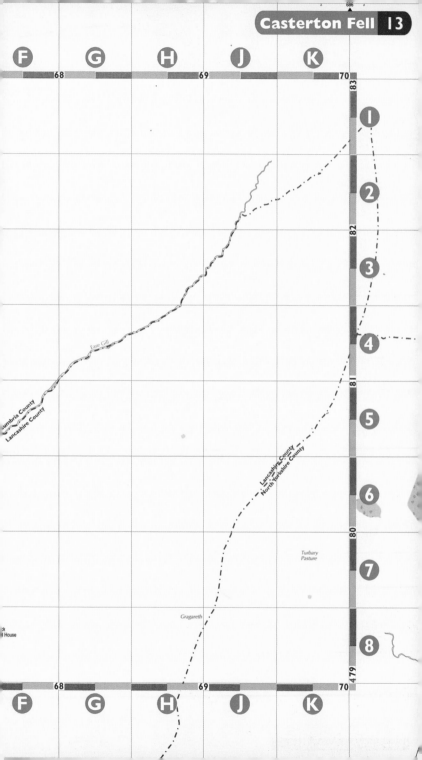

F G H J K

68 69 70 83

1
2
82
3
4
81
5
6
80
7
79
8

Ease Gill

Cumbria County
Lancashire County

Lancashire County
North Yorkshire County

Turbary
Pasture

Gragareth

ck
l House

F G H J K

68 69 70

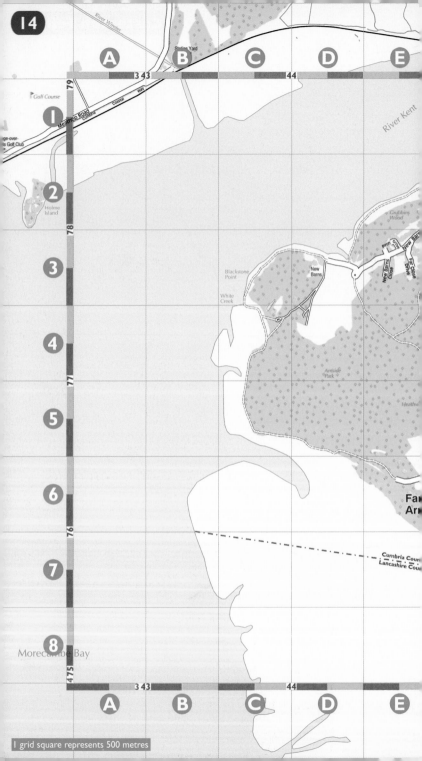

14

A B C D E

79

3 43   44

Golf Course

Meathop Road   Cumbria   Coastal   Way

I

ge-over-
s Golf Club

River Kent

78

2

Holme
Island

Grubbins
Wood

3

Blackstone
Point

New Barns

Barn
Close

New Barn

New Barns Close

Far Close Drive

White
Creek

77

4

Arnside
Park

5

Heathn

76

6

Fa
Arr

7

Cumbria Coun
Lancashire Cour

8

Morecambe Bay

475

3 43   44

A B C D E

1 grid square represents 500 metres

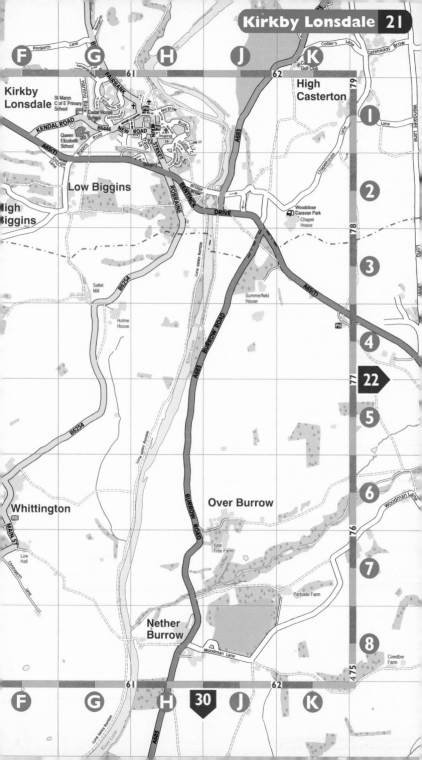

Smithy How

Collier's Lane

Casterton Golf Club

High Casterton

Well Lane

Gate

Brow

Fell Road

Fell Road

High Park

Bindloss Farm

A

B

C

D

E

3 63

64

1

Chapelhouse Lane

Wandales Lane

Long Level

2

Woodclose Caravan Park
Chapel House

Gowrey

Cumbria County
Lancashire County

Spring Wood

LA6

79

78

3

A65(T)

4

PH

▶ 21

77

Ellen Beck

Fairthwaite Park House

5

New House Caravan Park

High Gale

Low Lane

Leck

Leck C of E School

Overtown

Woodman Lane

Woodman Lane

Cowan Bridge

Coulter Beck Lane

Heber Hill

6

76

7

Parkside Farm

A65(T)

Hotel

Low House Farm

8

475

Cowdber Farm

A

B

▼ 31

C

D

E

3 63

64

Collingholme

Ireby Hi Farm

I grid square represents 500 metres

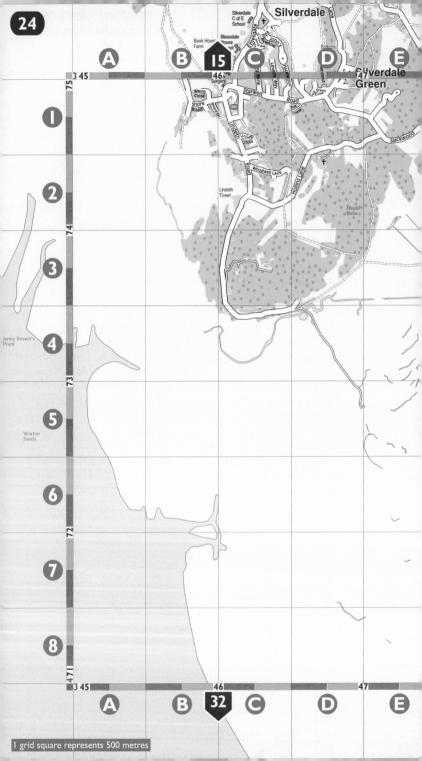

28

A   B   19   C   D   E

355   56   Wash Dub Wood   57   Docker Hall

75

1

Dalton Park Wood

Cumbria County
Lancashire County

Keer Holme Lane

2

74

Keer Holme

Keer Holme Lane

Docker Park

Do

Brown Edge

3

Starricks Farm

River Keer

Gunnerthwaite

Sr
Fa

4

73

The High Farm

27

5

Cinder Hill

Locka Lane

Craven View

6

72

Kitchlow Farm

wray
Road

7

142 ▲

Locka Farm

Locka L

Havelock House

8

471

355   56   B6254   57   Gowan Hall

A   B   36   C   D   E

Sunny Bank Farm

Borwick Road

B6254

1 grid square represents 500 metres

F G H 20 J K B6254

58 59 60 75

Newton

I

Outfield
Farm

Docker Lane

Newton
Green

Lane Foot
Farm

2

74

Lune Valley Ramble

Corsebarth

3

B6254

4

73

30

Beckerthwaite Beck

Higher
Broomfield

Lune Valley Ramble

5

B6254

River Lane

6

A683

Arkholme C of E
Primary School

Arkholme

72

Crook
Park

7

B6254

Vicar Lane

Storrs
Hall

Lune Valley Ramble

Melling

A683

ng with
C of E

8

A683

A471

Moordale Cl

58 59 37 60

F G H J K

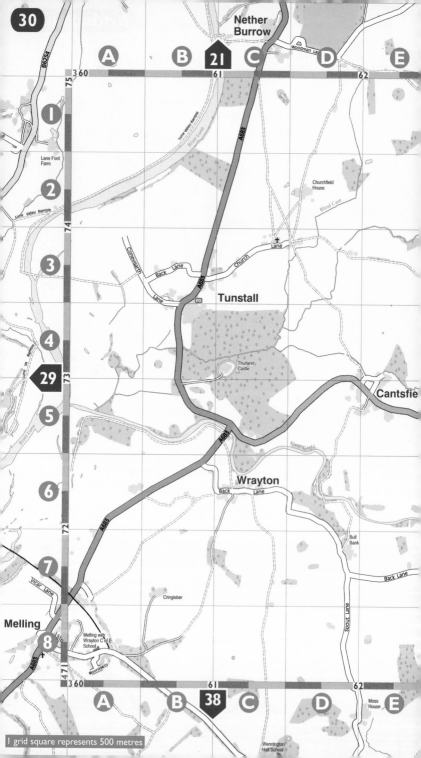

30

Nether Burrow

Woodman Lane

21

A683

Lune Valley Ramble

River Lune

Lane Foot Farm

Churchfield House

Blind Cant

Lune Valley Ramble

Connaught

Back Lane

Church Lane

Lane

Tunstall

PO

Lune via Ramble

29

River Lune

Thurland Castle

Cantsfie

A683

River Greta

Wrayton

Back Lane

Bull Bank

6

Back Lane

A683

Spout Lane

7

Vicar Lane

Cringleber

Melling

Melling with Wrayton C of E School

8

A683

Moorside Cl

38

Moss House

Wennington Hall School

B6254

1 grid square represents 500 metres

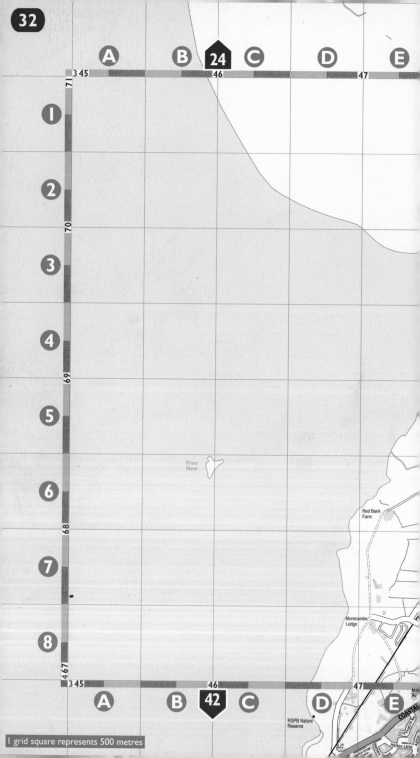

32

A B 24 C D E

3 45 46 47

71

1

2

70

3

4

69

5

Priest
Skear

6

Red Bank
Farm

68

7

Morecambe
Lodge

8

467

3 45 46 47

A B 42 C D E

RSPB Nature
Reserve

COASTAL

1 grid square represents 500 metres

I grid square represents 500 metres

I grid square represents 500 metres

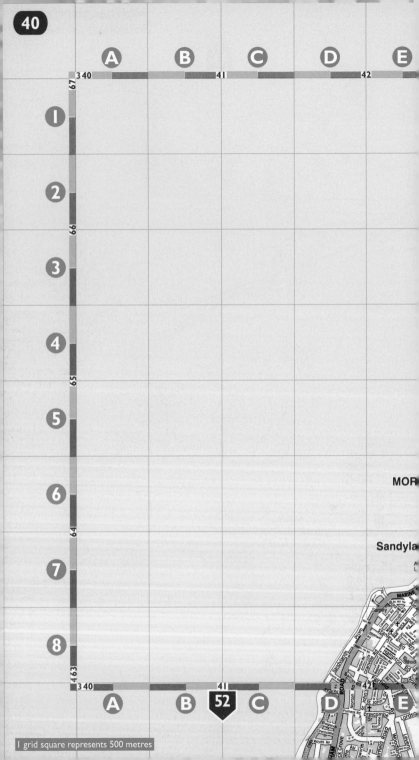

F G H **37** J K

58 59 60 67

Curwen Hall Farm

Scale House Barn

Moor Lane

Cold Park Wood

Hindburn Gill

Manor House

Nooby Gill Beck

eton

66

Back Farm

48

Barkin Gate

65

Thornbush

Claughton Moor

Whit Moor

Winder Wood

River Roeburn

64

7 Lower Salter

Winder

8 Mid Sal

Hornby Road

A 683

Roeburndale Road

F G H **59** J K

58 59 60

Ⓐ   Ⓑ   **38**   Ⓒ   Ⓓ   Ⓔ

Endowed School
Street
Abb
Be

360   67   **61**   **62**

River Hindburn

Cold
Park
Wood

Higher
Broadwood

1

Alcocks
Farm

2

66

Hindle Gill Beck

Bellhurst

Smeer
Hall

3

Outhwaite

4

Outhwaite
Wood

Wray
Wood
Moor

Scale

Back
Farm

65

◀ 47

River Roeburn

Barkin
Gate

5

6

64

Stauvin

7

Lower
Salter

Harterbeck

8

463

Winder

Hornby Road

**Middle
Salter**

Winder

360   64   **61**   **62**

Ⓐ   Ⓑ   **60**   Ⓒ   Ⓓ   Ⓔ

Hornby
Road

High Salter

Goodber Beck

1 grid square represents 500 metres

Thimble Hall

Spen Brow

F   G   H   39   J   K

63   64   65   67

Furness Ford

Plain House Lane

Spens Farm

Birks Farm

1

Thwaite Lane

High

Lower Stock Br

River Hindburn

Park House

2

Fairbeath Road

66

Lower Houses

3

ll Farm

+

Over Houses

4

Mill Lane

Tatham Fells School

50

Low

65

5

Coxwall Lane

+

White Moss

Ivah

6

Helks Bank Farm

Hollinhurst Brow

64

River Hindburn

Helks   Brow

Mill Brow

7

Botton Mill

Goodber Common

Summersgill

Botton Road

8

463

F   G   H   61   J   K

63   64   65

Lower Thrushgill

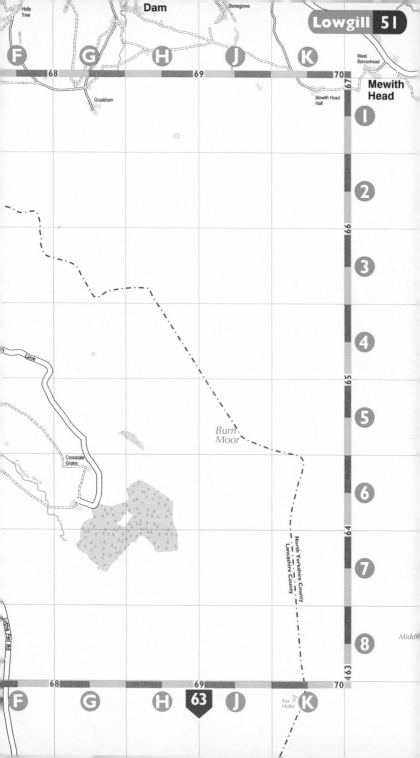

Dam

Stonegrove

Holly
Tree

F
G
H
J
K

West
Borronhead

68
69
70

67

Mewith
Head

Mewith Head
Hall

Gruskham

I

2

66

3

4

65

Lane

5

Burn
Moor

Croesdale Beck

Croesdale
Grains

6

64

North Yorkshire County
Lancashire County

7

Lyne Fell Rd

8

Middl

463

68
69
70

F
G
H
63
J
K

Fox
Holes

Quernmore Road

Roeburnd

Gresgarth
Hall

Ravenscar
Farm

F **G** **H** **45** **J** **K**

Hawkshead

53 54 55

Littled

Potts
Wood

1

Littled

Heights
Farm

Potts
Yeats

Intack

2

Baines
Crag

The
Crag

3

Littledale Road

Craig
Wood

4

ledale

58

5

Windy
Clough

Conder
Head

6

Clougha
Scar

7

Fell End
Farm

Rowton
Brook
Fell

8

F **G** **H** **69** **J** **K**

53 54 55

Shoote
Pile

Goodber
Common

F **G** **H** **49** **J** **K**

63 64 65 63

Summersgill

Cotton Road

Lower Thrushgill

1

Higher
Thrushgill

2

62

Green
Bank

3

Summersgill
Fell

Goodber
Fell

Thrushgill
Fell

4

61 **62**

5

Greenbank
Fell

6

60

River Roeburn

Salter
Fell

7

8

459

F G H **73** J K

63 64 65

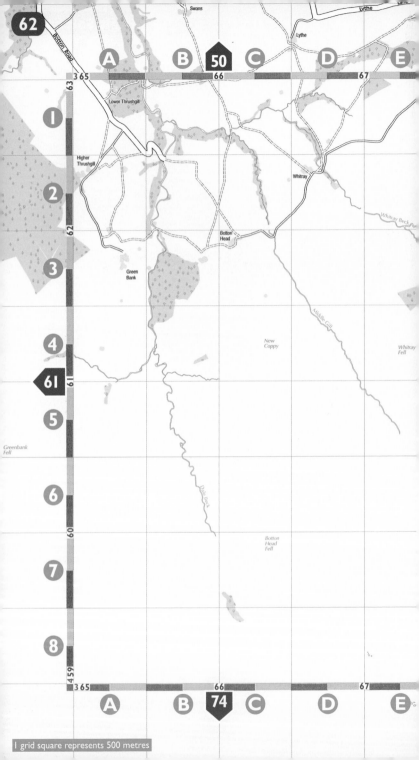

Barton Road

Swans

Lythe

Lythe

Lythe

A **B** **50** **C** **D** **E**

3 65 66 67

Lower Thrushgill

I

Higher
Thrushgill

2

Whitray

Whitray Beck

Green
Bank

3

Botton
Head

Middle Gill

4

New
Coppy

Whitray
Fell

61

61

5

Greenbank
Fell

6

Dale Beck

60

Botton
Head
Fell

7

8

459

3 65 66 67

A **B** **74** **C** **D** **E**

I grid square represents 500 metres

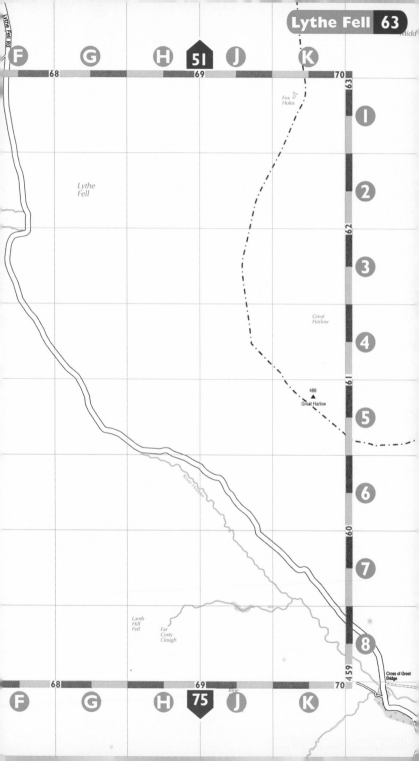

F G H 51 J K

68 69 70

63

1

Lythe Fell

2

62

3

Great Harlow

4

61

▲ 488
Great Harlow

5

River Hodder

6

60

7

Lamb Hill Fell
Far Costy Clough

8

459

Cross of Greet Bridge

Fox Holes

52

A **B** **C** **D** **E**

3 40   41   42

59

Red
Nab

Ocean Edge
Caravan Park

1

Walkers
Industrial
Estate

Middleton Road

Middleton
Business Park

Heysham
Business Park

Mill Hill
Grove
Westbourne
Road

Carr Lane
PO
Westmoor
House

2

58

Melbreak
Caravan
Park

Carr Lane

3

Brows

Trumley Farm

4

Potts
Corner

57

5

6

Sunderland
Brows

56

The

7

8

455

Hall End
Skear

3 40   41   42

A **B** **C** **D** **E**

1 grid square represents 500 metres

68

Quernmore

Narr Lodge

Wyresdale

A **B** **56** **C** **D** **E**
59 350 51 52 Quernmore

Brow Top Farm

I

Mount Vernon

Conderside Farm

Long Lane

58 Terrace Farm

Gibson's Farm

Lowe Brow

3

Dam Head

Moss Road

Long Lane

Bay Horse Road

4

Banton House

Blackwood End

Procter Moss Road

67

57

5

Kit Brow

Yeat House

Bay Horse Rd

6

Langshaw

56 Knowe Hill

Procter Moss Road

Gate House Bridge

7

Crag End

8

455

350 51 52

A **B** **81** **C** **D** **E**

Bay Horse Road

Borbles Hall

Ellel Crag

Middle

1 grid square represents 500 metres

Fell End Farm

F G H 57 J K

Rowton Brook Fell

53 54 55

59

Shooters Pile

1

2

58

Hare Appletree

Hare Appletree Fell

3

Damas Gill Reservoir

Damas Gill

4

Westfield House

Rotten Hill

57 70

Castle o' Trim

5

High Cross Moor

Higher Moor Head

6

Low Moor Head

56

Balderstones

7

Abbeystead Lane

Till's Farm

Lower Castle o' Trim

Borwicks

Brook House

8

4 55

55 Road

Chapel House Farm

53 54 55

F G H 82 J K

Plantation Lane

Abbeystead Road

F   G   H   59   J   K

58   560   59   60   59
Ward's
Stone

1

Ward's
Stone
Breast

2

58

Dunkenshaw
Fell

3

4

Luncheon
Huts

57   72

Coppy
Heads   Tarnsyke
Clough

Black Side
of Tarnbrook
Fell

5

Thrush
Clough

Tarnsyke
Barn

6

56

Tarnbrook

7

Tarnbrook Wyre   Higher Syke   Higher Syke

Ouzel
Thorn

8

4 55

58   59   60

F   G   H   84   J   K

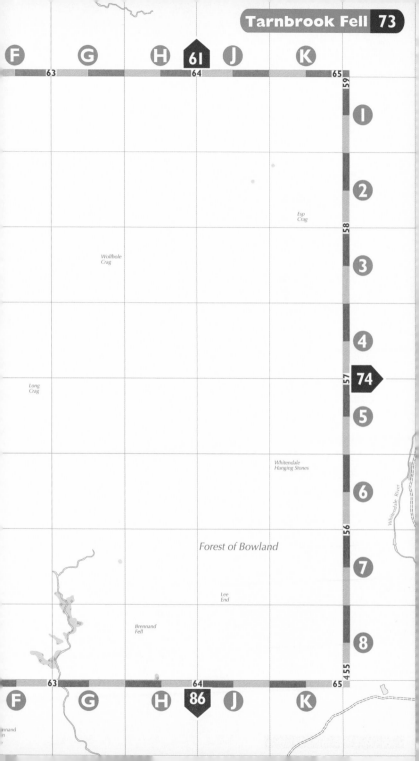

F   G   H   **61**   J   K

63   64   65

59

1

2

Esp Crag

58

Wolfhole Crag

3

4

57   **74** ▶

Long Crag

5

Whitendale Hanging Stones

6

Whitendale River

56

Forest of Bowland

7

Lee End

Brennand Fell

8

55

54

63   64   65

F   G   H   **86**   J   K

Brennand

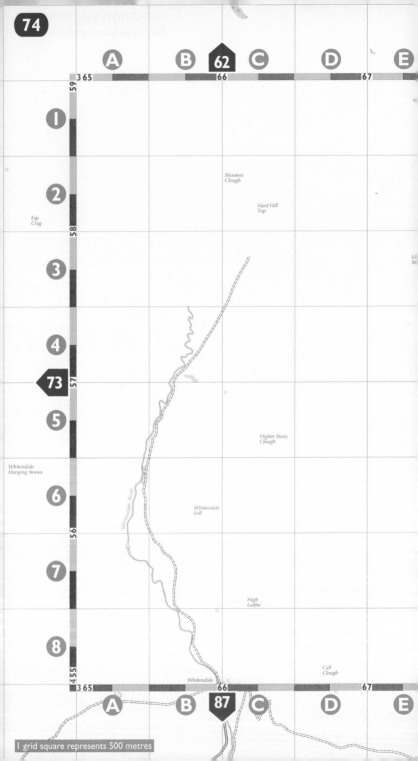

74

A B 62 C D E

365 66 67

59

1

2

Shooters
Clough

58

Esp
Crag

Hard Hill
Top

3

Li
St

4

73 57

5

Higher Stony
Clough

Whitendale
Hanging Stones

6

Whitendale
Fell

7

High
Laithe

8

Calf
Clough

455

Whitendale

365 66 67

A B 87 C D E

1 grid square represents 500 metres

F G H **63** J K

68 **69** **70**

59

1

Cross of Greet
Bridge

Lamb
Hill
Fell

Far
Costy
Clough

Bloe
Greet

Near
Costy
Clough

2

58

Lamb Hill
Farm

Great Bull
Stones

3

Reeves
Edge

4

57 **76**

Croasdale Fell

Croasdale Brook

5

Fell
Side

6

Fell
End

56

Clough

7

8

455

Low
Fell

Croasdale
House

F G H **88** J K

68 **69** **70**

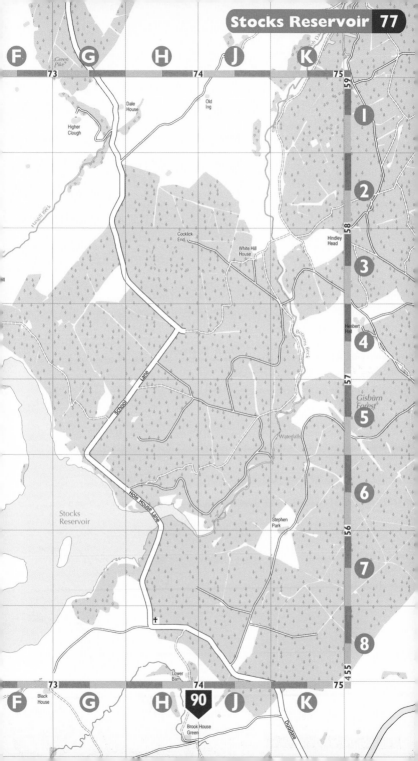

F
G
H
J
K

73
74
75

59

I

2

58

3

Green Pike

Dale House

Old Ing

Higher Clough

Haskill Beck

Cocklick End

White Hill House

Hindley Head

Hesbert Hall

4

57

Gisburn Forest

5

Bottoms Beck

Waterfalls

6

56

Stephen Park

Stocks Reservoir

Hole House Lane

School Lane

†

7

8

455

73
74
75

F
G
H
J
K

Black House

Lower Barn

90

Brook House Green

Dunsop

Galgate

Selleriey Farm

Smith Gre[...]

A   B   67   C   D   E

3 48   55   49

1

River Conder

2

54

Hampson Green

Junction 33

Hotel

Hampson Lane

Nuthurst

Chatburn House

River Cocker[...]

Cock Hall Farm

3

Ellel Grange

Lancaster Canal

Crag Hall

Hang Yeat

Whams Lane

M6

4

River Cocker

Hay Carr

79   53

PH

Works

Foxholes

5

Holly House

Bay Horse

A6

Potters Brook

6

Centre Farm

52

Cockerham Road

Lane

Cocker House Bridge

7

Lancaster Canal

Tansy Lane

Killcrash

Stony Lane

Wallace Lane

A6

Willow Close

Whinney Brow

Ribblesdale Drive

Lancaster Dr

Forton

Crookhey Gardens

Crookhey Hall

8

Stony Lane

Crookhey Hall Special School

School Lane

Forton CP School

Stony Lane

PRESTON LANCASTER ROAD

451

3 48   49

A   B   103   C   D   E

PRESTANG ROAD

Goose Green

Works

Hollins Lane

Deer
Clough

F G H **72** J K

61 62

55

1
Brennand
Tarn

White
Moor

Threaphaw
Fell **2**

54

Tower
Lodge **3**

Winfold
Fell

4

Blaze
Moss

53 **86** ▶

*Trough of
Bowland* **5**

Sniddle
Holes

Marshaw
Fell

Black
Clough

6

52

7

Holdron
Moss

Stake
End

8

451

F G H **108** J K

61 62

Holdron
Castle

Langden Brook

F G H **74** J K

Whitendale 66 Clough 67

55

1

2

54

Costy
Clough

3

Burn
Fell

4

53 **88**

5

Beatrix
Fell

6

52

Glenhurst

7

Rough Syke

8

Bishops
House

Beatrix Back of Hil
Barn

4 51

F G H **110** J K

Closes Barn ower or
arn Loaf

Moor
End

River Dunsop

North Yorkshire County
Lancashire County

F G H J K

76 B6478 **77**

Hartleys Farm

Higher Ghylls

Boon Beck

Knotts Lane

Cracoe Hill

Ghylls

I

2

Marl Barn

Stephen Moor Lodge

Far Knotts

Shays

Knotts

Beckfoot

3

Fells

Ling Hill

Spring Side

Knotts Lane

4

53 **92**

Lodge

5

Brow

6

Threap Green

Holden Lane

Anna Lane Head

7

Dugdales

Champion Farm

Broad Ing

8

Stephensons

Westmoor

451

76 **77**

Greaves

F G H **114** J K

55

54

53

52

94

A   B   C   D   E

3 83   84

1   Cow Hill

Worthy Hill Plantation

Halton West   Old Hall

2   Long Bank

Long Bank Lane

3   New House

North Yorkshire County

Lancashire County

4   Paythorne Moor

93

5   Carholme   Englands Head

Paa Lane

River Ribble

6   Higher Houses   Paa Farm

Ribble Way   Adams

Paa Lane

7   Loftrans   **Paythorne**   A682

Newsholme

8   Paythorne Bridge

Desmesne Farm

A682   LC

A   B   **117**   C   D   E

3 83   84

Knot Lane

1 grid square represents 500 metres

F G H J K

86 87

55

1

Haugh
Field

2

54

3

Swinden Gill Wood

Cobers
Laithe

Ash Tree
Farm

4

Swinden Moor
Head

53

5

6

North Yorkshire County
Lancashire County

52

7

Varley
Field

Horton
Pasture

451

8

86 87

F G H **118** J K

Pasture

Swinden

River Ribble

Mill

Lane

Nappa
ials

Nappa

Coneyber Lane

A682

Hayber

A682

alton
lace

Lane

U.
P.

F G H **78** J K

Cockerham Marsh

A588

Braides

Breck's Bridge

Sweetings

51

1

Gulf Lane

2

Sand Villa

50

Mill House

3

A588

Moss Edge

Gulf Lane

Tarn Farm

4 Moss Side Stables

Cockerham Moss

49 **102**

5

Gull Moss

Crawley's Dyke

6

Caunce Grange

48

7 marleigh Moss

8

47 Gibstick Hall

43 44 **127** 45

F G H J K

Island Lane

Cogie Hill Farm

Pilling Water

Bone

Brick

104

A
Shireshead
B
81
C
D
E

Holdings
White
Stony Lane
Snowhill
350
51
51
River Wyre
Foxhouses
52
Long L

1
Cleveley Bank Lane
PO

Webster's

2
50
Cleveleymere
M6
Lea Green
Cliftons
Long Lane
Syke's Farm

3
Wyre Bridge
Park Gate
Sands Bottom
Wyresdale Lake

4
Scorton
Brook Avenue
Snow Lane
Factory Lane
Wyresdale Park
The Tarn
103
49
M6
Scorton Bank

5
The Square
Scorton C of E School
Snowhill Lane
Clayands Caravan Park

6
48
Gubberford Lane
Mytten Hall
Barn Lane
Higher Lane
Grize Dale
Grizedale Brook

7
M6
Broad Fall
Slean End
Woodacre Pasture

8
447
Woodacre Hall
Higher Lane
Burns Farm
350
51
52

A
Birkhead Lane
LC
M6
B
130
C
D
E
River
Keeper's Lane
Barnacre Lodge
Birks F

1 grid square represents 500 metres

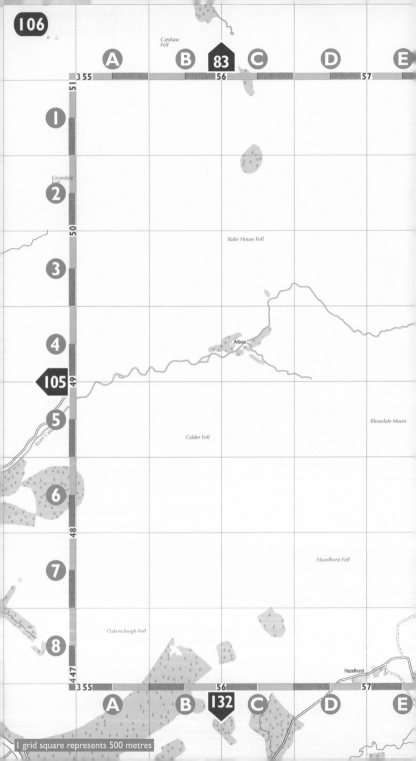

A B 83 C D E

3 55 56 57

51

1

Catshaw
Fell

Grizedale
Fell

2

50

Stake House Fell

3

4

Arbour

105 49

5

River Calder

Bleasdale Moors

Calder Fell

6

48

Hazelhurst Fell

7

Oakenclough Fell

8

447

Hazelhurst

3 55 56 57

A B 132 C D E

I grid square represents 500 metres

Langden
Head

F **G** **H** 84 **J** **K**

58 59 60

51

I

Lingy Pits
Moss

Raven
Scars

2

50

Bleadale
Nab

ster's Clough

3

Bleadale
Ridge

Fiendsdale

4

49 108 Bleadale
Moss

Luddock's Fell

5

Webster's Meadow

6

48

Home House Fell

Brown
Berry
Plain

7

8

447

58 59 60

F **G** **H** 133 **J** **K**

Fair
Snape
Fell

Fairsnape
Fell

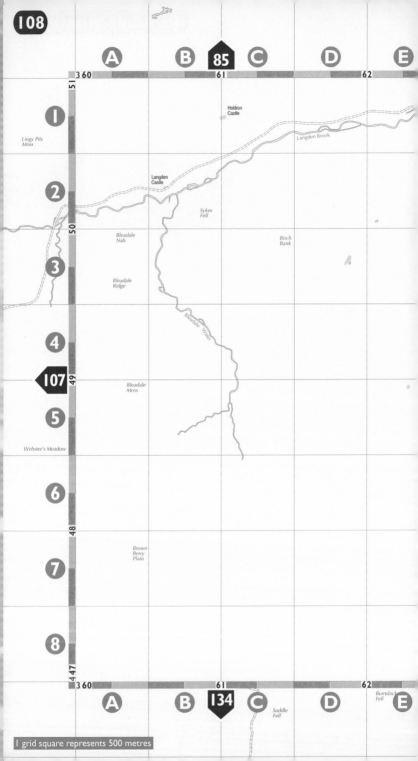

108

85

A   B   85   C   D   E

3 60   61   62

51

1

Lingy Pits
Moss

Holdron
Castle

Langden Brook

2

Langden
Castle

50

Sykes
Fell

Bleadale
Nab

Birch
Bank

3

Bleadale
Ridge

Bleadale Water

4

49

107

Bleadale
Moss

5

Webster's Meadow

6

48

Brown
Berry
Plain

7

8

47

3 60   61   62

A   B   134   C   D   E

Saddle
Fell

Burnslack
Fell

I grid square represents 500 metres

Sykes
Nab

Bishops

F   **G**   **H**   **86**   **J**   **K**

63   64   65

51

1

Dur
Brie

†

Hareden

Hareden Brook

Brown
Nab

50

2

3

4

New Hay
Farm

49   **110**

o

497
▲
Totridge Fell

5

6

Hodder
Bank

Whitmore

48

7

Lower Fence
Woods

Fair Oak
Fell

Reed
Barn

447

8

F   **G**   **H**   **135**   **J**   **K**

63   64   65

110

A   B   **87**   C   D   E

3 65   66   67

Bishops House

Beatrix

Back of Hil Barn

Roughh Syke

51

1

Knot or Sugar Loaf

Lower Barn

Closes Barn

Dunsop Bridge

50

2

Thorneyholme RC School

PO

Mossth

E

Root

Thorneyholme

Langden Brook

3

Langden Bridge

4

49

109

New Farm

5

Burholme

Hodder Bank

6

48

Burholme Bridge

Lower Fence Wood

7

Reed Barn

Higher Whitewell

8

47

New Laund

3 65   66   67

A   B PH **136** C Hall Hill D   E

Whitewell

1 grid square represents 500 metres

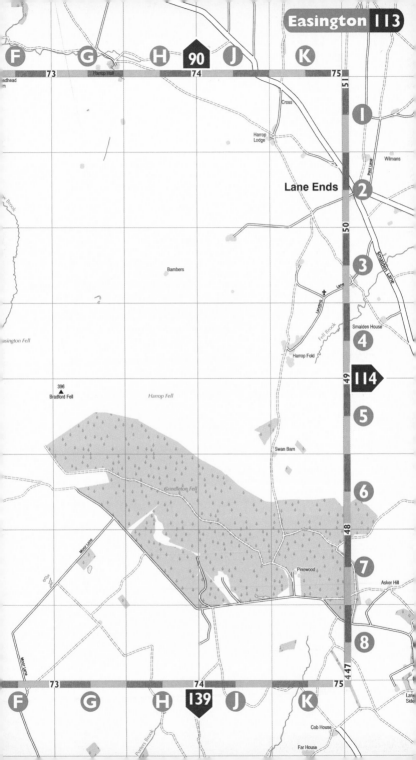

114

91

A   B   C   D   E

Westmoor

Step

Greaves

Cross

1

Wilmans

Alder Home

Lane 's   **2**

Clough Wood

Holden Clough

3

Barret Hill Brow

Bay Gate

Smalden Lane

Smalden House

Fat Hill

4

Harrop Fold

Cottams

◄ **113**

Swan Barn

5

Higher Heights

Springs Wood

Barret H

Lane

Rodhill

6

7

Pinewood

Scriddles Farm

Till House

Rodhill Gate

Asker Hill

Herris's

8

Smalden Lane

Broom Hill

Lawson Ho

1 grid square represents 500 metres

A   B   C   D   E

Lane Side

Cob House

Steelands

Hill House

140

F 78 G H 92 J K 80 51

Fore Becks

Monubent Head

Sturnd Cross Lane

Closes Hall

New Ing

Spring Head Farm

Eller Head

Park Nook

Hellifield Road

Fox Ghyll

Admiral's Wood

50

3

Bolton Close Plant

Gisburn Road

Fooden Lane

Barret Hill Brow

Main Street

Bolton-by-Bowland C of E School

Cisburn Road

Cemetery

Ouzel Hall Bridge

Bolton-by-Bowland

Fooden

Fawcett's Plantation

49

116

Holden Beck

Scott Lane

Scott Laithe

Skirden Beck

Bolton Park

Ribble Way

Cold Park Wood

Steep Wood

6

Bolton Hall Farm

Ribble Way

48

Huggan Ing

7

Gisb Cote

River Ribble

Kiln Way

Laithe

Rainsbar Wood

Ribble Way

Sawley Lodge

Dockber

8

447

Great Dudland

Laneside Farm

Sawley Grange

A59(T)

Cow Gill

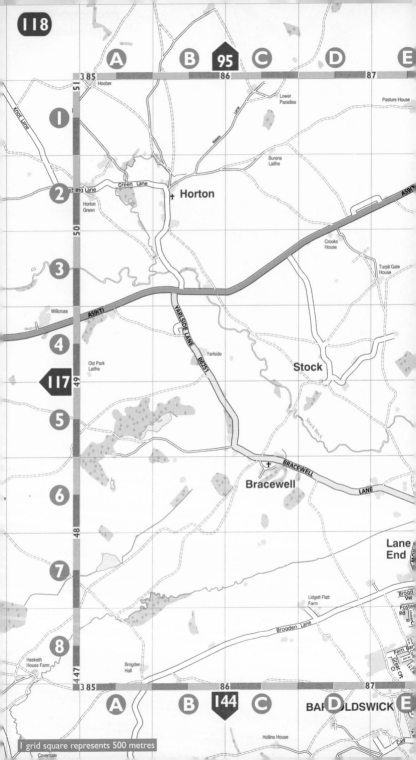

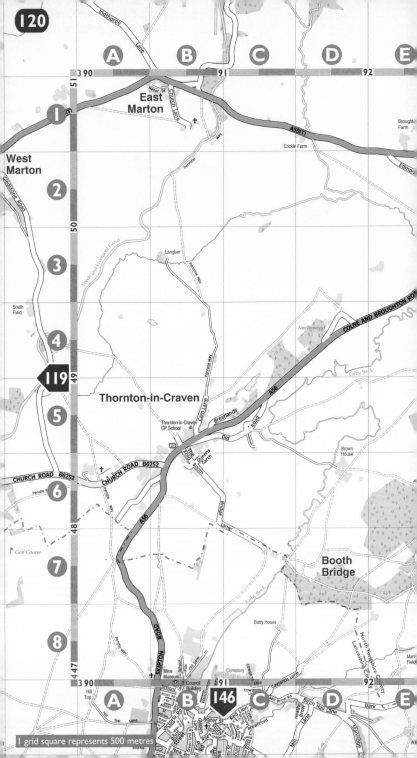

A   B   C   D   E

390   91   92
51

Ingthorpe Lane

East Marton

Church Lane

Heber Dr

A59(T)

Brought Farm

Crickle Farm

Edmon

West Marton

Gledstone Road

50

Leeds and Liverpool Canal

Langber

Pennine Way

South Field

Colne and Broughton Rd

Merlinwood

Earby Beck

119

49

Thornton-in-Craven

Carr Lane

Pennine Way

A56

Brearlands

Old Road

Thornton-in-Craven CP School

Brown House

PO

CHURCH ROAD   B6252   CHURCH ROAD   B6252

48

Pendle Way

Queens Garth

Booth Lane

School

A6068

Cragg Lane

Earby Beck

Booth Bridge

Golf Course

47

A56

SKIPTON ROAD

Pennine Way

Batty House

Cemetery

Cowgill Lane

North Yorkshire County Lancashire County

Marl Field

390   91   92

A   B   146   C   D   E

Hill Top

Mill Top Lane

Mine Museum

Council Building

Water St

Cemetery

Red Lion

Cowgill Lane

Cavlands Lane

Mill Brow Rd

Birch Hall Lane

Dark

Heather La

Stanridge C

Brownroyd

Chapel St

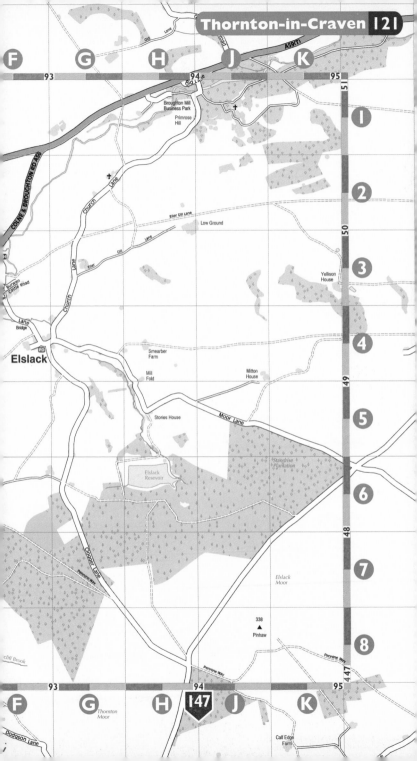

F G H J K

93

A59(T)

94e
Old Lane

Broughton Mill
Business Park

Primrose
Hill

Church Lane

Eller Gill Lane

Low Ground

Eller Gill Lane

Yellison
House

COLNE & BROUGHTON RD A456

Bracken
Castle Road

Lane
Bridge

Elslack

Church Lane

Smearber
Farm

Mill
Fold

Milton
House

Stories House

Moor Lane

Elslack
Reservoir

Standrise
Plantation

Copper Lane

Pennine Way

Elslack
Moor

cliff Brook

338
▲
Pinhaw

Pennine Way

Pennine Way

F G H J K

93 94 95

Thornton
Moor

147

Doggson Lane

Call Edge
Farm

51

50

49

48

447

1 2 3 4 5 6 7 8

A   B   96   C   D   E

330   31   32

47

1

46

2

3

45

4

5

44

6

7

443

8

CLEVELEYS

330   31

A   B   148   C   D   E

Golf Course   Fleetwood Golf Club

Princes Way

Sea Wall

A587

BROADWAY

Larkholme County Secondary School

Fleetwood Cricket Club

Larkholme Lane

Cardinal Allen RC School

St Edmunds RC Junior School

Larkholme CP School

Rossall Hospital

B5409 ROSSALL LANE

Fleetwood Farm

Rossall School

BROADWAY

ROSSALL ROAD

Northfold CP School

Westbourne Road

Promenade

Carr Gate

I grid square represents 500 metres

F G H **101** J K

I
2
3
4
5
6
7
8

128

Gibstick
Hall

43 44 45 47

Island   Lane
Cogie Hill
Farm

Pilling Water

Bone
Hill
Lane

Bone Hill
Farm

Birk   Lane

Kentucky
Farm

Black Hill
Farm

North Wood's
Hill Farm

**Eagland
Hill**

New   Lane

South Wood's
Hill Farm

Bradshaw Lane

Cocker   Lane

Birk's Farm

46

45

44

4 43

Cumming
Carr

Copthorne

Trashy
Hill

Skitham Lane

Eskham House

New
Eskham

Rigby Pool

Skitham

Cuckoo Lane

Rawcliffe
Moss

43 44 45

F G H **153** J K

Crab Tree Lane

132

Oakenclough Fell

A   B   106   C   D   E

3 55   56   57   Hazelhurst

47

1

Delph Lane

Fell End   Bleasdale
Tower   Clough
Heads
Cotts   River Brook

2

46   Brooks

3   Broadgate

Bleasdale
Bleasdale
C of E
School

4   High
Moor   Jack
Anderton
Bridge
Brock Rakes

131

45   Lane   Tootle
Hall

5

PC

6   Brock
Close

Wickins
Lane
End

Snape
Rake
Lane   Woodtop Farm

7   Brock Cott
Farm   Bleasdale Road
Crow Trees
Farm

Lickhurst

Brockmill

8   Hea
Fai

White Lane
143

3 55   56   57

Mill Lane   A   B   158   C   D   E

White
Lee   Fell
Side

Beacon Fell
Country Park

1 grid square represents 500 metres

F G H **107** J K

58 59 60

47

I

511
▲
Fairsnape
Fell

Wolf
Fell

2

46

Blindhurst
Fell

3

Higher
Fair Snape

Lower
Fair
Snape

432
▲
Parlick

4

45 **134**

5

Blindhurst

Fell Foot

6

Higher
Core

Lower Core

Startifants Lane

44

Bailey
Hey

Woodgates

7

Watery Gate
Farm

Fidlers
Lane

8 Collins Hill Lane

58 59 60

443

F G H **159** J K

Bro
Broo
Farm

Richmond Houses

Fair Oak Fell

Reed

F   G   H   **109**   J   K

63   64   65   47

1

Dinkling Green Farm

2

Fair Oak   46

Lickhurst Farm

Greystoneley   3

Works

Park Gate   Park Style   4

Leagram Brook   45   **136**

Chipping Lawn   5

6   Lower Lees

44

River Hodder   7

Stakes

Dairy Barn   8

ne   43   Doeford Bridge

F   G   H   **161**   J   K

63   64   65

Works   Green Farm

136

A   New Laund   B   **110**   C   D   E

365   66   67

1

+ PH
Whitewell

Hall Hill

Reed Barn

Higher Whitewell

47

I

2

Fair Oak

46

3

Greystoneley

Works

Radholme Laund

4

Ing Wood

Crane Wood House

135

45

5

Higher Lees Farm

Lees

6

Lower Lees

Lees House Farm

44

7

River

Stakes

8

43

Doeford Bridge

365   66   67

A   B   **162**   C   Plantation Farm   D   E

Yew Tree Farm

I grid square represents 500 metres

Marl Hill

Crimpton

F G H J K

68 **69** **70**

Tyne Moor

47

1

2

Spire Farm

Seedalls

Elm Clough Wood

46

3

Hare Clough

Flatts

4

45 **138**

Rabbit Lane

5

Braddup Farm

Ayxa Farm

Kitchens

6

Talbot Bridge

Cross Lane

44

Sandal Holme Farm

Mason House

Clow Bo

7

Bashall Eaves

Rugglesmere

8

443

Agden Farm

F G H J K

68 **69** **70**

163

Horse Hey Farm

Bashall Brook

138

A B 112 C D E

370 71 72

47

1

Browsholme Moor

FELL ROAD

B678

Moorcock Inn

2

New-o-Nook

46

3

Browsholme Road

Hodgson Moor

Daisy Hill

Buckstall

Leemings

B678

Mill Farm

Mill

Hare Clough

Freeholds Lane

4

137

45

5

Whitley Lane

Freeholds Lane

Braddup Farm

Cross Lane

Cross Lane

Colthurst Hall

Kitchen

6

Talbot Bridge

Braddup House

44

7

Clough Bottom

Page Fold

Lower New House

PO

Rugglesmere

8

443

Cow Hey

Backridge

370 71 72

A B 164 C D E

Brook

I grid square represents 500 metres

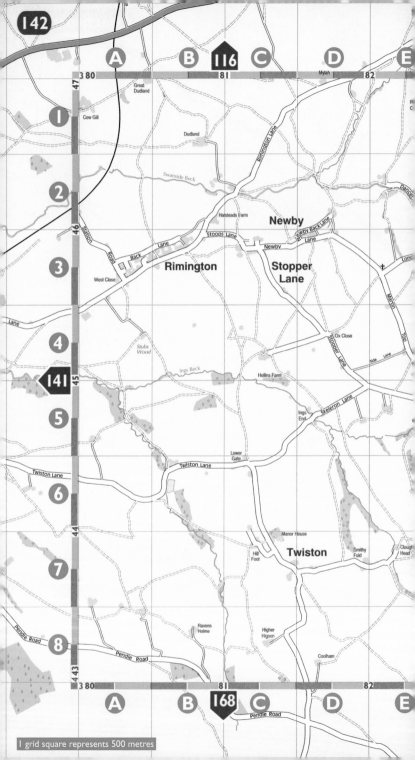

F G H **117** J K

What ose

New Ing

Coal Pit

Hey Hea

Brogden Hall

83   84   85

47

I

Bonny Blacks

Coverdale

Brogden Lane

2

Flas

46

Coppy House

3

r gh

Great Todber

Howgill Lane

Little Middop

Lane Side

gill

A682

Stocks House

Gisburn Old Road

Newfield Edge Hall Farm

4

Middop Hall

Stocks Lane

45   **144**

Whytha Road

Whytha

5

Middop Wood

Cold Weather House

A682

6

44

Higher Gills

Craven Laithe

7

Rimington Moor

Burn Moor

8

443

Jackson's House

83   84   **169**   85

F G H **169** J K

rn Moor End

Higher Wheathead

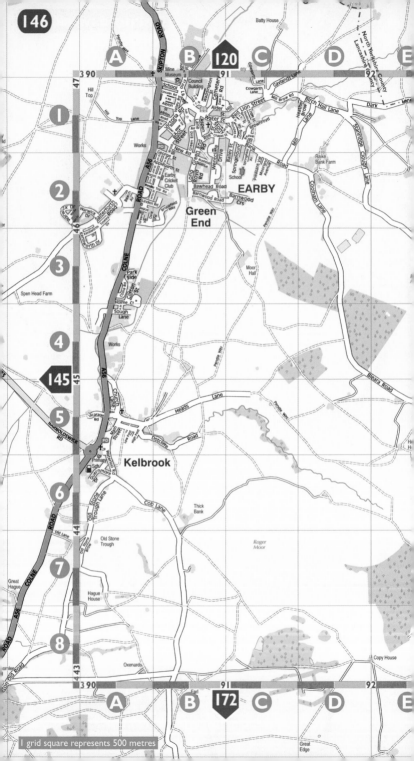

127

154

181

F G H J K

43 44 45 43

1
2
3
4
5
6
7
8

Curlew Farm

Crab Tree Lane

Crabtree Farm

Fir Tree Farm

Moss House

Wild Boar Farm

Hudsons Farm

White Hall

Rawcliffe Road

Turnover Hall

Rawcliffe Road

A586

River Wyre

Great Eccleston Health Centre

RAIKES ROAD

LANCASTER AV

B5295

Barrows Lane

St. Mary's Road

School

Ripon Close

Lancaster Close

Great Eccleston

A586

White House Lane

Cross House

Moss Side Lane

Thatcher House

Hall Lane

White House

White House Lane

Brock Road

Hollyovenbeck House

White Crosses

Lane Heads

Hornby Lane

Inskip Moss Side

Elswick Manor

Hornby

n Row

F
G
H
129
J
K

Works
Meadowcroft Av
Stones Lane

48
THE AVENUE
Park
Catterall
Gates
50
43

hurchtown
River Wyre
Old Lancaster Road
PRESTON LANCASTER NEW ROAD
Catterall
Stu

Church Street
Almshouses
the Green
St Helen's Close

Ripon Hall Farm
A6
Cook
Robin Lane
Gayton Drive
Rover Av
Bowey Av
Joe Lane
Ashfield Rd
GARSTANG RD B6430
Terrace
Stubbins
I

Catterall Lane
Catterall Lodge
PRESTON LANCASTER NEW ROAD
Claughton Industrial Estate
2
42

Westfield
3

Higher Silcock
Roe Farm
Myerscough House
4

Roe Bridge
Farther Light Ash
Banners Farm
41
Stanzaker Hall Farm
156
5

New Draught
Nearer Light Ash
River Brook
Lancashire College of Agriculture
6
Myerscough

New Draught Bridge
St Michael's Road
Myerscough College
40
7
Myerscough Lodge
St Michael's Road

New Draught
Carefoot
8

Lee Farm
439

48
49
183
50

F
G
H
J
Hallidays Farm
Moss Lane
K

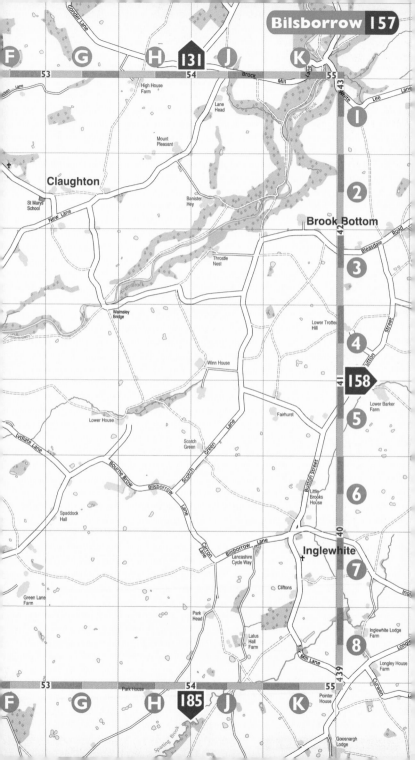

F G H 135 J K

Doeford Bridge

63 64 65 43

1

Greenlands Farm

Dairy Barn

Moss Lane

Works

Hotel

Gibbon Bridge

Loud Carr

Carr Side Farm

Loud Carr

2

Pale Farm

River Loud

42

3

Bradley Hall

Leach House

Clough Lane

Thornley Hall

Rock Brow

Forty Acre Lane

Brook House

Rams Clough

4

41 162

Four Acre Lane

5

Giles Farm

6

Cardwell House

Dale House

40

Lennox Farm

Myers's Farm

Forty Acre Farm

Golf Course

7

Cuckoo Hall

8

Golf Club

High House

Old Clitheroe Rd

PH

439

63 64 65

F G H 189 J K

Hoardsall

Moor Hey

A B 138 C D E

370 71 72

138

1

Rugglesmere

Cow Hey

Bashall Brook

Backridge

2

42

Bashall Town

Cheetail Farm

3

4

Thirty Acres

163

163 41

Withgill

NEW LANE

Mitton Lane

5

Sagar Fold

B6243

Rydding's Farm

Scott House

6

Angerham

Eastham House Farm

Over Hacking

40

7

Mitton Green

CHURCH

8

Woodfields

B6243

Lower Hodder Bridge

Lane

B6246

Great Mitton

439

370 71 72

A B 192 C D E

192

WHALLEY RD

River Hodder

Ribble Way

Ribble

Winckley Hall

1 grid square represents 500 metres

Stubbing Hill

Crag
End

Crag
Side

Brush

F   G   H   J   K

New Road Side   98   99   400   43

Crag
Top

Clough
Head

Hallan
Hill

New
Bridge

Lane   Buck Stone Lane

Fair
Place

Hill
top

Starr Farm

Over
Dean

Kid
Stone

Hitching
Stone

Stott
Hill
Moor

The New
Allotment

North Yorkshire County
Bradford

Maw
Stones

Long Gate

Copy Lane

Sykes Fork

White

Keighley
Moor

Keighley
Moor
Reservoir

Clough
Hey

Old
Bess

Clough Hey
Allotment

F   G   H   J   K

98   99   400   439

203

orth
oe

Flask

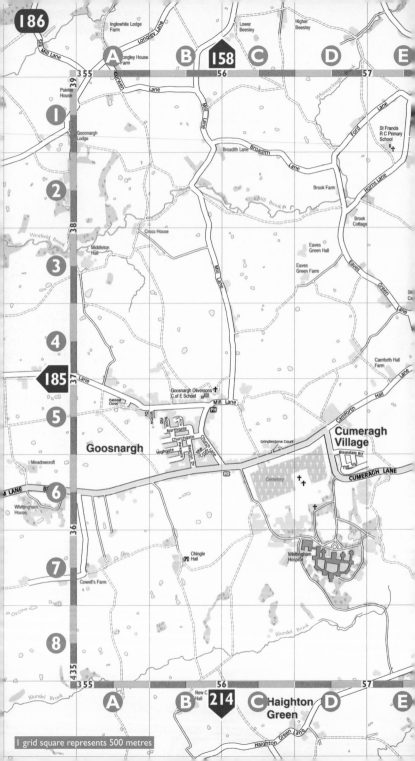

F G H **167** J K

78 79 80 39

I

Churn Clough Reservoir

Sabden Fold

2

Wood House

38

Ratten Clough

3

Dry Corner

Trefoil Road
Crowtrees Rd

Wesley Street
Stubbins Lane

Sabden CP School

Dean

den

Surgery
Works
Pendle St East
Sabden RC School

Sabden Brook

4

Stump Hall Road

Heyhouses

Back Lane

37

196

Padiham Road

5

Copthurst

Simonstone Road

Back Lane

The Cavaliers

Sabden Road

Barkerfield Close

6

A6

Fir Trees La

36

Northwood

Priddy Bank Farm

7

Northwood Farm

High House

Trapp Lane

Barrowford Road

8

Whins Lane

Sabden Rd

Old Moss

Higham Road

Pendle St

A6068

Law Farm

Huntroyde

High Whittaker Farm

A35

78 79 80

F G H **223** J K

A6068

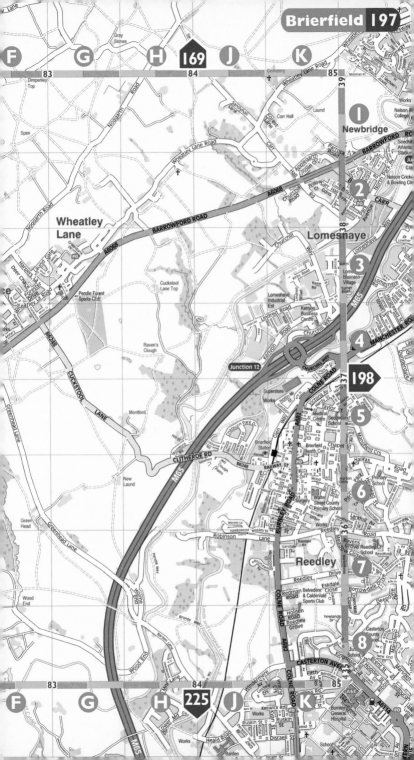

F G H 175 J K

I
2
3
4
5
6
7
8

Keighley
Moor
Reservoir

Old Bess

Oakworth
Moor

Flask

Dean
Clough
Head

Clough Head
Allotme

Harehills Lane

Works

Hill Top

Oldfield
First School

Cragg
Moor
Lodge Farm

Bottom   Road

Crag
Bottom

Dean Edge Road

New   Laithe   Road

Pennine Way

Old Snap

Scar Top Road

Scar
Top

Whitestone
Farm

Ponden
Reservoir

Hob Lane

Flush Isles

Ponden   Lane

Buckley

Pennine Way

Ponden
Clough

noll

Back

Bully Trees
Farm

Master
Stones

Bottoms

Stanbury
Moor

The Height

Black
Leech

Withins
Slack

Pennine Way

South
Dean

Brontë Way

Haworth
Moor

Withins   Hepton Bridge   Walk

Haworth   rd.

Harbour
Lodge

Withins
Flat

Brontë Way

98   99   400   435

39
38
37
36

204

A   B   176   C   D   E
     31

35 30   32

I

II

2

34

III

Central Pier

Princess Street

PROMENADE

A584

Stallfe
Centre

ST. CHAD'S ROAD

Bloomfield Road

St Chad's Road

Crystal Rd

Alexandra Rd

Library

LYTHAM ROAD

B5262

Coach
Station

Lonsdale Rd

Bloomfield Rd
(Bloomfield Road)

Field St

Bloomfield Road

CENTRAL DRIVE

Seasiders Way

Eaton

Bloomfield Rd

Bloomfield
Medical
Cen

Bloomfield

A5099

ANSDELL ROAD

WATERLOO   ROAD

The Waterloo
Crown Bowling Green

Waterloo
Medical Centre

Primary
School

B5261

WATERLOO ROAD

HAWES SIDE LANE

4 A5073

Blackpool
South Stn.

Chislehurst

5

34

3

South
Pier

Sandcastle
Leisure Centre

PROMENADE

Rawcliffe Street

Dean

Market

Withnell Road

Osbourne Road

Balmoral

Station Road

Hampton Rd

Windermere rd

Robinson

Yeadon Way

Hemingway

Marsden

Harcourt

Powell

St Cuthberts
Primary School

Fire
Station

South
Shore

Hotel

Avenue

Road

Avenue

Watson Av

Loftos

Yeadon Way

Avenue

B5262

4

33

Ripleys
Believe It or Not
Museum

Blackpool
Pleasure Beach

Blackpool
Pleasure Beach
Blackpool Ice
Drome

Watson

Woodstock Gdns

Kenilworth
Gardens

Burlington Road

LYTHAM ROAD

Severn Rd

Dinmore

School

Arnold
Gardens

Arnold

Broadway

Surgery

Luke's

St James'
Road

Martin's

Beverley Drive

Stamford Av

Ayrton

Rd

Road

Surgery

Arnal
Medical
Centre

Lennox
Av

Pedder's
Lane

Primary
School

Highfield

Lane

B5262

5

Blackpool
Pleasure
Beach Station

Wimbourne Pl

Hotel

Roseberry Rd

Horncliffe Road

Boscombe Rd

Bournemouth Rd

Harrowside

St James'
Road

Highfield Road

Scarsdale Av

Abbey
Road

Primrose Av

Cheddar Av

Belvere Av

Abbeyville

Clinic

Endsleigh Gardens

Lostock Gardens

Helen's Cl

Helen's Av

Stadium Av

6

32

PROMENADE

A584

Clifton Drive

Bennett Av

Waldock Av

Abercorn

Albany Av

Hillcrest Av

Lindsay Av

Hampton Hill

Preston
Avenue

Lancashire Area
Health Authority

Allandale

Rosemary

Roseacre

Kingston Av

Dalton Av

SQUIRES   GATE   LANE

Squires Gate

Tewkesbury Av

Sawley Av

Blackpool
Business Park

Farrington

Gate

7

32

Squires
Gate Stn

STARR GATE

SQUIRES GATE LANE

A584

Bosworth Pl

Crichton Av

Squires
Gate
Station

Westgate Road

Airport Hotel
Terminal

Works

Avroe Crs

Industrial Esta

31 30   32

4 31

8

A   B   230   C   D   E
     31

Blackpool
Airport

CLIFTON   DRIVE

I grid square represents 500 metres

A 335 35 B 36 C 178 D 37 E

Chain Lane

178

Mythop

Mythop Road

1

Mythop Road

Little
Marton

PRESTON NEW

2

Cartmell Rd

Langdale Road
Rusland
Road

34 A583

Troutbeck

3

Road
Works

Council Building

Clifton
Retail Park

Junction 4

M55

M55

Peel Hill

4

House

Superstore

205 33

Moss House Farm

Moss House Lane

Moss House La

Peel Hill

5

Road

Whitehill

Mariclough
Hampsfield
Camping Site

Lytham Drive

Pipers Height
Caravan Park

Peel Hill
Bridge

PRESTON NEW ROAD A583

Staining Wood Farm

6

Wild Lane

32

Peel Road

7

Peel

8 431

Division Lane

Peel Road

Brickworks

Anna's Road

A 335 35 B 36 C 232 D Lower Ballam E 37

Ballam Road

232

Lane

Peel Road

Bryers Rd

220

A · B · 192 · C · D · E

Lower Fold Farm
Chapel Lane
Langholme
Northcote Road
370 · 35 · 71 · 72
Hotel
St Leonards C of E & Langho Primary School
Whalley Road
Whalley Road
Higher Elker
New Road · Whalley Road
Pasturelands Drive
A59(T)

1
A59(T) LONGSIGHT ROAD · A666
Whalley Rd
Longsight Road
Mytton Fold Hotel & Golf Complex
Hotel
Hollin Hall

2
Langho Station
Clayton Row
Golf Course
Cronshaw
Moor Lane
Roscoes Head
Buanholm Dr · Moorgate Road
34
A666
Whinney Lane
York Road

3
St Mary's RC School
York
Whalley Old Road
Whittle Hall
Hillcrest Rd
Langho
Hawthorn Close

4
A666
WHALLEY ROAD
Carr Hall
Snodworth Road
York Road
Dean Clough Reservoir

219 · 33
Snodworth

5

6
Rishton Road
Wilpshire Road
32
Parsonage Reservoir
York Road
Blackburn Old Road
Clinkham
Bill

7
Harwood Road
New Inns
Wilpshire Road
Wilpshire Road

8
Upper Mickle Hey
431
370 · 35 · 71 · Dunscar · 72
Pede Road
Old Road
HARWOOD

A · B · 246 · C · D · E
Lower Cunliffe
Leeds & Liverpool Canal
Daniel St

1 grid square represents 500 metres

222

Easterley Farm

Old Roman Road

High House Farm

Back Lane

A

B

194

C

Whins Lane

D

E

35 75

76

Slater Sq

77

Windsor Close

Berkeley Dr

Parkhead

1

Read Hall Golf & Country Club

Hammond Drive

Hammond Drive

George Lane

Woodhead Road

St. Johns C of E School

Straits

Windhead Road

Haredock Close

A680

ACCRINGTON ROAD

Read Park

Golf Course

Tennyson Av

St. Johns C of E

Read

WHALLEY ROAD

Hambledon Av

Kirkstall Avenue

Read Cricket Club

Westminster

Tintern

2

34

WHALLEY ROAD A671

Sawley

Tumers

Simonsto

Cock Bridge

A680

Lane

Conyers

3

Martholme

LANE

Dunkirk

Cranberry

River Calder

Works

4

Altham Bridge

Great Harw Golf Club

221

33

Syleside Brook

Calder

Altham

Mill

LANE

Brownsills

BURNLEY ROAD

Syke

Altham Lane

Shorte

5

Altham St James C of E Primary School

Metcalf

Drive

Altham Industrial Estate

A680

WHALLEY ROAD

Syke Side

Syke Side

Metcalf

6

Hyndburn Bridge

Water St

Venture Court

Barnfield Way

32

A678

Spring Hill

Trout Beck

Clayton Dr

Leeds and Liverpool Canal

7

AV

Lynwood

Hotel

8

Lancaster Dr

Mount Pleas

Hopwood Ct

BURNLEY ROAD

Moorfield Way

Moorfield Dr

M65

Devonshire

St Marys

Moorfield Industrial Estate

Warwick Rd

CLAYTON-LE-MOORS

Church St

Victoria St

Chequers

WHALLEY ROAD

Mill St

Works

Gordon St

Gold Venture Farm

35 75

76

248

77

A

B

C

D

E

Huncoa Station

LLC

Enfield Cl

Brickwall

Mill St

I grid square represents 500 metres

F   G   H   201   J   K

93   94   35   95

I

The Plain

Rushy Clough

Hole Sike

Foul Sike

Dove Stones

2

Mere Stones

Field of the Mosses

County / ...erdale

34

3

Widdop Moor

Greave Clough

Pisser Clough

4

Widdop

33

Widdop Lodge

Widdop Reservoir

5

6

Flask

32

7

PH

Black Moor

Gorple Lower Reservoir

8

Graining Water

431

93   94   95

F   G   H   255   J   K

Raistrick Greave

Heptonstall

230

A B 204 C D E

330 31 32

31

1

Blackpool
Airport

DRIVE

2

NORTH

Duncan
Cl
Drake Cl
Frobisher
Drive
Golf Course

Napier Cl

St Anne's
Old Links
Golf Club

St Anne's
Cricket Club
Surgery

30

Stamford Rd
Salcombe
Cres

Highbury Road West
Highbury Road
Heeley
Road

Kilgrimol Gdns

Seaton Cres

ASDA

Lime Grove

Mayfield
County
School

3

CLIFTON

Hilda's Rd
Lime Grove

Council
Building

St A

West

PO

St Leonard's

St Andrew's Road

Cavendish

Evelyn's
Road

Clitheroe
Road
Grange

NORTH

Chestnut Road

Sandhurst

4

DRIVE

Beach

Toy & Teddy
Bear Museum

St Anne's Station

Clifton
Street

29

NORTH

Promenade

Todmorden Road

Hotel

Hotel

ST ANNE'S

St George's

St George's Lane

Council
Building
PO

CLIFTON

Hotel

5

Salter's
Bank

St Anne's
Pier

Fernlea Hotel &
Leisure Complex

Bank

Hotel

St Anne's
Swimming
Pool

Pleasure
Island

6

28

7

427

8

330 31 32

A B C D E

I grid square represents 500 metres

I grid square represents 500 metres

I grid square represents 500 metres

254

A   B   228   C   D   E

3 90   31   91   92

31

Cant Clough
Reservoir

Gorple Upp
Reservoir

1

Worsthorne
Moor

2

30

3

4

253   29

Stiperden
Moor

limestone

5

Stiperden
Bar House

The Long Causeway

6

Coal Clough
Wind Farm

Burnley Way

7

28

Bank Top
Farm

Lancashire County
Calderdale

Star
M

8

427

Coal Clough
Farm

Burnley Way

Coal Clough Road

Gail Lane

Mount Lane

Dell Lane

Lane

Sahar Lane

Hawks
Stones

Dean Farm

3 90

91   92

A   B   277   C   D   E

Pudsey

Shore
Road

Pudding
Shore

Shore Green

Blue
Bell
Lane

Hartley

I grid square represents 500 metres

F **G** **H** **229** **J** **K**

93 94 95

31

1

Raistrick
Greave

*Heptonstall
Moor*

2

30

Egypt

3

Colden Water

*Hoar Side
Moor*

4 **Rodmer
Clough**

Noah Dale

Greenland

29

Greenland Road

5

Four
Gates End

Moorcock Road

Earnshaw
Hole

Moorhall
Farm

6

28

Burnt Edge Lane

Brown

Halifax Lane

7 Higher

Long Cau

Kebs Road

Lower Lane

8

4 27

Eastwood Road

93 94 95

F **G** **H** **J** **K**

Lane

Staups
Moor

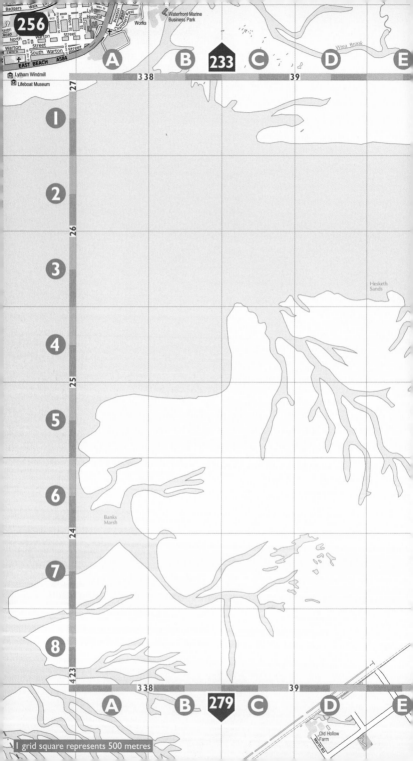

Lytham Windmill
Lifeboat Museum

Badgers Walk
North
Warton
South Warton
EAST BEACH A584

Waterfront Marine
Business Park

Wrea Brook

Hesketh
Sands

Banks
Marsh

Old Hollow
Farm

1 grid square represents 500 metres

F G H **234** J K

41 42

27

I

2

26

3 Hesketh
Out Marsh

4

25 **258**

5

6

24

7

Hundred End Gutter

Marsh
Farm

Shore Road

8

Ribble View
Farm

4 23

F G H **280** J K

41 42

Hundred

A 343 B 235 C D E

27

I

2

26

3

Hesketh
Out Marsh

Ribble Bank
Farm

4

257 25

Hesketh
New Marsh

5

Anchorage
Farm

Carr Hey Watercourse

6

24

Hesketh with Becconsall
All Saints C of E School

Marsh Road

7

Shore Road

Hesketh

8

Ribble View
Farm

Newarth

Silverda

Becc

A 343 B 281 C D E

Becconsall

Cherry Vale

Moss Lane

Hesketh

Kingsfold
Christian
School

I grid square represents 500 metres

I grid square represents 500 metres

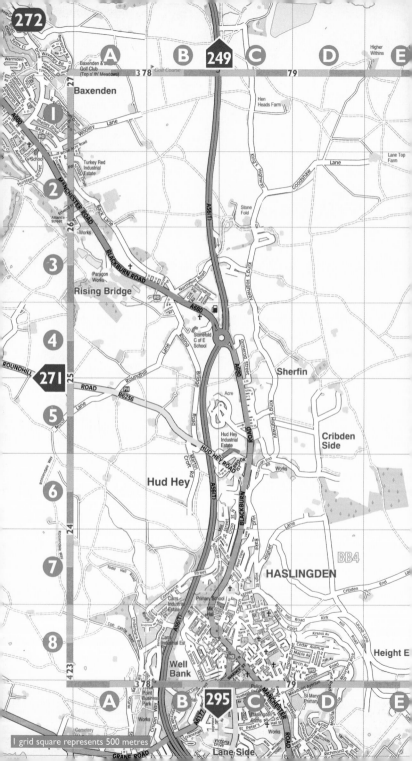

276

A B 253 C D E

27

3 88 89

1

Burnley Way

Heald
Moor

2

Irwell Valley Way

26

Burnley Way

Heald Lane

Rossendale Way

3

The Moorlands

Heald Ct

Heald
Lane

Bankfort Road

Wambs Farm

Works

4

Well La

Lane

BURNLEY ROAD

A646/11

25

275

River Irwell

Flower   Scar   Road

5

Irwell Valley Way

Todmorden
Moor

Scar Rd

Bacup Rd

Todmorden Old Road

Sharneyford
County
School

A681

Sharneyford

Holden
Gate

6

Works

Broad
Clough

BACUP

24

OL13

Higher
Change

ROAD

Rossendale Way

Uppers Gate

7

TODMORDEN

Old Rd

OAD

Green

ROAD

Lower

Greave

Greave

8

SHIRE STREET

Industrial
Est

Lower Coal Rd

Lowers
Reaps

A123

Wascoe Lane

3 88 89

A B 299 C D E

St Marys RC
Primary School

Lancashire County
Calderdale

Reaps
Moss

1 grid square represents 500 metres

F G H **254** J K

Hawks Stones

Orchan House Farm

1

Stony Lane

Pudsey

Shore

Hartley

smouth

Parkside

BURNLEY ROAD A646

2

Cornholme

Vale

Knotts Road

BURNLEY ROAD

Works

3

PH

Lower Moor

Works

Lydgate

4

River Calder

A646

Tower Causeway

Flower Scar Road

Todmorden High School

Flower Scar Road

Woodfield

5

Ewood La

Southall

Parkin Lane

Southall Ct

6

High Barn

Southall Road

Midgelden

Parkin Lane

Clough Foot

BACUP ROAD A681

7

Stones Lane

Dobroyd Castle Sc

Stones Rd

Stones

8

Works

A681

Industrial Estate

Gorpley Reservoir

F G H J K

Inchfield Moor

F **G** **H** **256** **J** **K**

38 39 40 23

I

2

Marsh Road

3 Far Banks

Taylor's Farm

New Lane

4 Gorsey

Pace

280

Moss Lane

5

6

7 Super Stubble Lane

Gravel La

Boundary Farm

Dalweb Industrial Park

8

419

38 39 40

F **G** **H** **303** **J** **K**

Old Hollow Farm

High Brow

Goose Dub Farm

Chorley's Lane

Bond's Lane

Chapel Lane

Banks Methodist Primary School

Vicarage Lane

George's Lane

Church Road

Works

Long Lane

Ralph's Wife's Lane

Church

St Stephens School

Fleetwood

Hesketh Av

Hoole Lane

Schwartzman Drive

Banks Health Centre

Banks

Aveling Drive

Station Road

Guinea Hall Lane

The Avenue

Rufford Drive

Lancaster

Abrams Fold

Abrams Green

St Stephens Primary School

North Meols Community Leisure Centre

Westsdale Drive

Brightstone Close

Avenham

Gravel Lane

Greaves Hall Avenue

The Close

Green Lane

Banks Road

The Sluice

WATER LANE A565(T)

A565(T) SOUTHPORT NEW ROAD

Hollywood Farm

Gravel Lane

Bobbiners Lane

Gravel Lane

Mere Lane

Cabin Lane

New Lane

PR9

Three Pools Waterway

The Sluice

Common

Lane

282
259
281
306

A B C D E

Silverdale

Becconsall Lane

Slone's Avenue

y Vale

PD

Attand Gardens

Greenways

Fulwood Av

Douglas Av

Tarleton CP School

Carr Lane

Carr Lane

Spencer's Drive

River View

River View

Hillcrest Drive

Holly Grove

Sutton Avenue

Howard Dr

Mason Close

Haig Av

Tarleton High School

The Beeches

The Spinney

Meolsgate Avenue

Firbank Avenue

Oaklands Avenue

Kearsley Av

Sandringham Av

Hunter Av

Latham Crescent

Plox Brow

TARLETON

Gorse Lane

Bannistre Health Centre

Sutton Lane

Church Rd

The Fosters

Bridge Close

Coe Lane

Tarleton C of E Primary School

Meadows

Trinity Walks

Churchview

Heritage

WINDGATE BANK BRIDGE

LIVERPOOL ROAD A59(T)

Works

Mill Hill

Saunders Lane

Saunders Lane

Much Hoole School

Liverpool Old Road

Liverpool Old Road

Much Hoole

Liverpool Old Road

Northern Avenue

Green

Liverpool Road

Park Av

Northall

Town Lane

Lunds Lane

Much H Town

Allum Lane

Carr House

B5248

CARR HOUSE LANE

B5248

Pompian Brow

Plocks Farm

Ashcroft's Farm

Bank Lane

Bank Hall

Leeds & Liverpool Canal

River Douglas

Eyes Lane

Eyes Lane

Back Lane

LIVERPOOL ROAD A59(T)

Sollom

Lock Lane

Sollom Lane

Red Bridge

Riverbosto...

LIVERPOOL ROAD

A B C D E

1 grid square represents 500 metres

294

A **B** **271** **C** **D** **E**

GRANE ROAD
A6177
GRANE ROAD

23
3 75 76 77

Haslingden Grane

1

Calf Hey Road

Ogden Reservoirs

Holden Wood Reservoirs

2

Calf Hey Reservoirs

Rossendale Way

22

Musbury Heights

3

4

Lancashire County
Blackburn

Rossendale Way

Musbury Brook

293 21

5

Cote's Farm

Brookfield Road

Musden Head Moor

Rossendale Way

6

20

Long Grain

Rossendale Way

7

8

Lancashire County
Blackburn

Wet Moss

Rossendale Way

4 19
3 75 76 77

A **B** **318** **C** **D** **E**

1 grid square represents 500 metres

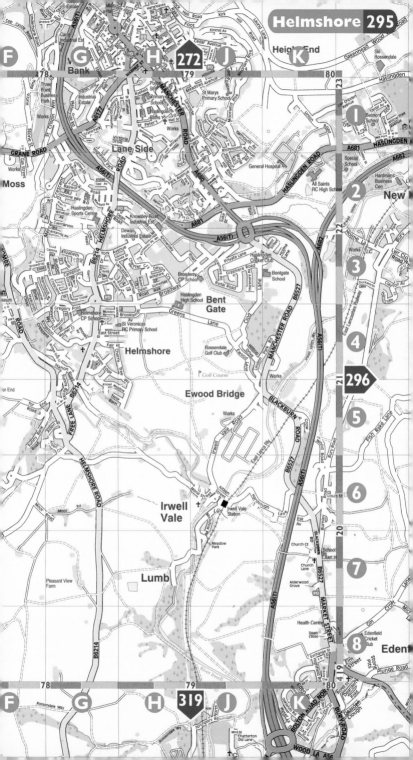

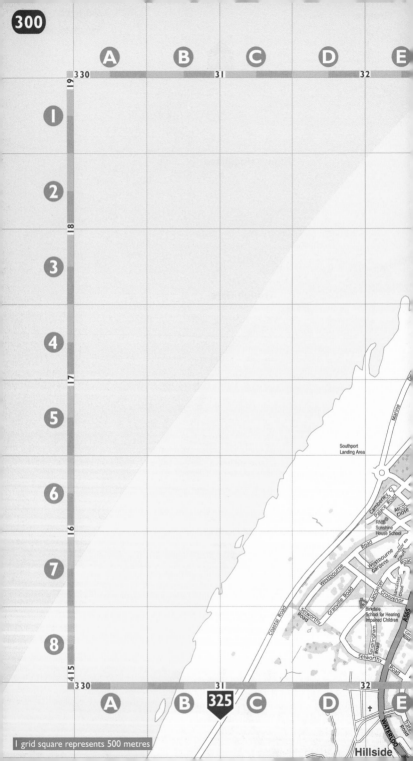

A B C D E

330 31 32

1

2

3

4

5

6

7

8

Southport
Landing Area

Camberley Ct
Prince Road
Ascot Close

RNIB
Sunshine
House School

Road

Westbourne

Westbourne
Gardens

Windsor
Road

Road

Grosvenor

Lancaster
Close

Birkdale
School for Hearing
Impaired Children

Selworthy
Road

Granville Road

Coastal Road

Southmingham

Selworthy

Road

A85

Road

Road

A B 325 C D E

330 31 32

WATERLOO
Road

Greenloans
Circle

Road

Hillside

I grid square represents 500 metres

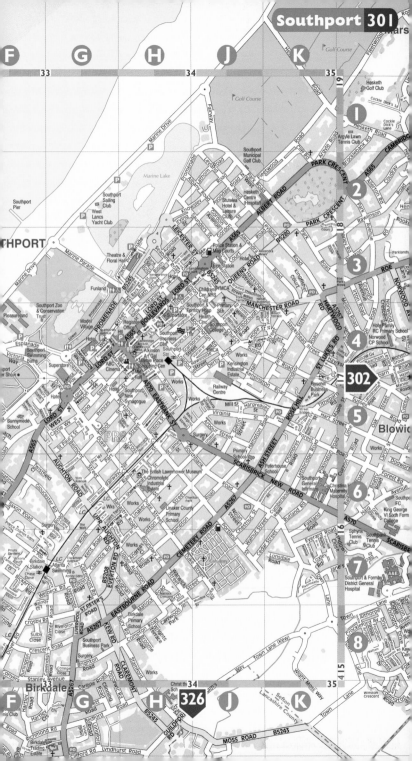

3 45   19   46   47

Sollom

Green Lane

Red Bridge

River Douglas

I

Lock Lane

Smith's Lane

Liverpool Old Road

Sollom Lane

MEADOW LANE

2

Moss Side Farm

THE STRINE

18

3

Lane

A581

Great Hanging Bridge

Sandy

A581

CROSTON ROAD

River Douglas

4

◄305

LIVERPOOL ROAD

Spark Lane

Leeds & Liverpool Canal

5

Croston Drive

Springwood Dr

Longshaw Cl

Meadow Lane

6

HOLMESWOOD ROAD

16

Rufford Park La

Works

LC

Little

White Bridge

B5246

7

Mere Sands Wood

Rufford Old Hall (NT)

Lane

DIAMOND JUBILEE ROAD

STATION ROAD

Rufford Station

MEADOW LANE

B5246

8

Tooth

Brick

Kiln

Albert Road

Highcrest

Hawthorne

Avenue

Rufford CE School

Flash Lane

New Road

A581

Holly Lane

Douglas Close

Mill Hey Lane

Rufford

3 45   46   47

CAUSEWAY L

River Douglas

I grid square represents 500 metres

F G H **289** J K

63 64 65 19

I

Round
Loaf

2

Anglezarke
Moor

18

3

4

314

17

5

Lead Mines
Clough

6

River Yarrow

16

Alance
Bridge

7

Wilcock's
Farm

8

Moses
Cocker's

Belmont Road

415

63 64 65

F G H **338** J K

ngton

Rivington
Moor

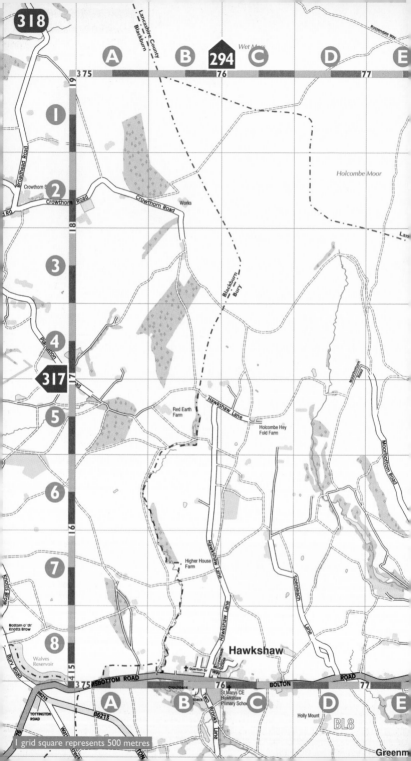

A B C D E

3 27 28 29

I 5

1

2

14

3

4

13

5

6

12

7

8

4 II

3 27 28 29

A B 343 C D E

Ainsdale
Sand Dune

I grid square represents 500 metres

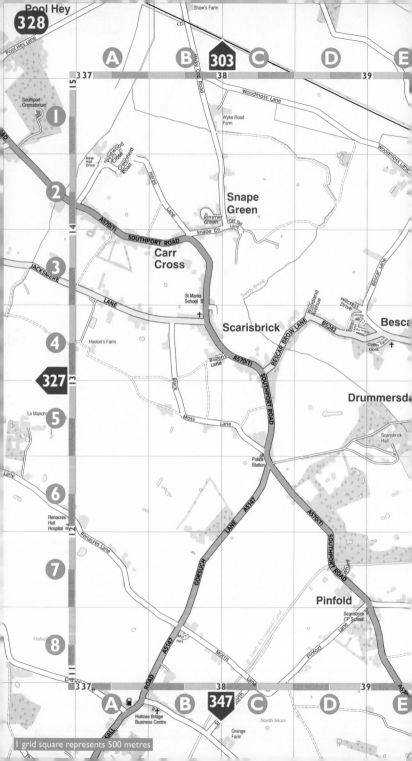

F
G
H
304
J
K

40
41
42

I

2

3

4

330

5

6

7

8

F
G
H
348
J
K

40
41
42

Crossings Lane

Midge Hall Lane

Wholesome Lane

Bescar Lane

escar Lane Station

White House Lane

dale Lane

Copelands

Shore Lane

LC

Martin Lane

LC

Highfield Lane

Drummersdale Lane

Merscar Lane

Corsit Lane

Works

DAM WOOD LANE

Leeds & Liverpool Canal

Shaw Hall
Caravan Park

**Heatons
Bridge**

Martin Lane

Rabbit Lane

Road

Edge Farm

urlston
reen

Moorfield

Smithy Lane

HEATONS BRIDGE ROAD

Briars Lane

Moorfield

Lane

B5242

BARRISON GREEN

PIPPIN STREET

Stan Lane

Hurlston Hall
Golf Club

Hurlston Hall
Country Caravan Park

Narrow

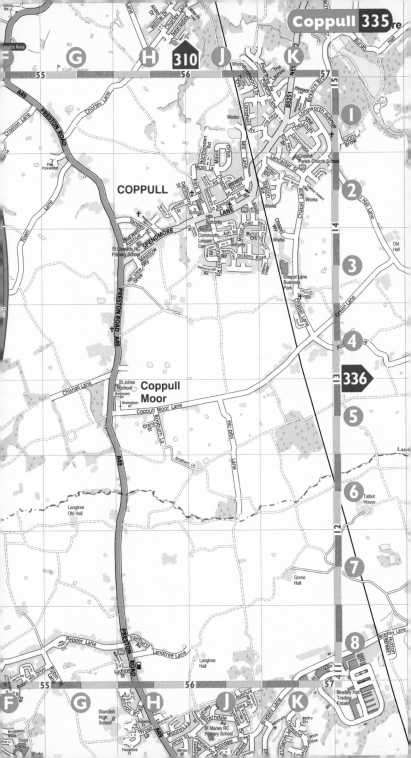

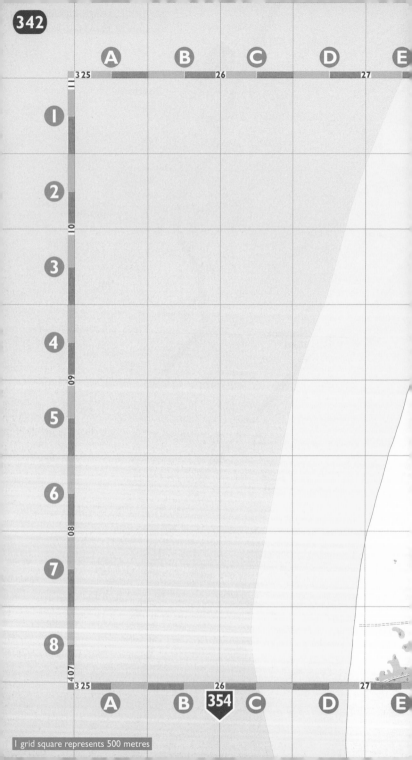

342

354

344

A B 325 C D E

330 31 32

I

Wood
Ainsdale Clinic
Woodvale
CP Sch

Pinfold
Lane
Meadow
Lane

Somerset Dr
Dorset
Avenue
Cornwall
Rose Cr
St John Stone
RC Primary School
Cherry
LIAC AV
Heather RI

Willowbank Holiday
Home & Touring Park
Woodvale Road
Vale Crescent

2
Dunlop
Avenue
Liverpool Old
Road
Moss Lane
Lancashire C
Hotel
Sefton

3
Golf Course
Woodvale
Airfield
Formby Hall
Golf Club
Broad Lane

4
North Moss Lane

343

Brewery Lane
Eight Acre
Lane
Southport Old Road

5
St Anne's
St Anne
Sefton
Lancashire County
Downholland Brook

St Peters
Cof E
Primary School
SOUTHPORT ROAD B542A

6
Cricket
Path
Cronton
Club
Formby Lawn
Tennis Club
The Paddock
Formby
Junior
Sports Club
Clifton Rd

7
Piercefield Road
New Road
L37
Freshfield
Primary
School
Moss Side
Moss Lane
Formby
High Lower
School

8
Church Hall
Whitehouse Lane
Police
Sta
Gardner
Our Lady of Compassion
RC Primary School
Sefton
Lancashire County
Formby's
Farm

Formby
AFC
Works
War
Memorial
ALTCAR ROAD BS195

330 31 32

A B 356 C D E

LORD
SEFTON
WAY

grid square represents 500 metres

I grid square represents 500 metres

350

331

349

362

A5209

BRIARS LANE

Leeds & Li...

Ellerbrook

Broadlands Grove

Flax Lane

Brook

A5209

Three Oaks CARR

Ring O' Bells Lane

Hollowford

Lane

Ring o' Bells

LOWRY HILL LANE

Moss Ridge

Back

Lane

Hobcross Lane

A5209

COURSE LANE

B5240

Lathom Park
Church of England
Primary School

Cranes Lane

HALL LANE

Halsall's Lodge
Farm

Dick's

Spa Lane

Holland
Business
Park   Spa
Farm

Cock Farm

Spa Lane

Firswood

Road

Stanley
Piece

Seddon

Works

Seddon Place

PLOUGH LANE

B5240

ROAD

B5240

A5... Dick's Lane

Statham Road

Works

Slate

Lane

Chapel House

NEVERSTITCH ROAD

DICK... LANE

A5... BLAGUEG...

Osprey... bine Lane

Works

Black Moss
Special
School

Brookfield
CP School

Kinsbur...

Tintagel

Hoscar
Station

Moss

Meadow

Carr Lane

Hoscar

LC

Lane

Frog

Lane

3 45

46

47

I

2

3

4

5

6

7

8

A   B   C   D   E

10

09

08

07

1 grid square represents 500 metres

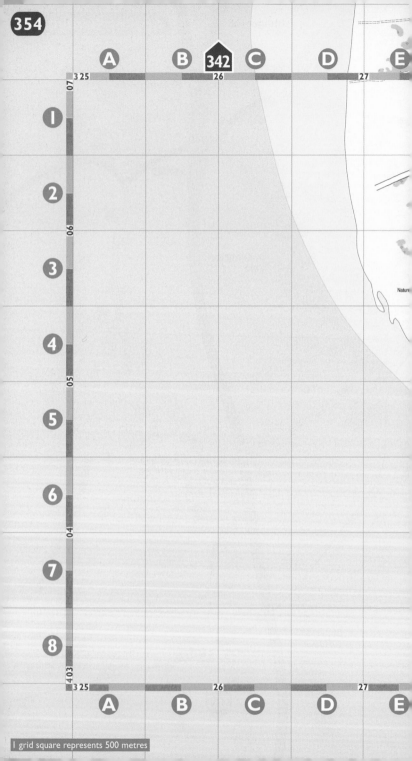

A **B** **362** **G** **D** **E**

03 45 46 47

I

Ben
Lane
Farm

Ben Lane Court

Intake Lane

Ormskir

**Park
Hill**

Busher Lane

Lane

Lodge Lane

Ben Lane

Coxbin Road

2

RAINFORD ROAD

Ormskir Road

Red Delph Lane

02

Works

Siding Lane

3

Walkden House
Farm

Lancashire County
St. Helens

ORMSKIRK

Grove Close

Works

4

Moss
Farm

Dairy Farm Road

RAINFORD

Works

01

367

A5077

5

Coach Road

BY-PASS

Moss Nook

Inglenook Farm

6

400

7

Simonswood
Moss

Lancashire County
St Helens

Coach Road

Moor
Game
Farm

ROAD

8

Brown
Birch Farm

Coach Road

MOSSBOROUGH

03 99

03 45 46 47

A **B** **C** **D** **E**

Boundary Lane

Mossborough Hall Lane

Coach

New Cut Lane

F   G   H   363   J   K

48   49   50   03   Long

Rainford
Junction

Crawford County Sch

Manor House

I

Crawford   Crawford Road   Works   Oakleigh   Holland Court

PO

Rainford Station

News Lane

Nook Road

Works

Maggots

Henderson Drive

Hey's Brow

2

Brow

Langwood   Lane

02

Reeds

3

Graysons Road   Brook Lodge Primary School   Rainford High School

Holiday Moss

Pim

Pasdale Drive

Christian

Crofters Drive

Muncaster   Drive

RAINFORD

4

370

01

CROSS PIT   LANE

Heyes Avenue   Hayes Grove

Rainford CE Primary School   Rainford Health Centre

B5205

Lakeside Court

5

CHURCH   ROAD

Council Buildings

The Kenneth Macrae Medical Centre   PO

Rookery Lane

HIGHER

LANE

Fire Clay Farm

MOSBOROUGH ROAD B5205

Thickwood Moss Lane

Church Road

Holly Lane

Rose Drive

Hopwood Crescent

Wellfield

Diamond Business Park

6

Moss Lane

RED CAT LANE

Hatchery Drive

CRANK

Pasture Lane

RAINFORD

A570(T)

Sandyway

Hazel Business Park

Mill Lane

HIGHER   LANE B5205

400

7

Crank

CRANK ROAD

B5201

Fairfield Gdns

Rainford Industrial Estate

Millbrook Business Centre

8

399

WA11   BYPASS

Reeds Lane

48   49   50

F   G   H   J   K   CRANK   Fairfield Drive

Hill Top House   Helena Road   Berrington's Lane   Rainford Brook

Winsta

Winstanley College

365

F G H J K

53 54 55

Tracks Lane

Billinge Hospital

Mendip

School

Pennine

AS71

Springpool

Beech Wa

PEMBERTON ROAD

Pine View

Longshaw

New Houses

Park Road

M6

Park Road

Longshaw Avenue

A571

1

2

02

3

AS71

Works

Ashton Road

4

Maddox Farm

Winstanley Road

01

Oakley

Wigan St. Helens

Beacon Road

St Aidan's CI

A571

5

Garswood United FC

Leyland Green

Brownall Green

NEWTON ROAD

Main Street

St Aidan's CE Priman School

B5207

BILLINGE ROAD

6

B5207

BILLINGE

Simm's Lane End

Thornhill

7

Blackleyhurst Av

Blackley Hurst Hall

Chapel End CP School

Garswood Road

Chadwick Green

Nugent House Sch

Carr Mill Road

Greenfield House

Works

Arch Lane

8

Station Road

Garswood

53 54 55

F G H J K

Tithe

Abbeystead 83 G2
Abbey Village 289 J1
Abraham Heights 2 A4
Accrington 248 A5
Adlington 337 H4
Ainsdale 325 J6
Ainsdale-on-Sea 324 E6
Aldcliffe 2 B6
Altham 222 D5
Anchorsholme 149 F2
Anderton 337 H3
Andertons Mill 333 H2
Ansdell 231 J6
Appley Bridge 352 E3
Arkholme 29 H6
Arnside 15 F1
Ashurst 351 H7
Astley Bridge 341 J7
Aughton 36 A8
Aughton 359 H4
Aughton Park 360 C1
Bacup 298 C1
Bailrigg 67 G2
Balderstone 217 G6
Balladen 296 C4
Bamber Bridge 263 G2
Bank Fold 269 H6
Bank Hey 245 K2
Bank Houses 78 B4
Bank Lane 319 K4
Banks 279 H5
Bank Top 352 E7
Bare 42 A5
Barley 168 E5
Barley Green 168 D6
Barnoldswick 144 D1
Barrow 193 H1
Barrow Bridge 340 E7
Barrowford 169 K7
Barrow Nook 367 J1
Barton 184 D4
Barton 346 B5
Bashall Eaves 137 J8
Baxenden 271 K1
Bay Gate 114 B3
Bay Horse 80 D5
Beardwood 244 B3
Becconsall 281 H1
Belgrave 298 D4
Belmont 315 F6
Belthorn 269 H5
Bent Gate 295 J3
Bescar 328 E4
Bickerstaffe 361 J6
Billinge 371 H6
Billington 192 E8
Bilsborrow 156 C7
Birch Green 363 J1
Birkacre 310 E8
Birkdale 326 B1
Bispham 148 B6
Bispham Green 332 E4
Blackburn 8 C1
Blackleach 210 E1
Blacko 170 B3
Black Pole 183 J6
Blackpool 5 E2
Blackrod 337 J8
Blacksnape 292 B3
Blaguegate 362 B2
Bleasdale 132 D4
Blowick 302 A5
Boarsgreave 297 J6
Bolton-by-Bowland 115 H4
Bolton Green 310 B4
Bolton-le-Sands 33 H7
Bolton Town End 33 F7
Bonds 129 K5
Booth Bridge 120 D7
Borwick 27 F4
Bottom of Hutton 236 E8
Bottom o' th' Moor 339 G8
Bowgreave 129 J7
Bowker's Green 360 B6
Bracewell 118 C6
Breedy Butts 149 K5
Bretherton 282 E5
Brierfield 198 B6
Brindle 264 E7
Brinscall 288 E4
Britannia 299 G3
Broad Clough 275 K6
Broadfield 247 K8
Broadfield 285 G2
Broadley 323 G6

Brock 156 B6
Brockhall Village 192 A5
Brook Bottom 157 K2
Brookfield 214 C7
Brookhouse 8 C3
Brookhouse 45 J5
Brooksbottoms 319 J8
Broughton 185 F8
Brown Edge 327 J1
Brownhill 219 G8
Brownlow 370 D3
Brownside 226 E5
Brunshaw 11 F3
Bryning 234 A3
Burnley 11 E3
Burnley Lane 225 H2
Burnley Wood 11 F5
Burn Naze 123 H7
Burscough 349 G1
Burscough Bridge 330 D5
Burton-in-Kendal 18 B6
Cabus 103 J7
Cadley 212 E7
Cadshaw 316 A2
Calder Vale 131 G3
Cantsfield 30 E5
Capernwray 27 G7
Carleton 149 H8
Carnforth 33 J1
Carr 319 H4
Carr Bank 15 K1
Carr Cross 328 B3
Carr Houses 357 F7
Catforth 183 F7
Catley Lane Head 322 E7
Caton 45 H5
Caton Green 45 K4
Catterall 155 J1
Chadwick Green 371 G7
Chapel House 362 D1
Chapels 268 E8
Chapeltown 317 H8
Charnock Green 309 K5
Charnock Richard 310 A7
Chatburn 140 D6
Chatterton 319 H2
Cherry Tree 266 E2
Chipping 134 D8
Chorley 311 F2
Church 247 K3
Church Clough 171 J8
Churchtown 155 F1
Churchtown 302 D2
Claughton 46 C1
Claughton 157 G2
Clawthorpe 18 C3
Clayton Brook 263 K6
Clayton Green 263 K7
Clayton Le Dale 218 E4
Clayton-le-Moors 221 K8
Clayton-le-Woods 286 B1
Cleveleys 122 B8
Cliffe 221 F5
Clifton 236 D2
Clitheroe 165 H2
Cliviger 252 E4
Cloughfold 296 C2
Clough Foot 277 G7
Clow Bridge 250 D6
Coates 119 H8
Cockden 226 E1
Cocker Bar 284 B2
Cockerham 79 H6
Cold Row 124 E6
Colne 171 G5
Colne Edge 171 G4
Common Edge 205 F5
Conder Green 66 C7
Constable Lee 273 H7
Copp 152 E8
Coppull 335 H2
Coppull Moor 335 H5
Copster Green 219 F3
Corner Row 208 C1
Cornholme 277 G2
Cottam 212 A5
Coup Green 241 H7
Cowan Bridge 22 B6
Cow Ark 136 E3
Cow Hill 214 E2
Cowling 174 E1
Cowling 311 J5
Cowpe 297 H5
Cox Green 341 K2
Crag Bank 33 J1

Crag Foot 3
Crank 3
Crawford 3
Crawshawbooth 2
Cribden Side 2
Crossens 2
Crossgill ....
Crossmoor 1
Croston 3
Cuddy Hill 1
Cuerden Green 2
Cumeragh Village 1
Dalton ....
Dalton 3
Dam Side 1
Dangerous Corner 3
Darwen 2
Dean 2
Digmoor 3
Dill Hall 2
Dimple 3
Dinckley 1
Docker ....
Dolphinholme ....
Dowbridge 2
Downham 1
Downholland Cross 3
Drummersdale 3
Duncombe 1
Dunnockshaw 2
Dunscar 3
Dunsop Bridge 1
Eagland Hill 1
Eagley 3
Earby 1
Earcroft 2
Earnshaw Bridge 2
Easington 1
East Marton 1
Eccleston 3
Edenfield 2
Edge End 2
Edge Fold 3
Edgeside 2
Edgworth 3
Egerton 3
Ellel ....
Elmers Green 3
Elmslack ....
Elslack 1
Elston 2
Elswick 1
Elswick Leys 1
Esprick 1
Euxton 3
Ewood 2
Ewood Bridge 2
Facit 3
Fair Oak 1
Far Arnside ....
Far Banks 2
Farington 2
Farington Moss 2
Farleton ....
Far Moor 3
Fence 1
Feniscliffe 2
Feniscowles 2
Fiddler's Ferry 2
Fisher's Row 1
Fishwick 2
Five Lane Ends ....
Flax Moss 2
Fleetwood ....
Fold Head 3
Ford Green 1
Forest Becks ....
Forest Holme 2
Formby 3
Forton ....
Foulridge 1
Four Lane Ends ....
Frances Green 1
Freckleton 2
Frenchwood ....
Freshfield 3
Fulwood 2
Galgate ....
Garstang 1
Garswood 3
Gathurst 3
Gisburn 1
Glasson ....
Goodshaw 2
Goodshaw Chapel 2
Goodshaw Fold 2

se Green	283 F1	
snargh	186 A5	
ge	214 E7	
t Altcar	357 F2	
t Eccleston	153 H6	
t Harwood	220 E5	
t Marton	5 F4	
t Marton Moss	205 H7	
t Marton Moss Side	205 H4	
t Mitton	192 D1	
t Plumpton	207 H4	
ve	276 A8	
en End	146 B2	
enhalgh	180 A6	
n Haworth	271 G2	
son Lane	264 D1	
singham	36 E3	
eford Village	338 A5	
sargh	215 H2	
shaw	269 F6	
shaw Green	332 D6	
dleton	140 C3	
sagill	92 B2	
le	269 G3	
ergham	224 B4	
gate	198 E8	
hton Green	214 C1	
hton Top	213 K2	
	17 F2	
Nook	125 J6	
Cross	235 F2	
Green	259 J5	
Green	364 C4	
well	341 J8	
all	346 E2	
on	44 A4	
on Green	44 D4	
on West	94 D1	
ableton	150 E2	
ableton Moss Side	151 F1	
pson Green	80 D2	
ton	223 J7	
horn	178 A3	
e Appletree	69 F3	
e Syke	198 C8	
wood	311 G1	
kayne	346 A6	
es Side	5 E6	
ingden	272 C7	
kshaw	318 C8	
ks Stones	254 E8	
elhurst	319 F7	
elslack	16 A1	
ley	323 J7	
th Charnock	336 E1	
ton	53 J6	
ton's Bridge	329 H7	
ht End	272 E8	
nshore	295 H4	
keth Bank	258 E7	
keth Lane	160 D4	
keth Moss	281 G2	
kin Green	309 F8	
k Bank	43 F2	
	145 G8	
Houses	231 J3	
sham	52 A4	
am	196 B6	
Biggins	21 F2	
Casterton	21 K1	
er Audley	9 D5	
er Ballam	232 C2	
er Bartle	212 A3	
er Croft	268 C2	
er End	364 E8	
erford	170 B5	
er Heysham	52 D5	
er Hogshead	299 H2	
er Penwortham	6 A6	
er Walton	241 G8	
er Wheelton	288 B2	
Moor	333 H7	
Park	302 B3	
Salter	60 B1	
town	355 J8	
Dale	333 F6	
ck Vale	248 C3	
ide	325 K1	
le Fold	221 G5	
dlesden	292 E2	
nton	265 H1	
ombe	319 G6	
ombe Brook	319 F8	
en	115 F4	
and Lees	352 D6	
n Hall	200 C2	
Hollins Lane	103 J1	
Holme	17 K1	
Holme Chapel	252 E5	
Holme Mills	17 K2	
Holmes	281 F8	
Holme Slack	214 B7	
Holmeswood	305 G5	
Holt Green	359 K4	
Hoohill	176 D4	
Hornby	37 H5	
Horrocks Fold	341 G4	
Horrocksford	139 K7	
Horton	118 B2	
Horwich	338 D7	
Hoscar	331 K7	
Houghwood	370 D5	
Howgill	143 F2	
Howick Cross	238 B7	
Hud Hey	272 B6	
Hugh Mill	297 F3	
Huncoat	249 F1	
Hundred End	280 D2	
Hunger Hill	334 D8	
Hurlston Green	329 F8	
Hurst Green	191 H2	
Hurstwood	227 G7	
Huttock Top	298 B2	
Hutton	260 D1	
Hutton Roof	19 K2	
Ince Blundell	356 E8	
Inglewhite	157 K7	
Ingol	212 C7	
Inskip	182 D3	
Inskip Moss Side	154 A8	
Intack	246 A6	
Ireby	23 G8	
Irwell Vale	295 H6	
Jack Green	264 D3	
Johnson Fold	340 B8	
Johnson's Hillock	287 H5	
Kelbrook	146 A6	
Kellamergh	234 B4	
Kingsfold	262 A2	
Kings Moss	370 B4	
Kirkby Lonsdale	21 F1	
Kirkham	208 E5	
Knott End-on-Sea	97 K5	
Knotts	91 J3	
Knowle Green	189 H3	
Knuzden Brook	246 D7	
Lady Green	356 E7	
Lamberhead Green	365 J6	
Lammack	244 D3	
Lancaster	2 B4	
Lane Bottom	198 E7	
Lane End	118 E7	
Lane Ends	113 K2	
Lane Ends	223 J8	
Lane Heads	153 H8	
Laneshaw Bridge	172 E4	
Lane Side	295 G1	
Langho	220 A3	
Larbreck	152 A5	
Larches	238 B2	
Laund	275 G7	
Layton	5 E1	
Lea	237 K2	
Lea Town	211 G8	
Leck	22 D5	
Leemings	138 D4	
Lees	136 C5	
Lewth	183 G5	
Leyland	285 H4	
Lightfoot Green	212 C2	
Limbrick	312 A6	
Little Altcar	356 A2	
Little Bispham	148 B3	
Little Carleton	177 F2	
Little Eccleston	152 E5	
Little Harwood	9 E2	
Little Hoole Moss Houses	260 C8	
Little Layton	177 F3	
Little Marsden	198 C4	
Little Marton	205 K2	
Little Moor	165 K5	
Little Moor End	270 D1	
Little Plumpton	207 G6	
Little Poulton	150 C8	
Little Singleton	151 G8	
Little Thornton	150 A4	
Little Town	190 C8	
Lomeshaye	197 K3	
Longridge	188 A4	
Longshaw	371 G2	
Longton	260 B3	
Lostock Hall	262 D4	
Love Clough	250 B8	
Low Biggins	21 G2	
Lower Ballam	232 D1	
Lower Bartle	211 K4	
Lower Copthurst	287 J3	
Lower Darwen	268 D4	
Lowerford	169 K7	
Lower Heysham	52 A4	
Lower Hodder Bridge	164 A8	
Lowerhouse	224 B5	
Lower Penwortham	6 C5	
Lower Salter	48 A7	
Lower Thurnham	79 H1	
Lowgill	50 A5	
Low Moor	165 G3	
Lucas Green	287 F5	
Lumb	274 C3	
Lumb	295 H7	
Lydgate	277 K4	
Lydiate	358 C6	
Lytham	233 F7	
Lytham St Anne's	231 G8	
Marsden Height	198 C6	
Marsh Houses	79 G7	
Marshside	278 A8	
Masongill	23 J8	
Matshead	156 C5	
Mawdesley	332 E1	
Medlar	180 D7	
Melling	29 K8	
Melling Mount	366 B4	
Mellor	218 A8	
Mellor Brook	217 J8	
Mere Brow	304 C1	
Mereclough	253 F2	
Mereside	205 J2	
Mere Side	305 F6	
Middleforth Green	6 B6	
Middle Salter	48 A8	
Middleton	65 F1	
Midge Hall	261 H8	
Milgate	299 G7	
Millhead	25 K7	
Mill Hill	267 H2	
Milnshaw	248 A4	
Montcliffe	339 H6	
Moor End	124 E5	
Moor Side	184 A7	
Moor Side	209 H2	
Morecambe	40 E6	
Moss Edge	126 D8	
Moss Side	233 G2	
Moss Side	284 D2	
Moss Side	359 J8	
Mossy Lea	334 D5	
Mowbreck	209 F4	
Much Hoole	259 J8	
Much Hoole Moss Houses	283 F1	
Much Hoole Town	282 E2	
Myerscough Smithy	216 E8	
Mythop	206 C1	
Nab's Head	242 E4	
Nangreaves	320 A8	
Nappa	95 F4	
Nateby	128 D5	
Nelson	198 D4	
Nether Burrow	21 H8	
Nether Kellet	34 B6	
Nethertown	192 E5	
Newbridge	198 A1	
Newburgh	351 F1	
Newby	142 C2	
Newchurch	297 G1	
Newchurch in Pendle	168 D8	
Newgate	364 C4	
New Hall Hey	296 A2	
New Houses	371 K2	
New Lane	330 B4	
New Longton	261 H3	
New Row	189 K2	
Newsham	184 C6	
Newsholme	94 D7	
Newton	29 J1	
Newton	111 J3	
Newton	177 J5	
Newton Fells	112 D7	
Newton with Scales	235 J1	
New Town	188 A6	
Newtown	308 C1	
Nog Tow	212 B4	
Norbreck	148 B4	
Norcross	149 G4	
Normoss	177 J4	

North Shore 176 C3	Salesbury 219 F5	Torrisholme 2
Northwood 367 F8	Saltcotes 232 E6	Tottleworth 2
Nun Hills 298 A4	Salterforth 145 J3	Tower Hill 3
Nuttall 319 H7	Salwick 210 E8	Town Green 3
Oakenclough 105 H7	Samlesbury 241 J1	Townsend Fold 2
Oakenshaw 221 H8	Samlesbury Bottoms 242 C5	Trawden 2
Old Langho 192 A7	Sandylands 40 E7	Treales 2
Ollerton Fold 265 J7	Sawley 140 E2	Trough Gate 2
Ormskirk 349 F7	Scaitcliffe 247 K6	Trunnah 1
Orrell 365 J4	Scale Hall 2 A1	Tunstall
Orrell Post 365 G4	Scarisbrick 328 C4	Turn 3
Ortner 82 B2	Scarth Hill 361 G1	Turner Green 2
Osbaldeston 217 K7	Scorton 104 A4	Turton Bottoms 3
Osbaldeston Green 217 K5	Scotforth 55 G7	Twiston 1
Oswaldtwistle 246 E8	Scronkey 100 B8	Up Holland 3
Out Rawcliffe 152 A2	Seed Lee 264 B4	Upper Thurnham
Over Burrow 21 J6	Shadsworth 246 A8	Vale 2
Over Kellet 34 E3	Sharneyford 276 B6	Waddington 2
Overton 65 H3	Sharoe Green 213 G4	Wade Hall 2
Overtown 22 B6	Sharples 341 H7	Walker Fold 1
Over Town 253 F3	Shawforth 299 H6	Walk Mill 2
Padiham 223 K3	Shaw Green 309 F1	Wallbank 3
Parbold 333 F8	Sherfin 272 C4	Wallsuches 3
Park Close 145 C5	Shevington 353 J6	Walmer Bridge 2
Park Hill 368 D7	Shevington Moor 353 J1	Walton-le-Dale 2
Paythorne 94 B7	Shevington Vale 353 H3	Walton Summit 2
Peel 206 B7	Shirdley Hill 327 H5	Warbreck 1
Peel Hill 206 A4	Shore 277 H1	Ward Green Cross 1
Pendleton 166 B7	Shuttleworth 320 A4	Warton 2
Pennylands 362 C3	Silverdale 15 H8	Warton 2
Penwortham Lane 262 C1	Silverdale Green 15 J8	Warton Bank 2
Pickup Bank 292 E1	Simm's Lane End 371 J6	Water 2
Pike Hill 226 C5	Simonstone 222 E2	Waterfoot 2
Pilling 100 A5	Singleton 179 F2	Waterloo 2
Pimlico 165 K1	Skelmersdale 363 G1	Waterside 2
Pincock 310 A3	Skerton 2 C1	Waterslack 2
Pinfold 328 D7	Skippool 149 K6	Weeton 2
Pippin Street 264 D5	Skitham 127 F7	Weir 2
Pleasington 266 D2	Slack Head 16 D1	Weld Bank 3
Pleckgate 245 F2	Slaidburn 89 H5	Well Bank 2
Pool Hey 302 D8	Slyne 43 F4	Wennington 2
Portsmouth 277 F2	Smallwood Hey 99 K6	Wesham 2
Potters Brook 80 C6	Smith Green 67 J8	West Bradford 2
Poulton-le-Fylde 178 A1	Snape Green 328 C2	Westby 2
Preesall 98 D6	Sollom 306 B1	West End 2
Preesall Park 124 E2	Southport 301 F3	West End 2
Preston 7 D4	South Shore 204 C3	Westhead 2
Priest Hutton 27 C3	Sower Carr 125 F7	West Marton 3
Primrose Hill 347 H3	Spring Green 147 C8	Whalley 2
Pudding Pie Nook 185 J8	Spring Hill 247 K6	Whalleys 3
Pudsey 277 G1	Squires Gate 204 C6	Wharles 2
Queen's Park 9 F5	Stacksteads 297 J3	Wheatley Lane 2
Queenstown 176 D4	Staining 178 A6	Wheelton 2
Quernmore 56 D8	Stake Pool 100 C7	Whin Lane End 2
Rainford 369 G4	Stalmine 125 F4	Whinny Heights 2
Rainford Junction 369 F1	Stalmine Moss Side 125 G4	Whitebirk 2
Rain Shore 322 A7	Stanah 150 A1	Whitechapel 2
Rake Head 297 G3	Stanhill 246 E7	White Coppice 3
Ramsbottom 319 F5	Stanley 350 E8	Whitehall 2
Ratten Row 153 F3	Stanley Gate 361 J4	Whiteholme 1
Rawtenstall 273 H8	St Annes 230 E3	White Lund 2
Raygill 147 H3	Staynall 124 C7	White Stake 2
Read 222 D1	St Michael's on Wyre 154 C4	Whitewell 2
Red Bridge 16 A7	Stock 118 C4	Whitewell Bottom 2
Red Lumb 321 K7	Stodday 66 C1	Whittington 2
Red Scar 215 F5	Stone Head 147 K8	Whittle-le-Woods 2
Reedley 197 K7	Stoneyholme 10 B1	Whittlestone Head 2
Reeds Holme 273 H5	Stopper Lane 142 C3	Whitworth 2
Revidge 8 A2	Street 81 K6	Wilderswood 3
Ribbleton 240 A1	Stubbins 156 A1	Willacy Lane End 2
Ribby 208 B7	Stubbins 319 J3	Wilpshire 2
Ribchester 189 J8	Stydd 189 K7	Winewall 2
Ridge 3 F2	Sunderland 65 F6	Winmarleigh 2
Riley Green 265 K3	Sunny Bower 246 A2	Wiswell 2
Rimington 142 B3	Sunnyhurst 291 G1	Withnell 2
Ring o' Bells 350 B1	Swillbrook 211 H1	Withnell Fold 2
Rishton 246 D2	Swinden 95 G1	Wolstenholme 3
Rising Bridge 272 A3	Syke 323 K7	Woodhey 3
Riversway Docklands 238 C3	Sykes 86 B7	Wood House 2
Rivington 338 B1	Tanhouse 363 J3	Woodnook 2
Roach Bridge 241 K5	Tanterton 212 D6	Woodplumpton 2
Robin Hood 333 K7	Tardy Gate 262 D3	Woodsfold 3
Roby Mill 352 D8	Tarleton 281 K5	Woodvale 2
Rockcliffe 298 D2	Tarleton Moss 281 C5	Worsthorne 2
Roe Lee 245 G2	Tarlscough 330 D2	Worston 2
Roseacre 181 H5	Tarnbrook 71 H7	Wray 2
Rose Grove 224 D6	Tatham 38 A3	Wrayton 2
Rose Hill 10 C5	Tewitfield 26 C3	Wrea Green 2
Rosehill 292 A3	Thistleton 180 A3	Wrightington Bar 2
Roughlee 169 J6	Thornton 150 A2	Wycoller 2
The Row 15 J7	Thornton-in-Craven 120 A5	Wymott 2
Royal Oak 360 D7	Thorpe Green 264 D7	Yealand Conyers
Rufford 306 C8	Tockholes 267 H8	Yealand Redmayne
Runshaw Moor 285 H7	Tontine 365 F5	Yealand Storrs
Sabden 195 F4	Top o'th' Lane 264 D8	York

SING THE STREET INDEX

et names are listed alphabetically. Each street name is followed by its postal town or area locality, the Postcode District,
page number, and the reference to the square in which the name is found.

ndard index entries are shown as follows:

org Pl *LANC* LA1 ....**3** D4

et names and selected addresses not shown on the map due to scale restrictions are shown in the index with an
erisk or with the name of an adjoining road in brackets:

esfield *COL** BB8 ....**172** A6

dale Ct
.*F/KEOS* (off Chester Av) FY6 ....**149** J7

ENERAL ABBREVIATIONS

...........................ACCESS	GA ....GATE	PL ....PLACE
...............................ALLEY	GAL ....GALLERY	PLN ....PLAIN
........................APPROACH	GDN ....GARDEN	PLNS ....PLAINS
...........................ARCADE	GDNS ....GARDENS	PLZ ....PLAZA
.....................ASSOCIATION	GLD ....GLADE	POL ....POLICE STATION
..........................AVENUE	GLN ....GLEN	PR ....PRINCE
............................BEACH	GN ....GREEN	PREC ....PRECINCT
.......................BUILDINGS	GND ....GROUND	PREP ....PREPARATORY
.............................BEND	GRA ....GRANGE	PRIM ....PRIMARY
.............................BANK	GRG ....GARAGE	PROM ....PROMENADE
...........................BRIDGE	GT ....GREAT	PRS ....PRINCESS
...........................BROOK	GTWY ....GATEWAY	PRT ....PORT
.........................BOTTOM	GV ....GROVE	PT ....POINT
.......................BUSINESS	HGR ....HIGHER	PTH ....PATH
......................BOULEVARD	HL ....HILL	PZ ....PIAZZA
..........................BYPASS	HLS ....HILLS	QD ....QUADRANT
.......................CATHEDRAL	HO ....HOUSE	QU ....QUEEN
.......................CEMETERY	HOL ....HOLLOW	QY ....QUAY
...........................CENTRE	HOSP ....HOSPITAL	R ....RIVER
............................CROFT	HRB ....HARBOUR	RBT ....ROUNDABOUT
..........................CHURCH	HTH ....HEATH	RD ....ROAD
............................CHASE	HTS ....HEIGHTS	RDG ....RIDGE
...................CHURCHYARD	HVN ....HAVEN	REP ....REPUBLIC
...........................CIRCLE	HWY ....HIGHWAY	RES ....RESERVOIR
..........................CIRCUS	IMP ....IMPERIAL	RFC ....RUGBY FOOTBALL CLUB
.............................CLOSE	IN ....INLET	RI ....RISE
...........................CLIFFS	IND EST ....INDUSTRIAL ESTATE	RP ....RAMP
.............................CAMP	INF ....INFIRMARY	RW ....ROW
..........................CORNER	INFO ....INFORMATION	S ....SOUTH
..........................COUNTY	INT ....INTERCHANGE	SCH ....SCHOOL
..........................COLLEGE	IS ....ISLAND	SE ....SOUTH EAST
..........................COMMON	JCT ....JUNCTION	SER ....SERVICE AREA
M ....COMMISSION	JTY ....JETTY	SH ....SHORE
........................CONVENT	KG ....KING	SHOP ....SHOPPING
.........................COTTAGE	KNL ....KNOLL	SKWY ....SKYWAY
........................COTTAGES	L ....LAKE	SMT ....SUMMIT
.............................CAPE	LA ....LANE	SOC ....SOCIETY
............................COPSE	LDG ....LODGE	SP ....SPUR
............................CREEK	LGT ....LIGHT	SPR ....SPRING
M ....CREMATORIUM	LK ....LOCK	SQ ....SQUARE
........................CRESCENT	LKS ....LAKES	ST ....STREET
Y ....CAUSEWAY	LNDG ....LANDING	STN ....STATION
............................COURT	LTL ....LITTLE	STR ....STREAM
..........................CENTRAL	LWR ....LOWER	STRD ....STRAND
...........................COURTS	MAG ....MAGISTRATE	SW ....SOUTH WEST
.......................COURTYARD	MAN ....MANSIONS	TDG ....TRADING
.........................CUTTINGS	MD ....MEAD	TER ....TERRACE
............................COVE	MDW ....MEADOWS	THWY ....THROUGHWAY
...........................CANYON	MEM ....MEMORIAL	TNL ....TUNNEL
.......................DEPARTMENT	MKT ....MARKET	TOLL ....TOLLWAY
.............................DALE	MKTS ....MARKETS	TPK ....TURNPIKE
.............................DAM	ML ....MALL	TR ....TRACK
.............................DRIVE	ML ....MILL	TRL ....TRAIL
............................DROVE	MNR ....MANOR	TWR ....TOWER
........................DRIVEWAY	MS ....MEWS	U/P ....UNDERPASS
S ....DWELLINGS	MSN ....MISSION	UNI ....UNIVERSITY
..............................EAST	MT ....MOUNT	UPR ....UPPER
.....................EMBANKMENT	MTN ....MOUNTAIN	V ....VALE
..........................EMBASSY	MTS ....MOUNTAINS	VA ....VALLEY
........................ESPLANADE	MUS ....MUSEUM	VIAD ....VIADUCT
...........................ESTATE	MWY ....MOTORWAY	VIL ....VILLA
........................EXCHANGE	N ....NORTH	VIS ....VISTA
.......................EXPRESSWAY	NE ....NORTH EAST	VLG ....VILLAGE
........................EXTENSION	NW ....NORTH WEST	VLS ....VILLAS
..........................FLYOVER	O/P ....OVERPASS	VW ....VIEW
....................FOOTBALL CLUB	OFF ....OFFICE	W ....WEST
.............................FORK	ORCH ....ORCHARD	WD ....WOOD
............................FIELD	OV ....OVAL	WHF ....WHARF
...........................FIELDS	PAL ....PALACE	WK ....WALK
.............................FALLS	PAS ....PASSAGE	WKS ....WALKS
.............................FLATS	PAV ....PAVILION	WLS ....WELLS
.............................FARM	PDE ....PARADE	WY ....WAY
.............................FORT	PH ....PUBLIC HOUSE	YD ....YARD
.........................FREEWAY	PK ....PARK	YHA ....YOUTH HOSTEL
.............................FERRY	PKWY ....PARKWAY	

POSTCODE TOWNS AND AREA ABBREVIATIONS

ACC .... Accrington
AIMK .... Ashton-in-Makerfield
AIRE .... Airedale
BBN .... Blackburn
BBNW .... Blackburn west
BCUP .... Bacup
BISP .... Bispham
BLY .... Burnley
BOL .... Bolton
BPOOL .... Blackpool
BPOOLE .... Blackpool east
BPOOLS .... Blackpool south
BRFD/BLYE .... Brierfield/Burnley east
BRSC .... Burscough
BURY .... Bury
BWCK/EAR .... Barnoldswick/Earby
CARN .... Carnforth
CHLY/EC .... Chorley/Eccleston
CHLYE .... Chorley east/Adlington/
                                    Whittle-le-Woods
CHTN/BK .... Churchtown/Banks
CLI .... Clitheroe
CLV/TH .... Cleveleys/Thornton
COL .... Colne

DWN .... Darwen
EDGW/EG .... Edgeworth/Egerton
FMBY .... Formby
FTWD .... Fleetwood
FUL/RIB .... Fulwood/Ribbleton
GAR/LONG .... Garstang/Longridge
GOS .... Grange-over-Sands
GTH/LHO .... Great Harwood/Langho
HBR .... Hebden Bridge
HEY .... Heysham
HGHB .... High Bentham
HOR/BR .... Horwich/Blackrod
HTWN .... Hightown
HWTH .... Haworth
KIRK/FR/WAR .... Kirkham/Freckleton/
                                          Warton
KKBY .... Kirkby
KKBYL .... Kirkby Lonsdale
LANC .... Lancaster
LEY/BBR .... Leyland/Bamber Bridge
LSTA .... Lytham St Anne's
MCMB .... Morecambe
MGHL .... Maghull
MTHPE .... Milnthorpe

NLSN .... Ne[...]
NWD/KWIPK .... Northw[...]
                                Knowsley Industrial
ORM .... Orm[...]
PDHM/BLYW .... Padiham/Burnley
PLF/KEOS .... Poulton-le-F[...]
                                      Knott End-o[...]
PRES .... Pre[...]
RAMS .... Ramsbo[...]
RAW/HAS .... Rawtenstall/Hasling[...]
RNFD/HAY .... Rainford/Haye[...]
ROCH .... Roch[...]
SFTN .... Se[...]
SKEL .... Skelmers[...]
SKP/WHF .... Skipton/Wharfe[...]
STHP .... South[...]
TOD .... Todmo[...]
TOT/BURYW .... Tottington/Bury [...]
WGN .... W[...]
WGNNW/ST .... Wigan northwest/Stan[...]
WGNS/IIMK .... Wigan so[...]
                                      Ince-in-Maker[...]
WGNW/BIL/O .... Wigan west/Billinge/C[...]
WHIT .... Whitw[...]

Aal - Air

Index - streets

A

Aalborg Pl *LANC* LA1 .... 3 D4
Aalborg Sq *LANC* LA1 .... 3 D4
Abberley Wy *WGNS/IIMK* WN3 .... 365 K7
Abbey Cl *FMBY* L37 .... 356 B1
    SKEL WN8 .... 364 E4
Abbey Crs *DWN* BB3 .... 292 A3
Abbey Dl *BRSC* L40 .... 331 F8
Abbeydale *HEY* LA3 .... 53 H1
Abbey Dr *WGNNW/ST* WN6 .... 353 F4
Abbey Fld *WGNW/BIL/O* WN5 .... 365 G5
Abbeyfield Cl *LANC* LA1 .... 55 G8
Abbey Flds *CLI* BB7 .... 193 F6
Abbey Fold *BRSC* L40 .... 330 D6
Abbey Gdns *STHP* PR8 .... 301 J1
Abbey Gv *CHLYE* PR6 .... 337 G4
Abbey La *BRSC* L40 .... 349 G3
Abbey Rd *BPOOLS* FY4 .... 204 C6
    CLI BB7 .... 193 G6
Abbeystead *SKEL* WN8 .... 363 J4
Abbeystead Dr *LANC* LA1 .... 55 G8
Abbeystead La *HGHB* LA2 .... 69 K6
Abbeystead Rd *HGHB* LA2 .... 81 K3
Abbey St *ACC* BB5 .... 248 C6
    FUL/RIB PR2 .... 6 B2
Abbeyville *BPOOLS* FY4 .... 204 C5
Abbey Wk *PRES* PR1 .... 262 A1
Abbeywood *SKEL* WN8 .... 363 J4
Abbot Brow *BBN* BB2 .... 217 K7
Abbots Cl *FMBY* L37 .... 356 A2
    KIRK/FR/WA PR4 .... 209 G7
    RAW/HAS BB4 .... 273 K1
Abbots Cft *HOR/BR* BL6 .... 338 D7
Abbotsford *ORM* L39 .... 348 E6
Abbotsford Av *BBN* BB2 .... 268 A2
Abbotsford Rd *BPOOLE* FY3 .... 5 F4
Abbotsgate *KKBYL* LA6 .... 21 G1
    LANC LA1 .... 2 A3
Abbotsway *PRES* PR1 .... 6 A5
Abbott Brow *BBN* BB2 .... 217 K7
Abbott Clough Av *BBN* BB1 .... 246 C6
Abbott Clough Cl *BBN* BB1 .... 246 C7
Abbott Cft *KIRK/FR/WA* PR4 .... 212 C4
Abbott St *HOR/BR* BL6 .... 338 D7
Abbotts Wy *FTWD* FY7 .... 97 G5
Abbotts Wy *WGNW/BIL/O* WN5 ...... 371 F8
Abbot Wk *CLI* BB7 .... 166 A3
Abel St *BRFD/BLYE* BB10 .... 11 D1
Abercorn Pl *BPOOLS* FY4 .... 204 B6
Abercorn Rd *BOL* BL1 .... 341 F8
Abercrombie Rd *FTWD* FY7 .... 97 F6
Aberdare Cl *BBN* BB1 .... 8 C2
Aberdeen Dr *BBN* BB1 .... 9 E5
Aberdeen Gdns *WHIT* OL12 .... 323 H7
Aberdeen Rd *LANC* LA1 .... 3 E4
Abingdon Dr *FUL/RIB* PR2 .... 238 C2
Abingdon Gv *HEY* LA3 .... 52 E4
Abingdon Rd *PDHM/BLYW* BB12 ... 223 H4
Abingdon St *BPOOL* FY1 .... 4 B1

Abinger St *BRFD/BLYE* BB10 .... 226 A2
Abington Dr *CHTN/BK* PR9 .... 279 J6
Abner Rw *COL* BB8 .... 171 K2
Abraham Altham Ct
    BRFD/BLYE (off Duke St) BB10 .... 197 K6
Abraham St *ACC* BB5 .... 248 B6
    BBN BB2 .... 268 B1
    HOR/BR BL6 .... 338 D7
Abrams Fold *CHTN/BK* PR9 .... 279 H6
Abrams Gn *CHTN/BK* PR9 .... 279 H6
Acacia Rd *FUL/RIB* PR2 .... 240 C1
Acacia Wk *BBN* BB1 .... 9 F4
Accrington Rd *BBN* BB1 .... 246 C6
    BLY BB11 .... 10 A4
    CLI BB7 .... 193 J7
Acer Gv *FUL/RIB* PR2 .... 214 D8
Ackhurst La *WGNW/BIL/O* WN5 ...... 353 J8
Ackhurst Rd *CHLY/EC* PR7 .... 310 D3
Ackroyd St *TOD* OL14 .... 277 C2
Acorn Av *ACC* BB5 .... 247 K8
Acorn Cl *LEY/BBR* PR5 .... 285 J5
Acorn Ms *BPOOLS* FY4 .... 205 K2
Acorn St *BBN* BB1 .... 9 F5
    BCUP OL13 .... 298 C1
Acre Av *BCUP* OL13 .... 298 B3
Acre Cl *RAMS* BL0 .... 295 K8
Acrefield *BBNW* BB2 .... 244 C4
    LEY/BBR PR5 .... 264 B7
    PDHM/BLYW BB12 .... 223 J2
    SKEL WN8 .... 351 C2
Acre Ga *BPOOLS* FY4 .... 204 E4
Acregate *SKEL* WN8 .... 363 J5
Acregate La *PRES* PR1 .... 240 B2
Acre Gv *KIRK/FR/WA* PR4 .... 260 A8
Acre Mill Rd *BCUP* OL13 .... 298 B4
Acre Moss La *MCMB* LA4 .... 41 C8
Acresbrook Rd
    PDHM/BLYW BB12 .... 196 B6
Acresfield *CHLY/EC* PR7 .... 337 F5
    COL BB8 .... 172 A6
Acresfield Cl *HOR/BR* * BL6 .... 337 J8
Acres La *FMBY* L37 .... 356 E4
    ORM L39 .... 358 A2
    PLF/KEOS FY6 .... 98 C3
Acre St *BRFD/BLYE* BB10 .... 225 K2
    WHIT OL12 .... 323 H2
Acreswood Cl *CHLY/EC* PR7 .... 335 J3
Acre Vw *BCUP* OL13 .... 298 B3
Active Wy *BLY* BB11 .... 10 C3
Acton Rd *BPOOLS* FY4 .... 5 E6
Adamson St *PDHM/BLYW* BB12 ...... 223 J2
    PDHM/BLYW BB12 .... 224 E5
Ada St *BBNW* BB2 .... 8 A4
    BRFD/BLYE BB10 .... 225 K2
    NLSN BB9 .... 198 C5
    RAMS BL0 .... 319 G6
Addington Rd *HGHB* LA2 .... 35 F6
Addington St *BBN* BB1 .... 9 E5
Addison Cl *BBNW* BB2 .... 8 A4
Addison Crs *BPOOLE* FY3 .... 5 D1
Addison Rd *FTWD* FY7 .... 97 G8
Addison St *ACC* BB5 .... 248 C6
    BBNW BB2 .... 8 A4

Addle St *LANC* LA1 .... 5[...]
Adelaide Av *CLV/TH* FY5 .... 14[...]
Adelaide St *ACC* BB5 .... 24[...]
    ACC BB5 .... 24[...]
    BLY * BB11 .... 22[...]
    BPOOL FY1 .... [...]
    FTWD FY7 .... 9[...]
    PRES PR1 .... [...]
    RAMS BL0 .... 31[...]
    RAW/HAS BB4 .... 27[...]
Adelaide St West *BPOOL* FY1 .... [...]
Adelaide Ter *BBNW* BB2 .... [...]
Adelphi Pl *PRES* PR1 .... [...]
Adelphi St *BLY* BB11 .... 1[...]
    BPOOL FY1 .... [...]
    LANC LA1 .... [...]
    PRES PR1 .... [...]
Adlington Av *PLF/KEOS* FY6 .... 14[...]
Adlington St *BLY* BB11 .... 1[...]
Admiral Cl *LSTA* FY8 .... 23[...]
Admiral St *BRFD/BLYE* BB10 .... 1[...]
Admiralty Cl *BRSC* * L40 .... 34[...]
Admiral Wy *FUL/RIB* PR2 .... 23[...]
Adstone Av *BPOOLE* FY3 .... 17[...]
Agate St *BBN* BB1 .... 24[...]
Agglebys Rd *PLF/KEOS* FY6 .... 12[...]
Agnes Ing La *HGHB* LA2 .... [...]
Agnes St *BBNW* * BB2 .... [...]
    PRES PR1 .... [...]
Agnew Rd *FTWD* FY7 .... 9[...]
Agnew St *LSTA* FY8 .... 23[...]
Aiken Ct *KIRK/FR/WA* PR4 .... 20[...]
Aikengill Rd *HGHB* LA2 .... [...]
Ailsa Av *BPOOLE* FY3 .... [...]
Ailsa Cl *GAR/LONG* PR3 .... 18[...]
Ailsa Rd *BBN* BB1 .... 24[...]
Ailsa Wk *HEY* LA3 .... [...]
Ainsdale Av *BISP* FY2 .... 14[...]
    BRFD/BLYE BB10 .... 19[...]
    CLV/TH FY5 .... 14[...]
    EDGW/EG BL7 .... 1[...]
    FTWD FY7 .... 12[...]
Ainsdale Cl *LANC* LA1 .... [...]
Ainsdale Dr *DWN* BB3 .... 29[...]
    FUL/RIB PR2 .... 23[...]
    WHIT OL12 .... 32[...]
Ainse Rd *HOR/BR* BL6 .... 33[...]
Ainslie Cl *GTH/LHO* * BB6 .... 22[...]
Ainslie Rd *FUL/RIB* PR2 .... 21[...]
Ainslie St *PDHM/BLYW* * BB12 .... 22[...]
Ainspool La *GAR/LONG* PR3 .... 12[...]
Ainsworth Ml *BBN* BB1 .... [...]
Ainsworth St *BBN* BB1 .... [...]
Aintree Crs *STHP* PR8 .... 30[...]
Aintree Dr *DWN* BB3 .... 29[...]
Aintree Rd *BPOOLS* FY4 .... 20[...]
    CLV/TH FY5 .... 1[...]
Airdrie Crs *BLY* BB11 .... 1[...]
Airdrie Pl *BISP* FY2 .... 14[...]
Aire Cl *LANC* LA1 .... [...]
Airedale *HGHB* LA2 .... 6[...]
Airedale Av *BPOOLE* FY3 .... [...]

dale Ct
...F/LHO BB5 (off Chester Av) FY6 ......149 J7
y St ACC BB5......248 D8
on Garth NLSN BB9......170 A8
en Cl RAMS BL0......319 H6
en St ACC BB5......248 C4
IW/HAS BB4......295 J6
St ACC BB5 * BL0......319 H6
nein Rd CARN LA5......34 A2
ce Br CHLYE PR6......313 F7
dale Cl LEY/BBR PR5......285 K4
Gv HEY LA3......52 D5
Ramsbottom Wy
TH/LHO BB6......221 H7
st BOL BL1......341 H8
ka St BBNW BB2......268 B1
ny Av BPOOLE FY4......204 C6
ny Cl PLF/KEOS FY6......178 A3
ny Dr BBN BB1......218 E3
Y/BBR PR5......263 C1
ny Rd BBNW BB2......244 D5
WD FY7......97 F2
TA FY8......231 J6
CMB LA4......41 F7
RES PR1......239 K1
marie St CLI BB7......165 H3
rta Cl BBNW BB2......244 D3
rt Pl DWN BB3......268 C4
HP PR8......301 H3
ert Rd BPOOL FY1......4 B3
RSC L40......306 A8
TN/BK PR9......301 J2
MBY L37......355 F3
JL/RIB PR2......213 H7
NC LA1......3 D2
Y/BBR PR5......286 E1
TA FY8......231 J6
CMB LA4......41 F7
RES PR1......239 H1
IW/HAS BB4......273 H3
st ACC BB5......247 J5
CC BB5......247 K1
CC BB5......247 K1
CC BB5......248 C6
BN BB1......247 F2
BNW BB2......267 K1
LY BB11......11 E3
WCK/EAR BB18......146 B1
ARN LA5......25 K8
HLY/EC PR7......311 H4
HLYE PR6......288 A4
WN BB3......291 K6
GW/EG BL7......316 D8
TWD FY7......97 H7
TH/LHO BB6......221 H7
OR/BR BL6......338 D7
RK/FR/WA PR4......208 D5
TA FY8......232 E4
LSN BB9......197 K6
LSN BB9......198 B3
HM/BLYW BB12......223 J3
AMS BL0......319 H5
IW/HAS BB4......274 A5
HIT OL12......323 C3
ert Ter BCUP OL13......275 J8
RES PR1......7 E1
HP PR8......301 G6
on Av BPOOLE FY3......5 F1
on Ct BLY BB11......10 B5
LI* BB7......165 K2
on Ms LANC LA1......3 E2
on Rd BBNW BB2......268 A2
WCK/EAR BB18......146 B1
on St ACC * BB5......248 B5
BNW BB2......267 K2
CUP OL13......275 K8
LY BB11......10 B4
WCK/EAR BB18......146 B1
HLY/EC PR7......311 G4
J BB7......165 K3
NC LA1......3 E2
LSN BB9......197 J6
LSN BB9......198 B3
HM/BLYW BB12......223 K4
on Ter BLY BB11......10 B4
righton Pl LEY/BBR PR5......262 E4
righton Crs LEY/BBR PR5......262 E4
righton St East LEY/BBR PR5......262 E4
m Bank Rd PRES * PR1......7 F3
m St East PRES PR1......7 F3
ester Av PRES PR1......6 A5
onbury Crs CLV/TH FY5......148 C1
te Gv FUL/RIB PR2......238 C1
cliffe Ct MCMB LA4......41 H8
cliffe Ms LANC LA1......2 B6

Aldcliffe Rd FUL/RIB PR2......238 A2
LANC LA1......2 B6
Alden Cl RAW/HAS BB4......295 G5
Alden Ri RAW/HAS BB4......295 G5
Alden Rd TOT/BURYW BL8......295 F7
Alder Ter
LANC (off Clarendon Rd) LA1......43 F8
Alder Av RAW/HAS BB4......296 D1
WGNW/BIL/O* WN5......371 F6
Alder Bank BBNW BB2......244 D7
RAW/HAS BB4......273 J8
Alderbank HOR/BR BL6......338 B8
Alderbrook Dr SKEL WN8......351 J4
Alder Cl CLV/TH FY5......149 J2
KIRK/FR/WA PR4......236 A1
LEY/BBR PR5......284 D4
Alder Coppice FUL/RIB PR2......212 A8
Alder Ct FTWD FY7......122 C1
LANC (off Alder Gv) LA1......2 B3
Alder Crs LEY/BBR PR5......264 C2
Alderdale Av STHP PR8......325 G6
Alder Dr CHLY/EC PR7......310 B8
LEY/BBR PR5......264 C2
Alderfield PRES PR1......239 F8
Alderford Cl CLI BB7......165 G4
Alder Gv ACC BB5......248 E1
BPOOLE FY3......176 E4
CHLY/EC PR7......335 K2
LANC LA1......2 B3
LSTA FY8......232 C8
PLF/KEOS FY6......177 K1
Alder Hill St BWCK/EAR BB18......146 B1
Alder La GAR/LONG PR3......152 E2
ORM L39......344 B3
RNFD/HAY WA11......370 B6
SKEL WN8......351 J4
Alderley SKEL WN8......363 J5
Alderley Av BOL BL1......341 J8
BPOOLE FY4......204 B6
Alderley Hts LANC LA1......43 F8
Alderney Cl BBNW BB2......267 J2
Alder Rd FUL/RIB PR2......214 F3
Aldersleigh Crs LEY/BBR PR5......264 C2
Alderson Crs FMBY L37......343 H7
The Alders GAR/LONG PR3......129 J2
Alder St BBN BB1......9 C1
BCUP OL13......275 J8
PDHM/BLYW BB12......224 E5
RAW/HAS BB4......273 J8
Alderville Cl KIRK/FR/WA PR4......234 D5
Alderwood Gv RAMS BL0......295 K2
Aldfield Av FUL/RIB PR2......237 J2
Aldingham Ct MCMB LA4......41 H8
Aldingham Wk MCMB LA4......41 G6
Aldon Gv KIRK/FR/WA PR4......260 B2
Aldon Rd PLF/KEOS FY6......150 B5
Aldren's La LANC LA1......3 D1
Aldwych Av BPOOLE FY3......5 D4
Aldwych Dr FUL/RIB PR2......238 D1
LEY/BBR PR5......262 E4
Alert St FUL/RIB PR2......6 A1
Alexander Cl BRSC L40......331 F8
Alexander Dr MGHL L31......359 F8
Alexander Gv PDHM/BLYW BB12......224 D5
Alexander Pl FUL/RIB PR2......215 F7
Alexander St NLSN BB9......198 E1
Alexandra Ms LANC LA1......3 E2
Alexandra Pavilions
PRES (off Stanleyfield Cl) PR1......7 E1
Alexandra Rd BBNW BB2......8 A3
BPOOL FY1......4 B6
BRSC L40......330 D7
CARN LA5......33 K2
CHTN/BK PR9......301 J3
CLV/TH FY5......149 J3
DWN BB3......291 H1
FMBY L37......355 F5
GAR/LONG PR3......188 A4
HEY LA3......40 F7
KIRK/FR/WA PR4......208 E5
LANC LA1......43 F8
LEY/BBR PR5......240 A3
LSTA FY8......231 F4
Alexandra St ACC BB5......221 J7
PRES PR1......240 A4
Alexandria Dr LSTA FY8......231 F6
Alexandria St RAW/HAS BB4......273 G7
Alford Fold FUL/RIB PR2......213 F4
Alfred St BPOOL FY1......4 C2
DWN* BB3......291 K5
EDGW/EG BL7......316 D8
LANC LA1......3 E2
RAMS BL0......319 H6
RNFD/HAY WA11......369 F4
WHIT OL12......323 H1

Algar St NLSN BB9......198 D1
Alice Av LEY/BBR PR5......285 J2
Alice Sq PRES PR1......7 E1
Alice St ACC BB5......247 J8
ACC BB5......248 D4
BWCK/EAR BB18......145 F1
DWN BB3......291 J3
MCMB LA4......41 J6
Alisan Rd PLF/KEOS FY6......149 H6
Alker La CHLYE PR6......286 E8
Alker St CHLY/EC PR7......311 G4
Alkincoats Rd COL BB8......171 G5
Allandale BPOOLS FY4......204 C6
Allandale Av CLV/TH FY5......123 F7
Allan St BCUP OL13......298 D2
Allenbury Pl BPOOLE FY3......205 G1
Allenby Av FUL/RIB PR2......213 K7
Allenby Rd LSTA FY8......230 E4
Allen Cl CLV/TH FY5......148 D2
Allen Ct BRFD/BLYE BB10......11 D1
Allendale Gv BRFD/BLYE BB10......226 D7
Allendale St COL BB8......171 K6
PDHM/BLYW BB12......224 D5
Allengate FUL/RIB PR2......213 H7
Allen St BRFD/BLYE BB10......11 D1
Allen Wy FTWD FY7......122 C1
Allerton Cl DWN BB3......291 J1
Allerton Dr PDHM/BLYW BB12......10 A3
Allerton Rd CHTN/BK PR9......302 A2
LEY/BBR PR5......240 B8
Alleys Gn CLI BB7......165 J2
Alleytroyds ACC BB5......247 J6
All Hallows Rd BISP FY2......148 D6
Alliance St ACC BB5......271 C2
Allison Gv COL BB8......171 J5
Allonby Av CLV/TH FY5......122 E7
Allotment La GAR/LONG PR3......154 C4
All Saint's Cl ACC BB5......247 F7
PDHM/BLYW BB12......224 B4
RAW/HAS BB4......273 H2
All Saints Rd BISP FY2......148 D5
LSTA FY8......230 E5
Allsprings Cl GTH/LHO BB6......221 H5
Allsprings Dr GTH/LHO BB6......221 H4
Alma Av COL BB8......171 H2
Alma Cl SKEL WN8......363 J5
Alma Ct SKEL WN8......364 E4
Alma Dr CHLY/EC PR7......310 C7
Alma Hl SKEL WN8......364 E4
Alma Pl CLI BB7......165 H4
Alma Rd COL BB8......172 D5
LANC* LA1......3 D5
SKEL WN8......364 E4
STHP PR8......301 G7
Alma Rw LEY/BBR PR5......264 D2
Alma St ACC BB5......221 K8
BBNW BB2......8 B4
BCUP OL13......298 E1
PDHM/BLYW BB12......223 J3
PRES PR1......7 E1
Almond Av BRSC L40......330 E5
Almond Brook Rd
WGNNW/ST WN6......353 K1
Almond Cl BBNW * BB2......289 J1
FUL/RIB PR2......214 A5
PRES PR1......238 D8
Almond Crs RAW/HAS BB4......296 B2
Almond Gv BOL * BL1......341 K8
Almond St BOL BL1......341 K7
DWN BB3......291 J3
Annwick Cl PDHM/BLYW BB12......10 B2
Alpha St BWCK/EAR BB18......145 J3
DWN BB3......291 K3
NLSN BB9......198 D1
Alpic Dr CLV/TH FY5......148 C4
Alpine Av BPOOLS FY4......204 E6
LEY/BBR PR5......262 E4
Alpine Cl DWN BB3......292 C2
LEY/BBR PR5......262 E4
Alpine Gv BBNW BB2......267 J3
Alpine Rd CHLYE PR6......287 J8
Alpine Vw CARN LA5......33 G5
Alsop St PRES PR1......239 G1
Alston Av CLV/TH FY5......122 D7
Alston Cl CLI BB7......195 F4
Alston Dr MCMB LA4......42 B6
Alston La GAR/LONG PR3......188 A8
Alston Rd BISP FY2......176 E1
Alston St PRES PR1......240 B2
Altcar La FMBY L37......355 K2
LEY/BBR PR5......285 F2
MGHL L31......358 C7
ORM L39......358 B2
Altcar Rd FMBY L37......356 B1
Altham Br ACC BB5......222 E4
Altham La ACC BB5......222 E5
Altham Rd MCMB LA4......41 J7

STHP PR8 ....327 G1
Altham St BRFD/BLYE BB10 ....11 D1
 PDHM/BLYW BB12 ....223 K3
Altham Wk MCMB LA4 ....41 J8
Althorpe Cl BPOOL FY1 ....176 C6
Althorpe Dr STHP PR8 ....302 A8
Altom St BBN BB1 ....8 C3
Alt Rd FMBY L37 ....356 A2
 HTWN L38 ....355 K7
Altys La ORM L39 ....348 D8
Alum Scar La BBNW BB2 ....243 F5
Alvanley Cl NWD/KWIPK/BIL/O WN5 .365 K2
Alvern Av FUL/RIB PR2 ....213 F7
Alvern Crs FUL/RIB PR2 ....213 F7
Alvina La NWD/KWIPK L33 ....366 E6
Alwin St BLY * BB11 ....10 B4
Alwood Av BPOOLE FY3 ....5 F1
Amber Av BBN BB1 ....245 G1
Amberbanks Gv BPOOL FY1 ....4 B5
Amber Ga FUL/RIB PR2 ....212 B5
Ambergate SKEL WN8 ....363 H4
Amberley St BBNW BB2 ....267 K1
Amberwood KIRK/FR/WA PR4 ....208 D6
Ambleside Av BWCK/EAR BB18 ....118 E8
 CHLY/EC* PR7 ....310 B2
 PLF/KEOS FY6 ....98 B5
 RAW/HAS BB4 ....296 A1
Ambleside Cl ACC BB5 ....248 C3
 BBN BB1 ....9 E3
 LEY/BBR PR5 ....263 H1
Ambleside Dr DWN BB3 ....269 F8
Ambleside Rd BPOOLS FY4 ....205 K2
 FUL/RIB PR2 ....214 C6
 LANC LA1 ....3 F1
Ambleway LEY/BBR PR5.....................240 B7
Ambrose Hall La KIRK/FR/WA PR4....184 A8
Ambrose St LEY/BBR PR5 ....285 K1
Amelia St BBN BB1 ....9 F3
Amersham SKEL WN8 ....363 H4
Amersham Cl KIRK/FR/WA PR4 ....261 G3
Amethyst St BBN BB1 ....245 G1
Amounderness Ct
 KIRK/FR/WA
 (off Marsden St) PR4 ....209 J4
Amounderness Wy CLV/TH FY5......149 J4
 FTWD FY7 ....123 J5
Ampleforth Dr LEY/BBR PR5 ....262 D2
Amy Johnson Wy BPOOLS FY4 ....204 D4
Ancenis Ct KIRK/FR/WA PR4 ....209 F6
Anchorage Ms FTWD FY7 ....97 H8
Anchorage Rd FTWD FY7 ....97 H8
Anchor Av DWN BB3 ....268 C7
Anchor Ct PRES PR1 ....7 D3
Anchor Cl KIRK/FR/WA PR4 ....260 E1
Anchor Gv DWN BB3 ....268 C7
Anchor House
 BBN (off Merchants Landing) BB1.......9 D5
Anchor Rd DWN BB3 ....268 C7
Anchorsholme La CLV/TH FY5 ......149 F3
Anchorsholme La East
 CLV/TH FY5.....................................148 D2
Anchorsholme La West
 CLV/TH FY5.....................................148 C2
Anchor St CHTN/BK PR9 ....301 H4
Anchor Wy LSTA FY8 ....230 E2
Ancliffe La HGHB LA2 ....43 G3
Ancrum Rd NWD/KWIPK L33 ....366 B5
Andelen Cl BLY BB11 ....223 J8
Anders Dr NWD/KWIPK L33 ....366 B6
Anderson Cl LANC LA1 ....3 F5
Anderson Rd BBN BB1 ....219 J4
Anderson St BPOOL FY1 ....4 C3
Anderton Cl RAW/HAS BB4 ....297 H4
Anderton Ct
 HOR/BR (off Bolton Rd) BL6 ....338 C6
Anderton La CHLYE PR6 ....338 A6
Anderton Rd CHLY/EC PR7 ....310 B2
 PDHM/BLYW BB12 ....196 B6
Anderton St CHLY/EC PR7 ....311 G4
 CHLYE PR6 ....337 G4
Andertons Wy FUL/RIB PR2 ....214 A6
Anderton Wy GAR/LONG PR3 ....129 K5
Andreas Cl STHP PR8 ....301 H7
Andrew Av BBNW BB2 ....267 J3
Andrew La BOL BL1 ....341 K5
Andrew Rd NLSN BB9 ....199 J4
Andrews Cl LEY/BBR PR5 ....355 J2
Andrews La FMBY L37 ....355 J2
Andrew St PRES PR1 ....240 A2
Andrews Yort FMBY L37 ....355 J2
Anemone Dr RAW/HAS BB4 ....295 F3
Angela St BBNW BB2 ....267 J2
Angelo St BOL BL1 ....341 H8
Anger's Hill Rd BPOOLS FY4 ....5 E6
Anglesey St BBNW BB2 ....267 J3
Angle St BRFD/BLYE BB10 ....11 D1
Anglezarke Rd CHLYE PR6 ....337 G4
Anglian Cl ACC BB5 ....247 G6
Aniline Cl CHLYE PR6 ....311 J3
Annan Crs BPOOLS FY4 ....205 J2
Annandale Cl NWD/KWIPK L33..........366 B5
Annandale Gdns SKEL WN8 ....364 C4
Annarly Fold BRFD/BLYE BB10 ....226 E6
Annaside Cl BPOOLS FY4 ....204 E4
Anna Av STHP PR8 ....326 A5
Anna's Rd BPOOLS FY4 ....232 A1
Anne Cl BRFD/BLYE BB10 ....11 E4
Annesley Av BPOOLE FY3 ....176 E3
Anne St BRFD/BLYE BB10 ....11 E4
Annie St ACC BB5 ....248 C4
 RAMS BL0 ....319 G7
 RAW/HAS BB4 ....296 C1
Annis St PRES PR1 ....240 A3
Ann St ACC BB5 ....221 K8
 LANC LA1 ....3 D4
 NLSN BB9 ....170 B8
 NLSN BB9 ....197 K5
 SKEL WN8 ....362 E2
Ansbro Av KIRK/FR/WA PR4 ....235 C5
Ansdell Gv CHTN/BK PR9 ....278 C7
 FUL/RIB PR2 ....212 E8
Ansdell Rd BPOOL FY1 ....5 D5
 HOR/BR BL6 ....338 E7
Ansdell Rd North LSTA FY8 ....231 K7
Ansdell Rd South LSTA FY8 ....231 K8
Ansdell St PRES * PR1 ....240 A2
Ansdell Ter BBN BB2 ....268 B2
Anshaw Cl EDGW/EG BL7 ....314 E3
Anson Cl LSTA FY8 ....230 D2
Anson Rd LSTA FY8 ....230 D2
Anson St BOL BL1 ....341 K8
Anstable Rd MCMB LA4 ....41 J8
Anthony Rd LANC LA1 ....2 C4
Antrim Rd BISP FY2 ....176 C2
Anvil Cl WGNW/BIL/O WN5 ....365 F6
Anvil Rd BCUP OL13 ....298 C3
Anyon St DWN BB3 ....291 K1
Anyon Vls
 HOR/BR
 (off Catherine St East) BL6 ....338 D7
Anzio Rd KIRK/FR/WA PR4 ....179 G6
The Apiary LEY/BBR PR5 ....283 C5
Apollo Crs NWD/KWIPK L33 ....366 C1
Apostles Wy NWD/KWIPK L33 ....366 B6
Appealing La LSTA FY8 ....230 E1
Appleby Cl ACC BB5 ....248 D6
 LEY/BBR PR5 ....264 D2
Appleby Dr NLSN BB9 ....170 B7
Appleby Rd BISP FY2 ....176 C2
 NWD/KWIPK L33 ....366 C7
Appleby St BBN BB1 ....9 E4
 NLSN BB9 ....198 B3
 PRES PR1 ....7 D1
Apple Cl BBNW BB2 ....8 A5
Applecross Dr BRFD/BLYE BB10 ....226 C3
Applefields LEY/BBR PR5 ....285 K4
Applegarth BWCK/EAR BB18 ....119 C3
 NLSN BB9 ....197 K2
Applegarth Rd HEY LA3 ....52 E1
Applegarth St BWCK/EAR BB18 ....146 B2
Applesike KIRK/FR/WA PR4 ....260 A2
Appley St BBNW BB2 ....244 D7
Appleton Cl PLF/KEOS FY6 ....177 G1
Appleton Rd SKEL WN8 ....363 F1
Apple Tree Cl GAR/LONG PR3 ....154 C3
Appletree Cl LANC LA1 ....55 C8
 PRES PR1 ....261 J1
Appletree Dr LANC LA1 ....55 C8
Apple Tree Wy ACC BB5 ....247 J6
Appley Cl WGNNW/ST WN6 ....352 E1
Appley La North
 WGNNW/ST WN6 ....352 E1
Appley La South SKEL WN8 ....352 E5
Approach Wy BLY BB11 ....251 G1
Apsley Fold GAR/LONG * PR3 ....188 B5
Aqueduct Rd BBNW BB2 ....267 K1
Aqueduct St FUL/RIB PR2 ....6 B1
Aragon Cl MGHL L31 ....359 G8
Arago St ACC BB5 ....248 C4
Arbories Av PDHM/BLYW BB12 ....223 H3
Arbory Dr PDHM/BLYW BB12 ....223 H2
The Arbory KIRK/FR/WA PR4 ....207 G4
Arbour Dr DWN BB3 ....268 A5
Arbour La WGNNW/ST WN6 ....353 K2
Arbour St STHP PR8 ....301 J5
Arboury St PDHM/BLYW BB12 ....223 H3
Arcadia Av MGHL L31 ....359 F8
Archery Av COL BB8 ....171 H3
Arch La AIMK WN4 ....371 J8
Arch St BLY * BB11 ....10 C3
Arcon Rd CHLY/EC PR7 ....335 J2

Ardee Rd PRES PR1 4
Arden Cl HGHB LA2 4
 STHP PR8 32
Ardengate LANC LA1 5
Arden Gn FTWD FY7 9
Ardleigh Av STHP PR8 30
Ardley Rd HOR/BR BL6 33
Ardmore Rd BISP FY2 17
Ardwick St BRFD/BLYE BB10 1
Argameols Cl STHP PR8 30
Argameols Gv FMBY L37 34
Argameols Rd FMBY L37 34
Argosy Av BPOOLE FY3 17
Argyle Rd CHTN/BK PR9 30
 LEY/BBR PR5 28
 PLF/KEOS FY6 15
Argyle St ACC BB5 24
 COL BB8 17
 DWN BB3 26
 LANC LA1 ....
Argyll Rd BISP FY2 17
 PRES PR1 ....
Ariel Wy FTWD FY7 9
Arkholme Av BPOOL FY1.........................
Arkholme Cl CARN LA5 3
Arkholme Ct MCMB * LA4 4
Arkholme Dr KIRK/FR/WA PR4 26
Arkwright Ct BPOOLS FY4 20
Arkwright Fold BBNW BB2 26
Arkwright St PDHM/BLYW BB12 22
Arley Gdns PDHM/BLYW BB12 1
Arley Ri BBNW BB2 24
Arley St CHLY/EC PR7 31
Arlington Av BPOOLS FY4 20
Arlington Cl STHP PR8 32
Arlington Rd DWN BB3 29
Armadale Rd BISP FY2 17
Armitstead Ct FTWD * FY7 12
Armitstead Wy FTWD FY7 12
Armstrong St FUL/RIB PR2 23
Arncliffe Av ACC BB5 24
Arncliffe Gv NLSN BB9 17
Arncliffe Rd BRFD/BLYE BB10 22
 HEY LA3 5
Arncot Rd BOL BL1 34
Arndale Cl FTWD FY7 12
Arndale Rd GAR/LONG PR3 18
Arnhem Rd CARN LA5 3
 PRES PR1 24
Arnian Rd RNFD/HAY WA11 36
Arnian Wy RNFD/HAY WA11 36
Arnold Av BPOOLS FY4 20
Arnold Cl BLY BB11 25
 FUL/RIB PR2 24
Arnold Pl CHLY/EC PR7 31
Arnold Rd EDGW/EG BL7 34
 LSTA FY8 23
Arnold St ACC BB5 24
Arno St PRES PR1 ....
Arnott Rd BPOOLS FY4 ....
 FUL/RIB PR2 23
Arnside Av BPOOL FY1...........................
 LSTA FY8 ....
Arnside Cl ACC BB5 24
 LANC LA1 ....
 LEY/BBR PR5 ....
Arnside Crs BBNW BB2 26
 MCMB LA4 4
Arnside Rd CHTN/BK PR9 30
 FUL/RIB PR2 23
 WGNW/BIL/O WN5 36
Arnside Ter CHTN/BK PR9 30
Arnside Vw
 PLF/KEOS (off Promenade) FY6 98
Arran Av BBN BB1 26
Arran Cl HEY LA3 5
Arran St BLY BB11 10
Arrow La HGHB LA2 44
Arrowsmith Cl LEY/BBR PR5 26
Arrowsmith Dr LEY/BBR PR5 26
Arrowsmith Gdns CLV/TH FY5 12
Arroyo Wy FUL/RIB PR2 21
Arthurs La PLF/KEOS FY6 15
Arthur St ACC BB5 24
 BBNW BB2 ....
 BCUP OL13 27
 BLY* BB11 10
 BWCK/EAR BB18 11
 BWCK/EAR BB18 14
 FTWD FY7 9
 GTH/LHO BB6 22
 NLSN BB9 19
 NLSN BB9 19
 PRES PR1 ....
Arthur Wy BBNW BB2 ....
Artillery St ACC BB5 24

Augusta St *ACC* BB5 ....248 C7
Auster Crs *KIRK/FR/WA* PR4 ....235 F1
Austin Crs *FUL/RIB* PR2 ....212 D7
Austin Gv *BPOOL* FY1 ....4 B6
Austins Cl *LEY/BBR* PR5 ....285 J3
Austin St *BCUP* OL13 ....298 D1
  BLY BB11 ....10 B1
Austin Wy *BPOOLS* FY4 ....206 C4
Austwick Rd *LANC* LA1 ....2 B1
Austwick Wy *ACC* BB5 ....248 E6
Avallon Wy *DWN* BB3 ....292 A2
Avalon Cl *PDHM/BLYW* BB12 ....224 B4
Avalon Dr *KIRK/FR/WA* PR4 ....235 G4
Avalwood Av *KIRK/FR/WA* PR4 ....260 C5
Avebury Cl *BBNW* BB2 ....268 D3
Aveling Dr *CHTN/BK* PR9 ....279 J5
Avelon Cl *MGHL* L31 ....358 D6
Avenham Cl *CHTN/BK* PR9 ....279 K6
Avenham Colonnade *PRES* PR1 ....7 E4
Avenham La *PRES* PR1 ....7 E4
Avenham Pl *PRES* PR1 ....7 E4
Avenham Rd *CHLY/EC* PR7 ....311 G4
  PRES PR1 ....7 E3
Avenham St *PRES* PR1 ....7 E3
Avenue Pde *ACC* BB5 ....248 C5
Avenue Rd *BPOOLE* FY3 ....177 H3
  CLI BB7 ....191 G2
The Avenue *BLY* BB11 ....252 B1
  CHLYE PR6 ....337 G3
  CHTN/BK PR9 ....279 H6
  CHTN/BK PR9 ....303 H6
  FUL/RIB PR2 ....212 C5
  FUL/RIB PR2 ....237 K2
  GAR/LONG PR3 ....129 G8
  GAR/LONG PR3 ....129 H2
  LEY/BBR PR5 ....285 H5
  ORM L39 ....348 C5
  PDHM/BLYW BB12 ....168 E6
  PLF/KEOS FY6 ....149 J7
  PRES PR1 ....238 D6
  RNFD/HAY WA11 ....369 F5
  WGNW/BIL/O WN5 ....365 F8
Avon Av *FTWD* FY7 ....122 D3
Avon Br *FUL/RIB* PR2 ....212 E8
Avoncliff Cl *BOL* BL1 ....341 H8
Avon Cl *NWD/KWIPK* L33 ....366 C5
Avon Ct *PDHM/BLYW* BB12 ....10 A2
Avondale Av *BBN* BB1 ....246 C6
  PDHM/BLYW BB12 ....224 E4
Avondale Cl *DWN* BB3 ....291 G1
Avondale Crs *BPOOLS* FY4 ....205 F4
Avondale Dr *KIRK/FR/WA* PR4 .....282 A3
  LEY/BBR PR5 ....262 E3
Avondale Ms *DWN* BB3 ....268 B8
Avondale Rd *CHLY/EC* PR7 ....311 G4
  CHTN/BK PR9 ....301 H6
  DWN BB3 ....291 G1
  HEY LA3 ....40 E8
  LANC LA1 ....3 E5
  LSTA FY8 ....230 C3
  NLSN BB9 ....198 B4
Avondale Rd North *CHTN/BK* PR9 ...301 J2
Avondale St *COL* BB8 ....172 A6
Avon Dr *BWCK/EAR* BB18 ....119 C8
Avon Gdns *KIRK/FR/WA* PR4 ....211 K6
Avon Gv *FTWD* FY7 ....96 E7
Avonhead Cl *HOR/BR* BL6 ....338 D8
Avon Pl *BPOOL* FY1 ....176 C3
Avonside Av *CLV/TH* FY5 ....123 G8
Avon St *LSTA* FY8 ....230 E5
Avonwood Cl *DWN* BB3 ....291 G1
Avroe Crs *LSTA* FY8 ....204 D7
Aylesbury Av *BPOOLS* FY4 ....5 D6
Aylesbury Wk *BRFD/BLYE* BB10 ...198 B3
Ayr Cl *STHP* PR8 ....302 B7
Ayr Ct *FTWD* FY7 ....122 A4
Ayrefield Gv *WGNW/ST* WN6 ....353 F5
Ayrefield La *SKEL* WN8 ....352 E7
Ayr Gv *BLY* BB11 ....10 A6
Ayr Rd *BBN* BB1 ....246 B8
Ayr St *LANC* LA1 ....3 E4
Ayrton Av *BPOOLS* FY4 ....204 C5
Ayrton St *COL* BB8 ....171 J6
Aysgarth Av *FUL/RIB* PR2 ....213 H4
Aysgarth Ct *BPOOLS* FY4 ....205 F4
Aysgarth Dr *ACC* BB5 ....248 D5
  DWN BB3 ....291 G1
  LANC LA1 ....43 F7
Aysgarth Rd *LANC* LA1 ....2 B3
Ays-Garth Rd *LANC* LA1 ....2 B3
Azalea Cl *FUL/RIB* PR2 ....214 A3
  LEY/BBR PR5 ....286 C1
Azalea Gv *MCMB* LA4 ....42 A6
Azalea Rd *BBNW* BB2 ....244 D5

B

Babbacombe Av *BPOOLS* FY4 ....204 B5
Babylon La *CHLYE* PR6 ....337 J2
Back Ainsworth St *BOL* * BL1 ....341 G8
Back Albert Rd *COL* * BB8 ....171 H7
Back Albert St *PDHM/BLYW* BB12 ...223 J3
Back Altham St
  PDHM/BLYW BB12 ....223 K3
Back Anson St *BOL* * BL1 ....341 K8
Back Arthur St *ACC* BB5 ....221 K8
Back Ashbee St *BOL* BL1 ....341 J8
Back Ashburton Rd *BPOOL* FY1 ....176 B4
Back Ashby St *CHLY/EC* PR7 ....311 G5
Back Ashworth La *BOL* BL1 ....341 K6
Back Atkinson St *COL* BB8 ....171 G7
Back Avondale Rd East *HEY* LA3 .....40 E8
Back Bath St *STHP* PR8 ....301 H3
Back Baxendale St *BOL* BL1 ....341 J7
Back Baytorpe St North
  BOL * BL1 ....341 K8
Back Belmont Rd *BOL* * BL1 ....341 J6
Back Belmont Rd East *BOL* BL1 ....341 J6
Back Birley St *BOL* BL1 ....341 J7
Back Blackburn Rd East
  EDGW/EG BL7 ....316 B8
Back Blackburn Rd West *BOL* BL1 ...341 J7
  EDGW/EG * BL7 ....341 J3
Back Bond St *BOL* BL1 ....341 K8
Back Boundary St *COL* * BB8 ....171 H7
Back Bourne's Rw *LEY/BBR* PR5 ...264 D2
Back Bridge St *RAMS* BL0 ....319 J5
Back Brindley St *BOL* BL1 ....341 K7
Back Broad o' th' La *BOL* * BL1 .....341 J7
Back Brown St *COL* * BB8 ....171 G7
Back Burnley Rd *ACC* * BB5 ....248 C5
Back Calton Ter *MCMB* LA4 ....41 H5
Back Cambridge St *COL* BB8 ....171 H7
Back Canada St *HOR/BR* BL6 ....338 D8
Back Carr Mill St *RAW/HAS* * BB4 ...272 C6
  HOR/BR BL6 ....338 E8
Back Chapel St *COL* BB8 ....171 H7
Back Church St *BPOOL* FY1 ....4 B2
  NLSN BB9 ....170 B8
  PDHM/BLYW * BB12 ....223 J7
  RAW/HAS BB4 ....297 G1
Back Clarendon Rd *BPOOL* * FY1 ......4 B5
Back Clayton St *NLSN* BB9 ....198 D2
Back Club St *LEY/BBR* PR5 ....263 H4
Back Cobden St *BOL* BL1 ....341 H8
Back Commercial St *NLSN* BB9 .....197 K5
Back Commons *CLI* BB7 ....165 H2
Back Coniston St *BOL* * BL1 ....341 K8
Back Cookson St *BPOOL* * FY1 ....4 C1
Back Cop La *FTWD* FY7 ....97 G7
Back Cowm La *WHIT* OL12 ....299 F6
Back Cox Green Rd North
  EDGW/EG BL7 ....341 K3
Back Crescent St *MCMB* LA4 ....41 G6
Back Crown St *HOR/BR* BL6 ....338 C7
Back Crumpsall St North *BOL* BL1 ...341 J8
Back Cunliffe Rd *BPOOL* FY1 ....5 D5
Back Darwen Rd North
  EDGW/EG BL7 ....341 J2
Back Drinkhouse La
  LEY/BBR PR5 ....307 G1
Back Drummond St *BOL* * BL1 ....341 J7
Back Duckworth St *DWN* BB3 ....291 J2
Back Duke St *COL* BB8 ....171 H7
Back Duncan St *HOR/BR* * BL6 ......338 E8
Back Earl St *COL* BB8 ....171 H7
Back East Bank *NLSN* * BB9 ....170 B7
Back Eastbank St *BOL* BL1 ....341 K8
Back Eaves St *BPOOL* FY1 ....176 B4
Back Eckersley Rd *BOL* BL1 ....341 J8
Back Eden St *BOL* BL1 ....341 J7
Back Emmett St *HOR/BR* BL6 ....338 D4
Back Epsom St *CLV/TH* FY5 ....149 F3
Back Fairhaven Rd *BOL* BL1 ....341 K8
Back Florence Av *BOL* BL1 ....341 K7
Back Forest St *STHP* PR8 ....301 K5
Back Gaythorne St *BOL* * BL1 ....341 K8
Back George St *HOR/BR* BL6 ....338 E8
Back Glen Eldon Rd *LSTA* FY8 ......230 E4
Back Green St *MCMB* LA4 ....41 H5
Back Gresham St *BOL* * BL1 ....341 K8
Back Grimshaw St *PRES* PR1 ....7 E3
Back Hall St *COL* BB8 ....171 H7
Back Harry St *NLSN* BB9 ....170 B8
Back Heys *ACC* * BB5 ....247 J8
Back High St *BPOOL* FY1 ....4 B1
  EDGW/EG BL7 ....314 E6
  EDGW/EG BL7 ....317 G7

Back Hill St *RAW/HAS* BB4 27
Back Holland St *BOL* BL1 34
Back Holland St East *BOL* * BL1 34
Back Holly Pl *BOL* BL1 34
Back Holly St *BOL* BL1 34
Back Hope St *BCUP* OL13 27
Backhouse St *ACC* BB5 24
Back Howarden St *BOL* * BL1 34
Back Irlam St *BOL* BL1 34
Back Irlam St North *BOL* * BL1 34
Back Ivy Bank Rd *BOL* BL1 34
Back King St North
  EDGW/EG BL7 34
Back Knowlys Rd *HEY* * LA3 5
Back La *ACC* BB5 24
  BRFD/BLYE BB10 19
  BRFD/BLYE BB10 20
  BRSC L40 33
  BRSC L40 33
  BRSC L40 35
  CARN LA5 1
  CHLY/EC PR7 28
  CHLY/EC PR7 30
  CHLYE PR6 28
  CLI BB7 8
  CLI BB7 14
  CLI BB7 14
  CLI BB7 19
  COL BB8 20
  GAR/LONG PR3 15
  GAR/LONG PR3 15
  GAR/LONG PR3 18
  HGHB LA2 4
  KIRK/FR/WA PR4 18
  KIRK/FR/WA PR4 20
  KIRK/FR/WA PR4 25
  KKBYL LA6 4
  KKBYL LA6 5
  KKBYL LA6 9
  LEY/BBR PR5 28
  MTHPE LA7 1
  ORM L39 34
  ORM L39 35
  ORM L39 36
  PDHM/BLYW BB12 19
  PDHM/BLYW BB12 19
  PLF/KEOS FY6 12
  PLF/KEOS FY6 12
  RAW/HAS BB4 27
  RNFD/HAY WA11 37
  SKEL WN8 35
  SKEL WN8 36
  WGNNW/ST WN6 35
  WHIT OL12 32
Back La East *BRSC* L40 33
Back Leachfield St *BOL* BL1 34
Back Leach St *COL* * BB8 17
Back Lee St *RAW/HAS* BB4 29
Back Lines St *MCMB* LA4 4
Back Longworth Rd
  EDGW/EG BL7 31
Back Lord St *BPOOL* FY1 4
  RAW/HAS BB4 27
Back Lune St *COL* * BB8 17
Back Mackenzie St *BOL* BL1 34
Back Marine Rd *MCMB* LA4 4
Back Marine Rd East *MCMB* * LA4 4
Back Maxwell St *BOL* * BL1 34
Back Mcdonna St *BOL* BL1 34
Back Miller St *BOL* * BL1 34
Back Mill St North
  EDGW/EG * BL7 34
Back Mill St South
  EDGW/EG * BL7 34
Back Moon Av *BPOOL* FY1 4
Back Morecambe St *MCMB* LA4 4
Back Moss La *BRSC* L40 33
Back Mt *CHLY/EC* * PR7 31
Back Murton Ter *BOL* * BL1 34
Back Nelson St *HOR/BR* * BL6 33
Back North Crs *LSTA* FY8 23
Back O the Town La *HTWN* L38 35
Back Owen St *ACC* BB5 24
Back Palm St *BOL* BL1 34
Back Park Vw *EDGW/EG* BL7 34
Back Peter St *NLSN* BB9 17
Back Pleasant St *BPOOL* * FY1 17
Back Poplar Av *BOL* BL1 34
Back Primrose St *BOL* * BL1 34
Back Primula St *BOL* BL1 34
Back Queen St *GTH/LHO* BB6 22
  LANC LA1 4
  MCMB LA4 4
Back Railway Vw *CHLY/EC* PR7 33
Back Raimond St *BOL* BL1 34
Back Rainshaw St *BOL* BL1 34
Back Rawlinson St *HOR/BR* * BL6 33

k Read's Rd BPOOL FY1 ....4 C3
k Rhoden Rd ACC BB5...270 C1
k Rings Rw RAW/HAS BB4 ...273 H1
k Rock Av BOL BL1....341 G8
k Rossini St BOL * BL1 ....341 H8
k RW SKEL * WN8 .....364 K4
HIT (off Knacks La) OL12 ...323 F5
k Rushton St BCUP * OL13 ...298 C3
k St Anne's Rd West LSTA FY8 ..230 E5
k St John St BCUP * OL13 ...275 J8
k Sandy Bank Rd
DCW/EG BL7 ......317 H6
k School La SKEL WN8....362 C1
EL WN8......364 K4
k Scotland Rd NLSN * BB9 ...198 B3
k Seed St PRES * PR1 .....7 D2
k Seymour St BOL BL1....341 K8
k Shannon St BPOOL * FY1 .....4 B4
k Sherwood St BOL * BL1...341 K8
k Somerville St BOL * BL1...341 G8
k Spencer St RAW/HAS BB4 ...273 H3
k Springfield Rd North
TA FY8 .....230 E5
k Square St RAMS BLO....319 J5
k Stanley St RAMS * BLO...319 H6
k Starkie St PRES PR1 .....7 D3
Backs GAR/LONG PR3...188 A3
k St HEY LA3 ......65 H3
k Sun St LANC LA1.....3 D3
k Talbot St BOL BL1 .....341 K7
k Thorns Rd BOL BL1.....341 J8
k Viola St BOL BL1.....341 J8
k Virginia St STHP PR8....301 H5
k Walnut St BOL BL1.....341 K8
k Warbreck Rd BPOOL FY1....4 B1
k Waterloo St BOL * FY1....4 B6
k Water St ACC * BB5.....248 C6
DCW/EG BL7......341 H1
k Waverley St BOL BL1.....341 J8
k Wellington St ACC BB5....248 C6
k West Crs LSTA * FY8 .....230 E5
k Willow St PDHM/BLYW BB12...10 B2
k Wilmot St BOL * BL1....341 G8
k Wilton St BOL BL1....341 K8
k Windermere St BOL BL1....341 K8
k Winterdyne Ter HEY LA3....40 E7
k Woodfield Rd BPOOL * FY1....4 B5
k Wood St HOR/BR BL6....338 D7
k Wright St HOR/BR BL6....338 D7
k York St CLI * BB7....165 J3
AW/HAS BB4 ......273 H4
k Zion St COL * BB8....171 H4
on St NLSN BB9 ......198 C3
up Old Rd BCUP OL13....275 J2
up BLY BB11......252 A2
AW/HAS BB4......296 C1
OD OL14......276 D6
by Wd NWD/KWIPK L33...366 D7
don Ct MCMB LA4 ......41 J8
en Ter BBNW BB2....267 K2
ge Brow ACC BB5......247 J6
gers Cft FUL/RIB PR2....240 D2
gers Rake FMBY L37....343 C6
gers Wk CHLY/EC PR7....287 F6
gers Wy LEY/BBR PR5....239 K8
ganley La CHLYE PR6.....311 J1
ot St BPOOL FY1 ......4 B6
ey Bank CLI BB7....163 J4
ey Ct BPOOLE FY3 .....5 E1
ey La HEY LA3....52 C3
ey St BLY BB11......10 B4
NCK/EAR BB18......146 C2
rigg La LANC LA1....67 G2
nes Av BPOOLE FY3....177 F2
NCK/EAR BB18......119 F8
RES PR1 ......7 D3
ers Ct BPOOLE FY4....205 F4
er's La CHTN/BK PR9....278 B8
er St BBN BB1......9 F5
CUP OL13......275 J8
LY BB11......10 B4
ANC LA1......43 F8
EY/BBR PR5......285 K1
LSN BB9......198 C3
AMS BLO......319 H6
aclava St BBN BB1......8 C3
CI BBN BB1......8 C3
arres Ct LEY/BBR PR5....285 J2
arres PI LEY/BBR PR5....285 J3
arres Rd CHLY/EC PR7....311 F6
JL/RIB PR2......212 E8
EY/BBR PR5......285 J3
derstone CI BRFD/BLYE BB10...226 B1
derstone Hall La BBNW BB2...216 C5

Balderstone La BRFD/BLYE BB10 ....226 C2
Balderstone Rd KIRK/FR/WA PR4 ....235 F4
PRES PR1......6 B5
Baldwin Gv BPOOL FY1 ......5 D5
Baldwin HI CLI BB7......165 H3
Baldwin Rd CLI BB7......165 H3
Baldwin St BBNW * BB2......8 A6
BCUP OL13......297 K3
LEY/BBR PR5......263 H5
WGNW/BIL/O WN5......365 K6
Balfour Cl CLV/TH FY5......149 K4
NLSN BB9......198 B6
Balfour St FUL/RIB PR2......213 G8
STHP PR8......302 A6
Balfour St BBNW BB2......8 A5
GTH/LHO BB6......221 H6
LEY/BBR PR5......285 J2
Balham Av BPOOLS FY4......204 E6
Ballam Rd FUL/RIB PR2......238 A2
LSTA FY8......232 C1
Ballam St BLY BB11......11 D5
Ballantrae Rd BBN BB1......246 B8
Ballater St BLY BB11......10 A6
Balle St DWN BB3......291 J3
Ballet Hill Crs GAR/LONG PR3....156 C6
Ball Grove Dr COL BB8......172 B6
Balliol Cl PDHM/BLYW BB12....223 K5
Ball La HGHB LA2......45 C5
Ball's Pl STHP PR8......301 H4
Ball St BPOOL FY1......4 B6
NLSN* BB9......198 B2
PLF/KEOS FY6......149 K3
Balmer Gv BPOOL FY1......5 D4
Balmoral Av CHLY/EC PR7......336 E5
CLI BB7......165 G5
HEY LA3......40 E8
LEY/BBR PR5......286 A3
Balmoral Av BBN BB1......219 J7
Balmoral Crs BBN BB1......246 D7
Balmoral Dr CHLYE PR6......288 E3
CHTN/BK PR9......278 D8
FMBY L37......355 J2
Balmoral Pl CLV/TH FY5......149 J3
Balmoral Rd ACC BB5......248 D4
BPOOLS FY4......204 B3
CHLY/EC PR7......308 E4
CHLY/EC PR7......311 F5
DWN BB3......291 K5
HEY LA3......40 E8
KIRK/FR/WA PR4......261 H2
LANC LA1......3 E4
LEY/BBR PR5......240 B8
LSTA FY8......231 G6
RAW/HAS BB4......295 G2
Balmoral Ter FTWD FY7......97 H5
Balm St RAMS BLO......319 G7
Balniel Cl CHLY/EC PR7......311 F4
Balshaw Crs LEY/BBR PR5......285 H1
Balshaw La CHLY/EC PR7......310 B2
Balshaw Rd HGHB LA2......50 E6
LEY/BBR PR5......285 H2
Balshaw St LEY/BBR * PR5......263 H1
Balshaw Ter
KIRK/FR/WA
(off Marsden St) PR4......209 F7
Baltic Buildings
RAW/HAS (off Schofield St) BB4...297 G3
Baltic Rd RAW/HAS BB4......297 G3
Baltimore Rd LSTA * FY8......231 H5
Bamber Av BISP FY2......148 C7
Bamber Gdns CHTN/BK PR9......302 C5
Bambers La BPOOLS FY4......205 J4
Bamber St CHLY/EC PR7......311 F6
Bamburgh Cl BPOOLS FY4......205 G4
Bamburgh Dr PDHM/BLYW BB12...10 B2
Bamford Crs ACC BB5......248 D7
Bamford Rd RAMS BLO......320 A3
Bamfords Fold LEY/BBR PR5......283 F6
Bamford St BLY BB11......11 D3
NLSN BB9......198 B3
Bamton Av BPOOLS FY4......204 C5
Banastre CHLY/EC PR7......310 E1
Banastre St STHP PR8......301 G6
Banastre St ACC BB5......248 A2
Banbury Av ACC BB5......247 G7
BISP FY2......176 D3
Banbury Cl BBNW BB2......267 C3
Banbury Dr FUL/RIB PR2......213 C7
Banbury Rd HEY LA3......41 J8
LSTA FY8......231 F5
WGNW/BIL/O WN5......371 F1
Bancroft Av CLV/TH FY5......149 H1
Bancroft Fold BWCK/EAR BB18...144 E2
Bancroft Rd BRFD/BLYE BB10...11 F1
Bancroft St BBN BB1......9 D4

Band La GAR/LONG PR3......154 D2
Bangor Av BISP FY2......148 D7
Bangor St BBN BB1......9 D7
Bank Av WGNW/BIL/O WN5......365 F6
Bank Bottom DWN BB3......291 J3
Bank Br KIRK/FR/WA PR4......282 B6
Bank Brow SKEL WN8......352 E6
Bank Cl HGHB LA2......67 F7
KIRK/FR/WA PR4......260 B3
Bank Cft KIRK/FR/WA PR4......260 B3
Bankcroft Cl PDHM/BLYW BB12...224 A3
Bankes Av WGNW/BIL/O WN5......365 J5
Bankfield BLY BB11......11 D3
SKEL WN8......363 J4
Bankfield Ct CLV/TH FY5......149 H3
Bankfield Gv BPOOL FY1......5 E4
Bankfield La CHTN/BK PR9......302 D1
Bankfield St BCUP OL13......298 A3
COL BB8......171 F7
COL BB8......172 B7
Bank Fold NLSN BB9......170 C7
Bankhall Ter BRFD/BLYE BB10...11 D2
Bank Head La LEY/BBR PR5......264 B3
Bank Hey La North BBN BB1......219 H8
Bank Hey La South BBN BB1......245 J2
Bank Hey St BPOOL FY1......4 B3
Bank House La BCUP OL13......298 D1
Bankhouse Rd NLSN BB9......198 C2
Bankhouse St BLY BB11......10 C3
Bank House St NLSN BB9......170 C7
Bank La BBN BB1......246 B7
KIRK/FR/WA PR4......234 A7
MGHL L31......366 A5
NWD/KWIPK L33......366 B7
Bank Meadow HOR/BR BL6......338 E7
Bank Nook
CHTN/BK (off Radnor Dr) PR9...278 B8
Bank Pde BLY BB11......11 D3
PRES PR1......7 E4
Bank Pl FUL/RIB PR2......6 A1
Bank Rd LANC LA1......43 F8
SKEL WN8......352 E6
Banksbarn SKEL WN8......363 J4
Banks Bridge Cl BWCK/EAR BB18...119 G7
Banks Crs HEY LA3......52 D5
Banksfield Av FUL/RIB PR2......212 E8
Banksfield Pl LEY/BBR PR5......263 J4
Banks Hl BWCK/EAR BB18......118 E7
Bankside BBNW BB2......268 B1
CHLYE PR6......287 F2
HTWN L38......355 K8
SKEL WN8......351 H1
Bankside Cl BCUP OL13......298 C2
Bankside La BCUP OL13......298 C2
Bank Sq CHTN/BK PR9......301 H3
Banks St BPOOL FY1......4 B1
BRFD/BLYE BB10......199 F8
Bank St ACC BB5......247 J5
ACC* BB5......248 C6
BCUP OL13......298 D1
BWCK/EAR BB18......145 G1
CHLY/EC PR7......311 G3
CHLY/EC PR7......337 F4
COL BB8......200 C3
DWN BB3......291 J2
EDGW/EG BL7......317 G7
NLSN BB9......197 K5
NLSN BB9......198 C2
PDHM/BLYW BB12......223 J2
RAMS BLO......320 A4
RAW/HAS BB4......272 C8
RAW/HAS BB4......296 C1
Bank Top BBNW BB2......8 A6
BLY BB11......11 D2
Bankwood WGNNW/ST WN6......353 G5
Banner Cl CHLY/EC PR7......308 D4
Bannerman Ter CHLYE PR6......311 H4
Bannister Cl COL BB8......172 B8
LEY/BBR PR5......241 F7
Bannister Ct
NLSN (off Yorkshire St) BB9......198 C4
Bannister Dr LEY/BBR PR5......285 C2
Bannister Gn CHLY/EC PR7......308 E8
Bannister Hall Crs LEY/BBR PR5...241 F7
Bannister Hall Dr LEY/BBR PR5...241 F7
Bannister Hall La LEY/BBR PR5...241 F7
Bannister La BRSC L40......333 C5
LEY/BBR PR5......262 A7
Bannister's Bit PRES PR1......261 K1
Bannister St CHLY/EC PR7......311 G4
LSTA* FY8......232 D8
Bannistre Cl LSTA FY8......231 G3
Bannistre Ct KIRK/FR/WA PR4......282 A5
Barbara Castle Wy BBN BB1......8 C4
Barberry Bank EDGW/EG BL7......341 H1

Barbondale Rd KKBYL LA6 ....12 B1
Barbon Pl LANC LA1 ....42 E8
Barbon St BRFD/BLYE BB10 ....226 A1
Barbrook Cl WGNNW/ST WN6 ......353 K1
Barclay Av BLY BB11 ....224 E7
  BPOOLE FY3 ....5 F5
Barclay Rd GAR/LONG PR3 ....188 A4
Barcroft Gn BRFD/BLYE BB10 ....252 C2
Barcroft St COL BB8 ....171 G6
Barden Cft ACC BB5 ....221 K7
Barden La PDHM/BLYW BB12 ....197 H8
Barden Pl FUL/RIB PR2 ....214 B7
Barden Rd ACC BB5 ....247 K7
Barden St BRFD/BLYE BB10 ....11 E1
Bardsea Pl FUL/RIB PR2 ....212 B8
Bardsley Cl WGNW WN8 ....364 C4
Bardsway CLV/TH FY5 ....123 G8
Bardsway Av BPOOLE FY3 ....5 E1
Bare Av MCMB LA4 ....42 A5
Bare La MCMB LA4 ....42 A5
Barford Cl SKEL WN8 ....364 C4
  STHP PR8 ....325 G5
Bargee Cl BBN BB1 ....9 D6
Barham St BPOOL FY1 ....4 B5
Barker Brow GAR/LONG PR3 ....190 C8
Barker Cl KKBYL LA6 ....18 A5
Barkerfield Cl PDHM/BLYW BB12 ...196 A6
Barkerhouse Rd NLSN BB9 ....198 D3
Barker La BBNW BB2 ....244 D1
Barkfield Av FMBY L37 ....343 J7
Barkfield La FMBY L37 ....343 H7
Bar La BOL BL1 ....341 J6
Barley Bank St DWN BB3 ....291 H1
Barley Cl BBNW BB2 ....8 B4
Barley Cop La LANC LA1 ....42 C7
Barleydale Rd NLSN BB9 ....170 C6
Barleyfield CHLYE PR6 ....264 B8
Barley Gv BRFD/BLYE BB10 ....11 F3
Barley Holme Rd RAW/HAS BB4 ....273 H3
Barley La BBNW BB2 ....8 B4
  NLSN BB9 ....168 C2
  PDHM/BLYW BB12 ....168 B5
Barley New Rd
  PDHM/BLYW BB12 ....169 F6
Barley St PDHM/BLYW BB12 ....223 J4
Barley Wy BBNW * BB2 ....8 B4
Barlow Crs BPOOLE FY3 ....5 E3
Barlow Park Av BOL BL1 ....341 H6
Barlow's Cl ORM L39 ....327 F6
Barlow St ACC BB5 ....248 A5
  PRES PR1 ....6 C1
  RAW/HAS BB4 ....273 H8
Barmouth Av BPOOLE FY3 ....205 H1
Barmouth Crs BBN BB1 ....245 F2
Barmskin La CHLY/EC PR7 ....333 K1
Barnacre Cl FUL/RIB PR2 ....213 J3
  LANC LA1 ....67 H1
Barnacre Rd GAR/LONG PR3 ....188 A3
Barnard Cl ACC BB5 ....247 G7
Barn Cft LEY/BBR PR5 ....284 D2
  PRES PR1 ....238 D7
Barncroft Dr HOR/BR BL6 ....339 H8
Barnes Av CLV/TH FY5 ....122 E6
  RAW/HAS BB4 ....296 B1
Barnes Cl RAMS BL0 ....319 G8
Barnes Ct BRFD/BLYE BB10 ....226 B7
Barnes Dr MGHL L31 ....358 E7
Barnes Rd HEY LA3 ....40 E8
  ORM L39 ....348 C8
  SKEL WN8 ....362 D2
Barnes Sq ACC BB5 ....221 K8
Barnes St ACC BB5 ....221 K8
  ACC BB5 ....247 J4
  ACC BB5 ....248 C5
  BLY BB11 ....11 D3
  RAW/HAS BB4 ....272 C5
Barnfield KIRK/FR/WA PR4 ....208 E6
  KIRK/FR/WA PR4 ....282 C1
  LEY/BBR PR5 ....262 D3
Barnfield Av BRFD/BLYE BB10 ....226 B5
Barnfield Cl CLV/TH FY5 ....123 F7
Barn Field Cl COL BB8 ....172 B6
Barnfield Cl EDGW/EG BL7 ....341 J1
Barnfield Dr SKEL WN8 ....364 A4
Barnfield Mnr
  PLF/KEOS (off Lodge La) FY6 ....151 H3
Barnfield St ACC BB5 ....248 C5
Barnfield Wy ACC BB5 ....222 E6
Barn Gill Cl BBN BB1 ....9 D6
Barn Hey KIRK/FR/WA PR4 ....260 B2
Barn Meadow EDGW/EG BL7 ....317 H6
  LEY/BBR PR5 ....264 C5
Barn Meadow Crs BBN BB1 ....247 G2
Barnmeadow La GTH/LHO BB6 ....221 G6
Barnoldswick Rd BWCK/EAR BB18 ..145 K5
  NLSN BB9 ....170 D4

Barnsfold FUL/RIB PR2 ....213 F5
Barnside CHLY/EC PR7 ....286 A8
Barns La GAR/LONG PR3 ....159 G4
Barnston Cl BOL BL1 ....341 K7
Barnwood Crs BWCK/EAR BB18 ......146 A8
Barnwood Rd BWCK/EAR BB18 ....146 B2
Baron Rd BPOOL FY1 ....4 C6
Barons Cl DWN BB3 ....268 D4
Baron St DWN BB3 ....291 G1
  RAW/HAS BB4 ....297 F2
Barons Wy CHLY/EC PR7 ....310 B1
  DWN BB3 ....268 D5
Barracks Rd BLY BB11 ....10 A3
Barret Hill Brow CLI BB7 ....114 B5
Barret St BWCK/EAR BB18 ....146 A4
Barrett Av STHP PR8 ....326 C1
Barrett St STHP PR8 ....326 C1
Barrett St BRFD/BLYE BB10 ....11 D1
Barrington Dr STHP PR8 ....325 H6
Barrison Gn BRSC L40 ....348 C1
Barritt Rd RAW/HAS BB4 ....296 B1
Barronwood Ct KIRK/FR/WA PR4 ....282 A6
Barrow Bridge Rd BOL BL1 ....340 D7
Barrowford Rd COL BB8 ....170 E6
  NLSN BB9 ....198 A2
  PDHM/BLYW BB12 ....195 K8
Barrow Nook La ORM L39 ....361 J8
Barrow's La GAR/LONG PR3 ....153 F6
  HEY LA3 ....52 B5
Barrows La East GAR/LONG PR3 .....153 F6
Barry Av FUL/RIB PR2 ....212 B8
Barry Gv HEY LA3 ....52 D5
Barry St PDHM/BLYW BB12 ....224 D5
Bar St BRFD/BLYE BB10 ....11 E1
Bar Ter WHIT OL12 ....323 G4
Bartholomew Rd MCMB LA4 ....41 J7
Bartle La KIRK/FR/WA PR4 ....211 J4
Bartle Pl FUL/RIB PR2 ....238 A2
Bartle Rd LSTA FY8 ....231 G3
Bartle St BLY BB11 ....224 E6
Barton Av BPOOL FY1 ....4 B5
  PLF/KEOS FY6 ....98 A6
Barton Clough
  WGNW/BIL/O WN5 ....371 G6
Barton Ct
  LANC (off Barton Rd) LA1 ....55 C7
Barton Heys Rd FMBY L37 ....355 H2
Barton La GAR/LONG PR3 ....184 E5
Barton Rd LANC LA1 ....55 G7
  LSTA FY8 ....230 E3
Bartons Cl CHTN/BK PR9 ....279 F6
Barton Sq PLF/KEOS FY6 ....98 A6
Barton St BBNW BB2 ....8 B4
  WGNW/BIL/O WN5 ....365 K6
Bashall Gv LEY/BBR PR5 ....262 E8
Basil St COL BB8 ....171 H7
Basil St COL BB8 ....171 H7
  PRES PR1 ....240 A1
Basnett St BRFD/BLYE BB10 ....226 B7
Bassenthwaite Av
  NWD/KWIPK L33 ....366 B7
Bassenthwaite Rd BPOOLE FY3.......205 H1
Bass La BURY BL9 ....320 A8
Bastwell Rd BBN BB1 ....9 D2
Bateman Gv MCMB LA4 ....41 H6
Bateman Rd MCMB LA4 ....41 H6
Bates St ACC BB5 ....221 J8
Bathgate Wy NWD/KWIPK L33........366 B5
Bath Mill La LANC LA1 ....3 E3
Bath Mill Sq LANC LA1 ....3 E3
Bath Rd LSTA FY8 ....232 D8
Bath Springs ORM L39 ....348 D6
Bath St ACC BB5 ....248 B7
  BBNW BB2 ....8 A5
  BCUP OL13 ....298 E1
  BPOOLS FY4 ....4 B6
  COL BB8 ....171 J6
  FUL/RIB PR2 ....6 B1
  LANC LA1 ....3 E3
  LSTA FY8 ....232 D8
  MCMB LA4 ....41 G6
  NLSN BB9 ....198 D3
  STHP PR8 ....301 H3
Bath St North CHTN/BK PR9 ....301 H3
Bathurst Av BPOOLE FY3 ....177 G4
Bathurst St BBNW BB2 ....8 B4
Batridge Rd EDGW/EG BL7 ....316 E4
Battismore Rd MCMB LA4 ....41 G6
Battle Wy FMBY * L37 ....356 B1
Bawdlands CLI BB7 ....165 H3
Bawhead Rd BWCK/EAR BB18 ....146 B2
Baxendale St BOL BL1 ....341 J7
Baxtergate MCMB LA4 ....41 H5
Bayard St PDHM/BLYW * BB12 ....224 C5
Baycliffe Crs MCMB LA4 ....41 G6
Bay Cl HEY LA3 ....52 B5
Bay Horse Dr LANC LA1 ....55 H8
Bay Horse La KIRK/FR/WA PR4 ....182 C7

Bay Horse Rd HGHB LA2 ....8[?]
Bayley Fold CLI BB7 ....1[?]
Bayley St ACC BB5 ....22[?]
Bayliss Cl FUL/RIB PR2 ....21[?]
Baylton Dr GAR/LONG PR3 ....15[?]
Baynes St DWN BB3 ....29[?]
Bay Rd FUL/RIB PR2 ....24[?]
  LANC LA1 ....[?]
Bayside FTWD FY7 ....[?]
Bay St BBN BB1 ....[?]
Bayswater BISP * FY2 ....14[?]
The Bay CLV/TH FY5 ....12[?]
Baythorpe St BOL BL1 ....34[?]
Baytree Cl CHTN/BK PR9 ....27[?]
  LEY/BBR PR5 ....26[?]
Bay Tree Farm
  FUL/RIB (off Sutton Dr) PR2 ....23[?]
Bay Tree Rd CHLYE PR6 ....28[?]
Baytree Wk WHIT OL12 ....32[?]
Bay Vw KKBYL LA6 ....[?]
Bay View Av HGHB LA2 ....[?]
Bay View Ct
  LANC (off Station Rd) LA1 ....[?]
Bay View Crs HGHB LA2 ....[?]
Bazil Gv HEY LA3 ....[?]
Bazil La HEY LA3 ....[?]
Bazley Rd LSTA FY8 ....23[?]
Bazley St BOL BL1 ....34[?]
Beacham Rd STHP PR8 ....30[?]
Beach Av CLV/TH FY5 ....12[?]
  LSTA FY8 ....23[?]
Beachcomber Dr CLV/TH FY5 ....12[?]
Beach Ct
  LSTA (off East Beach) FY8 ....23[?]
Beachley Rd FUL/RIB PR2 ....21[?]
Beachley Sq PDHM/BLYW BB12 ....31[?]
Beach Priory Gdns STHP PR8...............30[?]
Beach Rd CLV/TH FY5 ....12[?]
  FTWD FY7 ....[?]
  GAR/LONG PR3....................................[?]
  LSTA FY8 ....23[?]
  STHP PR8 ....30[?]
Beach St LSTA FY8 ....23[?]
  MCMB LA4 ....[?]
Beachwood La CARN LA5 ....1[?]
Beacon Av FUL/RIB PR2 ....21[?]
Beacon Cl COL BB8 ....17[?]
Beacon Crossing
  SKEL (off The Common) WN8 ....35[?]
Beacon Dr GAR/LONG PR3 ....18[?]
Beacon Gv FUL/RIB PR2 ....21[?]
  GAR/LONG PR3....................................12[?]
Beacon Hl
  WGNW/BIL/O
  (off Beacon Rd) WN5 ....37[?]
Beacon La BRSC L40 ....35[?]
  SKEL WN8 ....35[?]
Beacon Rd PLF/KEOS FY6 ....15[?]
  WGNNW/ST WN6 ....35[?]
  WGNW/BIL/O WN5 ....37[?]
Beaconsfield Av PRES PR1 ....24[?]
Beaconsfield Rd CHTN/BK PR9 ....30[?]
Beaconsfield St ACC BB5 ....22[?]
  GTH/LHO BB6 ....22[?]
  RAW/HAS BB4 ....27[?]
Beaconsfield Ter CHLYE PR6 ....31[?]
  GAR/LONG PR3....................................15[?]
The Beacons WGNNW/ST WN6............35[?]
Beacon St CHLY/EC PR7 ....31[?]
Beacon Vw WGNNW/ST WN6 ....35[?]
Beacon View Dr SKEL WN8 ....36[?]
Beaford Cl WGNW/BIL/O WN5 ....36[?]
Beale Rd NLSN BB9 ....19[?]
Beamont Dr PRES PR1 ....2[?]
Bean Av BPOOLS FY4 ....20[?]
Beardshaw Av BPOOL FY1 ....[?]
Beardsworth St BBN BB1 ....[?]
Beardwood BBNW BB2 ....24[?]
Beardwood Brow BBNW BB2 ....24[?]
Beardwood Meadow BBNW BB2 ....24[?]
Beardwood Pk BBNW BB2 ....24[?]
Bearncroft SKEL WN8 ....36[?]
Bear St PDHM/BLYW BB12 ....22[?]
Bearswood Cft CHLYE PR6 ....24[?]
Beatie St NLSN * BB9 ....19[?]
Beatrice Av PDHM/BLYW BB12 ....22[?]
Beatrice Pl BBNW BB2 ....26[?]
Beattock Cl NWD/KWIPK L33 ....36[?]
Beattock Pl BISP * FY2 ....14[?]
Beatty Av CHLY/EC PR7 ....31[?]
Beatty Cl LSTA FY8 ....23[?]
Beatty Rd STHP PR8 ....30[?]
Beauclerk Rd LSTA FY8 ....23[?]
Beaufort Cl FMBY L37 ....35[?]
Beaufort Av BISP FY2 ....14[?]
Beaufort Cl ORM L39 ....35[?]

M/BLYW BB12 ... 222 E1
ort Gv MCMB LA4 ... 41 K6
ort Rd BCUP OL13 ... 275 K4
MB LA4 ... 42 A6
ort St NLSN BB9 ... 198 B4
ey Av PDHM/BLYW BB12 ... 222 E1
naris Av BBNW BB2 ... 267 H2
naris Rd LEY/BBR PR5 ... 286 A3
nont Av HOR/BR BL6 ... 338 E7
nont Cl BBN BB1 ... 360 B1
nont Gdns PLF/KEOS FY6 ... 149 G6
nont Av WGNW/BIL/O WN5 ... 365 K3
nont Pl LANC LA1 ... 43 F7
nont Rd HOR/BR BL6 ... 338 D7
nont St LANC LA1 ... 43 F7
r Cl BBN BB1 ... 219 H6
rs La SKEL WN8 ... 363 K5
s Rd ORM L39 ... 348 A8
nsall La KIRK/FR/WA PR4 ... 258 E8
ct FTWD FY7 ... 122 D2
lean Av PLF/KEOS FY6 ... 177 K1
nham Ct BRFD/BLYE BB10 ... 198 B8
tt Ct PRES PR1 ... 7 D1
Gv CLV/TH FY5 ... 122 E7
ide COL BB8 ... 172 B8
side HGHB LA2 ... 45 C4
Vw
C (off Hala Sq) LA1 ... 55 G8
vay Av BPOOLE FY3 ... 177 F4
e Rd KKBYL LA6 ... 21 C1
e Pl CLV/TH FY5 ... 148 E2
ngton St NLSN * BB9 ... 198 B2
rd Av CLV/TH FY5 ... 122 D7
rd Cl ACC BB5 ... 247 G5
rd Ms DWN BB3 ... 268 C7
rd Pl LANC LA1 ... 55 C7
M/BLYW BB12 ... 223 K4
rd Rd BPOOL FY1 ... 176 C3
/RIB PR2 ... 213 J7
FY8 ... 233 F7
P PR8 ... 326 C1
rdshire Av
M/BLYW BB12 ... 224 D4
rd St BBNW BB2 ... 267 K1
V BB3 ... 268 C7
/E/EG BL7 ... 341 H1
V* BB9 ... 197 K2
OL14 ... 277 K4
rd Ter RAW/HAS BB4 ... 295 C3
acre RAMS BLO ... 319 K6
am St MCMB LA4 ... 41 H5
Av BPOOLE FY3 ... 5 E2
K/EAR BB18 ... 146 A2
/EC PR7 ... 285 K8
YE PR6 ... 337 H3
V BB3 ... 291 K1
/B LA2 ... 67 F7
K/FR/WA PR4 ... 208 E7
K/FR/WA PR4 ... 234 B5
/BBR PR5 ... 285 J3
/KEOS FY6 ... 149 K7
WN8 ... 351 J2
Cl ACC BB5 ... 270 B1
BB1 ... 219 C5
BB1 ... 247 F3
P OL13 ... 275 K8
C L40 ... 306 C7
B7 ... 165 H3
Y L32 ... 366 A8
WN8 ... 362 E2
T OL12 ... 323 G2
Crs ACC BB5 ... 248 A2
croft CLV/TH * FY5 ... 122 C7
Dr FMBY L37 ... 343 H7
/RIB PR2 ... 213 F3
/LONG PR3 ... 188 A4
K/FR/WA PR4 ... 234 E6
K/FR/WA PR4 ... 235 K1
/KEOS FY6 ... 177 K1
/HAS BB4 ... 295 J1
eeches BOL BL1 ... 341 H5
YE PR6 ... 264 B8
K/FR/WA PR4 ... 282 A4
/KEOS FY6 ... 179 F2
field LANC LA1 ... 2 B3
L WN8 ... 332 E6
field Av BPOOLE FY3 ... 5 E4
K/FR/WA PR4 ... 208 A8
/KEOS FY6 ... 98 C6
field Ct LEY/BBR PR5 ... 285 K3
field Gdns STHP PR8 ... 301 F5
field Rd LEY/BBR PR5 ... 285 J4
fields CHLYE/EC PR7 ... 308 D5
Gdns CHLYE PR6 ... 287 F2
D/HAY WA11 ... 368 E4

Beech Gv ACC BB5 ... 248 A7
BRFD/BLYE BB10 ... 198 A7
CHTN/BK PR9 ... 302 A4
DWN BB3 ... 140 D6
FUL/RIB PR2 ... 238 D2
MCMB LA4 ... 42 A6
PLF/KEOS FY6 ... 98 A5
Beech Hill Cl LEY/BBR PR5 ... 240 C8
Beeching Cl LANC * LA1 ... 3 D5
Beech Meadow ORM L39 ... 348 A7
Beech Mt BBN BB1 ... 219 H8
Beech Rd GAR/LONG PR3 ... 129 H3
HGHB LA2 ... 44 A4
KIRK/FR/WA PR4 ... 180 D2
LEY/BBR PR5 ... 285 J1
ORM L39 ... 359 J5
Beech St ACC * BB5 ... 248 C6
ACC BB5 ... 248 C6
BBN BB1 ... 9 E2
BCUP OL13 ... 275 K8
CLI BB7 ... 165 J5
EDGW/EG BL7 ... 317 H6
GTH/LHO BB6 ... 221 G5
LANC LA1 ... 2 B3
NLSN BB9 ... 198 C2
PDHM/BLYW BB12 ... 223 K4
PRES PR1 ... 6 A4
RAMS BLO ... 319 J8
RAW/HAS BB4 ... 273 G8
Beech St South PRES PR1 ... 6 C4
Beech Ter PRES PR1 ... 6 C4
Beechthorpe Av CLI BB7 ... 139 F7
Beech Tree Av WGNNW/ST WN6 ... 353 F5
Beech Tree Cl NLSN BB9 ... 198 C4
Beechtrees SKEL WN8 ... 363 J4
Beechway FUL/RIB * PR2 ... 213 J7
PRES PR1 ... 238 D8
Beechwood SKEL WN8 ... 351 J8
Beechwood Av ACC BB5 ... 248 D8
BLY BB11 ... 10 B6
CLI BB7 ... 165 J5
FUL/RIB PR2 ... 212 E7
LEY/BBR PR5 ... 240 A7
RAMS BLO ... 319 K5
WGNNW/ST WN6 ... 353 H6
Beechwood Ct
CHLY/EC (off Chapel La) PR7 ... 335 K3
Beechwood Crs
WGNW/BIL/O WN5 ... 365 G5
Beechwood Cft CHLYE PR6 ... 265 K8
Beechwood Dr BBNW BB2 ... 267 F3
CLV/TH FY5 ... 149 H3
FMBY L37 ... 355 G2
ORM L39 ... 348 B7
Beechwood Gdns LANC LA1 ... 67 G1
Beechwood Gv BISP FY2 ... 148 E6
Beechwood Ms BBNW BB2 ... 268 D3
Beechwood Rd BBN BB1 ... 9 H1
CHLY/EC PR7 ... 311 H5
Bee La PRES PR1 ... 262 A2
Beenland St PRES PR1 ... 240 B2
Beeston Av PLF/KEOS FY6 ... 149 J6
Beetham Ct ACC BB5 ... 221 J8
Beetham Pl BPOOLE FY3 ... 5 E1
Begonia Gv DWN BB3 ... 291 H3
Bela Gv BPOOL FY1 ... 4 C5
Beldale Pk KKBY L32 ... 366 A7
Belfield SKEL WN8 ... 363 K5
Belfield Rd ACC BB5 ... 248 B6
Belford Av CLV/TH FY5 ... 123 F7
Belford St PDHM/BLYW BB12 ... 10 C2
Belfry Cl CHLYE PR6 ... 286 B7
Belfry Man
GTH/LHO
(off St Andrews Rd) BB6 ... 192 A5
The Belfry
DWN (off Chapter Rd) BB3 ... 292 A3
LSTA FY8 ... 233 F6
Belgarth Rd ACC BB5 ... 248 C4
Belgrave Av KIRK/FR/WA PR4 ... 208 A4
PRES PR1 ... 238 D8
Belgrave Cl BBNW BB2 ... 8 A6
LSTA FY8 ... 231 K5
Belgrave Ct
FUL/RIB (off Caxton Rd) PR2 ... 213 K4
Belgrave Crs HOR/BR BL6 ... 339 F8
Belgrave Pl PLF/KEOS FY6 ... 177 H1
Belgrave Rd BPOOLS FY4 ... 5 E6
COL BB8 ... 171 H5
DWN BB3 ... 291 H3
LEY/BBR PR5 ... 285 J3
PLF/KEOS FY6 ... 177 H1
STHP PR8 ... 301 F7
Belgrave Sq DWN * BB3 ... 291 J2
Belgrave St ACC BB5 ... 272 B3
NLSN BB9 ... 197 J5

NLSN BB9 ... 198 D3
PDHM/BLYW BB12 ... 10 C2
Bellamy Av MCMB LA4 ... 41 G8
Belle Isle Av WHIT OL12 ... 323 G5
Belle Vue Av LANC LA1 ... 3 E6
Belle Vue Dr LANC LA1 ... 3 E5
Belle Vue La CLI BB7 ... 139 F7
Belle Vue Pl BLY * BB11 ... 10 B3
BPOOLE FY3 ... 5 D2
Belle Vue St BBNW BB2 ... 8 A4
BLY BB11 ... 10 B3
Bellfield Rd MCMB LA4 ... 41 J6
Bellingham Rd LSTA FY8 ... 232 D6
Bellis Av CHTN/BK PR9 ... 302 A1
Bellis Gv NWD/KWIPK * L33 ... 366 B6
Bellis Wy LEY/BBR PR5 ... 262 E1
Bell La ACC BB5 ... 222 B7
GAR/LONG PR3 ... 130 D7
WGNW/BIL/O WN5 ... 365 K3
Bell's Ar BRFD/BLYE BB10 ... 11 D1
Bell's Br GAR/LONG PR3 ... 129 F1
Bell's Cl MGHL L31 ... 358 E7
Bells La LEY/BBR PR5 ... 264 D1
MGHL L31 ... 358 C8
Bell St RAW/HAS BB4 ... 272 C8
Belmont Av BPOOL FY1 ... 4 C4
FUL/RIB PR2 ... 214 B8
PLF/KEOS FY6 ... 149 H8
WGNW/BIL/O WN5 ... 365 F8
Belmont Cl BRSC L40 ... 330 E8
CHLYE PR6 ... 288 E3
FUL/RIB PR2 ... 240 B1
LANC LA1 ... 42 D8
Belmont Ct GAR/LONG PR3 ... 188 B4
Belmont Crs FUL/RIB PR2 ... 240 B1
Belmont Dr CHLYE PR6 ... 311 J2
Belmont Gv BRFD/BLYE BB10 ... 226 B6
Belmont Pl CHLY/EC PR7 ... 335 G5
Belmont Rd BOL BL1 ... 341 H5
CHLYE PR6 ... 290 B6
CHLYE PR6 ... 337 H4
EDGW/EG BL7 ... 314 D4
FTWD FY7 ... 97 G8
FUL/RIB PR2 ... 238 E1
GTH/LHO BB6 ... 221 F6
HOR/BR BL6 ... 338 E2
LEY/BBR PR5 ... 285 F2
LSTA FY8 ... 231 J6
Belmont St STHP PR8 ... 301 G5
Belper St BBN BB1 ... 9 E3
Belsfield Dr KIRK/FR/WA PR4 ... 258 D7
Belthorn Rd BBN BB1 ... 269 G3
Belton Hl FUL/RIB PR2 ... 213 F3
Belvedere Av RAW/HAS BB4 ... 297 J2
Belvedere Dr CHLY/EC PR7 ... 311 F5
FMBY L37 ... 355 K2
Belvedere Pk ORM L39 ... 360 A4
Belvedere Rd BBN BB1 ... 219 J8
BRFD/BLYE BB10 ... 11 E3
CHLYE PR6 ... 337 H5
CLV/TH FY5 ... 149 J3
LEY/BBR* PR5 ... 285 K1
STHP PR8 ... 325 J6
Belverdale Gdns BPOOLS FY4 ... 205 F6
Belvere Av BPOOLS FY4 ... 204 D6
Benbow Cl LSTA FY8 ... 230 D2
Bence Rd PRES PR1 ... 7 F3
Bence St COL BB8 ... 171 J6
Benenden Pl CLV/TH * FY5 ... 149 G1
Bengal St CHLY/EC PR7 ... 311 G2
Bengarth Rd CHTN/BK PR9 ... 302 B5
Ben La BWCK/EAR BB18 ... 119 H8
RNFD/HAY WA11 ... 368 B1
Ben Lane Ct ORM L39 ... 368 B1
Bennett Av BPOOL FY1 ... 4 C3
Bennett Dr WGNW/BIL/O WN5 ... 365 F7
Bennett Rd CLV/TH FY5 ... 123 G8
Bennett's La BPOOLS FY4 ... 205 F5
Bennett St NLSN BB9 ... 198 D1
Bennington St BBNW BB2 ... 9 D6
Benson Av MCMB LA4 ... 41 K7
Benson La KIRK/FR/WA PR4 ... 182 E8
Benson Rd BPOOLE FY3 ... 176 E3
Benson's La GAR/LONG PR3 ... 183 J2
Benson St BBN BB1 ... 9 F2
EDGW/EG* BL7 ... 317 J6
Bent Gap La BBNW BB2 ... 8 A5
Bentham Av BRFD/BLYE BB10 ... 197 K8
FTWD FY7 ... 122 C2
Bentham Cl BBNW BB2 ... 267 J2
Bentham Rd BBNW BB2 ... 267 J2
LANC LA1 ... 67 G1
Bentham St CHLY/EC PR7 ... 335 J2
STHP PR8 ... 301 H6
Bentham's Wy STHP PR8 ... 326 E1
Bentinck Av BPOOLS FY4 ... 204 B6
Bentinck Dr KKBYL LA6 ... 21 H2

Bentinck Rd *LSTA* FY8 ....**230** C3
Bent La *COL* BB8 ....**172** B5
   LEY/BBR PR5 ....**285** K2
Bentlea Rd *CLI* BB7 ....**117** F5
Bentley Dr *BPOOLS* FY4 ....**206** C7
   KIRK/FR/WA PR4 ....**208** C6
Bentley La *BRSC* L40 ....**333** F4
Bentley Mnr
   FUL/RIB (off Hareden Rd) PR2 .....**240** D1
Bentley Park Rd *KIRK/FR/WA* PR4 ...**260** A4
Bentley St *BBN* BB1 ....**246** A6
   BCUP OL13 ....**275** K8
   DWN BB3 ....**291** K4
   NLSN BB9 ....**198** B4
Bentley Wood Wy *BLY* BB11............**224** A7
Benton Rd *FUL/RIB* PR2 ....**214** B7
Bents
   COL (off Skipton Old Rd) BB8......**172** B5
Bent St *ACC* BB5 ....**247** H8
   BBNW BB2 ....**8** B5
   RAW/HAS BB4 ....**295** K3
Bentwood Rd *RAW/HAS* BB4 ....**272** B8
Beresford Dr *CHTN/BK* PR9 ....**302** B2
Beresford Gdns *CHTN/BK* PR9 ....**302** B1
Beresford Rd *BLY* * BB11 ....**10** A4
   BPOOL FY1 ....**176** C4
Bergen St *BLY* BB11 ....**224** D6
Bergerac Crs *BISP* FY2 ....**149** F5
Berkeley Cl *CHLY/EC* PR7 ....**311** H6
   NLSN * BB9 ....**198** C4
Berkeley Crs *PDHM/BLYW* BB12 ......**223** J2
Berkeley Dr *LEY/BBR* PR5 ....**263** H1
   PDHM/BLYW BB12 ....**222** H2
Berkeley Rd *BOL* BL1 ....**341** J7
Berkeley St *NLSN* BB9 ....**197** J6
   NLSN BB9 ....**198** C5
   PRES PR1 ....**6** C1
Berkley Cl *KIRK/FR/WA* PR4 ....**208** C6
Berkshire Av *PDHM/BLYW* BB12 ......**224** D4
Berkshire Cl *BBN* BB1 ....**219** H5
Bernard St *WHIT* OL12 ....**323** J8
Berne Av *HOR/BR* BL6 ....**338** C8
Berridge Av *PDHM/BLYW* BB12 ....**224** C5
Berriedale Rd *NLSN* BB9 ....**198** E2
Berry Cl *SKEL* WN8 ....**363** F1
Berry Fld *PRES* PR1 ....**238** E8
Berry House Rd *BRSC* L40 ....**304** E7
Berry La *GAR/LONG* PR3 ....**188** A3
Berrys La *CLI* BB7 ....**221** G1
   PLF/KEOS FY6 ....**149** J7
Berry St *BLY* BB11 ....**10** C4
   CHLYE PR6 ....**337** C3
   LEY/BBR PR5 ....**262** D3
   NLSN * BB9 ....**197** K6
   PRES PR1 ....**7** E3
   SKEL WN8 ....**362** E1
Bertha St *ACC* BB5 ....**248** D5
Bertram Av *MCMB* LA4 ....**41** C7
Bertrand Av *BPOOLE* FY3 ....**177** G4
   STHP PR8 ....**325** J5
Berwick Dr *FUL/RIB* PR2 ....**213** F7
   PDHM/BLYW BB12 ....**10** B2
Berwick Rd *BPOOLS* FY4 ....**204** C7
   LSTA FY8 ....**231** F4
   PRES PR1 ....**7** E3
Berwick St *PRES* * PR1 ....**240** C2
Berwyn Av *MCMB* LA4......................**41** K6
Berwyn Cl *HOR/BR* BL6 ....**338** E6
Beryl Av *BBN* BB1 ....**245** H1
   CLV/TH FY5 ....**148** E2
Beryl St *BOL* BL1 ....**341** K8
Bescar Brow La *BRSC* L40 ....**328** D4
Bescar La *BRSC* L40 ....**328** E3
Bescot Wy *CLV/TH* FY5 ....**149** F4
Bessie St *BWCK/EAR* BB18 ....**145** F1
Bethel Av *BISP* FY2 ....**148** D7
Bethel Rd *BBN* BB1 ....**9** E2
Bethel St *BWCK/EAR* BB18 ....**119** H8
Bethesda Cl *BBNW* BB2 ....**8** B6
Bethesda Rd *BPOOL* FY1 ....**4** B3
Bethesda St *BLY* BB11 ....**10** C3
   BWCK/EAR BB18 ....**145** F2
Betony *MCMB* LA4 ....**42** B4
Betony Cl *WHIT* OL12 ....**323** H8
Bett La *CHLYE* PR6 ....**288** C2
Beulah Av *MCMB* LA4 ....**41** K6
   WGNW/BIL/O WN5 ....**371** F7
Bevan Pl *NLSN* BB9 ....**198** D1
Beverley Av *PLF/KEOS* FY6 ....**177** K3
   WGNW/BIL/O WN5 ....**371** G3
Beverley Cl *CHTN/BK* PR9 ....**278** E6
   FUL/RIB PR2 ....**6** A1
   KIRK/FR/WA PR4 ....**207** J8
Beverley Dr *CLI* BB7 ....**165** H5

Beverley Gv *BPOOLS* FY4 ....**204** C4
Beverley Rd *NLSN* BB9 ....**170** C3
   WGNW/BIL/O WN5 ....**365** K3
Beverley Rd North *LSTA* FY8 ....**231** C3
Beverley Rd South *LSTA* FY8 ....**231** H3
Beverley St *BBNW* BB2 ....**267** J2
   BLY BB11 ....**10** B4
Beverly Cl *CLV/TH* FY5 ....**149** H3
Bevington Cl *BLY* BB11 ....**10** B4
Bewcastle Dr *BRSC* L40 ....**349** F8
Bexhill Rd *FUL/RIB* PR2 ....**212** C4
Bexley Av *BPOOLE* FY3 ....**176** D3
Bexley Pl *LSTA* FY8 ....**231** K6
Bezza La *BBNW* BB2 ....**216** C6
   LEY/BBR PR5 ....**216** B7
Bhailok St *PRES* PR1 ....**6** C2
Bibby Dr *BPOOLE* FY3 ....**178** A7
Bibby Rd *CHTN/BK* PR9 ....**302** C2
Bibby's La *BISP* FY2 ....**148** D8
Bickerstaffe St *BPOOL* FY1 ....**4** B4
Bickerton Rd *STHP* PR8 ....**301** F7
Bicknell St *BBN* BB1 ....**8** C3
Bideford Av *BPOOLE* FY3 ....**177** G5
Bidston St *PRES* PR1 ....**240** C3
Bigdale Dr *NWD/KWIPK* L33 ....**366** E8
Biggins La *KKBYL* LA6 ....**20** E4
Biggins Rd *KKBYL* LA6 ....**21** C2
Billinge Av *RAW/HAS* BB4 ....**273** H6
Billinge Cl *BBNW* BB2 ....**244** D6
Billinge End Rd *BBNW* BB2 ....**243** H6
Billinge Rd *AIMK* WN4 ....**371** K6
Billinge St *BBN* BB1 ....**9** E5
Billington Av *RAW/HAS* BB4 ....**273** H6
Billington Gdns *CLI* BB7 ....**192** E7
Billington Rd *BLY* BB11 ....**224** C8
Billington St *KIRK/FR/WA* PR4 ....**208** D5
Billington St East
   KIRK/FR/WA PR4 ....**208** D5
Bilsborough Hey *PRES* PR1 ....**262** B2
Bilsborough Meadow
   FUL/RIB PR2 ....**212** A8
Bilsborrow La *GAR/LONG* PR3 ....**156** D7
Binbrook Pl *CHLY/EC* PR7 ....**310** E3
Binfold Cft *KKBYL* LA6 ....**21** H2
Bingley Av *BPOOLE* FY3 ....**5** F1
Bingley Cl *CHLYE* PR6 ....**287** G1
Binns St *RAW/HAS* BB4 ....**273** H4
Binyon Ct *LANC* LA1 ....**3** D5
Binyon Rd *LANC* LA1 ....**3** D5
Birbeck Rd *NWD/KWIPK* L33 ....**366** E8
Birch Av *BRSC* L40 ....**330** E7
   CHLY/EC PR7 ....**286** A7
   CLV/TH FY5 ....**148** E1
   FUL/RIB PR2 ....**238** C1
   HGHB LA2 ....**67** F7
   KIRK/FR/WA PR4 ....**209** K8
   LEY/BBR PR5 ....**263** H8
   PRES PR1 ....**238** C8
   RAW/HAS BB4 ....**272** D8
Birchbank Gdns *BBN* BB1 ....**9** E2
Birch Cl *ACC* BB5 ....**248** E1
   WHIT OL12 ....**323** C6
Birch Crs *ACC* BB5 ....**247** K8
   LEY/BBR PR5 ....**264** D2
Birch Dr *CARN* LA5 ....**15** G7
Birchenlee La *COL* BB8 ....**171** H8
Birches Rd *EDGW/EG* BL7 ....**317** J8
The Birches *FMBY* L37 ....**343** J6
Birch Fld *CHLYE* PR6 ....**264** C8
Birchfield *KIRK/FR/WA* PR4 ....**259** K7
Birchfield Dr *GAR/LONG* PR3 ....**188** A3
Birchfield Wy *MGHL* L31 ....**358** D6
Birch Gn *FMBY* L37 ....**343** H6
Birch Green Rd *SKEL* WN8 ....**351** J8
Birch Gv *CARN* LA5 ....**14** E3
   CLI BB7 ....**193** H3
   LANC LA1 ....**2** B2
   PLF/KEOS FY6 ....**125** F4
   TOT/BURYW BL8 ....**319** C8
Birch Hall Av *DWN* BB3 ....**268** D7
Birch Hall La *BWCK/EAR* BB18 ....**146** B1
Birchin La *CHLYE* PR6 ....**287** H2
Birch La *GAR/LONG* PR3 ....**159** C3
Birchley Av *WGNW/BIL/O* WN5 ....**370** E8
Birchley Rd *WGNW/BIL/O* WN5 ....**370** E8
Birchover Cl *FUL/RIB* PR2 ....**212** C6
Birch Rd *CHLY/EC* PR7 ....**335** J2
   CHLYE PR6 ....**311** H1
   GAR/LONG PR3..........................**129** G4
Birch St *ACC* * BB5 ....**248** B5
   BCUP OL13 ....**275** J8
   FTWD FY7 ....**97** G7
   LSTA FY8 ....**232** E3
   SKEL WN8 ....**362** E2
   STHP PR8 ....**301** H7
Birchtree Av *HEY* LA3 ....**52** E2
Birch Tree Gdns *BPOOLE* FY3 ....**205** H1

Birch Wk *BBN* BB1 ....
Birch Wy *PLF/KEOS* FY6 ....
Birchway Av *BPOOLE* FY3 ....
Birchwood Cl *BBN* BB1 ....
Birchwood Av *KIRK/FR/WA* PR4.......
Birchwood Cl *LSTA* FY8 ....
Birchwood Dr *CHLY/EC* PR7 ....
   FUL/RIB PR2..............................
   PLF/KEOS FY6 ....
Birchwood Wy *NWD/KWIPK* L33 .....
Bird St *NLSN* BB9 ....
   PRES PR1 ....
Birdy Brow *CLI* BB7 ....
Birkacre Brow *CHLY/EC* PR7 ....
Birkacre Rd *CHLY/EC* PR7 ....
Birkbeck Pl *FTWD* FY7 ....
Birkbeck Wy *BRFD/BLYE* BB10........
Birkdale Av *BISP* FY2 ....
   FTWD FY7 ....
   KIRK/FR/WA PR4 ....
   LSTA FY8.................................
Birkdale Cl *CLV/TH* FY5 ....
   KIRK/FR/WA PR4 ....
   LANC LA1.................................
Birkdale Cop *STHP* PR8 ....
Birkdale Dr *FUL/RIB* PR2 ....
Birkett Cl *BOL* BL1 ....
Birkett Dr *BOL* BL1 ....
   FUL/RIB PR2..............................
Birkett Pl *FUL/RIB* PR2 ....
Birkett Rd *ACC* BB5 ....
Birkey La *FMBY* L37 ....
Birklands Av *MCMB* LA4 ....
Birkrig *SKEL* WN8 ....
Birks Brow *GAR/LONG* PR3 ....
Birkside Wy *BPOOLS* FY4 ....
Birk St *PRES* PR1 ....
Birley Bank *PRES* PR1 ....
Birley Cl *WGNNW/ST* WN6 ....
Birley Pl *BRFD/BLYE* BB10 ....
Birley St *BBN* BB1 ....
   BPOOL * FY1............................
   KIRK/FR/WA PR4 ....
   PRES PR1 ....
Birleywood *SKEL* WN8 ....
Birnam Gn *FTWD* FY7......................
Birtwhistle Cl *NLSN* * BB9 ....
Birtwhistle Av *COL* BB8 ....
Birtwistle Cl *COL* BB8.....................
Birtwistle Hyde Pk *COL* * BB8 ....
Birtwistle St *ACC* BB5 ....
   GTH/LHO BB6 ....
   LEY/BBR PR5 ....
Bisham Cl *DWN* BB3 ....
Bishopdale Cl0se *LANC* LA1 ....
Bishopdale Cl *BBNW* BB2 ....
Bishopdale Rd *LANC* LA1 ....
Bishopgate *PRES* * PR1 ....
Bishopsgate *BPOOLE* FY3 ....
   LANC LA1.................................
Bishops Ga *LSTA* FY8 ....
Bishopstone Cl *BBNW* BB2 ....
Bishop St *ACC* * BB5 ....
   BRFD/BLYE BB10 ....
   NLSN BB9.................................
Bishopsway *PRES* PR1 ....
Bison Pl *LEY/BBR* PR5 ....
Bispham Av *LEY/BBR* PR5................
Bispham Rd *BISP* FY2 ....
   BPOOLE FY3..............................
   CHTN/BK PR9 ....
   CLV/TH FY5 ....
   NLSN BB9.................................
Bispham St *PRES* PR1 ....
Bittern Cl *BPOOLE* FY3....................
Bivel St *PDHM/BLYW* BB12 ....
Black Abbey St *ACC* BB5 ....
Blackacre La *BRSC* L40 ....
Black-a-Moor La *ORM* L39 ....
Blackamoor Rd *BBN* BB1 ....
Blackberry Hall Crs *HEY* LA3...........
Blackberry Wy *PRES* PR1 ....
Blackbrook Cl *CHLYE* PR6 ....
Black Bull La *FUL/RIB* PR2 ....
Blackburn Brow *CHLYE* PR6 ....
Blackburn Old Rd *BBN* BB1 ....
   GTH/LHO BB6 ....
Blackburn Rd *ACC* BB5 ....
   ACC BB5 ....
   BBN BB1 ....
   BOL BL1....................................
   CHLYE PR6 ....
   DWN BB3 ....
   EDGW/EG BL7 ....
   GAR/LONG PR3..........................
   GAR/LONG PR3..........................
   GTH/LHO BB6 ....

/BBR PR5.....241 F7
HM/BLYW BB12.....223 G4
MS BLO.....295 K7
//HAS BB4.....272 C6
burn St BBN BB1.....8 C3
BB11.....10 C3
LYE PR6.....311 H4
car La SFTN L29.....357 C8
Cft CHLYE PR6.....264 A8
Dyke La CARN LA5.....15 H1
er St BRFD/BLYE BB10.....225 J1
fen Pl BISP FY2.....176 D3
field Rd KIRK/FR/WA PR4.....235 F5
gate La KIRK/FR/WA PR4.....281 G8
horse La HOR/BR BL6.....337 J8
Horse St CHLY/EC * PR7.....311 F5
R/BR BL6.....337 J8
House La BRFD/BLYE BB10.....199 H8
/LONG PR3.....160 B3
hurst St KIRK/FR/WA PR4.....260 C3
hurst Rd MGHL L31.....358 E6
La GAR/LONG PR3.....127 J1
MS BLO.....320 D4
ane Cft CLI BB7.....165 J2
each Av FUL/RIB PR2.....215 H2
each La KIRK/FR/WA PR4.....211 F1
ledge Cl WGNW/BIL/O WN5.....365 G6
ley Gv NWD/KWIPK * L33.....366 E5
leyhurst Av
NW/BIL/O WN5.....371 C6
Moor Rd BRSC L40.....332 C1
Moss La BRSC L40.....328 B4
M L39.....360 B1
Moss Rd NLSN BB9.....169 F2
o Bar Rd NLSN BB9.....169 K5
pool Old Rd BPOOLE FY3.....177 C1
R/LONG PR3.....152 D6
pool Rd BISP FY2.....148 D7
R/LONG PR3.....154 B5
R/LONG PR3.....188 A4
K/FR/WA PR4.....208 A5
K/FR/WA PR4.....236 D3
A FY8.....231 H3
/KEOS FY6.....149 G7
ES PR1.....213 J8
pool Rd North LSTA FY8.....231 H5
pool St ACC BB5.....247 J6
N BB3.....291 K5
rod Brow HOR/BR BL6.....337 H7
snape Rd DWN BB3.....292 A1
stone Rd CHLYE PR6.....311 J2
thorn Cl CLV/TH FY5.....123 F6
/RIB PR2.....237 K2
K/FR/WA PR4.....235 K1
thorn Crs BCUP OL13.....275 J8
thorn Cft CHLYE PR6.....286 E1
thorn Dr PRES PR1.....238 C8
wood Pl LANC LA1.....3 F6
wood Rd BCUP OL13.....297 K4
s St LANC LA1.....2 C3
legate La SKEL WN8.....362 B1
scough Rd CHLY/EC * PR7.....335 J3
owrie Gdns ORM L39.....348 E7
Gv CHTN/BK PR9.....302 B4
EG BL7.....341 K3
way Av BPOOLE FY3.....5 F1
Av LEY/BBR PR5.....262 D4
hall SKEL WN8.....363 K4
ley Crs BWCK/EAR BB18.....118 E7
St ACC BB5.....248 B5
water Rd BBN BB1.....9 F2
y Moor BBNW BB2.....8 B4
y St BLY BB11.....11 E5
ston St FTWD FY7.....97 G7
he St FUL/RIB * PR2.....6 A1
lford Av CLV/TH FY5.....148 C2
lford Cl STHP PR8.....300 E6
el St BLY BB11.....10 B3
aw La PRES PR1.....238 C1
ike Moss LEY/BBR PR5.....284 D2
on Av CLV/TH FY5.....122 E7
on Pk SKEL WN8.....363 K4
hers Dr LEY/BBR PR5.....285 G2
Cl PDHM/BLYW BB12.....224 E3
holt Rd RAMS BLO.....320 B2
La BRSC L40.....331 K6
a Rd BWCK/EAR BB18.....146 D4
dale Av BPOOLE FY3.....178 A6
BB7.....165 G4
/TH FY5.....148 D2
/KEOS FY6.....149 G6
dale Cl LEY/BBR PR5.....263 J3
/BBR PR5.....285 K4
M L39.....360 B4
dale Gv HEY LA3.....52 E2
dale Rd GAR/LONG PR3.....158 A3

GAR/LONG PR3.....186 D5
LSTA FY8.....232 E7
PLF/KEOS FY6.....97 K6
Bleasdale St East PRES * PR1.....7 F1
Blea Tarn Pl MCMB LA4.....41 K7
Blelock St PRES PR1.....7 E3
Blenheim Av BPOOL FY1.....5 D3
KIRK/FR/WA PR4.....208 D6
Blenheim Cl BBN BB1.....245 G2
LEY/BBR PR5.....263 F3
Blenheim Dr CLV/TH FY5.....149 J1
KIRK/FR/WA PR4.....234 B5
Blenheim Pl LSTA FY8.....230 E2
Blenheim Rd STHP PR8.....325 H5
Blenheim St COL BB8.....172 A6
Blenheim Wy KIRK/FR/WA PR4.....212 A5
Blesma Ct
BPOOLS (off Lytham Rd) FY4.....204 C5
Blind La CLI BB7.....117 F6
PDHM/BLYW BB12.....196 C5
Blindman's La ORM L39.....348 K5
Bloomfield Ct PRES PR1.....239 G1
Bloomfield Gra PRES PR1.....261 K1
Bloomfield Rd BPOOL FY1.....4 C5
CHLYE PR6.....289 G2
Bloomfield St BOL BL1.....341 J8
Bloom St RAMS BLO.....319 G7
Blossom Av BPOOLS FY4.....205 F4
The Blossoms FUL/RIB PR2.....214 A5
Blucher St COL BB8.....171 J7
Bluebell Av RAW/HAS BB4.....295 G3
Bluebell Cl CHLYE PR6.....287 F6
CLV/TH FY5.....123 F6
KIRK/FR/WA PR4.....258 D7
Bluebell Gv BLY BB11.....224 C6
Blue Bell La TOD OL14.....277 H1
Blue Bell Pl PRES PR1.....7 E2
Bluebell Wy FUL/RIB PR2.....214 C5
Blue Moor KIRK/FR/WA PR4.....209 K2
Blue Scar La CLI BB7.....92 C5
Blue Stone La BRSC L40.....308 A8
Blundell Av FMBY L37.....343 F7
HTWN L38.....355 K8
STHP PR8.....326 B1
Blundell Crs STHP PR8.....326 B1
Blundell Dr STHP PR8.....326 B1
Blundell Gv HTWN L38.....355 K8
Blundell La CHTN/BK PR9.....302 C1
PRES PR1.....238 D5
Blundell Rd FUL/RIB PR2.....213 G8
LSTA FY8.....231 F2
Blundell St BPOOL FY1.....4 C4
Blythe Av CLV/TH FY5.....122 E6
Blythe La BRSC L40.....349 J2
Blythewood SKEL WN8.....363 J4
Boar Clough NLSN BB9.....168 A5
Boarded Barn CHLY/EC PR7.....286 A8
Boardman Av BPOOL FY1.....5 D5
Board St BRFD/BLYE BB10.....225 J2
Boarsgreave La RAW/HAS BB4.....297 H5
Bobbin Cl ACC * BB5.....248 A6
Bobbiners La CHTN/BK PR9.....279 J8
Bobbin Mill Ct TOD OL14.....277 G2
Bobby Langton Wy BRSC L40.....330 E6
Bocholt Wy RAW/HAS BB4.....296 C1
Bodie Hl HGHB LA2.....65 J6
Bodkin La GAR/LONG PR3.....151 H4
Bodmin Av CHTN/BK PR9.....278 D6
Bodmin St PRES PR1.....240 B2
Boegrave Av LEY/BBR PR5.....262 D3
Bogburn La CHLY/EC PR7.....335 H6
Bog Height Rd DWN BB3.....267 K5
Boland St BBN BB1.....9 E2
Bold La ORM L39.....359 K4
Bold St ACC BB5.....248 D5
BBN BB3.....8 C3
BCUP OL13.....298 D2
CHTN/BK PR9.....301 H3
COL BB8.....171 J7
FTWD FY7.....97 H6
HEY LA3.....40 E7
PRES PR1.....239 F1
The Boleyn MGHL L31.....359 G8
Bolland Prospect CLI BB7.....165 K3
Bolland St BWCK/EAR BB18.....119 F8
Bolton Av ACC BB5.....248 D2
LANC LA1.....43 F7
PLF/KEOS FY6.....149 J6
Bolton Cv NLSN BB9.....170 B8
Bolton La CARN LA5.....33 J7
Bolton Meadow LEY/BBR PR5.....284 C3
Bolton Rd BBNW BB2.....8 C6
BBNW BB2.....266 B7
CHLY/EC PR7.....311 H5

CHLYE PR6.....337 J4
DWN BB3.....291 K6
EDGW/EG BL7.....317 H7
LEY/BBR PR5.....265 K4
STHP PR8.....301 G7
Bolton Rd North RAMS BLO.....319 J2
Bolton Rd West RAMS BLO.....319 G7
Bolton's Cop CHTN/BK PR9.....280 B5
Boltons Ct PRES PR1.....7 E3
Bolton's Meanygate
KIRK/FR/WA PR4.....281 G4
Bolton St BPOOL FY1.....4 B5
CHLY/EC PR7.....311 G4
COL BB8.....171 F7
RAMS BLO.....319 H6
RAW/HAS BB4.....297 G2
Bombay St BBNW BB2.....8 A6
Bonchurch St BBN * BB1.....246 A7
Bond Cl HOR/BR BL6.....338 E8
Bond's La CHLY/EC PR7.....337 F4
CHTN/BK PR9.....279 J4
GAR/LONG PR3.....129 J5
KIRK/FR/WA PR4.....180 E1
Bond St BRFD/BLYE BB10.....11 D1
COL BB8.....171 H6
DWN BB3.....268 D8
LANC LA1.....3 E3
NLSN* BB9.....198 B4
RAMS BLO.....320 A1
Bone Cft CHLYE PR6.....287 F1
Bone Hill La GAR/LONG PR3.....127 G1
Bonfire Hill Cl RAW/HAS BB4.....273 H4
Bonfire Hill Rd RAW/HAS BB4.....273 H4
Bonney St CLV/TH FY5.....123 H8
Bonny St BPOOL FY1.....4 B3
Bonsall St BBNW BB2.....267 J1
Boome St BPOOLS FY4.....204 C5
Boon Town KKBYL LA6.....18 B6
Boon Wks KKBYL LA6.....18 B5
Booth Bridge La SKP/WHF BD23.....120 B6
Booth Ct BRFD/BLYE BB10.....11 D1
Booth Crs RAW/HAS BB4.....297 H2
Boothley Rd BPOOL FY1.....4 C1
Boothman Pl NLSN BB9.....198 C1
Boothman St BBNW * BB2.....268 A1
Booth Rd RAW/HAS BB4.....297 H2
Boothroyden BPOOL FY1.....176 B3
Booth's La ORM L39.....347 H6
Booth St ACC BB5.....248 C6
BCUP OL13.....298 E1
BOL BL1.....341 G8
CARN LA5.....33 K2
CHTN/BK PR9.....301 H3
NLSN BB9.....198 B3
RAW/HAS BB4.....272 B7
RAW/HAS BB4.....297 G3
Bootle St PRES PR1.....240 A2
Boot St BWCK/EAR BB18.....146 B1
Borage Cl CLV/TH FY5.....123 C6
Border Ct LANC LA1.....2 B3
Bores Hl WCN WN1.....336 C7
Borough Rd DWN BB3.....291 H3
Borron La KKBYL LA6.....27 H7
Borrowdale FMBY L37.....343 K6
Borrowdale Av BBN BB1.....246 A8
FTWD FY7.....96 E7
Borrowdale Cl ACC BB5.....248 D2
BRFD/BLYE BB10.....198 A8
Borrowdale Dr BRFD/BLYE BB10.....198 A7
Borrowdale Gv MCMB LA4.....41 K6
Borrowdale Rd BPOOLS FY4.....205 H2
LANC LA1.....3 E4
LEY/BBR PR5.....285 K4
WGNW/BIL/O* WN5.....365 K4
Borwick Av CARN LA5.....26 A5
Borwick Cl CARN LA5.....26 A6
Borwick St KKBYL LA6.....26 E4
MCMB* LA4.....41 H8
Borwick Dr LANC LA1.....2 B1
Borwick La CARN LA5.....26 B5
Borwick Rd KKBYL LA6.....27 J6
Bosburn Dr BBNW BB2.....243 J1
Boscombe Av HEY LA3.....52 E1
Boscombe Rd BPOOLS FY4.....204 B5
Bosley Cl DWN BB3.....292 B3
Bostock St PRES PR1.....7 E3
Boston Av BISP FY2.....148 D5
Boston Rd BCUP OL13.....275 J8
LSTA FY8.....231 H5
Bostons GTH/LHO BB6.....221 F6
Boston St NLSN BB9.....198 D5
Bosworth Dr STHP PR8.....325 H7
Bosworth Pl BPOOLS FY4.....204 B7
Bosworth St HOR/BR BL6.....338 D7
Botanic Rd CHTN/BK PR9.....302 D1
Botany Brow CHLYE PR6.....311 J1
Bott House La NLSN BB9.....198 E1

Bottomdale Rd HGHB LA2 ... 43 F3
Bottomgate BBN BB1 ... 9 E4
Bottomley Bank La
  RAW/HAS BB4 ... 273 J3
Bottomley St NLSN BB9 ... 198 C3
Bottomley Yd
  NLSN (off Bottomley St) BB9 ... 198 C3
Bottom o' th' Knotts Brow
  EDGW/EG BL7 ... 317 K8
Bottom o' th' Moor HOR/BR BL6 ... 339 H8
Bottoms La CARN LA5 ... 15 J7
Botton Rd HGHB LA2 ... 49 K8
Boulder St RAW/HAS BB4 ... 273 H4
Bouldsworth Rd
  BRFD/BLYE BB10 ... 226 C6
Boulevard PRES PR1 ... 7 F5
The Boulevard LSTA FY8 ... 231 G7
Boulsworth Cl
  BWCK/EAR
  (off Dales View Pk) BB18 ... 145 F4
Boulsworth Crs NLSN BB9 ... 199 F2
Boulsworth Dr COL BB8 ... 200 C2
Boulsworth Gv COL BB8 ... 172 A6
Boulview Ter COL BB8 ... 172 A6
Boundary Cl CHLY/EC PR7 ... 308 C5
  KIRK/FR/WA PR4 ... 261 G3
Boundary La BRSC L40 ... 331 F8
  CHTN/BK PR9 ... 280 B6
  GAR/LONG PR3 ... 125 K4
  KIRK/FR/WA PR4 ... 281 J2
  WCNNW/ST WN6 ... 334 E8
Boundary Meanygate
  KIRK/FR/WA PR4 ... 280 C4
Boundary Rd ACC BB5 ... 248 C4
  FUL/RIB PR2 ... 213 F8
  LANC LA1 ... 3 D5
  LSTA FY8 ... 233 G6
Boundary St BRFD/BLYE BB10 ... 226 A1
  COL BB8 ... 171 H7
  LEY/BBR PR5 ... 285 K1
  STHP PR8 ... 301 H7
Bourble's La GAR/LONG PR3 ... 99 F8
Bourne Brow GAR/LONG PR3 ... 157 G6
Bourne May Rd PLF/KEOS FY6 ... 97 K6
Bournemouth Rd BPOOLS FY4 ... 204 B5
Bourne Rd CLV/TH FY5 ... 123 H6
Bournesfield LEY/BBR PR5 ... 264 D2
Bourne's Rw LEY/BBR PR5 ... 264 D2
Bourne Wy CLV/TH FY5 ... 123 F7
Bovington Av CLV/TH FY5 ... 149 F3
Bow Brook Rd LEY/BBR PR5 ... 285 K2
Bowden Av BBNW BB2 ... 266 D2
Bowen St BBNW BB2 ... 267 J1
Bower Cl BBNW BB2 ... 267 J1
Bowerham La HGHB LA2 ... 55 H8
Bowerham Rd LANC LA1 ... 3 E5
Bowerham Ter LANC LA1 ... 3 E4
Bowers La GAR/LONG PR3 ... 128 C4
The Bowers CHLY/EC PR7 ... 311 H7
Bower St BBNW BB2 ... 267 J1
Bowes Lyon Pl LSTA * FY8 ... 231 J4
Bowfell Av MCMB LA4 ... 41 K6
Bowfell Cl BPOOLS FY4 ... 205 K2
Bowfield's La BBNW BB2 ... 217 F7
Bowgreave Cl BPOOLS FY4 ... 205 K2
Bowgreave Dr GAR/LONG PR3 ... 129 K7
Bow Hills La CLI BB7 ... 94 B7
Bowker's Green La ORM L39 ... 360 C6
Bowland Av BRFD/BLYE BB10 ... 226 C6
  CHLYE PR6 ... 311 H3
  FTWD FY7 ... 122 D3
Bowland Cl CARN LA5 ... 33 J2
  GAR/LONG PR3 ... 188 B3
Bowland Crs BPOOLS FY3 ... 177 J3
Bowland Dr LANC LA1 ... 2 B1
Bowland Gate La CLI BB7 ... 139 C1
  LSTA FY8 ... 231 J5
Bowland Rd FUL/RIB PR2 ... 214 E8
  GAR/LONG PR3 ... 129 J2
  HEY LA3 ... 52 E3
Bowland Vw GAR/LONG PR3 ... 129 J2
  HGHB LA2 ... 65 J6
  NLSN BB9 ... 198 B7
Bowland View Ct
  PLF/KEOS (off Stricklands La) FY6 ... 125 F5
Bow La LEY/BBR PR5 ... 285 K2
  PRES PR1 ... 6 C3
Bowlers Cl FUL/RIB PR2 ... 214 A6
Bowlingfield FUL/RIB PR2 ... 212 C5
Bowling Green Cl DWN BB3 ... 291 K4
  STHP PR8 ... 302 B6
Bowman St BBN BB1 ... 9 D4
Bowness Av BPOOLS FY4 ... 205 J3
  CLV/TH FY5 ... 149 H1
  LSTA FY8 ... 231 F2
  NLSN BB9 ... 198 C5
  STHP PR8 ... 325 J8
Bowness Cl BBN BB1 ... 9 E3
Bowness Pl FTWD FY7 ... 122 C2
Bowness Rd LANC LA1 ... 3 E2
  PDHM/BLYW BB12 ... 223 J1
  PRES PR1 ... 240 E2
Bowood Ct BPOOLE FY3 ... 177 H4
Bowran St PRES PR1 ... 7 D2
Bow St LEY/BBR PR5 ... 285 K1
Boxer Pl LEY/BBR PR5 ... 284 E1
Box St RAMS * BL0 ... 319 K5
Boxwood Dr BBNW BB2 ... 267 G3
Boxwood St BBN BB1 ... 9 D1
Boyes Av GAR/LONG PR3 ... 155 K1
Boyes Brow NWD/KWIPK L33 ... 366 B7
Boyle St BBN BB1 ... 9 D3
Boys La FUL/RIB PR2 ... 212 E6
Brabiner La FUL/RIB PR2 ... 187 F8
Bracebridge Dr STHP PR8 ... 327 H1
Bracewell Av PLF/KEOS FY6 ... 150 C8
Bracewell Cl NLSN * BB9 ... 198 C3
Bracewell La SKP/WHF BD23 ... 118 C6
Bracewell Rd FUL/RIB PR2 ... 214 C6
Bracewell St BRFD/BLYE BB10 ... 225 K2
  BWCK/EAR BB18 ... 119 F8
  NLSN BB9 ... 198 D3
Brackenbury Cl LEY/BBR PR5 ... 262 D4
Brackenbury Rd FUL/RIB * PR2 ... 213 G8
  PRES PR1 ... 213 G8
Brackenbury St PRES PR1 ... 239 H1
Bracken Cl BBNW BB2 ... 267 G3
  BOL BL1 ... 341 H5
  CHLYE PR6 ... 311 J3
Bracken Dr KIRK/FR/WA PR4 ... 235 H4
Bracken Gv RAW/HAS BB4 ... 295 H4
Bracken Hey CLI BB7 ... 166 A3
Brackenthwaite Rd CARN LA5 ... 16 D4
Brackenway FMBY L37 ... 344 A5
Bracknell Wy ORM L39 ... 359 J2
Braconash Rd LEY/BBR PR5 ... 285 C1
Bradda Rd BBNW BB2 ... 268 B2
Braddon St PRES PR1 ... 240 B2
Brades Av CLV/TH FY5 ... 149 K1
Brades La KIRK/FR/WA PR4 ... 235 H4
Brade St CHTN/BK PR9 ... 278 E7
Bradford Gv HEY LA3 ... 52 D5
Bradford St ACC BB5 ... 248 D5
Bradkirk La LEY/BBR PR5 ... 264 A3
Bradkirk Pl LEY/BBR PR5 ... 263 K4
Bradley Cl CHLY/EC PR7 ... 309 F5
Bradley Fold NLSN * BB9 ... 198 C2
Bradley Gdns PDHM/BLYW BB12 ... 224 D6
Bradley Hall Rd NLSN BB9 ... 198 D2
Bradley La CHLY/EC PR7 ... 309 F5
Bradley Rd NLSN BB9 ... 198 C2
Bradley Rd East NLSN BB9 ... 198 C2
Bradley St CHTN/BK PR9 ... 301 J3
  COL BB8 ... 171 K6
Bradley Vw NLSN * BB9 ... 198 C2
Bradman Rd NWD/KWIPK L33 ... 367 G8
Bradshaw Brow BRSC L40 ... 333 G1
Bradshaw St BBN BB1 ... 8 C1
  NLSN BB9 ... 198 C4
Bradshawgate Dr CARN LA5 ... 15 G7
Bradshaw La BRSC L40 ... 333 G1
  GAR/LONG PR3 ... 126 C1
  KIRK/FR/WA PR4 ... 179 K8
  SKEL WN8 ... 351 J2
Bradshaw Rw ACC BB5 ... 247 K5
Bradshaw's La STHP PR8 ... 325 K5
Bradshaw St ACC * BB5 ... 247 K5
  LANC LA1 ... 3 E4
  NLSN BB9 ... 198 C3
  WCNNW/BIL/O WN5 ... 365 J5
Bradshaw St East ACC * BB5 ... 248 C5
Bradshaw St West ACC * BB5 ... 247 K5
Bradyll Ct GTH/LHO BB6 ... 192 A5
Brady St HOR/BR BL6 ... 338 C6
Braefield Crs FUL/RIB PR2 ... 214 D8
Braemar Av CHTN/BK PR9 ... 302 A1
  CLV/TH FY5 ... 149 J4
Braemar Wk BISP FY2 ... 149 F5
Braeside BBNW BB2 ... 8 A3
Braeside Crs WGNNW/BIL/O WN5 ... 371 F6
Braganza Wy LANC LA1 ... 2 A3
Braidhawn WGNNW/ST WN6 ... 353 C4
Braid's La GAR/LONG PR3 ... 130 C4
Braintree Av PRES PR1 ... 262 B1
Braith Cl BPOOLS FY4 ... 205 F3
Braithwaite WGNNW/ST WN6 ... 353 J5
Braithwaite St BPOOL FY1 ... 176 B4
Bramble Cl KIRK/FR/WA PR4 ... 208 C5
Bramble Ct CLV/TH FY5 ... 149 G1
  PRES PR1 ... 262 B1
Bramble Gdns PLF/KEOS FY6 ... 177 G5
The Brambles BBNW BB2 ... 244 C3
  CHLY/EC PR7 ... 335 K1
CLI BB7 ...
FUL/RIB PR2 ...
Bramble St BRFD/BLYE BB10 ...
Bramble Wy SKEL WN8 ...
Bramblewood LEY/BBR PR5 ...
The Bramblings PLF/KEOS FY6 ...
Bramcote Cl NWD/KWIPK L33 ...
Bramcote Rd NWD/KWIPK L33 ...
Bramcote Wk NWD/KWIPK L33 ...
Bramhall Rd SKEL WN8 ...
Bramley Av FTWD FY7 ...
  PDHM/BLYW BB12 ...
Bramley Cl ACC BB5 ...
Bramley Rd EDGW/EG BL7 ...
Bramley St ACC BB5 ...
Brampton Av CLV/TH FY5 ...
Brampton Dr MCMB LA4 ...
Brampton St FUL/RIB PR2 ...
Bramwell Rd KIRK/FR/WA PR4 ...
Bramworth Av RAMS BL0 ...
Branch Rd BBNW BB2 ...
  BLY BB11 ...
  CLI BB7 ...
  DWN BB3 ...
  NLSN BB9 ...
Brancker St CHLY/EC PR7 ...
Brandiforth St LEY/BBR PR5 ...
Brandon Cl SKEL WN8 ...
Brandreth Delph SKEL WN8 ...
Brandreth Dr SKEL WN8 ...
Brandreth Pk SKEL WN8 ...
Brandwood PRES PR1 ...
  RAW/HAS (off Staghills Rd) BB4 ...
Brandwood Gv BRFD/BLYE BB10 ...
Brandwood Pk BCUP OL13 ...
Brandwood Rd BCUP OL13 ...
Brandwood St DWN BB3 ...
Brandy House Brow BBNW BB2 ...
Branksome Av CLV/TH FY5 ...
Branksome Dr MCMB LA4 ...
Branston Rd BPOOLS FY4 ...
Branstree Rd BPOOLS FY4 ...
Brant Ct FTWD FY7 ...
Brantfell Dr PDHM/BLYW BB12 ...
Brantfell Rd BBN BB1 ...
  GTH/LHO BB6 ...
Brant Rd PRES PR1 ...
Brantwood ACC BB5 ...
Brantwood Av BBN BB1 ...
  MCMB LA4 ...
Brantwood Dr LANC LA1 ...
  LEY/BBR PR5 ...
Brassey St PDHM/BLYW BB12 ...
Brathay Rd FTWD FY7 ...
Braxfield Ct
  LSTA (off St Anne's Rd West) FY8 ...
Brays Heys
  CLV/TH (off Lawsons Rd) FY5 ...
Brays Rd LSTA FY8 ...
Bray St FUL/RIB * PR2 ...
Brazil Cl HEY LA3 ...
Bread St PDHM/BLYW * BB12 ...
Brearlands SKP/WHF BD23 ...
Brearley St BCUP OL13 ...
Breck Cl PLF/KEOS FY6 ...
Breck Dr PLF/KEOS FY6 ...
Breck Rd BPOOLE FY3 ...
  PLF/KEOS FY6 ...
Breck's Br HGHB LA2 ...
Breckside Cl PLF/KEOS FY6 ...
Brecon Av ACC BB5 ...
Brecon Cl BPOOL FY1 ...
Brecon Rd BBN BB1 ...
Bredon Av CHLY/EC PR7 ...
Bredon Cl LSTA FY8 ...
Breeze Cl CLV/TH FY5 ...
  COL BB8 ...
Breeze Mt LEY/BBR PR5 ...
Breeze Rd STHP PR8 ...
Brenbar Crs WHIT * OL12 ...
Brendjean Rd MCMB LA4 ...
Brennand Cl LANC LA1 ...
  LEY/BBR PR5 ...
Brennand St BRFD/BLYE BB10 ...
  CLI BB7 ...
Brentlea Av HEY LA3 ...
Brentlea Crs HEY LA3 ...
Brent St BRFD/BLYE BB10 ...
Brentwood FTWD FY7 ...
Brentwood Av BLY BB11 ...
  CLV/TH FY5 ...
  PLF/KEOS FY6 ...
Brentwood Ct CHTN/BK PR9 ...
Brentwood Rd CHLYE PR6 ...
  NLSN BB9 ...
Bretherton Cl LEY/BBR PR5 ...

erton Rd LEY/BBR PR5 .....283 G7
erton Ter LEY/BBR PR5 .....285 J2
arch Dr LANC LA1 .....2 C6
argh Cl LANC LA1 .....2 C5
argh Dr LANC LA1 .....2 C5
Cl CLI BB7 .....166 A4
on Fold STHP PR8 .....302 B6
ery La FMBY L37 .....343 K5
C LA1 .....3 D3
ery St GAR/LONG PR3 .....188 B4
OL14 .....277 K3
orth Fold La CHLYE PR6 .....264 E8
Av CHLY/EC PR7 .....286 A7
Bank Rw FUL/RIB PR2 .....213 H3
Cft KIRK/FR/WA PR4 .....260 B4
Fld BISP FY2 .....149 F5
ield CHLY/EC BL7 .....341 H1
ield Rd PLF/KEOS FY6 .....149 H5
Gv FUL/RIB PR2 .....212 C7
Hill Cl BBN BB1 .....9 E5
Lea Rd KKBYL LA6 .....34 A6
Ms CLV/TH FY5 .....149 J2
Rd BBN BB1 .....9 D1
/TH FY5 .....149 H2
P PR8 .....325 K7
Brook BRSC L40 .....331 G8
Gn SKEL WN8 .....351 G7
La BRSC L40 .....331 G8
riars CHLY/EC PR7 .....308 E5
/RIB PR2 .....214 B5
P PR8 .....326 B2
St BCUP OL13 .....298 E2
wood KIRK/FR/WA PR4 .....234 E5
wood Cl KIRK/FR/WA PR4 .....207 G1
/BBR PR5 .....285 F3
wood Dr CLV/TH FY5 .....149 H4
wood Dr BISP FY2 .....148 E6
Cft HTWN L38 .....355 K8
croft La LEY/BBR PR5 .....283 G8
house Gdns
/LONG (off Garstang Rd) PR3 .....134 E8
House La PLF/KEOS FY6 .....124 D7
house La PLF/KEOS FY6 .....124 E7
Kiln La BRSC L40 .....306 A8
e Av ORM L39 .....348 C7
e Bank FUL/RIB PR2 * PR5 .....240 A5
e Brow KKBYL LA6 .....21 H7
e Cl LEY/BBR PR5 .....262 D3
e Cft ACC BB5 .....221 K7
N LA5 .....33 G7
e End LEY/BBR PR5 .....263 F4
e End La RAW/HAS BB4 .....295 G4
e End St TOD * OL14 .....277 H2
efield St PDHM/BLYW BB12 .....223 J7
ehall Dr SKEL WN8 .....364 D4
e House Rd BPOOLS FY4 .....205 F3
e La LANC LA1 .....3 D3
emill Rd BBN BB1 .....9 D1
e Mill Rd NLSN BB9 .....198 A3
e Rd CLI BB7 .....140 D6
/D FY7 .....97 H7
/RIB PR2 .....238 E1
YL LA6 .....34 A7
C LA1 .....3 D6
/BBR PR5 .....263 F3
YL LA8 .....231 K7
eside LSTA FY8 .....204 B7
e st ACC BB5 .....247 J5
BB5 .....248 C5
N BB1 .....8 C5
N BB1 .....247 F1
BB11 .....11 D3
BB8 .....171 G7
R/LONG PR3 .....129 G5
LHO BB6 .....221 G6
R/BR BL6 .....338 E7
/BBR PR5 .....241 F8
/BBR PR5 .....263 H4
N BB9 .....197 K5
M L39 .....348 C7
HM/BLYW BB12 .....223 H3
MS BLO 319 J5
/HAS BB4 .....274 D3
/HAS BB4 .....297 H2
/HAS* BB4 .....297 G4
/P PR8 .....301 H5
/T* OL12 .....323 G2
e Ter LEY/BBR* PR5 .....240 A5
et St LANC * LA1 .....3 D3
eview Dr NWD/KWIPK L33 .....366 D7
ewater Av CLV/TH FY5 .....149 F4
ewater Cl BLY BB11 .....224 D3
eway LEY/BBR PR5 .....263 F3
e Wills La CHTN/BK PR9 .....278 E6

Bridleway RAW/HAS BB4 .....297 H1
Brief St BRFD/BLYE BB10 .....11 D1
Briercliffe Av BPOOLE FY3 .....5 F5
COL BB8 .....171 F8
Briercliffe Rd BRFD/BLYE BB10 .....11 E1
BRFD/BLYE BB10 .....226 A2
CHLYE PR6 .....311 H2
Briercliffe St COL BB8 .....171 F8
Brier Crs NLSN BB9 .....198 B5
Brierfield KIRK/FR/WA PR4 .....261 G3
SKEL WN8 .....363 K6
Brier St NLSN BB9 .....198 B6
Brierholme Av EDGW/EG BL7 .....341 J2
Brierley Av BPOOLE FY3 .....5 E1
Brierley La KIRK/FR/WA PR4 .....183 H3
Brierley Rd LEY/BBR PR5 .....263 K4
Brierley St PRES PR1 .....6 B1
Briers Brow CHLYE PR6 .....288 B4
Briery Bank CARN LA5 .....15 H2
Briery Cl FUL/RIB PR2 .....214 A7
Brieryfield Rd PRES PR1 .....6 B2
Briery Hey LEY/BBR PR5 .....264 B5
Brigg Fld ACC BB5 .....221 K7
Briggs Fold Cl EDGW/EG BL7 .....341 J1
Briggs Fold Rd EDGW/EG BL7 .....341 J1
Briggs Rd FUL/RIB PR2 .....238 C1
Brighouse Cl ORM L39 .....348 B5
Brighton Av BPOOLS FY4 .....204 B3
CLV/TH FY5 .....148 D1
LSTA FY8 .....231 F4
Brighton Crs FUL/RIB PR2 .....212 C8
Brighton Rd BRFD/BLYE BB10 .....198 A8
STHP PR8 .....301 G8
Brighton St CHLYE * PR6 .....311 J3
TOD OL14 .....277 H2
Brighton Ter BBNW BB2 .....244 D5
DWN BB3 .....291 G1
Bright's Cl CLI BB7 .....111 K1
Brightstone Cl CHTN/BK PR9 .....279 K6
Bright St ACC BB5 .....247 K8
BBN BB1 .....9 F3
BPOOLS FY4 .....204 B5
BRFD/BLYE BB10 .....225 J2
CHTN/BK PR9 .....302 B4
CLI BB7 .....165 K3
COL BB8 .....171 H6
COL BB8 .....172 B6
DWN BB3 .....291 H1
RAW/HAS BB4 .....273 H8
Bright Ter COL BB8 .....200 B1
Brigsteer Cl ACC BB5 .....247 J1
Brindle Cl GAR/LONG PR3 .....188 B4
LANC LA1 .....2 A1
LEY/BBR PR5 .....264 A3
Brindle Fold LEY/BBR PR5 .....264 B4
Brindle Hts CHLYE PR6 .....264 E6
Brindle Rd CHLYE PR6 .....264 C5
LEY/BBR PR5 .....263 J1
Brindle St BBNW BB2 .....267 J2
CHLY/EC PR7 .....311 G5
PRES PR1 .....240 A3
Brindley Cl BLY BB11 .....224 B7
Brinklow Cl STHP PR8 .....325 G6
Brinks Rw
HOR/BR (off Wildererswood) BL6 .....339 F6
Brinwell Rd BPOOLS FY4 .....205 H2
Brisbane Pl CLV/TH FY5 .....149 F4
Brisbane St ACC BB5 .....248 A2
Bristol Av BISP FY2 .....148 E7
FTWD FY7 .....122 C3
LEY/BBR PR5 .....263 F7
Bristol Cl BBN * BB1 .....9 E5
Bristol St BLY BB11 .....10 A5
COL BB8 .....171 J6
MCMB LA4 .....41 J7
Bristow Av FUL/RIB PR2 .....238 D1
Britannia Av BCUP OL13 .....298 E1
Britannia Dr FUL/RIB PR2 .....238 D3
Britannia Pl BPOOLE FY1 .....4 B4
Britannia St GTH/LHO BB6 .....221 G6
Britannia Wk BLY BB11 .....11 E5
LSTA FY8 .....231 J3
Britannia Wy RAW/HAS BB4 .....295 G3
Britten Cl BBNW BB2 .....268 D1
Britten St DWN BB3 .....291 H1
Britwell Cl BBNW BB2 .....268 D3
Brixey St PRES PR1 .....6 B4
Brixham Pl BPOOLS FY4 .....204 B5
Brixton Rd PRES PR1 .....7 F4
Broadacre HGHB LA2 .....45 G6
SKEL WN8 .....364 C5
WCNNW/ST WN6 .....353 H1
Broadacre Cl HGHB LA2 .....45 G6
Broadacre Pl HGHB LA2 .....45 F6
Broadacre Vw HGHB LA2 .....45 G6
Broad Cft KIRK/FR/WA PR4 .....260 B2
Broadfield ACC BB5 .....270 E1

KIRK/FR/WA PR4 .....212 D1
Broadfield Av BPOOLS FY4 .....204 E6
PLF/KEOS FY6 .....150 B8
Broadfield Dr LEY/BBR PR5 .....285 G2
PRES PR1 .....262 A1
Broadfield Rd ACC BB5 .....248 A8
Broadfields CHLY/EC PR7 .....311 F1
Broadfield St ACC BB5 .....247 K8
Broadfleet Cl GAR/LONG PR3 .....100 A5
Broadfold Av BBN BB1 .....9 E2
Broad Ga DWN BB3 .....291 K1
Broadgate PRES PR1 .....6 B4
Broadgreen Cl LEY/BBR PR5 .....285 H2
Broadhead Rd DWN BB3 .....293 G2
EDGW/EG BL7 .....317 J4
RAW/HAS BB4 .....293 G3
Broadhurst La WCNNW/ST WN6 .....334 D5
Broadhurst Rd CLV/TH FY5 .....148 E3
Broadhurst Wy BRFD/BLYE BB10 .....198 A7
Broad Ing Cl BRFD/BLYE BB10 .....252 C2
Broadith La GAR/LONG PR3 .....186 C1
Broadlands STHP PR8 .....300 E8
WCNNW/ST WN6 .....353 K5
Broadlands Dr CARN LA5 .....33 F8
Broadlands Pl LSTA FY8 .....232 B7
Broad La CLI BB7 .....193 F6
FMBY L37 .....344 C4
FMBY L37 .....344 D8
FMBY L37 .....356 E1
GAR/LONG PR3 .....103 F6
ORM L39 .....358 E1
Broadley St RAW/HAS BB4 .....273 H8
Broadmead SKEL WN8 .....351 H1
Broad Meadow GAR/LONG PR3 .....134 D8
LEY/BBR PR5 .....262 D3
Broad Meadow La LEY/BBR PR5 .....282 E8
Broadness Dr NLSN BB9 .....198 C5
Broad Oak Av GAR/LONG PR3 .....129 K5
Broad Oak Cl CHLYE PR6 .....337 G3
Broad Oak Gn PRES PR1 .....238 D8
Broad Oak La BPOOLE FY3 .....177 K6
KIRK/FR/WA PR4 .....261 J1
PRES PR1 .....238 D8
Broad Oak Rd ACC BB5 .....248 C6
Broad o' th' La BOL BL1 .....341 J7
WCNNW/ST WN6 .....353 J5
Broadpool La PLF/KEOS FY6 .....150 E2
Broadriding Rd WCNNW/ST WN6 .....353 G5
Broad Sq LEY/BBR PR5 .....285 J3
Broad St LEY/BBR PR5 .....285 J3
NLSN BB9 .....198 B3
Broadtree Cl BBNW BB2 .....217 J8
Broadwater Av FTWD FY7 .....122 E3
Broadwater Gdns
FTWD (off Broadwater Av) FY7 .....122 E3
Broadway ACC * BB5 .....248 B5
BBN BB1 .....245 G1
BPOOLS FY4 .....204 C4
FTWD FY7 .....122 D5
FUL/RIB PR2 .....213 F5
FUL/RIB PR2 .....238 E1
HOR/BR BL6 .....339 F8
LANC LA1 .....3 D1
LEY/BBR PR5 .....285 K3
MCMB LA4 .....41 K6
NLSN BB9 .....198 B3
RAW/HAS BB4 .....295 H3
Broadway Cl STHP PR8 .....325 H6
Broadway Crs RAW/HAS BB4 .....295 G3
Broadway Pl NLSN BB9 .....170 B8
NLSN BB9 .....198 E2
Broadway St BBNW BB2 .....267 J2
Broadwood Cl PRES PR1 .....238 D7
Broadwood Dr FUL/RIB PR2 .....213 G4
Broadwood Wy LSTA FY8 .....232 A7
Brock Av FTWD FY7 .....122 D1
Brockbank Av LANC LA1 .....54 B3
Brock Cl LANC LA1 .....42 E8
Brock Clough Rd RAW/HAS BB4 .....274 C7
Brockenhurst St BRFD/BLYE BB10 .....11 F4
Brockholes Brow PRES PR1 .....240 D2
Brockholes Crs PLF/KEOS FY6 .....178 A1
Brockholes Vw PRES PR1 .....240 A4
Brockholes Wy GAR/LONG PR3 .....156 A2
Brocklebank Rd CHTN/BK PR9 .....302 A2
Brocklehurst Av ACC BB5 .....248 B8
Brocklewood Av PLF/KEOS FY6 .....177 K3
Brock Mill La GAR/LONG PR3 .....131 J8
Brock Rakes GAR/LONG PR3 .....132 D4
Brock Rd CHLYE PR6 .....311 H2
GAR/LONG PR3 .....153 J7
Brock Side GAR/LONG PR3 .....156 D5
Brock St LANC LA1 .....3 D3
Brockway PLF/KEOS FY6 .....177 K1
Brockway Av BPOOLE FY3 .....5 F1
Broderick Av BISP FY2 .....176 E2
Brodick Rd BBN BB1 .....246 B8

Brogden La *BWCK/EAR* BB18 .....144 A2
Brogden St *BWCK/EAR* BB18 .....119 F8
Brogden Vw *BWCK/EAR* BB18 .....118 E7
Broken Bank Head *CLI* BB7 .....88 D1
Broken Banks *COL* BB8 .....171 J7
Broken Stone Rd *SKEL* WN8 .....362 C2
Bromilow Rd *SKEL* WN8 .....362 C2
Bromley CI *BISP* FY2 .....176 E2
Bromley Gn *CHLYE* PR6 .....287 K7
Bromley Rd *LSTA* FY8 .....231 F5
Bromley St *BBNW* BB2 .....8 A4
  PRES PR1 .....6 B2
Brompton CI *LSTA* FY8 .....231 K5
Brompton Rd *PLF/KEOS* FY6 .....177 K2
  STHP PR8 .....302 A2
Bromsgrove Av *BISP* FY2 .....148 C7
Bromsgrove Rd *BRFD/BLYE* BB10 .....11 E1
Bronte Av *BRFD/BLYE* BB10 .....226 B5
Bronte Wy *BRFD/BLYE* BB10 .....227 H3
  COL BB8 .....173 F7
  HWTH BD22 .....205 K7
  PDHM/BLYW BB12 .....224 B3
Brooden Dr *BRFD/BLYE* BB10 .....198 A4
Brook Av *GAR/LONG* PR3 .....104 A4
  HEY LA3 .....41 F8
  MGHL L31 .....359 G8
Brook Cft *FUL/RIB* PR2 .....212 D8
Brookdale *CHLYE* PR6 .....337 G2
  EDGW/EG BL7 .....314 E7
  KIRK/FR/WA PR4 .....261 H5
  WHIT OL12 .....323 J8
Brookdale Av *CLV/TH* FY5 .....148 E3
Brookdale CI *LEY/BBR* PR5 .....285 K5
Brookdean CI *BOL* BL1 .....341 G8
Brooke CI *ACC* BB5 .....271 K1
  CHTN/BK PR9 .....302 D4
Brookes St *BCUP* OL13 .....298 B3
Brooke St *CHLYE* PR6 .....311 H4
Brook Farm *ORM* L39 .....348 C2
Brookfield *BBNW* BB2 .....244 A1
  BRSC L40 .....332 E1
  LEY/BBR PR5 .....283 H8
  SKEL WN8 .....351 J1
Brookfield Av *BPOOLE* FY4 .....205 G5
  CLV/TH FY5 .....149 J1
  FUL/RIB PR2 .....214 A7
Brookfield CI *CARN* LA5 .....33 H6
  KKBYL LA6 .....18 A1
Brookfield Ct *GAR/LONG* PR3 .....134 E8
Brookfield Dr *FUL/RIB* PR2 .....213 G3
Brookfield La *ORM* L39 .....359 J6
Brookfield PI *LEY/BBR* PR5 .....263 K5
Brookfield Rd *CLV/TH* FY5 .....149 J1
  SKEL WN8 .....364 E5
  WGNW/ST WN6 .....353 K1
Brookfields
  WGNW/BIL/O (off Brook La) WN5 .....365 K6
Brookfield St *BBN* BB1 .....8 C3
  PRES PR1 .....7 D1
  TOD OL14 .....277 H2
Brookfield Wy *BWCK/EAR* BB18 .....146 B2
Brookford CI *PDHM/BLYW* BB12 .....10 A1
Brook Gv *CLV/TH* FY5 .....122 E7
  HEY LA3 .....41 F8
Brook Hey *KIRK/FR/WA* PR4 .....260 A3
Brook Hey Dr *NWD/KWIPK* L33 .....366 D7
Brookhouse CI *LEY/BBR* PR5 .....264 E1
Brookhouse Dr *LEY/BBR* PR5 .....264 E1
Brookhouse La *BBN* BB1 .....9 D3
Brookhouse Rd *HGHB* LA2 .....45 C6
  ORM L39 .....348 B5
Brookhouse St *FUL/RIB* PR2 .....6 B1
Brookland CI *ACC* BB5 .....221 J7
Brooklands *FUL/RIB* PR2 .....238 C2
  GAR/LONG PR3 .....135 F8
  HOR/BR BL6 .....338 E8
  ORM L39 .....348 D5
Brooklands Av *BLY* BB11 .....11 E6
  FUL/RIB PR2 .....213 G4
  KIRK/FR/WA PR4 .....208 E6
  RAW/HAS BB4 .....295 H4
Brooklands Ct
  LANC (off Lentworth Dr) LA1 .....55 G7
Brooklands Dr *GAR/LONG* PR3 .....129 J5
  HEY LA3 .....52 C5
  WGNW/BIL/O WN5 .....365 F6
Brooklands Gv *BRSC* L40 .....331 F5
Brooklands Rd *BLY* BB11 .....11 E6
  LSTA FY8 .....231 F5
  SKEL WN8 .....364 E4
Brooklands Ter *BBN* * BB1 .....9 E2
The Brooklands *KIRK/FR/WA* PR4 .....207 J7
Brookland St *RAW/HAS* BB4 .....297 F2
Brook La *CHLY/EC* PR7 .....309 K2
  KIRK/FR/WA PR4 .....259 K8
  KIRK/FR/WA PR4 .....262 A4
  LEY/BBR PR5 .....262 A5

  ORM L39 .....348 C7
RNFD/HAY WA11 .....370 B4
SKP/WHF BD23 .....94 C1
  WGNW/BIL/O WN5 .....365 J6
Brooklyn Av *BPOOLE* FY3 .....176 E3
Brooklyn Rd *BBN* BB1 .....219 G6
Brook Meadow *KIRK/FR/WA* PR4 .....212 B5
Brook PI *FUL/RIB* PR2 .....237 K1
Brook Rd *HEY* LA3 .....41 F8
  LSTA FY8 .....232 E7
Brook Rd North *FUL/RIB* PR2 .....213 F8
Brooksbottom CI *RAMS* BL0 .....319 J7
Brookside *CHLY/EC* PR7 .....310 A1
  CHLY/EC PR7 .....335 K2
  CLV/TH FY5 .....123 J8
  GTH/LHO BB6 .....192 A6
  KIRK/FR/WA PR4 .....208 D5
Brookside Av *RNFD/HAY* WA11 .....368 E4
Brookside CI *LEY/BBR* PR5 .....262 B8
  TOT/BURYW BL8 .....319 G8
  WGNW/BIL/O WN5 .....371 G7
Brookside Crs *CLI* BB7 .....139 H4
Brookside Dr *HGHB* LA2 .....81 J2
Brookside La *ACC* BB5 .....246 D8
Brookside Rd *FUL/RIB* PR2 .....213 F4
  STHP PR8 .....326 E2
Brookside St *ACC* BB5 .....247 G8
Brookside Vw *ACC* BB5 .....247 F7
Brooks Rd *FMBY* L37 .....355 H1
Brook St *ACC* BB5 .....247 J8
  BBN BB1 .....247 F2
  BBNW BB2 .....267 J1
  BPOOLS FY4 .....5 E6
  BWCK/EAR BB18 .....145 F3
  BWCK/EAR BB18 .....146 B1
  CHLYE PR6 .....337 G2
  CHTN/BK PR9 .....278 E7
  CLI BB7 .....165 K2
  COL BB8 .....171 H6
  FTWD FY7 .....122 E3
  FUL/RIB PR2 .....213 F8
  KIRK/FR/WA PR4 .....208 D5
  LANC LA1 .....2 C4
  LEY/BBR PR5 .....241 F8
  NLSN BB9 .....198 C3
  RAW/HAS BB4 .....272 C6
Brooks Wy *FMBY* L37 .....355 H1
Brookview *FUL/RIB* PR2 .....213 K6
Brookway *BBNW* BB2 .....267 J3
  KIRK/FR/WA PR4 .....260 A3
Brooky Moor
  EDGW/EG (off Bury Rd) BL7 .....317 J5
Broome Rd *STHP* PR8 .....301 H8
Broom Fld *GAR/LONG* PR3 .....129 K7
Broomfield Mill St *PRES* PR1 .....7 D1
Broomfield PI *BBNW* BB2 .....244 D8
Broomfield Rd *FTWD* FY7 .....97 F8
Broomholme *WGNW/ST* WN6 .....353 F4
Brotherton Mdw *CLI* BB7 .....165 K3
Brougham St *PDHM/BLYW* BB12 .....10 C2
Brough Av *BISP* FY2 .....176 E1
Broughton Av *BPOOLE* FY3 .....176 E4
  STHP PR8 .....301 K7
Broughton CI *BBNW* BB2 .....268 D2
Broughton Gv *HEY* LA3 .....41 J8
Broughton St *DWN* BB3 .....291 H1
  *PDHM/BLYW** BB12 .....10 A3
  PRES PR1 .....213 G8
Broughtons Yd
  ACC (off Oak St) BB5 .....248 C5
Broughton Tower Wy
  FUL/RIB PR2 .....213 J3
Broughton Wy *PLF/KEOS* FY6 .....149 J5
Brow CI *GAR/LONG* PR3 .....152 E5
Brow Ct *RAW/HAS* BB4 .....272 C2
Brow Edge *RAW/HAS* BB4 .....297 F2
Browfoot CI *CARN* LA5 .....34 B1
Browgate *CLI* BB7 .....141 F3
Browgill PI *LANC* LA1 .....2 A2
Browhead Rd *BRFD/BLYE* BB10 .....11 E1
Brow Hey *LEY/BBR* PR5 .....264 K5
Brownedge CI *LEY/BBR* PR5 .....263 G2
Brownedge La *LEY/BBR* PR5 .....263 H2
Brownedge Rd *LEY/BBR* PR5 .....262 E3
Brown Heath Av
  WGNW/BIL/O WN5 .....371 F8
Brownhill Av *BRFD/BLYE* BB10 .....11 F3
Brownhill Dr *BBN* BB1 .....9 E1
Brown Hill La *COL* BB8 .....171 K4
Brownhill La *KIRK/FR/WA* PR4 .....260 A4
Brownhill Rd *BBN* BB1 .....219 H8
  LEY/BBR PR5 .....285 K7
Browning Av *ACC* BB5 .....247 G6
  CLV/TH FY5 .....123 G8

  LSTA FY8 2
Browning CI *COL* BB8 1
Browning Crs *PRES* * PR1 1
Browning Rd *PRES* PR1 1
Browning St *DWN* BB3 1
Brown La *LEY/BBR* PR5
Brownley St *CHLYE* PR6
  CHLYE PR6
Brownlow La *WGNW/BIL/O* WN5
Brownlow Rd *HOR/BR* BL6
Brownlow St *BBN* BB1
  CLI BB7
Brownroyd *BWCK/EAR* BB18
Browns Hey *CHLY/EC* PR7
Brownside Rd *BRFD/BLYE* BB10
Brown's La *KIRK/FR/WA* PR4
  PLF/KEOS FY6
Brown Sq *BLY* BB11
Brown St *ACC* BB5 2
  BBN BB1
  BCUP OL13
  BLY BB11
  CHLYE PR6
  CLI BB7
  CLV/TH FY5
  FTWD FY7
  LEY/BBR PR5
  RAMS BL0
Brown St East *COL* BB8 1
Brown St West *COL* * BB8 1
Brows CI *FMBY* L37
Browsholme *LANC* LA1
Browsholme Av *BRFD/BLYE* BB10
  FUL/RIB PR2
  CARN LA5
Browsholme Rd *CLI* BB7 1
Brows La *FMBY* L37 3
The Brow *KIRK/FR/WA* PR4
Brow Vw *BRFD/BLYE* * BB10
Broxton Av *WGNW/BIL/O* WN5 3
Broyd Vw *LANC* LA1
Bruce St *BBN* BB1
  BLY BB11
  BWCK/EAR BB18
Bruna La *GAR/LONG* PR3 1
Brundhurst Fold *BBNW* BB2
Brunel Dr *BBN* BB1
Brunel St *BOL* BL1
  PDHM/BLYW BB12
Brunel Wk *BBN* BB1
Brunel Wy *BPOOLS* FY4
Brungerley Av *CLI* BB7
Brungerley Br *CLI* BB7
Brun Gv *BPOOL* FY1
Brunshaw Av *BRFD/BLYE* BB10
Brunshaw Rd *BRFD/BLYE* BB10
Brun St *BLY* BB11
Brunswick Dr *COL* BB8 1
Brunswick PI *FUL/RIB* PR2
Brunswick Rd *HEY* LA3
Brunswick St *BBNW* BB2
  BLY BB11
  CHLY/EC PR7
  DWN BB3
  NLSN BB9
Brunswick Ter *ACC* BB5
  BCUP OL13
Brunton Rd *LANC* LA1
Brush St *BLY* BB11
Brussells Rd *DWN* BB3
Bryan Rd *BPOOLE* FY3
Bryan St *BBNW* BB2
Brydeck Av *PRES* PR1
Bryer St *LANC* LA1
Bryn Gv *CARN* LA5
Bryning Av *BISP* FY2
  KIRK/FR/WA PR4
Bryning Fern La *KIRK/FR/WA* PR4
Bryning Hall La *KIRK/FR/WA* PR4
Bryning La *KIRK/FR/WA* PR4
  KIRK/FR/WA PR4
Bryn Lea Ter *BOL* BL1
Bryony CI *CLV/TH* FY5
  WGNW/BIL/O WN5
Buccleuch Av *CLI* BB7
Buccleuch CI *CLI* BB7
Buccleuch St *BLY* BB11
Buchanan St *BPOOL* FY1
  CHLYE PR6
  RAMS BL0
Buckden CI *CLV/TH* FY5
Buckden Ga *NLSN* * BB9
Buckden PI *HEY* LA3
Buckden Rd *ACC* BB5
Buckfast Dr *FMBY* L37

...holes La CHLYE PR6......288 C2
...hurst La BURY BL9......320 D8
...ngham Av PRES PR1......262 A1
...ngham Ct RAW/HAS BB4......295 G2
...ngham Ct NWD/KWIPK L33......366 D8
...ngham Dr
...HM/BLYW BB12......222 D1
...ngham Gv ACC BB5......247 K4
...BY L37......355 J1
...ngham Pl HEY LA3......41 E8
...ngham Rd HEY LA3......41 E8
...A FY9......231 K7
...ngham St CHLYE PR6......311 H4
...ingham Wy PLF/KEOS FY6......149 J6
...and Dr WGNW/BIL/O WN5......365 K3
...ands Av FUL/RIB PR2......239 F1
...ands La HWTH BD22......175 G1
...ey Crs CLV/TH FY5......148 C4
...nell Fl CLV/TH FY5......148 E4
...nshaw Hall La CHLY/EC PR7......311 F1
...Stone La HWTH BD22......175 G1
...t St BLY BB11......10 B4
...BB7......140 B4
...BB8......171 J6
...ton Cl CHLYE PR6......287 G5
...Cl KIRK/FR/WA PR4......212 B5
...st DWN BB3......291 J3
...ock St BRFD/BLYE BB10......225 K2
...Rd LANC LA1......3 D2
...St LANC * LA1......3 D3
...op FMBY L37......344 B8
...ns La BRSC L40......328 B4
...r Av PRES PR1......6 C6
...r St LANC LA1......43 F8
...W/HAS BB4......296 C1
...inch St PRES * PR1......7 F1
...ugh Cl ACC BB5......248 A6
...Park La PLF/KEOS FY6......150 B5
...nape La GAR/LONG PR3......158 D5
...St BLY BB11......11 D3
...er St FUL/RIB PR2......238 E1
...er La BBNW BB2......244 C7
...Bungalows BWCK/EAR
...E Wentcliffe Dr) BB18......146 B2
...kers Hill Cl BBNW BB2......267 J3
...ker St KIRK/FR/WA PR4......235 C5
...ting Pl CLV/TH FY5......149 G5
...ank Cl BPOOLS FY4......205 F6
...ock Wk HEY LA3......53 H1
...ett St BLY BB11......10 A4
...ord Cl BBNW BB2......267 F3
...POOLE FY3......177 G4
...ord Dr HEY LA3......52 E4
...late BPOOLS FY4......204 D6
...ess Av BPOOLS FY4......204 E4
...ess' La FMBY L37......357 G2
...ess St BBN BB1......246 A6
...gh Hall Rd CHLY/EC PR7......310 E8
...h La CHLY/EC PR7......311 D7
...h La South CHLY/EC PR7......336 B1
...hley Cl CHLYE PR6......287 C6
...hley Ct LEY/BBR * PR5......285 K2
...h Mdw CHLY/EC PR7......311 F7
...undy Crs BISP FY2......149 F4
...olme Br CLI BB7......110 B7
...olme Cl FUL/RIB PR2......240 E1
...olme Pl FUL/RIB PR2......240 E1
...olme Rd FUL/RIB PR2......240 E1
...eigh Rd PRES PR1......6 C3
...eigh St PDHM/BLYW BB12......10 C1
...CMB LA4......41 K6
...ington Av FMBY L37......344 B8
...ington Gv MCMB LA4......41 K6
...ington Rd BPOOLS FY4......204 B5
...HP PR8......301 F8
...ington Rd West BPOOLS FY4......204 A5
...ington St BBNW BB2......8 A4
...HLY/EC PR7......311 H4
...LSN BB9......198 A4
...nage Gdns BPOOLS FY4......204 D4
...ned House La PLF/KEOS FY6......124 E2
...nfell Rd LANC LA1......2 B1
...n Gv CLV/TH FY5......122 D7
...nham Cl BLY BB11......10 B4
...nham Ct HEY LA3......52 B7
...nham Ga BLY BB11......10 B4
...nley Cl BBN BB1......9 F4
...nley La ACC BB5......249 F1
...nley Rd ACC BB5......248 C4
...CC BB5......248 D3
...CC BB5......249 F6
...CC BB5......249 F2
...CUP OL13......275 J6
...LY BB11......252 B8
...LY BB11......252 B2
...RFD/BLYE BB10......197 K7
...RFD/BLYE BB10......198 D8

...CLI BB7......117 F6
...COL BB8......198 E1
...COL BB8......200 B2
...PDHM/BLYW BB12......224 A4
...RAMS BLO......295 K6
...RAW/HAS BB4......273 G6
...STHP PR8......325 J6
...TOD OL14......276 D1
Burnley Rd East RAW/HAS BB4......274 C8
Burnley St BBN BB1......246 B5
Burnley Wy BCUP OL13......276 A1
...BLY BB11......223 H8
...BRFD/BLYE BB10......11 E2
...HBR HX7......228 D6
...PDHM/BLYW BB12......224 A2
...TOD OL14......254 B6
Burnsall Av BPOOLE FY3......177 G2
...HEY LA3......52 D3
Burnsall Cl BRFD/BLYE BB10......198 C8
Burnsall Fl FUL/RIB PR2......214 C7
...NLSN BB9......170 A8
Burnsall Rd ACC BB5......247 K7
...CLV/TH FY5......149 F1
...LSTA FY8......233 F7
Burns Av ACC BB5......247 G6
Burns Cl WGNW/BIL/O WN5......371 F2
Burns Dr ACC BB5......271 K1
Burnside RAMS BLO......319 K1
...SKEL WN8......351 H1
Burnside Av BPOOLS FY4......204 E3
...FTWD FY7......122 C1
...FUL/RIB PR2......214 D8
...GAR/LONG PR3......131 G3
Burnside Wy PRES PR1......239 F8
Burnslack La FUL/RIB PR2......214 D8
Burns Pl BPOOLS FY4......205 F3
Burns Rd FTWD FY7......97 J3
Burns St NLSN BB9......198 B2
...PDHM/BLYW BB12......10 C1
...PDHM/BLYW BB12......223 K4
...PDHM/BLYW* BB12......223 J7
...PRES PR1......240 B1
Burns Wk DWN BB3......292 A2
Burns Wy GTH/LHO BB6......221 F7
Burnt Edge La BOL BL1......339 K6
...HBR HX7......255 K7
Burrell Av COL BB8......171 H5
Burrington Cl FUL/RIB PR2......214 B5
Burrow Heights La HGHB LA2......67 F5
Burrow Rd KKBYL LA6......21 H6
...PRES PR1......7 E1
Burrow's La PLF/KEOS FY6......124 B5
Burscough Rd ORM L39......348 D5
Burscough St ORM L39......348 C6
Burton Av LANC LA1......42 C8
Burton Ct FTWD FY7......122 C1
Burton Gdns NLSN BB9......197 K6
Burton Pk KKBYL LA6......18 A5
Burton Rd BPOOLS FY4......205 F3
...KKBYL LA6......18 A1
Burton St BBN BB1......247 G2
...BLY BB11......11 D5
Burwains Av COL BB8......171 H2
Burwell Av CHLY/EC PR7......335 H3
...FMBY L37......355 H2
Burwell Cl WHIT OL12......323 H4
Burwen Castle Rd
...SKP/WHF BD23......121 F3
Burwen Cl BLY BB11......10 A6
Burwood Cl PRES PR1......262 C1
Burwood Dr BPOOLE FY3......177 G5
...FUL/RIB PR2......240 C1
Bury Fold La DWN BB3......291 J5
Bury New Rd RAMS BLO......319 K6
Bury Old Rd RAMS BLO......320 B7
Bury Rd EDGW/EG BL7......317 J5
...RAMS BLO......319 J6
...RAW/HAS BB4......272 C8
...RAW/HAS BB4......295 K6
...STHP PR8......301 G8
Bury St ACC BB5......247 H8
...DWN BB3......291 J2
Buseph Cl MCMB LA4......42 B7
Buseph Dr MCMB LA4......42 B7
Bushburn Cl GTH/LHO BB6......220 A2
Bushby's La FMBY L37......355 G1
Bushby's Pk FMBY L37......355 G1
Bushell Pl PRES PR1......7 E4
Bushell St PRES PR1......7 D1
Bushey La RNFD/HAY WA11......368 E1
Bush La KIRK/FR/WA PR4......235 F7
Bush St BRFD/BLYE BB10......11 D1
Bussel Rd PRES PR1......262 B1
Butcher Brow LEY/BBR PR5......240 C6
Butchers La ORM L39......359 H6
Bute Av BPOOL FY1......176 B4

Bute Rd BBN BB1......269 G1
Bute St BLY BB11......10 A6
Butler Pl PRES PR1......239 H1
Butler Rd BPOOL FY1......4 B4
Butler St BBN BB1......247 G2
...BPOOL FY1......4 C1
...BRFD/BLYE* BB10......11 D1
...PRES PR1......6 C3
...RAMS BLO......319 G7
Buttercross Cl BLY BB11......251 F1
Butterfield Gdns ORM L39......348 B8
Butterfield St LANC LA1......3 D3
Butterlands PRES PR1......240 D3
Buttermere Av ACC BB5......247 H6
...CHLY/EC PR7......310 E5
...COL BB8......171 K5
...FTWD FY7......122 C2
...MCMB* LA4......41 K7
Buttermere Cl BBN BB1......9 D3
...FMBY L37......343 H8
...FUL/RIB PR2......214 A7
...LEY/BBR PR5......263 G1
...NWD/KWIPK L33......366 B7
Buttermere Ct LANC * LA1......3 F2
Buttermere Crs RNFD/HAY WA11......369 F1
Buttermere Dr PLF/KEOS FY6......98 B6
...RAMS BLO......319 H4
Buttermere Rd BRFD/BLYE BB10......226 C6
...GAR/LONG PR3......187 K6
...LANC LA1......3 F2
Butterworth Brow CHLY/EC PR7......310 D7
...CHLYE PR6......289 F4
Butterworth Cl KIRK/FR/WA PR4......208 E5
Butt Hill La GAR/LONG PR3......131 F7
Button St GAR/LONG PR3......157 K6
Butts BWCK/EAR BB18......145 F1
...GTH/LHO BB6......221 F6
Butts Cl CLV/TH FY5......123 J7
...GAR/LONG PR3......165 J1
Butt's La GAR/LONG PR3......153 F5
...STHP PR8......302 B6
Butts Mt GTH/LHO BB6......221 G6
Butts Rd CLV/TH FY5......123 H7
Buxton Av BISP FY2......148 D7
Buxton St ACC BB5......248 A6
...MCMB LA4......41 J7
...WHIT OL12......299 H8
Bye La ORM L39......346 E8
Bye Rd RAMS BLO......320 A4
Byerworth Rd North
...GAR/LONG PR3......129 J6
Byerworth Rd South
...GAR/LONG PR3......129 J6
Byfield Av CLV/TH FY5......148 E4
Byland Cl BPOOLS FY4......204 C6
...FMBY L37......356 B1
...PDHM/BLYW BB12......222 D2
Bymbrig Cl LEY/BBR PR5......263 H3
By-Pass Rd CARN LA5......33 G7
Byrom St CARN LA5......33 G7
Byrom St BBNW BB2......8 B5
...CHTN/BK PR9......302 B5
Byron Av CARN LA5......33 G6
...CLV/TH FY5......123 G8
...KIRK/FR/WA PR4......234 C5
...LSTA FY8......233 F7
Byron Cl ACC BB5......247 G7
...FMBY L37......343 K7
...KIRK/FR/WA PR4......281 K6
...WGNW/BIL/O WN5......365 H4
Byron Crs CHLY/EC PR7......335 J3
Byron Gv BWCK/EAR BB18......118 E8
Byron Rd COL BB8......171 G6
...HEY LA3......40 E8
...MGHL L31......359 G8
Byron Sq GTH/LHO * BB6......221 F7
Byron St BPOOLS FY4......4 B6
...CHLY/EC PR7......311 G3
...FTWD FY7......97 G4
...PDHM/BLYW BB12......224 B4

C

Cabin La CHTN/BK PR9......279 G8
...KIRK/FR/WA PR4......304 E5
...MGHL L31......358 B7
...ORM L39......327 F6
Cable St FMBY L37......344 A7
...LANC LA1......3 D3
...STHP PR8......301 H4
Cabus Nook La GAR/LONG PR3......103 H4
Cadby Av BPOOLE FY3......5 F5
Cadley Av FUL/RIB PR2......212 D8
Cadley Cswy FUL/RIB PR2......212 E7
Cadley Dr FUL/RIB PR2......212 D8
Cadogan Pl PRES PR1......7 E4

Cadogan St NLSN BB9 ....198 B1
Cadshaw Cl BBN BB1 ....8 C1
Cadwell Rd MGHL L31 ....358 D6
Caernarfon Cl CLV/TH FY5 .....149 K1
Caernarvon Av
   PDHM/BLYW BB12 ....224 C4
Caernarvon Rd RAW/HAS BB4 ...295 G2
Cage La KIRK/FR/WA PR4 ....261 J3
Cairndale Dr LEY/BBR PR5 ......285 K5
Cairn Gv BPOOLS FY4 ....204 C7
Cairns Cl NLSN BB9 ....170 A8
Cairnsmore Av PRES PR1 ....240 D2
Cairo St PDHM/BLYW BB12 ....10 A3
Caister Cl SKEL WN8 ....363 K3
Calcott St BLY BB11 ....251 G1
Caldbeck Cl NLSN BB9 ....198 C5
Caldbeck Rd LANC LA1 ....3 F2
Calder Av CHLY/EC PR7 ....311 F6
   CHLYE PR6 ....289 C2
   CLI BB7 ....192 E7
   CLV/TH FY5 ....149 F1
   DWN BB3 ....268 A7
   FTWD FY7 ....122 D1
   FUL/RIB PR2 ....213 H5
   GAR/LONG PR3 ....188 A4
   KIRK/FR/WA PR4 ....234 D6
   ORM L39 ....348 C7
Calder Bank BBN BB1 ....8 C2
Calder Banks BBN BB1 ....8 C2
Calderbrook Av BLY BB11 ....10 B6
Calderbrook Pl BLY BB11 ....10 B6
Calder Cl CARN LA5 ....33 H2
   KIRK/FR/WA PR4 ....209 F6
   LSTA FY8 ....231 F1
   NLSN BB9 ....198 B2
   NWD/KWIPK L33 ....366 D5
Calder Ct ACC BB5 ....222 E5
Calder Dr GAR/LONG PR3 ....155 K1
Calder House La GAR/LONG PR3 ...129 K7
Calder Pl GTH/LHO BB6 ....221 J5
Calder Rd BISP FY2 ....176 C2
   RAW/HAS BB4 ....273 H7
Calder St BBN BB1 ....9 D2
   BLY BB11 ....10 C3
   COL BB8 ....171 G7
   FUL/RIB PR2 ....6 A2
   NLSN BB9 ....198 B2
   PDHM/BLYW BB12 ....223 J3
Calder V CLI BB7 ....193 G7
   NLSN BB9 ....198 B1
Caldervale Av PLF/KEOS FY6 ...149 J8
Calder Vale Rd BLY BB11 ....10 C3
Calder Wy LANC LA1 ....54 B1
Caldicott Wy PLF/KEOS FY6 ....149 J5
Caldwell St NWD/KWIPK * L33 ...366 D6
Caldy Dr TOT/BURYW BL8 ....319 G8
Caleb St NLSN BB9 ....198 C2
Caledonian Av BPOOLE FY3 .....176 D4
Calfcote La GAR/LONG PR3 ......188 B4
Calf Croft Pl LSTA FY8 ....232 C7
Calf Hall La BWCK/EAR BB18 ...144 E1
Calf Hey ACC BB5 ....221 K7
Calf Hey Rd RAW/HAS BB4 ......294 B1
Calf Wood La AIRE BD20 ....147 K2
Calgary Av BBNW BB2 ....244 D3
Calico Cl ACC BB5 ....247 F7
Calico Dr GAR/LONG PR3 ....129 K8
Calico St BRFD/BLYE BB10 ....268 A2
Calico Wood Av WGNNW/ST WN6 ...353 H5
Calkeld La LANC LA1 ....3 D3
Calla Dr GAR/LONG PR3 ....129 J3
Callender St RAMS BL0 ....319 H5
Callon St PRES PR1 ....240 C3
Caltha St RAMS BL0 ....319 H5
Calva Cl PDHM/BLYW BB12 .....224 D3
Calverley St PRES PR1 ....240 B2
Calverley Wy WHIT OL12 ....323 J7
Calvert Pl BPOOLE FY3 ....177 G3
Cambell's Ct LSTA FY8 ....230 E4
Camberley Cl STHP PR8 ....300 E6
Camborne Av CARN LA5 ....33 J3
Camborne Ct BPOOLE FY3 ....205 H1
Camborne Pl KIRK/FR/WA PR4 ...234 E5
Cambray Dr BPOOL FY1 ....176 C3
Cambrian Cl BBN BB1 ....219 H8
Cambrian Wy RAW/HAS BB4 ....295 H2
Cambridge Ar STHP PR8 ....301 H4
Cambridge Av CHTN/BK PR9 ...302 B1
   LANC LA1 ....3 F6
Cambridge Cl BBN * BB1 ....9 D5
   PDHM/BLYW BB12 ....223 K4
   PRES PR1 ....239 G1
Cambridge Dr BBN BB1 ....246 E2
   GAR/LONG PR3 ....129 H4
   PDHM/BLYW BB12 ....223 K4
Cambridge Gdns CHTN/BK PR9 ...302 B1
Cambridge Rd BPOOL FY1 ....5 D2

CHTN/BK PR9 ....302 A2
CLV/TH FY5 ....122 C8
FMBY L37 ....355 H2
FTWD FY7 ....96 E8
HEY LA3 ....40 E8
LEY/BBR PR5 ....263 J3
LSTA FY8 ....231 K7
SKEL WN8 ....362 E2
WGNW/BIL/O WN5 ....365 G3
Cambridge St ACC * BB5 ....248 C4
   BBN BB1 ....9 D5
   BLY* BB11 ....10 A4
   CHLY/EC PR7 ....311 G4
   COL* BB8 ....171 H7
   DWN BB3 ....292 A2
   GTH/LHO BB6 ....221 H6
   NLSN* BB9 ....197 K6
   PRES PR1 ....239 C1
Cambridge Wk PRES * PR1 ....239 C1
Cambridge Wks STHP PR8 ....301 H4
Cam Cl LEY/BBR PR5 ....263 J3
Camden Pl PRES PR1 ....7 D3
Camden Rd BPOOLE FY3 ....5 E1
Camden St NLSN * BB9 ....170 B8
Camellia Dr LEY/BBR PR5 ....286 C1
Cameron Av BPOOLE FY3 ....176 E4
Cameron Cft CHLYE * PR6 ....311 H3
Cameron St BOL BL1 ....341 H6
   BRFD/BLYE BB10 ....225 J2
Camforth Hall La GAR/LONG PR3 ...186 D5
Cam La LEY/BBR PR5 ....263 K8
   SKP/WHF BD23 ....120 B5
Camms Vw RAW/HAS BB4 ....295 G3
Camomile Cl CHLY/EC * PR7 .....286 E8
Campbell Av BPOOLE FY3 ....176 E4
Campbell St BBN BB1 ....245 C2
   PDHM/BLYW BB12 ....222 D2
   PRES PR1 ....7 F2
Campion Cl CLV/TH FY5 ....123 F6
Campion Dr FUL/RIB PR2 ....237 J2
   RAW/HAS BB4 ....295 G3
The Campions FUL/RIB PR2 ......237 J2
Campion Wy HEY LA3 ....53 H1
   WHIT OL12 ....323 C8
Camp St BRFD/BLYE BB10 ....198 C8
Cam St PRES PR1 ....240 A1
Camwood LEY/BBR PR5 ....264 A7
Camwood Dr LEY/BBR PR5 ....262 E7
Cam Wood Fold CHLYE PR6 ......263 K8
Canada Crs BISP FY2 ....148 E8
Canada St HOR/BR BL6 ....338 D8
Canal Bank
   BRSC (off New La) L40 ....330 B5
Canal Bank Pygons Hl MGHL L31 ...358 E4
Canal Gdns CARN LA5 ....33 H5
Canalside BBN BB1 ....9 D6
Canal Side NLSN BB9 ....198 B1
Canal St ACC BB5 ....247 J5
   BBNW BB2 ....267 J2
   BLY* BB11 ....10 C3
   CHLY/EC PR7 ....337 G5
Canal Wk CHLYE PR6 ....311 G3
   LANC* LA1 ....3 E3
Canberra Cl CLV/TH FY5 ....149 F4
Canberra Ct
   BPOOLS
   (off Amy Johnson Wy) FY4 .....204 E7
Canberra Rd LEY/BBR PR5 ....285 K2
Canberra Wy KIRK/FR/WA PR4 ...234 C5
Candlemakers Ct CLI BB7 ....165 J3
Cann Bridge St LEY/BBR PR5 ...240 E7
Canning Rd CHTN/BK PR9 ....302 C4
Canning St PDHM/BLYW BB12 ...10 C2
Cannock Av BPOOLE FY3 ....176 E3
Cannon Hl FUL/RIB * PR2 ....6 A1
   LANC (off Westbourne Rd) LA1 ...3 A2
Cannon St ACC BB5 ....248 B6
   NLSN BB9 ....198 D2
   PRES PR1 ....7 D3
   RAMS BL0 ....319 G7
Canterbury Av BPOOLE FY3 ....5 F4
   LANC LA1 ....3 F5
Canterbury Cl CHLYE PR6 ....288 C3
   FMBY L37 ....343 K6
   GAR/LONG PR3 ....129 J3
   PLF/KEOS FY6 ....149 J6
   STHP PR8 ....301 F7
Canterbury St BBNW BB2 ....8 B5
   CHLYE PR6 ....311 J3
Canterbury Wy GAR/LONG PR3 ...129 G4
Cantlow Fold STHP PR8 ....325 D7
Cantsfield Av FUL/RIB PR2 ....212 D7
Canute St PRES PR1 ....7 E1
Capernwray Rd KKBYL LA6 ....35 F1
Cape St RAW/HAS BB4 ....296 C1
Capilano Pk ORM L39 ....360 A3
Capitol Wy LEY/BBR PR5 ....240 A6

Capstan Cl LSTA FY8 2
Captains Rw LANC LA1 2
Captain St BCUP OL13 2
   HOR/BR BL6 3
Carawood Cl WGNNW/ST WN6 ...3
Carcroft Av BISP FY2 1
Cardale KIRK/FR/WA PR4 2
Cardiff St SKEL WN8 3
Cardigan Av ACC BB5 2
   CLI BB7 1
   PDHM/BLYW BB12 2
Cardigan Cl CLI BB7 1
Cardigan Pl BPOOLS FY4 1
Cardigan Rd STHP PR8 3
Cardigan St FUL/RIB PR2 2
   WHIT OL12 3
Cardinal Gdns LSTA FY8 2
Cardinal Pl CLV/TH FY5 1
Cardinal St BRFD/BLYE BB10 2
Cardwell Cl KIRK/FR/WA PR4 2
Cardwell Pl BBNW BB2 2
Cardwell St PDHM/BLYW BB12 ...2
Carfax Rd NWD/KWIPK L33 3
Carham Rd BBN BB1 2
Carholme Av BRFD/BLYE BB10 ...2
Carisbrooke Av BPOOLS FY4 2
Carisbrooke Cl PLF/KEOS FY6 1
Carisbrooke Dr BOL BL1 1
   CHTN/BK PR9 2
Carleton Av BPOOLE FY3 1
   FUL/RIB PR2 2
   PDHM/BLYW BB12 2
Carleton Dr PRES PR1 1
Carleton Gdns PLF/KEOS FY6 1
Carleton Ga PLF/KEOS FY6 1
Carleton Rd CHLYE PR6 1
   COL BB8 2
Carleton St MCMB LA4 1
   NLSN BB9 2
Carleton Wy PLF/KEOS FY6 1
Carley St DWN BB3 2
Carlile Wy NWD/KWIPK L33 3
Carlin Ga BISP FY2 2
Carlinghurst Rd BBNW BB2 2
Carlisle Av FTWD FY7 2
   PRES PR1 3
Carlisle Gv CLV/TH FY5 2
Carlisle Pl CHLYE PR6 3
Carlisle Rd ACC * BB5 2
   STHP PR8 3
Carlisle St BBN BB1 1
   PRES PR1 2
   WHIT OL12 3
Carloway Av FUL/RIB PR2 3
Carl's Wy NWD/KWIPK L33 3
Carlton Av CHLYE PR6 2
   SKEL WN8 3
Carlton Dr PRES PR1 2
Carlton Gdns BBN BB1 1
Carlton Gv BISP FY2 1
Carlton Pl CLI BB7 2
Carlton Rd BBN BB1 2
   BLY BB11 2
   LEY/BBR PR5 2
   LSTA FY8 2
   STHP PR8 2
Carlton St BCUP OL13 2
   FUL/RIB PR2 2
   NLSN BB9 1
Carluke St BBN BB1 1
Carlyle Av BPOOLS FY4 2
Carmel Cl ORM L39 3
Carnarvon Rd BBNW BB2 2
   PRES PR1 3
   STHP PR8 3
Carnfield Pl LEY/BBR PR5 2
Carnforth Av BISP FY2 2
Carnforth Brow CARN LA5 3
Carnforth Cl BBNW BB2 2
Carnoustie Cl FUL/RIB PR2 2
   STHP PR8 3
Carnoustie Ct PRES PR1 2
Carnoustie Dr RAMS BL0 3
Caroline Cl HEY LA3 3
Caroline St BPOOL FY1 2
   PRES PR1 2
Carradice Cl NLSN BB9 3
Carr Bank Av RAMS BL0 3
Carr Bank Dr RAMS BL0 3
Carr Bank Rd RAMS BL0 3
Carr Barn Brow LEY/BBR PR5 2
Carr Cl GAR/LONG PR3 3
   PLF/KEOS FY6 1
Carr Dr KIRK/FR/WA PR4 2
Carr End La PLF/KEOS FY6 1
Carr Fld LEY/BBR PR5 2
Carr Fold RAMS * BL0 3

Ga CLV/TH FY5 ....122 C7
Hall Dr NLSN BB9 ....197 K2
Hall Gdns NLSN BB9 ....197 K2
Hall Rd NLSN BB9 ....197 K1
Head La PLF/KEOS FY6 ....178 A1
Hey
 /TH (off Gaskell Crs) FY5 ....149 G5
House La HTWN L38 ....356 E7
2K/FR/WA PR4 ....282 D4
VC LA1 ....2 C4
GNNW/ST WN6 ....334 D3
er's Rw COL BB8 ....172 E5
ngton Gv MCMB LA4 ....42 A6
LY/EC PR7 ....337 F4
La BBNW BB2 ....244 B5
*SC L40 ....307 H4
SC L40 ....331 H8
R/LONG PR3 ....100 A7
Y LA3 ....52 C4
Y LA3 ....64 D3
2K/FR/WA PR4 ....209 H5
2K/FR/WA PR4 ....233 K5
2K/FR/WA PR4 ....281 K3
2K/FR/WA PR4 ....283 G2
Y/BBR PR5 ....262 D8
Y/BBR PR5 ....307 H3
GHL L31 ....358 B6
F/KEOS FY6 ....124 E8
F/KEOS FY6 ....178 D2
W/HAS BB4 ....296 C3
W/HAS BB4 ....297 G4
-P PR8 ....326 B4
Meadow LEY/BBR PR5 ....264 B5
Mill Crs WGNW/BIL/O WN5 ....371 G7
Mill Ms HWTH BD22 ....174 E1
Mill Rd WGNW/BIL/O WN5 ....371 G8
Moss La ORM L39 ....326 E8
oll Cm ORM L39 ....348 D4
ol St PRES PR1 ....7 F1
on La GAR/LONG PR3 ....157 J7
Rd BLY BB11 ....10 B1
VCK/EAR BB18 ....118 E8
LYE PR6 ....287 F1
LBB8 ....171 J5
VN BB3 ....291 K3
WD FY7 ....97 G6
2R/BR BL6 ....338 D6
2K/FR/WA PR4 ....209 F7
SN BB9 ....198 A2
F/KEOS FY6 ....150 E1
W/HAS BB4 ....274 E3
W/HAS BB4 ....296 B2
D OL14 ....277 F3
s Crs FMBY L37 ....355 H2
s Crs West FMBY L37 ....355 H2
Side La HTWN L38 ....357 G8
St BBN BB1 ....8 C3
LYE PR6 ....311 J2
Y/BBR PR5 ....263 H5
ES PR1 ....7 F3
MS BLO 319 H4
s Wd BBNW BB2 ....244 B5
wood Dr KIRK/FR/WA PR4 ....209 F7
wood Gn PDHM/BLYW BB12 ....223 J3
wood Hey RAMS BLO 319 G7
wood Pk STHP PR8 ....301 H8
wood Wk LEY/BBR PR5 ....239 K8
wood Wy LEY/BBR PR5 ....262 E1
y La COL BB8 ....171 J6
shalton Rd BPOOL FY1 ....176 B4
luith Av BPOOL FY3 ....5 E4
son Rd BPOOLS FY4 ....205 G2
er Av BLY BB11 ....223 J7
VFD/HAY WA11 ....369 C6
er Fold BBNW BB2 ....244 A1
er Pl
 LSN (off Woodlands Rd) BB9 ....198 D3
er's La CLI BB7 ....93 G7
er St ACC BB5 ....248 B7
POOL FY1 ....4 B2
OHM/BLYW BB12 ....224 E4
erville Cl BPOOLS FY4 ....205 G4
cford Br GAR/LONG PR3 ....152 E5
cford La GAR/LONG PR3 ....152 E5
cford La GAR/LONG PR3 ....152 E5
cford Pk
AR/LONG (off Cartford La) PR3 ....152 E5
Ga PLF/KEOS FY6 ....98 D8
mel Av ACC BB5 ....248 A8
WD FY7 ....122 C7
mel Cl STHP PR8 ....302 B8
mel Dr FMBY L37 ....356 B1

LEY/BBR PR5 ....241 J8
PDHM/BLYW BB12 ....224 D3
Cartmell La GAR/LONG PR3 ....128 B3
LSTA FY8 ....233 F4
Cartmell Rd BBNW BB2 ....244 D3
BPOOLS FY4 ....205 K2
LSTA FY8 ....231 F7
Cartmel Pl FUL/RIB PR2 ....238 A1
MCMB LA4 ....41 J7
Cartmel Rd LANC LA1 ....3 F1
LEY/BBR PR5 ....285 F3
Cartwright Ct LANC LA1 ....2 C6
Carus Av DWN BB3 ....292 C3
Carus Pk KKBYL LA6 ....29 H7
Carus St DWN BB3 ....292 D2
Carvers Brow LEY/BBR PR5 ....307 H2
Carwood La CHLYE PR6 ....287 G4
Caryle Gv MCMB LA4 ....42 A5
Caryl Rd LSTA FY8 ....230 C3
Cascades SKEL (off Daniels La) WN8 ....363 J4
Casserley Rd COL BB8 ....171 K5
Castercliffe Rd NLSN BB9 ....199 F3
Casterton CHLY/EC PR7 ....310 A1
Casterton Av BRFD/BLYE BB10 ....197 K8
Castle Av PLF/KEOS FY6 ....149 H5
Castle Bank CARN LA5 ....15 H7
Castle Cl COL BB8 ....171 J5
Castle Crs HOR/BR BL6 ....338 E6
Castle Dr CHLY/EC PR7 ....336 E5
FMBY L37 ....355 K2
Castle Fold PRES PR1 ....262 C1
Castlegate BPOOL FY1 ....4 B6
Castle Gate CLI BB7 ....165 J3
Castle HI LANC LA1 ....2 C3
Castle House La CHLY/EC PR7 ....336 E5
Castle La BPOOLE FY3 ....177 K6
BRSC L40 ....349 H1
GAR/LONG PR3 ....129 K5
Castle Mt FUL/RIB PR2 ....213 H4
Castle Pk LANC LA1 ....2 C3
Castlerigg Dr PDHM/BLYW BB12 ....224 D3
Castlerigg Pl BPOOLS FY4 ....205 J2
Castle Rd COL BB8 ....171 J5
Castle St BBN BB1 ....9 F4
CHLY/EC PR7 ....311 H4
CHTN/BK PR9 ....301 H4
CLI BB7 ....165 J3
NLSN* BB9 ....197 K5
NLSN BB9 ....198 D3
PDHM/BLYW BB12 ....10 C2
PDHM/BLYW BB12 ....223 J7
PRES PR1 ....7 D1
Castleton Rd PRES PR1 ....7 F1
Castletown Dr BCUP OL13 ....299 F3
Castle Vw BWCK/EAR BB18 ....145 F2
CLI BB7 ....165 J3
Castle Wk PRES PR1 ....6 A4
STHP PR8 ....301 G5
Catforth Av BPOOLS FY4 ....205 H2
Catforth Rd FUL/RIB PR2 ....238 A2
KIRK/FR/WA PR4 ....185 F6
Catharine's La ORM L39 ....360 D1
Cathedral Cl BBN BB1 ....8 C5
Cathedral Dr HEY LA3 ....53 H1
Catherine Cl KIRK/FR/WA PR4 ....208 D4
Catherine St CHLY/EC * PR7 ....311 G5
KIRK/FR/WA PR4 ....208 D5
PRES PR1 ....7 F2
Catherine St East HOR/BR BL6 ....338 D6
Catherine St West HOR/BR BL6 ....338 C6
Cathrow Br KIRK/FR/WA PR4 ....261 H4
Cathrow Wy CLV/TH FY5 ....149 K1
Catley Cl CHLYE PR6 ....287 G6
Catlow Hall St ACC BB5 ....247 J8
Caton Av FTWD FY7 ....122 D2
Caton Cl CHTN/BK PR9 ....278 B7
GAR/LONG PR3 ....188 B5
Caton Green Rd HGHB LA2 ....45 J5
Caton Gv BPOOLE * FY3 ....177 K4
Caton Rd LANC LA1 ....3 E2
Cato St RAMS * BLO 319 G7
Cat Tail La STHP PR8 ....328 C2
Catterall Cl BPOOL FY1 ....176 D4
Catterall Gates La GAR/LONG PR3 ....155 J1
Catterall La GAR/LONG PR3 ....155 H2
Catterall St BBNW BB2 ....267 K3
Catterick Fold STHP PR8 ....302 B8
Cattle St GTH/LHO BB6 ....221 F6
Caunce Av CHTN/BK PR9 ....279 J5
Caunce's Rd CHTN/BK PR9 ....304 B5
Caunce St BPOOL FY1 ....4 C1
BPOOLE FY1 ....5 E1
Causeway COL BB8 ....171 J2
GTH/LHO BB6 ....221 F6
Causeway Av FUL/RIB PR2 ....212 D7
Causeway Cft CLI BB7 ....165 K2

Causeway End
RAW/HAS (off Gregory Fold) BB4 ....295 G4
Causeway Head RAW/HAS BB4 ....295 G3
Causeway La BRSC L40 ....331 H2
FMBY L37 ....357 H2
The Causeway CHLYE PR6 ....311 J3
CHTN/BK PR9 ....278 E6
LEY/BBR PR5 ....284 B5
Causey Foot NLSN BB9 ....198 B4
Cavalry Wy PDHM/BLYW BB12 ....10 A3
Cavendish Ct CARN LA5 ....33 G6
Cavendish Crs FUL/RIB PR2 ....214 D8
Cavendish Dr FUL/RIB PR2 ....214 D8
Cavendish Man
CLV/TH (off Green Dr) FY5 ....122 C8
Cavendish Pl BBNW BB2 ....244 D8
LEY/BBR PR5 ....240 B8
Cavendish Rd BISP FY2 ....148 C7
HEY LA3 ....40 E8
LSTA FY8 ....230 C3
PRES PR1 ....240 C2
STHP PR8 ....301 F8
Cavendish St BWCK/EAR BB18 ....144 E2
CHLYE PR6 ....311 J4
DWN BB3 ....268 C8
LANC LA1 ....2 B3
Cave St BBNW BB2 ....267 J2
Cavour St PDHM/BLYW BB12 ....10 C2
Cawthorne St LANC LA1 ....2 C3
Caxton Av BISP FY2 ....148 C6
Caxton Rd FUL/RIB PR2 ....213 K3
Cecilia Rd BBNW BB2 ....267 G1
Cecilia St PRES PR1 ....240 B2
Cecil St ACC BB5 ....247 J7
BBN BB1 ....247 G2
BPOOL FY1 ....176 C4
BWCK/EAR BB18 ....118 E8
LSTA FY8 ....232 C8
Cedar Av CHLY/EC PR7 ....286 A7
CLV/TH FY5 ....148 E1
FTWD FY7 ....122 E3
FUL/RIB PR2 ....238 C1
KIRK/FR/WA PR4 ....234 B5
LEY/BBR* PR5 ....262 E3
PLF/KEOS FY6 ....98 C6
PLF/KEOS FY6 ....177 K3
RAW/HAS BB4 ....272 D8
Cedar Cl BBN BB1 ....247 F3
FUL/RIB PR2 ....215 H2
GAR/LONG PR3 ....129 H3
KIRK/FR/WA PR4 ....210 A8
Cedar Crs KIRK/FR/WA PR4 ....208 E7
ORM L39 ....348 A7
RAMS BLO 319 J4
Cedar Dr FMBY L37 ....355 G2
Cedar Fld CHLYE PR6 ....287 G1
Cedar Gv KIRK/FR/WA PR4 ....260 B2
SKEL WN8 ....362 E2
WGNW/BIL/O WN5 ....365 H5
Cedar Rd CHLYE PR6 ....311 H1
FUL/RIB PR2 ....240 C1
LANC LA1 ....2 B3
Cedars Cl BWCK/EAR BB18 ....144 E2
Cedar Sq BPOOL FY1 ....4 B2
The Cedars CHLY/EC PR7 ....308 D4
CHLY/EC PR7 ....311 F7
KIRK/FR/WA PR4 ....261 G3
Cedar St ACC BB5 ....248 D5
BBN BB1 ....9 D1
BLY BB11 ....11 E4
MCMB LA4 ....41 F7
STHP PR8 ....301 J7
Cedar Wk KIRK/FR/WA PR4 ....180 D2
Cedar Wy PRES PR1 ....238 D8
Cedarwood Cl LSTA FY8 ....232 A7
Cedarwood Dr LEY/BBR PR5 ....285 G3
Cedric Pl BISP FY2 ....148 C2
Celandine Cl CLV/TH FY5 ....123 F6
Celandine Wk WGNS/IIMK WN3 ....365 K7
Celia St BRFD/BLYE BB10 ....11 F4
Cemetery La BLY BB11 ....224 C7
PLF/KEOS FY6 ....124 D2
Cemetery Rd BWCK/EAR BB18 ....146 B1
PRES PR1 ....240 A2
RAMS BLO 319 D2
STHP PR8 ....301 H7
Cemetery Vw CHLY/EC PR7 ....337 F5
Centenary Rd BLY BB11 ....11 D4
Central Av ACC BB5 ....247 G2
CLI BB7 ....165 H4
KIRK/FR/WA PR4 ....208 C5
LANC LA1 ....43 H7
LEY/BBR PR5 ....264 D1
RAMS BLO 319 K1
Central Av North CLV/TH FY5 ....123 F8
Central Avnue STHP PR8 ....326 B3

Central Beach *LSTA* FY8 ....232 D8
Central Dr *BPOOL* FY1 ....4 B3
 LSTA FY8 ....231 J6
 MCMB LA4 ....41 C6
 PRES PR1 ....238 C7
 RNFD/HAY WA11 ....369 F4
 WGNNW/ST WN6 ....353 K5
Central St *RAMS* BL0 ....319 H5
Central Vw *BCUP* OL13 ....298 E1
Centre Dr *LEY/BBR* PR5 ....264 A7
Centre Rd *AIRE* BD20 ....147 H5
Centurian Wy *BBN* BB1 ....268 E5
Centurion Cl *BBN* BB1 ....268 E4
Centurion Ct *BBN** BB1 ....268 E5
 FUL/RIB
 (off Watling Street Rd) PR2 ....213 H7
Centurion Wy *LEY/BBR* PR5 ....262 D7
Ceres Wy *LANC* LA1 ....2 A3
Chaddock St *PRES* PR1 ....7 D3
Chadfield Rd *BPOOL* FY1 ....5 D5
Chad St *NLSN** BB9 ....198 E1
Chadwell Rd *NWD/KWIPK* L33 ....366 D7
Chadwick Gdns *LEY/BBR* PR5 ....262 D4
Chadwick St *BBNW* BB2 ....268 A1
 *BPOOL** FY1 ....4 C4
Chaffinch Cl *CLV/TH* FY5 ....123 F6
Chaffinch Ct *BPOOLE** FY3 ....177 H5
Chaigley Ct *CLI* BB7 ....163 J3
Chaigley Rd *KIRK/FR/WA* PR4 ....188 B3
Chain Caul Rd *FUL/RIB* PR2 ....238 A4
Chain Caul Wy *FUL/RIB* PR2 ....238 A3
Chain House La
 KIRK/FR/WA PR4 ....261 K4
Chain La *BPOOLE* FY3 ....178 A7
Chalfont Rd *FUL/RIB* PR2 ....212 E6
Challenge Wy *BBN* BB1 ....246 A4
Chambres Rd *STHP* PR8 ....301 K6
Chambres Rd North *STHP* PR8 ....301 K5
Champagne Av *BISP* FY2 ....149 F5
Chancellors Whf
 LANC (off Aldcliffe Rd) LA1 ....3 D4
Chancel Pl *DWN* BB3 ....292 A2
Chancel Wy *DWN* BB3 ....292 A3
Chancery Rd *CHLY/EC* PR7 ....310 E2
Chandlers Cft *KIRK/FR/WA* PR4 ....258 D8
Chandlers Rest *LSTA* FY8 ....233 F8
Chandler St *PRES* PR1 ....6 C2
Chandley Cl *STHP* PR8 ....325 C6
Change Cl *BCUP* OL13 ....276 A7
Changford St *NWD/KWIPK* L33 ....366 E8
Channel Wy *FUL/RIB* PR2 ....6 A2
Channing Rd *LSTA* FY8 ....231 J7
Chapel Brow *GAR/LONG* PR3 ....188 B5
 LEY/BBR PR5 ....285 K2
Chapel Cl *CLI* BB7 ....139 J6
 HEY LA3 ....65 G3
 HGHB LA2 ....42 D2
 KIRK/FR/WA PR4 ....208 D4
Chapel Flds *EDGW/EG* BL7 ....317 G7
Chapelfield St *BOL* BL1 ....341 J8
Chapel Fold *CLI* BB7 ....193 K4
 *COL** BB8 ....171 H7
Chapel Gdns
 GAR/LONG
 (off Cock Robin La) PR3 ....155 K1
 KIRK/FR/WA PR4 ....258 K1
Chapel Gra *EDGW/EG* BL7 ....317 G7
Chapel HI *BWCK/EAR* BB18 ....145 H4
 GAR/LONG PR3 ....188 B5
Chapel Hill La *RAW/HAS* BB4 ....273 J7
Chapelhouse La *KKBYL* LA6 ....21 K2
Chapel House Rd *NLSN* BB9 ....198 B5
Chapelhouse Wk *FMBY* L37 ....344 A8
Chapel La *BRSC* L40 ....349 J1
 CARN LA5 ....15 G1
 CHLY/EC PR7 ....335 K3
 CHLYE PR6 ....288 A6
 CHTN/BK PR9 ....279 K5
 CLI BB7 ....139 J6
 CLI BB7 ....140 B3
 FMBY L37 ....343 K8
 GAR/LONG PR3 ....151 K1
 GTH/LHO BB6 ....219 K1
 HEY LA3 ....65 H3
 HGHB LA2 ....67 G4
 KIRK/FR/WA PR4 ....182 D7
 KIRK/FR/WA PR4 ....209 F7
 KIRK/FR/WA PR4 ....260 D3
 KIRK/FR/WA PR4 ....305 F6
 LEY/BBR PR5 ....265 J1
 SKEL WN8 ....351 K2
 TOT/BURYW BL8 ....319 G5
Chapel Meadow *KIRK/FR/WA* PR4 ....260 D3
Chapel Mdw *KIRK/FR/WA* PR4 ....282 A6
Chapel Ms
 BWCK/EAR (off James St) BB18 ....146 B2
 ORM L39 ....348 C7

Chapel Park Rd *KIRK/FR/WA* PR4 ....260 D3
Chapel Ri *CLI* BB7 ....193 F7
Chapel Rd *BPOOLS* FY4 ....205 G4
 FUL/RIB PR2 ....213 J7
 KIRK/FR/WA PR4 ....258 D8
Chapels *DWN* BB3 ....268 D8
Chapels Brow *DWN* BB3 ....268 D8
Chapelside Cl *GAR/LONG* PR3 ....155 K1
Chapels La *DWN* BB3 ....267 G8
Chapel St *ACC* BB5 ....221 J8
 ACC BB5 ....247 J7
 ACC BB5 ....248 C6
 BBN BB1 ....247 G2
 BBN BB1 ....269 J5
 BBNW BB2 ....8 B5
 BCUP OL13 ....298 A3
 BLY BB11 ....11 D3
 BPOOL FY1 ....4 B3
 BRFD/BLYE BB10 ....226 E6
 BWCK/EAR BB18 ....146 B1
 CHLY/EC PR7 ....311 G1
 CHLY/EC PR7 ....335 J2
 CHLY/EC PR7 ....337 F5
 CHLYE PR6 ....288 E3
 CLI BB7 ....89 H6
 COL BB8 ....171 H1
 COL BB8 ....171 H2
 DWN BB3 ....291 J3
 EDGW/EG BL7 ....314 E6
 EDGW/EG BL7 ....316 B3
 GAR/LONG PR3 ....153 F6
 GAR/LONG PR3 ....188 A4
 HGHB LA2 ....67 G8
 HOR/BR BL6 ....338 E6
 LANC LA1 ....3 D3
 LSTA FY8 ....232 C8
 *MCMB** LA4 ....41 G6
 NLSN BB9 ....197 K5
 NLSN BB9 ....198 C3
 ORM L39 ....348 D6
 PDHM/BLYW BB12 ....196 B6
 PLF/KEOS FY6 ....149 K7
 PRES PR1 ....7 D3
 RAW/HAS BB4 ....272 C8
 RAW/HAS BB4 ....273 H3
 RAW/HAS BB4 ....297 G3
 *STHP** PR8 ....301 H4
 WGNNW/BIL/O WN5 ....365 K5
Chapel Vw *HEY* LA3 ....65 H3
 RNFD/HAY WA11 ....370 B7
Chapel Vls
 BCUP (off Todmorden Rd) OL13 ....276 A7
Chapel Wk *KIRK/FR/WA* PR4 ....260 E3
 PDHM/BLYW BB12 ....223 J1
Chapel Wks *KIRK/FR/WA* PR4 ....209 F7
 *PRES** PR1 ....7 D3
Chapel Wy *CHLY/EC* PR7 ....335 K2
Chapel Yd *LEY/BBR* PR5 ....240 B6
Chapman Cl *GAR/LONG* PR3 ....153 G6
Chapman Ct *BWCK/EAR* BB18 ....119 F8
Chapman Rd *DWN* BB3 ....292 D2
 FUL/RIB PR2 ....213 J8
Chapter Rd *DWN* BB3 ....292 A3
Chardonnay Crs *BISP* FY2 ....149 F4
Charlbury Gv *HEY* LA3 ....52 E4
Charles Av *STHP* PR8 ....326 A5
Charlesbye Av *ORM* L39 ....348 E5
Charles Cl *KIRK/FR/WA* PR4 ....258 D8
Charles Ct *LANC* LA1 ....3 D5
Charles Crs *LEY/BBR* PR5 ....241 G8
Charles Gv *GAR/LONG* PR3 ....187 K4
Charles La *RAW/HAS* BB4 ....295 C1
Charles St *ACC* BB5 ....221 J8
 ACC BB5 ....247 J8
 BBNW BB2 ....268 A1
 BPOOL FY1 ....4 C1
 COL BB8 ....171 J2
 DWN BB3 ....291 H1
 EDGW/EG BL7 ....341 H1
 GTH/LHO BB6 ....221 G7
 LANC LA1 ....3 D5
 MCMB LA4 ....41 J6
 NLSN BB9 ....198 C1
 RAW/HAS BB4 ....297 H1
 WHIT OL12 ....323 H5
Charles Wy *KIRK/FR/WA* PR4 ....238 A2
Charlesway Ct
 FUL/RIB (off Lea Rd) PR2 ....238 A2
Charlesworth Cl *MGHL* L31 ....358 D6
Charlotte Pl *PRES* PR1 ....7 E3
Charlotte St *BBN* BB1 ....8 C3
 BLY BB11 ....10 C3
 EDGW/EG BL7 ....317 G7
 PRES PR1 ....7 E3
 *RAMS** BL0 ....319 H6
Charnley Cl *PRES* PR1 ....261 K1
Charnley Fold *LEY/BBR* PR5 ....263 J1

Charnley Fold La *LEY/BBR* PR5 2
Charnley Rd *BPOOL* FY1 ....
Charnley's La *CHTN/BK* PR9 2
Charnley St *BBNW* BB2 2
 LANC LA1 ....
 *PRES** PR1 ....
Charnock Av *PRES* PR1 2
Charnock Back La *CHLYE* PR6 3
Charnock Brow Preston Rd
 CHLY/EC PR7 3
Charnock Fold *PRES** PR1 2
Charnock St *CHLYE* PR6 3
 KIRK/FR/WA PR4 2
 LEY/BBR PR5 2
 PRES PR1 2
Charnwood Av *BPOOLE* FY3 1
Charnwood Cl *BBNW* BB2 2
Charter Brook
 GTH/LHO (off Princess St) BB6 2
Charterhouse Pl *BBNW* BB2 2
Charter La *CHLY/EC* PR7 3
Charter St *ACC* BB5 2
Chartwell Cl *CHLYE* PR6 2
Chartwell Ri *LEY/BBR* PR5 2
Chartwell Rd *STHP* PR8 3
Chase Cl *STHP* PR8 3
Chase Heys *CHTN/BK* PR9 3
The Chase
 BPOOLE (off Normoss Rd) FY3 1
 CARN LA5 ....
 CLV/TH FY5 1
 KIRK/FR/WA PR4 2
 LEY/BBR PR5 2
 PDHM/BLYW BB12 2
Chatburn Av *BRFD/BLYE* BB10 2
 CLI BB7 1
Chatburn Cl *GTH/LHO* BB6 2
 PLF/KEOS FY6 1
 RAW/HAS BB4 2
Chatburn Old Rd *CLI* BB7 1
Chatburn Park Dr *CLI* BB7 1
 NLSN BB9 1
Chatburn Rd *BOL* BL1 3
 CLI BB7 1
 FUL/RIB PR2 1
 GAR/LONG PR3 1
Chatburn St *BBNW* BB2 2
Chatham Av *LSTA* FY8 1
Chatham Crs *COL* BB8 1
Chatham Pl *CHLYE* PR6 3
 PRES PR1 2
Chatham St *COL* BB8 1
 NLSN BB9 1
Chatsworth Av *BISP* FY2 1
 FTWD FY7 1
 KIRK/FR/WA PR4 2
Chatsworth Cl *CHLY/EC* PR7 3
 CLV/TH FY5 1
 NLSN BB9 1
Chatsworth Ct *CHLYE* PR6 3
Chatsworth Rd *HEY* LA3 ....
 LANC LA1 ....
 LEY/BBR PR5 2
 LEY/BBR PR5 2
 LSTA FY8 2
 STHP PR8 3
Chatsworth St *PRES* PR1 3
 WHIT OL12 3
Chatteris Pl *CLV/TH* FY5 1
Chatterton Dr *ACC* BB5 2
Chatterton Old La *RAMS* BL0 3
Chatterton Rd *RAMS* BL0 3
Chaucer Av *CLV/TH* FY5 1
Chaucer Cl *CHLY/EC* PR7 3
Chaucer Gdns *GTH/LHO* BB6 2
Chaucer Rd *FTWD* FY7 ....
Chaucer St *PRES* PR1 2
Cheam Av *CHLY/EC* PR7 3
Cheapside *BPOOL* FY1 ....
 CHLY/EC PR7 3
 FMBY L37 3
 *LANC** LA1 ....
 PRES PR1 ....
Cheddar Av *BPOOLS* FY4 2
Cheddar Dr *FUL/RIB* PR2 2
Chedworth Av *HEY* LA3 ....
Cheetham Meadow
 LEY/BBR PR5 2
Cheetham St *BBNW* BB2 2
Chelburn Gv *BRFD/BLYE* BB10 1
Chelford Av *BOL* BL1 3
 BPOOLE FY3 1
Chelford Cl *PRES* PR1 2
Chelmsford Cl *LANC* LA1 3
Chelmsford Gv *CHLY/EC* PR7 3
Chelmsford Pl *CHLY/EC* PR7 3
Chelmsford Wk *LEY/BBR* PR5 2

...ea Av *BISP* FY2 ....**176** E2
...ton Dr *RAW/HAS* BB4 ....**295** G4
...enham Av *ACC* BB5 ....**248** C4
...enham Crs *CLV/TH* FY5 ....**149** K3
...A FY8 ....**233** F6
...enham Dr
...*NW/BIL/O* WN5 ....**371** F1
...enham Rd *BBNW* BB2 ....**8** A4
...OOL FY1 ....**176** B4
...IC LA1 ....**3** D6
...enham Wy *STHP* PR8 ....**302** B7
...wood Cl *BOL* BL1 ....**341** H4
...stow Rd *BPOOLE* FY3 ....**177** F3
...uer Cl *SKEL* WN8 ....**364** B6
...uer La *SKEL* WN8 ....**364** B5
...uers *ACC* BB5 ....**247** K1
...uers Av *LANC* LA1 ....**55** H7
...ton Fld *FUL/RIB* PR2 ....**212** E4
...ton Pk *STHP* PR8 ....**301** H6
...HP PR8 ....**302** A8
...ry Cl *BBN* BB1 ....**9** F4
...L/RIB PR2 ....**214** B5
...*K/FR/WA* PR4 ....**208** C3
...ryclough Wy *BBNW* BB2 ....**267** H3
...ry Crs *ACC* BB5 ....**270** C1
...W/HAS BB4 ....**296** B3
...rydale *BISP* FY2 ....**148** D6
...ryfields *CHLYE* PR6 ....**286** B7
...ry Gn *ORM* L39 ....**359** K2
...ry Gv *BRSC* L40 ....**330** E5
...LYE PR6 ....**289** H1
...R/LONG PR3 ....**188** A3
...ry Crs *CARN* LA5 ....**43** F1
...R/LONG PR3 ....**100** C6
...Y* LA3 ....**52** C5
...ry Tree Ct
...WD (off Aughton St) FY7 ....**97** H6
...ry Tree Dr *LANC* LA1 ....**55** F7
...ry Tree Gdns *BPOOLS* FY4 ....**205** G3
...ry Tree Gv *CHLYE* PR6 ....**287** G8
...ry Tree La *BBNW* BB2 ....**267** F3
...M L39 ....**359** K2
...ry Tree Ms *BLY* BB11 ....**10** A6
...ry Tree Rd *BPOOLS* FY4 ....**205** G2
...ry Tree Rd North
...OOLE FY3 ....**205** G2
...ry Trees *LEY/BBR* PR5 ....**239** K8
...ry Tree Wy *RAW/HAS* BB4 ....**295** G4
...ry V *KIRK/FR/WA* PR4 ....**281** J1
...sham Dr *KIRK/FR/WA* PR4 ....**261** G4
...sham St *GAR/LONG* PR3 ....**153** F6
...shire Cft *RAMS* BL0 ....**319** K5
...shire House La *LEY/BBR* * PR5...**262** E2
...shire Lines Pth *FMBY* L37 ....**345** F5
...smere Cft
...*PES* (off Chesmere Dr) PR1 ....**238** C4
...smere Dr *PRES* PR1 ....**238** D5
...snell Gv *NWD/KWIPK* L33 ....**366** C6
...ster Av *CHLYE* PR7 ....**311** J7
...TN/BK PR9 ....**302** B3
...* BB7 ....**165** J2
...V/TH FY5 ....**148** D1
...F/KEOS FY6 ....**149** J8
...ster Cl *BBN* BB1 ....**9** F5
...AR/LONG PR3..........................**129** H4
...ster Crs *RAW/HAS* BB4 ....**295** H3
...ster Dr *RAMS* BL0....................**319** G7
...sterfield Cl *STHP* PR8 ....**325** H7
...sterfield Dr *NWD/KWIPK* L33 ....**366** C6
...sterfield Rd *BPOOL* FY1 ....**176** B3
...HP PR8 ....**325** H7
...ster Pl *CHLYE* PR6 ....**337** C3
...R/LONG PR3..............................**153** G6
...NC LA1 ....**3** E4
...ster Rd *BPOOLE* * FY3 ....**176** D3
...TN/BK PR9 ....**302** B3
...*PES* PR1 ....**240** A2
...ster St *ACC* BB5 ....**248** A4
...RN BB1 ....**9** E4
...stnut Av *BPOOLS* FY4 ....**205** F6
...RN LA5 ....**33** G6
...*LY/EC* PR7 ....**286** A7
...*LYE* PR6 ....**311** J1
...GHB LA2 ....**45** H5
...RES PR1 ....**238** C7

Chestnut Cl *LEY/BBR* PR5 ....**263** H1
  ORM L39 ....**346** E2
Chestnut Ct *ORM* L39 ....**348** D5
Chestnut Crs *CLI* BB7 ....**193** H2
  FUL/RIB PR2 ....**240** C1
  KIRK/FR/WA PR4 ....**260** A3
Chestnut Dr *BWCK/EAR* BB18.....**144** E2
  FUL/RIB PR2 ....**213** F4
  MCMB LA4 ....**42** B4
  RAW/HAS BB4 ....**296** B3
Chestnut Gra *ORM* L39 ....**348** B8
Chestnut Gv *ACC* BB5 ....**222** A7
  ACC BB5 ....**248** A7
  DWN BB3 ....**291** J6
  LANC LA1 ....**2** B3
Chestnut Ri *BLY* BB11 ....**10** C5
The Chestnuts *CHLY/EC* PR7 ....**335** K1
Chestnut St *STHP* PR8 ....**301** J7
Chestnut Wk *BBN* BB1 ....**9** F4
Chestnut Wy *FMBY* L37 ....**355** G2
Chevassut Cl *NLSN* BB9 ....**198** A2
Cheviot Av *BRFD/BLYE* BB10 ......**226** C6
  CLV/TH FY5 ....**123** F7
  LSTA FY8 ....**233** G6
Cheviot Cl *BOL* BL1 ....**341** H6
  HOR/BR BL6 ....**338** E6
  RAMS BL0 ....**319** J7
Cheviot St *PRES* PR1 ....**6** A2
Cheviot Wy *NWD/KWIPK* L33 .....**366** D5
Chew Gdns *PLF/KEOS* FY6 ....**149** H8
Chichester Cl *BRFD/BLYE* BB10 ....**11** E3
  CLV/TH FY5 ....**149** G1
Chicken St *BBNW* BB2 ....**8** A5
Chiddlingford Ct
  BPOOL (off Somerset Av) FY1 ......**5** D4
Chilham St *WGNW/BIL/O* WN5 ...**365** J5
Chiltern Av *BPOOLS* FY4 ....**204** D8
  BRFD/BLYE BB10 ....**226** C6
  CHLY/EC PR7 ....**310** B2
  PLF/KEOS FY6 ....**149** J8
Chiltern Cl *HOR/BR* BL6 ....**338** E6
  LSTA FY8 ....**233** F6
  RAMS BL0 ....**319** J7
Chiltern Dr *KKBY* L32 ....**366** A4
Chiltern Meadow *LEY/BBR* PR5 ...**286** B2
Chiltern Rd *RAMS* BL0 ....**319** J7
  STHP PR8 ....**325** G5
The Chimes *KIRK/FR/WA* PR4 .....**208** B1
  KIRK/FR/WA PR4 ....**282** E6
China St *ACC* BB5 ....**247** K5
  LANC LA1 ....**3** D3
Chindit Cl *FMBY* L37 ....**355** H1
Chindits Wy *FUL/RIB* PR2 ....**213** K7
Chingford Bank *BRFD/BLYE* BB10...**198** B8
Chingle Cl *FUL/RIB* PR2 ....**214** C5
Chipping Av *STHP* PR8................**325** G6
  BRFD/BLYE BB10 ....**226** B7
Chipping Gv *BPOOLE* FY3 ....**177** G3
Chipping La *GAR/LONG* PR3 ....**188** A2
Chipping St *PDHM/BLYW* BB12 ...**223** K2
Chisacre Dr *WGNNW/ST* WN6 ....**353** F4
Chisholm Cl *WGNNW/ST* WN6....**335** F8
Chislehurst Av *BPOOLS* FY4 ....**4** C5
Chislehurst Gv *BRFD/BLYE* BB10 ...**198** B7
Chislehurst Pl *LSTA* FY8 ....**231** K5
Chislett Cl *BRSC* * L40 ....**330** D7
Chisnall Av *WGNNW/ST* WN6 ....**334** D6
Chisnall La *CHLY/EC* PR7 ....**334** E6
  CHLY/EC PR7 ....**334** D1
Chiswell Gv *CLV/TH* FY5 ....**150** A3
Chiswick Gv *BPOOLE* FY3 ....**205** H1
Chorley Cl *CHTN/BK* PR9 ....**279** G6
Chorley Hall Rd *CHLY/EC* PR7 ....**311** G1
Chorley La *CHLY/EC* PR7 ....**335** G1
Chorley New Rd *HOR/BR* BL6......**338** D8
  HOR/BR BL6 ....**339** G8
Chorley Old Rd *CHLYE* PR6 ....**287** G4
  HOR/BR BL6 ....**339** G8
Chorley Rd *BPOOLE* FY3 ....**177** F1
  CHLY/EC PR7 ....**337** G6
  CHLYE PR6 ....**265** J8
  CHLYE PR6 ....**337** G2
  HOR/BR BL6 ....**337** J8
  LEY/BBR PR5 ....**240** B8
  SKEL WN8 ....**332** E7
  WGN WN1 ....**336** C6
Chorley St *CHLYE* PR6 ....**337** H3
Choriton Cl *BRFD/BLYE* BB10 .....**226** B1
Chorlton St *BBN* BB1 ....**9** D2
Christ Church Sq *ACC* * BB5 ......**248** C6
Christ Church St *ACC* * BB5 ....**248** C6
  BCUP OL13 ....**275** K8
  PRES PR1 ....**6** C3
Christian Rd *PRES* PR1 ....**6** C3
Christie Av *MCMB* LA4 ....**41** K7
Christines Crs *BRSC* L40 ....**330** D7
Christleton *WGNNW/ST* WN6 .....**353** K5

Christleton Cl *BRFD/BLYE* BB10 ...**198** D8
Church Aly *ACC* * BB5 ....**247** K1
Church Av *ACC* BB5 ....**271** K2
  LANC LA1...................................**55** F7
  PRES PR1 ....**6** A4
  PRES PR1 ....**240** C3
Church Bank *KKBYL* LA6 ....**34** E3
Church Bank St *DWN* * BB3 ....**291** J2
Church Br
  ACC (off Mill St) BB5 ....**247** K5
Church Brow *CARN* LA5 ....**33** G8
  CLI BB7 ....**165** J2
  HGHB LA2 ....**43** K5
  LEY/BBR PR5 ....**240** B6
Church Brow Cl *CARN* LA5 ....**33** G8
Church Brow Gdns *CLI* BB7 ....**165** K2
Church Cl *BBNW* BB2 ....**244** A1
  CHTN/BK PR9 ....**302** C3
  CLI BB7 ....**139** F7
  CLI BB7 ....**165** J2
  FMBY L37 ....**344** A8
  HGHB LA2 ....**81** J4
  KIRK/FR/WA PR4 ....**234** E5
  PDHM/BLYW BB12 ....**222** C1
  RAMS BL0 ....**319** H6
Church Close Ct *FMBY* * L37 ......**344** A8
Church Ct *CARN* LA5 ....**33** G8
  PRES PR1 ....**240** A1
  RAMS BL0 ....**295** K7
Church Dr *LSTA* FY8 ....**232** B8
  WGNW/BIL/O WN5 ....**365** F6
Churchfield *FUL/RIB* PR2 ....**213** H5
  WGNNW/ST WN6 ....**353** J5
Church Flds *BRSC* L40 ....**328** D4
  ORM L39 ....**348** C6
Churchfields *STHP* PR8 ....**301** F8
Church Fold *CHLY/EC* PR7 ....**310** C7
  CHLY/EC PR7 ....**335** K3
Church Gdns *KIRK/FR/WA* PR4 ...**234** C5
Churchgate *CHTN/BK* PR9 ....**302** B2
  GAR/LONG PR3 ....**186** B5
Churchgate Ms *CHTN/BK* PR9 ....**302** C2
Church Gn *FMBY* L37 ....**355** G1
  KKBY L32 ....**366** C8
Church Gv *HEY* LA3 ....**65** J3
Church Hall *ACC* BB5 ....**247** K5
Church HI *CARN* LA5 ....**15** G1
  CHLYE PR6 ....**287** F4
  KKBYL LA6 ....**34** A6
Church Hill Av *CARN* LA5 ....**25** K6
Church Hill Rd *BBN* BB1 ....**9** E2
  ORM L39 ....**348** B5
Churchill Av *BBN* BB1 ....**246** E3
  CHTN/BK PR9 ....**302** B1
Churchill Cl *CLV/TH* FY5 ....**149** H1
Churchill Ct *BPOOLE* FY3................**5** D1
Churchill Dr *FUL/RIB* * PR2 ....**214** B7
Churchill Rd *CHLYE* PR6 ....**289** G3
  FUL/RIB PR2 ....**214** A7
  NLSN BB9 ....**197** K2
Churchill St *TOD* OL14 ....**277** K3
Churchill Wy *LEY/BBR* PR5 ....**285** J1
  NLSN BB9 ....**197** K4
  PDHM/BLYW BB12 ....**197** K3
Church La *ACC* BB5 ....**248** A2
  BBNW BB2 ....**244** A1
  BWCK/EAR BB18 ....**146** A5
  CHLY/EC PR7 ....**310** B7
  CLI BB7 ....**164** C8
  CLI BB7 ....**193** G6
  GAR/LONG PR3........................**102** D7
  GAR/LONG PR3........................**156** C1
  GAR/LONG PR3........................**158** B4
  GAR/LONG PR3........................**186** B5
  GAR/LONG PR3........................**213** F2
  GTH/LHO BB6..........................**221** G5
  KIRK/FR/WA PR4 ....**210** C8
  KIRK/FR/WA PR4 ....**262** B4
  KKBYL LA6 ....**30** C3
  MCMB LA4 ....**41** J5
  ORM L39 ....**358** B3
  ORM L39 ....**359** J4
  PLF/KEOS FY6 ....**151** F2
  RAMS BL0 ....**295** K7
  RAW/HAS BB4 ....**297** G2
  SKP/WHF BD23 ....**120** B1
  SKP/WHF BD23 ....**121** G2
  WGNNW/ST WN6 ....**334** B3
  WGNNW/ST WN6 ....**353** J5
Church Mdw *COL* BB8 ....**171** H6
Church Pk *HEY* LA3 ....**65** H3
  KIRK/FR/WA PR4 ....**211** F8
Church Raike *GAR/LONG* PR3 .....**134** E8
Church Rd *BRSC* L40 ....**306** C2
  CHTN/BK PR9 ....**279** J5
  CLV/TH FY5 ....**149** F1
  FMBY L37 ....**344** A7

KIRK/FR/WA PR4 ....**207** G1
KIRK/FR/WA PR4 ....**208** D4
KIRK/FR/WA PR4 ....**209** J4
KIRK/FR/WA PR4 ....**234** B4
KIRK/FR/WA PR4 ....**282** A6
LEY/BBR PR5 ....**263** H4
LEY/BBR PR5 ....**285** J3
LSTA FY8 ....**231** F4
LSTA FY8 ....**232** B8
ORM L39 ....**361** J5
PLF/KEOS FY6 ....**179** G2
RAMS BL0 ....**320** A3
RNFD/HAY WA11 ....**369** F5
SKEL WN8 ....**363** F2
SKP/WHF BD23 ....**119** K6
TOD OL14 ....**277** K3
Church Rw KIRK/FR/WA PR4 ....**207** K7
PRES PR1 ....**7** E2
Churchside KIRK/FR/WA PR4 ....**261** C3
Church St ACC BB5 ....**247** J5
ACC BB5 ....**247** H8
ACC BB5 ....**247** K1
ACC BB5 ....**248** C6
BBN BB1 ....**8** C4
BBN BB1 ....**246** E2
BCUP OL13 ....**298** A3
BLY BB11 ....**11** D2
BPOOL FY1 ....**4** B2
BRFD/BLYE BB10 ....**226** D1
BWCK/EAR BB18 ....**145** F1
CHLY/EC* PR7 ....**311** G4
CHLYE PR6 ....**337** G4
CHTN/BK PR9 ....**301** J4
CLI BB7 ....**89** H6
CLI BB7 ....**165** J3
COL BB8 ....**171** H6
COL BB8 ....**200** C1
DWN BB3 ....**291** J2
EDGW/EG BL7 ....**314** E7
FTWD FY7 ....**97** H7
GAR/LONG PR3 ....**129** H5
GAR/LONG PR3 ....**155** G1
GAR/LONG PR3 ....**188** B4
GAR/LONG PR3 ....**189** K7
GTH/LHO BB6 ....**221** C6
HGHB LA2 ....**43** K5
HOR/BR BL6 ....**338** E7
KIRK/FR/WA PR4 ....**209** F6
KKBYL LA6 ....**21** F6
LANC LA1 ....**3** D3
LEY/BBR PR5 ....**241** F8
LEY/BBR PR5 ....**285** K1
LEY/BBR PR5 ....**307** H2
MCMB LA4 ....**41** H5
NLSN BB9 ....**170** B7
NLSN BB9 ....**197** K6
ORM L39 ....**348** C6
PDHM/BLYW BB12 ....**222** D2
PDHM/BLYW BB12 ....**223** J7
PDHM/BLYW BB12 ....**223** H3
PLF/KEOS* FY6 ....**149** K8
PRES PR1 ....**7** E3
RAMS BL0 ....**319** J5
RAW/HAS BB4 ....**272** C8
RAW/HAS BB4 ....**273** H3
RAW/HAS BB4 ....**297** J2
SKEL WN8 ....**364** E4
WGNW/BIL/O WN5 ....**365** F6
WGNW/BIL/O WN5 ....**365** K5
WHIT OL12 ....**323** G3
Church Ter DWN * BB3 ....**291** J2
Churchtown Crs BCUP OL13 ....**298** E2
Church Vw KIRK/FR/WA PR4 ....**282** A6
ORM L39 ....**359** J4
Church Wk BBN BB1 ....**219** H8
CHLY/EC PR7 ....**310** A1
FUL/RIB PR2 ....**214** D6
KIRK/FR/WA PR4 ....**208** D4
KIRK/FR/WA PR4 ....**282** A6
Church Wy FMBY L37 ....**355** C1
KKBY L32 ....**366** C8
NLSN BB9 ....**198** B5
Churton Gv WGNNW/ST WN6 ....**353** K1
Chysden Cl CHLYE PR6 ....**287** G6
Cicely La BBN BB1 ....**9** D4
Cicely St BBN BB1 ....**9** D5
Cinderbarrow La KKBYL LA6 ....**26** E1
Cinder La HGHB LA2 ....**55** F8
KIRK/FR/WA PR4 ....**183** C5
KIRK/FR/WA PR4 ....**304** D1
Cinnamon Brow SKEL WN8 ....**364** E5
Cinnamon Ct PRES PR1 ....**261** C1
Cinnamon Hill Dr North
LEY/BBR PR5 ....**240** B8
Cinnamon Hill Dr South
LEY/BBR PR5 ....**240** B8
Cintra Av FUL/RIB PR2 ....**239** F1

Cirrus Dr ORM L39 ....**359** J2
City Heights Cl LANC * LA1 ....**3** E3
City Rd WGNW/BIL/O WN5 ....**365** K4
Clairane Av FUL/RIB PR2 ....**213** C5
Clancut La CHLY/EC PR7 ....**335** K1
Clanfield FUL/RIB PR2 ....**213** G4
Clara St PRES * PR1 ....**240** A4
WHIT OL12 ....**323** H2
Clare Av COL BB8 ....**198** E1
Claremont Av CHLY/EC PR7 ....**311** F4
CLI BB7 ....**165** K4
STHP PR8 ....**301** G7
Claremont Ct BPOOL FY1 ....**176** C4
Claremont Crs MCMB LA4 ....**41** F7
Claremont Dr CLI BB7 ....**165** A4
ORM L39 ....**348** B8
Claremont Gdns STHP PR8 ....**301** G7
Claremont Pl LSTA FY8 ....**230** E3
Claremont Rd ACC BB5 ....**248** B5
BPOOL FY1 ....**176** C4
CHLY/EC PR7 ....**311** F6
MCMB LA4 ....**41** F7
STHP PR8 ....**301** G7
WGNW/BIL/O WN5 ....**371** G6
Claremont St NLSN BB9 ....**197** J5
PDHM/BLYW BB12 ....**10** A3
Claremont Ter NLSN BB9 ....**198** B4
Claremount Av LEY/BBR PR5 ....**285** K3
Clarence Av CLV/TH FY5 ....**122** D8
PLF/KEOS FY6 ....**98** A6
Clarence Pk BBNW BB2 ....**244** D4
Clarence Rd ACC BB5 ....**248** A7
STHP PR8 ....**301** G7
Clarence St BBN BB1 ....**8** B3
BLY BB11 ....**11** E5
BWCK/EAR BB18 ....**145** G3
CHLY/EC* PR7 ....**311** H4
COL BB8 ....**172** A6
COL BB8 ....**200** C1
DWN BB3 ....**268** C8
GAR/LONG PR3 ....**188** A4
LANC LA1 ....**3** E4
LEY/BBR PR5 ....**285** K1
MCMB LA4 ....**41** H5
RAW/HAS BB4 ....**273** H4
Clarendon Gv MGHL L31 ....**358** E6
Clarendon Rd BBN BB1 ....**9** D1
BPOOL FY1 ....**4** B5
LANC LA1 ....**43** F8
LSTA FY8 ....**231** F3
Clarendon Rd East BBN BB1 ....**9** E1
MCMB LA4 ....**41** F7
Clarendon Rd North LSTA FY8 ....**231** F3
Clarendon Rd West HEY LA3 ....**40** E8
Clarendon St ACC BB5 ....**248** D5
CHLYE PR6 ....**311** J5
COL BB8 ....**172** B6
PRES PR1 ....**7** E4
Clare Rd LANC LA1 ....**42** E8
Clare St BLY BB11 ....**10** A3
BPOOL FY1 ....**4** B6
Claret St ACC BB5 ....**248** A6
Clarke Holme St RAW/HAS * BB4 ....**297** H1
Clarke St BBN BB1 ....**247** F7
Clarke Wood Cl CLI BB7 ....**193** K3
Clarkfield Cl BRSC L40 ....**331** F8
Clarkfield Dr MCMB LA4 ....**41** K6
Clarksfield Rd CARN LA5 ....**33** G7
Clark St MCMB LA4 ....**41** H5
PLF/KEOS FY6 ....**150** B8
Claughton Av LEY/BBR PR5 ....**286** C2
Claughton Dr LANC LA1 ....**55** C8
Claughton St BRFD/BLYE BB10 ....**225** K2
Claybank PDHM/BLYW BB12 ....**223** J2
Claybridge Cl WGNW/BIL/O WN5 ....**365** J2
Clay Brow Rd SKEL WN8 ....**364** A5
Clayburn Cl CHLYE PR6 ....**311** H1
Clay Gap La PLF/KEOS FY6 ....**125** H7
Clay Hill La GAR/LONG PR3 ....**189** H3
Claylands Dr CARN * LA5 ....**33** C7
Clay La HEY LA3 ....**53** F3
Clay St BLY BB11 ....**224** E6
Clayton Av LEY/BBR PR5 ....**285** F4
RAW/HAS BB4 ....**296** A3
Clayton Brook Rd LEY/BBR PR5 ....**264** A6
Clayton Cl NLSN BB9 ....**198** B2
Clayton Ct GAR/LONG PR3 ....**188** B4
Clayton Crs BPOOLS FY4 ....**204** D5
Clayton Gdns BRSC L40 ....**330** E7
Claytongate CHLY/EC PR7 ....**335** K1
Clayton Green Rd CHLYE PR6 ....**264** A8
Clayton Gv BBN BB1 ....**219** F5
Claytonhalgh GAR/LONG PR3 ....**190** A8
Clayton Hall Dr ACC BB5 ....**221** K7
Clayton Ms SKEL WN8 ....**362** D2
Clayton Rw GTH/LHO BB6 ....**220** B2
Clayton's Ga PRES PR1 ....**7** D2

Clayton St ACC BB5 ....**2**
BBNW BB2 ....**1**
BWCK/EAR BB18 ....**1**
COL BB8 ....**1**
GTH/LHO BB6 ....**2**
LEY/BBR PR5 ....**2**
NLSN BB9 ....**1**
SKEL WN8 ....**3**
Cleator Av BISP FY2 ....**1**
Cleaver St BBN BB1 ....**1**
BRFD/BLYE BB10 ....
Clecken La GAR/LONG PR3 ....**1**
Clegg Av CLV/TH FY5 ....**1**
Clegg St BRFD/BLYE BB10 ....
BRFD/BLYE BB10 ....
KIRK/FR/WA* PR4 ....**2**
NLSN BB9 ....**1**
NLSN BB9 ....**1**
RAW/HAS BB4 ....**3**
SKEL WN8 ....**3**
WHIT OL12 ....**3**
Clegg St East BRFD/BLYE * BB10 ....
Clematis Cl CHLY/EC PR7 ....**2**
Clematis St BBNW BB2 ....**2**
Clements Dr BRFD/BLYE BB10 ....**1**
Clement St ACC BB5 ....
DWN BB3 ....**2**
Clengers Brow CHTN/BK PR9 ....**2**
Clent Av MGHL L31 ....**3**
Clent Gdns MGHL L31 ....**3**
Clerkhill St BBN BB1 ....
Clevedon Rd BPOOL FY1 ....**1**
FUL/RIB PR2 ....**2**
Cleveland Av FUL/RIB PR2 ....**2**
Cleveland Cl KKBY L32 ....**3**
RAMS BL0 ....**3**
Cleveland Dr LANC LA1 ....**2**
Cleveland Rd LEY/BBR PR5 ....**2**
LSTA FY8 ....**2**
Clevelands Av CARN LA5 ....
HEY LA3 ....
Clevelands Gv BLY BB11 ....
HEY LA3 ....
Clevelands Mt BLY BB11 ....
Clevelands Rd BLY BB11 ....
Cleveland St CHLY/EC PR7 ....**3**
CHLY/EC* PR7 ....**3**
COL BB8 ....**1**
TOD OL14 ....**2**
Clevelands Wk HEY LA3 ....
Cleveleys Av CHTN/BK PR9 ....**2**
CLV/TH FY5 ....**1**
FUL/RIB PR2 ....**2**
LANC LA1 ....
Cleveleys Rd ACC BB5 ....**2**
BBNW BB2 ....**2**
CHTN/BK PR9 ....**2**
LEY/BBR PR5 ....
The Cleves MGHL L31 ....**3**
Cleve Wy FMBY L37 ....**3**
Clieves Hills La ORM L39 ....**3**
Cliffe Ct PRES PR1 ....**2**
Cliffe Dr CHLYE PR6 ....**2**
Cliffe La GTH/LHO BB6 ....**2**
Cliffe St NLSN BB9 ....**1**
Clifford Av KIRK/FR/WA PR4 ....**2**
MCMB LA4 ....**2**
Clifford Rd BPOOL FY1 ....**1**
STHP PR8 ....**3**
Clifford St BWCK/EAR BB18 ....**1**
CHLY/EC PR7 ....**3**
COL BB8 ....**1**
Cliff Pl BISP FY2 ....**1**
Cliff Rd CHTN/BK PR9 ....**3**
The Cliffs HEY LA3 ....
Cliff St BBN BB1 ....**2**
COL BB8 ....**1**
PDHM/BLYW BB12 ....**2**
PRES PR1 ....
Clifton Av ACC BB5 ....**2**
BPOOLE FY3 ....**2**
FUL/RIB PR2 ....**2**
KIRK/FR/WA PR4 ....**2**
LEY/BBR PR5 ....**2**
Clifton Cl CLV/TH FY5 ....**1**
Clifton Ct
LSTA (off Victoria St) FY8 ....**2**
Clifton Crs BPOOLE FY3 ....**2**
PRES PR1 ....**2**
Clifton Dr BPOOLS FY4 ....**2**
GTH/LHO BB6 ....**2**
HOR/BR BL6 ....**3**
LSTA FY8 ....**2**
MCMB LA4 ....
PRES PR1 ....
Clifton Dr North LSTA FY8 ....**2**
Clifton Dr South LSTA FY8 ....**2**

on Flds
RK/FR/WA (off Lytham Rd) PR4 236 B4
on Gdns LSTA FY8 231 J5
on Gn KIRK/FR/WA PR4 236 C2
on Gv CHLY/EC PR7 311 F4
ES PR1 214 A8
on La KIRK/FR/WA PR4 210 C8
on Pl FUL/RIB * PR2 238 D1
RK/FR/WA PR4 235 F5
on Rd BPOOLS FY4 205 J3
IBY L37 344 A6
WD FY7 97 G8
SN BB9 198 A7
DHM/BLYW BB12 224 E4
HP PR8 302 B5
GNW/BIL/O WN5 371 F7
on St ACC BB5 248 A7
3N BB1 247 F2
POOL FY1 4 B2
VCK/EAR BB18 146 A3
L BB8 171 H6
L BB8 200 B1
VN BB3 268 B7
TA FY8 232 D8
DHM/BLYW BB12 10 B3
RES PR1 6 B4
kham Rd GTH/LHO BB6 220 E6
ning Rd STHP PR8 326 C1
on Av BPOOL FY1 4 C3
on St BBN BB1 9 E3
pers Quay
3N (off Merchants Landing) BB1 9 D5
eroe Pl BPOOLS FY4 205 G3
eroe Rd CLI BB7 139 J6
I BB7 139 F7
I BB7 140 C8
I BB7 193 G6
I BB7 194 E2
TA FY8 231 J5
SN BB9 197 J5
DHM/BLYW BB12 197 H6
eroes La KIRK/FR/WA PR4 235 F5
eroe St PDHM/BLYW BB12 223 J3
RES PR1 240 A4
e Av LSTA FY8 230 E2
e Ldg STHP PR8 326 B1
e Rd PRES PR1 238 D5
HP PR8 326 B2
e St PDHM/BLYW BB12 10 C1
khouse Av BRFD/BLYE BB10 198 B8
khouse Ct BRFD/BLYE BB10 198 B8
khouse Gv BRFD/BLYE BB10 198 B8
l La RAW/HAS BB4 295 J4
ls Carr La PLF/KEOS FY6 98 B8
ger La SKP/WHF BD23 121 G7
ster Dr DWN BB3 292 A2
sters HEY LA3 53 H1
Cloisters BPOOLE FY3 5 E2
I BB7 193 H6
IBY (off Halsall La) L37 343 K8
JL/RIB PR2 6 B2
RK/FR/WA PR4 282 A5
Y/BBR PR5 286 A1
AW/HAS BB4 297 G3
ain Rd NWD/KWIPK L33 366 E8
e La HWTH BD22 174 E2
Close ACC BB5 221 K7
CC BB5 272 B3
HLYE PR6 288 C1
HTN/BK PR9 279 J6
LV/TH FY5 122 D7
JL/RIB PR2 214 C5
AR/LONG PR3 129 H2
TWN L38 356 E8
RK/FR/WA PR4 207 G1
RK/FR/WA PR4 209 F7
RK/FR/WA PR4 261 H4
gha Av HGHB LA2 44 B4
NC LA1 3 F5
gh Acre CHLY/EC PR7 310 E1
gh Av LEY/BBR PR5 239 K8
gh Bank CLI BB7 140 D6
gh End Rd RAW/HAS BB4 272 C6
ghfield PRES PR1 262 A2
gh La GAR/LONG PR3 161 F4
DHM/BLYW BB12 223 F1
gh Rd BCUP OL13 275 K8
SN BB9 198 E3
gh St BCUP OL13 298 B3
Y BB11 10 A4
WN BB3 292 A5
AW/HAS BB4 297 H2
Clough CHLYE PR6 263 K8
ghwood Crs
GNNW/ST WN6 353 F4
elly Av BISP FY2 148 C5
JL/RIB PR2 213 F8
Clovelly Dr PRES PR1 238 C6
SKEL WN8 351 G3
STHP PR8 326 A3
Clover Av LSTA FY8 231 G2
Clover Ct BISP FY2 149 F5
Clover Crs PDHM/BLYW BB12 10 A1
Clover Dr KIRK/FR/WA PR4 235 H4
Clover Fld CHLYE PR6 287 F1
Cloverfield PRES PR1 238 D7
Cloverfields BBN BB1 9 E3
Clover Hl
BCUP (off Greensnook La) OL13 275 K8
Clover Hill Rd NLSN BB9 198 D4
Clover Ms BPOOLE * FY3 5 E1
Clover Rd CHLY/EC PR7 310 E6
Clover St BCUP OL13 275 K8
Clover Ter DWN BB3 268 D8
Club La GAR/LONG PR3 134 E8
Club St LEY/BBR PR5 263 H4
TOD OL14 277 G2
Clucas Gdns ORM L39 348 C5
Clydesdale Pl LEY/BBR PR5 284 E1
Clyde St BBNW * BB2 244 D8
BPOOL* FY1 176 B4
FUL/RIB PR2 6 A2
Clyffes Farm Cl BRSC L40 328 E4
Coach House Cottages
RAW/HAS
(off Manchester Rd) BB4 295 H1
Coach House Ct BRSC L40 330 E8
Coach House Dr WGNNW/ST WN6 353 K5
Coach Ms
MCMB (off West End Rd) LA4 41 F7
Coach Rd ACC BB5 247 J6
ORM L39 367 K2
Coal Clough La BLY BB11 10 B4
Coal Clough Rd TOD OL14 254 A8
Coal Pit La ACC BB5 247 K7
BCUP OL13 276 A8
CLI BB7 117 J8
COL BB8 171 K7
DWN BB3 267 H8
ORM L39 362 C7
RAW/HAS BB4 274 D8
Coal Pit Rd BOL BL1 339 K4
Coal Rd RAMS BL0 320 C3
Coal St BLY BB11 10 C3
Coastal Dr HGHB LA2 42 D2
Coastal Ri HGHB LA2 42 D2
Coastal Rd CARN LA5 42 E1
MCMB LA4 42 B3
STHP PR8 325 G5
Coastline Ms
CHTN/BK (off Lytham Rd) PR9 278 C7
Coates Av BWCK/EAR BB18 119 G8
Coates Flds BWCK/EAR BB18 119 G7
Coates La BWCK/EAR BB18 119 G7
Cobb's Brow La SKEL WN8 351 G2
Cobb's Clough Rd BRSC L40 351 F6
Cobbs La ACC BB5 270 D3
Cob Castle Rd RAW/HAS BB4 272 A8
Cobden Ct BBN * BB1 8 C4
Cobden Rd CHTN/BK PR9 302 B5
Cobden St BCUP OL13 299 F3
BOL BL1 341 H8
BRFD/BLYE BB10 11 E1
BRFD/BLYE BB10 198 D8
BWCK/EAR BB18 145 F2
CHLYE PR6 311 J2
DWN BB3 291 J3
EDGW/EG* BL7 341 H1
NLSN BB9 198 B4
PDHM/BLYW BB12 223 J7
PDHM/BLYW BB12 223 K2
Cobham Rd ACC BB5 248 C6
Cob La BWCK/EAR BB18 146 A6
Cob Moor Av WGNW/BIL/O WN5 371 F2
Cob Moor Rd WGNW/BIL/O WN5 371 F2
Cobourg Cl BBNW BB2 268 C1
Cob Wall BBN BB1 9 E2
Cochran St DWN * BB3 291 J3
Cock Br GTH/LHO BB6 221 K2
Cocker Av PLF/KEOS FY6 178 C1
Cocker Bar Rd LEY/BBR PR5 283 J4
Cockerham Rd GAR/LONG PR3 129 G1
HGHB LA2 80 B7
Cocker Ho Br HGHB LA2 79 K7
Cockerill St RAW/HAS BB4 272 C7
Cocker La LEY/BBR PR5 284 E2
Cockermouth Cl DWN BB3 268 C4
Cocker Rd LEY/BBR PR5 263 K4
Cockersand Av KIRK/FR/WA PR4 260 D2
Cockersand Dr LANC LA1 55 G8
Cocker Sq BPOOL FY1 4 B1
Cocker St BPOOL FY1 4 B1
Cock Hall La WHIT OL12 323 F2
Cockhall La WHIT OL12 323 G2
Cockhill La COL BB8 172 B3
Cocking Yd KKBYL LA6 18 B6
Cockle Dick's La CHTN/BK PR9 302 A1
Cockridge Cl BBNW BB2 267 J4
Cock Robin Cottages
LEY/BBR (off Highfield Rd) PR5 307 J1
Cock Robin La GAR/LONG PR3 155 K1
Codale Av BISP FY2 148 D6
Coddington St BBN * BB1 9 F4
Coe La KIRK/FR/WA PR4 282 A5
Cog La BLY BB11 10 A5
Cog St BLY BB11 10 A4
Colbran St BRFD/BLYE BB10 225 K2
NLSN BB9 198 D1
Colburne Cl BRSC L40 331 F6
Colchester Av LANC LA1 3 F6
Colchester Rd BPOOLE FY3 5 F4
STHP PR8 327 H1
Coldale Ct
BPOOLS (off Harrowside) FY4 204 B5
Cold Bath St PRES PR1 6 C2
Coldstream Pl BBNW BB2 268 B1
Coldweather Av NLSN BB9 198 D6
Cold Well La MTHPE LA7 16 A2
Colebatch FUL/RIB PR2 213 F6
Cole Crs ORM L39 360 A3
Coleman St NLSN BB9 198 D3
Colenso Rd BBN BB1 8 B2
FUL/RIB PR2 238 E1
Coleridge Av CLV/TH FY5 123 F8
WGNW/BIL/O WN5 365 J5
Coleridge Cl COL BB8 171 H5
Coleridge Dr ACC BB5 271 K1
Coleridge Pl GTH/LHO BB6 221 F7
Coleridge Rd BPOOL FY1 5 D1
WGNW/BIL/O WN5 371 F2
Coleridge St BBNW BB2 8 A6
Colesberg Ct CARN LA5 15 G1
Coles Dr CARN LA5 15 G2
Coleshill Av BRFD/BLYE BB10 11 F4
Colesville Av CLV/TH FY5 149 H2
Colinmander Gdns ORM L39 348 A8
Colin St BLY BB11 10 A4
BWCK/EAR BB18 119 F8
College Av CLV/TH FY5 148 C2
FMBY L37 343 J7
College Cl FMBY L37 343 H7
GAR/LONG PR3 188 A6
PDHM/BLYW BB12 223 K5
STHP PR8 301 G8
College Ct PRES PR1 239 G1
College Ga CLV/TH FY5 122 C6
College Pth FMBY L37 343 H6
College Rd SKEL WN8 364 D2
College St ACC BB5 248 A5
TOD OL14 277 H2
Colliers Row Rd BOL BL1 340 B6
Colliers St ACC BB5 247 J6
Collier St ACC * BB5 271 K1
Collinge Fold La RAW/HAS BB4 273 G7
Collinge St PDHM/BLYW BB12 223 J4
Collingham Pk LANC LA1 67 F2
Colling St RAMS * BL0 319 H6
Collingwood ACC BB5 247 J1
Collingwood Av BPOOLE FY3 5 E1
LSTA FY8 230 E2
Collingwood Pl BPOOLE FY3 5 E1
Collingwood Rd CHLY/EC PR7 310 E4
Collingwood St COL BB8 171 F7
Collins Av BISP FY2 148 E8
Collins Dr ACC BB5 271 K1
Collin's Hill La GAR/LONG PR3 134 A8
Collinson St PRES PR1 240 A2
Collins Rd LEY/BBR PR5 263 J2
Collins Rd North LEY/BBR PR5 263 J1
Collisdene Rd WGNW/BIL/O WN5 365 F5
Collison Av CHLY/EC PR7 311 F3
Collyhurst Av BPOOLS FY4 204 E5
Colman Ct PRES PR1 6 B4
Colnbrook WGNNW/ST * WN6 353 K2
Colne & Broughton Rd
SKP/WHF BD23 120 D4
Colne La COL BB8 171 J7
Colne Rd BRFD/BLYE BB10 11 E1
BRFD/BLYE BB10 197 K8
BWCK/EAR BB18 144 E2
BWCK/EAR BB18 145 K7
COL BB8 200 A1
HWTH BD22 174 C1
NLSN BB9 170 C7
NLSN BB9 197 K6
SKP/WHF BD23 120 A6
Colt House Cl LEY/BBR PR5 285 J4
Colthurst Dr CLI BB7 166 A1
Coltsfoot Dr CHLYE PR6 311 H1
Coltsfoot Wk HEY LA3 53 H1
Columbia Wy BBNW BB2 244 D3

Columbine Cl CHLY/EC * PR7 ....286 E8
   WHIT OL12 ....323 G8
Colville Av BPOOLS FY4 ....204 C6
Colville Rd DWN BB3 ....268 B7
Colville St BRFD/BLYE BB10 ....11 D1
Colwyn Av BPOOLS FY4 ....5 E6
   MCMB LA4 ....41 K5
Colwyn Pl FUL/RIB PR2 ....212 C8
Colyton Cl CHLYE PR6 ....311 J3
Colyton Rd CHLYE PR6 ....311 J3
Colyton Rd East CHLYE PR6 ....311 J3
Combermere Gv HEY LA3 ....52 C6
Combermere Rd HEY LA3 ....52 C5
Comer Gdns MGHL L31 ....358 E8
Comet Rd LEY/BBR PR5 ....284 E1
Comet St BCUP OL13 ....275 J4
Commerce St BCUP OL13 ....298 D1
   RAW/HAS BB4 ....272 B7
Commercial Rd CHLY/EC PR7 ....311 G2
   GTH/LHO BB6 ....221 G6
   NLSN BB9 ....198 C3
Commercial St ACC BB5 ....247 H8
   ACC BB5 ....247 J5
   BBN BB1 ....247 F1
   BCUP OL13 ....298 B3
   BPOOLS FY4 ....4 B6
   BWCK/EAR BB18 ....145 F1
   RAW/HAS BB4 ....250 C8
Common Bank La CHLY/EC PR7 ....310 C4
Common Edge Rd BPOOLS FY4 ....204 E4
Common End CHLY/EC PR7 ....336 E7
Common Garden St LANC LA1 ....3 D3
Common La CHTN/BK PR9 ....303 K1
Commonside LSTA FY8 ....231 K7
Commons La BBNW BB2 ....217 C5
The Common CHLY/EC PR7 ....336 E6
   SKEL WN8 ....332 E8
Commonwealth Cl LSTA FY8 ....231 J3
Como Av BLY BB11 ....224 E7
Company St SBN * BB1 ....247 J2
Compass Cottages
   CHLYE (off Briers Brow) PR6 ....288 E8
Compley Av PLF/KEOS FY6 ....177 J1
Compley Gn PLF/KEOS FY6 ....177 J1
Compston Av RAW/HAS BB4 ....273 H2
Compton Cl PLF/KEOS FY6 ....149 J6
Compton Gn FUL/RIB PR2 ....212 E4
Compton Rd STHP PR8 ....301 H1
Comrie Crs BLY BB11 ....10 A6
Conder Av CLV/TH FY5 ....149 F1
Conder Brow CARN LA5 ....34 A1
Conder Green Rd HGHB LA2 ....67 F8
Conder Pl LANC * LA1 ....2 C1
Conder Rd FUL/RIB PR2 ....238 A2
Condor Gv BPOOLS FY1 ....5 D4
   LSTA FY8 ....230 D3
Conduit St NLSN BB9 ....198 B2
Coneygarth La KKBYL LA6 ....21 F7
   KKBYL LA6 ....30 A3
Congleton Cl BPOOLS FY4 ....205 H2
Congress St CHLY/EC PR7 ....311 G2
Conifer Cl NWD/KWIPK L33 ....366 C6
Conifer Ct FMBY L37 ....355 K1
The Conifers GAR/LONG PR3 ....184 D3
   KIRK/FR/WA PR4 ....209 F6
   MGHL L31 ....358 E8
   PLF/KEOS FY6 ....150 D1
Conisber Cl EDGW/EG BL7 ....341 J3
Coniston BOL * BL1 ....341 K8
Coniston Av ACC BB5 ....247 K7
   BWCK/EAR BB18 ....118 E8
   CHLY/EC PR7 ....310 B2
   CHLYE PR6 ....337 H3
   CLV/TH FY5 ....149 H1
   FTWD FY7 ....96 E7
   FUL/RIB PR2 ....239 F1
   LSTA FY8 ....231 F1
   PDHM/BLYW BB12 ....223 J1
   PLF/KEOS FY6 ....98 A5
   PLF/KEOS FY6 ....149 H1
   PLF/KEOS FY6 ....150 E1
   WGNW/BIL/O WN5 ....365 H3
Coniston Dr GAR/LONG PR3 ....188 A6
   NWD/KWIPK L33 ....366 B7
   RAMS BL0 ....319 J4
Coniston Dr DWN BB3 ....292 A1
   LEY/BBR PR5 ....263 H1
Coniston Gv COL BB8 ....171 K5
Coniston Rd BBN BB1 ....9 E2
   BPOOLS FY4 ....204 C3
   CARN LA5 ....33 G7
   CARN LA5 ....34 A3
   CHLY/EC PR7 ....311 F5
   FMBY L37 ....355 H1
   FUL/RIB PR2 ....214 A7
   HOR/BR BL6 ....337 K8
   LANC LA1 ....3 E1

MCMB LA4 ....41 J6
Coniston Crs PDHM/BLYW BB12 ....224 E5
Coniston Wy BBN BB1 ....246 D2
   BCUP OL13 ....275 K7
   LEY/BBR PR5 ....307 H1
   RNFD/HAY WA11 ....369 F1
Connaught Rd HEY LA3 ....52 B6
   LANC LA1 ....3 F6
   PRES PR1 ....6 C5
Conningsby Cl EDGW/EG BL7 ....341 K3
Consett Av CLV/TH FY5 ....122 C6
Constable Av BLY BB11 ....10 C6
   LEY/BBR PR5 ....262 D4
Constable Lee Crs RAW/HAS BB4 .....273 H7
Convent Cl LEY/BBR PR5 ....263 C2
   LEY/BBR PR5 ....286 A1
   ORM L39 ....360 B1
Convent Crs BPOOLE FY3 ....177 G3
Conway Av BBN BB1 ....8 C2
   BPOOLE FY3 ....177 H4
   CLI BB7 ....165 G4
   CLV/TH FY5 ....148 D1
   LEY/BBR PR5 ....262 C2
   LEY/BBR PR5 ....286 A3
Conway Cl CHLY/EC PR7 ....310 C2
   GAR/LONG PR3 ....155 K2
   NWD/KWIPK L33 ....366 B6
   RAMS BL0 ....319 H5
   RAW/HAS BB4 ....295 H2
Conway Ct LEY/BBR PR5 ....264 C1
Conway Crs BWCK/EAR BB18 ....145 G1
   WGNW/BIL/O WN5 ....371 G5
Conway Dr ACC BB5 ....247 F7
   FUL/RIB PR2 ....212 E5
   WGNW/BIL/O WN5 ....371 H6
Conway Gv BRFD/BLYE BB10 ....198 A8
Conway Rd CHLY/EC PR7 ....308 E4
   RAW/HAS BB4 ....273 K8
Conyers Av STHP PR8 ....301 F8
Cooke St HOR/BR BL6 ....339 F7
Cook Gdns BBN BB1 ....9 F5
Cook Green La GAR/LONG PR3 ....189 H4
Cook House Rd COL BB8 ....171 J5
Cookson Cl KIRK/FR/WA PR4 ....235 F5
Cookson Rd CLV/TH FY5 ....123 C8
Cookson St BPOOL FY1 ....4 C2
Coolham La BWCK/EAR BB18 ....146 D2
Coolidge Av LANC LA1 ....2 A4
The Coombes FUL/RIB PR2 ....213 H6
The Cooperage ACC BB5 ....247 H8
Co-operation St BCUP * OL13 ....298 C1
   RAW/HAS BB4 ....273 H4
   RAW/HAS BB4 ....296 D1
   RAW/HAS* BB4 ....297 H1
Co-operative La BWCK/EAR BB18 ......145 F1
   LEY/BBR PR5 ....263 H3
   RAW/HAS BB4 ....295 F4
Cooper Hill Cl LEY/BBR PR5 ....240 B6
Cooper Hill Dr LEY/BBR PR5 ....240 B6
Cooper Rd PRES PR1 ....6 B3
Coopers Cl
   ACC (off Peel St) BB5 ....247 H8
Cooper's La CHLY/EC PR7 ....333 K3
Cooper St BCUP OL13 ....275 J8
   BLY* BB11 ....11 D4
   HOR/BR BL6 ....338 D7
   NLSN BB9 ....198 D2
Cooper's Wy BPOOL * FY1 ....176 D4
Coop St BOL BL1 ....341 J7
   BPOOL FY1 ....4 B3
Coote La KIRK/FR/WA PR4 ....262 C4
Copeland Pl LSTA FY8 ....232 E7
Cop La FTWD FY7 ....97 C7
   PRES PR1 ....238 D6
Copperas Cl WGNNW/ST WN6 ....353 J4
Copper Beech Cl
   KIRK/FR/WA PR4 ....259 K8
Copper Beeches
   BBNW (off Meins Rd) BB2 ....246 D6
   PRES PR1 ....262 A1
Copperfield Cl BRFD/BLYE BB10 ....226 D5
Copperfield St BBN BB1 ....9 D6
Copperwood Wy CHLY/EC PR7 ....310 D4
Coppice Av ACC BB5 ....248 D4
Coppice Cl CHLYE PR6 ....311 J2
Coppice Ct WGNW/BIL/O WN5 ....371 F1
   NLSN* BB9 ....198 E1
Coppice Dr WGNW/BIL/O WN5 ....371 F1
   WHIT OL12 ....323 G4
Coppice La CHLYE PR6 ....288 C2
Coppice Leys FMBY L37 ....343 J8
The Coppice ACC BB5 ....221 K7
   BBNW BB2 ....244 C4
   FUL/RIB PR2 ....212 C7
   KIRK/FR/WA PR4 ....208 E5
   KIRK/FR/WA PR4 ....260 B5
   MCMB LA4 ....42 A6

RAMS BL0 31
Coppice V RAMS BL0 31
Coppins Gn PLF/KEOS FY6 17
Copp La GAR/LONG PR3 ....15?
   KIRK/FR/WA PR4 ....18€
Coppull Hall La CHLY/EC PR7 ....33€
Coppull Moor La CHLY/EC PR7 ....33?
Coppull Rd CHLY/EC PR7 ....31€
   MGHL L31 35
Copse Rd FTWD FY7 12
The Copse ACC BB5 24
   CHLY/EC PR7 31
   WGNW/BIL/O WN5 ....36€
Copster Dr GAR/LONG PR3 ....18?
Copthorne Av PDHM/BLYW BB12 .....19€
Copthurst La CHLYE PR6 28
Copthurst St PDHM/BLYW * BB12 .....22?
Coptrod Head Cl WHIT OL12 32
Copy La HGHB LA2 4
Copy Nook BBN BB1 ....?
Coral Cl BPOOLS FY4 20
Corbridge Cl BPOOLS FY4 20
   PLF/KEOS FY6 14
Corcas La PLF/KEOS FY6 12
Cork Rd LANC LA1 ....?
Corlass St NLSN BB9 17
Corncroft PRES PR1 ....23?
Cornel Gv BLY BB11 22
Cornelian St BBN BB1 24
Corner Bank La KIRK/FR/WA PR4 .....20€
The Corners CLV/TH FY5 12
Cornfield KIRK/FR/WA PR4 22
Cornfield Gv PDHM/BLYW BB12 ....22?
Cornfield St DWN BB3 29
Cornflower Cl CHLYE PR6 31
   KIRK/FR/WA PR4 ....25€
Cornford Rd BPOOLS FY4 20
Cornholme BRFD/BLYE BB10 ....22€
Corn Mill Yd ACC * BB5 24
Cornthwaite Rd FUL/RIB * PR2 21
   BISP FY2 ....17€
   CLV/TH FY5 ....12?
Cornwall Av BBN BB1 ....24€
   BISP FY2 ....17€
   CLV/TH FY5 ....12?
Cornwall Ms
   CLV/TH (off Cornwall Av) FY5 12
Cornwall Pl ACC * BB5 24
   BPOOLE FY3 ....20€
Cornwall Rd BBN BB1 24
Cornwall Wy STHP PR8 34
Corona Av MGHL L31 35
Coronation Av BBNW BB2 35
   FMBY L37 36
   GAR/LONG PR3 8
   PDHM/BLYW BB12 22
Coronation Crs PRES PR1 ....
Coronation Gv RAW/HAS BB4 29
Coronation Pl NLSN BB9 ....17€
Coronation Rd BRFD/BLYE BB10 ....19€
   CLV/TH FY5 ....14?
   KIRK/FR/WA PR4 20
   LSTA FY8 ....23?
   MGHL L31 35
Coronation St BPOOL FY1 ....
   BWCK/EAR BB18 14
   GTH/LHO BB6 ....22?
Coronation Wk STHP PR8 30
   WGNW/BIL/O WN5 37
Coronation Wy LANC LA1 4
Corporation St ACC BB5 ....24€
   BPOOL FY1 ....
   CHLYE PR6 31
   CLI BB7 16
   COL BB8 17
   PRES PR1 ....
Corranstone Cl HOR/BR BL6 ....33?
Corrib Rd BISP FY2 ....17€
Corringham Rd MCMB LA4 ....4?
Corwen Cl BBN BB1 ....
Cosford St KIRK/FR/WA PR4 ....17?
Cosgate Cl WGNW/BIL/O WN5 36
Cotford Rd BOL BL1 34
Cotswold Av CHLY/EC PR7 ....31€
   WGNW/BIL/O WN5 36
Cotswold Cl CHLY/EC PR7 ....30?
   RAMS BL0 31
Cotswold Dr HOR/BR BL6 ....33?
Cotswold Ms
   BBN (off Roman Rd) BB1 26
Cotswold Rd BISP FY2 17
   CHLY/EC PR7 31
   LSTA FY8 23
Cottage Cl ORM L39 34
Cottage Flds CHLY/EC PR7 31
Cottage La LEY/BBR PR5 26
   ORM L39 34
Cottage Ms ORM L39 34
Cottam Av FUL/RIB PR2 21

am Cl CLI BB7	193 G6
TA FY8	231 F1
am Gn KIRK/FR/WA PR4	212 A5
am Hall La KIRK/FR/WA PR4	212 A6
am La FUL/RIB PR2	212 C8
RK/FR/WA PR4	260 D5
RES PR1	7 E2
on Dr ORM L39	348 B4
on Rw	
.Y (off Manchester Rd) BB11	251 F6
ton St ACC BB5	248 B6
OHM/BLYW BB12	10 A3
OHM/BLYW BB12	223 J4
on Tree La COL BB8	172 A6
dray La CHTN/BK PR9	302 A2
lston Av BISP FY2	148 B8
lston Rd LANC LA1	3 F5
ltate St PDHM/BLYW BB12	224 C5
lthurst St RAMS BLO	319 H5
lton Rd NLSN BB9	197 K4
ltshead Av WGNW/BIL/O WN5	371 G5
nsell Ct CLV/TH FY5	149 H1
ntess Cl KIRK/FR/WA PR4	208 E4
ntess Crs BISP FY2	148 C8
ntess Rd DWN BB3	268 C4
ntess St ACC BB5	247 K5
ntess Wy CHLY/EC PR7	310 E1
ntessway LEY/BBR PR5	263 H2
nty Brook La COL BB8	145 G8
nty Rd KKBY L32	366 C8
RM L39	348 B6
nty St LANC LA1	2 C3
pe Gn LEY/BBR PR5	241 J7
pland St WHIT OL12	323 C3
rage Low La WGNNW/ST WN6	334 B7
urse La BRSC L40	350 E2
KEL WN8	351 G2
rtfield ORM L39	348 B4
rtfield Av BISP FY2	176 D3
rtgreen ORM L39	348 B4
rt Ms	
HTN/BK (off Mill Lane Crs) PR9	302 C2
rt Rd CHTN/BK PR9	301 J3
Court FUL/RIB PR2	212 E4
asin's La BRSC L40	306 A8
vgill St BWCK/EAR BB18	146 B2
w La BLY FY3	10 C3
vley Crs PDHM/BLYW BB12	224 A4
vley Rd BOL BL1	341 K6
POOLS FY4	205 F3
JL/RIB PR2	214 C8
vling Brow CHLYE PR6	311 G4
vling La LEY/BBR PR5	285 F2
vm Park Wy North WHIT OL12	323 H1
vm Park Wy South WHIT OL12	323 H1
vm St WHIT OL12	299 J6
vper Av CLI BB7	165 J2
vpe Rd RAW/HAS BB4	297 G4
vper St BBN BB1	9 D2
LY BB3	224 E6
vslip Wy CHLYE PR6	311 H1
vtoot La BCUP OL13	275 J8
v Well La CHLYE PR6	287 F3
field WGNNW/ST WN6	353 F4
Green EDGW/EG BL7	316 B8
Green Rd EDGW/EG BL7	316 B7
btree Av BCUP OL13	298 E2
RES PR1	238 C8
AW/HAS BB4	297 H1
btree Cl BRSC L40	330 D7

Crabtree La BRSC L40	330 C6
Crab Tree La GAR/LONG PR3	153 C1
Crabtree Orch CLV/TH FY5	123 H8
Crabtree Rd CLV/TH FY5	123 H8
Crabtree St BBN BB1	9 F4
COL BB8	171 G7
NLSN BB9	197 K6
RAW/HAS BB4	274 C7
Cracoe Gill NLSN * BB9	170 A8
Craddock Rd COL BB8	171 J6
Crag Bank Crs CARN LA5	33 J3
Crag Bank La CARN LA5	33 H2
Crag Bank Rd CARN LA5	33 J3
Cragg Bottom Rd HWTH BD22	203 F3
Craggs La HGHB LA2	50 C5
Cragg's Rw PRES PR1	7 D2
Cragg St BPOOL FY1	4 B1
COL BB8	171 G6
Crag La KKBYL LA6	19 J2
Crag Rd CARN LA5	25 F3
LANC LA1	3 F2
Craigflower Ct LEY/BBR PR5	264 B4
Craighall Rd BOL BL1	341 J5
Craiglands Av HEY LA3	52 D1
Craiglands Ct LANC LA1	2 A6
Craig St HEY LA3	40 D8
Crake Av FTWD FY7	122 C1
Crake Bank LANC LA1	2 A1
Cranberry Cl DWN BB3	292 B5
Cranberry La DWN BB3	292 B6
Cranberry Ri RAW/HAS BB4	273 H2
Cranborne Av PRES PR1	240 A4
Cranborne Ter BBNW BB2	8 A3
Cranbourne Dr ACC BB5	248 A3
CHLYE PR6	311 J4
Cranbourne Gv CLV/TH FY5	150 A4
Cranbourne St CHLYE PR6	311 H4
COL BB8	171 J5
LEY/BBR PR5	263 H5
Cranbrook Av ACC BB5	247 G7
BISP FY2	148 D6
Cranbrook St BBNW BB2	268 A1
Cranes La BRSC L40	349 K4
Crane St CHLY/EC PR7	335 H5
Cranfield Vw DWN BB3	292 A5
Crank HI RNFD/HAY WA11	370 A7
Crank Rd RNFD/HAY WA11	370 B4
Crankshaw St RAW/HAS BB4	273 H8
Cranleigh Av BISP FY2	148 C3
Cranmer St BLY BB11	10 B3
Cranshaw Dr BBN BB1	9 F4
Cranwell Av LANC LA1	3 F6
Cranwell Cl BBN BB1	9 D5
Cranwell St KIRK/FR/WA PR4	208 D5
Craven Cl FUL/RIB PR2	213 H4
Cravendale Av NLSN BB9	170 A4
Craven's Av BBNW BB2	268 A4
Cravens Hollow DWN BB3	268 D5
Craven St ACC BB5	248 A6
BLY BB11	11 D4
BWCK/EAR BB18	145 G1
CLI BB7	165 J4
COL BB8	172 A6
NLSN BB9	197 K6
RAW/HAS BB4	296 B1
Crawford Av BISP FY2	148 D6
CHLY/EC PR7	311 F4
CHLY/EC PR7	336 E6
LEY/BBR PR5	285 J3
MGHL L31	358 D8
PRES PR1	240 D7
Crawford Rd SKEL WN8	369 K1
Crawford St NLSN BB9	198 C3
Crawshaw Dr RAW/HAS BB4	273 H5
Crawshaw Gra RAW/HAS BB4	273 H5
Crawshaw La BRFD/BLYE BB10	199 H5
Crawshaw St ACC BB5	248 B5
Crediton Av CHTN/BK PR9	278 D6
Crediton Cl BBNW * BB2	267 K3
Crescent Av FMBY L37	355 J2
Crescent Gn ORM L39	359 K2
Crescent Rd PLF/KEOS FY6	150 A7
STHP PR8	301 F8
Crescent St PRES PR1	240 A2
The Crescent BBNW BB2	267 F2
BPOOLS FY4	204 B4
BRFD/BLYE BB10	197 K7
BRFD/BLYE BB10	226 E6
BWCK/EAR	
(off Dales View Pk) BB18	145 F4
CHLY/EC PR7	311 G1
CHTN/BK PR9	278 E8
CLI BB7	165 H4
CLI BB7	192 E5
COL BB8	171 H5
FTWD FY7	122 E3
FUL/RIB PR2	238 C1

HGHB LA2	42 D2
KIRK/FR/WA PR4	234 A7
KKBYL LA6	17 K1
LEY/BBR PR5	263 F3
LEY/BBR PR5	263 J1
PLF/KEOS FY6	98 D7
PLF/KEOS FY6	149 J7
WHIT (off Hall St) OL12	323 G3
Cressell Pk WGNNW/ST WN6	353 J1
Cressingham Wk LANC LA1	55 H8
Cresswood Av CLV/TH FY5	148 D2
Crestway BPOOLE FY3	5 F1
KIRK/FR/WA PR4	282 A3
Creswell Av FUL/RIB PR2	212 B8
Creswick Av BLY BB11	251 H1
Creswick Cl BLY BB11	10 C6
Crewdson St DWN BB3	291 H1
Crewgarth Rd HEY LA3	53 H1
Cribden End La RAW/HAS BB4	272 C7
Cribden La RAW/HAS BB4	273 F6
Cribden St RAW/HAS BB4	273 G7
Criccieth Cl RAW/HAS * BB4	295 H2
Crichton Pl BPOOLS FY4	204 B6
Cricketers Gn CHLY/EC PR7	308 D4
Cricket Pth FMBY L37	343 K6
STHP PR8	301 F8
Crimbles La HGHB LA2	79 F8
Crimea St BCUP OL13	298 E1
Crime Well La HEY LA3	52 C4
Cringle Wy CLI BB7	166 A1
Cripple Ga WGNNW/ST WN6	353 H1
Cripple Gate La LEY/BBR PR5	242 C7
Critchley Cl KIRK/FR/WA PR4	259 K8
Critchley Wy NWD/KWIPK L33	366 D6
Croasdale LANC LA1	2 A1
Croasdale Av BRFD/BLYE BB10	226 B1
FUL/RIB PR2	214 C6
Croasdale Cl CARN LA5	33 J2
Croasdale Dr CLI BB7	165 K4
CLV/TH FY5	123 F8
SKEL WN8	332 E8
Croasdale Sq BBN BB1	9 D6
Crockleford Av STHP PR8	302 A8
Crocus Cl RAW/HAS BB4	295 F3
Crocus Fld LEY/BBR PR5	285 J4
Croft Av BRSC L40	331 F8
HGHB LA2	42 E3
WGNW/BIL/O WN5	365 F6
Croft Bank PRES PR1	238 E8
Croft Butts La KIRK/FR/WA PR4	235 C5
Croft Cl RAW/HAS BB4	273 H6
Croft Ct	
CLV/TH (off Butts Cl) FY5	123 J7
FTWD (off The Croft) FY7	122 E1
Crofters Fold HEY LA3	52 E1
HGHB LA2	67 H7
Crofters Gn CHLY/EC PR7	286 A8
PRES PR1	239 G1
Crofters Ms BPOOL FY1	176 G1
Croftgate FUL/RIB PR2	213 H6
Croft Head Rd BBN BB1	245 K2
Croft Hey BRSC L40	306 B7
Croft Heys ORM L39	359 K2
Croftlands RAMS BLO	319 G8
WGNW/BIL/O WN5	365 F7
Croft La PDHM/BLYW BB12	196 B5
Croft Meadow LEY/BBR PR5	264 B5
Crofton Av BISP FY2	148 D6
Croft Pk	
LEY/BBR (off Wigan Rd) PR5	286 A2
Croft Rd CHLYE PR6	311 J4
Crofts Cl KIRK/FR/WA PR4	209 G6
Croftson Av ORM L39	348 D4
The Crofts KIRK/FR/WA PR4	260 B2
Croft St ACC * BB5	248 B5
BCUP OL13	275 J8
BLY BB11	11 D4
BWCK/EAR BB18	146 C1
CLI BB7	165 J4
DWN* BB3	291 J2
GTH/LHO BB6	221 G7
MCMB LA4	41 J7
PRES PR1	6 B2
The Croft BBN BB1	8 B2
CHLY/EC PR7	285 K8
CHLY/EC PR7	308 E4
CLV/TH FY5	148 D1
COL BB8	171 J4
FTWD FY7	122 D1
GAR/LONG PR3	129 H1
GAR/LONG PR3	186 B6
HGHB LA2	45 F5
LEY/BBR* PR5	265 C1
LSTA FY8	231 H2
MGHL L31	358 D6
PLF/KEOS* FY6	177 K1

WGNW/BIL/O WN5	365 F7
Croft Wy CLV/TH FY5	149 J3
Crombleholme Rd PRES PR1	240 C2
Cromer Av BRFD/BLYE BB10	226 A2
Cromer Gv BRFD/BLYE BB10	226 A2
Cromer Pl BBN BB1	8 C2
FUL/RIB PR2	212 C7
Cromer Rd BISP FY2	148 E7
LSTA FY8	231 G2
STHP PR8	326 A1
Cromfield ORM L39	360 A1
Cromford Dr WGNW/BIL/O WN5	365 K6
Cromford Wk PRES * PR1	240 C3
Crompton Av BPOOLS FY4	204 E4
Crompton Pl BBNW BB2	244 D6
Crompton St PRES PR1	240 A2
Cromwell Av PRES PR1	238 E8
Cromwell Cl ORM L39	360 A1
Cromwell Ms	
GAR/LONG	
(off Archery Gdns) PR3	129 K2
Cromwell St ACC BB5	248 B5
BBN BB1	9 E5
PDHM/BLYW BB12	10 C2
PRES PR1	7 E1
Cronkshaw St PDHM/BLYW BB12	11 D2
Cronshaw Dr GTH/LHO BB6	220 A2
Crookall Cl FTWD FY7	123 H1
Crook Dale La PLF/KEOS FY6	125 G4
Crooked La PRES PR1	7 E2
Crooked Shore BCUP OL13	275 J8
Crookfield Rd CHLYE PR6	290 C8
Crook Gate La GAR/LONG PR3	152 A2
Crookhalgh Av BRFD/BLYE BB10	226 D5
Crookhey Gdns HGHB LA2	79 K8
Crookhurst Av WGNW/BIL/O WN5	371 K5
Crookings La PRES PR1	238 C5
Crooklands Dr GAR/LONG PR3	129 J3
Crookleigh Pl HEY * LA3	52 D1
Crook St CHLY/EC PR7	311 F6
CHLY/EC PR7	337 F4
PRES PR1	7 F2
Croos St ACC BB5	248 C6
Cropper Gdns KIRK/FR/WA PR4	258 C8
Cropper Rd BPOOLS FY4	205 H4
Cropper's La ORM L39	360 E2
Cropton Rd FMBY L37	343 H8
Crosby Cl DWN BB3	291 K5
Crosby Gv BPOOLE FY3	5 F4
Crosby Pl FUL/RIB PR2	212 C7
Crosby Rd BBNW BB2	268 D2
LSTA FY8	231 F2
STHP PR8	301 F8
Crosier Wk KIRK/FR/WA PR4	212 A6
Crosland Rd North LSTA FY8	231 F2
Crosland Rd South LSTA FY8	231 G3
Crosley Cl ACC BB5	248 B8
Cross Barn Gv DWN BB3	291 K3
Cross Brow Preston Rd	
CHLY/EC PR7	310 A3
Crossdale Sq LANC * LA1	3 E3
Crosse Hall La CHLYE PR6	311 J4
Crosse Hall St CHLYE PR6	311 K4
Crossens Wy CHTN/BK PR9	278 E5
Cross Fld KIRK/FR/WA PR4	260 D2
Crossfield Rd SKEL WN8	363 J3
Crossfield St BBNW BB2	9 D6
Cross Flatts Crs BWCK/EAR BB18	145 J3
Cross Fold CLI BB7	140 B3
Cross Green Cl FMBY L37	356 A1
Cross Green Rd FUL/RIB PR2	213 G5
Cross Hagg St COL * BB8	171 G4
Cross Halls PRES PR1	238 D8
Cross Helliwell St COL * BB8	171 H3
Cross Hill La CLI BB7	143 F2
Crosshill Rd BBNW BB2	244 D6
The Crossing LEY/BBR PR5	265 G1
Crossland Rd BPOOLS FY4	5 E6
Crossland St ACC BB5	248 A6
Cross La BWCK/EAR BB18	145 J3
CLI BB7	138 A6
HGHB LA2	39 K3
KIRK/FR/WA PR4	209 H2
ORM L39	346 D2
PDHM/BLYW BB12	168 D7
TOT/BURYW BL8	319 G6
WGNW/BIL/O WN5	365 F8
Crossley Fold BLY BB11	10 A5
Cross Meanygate	
KIRK/FR/WA PR4	305 G6
Cross Pit La RNFD/HAY WA11	369 F5

Cross Rd HGHB LA2	39 J6
Cross School St COL * BB8	171 H7
Cross Skelton St COL BB8	171 J6
Cross St ACC BB5	247 H7
BPOOL FY1	176 B4
BRFD/BLYE BB10	226 D1
BRFD/BLYE* BB10	227 F5
BWCK/EAR BB18	146 A2
CHLY/EC* PR7	311 G2
CLI* BB7	165 H3
DWN BB3	268 C4
DWN BB3	291 K4
EDGW/EG BL7	341 K4
FTWD* FY7	97 H6
GAR/LONG PR3	187 K5
GTH/LHO BB6	221 H6
LEY/BBR PR5	285 K1
LSTA FY8	230 D3
MCMB LA4	41 J6
NLSN BB9	197 K6
NLSN BB9	198 B3
PDHM/BLYW BB12	196 B6
PRES PR1	7 D3
RAMS BL0	319 J5
RAW/HAS BB4	273 H4
STHP PR8	301 H5
WGNW/BIL/O* WN5	365 K5
Cross St North RAW/HAS BB4	272 C7
Cross St West COL BB8	171 F7
The Cross HTWN L38	356 D8
Cross Wy CLV/TH FY5	122 D7
Crossways CLI BB7	139 H4
Croston Av CHLYE PR6	337 G3
Croston Barn Rd GAR/LONG PR3	129 G3
Croston Dr BRSC L40	306 B5
Croston La CHLY/EC PR7	335 F2
Croston Rd BRSC L40	306 B5
GAR/LONG PR3	129 H3
LEY/BBR PR5	262 B8
Croston's Brow CHTN/BK PR9	278 B8
Croston St BBN * BB1	246 A6
Crowder Av CLV/TH FY5	149 H1
Crowell Wy LEY/BBR PR5	240 C3
Crow Hills Rd PRES PR1	238 C5
Crowland Cl CHTN/BK PR9	302 C5
Crowland St CHTN/BK PR9	302 C5
Crowland Wy FMBY L37	356 B1
Crow La GAR/LONG PR3	152 C4
RAMS BL0	319 J5
SKEL WN8	352 B8
Crowle St PRES PR1	240 B3
Crown Cl FMBY L37	356 A1
Crowndale EDGW/EG BL7	317 H4
Crownest Rd BWCK/EAR BB18	119 F8
Crown Gdns EDGW/EG BL7	317 H5
Crown La FTWD FY7	97 H1
HOR/BR BL6	338 B8
KIRK/FR/WA PR4	211 G1
Crownlee PRES PR1	238 C5
Crown Point Rd BLY BB11	251 G2
Crown St ACC BB5	248 A6
CHLY/EC PR7	311 G3
DWN BB3	291 J3
LEY/BBR PR5	262 E8
PRES PR1	7 D2
Crown Wy COL BB8	171 G7
Crow Orchard Rd	
WGNNW/ST WN6	353 H1
Crow Park La CLI BB7	117 H4
Crowshaw Dr WHIT OL12	323 J8
Crowther St ACC BB5	221 J8
BLY BB11	11 E4
Crowthorn Rd EDGW/EG BL7	317 K2
Crow Tree Av BCUP * OL13	297 K3
Crow Trees Brow CLI BB7	140 D1
Crowtrees Gv NLSN BB9	169 H6
Crow Trees La EDGW/EG BL7	317 G4
Crowtrees Rd CLI BB7	195 F3
Crowtrees Yd HGHB LA2	39 K5
Crow Wood Av PDHM/BLYW BB12	10 A2
Crow Wood Ct	
PDHM/BLYW	
(off Crow Wood Av) BB12	10 B2
Crow Wood Rd RAW/HAS BB4	295 K5
Croxteth Cl MGHL L31	359 G8
Croxteth Dr RNFD/HAY WA11	369 F4
Croyde Cl CHTN/BK PR9	278 C5
Croyde Rd LSTA FY8	231 G6
Croydon Rd BPOOLE FY3	176 E4
Croydon St BBNW BB2	8 A4
Crummock Pl BPOOLS FY4	205 J2
Crummock Rd PRES PR1	240 E2
Crumpax Av GAR/LONG PR3	188 A3
Crundale Rd EDGW/EG BL7	341 K5
Crystal Gv LSTA FY8	230 E3
Crystal Rd BPOOL FY1	4 B6
CLV/TH FY5	123 H6

Cuba St NLSN * BB9	198 ...
Cuckoo Brow BBN BB1	...
Cuckoo La GAR/LONG PR3	12 ...
Cuckstool La PDHM/BLYW BB12	19 ...
Cudworth Rd LSTA FY8	23 ...
Cuerdale La LEY/BBR PR5	26 ...
Cuerdale St BRFD/BLYE BB10	19 ...
Cuerden Av LEY/BBR PR5	28 ...
Cuerden Cl LEY/BBR PR5	26 ...
Cuerden Ri LEY/BBR PR5	26 ...
Cuerden St CHLYE PR6	31 ...
COL BB8	17 ...
Cuerden Wy LEY/BBR PR5	26 ...
Culbeck La CHLY/EC PR7	28 ...
Culham Cl CLV/TH FY5	14 ...
Culshaw St BRFD/BLYE BB10	1 ...
Culshaw Wy BRSC L40	32 ...
Culvert La SKEL WN8	35 ...
Cumberland Av ACC BB5	22 ...
BPOOL FY1	...
CLV/TH FY5	12 ...
LEY/BBR PR5	28 ...
PDHM/BLYW BB12	22 ...
Cumberland Rd STHP PR8	30 ...
Cumberland St BBN BB1	...
NLSN* BB9	19 ...
Cumberland View Rd HEY LA3	4 ...
Cumbria Coastal Wy GOS LA11	1 ...
Cumbrian Av BPOOLE * FY3	17 ...
Cumbrian Wy PDHM/BLYW BB12	22 ...
Cumeragh La GAR/LONG PR3	18 ...
Cumpstey St BBNW * BB2	...
Cunliffe Av RAMS BL0	31 ...
Cunliffe Cl BBN BB1	24 ...
Cunliffe La CLI BB7	19 ...
Cunliffe Rd BBN BB1	24 ...
BPOOL FY1	...
Cunliffe St CHLY/EC PR7	31 ...
PRES* PR1	...
RAMS BL0	31 ...
Cunnery Meadow LEY/BBR PR5	28 ...
Cunningham Av CHLY/EC PR7	31 ...
Cunningham Gv	
PDHM/BLYW BB12	22 ...
Cunscough La MGHL L31	36 ...
Curate St CHLYE PR6	31 ...
GTH/LHO BB6	22 ...
Curlew Cl ACC BB5	24 ...
BBN BB1	24 ...
CLV/TH FY5	12 ...
LEY/BBR PR5	28 ...
Curlew Gdns BLY BB11	22 ...
Curlew Gv HEY LA3	...
Curlew La BRSC L40	33 ...
Curteis St HOR/BR BL6	33 ...
Curtis Dr FTWD FY7	9 ...
Curtis St RAW/HAS BB4	27 ...
Curven Edge RAW/HAS BB4	29 ...
Curve St BCUP OL13	29 ...
Curwen La GAR/LONG PR3	15 ...
Curwen St PRES PR1	24 ...
Curzon Pl BBNW BB2	...
Curzon Rd LSTA FY8	23 ...
PLF/KEOS FY6	15 ...
STHP PR8	30 ...
Curzon St BLY BB11	1 ...
BRFD/BLYE BB10	19 ...
CLI BB7	16 ...
Custom House La FTWD FY7	9 ...
Customs Wy FUL/RIB PR2	...
Cut La BBN BB1	24 ...
BRSC L40	34 ...
Cutler Cl BBNW BB2	...
Cutler Crs BCUP OL13	29 ...
Cutler La BCUP OL13	29 ...
GAR/LONG PR3	16 ...
Cutt Cl LEY/BBR PR5	28 ...
Cutts La PLF/KEOS FY6	15 ...
Cygnet Cl ORM L39	36 ...
Cypress Av CLV/TH FY5	14 ...
Cypress Cl FUL/RIB PR2	21 ...
LEY/BBR PR5	26 ...
Cypress Gv BPOOLE * FY3	17 ...
LEY/BBR PR5	26 ...
Cypress Rdg BBNW BB2	26 ...
Cypress Rd STHP PR8	30 ...
Cyprus Av LSTA FY8	23 ...
Cyprus Rd HEY LA3	5 ...
Cyprus St DWN BB3	29 ...

D

Daffodil Cl RAW/HAS BB4	29 ...
WHIT OL12	32 ...
Daffodil St BOL BL1	34 ...

ger Rd KIRK/FR/WA PR4........210 C2
gers Hall La BPOOLS FY4........204 E3
gers La PLF/KEOS FY6........98 D8
lia Cl WHIT OL12........323 H8
ton Rd SKEL WN8........364 C4
y Farm Rd RNFD/HAY WA11........368 D4
y Bank BCUP * OL13........275 J8
y Bank Cl LEY/BBR PR5........285 F2
y Bank Crs BRFD/BLYE BB10........226 C6
y Bank St TOD OL14........277 C2
y Cft FUL/RIB PR2........237 K3
syfields LEY/BBR * PR4........212 B4
syfield St DWN BB3........268 B6
sy Fold CHLYE PR6........311 J1
sy Hi RAW/HAS BB4........273 H8
sy Hill Dr CHLYE PR6........337 C3
sy Hill Fold CHLY/EC PR7........310 B2
sy La BBN BB1........9 D3
RSC L40........331 H1
RES PR1........214 A8
sy Meadow LEY/BBR PR5........264 A6
sy St BBN BB1........9 E3
OL BB8........171 H7
La........43 F8
by Cl CLV/TH FY5........149 F3
RES PR1........214 B8
by Crs BBNW BB2........267 H2
by Lea BBNW BB2........267 G2
e Av CHLY/EC PR7........310 B3
GHB LA2........42 E3
RK/FR/WA PR4........259 K4
EL WN8........351 H1
ecrest WGNW/BIL/O WN5........371 F2
e Dyke Wk PLF/KEOS FY6........149 H8
egarth Cl BPOOLS FY4........205 J2
ehead Rd LEY/BBR PR5........285 K5
e La NWD/KWIPK L33........366 E7
e Ms BPOOL FY1........4 B4
esford RAW/HAS BB4........295 H2
esford Cl CLV/TH FY5........149 J3
eside NWD/KWIPK L33........366 D8
e Dales
WCK/EAR
ff Dales View Pk) BB18........145 F4
TH/LHO BB6........219 J3
e St ACC * BB5........247 J7
CC BB5........248 A5
BNW BB2........8 B5
CUP OL13........275 J8
POOL FY1........4 B4
WCK/EAR BB18........146 B1
OL BB8........171 C6
ANC LA1........3 E4
LSN BB9........197 J6
LSN BB9........198 A3
DHM/BLYW* BB12........10 A3
RES PR1........7 F2
AMS BL0........319 J3
AW/HAS BB4........272 C8
esview Crs HEY LA3........52 D4
esway NLSN BB9........170 A4
e Vw BWCK/EAR BB18........146 A2
HLY/EC PR7........311 G7
WN BB3........268 B5
ewood Av BPOOLS FY4........5 E6
glish Dr BBNW BB2........268 A4
keith Rd NLSN * BB9........198 A3
keith Rd HEY LA3........40 D8
ANC LA1........3 E3
ton Sq LANC LA1........3 D3
ton St BLY BB11........10 A6
STA FY8........230 D3
LSN BB9........198 C4
ne Fold PDHM/BLYW BB12........196 B5
DHM/BLYW* BB12........223 H5
n Head Rd BWCK/EAR BB18........145 F1
n Side COL BB8........171 H4
nside St LANC LA1........3 D3
n Wood La BRSC L40........329 G6
nbers SKEL WN8........364 B5
ncer La CLI BB7........142 E2

Dane Hall La CHLY/EC PR7........309 F1
Danesbury Cl WGNW/BIL/O WN5........371 G7
Danesbury Pl BPOOL FY1........4 C2
Danes Cl KIRK/FR/WA PR4........209 G6
Danes Dr LEY/BBR PR5........263 G2
Daneshouse Rd BRFD/BLYE BB10........11 D1
Dane St PDHM/BLYW BB12........11 D2
Danesway CHLY/EC PR7........337 F2
LEY/BBR PR5........263 G2
PRES PR1........238 C7
Daneswood Av WHIT OL12........323 G4
Daneswood Cl WHIT OL12........323 F3
Daneway STHP PR8........325 H5
Danewerke St PRES * PR1........7 E2
Daniel Fold La GAR/LONG PR3........155 J1
Daniell St BBN BB1........246 E1
Daniels La SKEL WN8........363 J4
Daniel St ACC BB5........221 J8
WHIT OL12........323 H2
Danson Gdns BISP FY2........176 D3
Danvers St BBN BB1........247 F1
Darbishire Rd FTWD FY7........97 F6
Daresbury Av STHP PR8........325 G6
Darfield SKEL WN8........364 B4
Darkinson La KIRK/FR/WA PR4........237 F1
Dark La BRSC L40........308 A8
BRSC L40........349 F5
BWCK/EAR BB18........146 D1
CHLYE PR6........287 J5
HOR/BR BL6........337 H7
RAW/HAS BB4........297 C3
Darkwood Crs CLI BB7........140 D6
Dark Wood La LEY/BBR PR5........242 B5
Darley Av BPOOLS FY4........204 D4
Darley St HOR/BR BL6........338 C2
Darlington St CHLY/EC PR7........335 H2
Darmond Rd NWD/KWIPK L33........366 E8
Darnbrook Rd BWCK/EAR BB18........144 E1
Darnley St BRFD/BLYE BB10........11 H3
Dartford Cl BBN BB1........9 D5
Dartmouth Cl KIRK/FR/WA PR4........208 D3
Dart St FUL/RIB PR2........6 A2
Darwen Cl GAR/LONG PR3........188 B4
Darwen Rd EDGW/EG BL7........341 K3
Darwen St BBNW BB2........8 C5
PDHM/BLYW* BB12........223 J3
PRES* PR1........240 A4
Darwen Vw LEY/BBR PR5........240 C6
Darwin St BRFD/BLYE BB10........225 J1
Daub Hall La LEY/BBR PR5........264 D1
Daub La BRSC L40........332 C3
Dauntesey Av BPOOLS FY3........177 G5
Davenham Rd DWN BB3........268 B8
FMBY L37........343 K7
Davenport Av BISP FY2........148 C6
Davenport Gv NWD/KWIPK L33........366 C7
Daventry Av BISP FY2........148 B7
Davidson St LANC LA1........3 E4
David St BCUP OL13........298 B3
BLY BB11........10 C5
NLSN BB9........170 B7
Davies Rd BBN BB1........246 B5
Davis St GAR/LONG PR3........188 A3
Davy Field Rd DWN BB3........268 D5
Dawber's La CHLY/EC PR7........309 G1
Dawlish Av BPOOLS FY3........177 F5
Dawlish Cl BBNW BB2........267 K3
Dawlish Dr CHTN/BK PR9........278 C6
Dawlish Pl FUL/RIB PR2........212 C8
Dawnay Rd FUL/RIB PR2........214 C8
Dawson Av CHTN/BK PR9........278 E6
PDHM/BLYW BB12........222 E1
Dawson La CHLYE PR6........286 C4
Dawson Pl LEY/BBR PR5........263 K4
Dawson Rd LSTA FY8........231 F2
ORM L39........348 D4
Dawson Sq BLY BB11........11 D2
Dawson Wk PRES* PR1........7 D1
Daybrook SKEL WN8........364 B5
Dayfield SKEL WN8........364 C4
Day St NLSN BB9........198 C4
Dayton Pl BPOOLS FY4........204 C5
Deal Pl LSTA FY8........231 F2
Deal St BBN BB1........9 D2
Dean Brow GAR/LONG PR3........190 B3
Dean Cl RAMS BL0........295 K8
SKEL WN8........364 A4
WGNW/BIL/O WN5........371 F8
Dean Ct FTWD FY7........122 D3
Dean Crs WGNW/BIL/O WN5........365 K3
Deancroft Av HEY LA3........52 E1
Dean Edge Rd HWTH BD22........203 J3
Dean Fold RAW/HAS BB4........274 D3
Dean Head La CHLYE PR6........313 C7
Dean La DWN BB3........290 C7
GTH/LHO BB6........221 F4
LEY/BBR PR5........215 K8

RAW/HAS BB4........274 D3
Dean Meadow CLI BB7........165 H4
Dean Rd RAW/HAS BB4........295 G2
Deans Ct FMBY L37........343 K6
Deansgate BPOOL FY1........4 B2
MCMB LA4........41 H6
Deansgate La FMBY L37........344 B6
Deansgate La North FMBY L37........344 A5
Deansgreave Rd BCUP OL13........299 F8
Deans La BRSC L40........332 A7
SKEL WN8........351 F1
Dean St BLY BB11........10 B3
BPOOLS FY4........204 B3
COL BB8........200 B1
DWN BB3........268 C7
LEY/BBR PR5........263 H2
PDHM/BLYW BB12........223 K2
Dean Wood Av
WGNW/BIL/O WN5........365 G2
Dearden Clough RAMS BL0........320 A1
Dearden Fold RAMS BL0........320 A1
Dearden Nook RAW/HAS BB4........296 C2
Deborah Av FUL/RIB PR2........213 J4
Dee Cl NWD/KWIPK L33........366 D5
Deepdale Av PLF/KEOS FY6........149 H6
Deepdale Cl MTHPE LA7........16 D1
Deepdale Ct NLSN BB9........170 A4
Deepdale Dr BRFD/BLYE BB10........198 A7
Deepdale Gn NLSN BB9........170 A4
Deepdale Houses
PRES (off Peel Hall St) PR1........7 F1
Deepdale La KIRK/FR/WA PR4........210 D8
Deepdale Mill St PRES * PR1........7 F1
Deepdale Pk
PRES (off Blackpool Rd) PR1........214 B8
Deepdale Rd BPOOLS FY4........205 J3
FTWD FY7........97 G8
PRES PR1........7 F1
Deepdale St PRES PR1........7 F2
Deerbolt Cl KKBY L32........366 A8
Deerbolt Crs KKBY L32........366 A8
Deerbolt Wy KKBY L32........366 A8
Deer Chace PDHM/BLYW BB12........197 F3
Deerfold CHLY/EC PR7........311 F1
Deerhurst Rd CLV/TH FY5........148 E4
Dee Rd LANC LA1........2 B1
Deer Pk ACC BB5........248 E3
Deer Park La HGHB LA2........37 G5
Deer Park Rd BRFD/BLYE BB10........226 B8
Deerplay Cl BRFD/BLYE BB10........226 C1
Deerstone Av BRFD/BLYE BB10........11 F3
Deerstone Rd NLSN BB9........199 F3
Deeside BPOOLS FY4........204 D6
Dee St LSTA FY8........230 E5
Deganwy Av BBN BB1........8 C2
Deighton Av LEY/BBR PR5........285 J3
Deighton Rd CHLY/EC PR7........311 F5
De Lacy St CLI BB7........165 H3
FUL/RIB PR2........239 F1
Delamere Av HEY LA3........52 C5
Delamere Cl BBNW BB2........267 J1
Delamere Pl CHLYE PR6........311 H3
Delamere Rd BRFD/BLYE BB10........198 D8
SKEL WN8........363 F1
STHP PR8........325 H6
Delamere Wy SKEL WN8........364 C4
Delany Dr KIRK/FR/WA PR4........234 E5
Delaware Crs KKBY L32........366 A8
Delaware Rd BPOOLS FY3........176 E2
Delaware St PRES PR1........240 A2
Delf La ORM L39........346 C6
TOD OL14........254 D8
Delius Cl BBNW BB2........268 D2
Dell Meadow WHIT OL12........323 G6
Dell Rd WHIT OL12........323 F7
The Dell CHLYE PR6........288 A8
DWN BB3........268 A5
FUL/RIB PR2........213 F4
KIRK/FR/WA PR4........207 K8
SKEL WN8........364 D4
WCNNW/ST WN6........353 F4
The Dellway KIRK/FR/WA PR4........237 K8
Delma Rd BRFD/BLYE BB10........226 C6
Delph Ap BBN BB1........246 A7
Delph Av EDGW/EG BL7........316 B8
Delph Brook Wy EDGW/EG BL7........341 H1
Delph Cl BBN BB1........246 A7
Delph Common Rd ORM L39........359 K2
Delph Ct GTH/LHO BB6........221 G6
Delphene Av BISP FY2........148 D5
CLV/TH FY5........148 D5
Delphinium Wy DWN BB3........268 D4
Delph La BBN * BB1........246 A8
CHLY/EC PR7........310 B5
FMBY L37........343 G5
GAR/LONG PR3........130 C3
GAR/LONG PR3........131 K2

ORM L39 ....360 A2
Delph Meadow Gdns
  WGNW/BIL/O WN5 ....370 A1
Delph Mt *GTH/LHO* BB6 ....221 F5
Delph Park Av *ORM* L39 ....359 K2
Delph Rd *GTH/LHO* BB6 ....221 F6
Delphside Cl *WGNW/BIL/O* WN5 ...365 H5
Delphside Rd *WGNW/BIL/O* WN5 ..364 E6
Delph St *DWN* * BB3 ....268 E8
The Delph *SKEL* WN8 ....332 E8
Delph Wy *CHLYE* PR6 ....287 G4
Delta Cl *FTWD* FY7 ....97 G7
Delta Park Av *KIRK/FR/WA* PR4 ...258 D7
Delta Park Dr *KIRK/FR/WA* PR4 ...258 D7
Delves La *BRFD/BLYE* BB10 ......199 G4
Demming Cl *FUL/RIB* PR2 ....237 J3
Denbigh Av *CHTN/BK* PR9 ....278 D8
  CLV/TH FY5 ....148 E2
Denbigh Cl *LEY/BBR* PR5 ....285 K2
Denbigh Dr *CLI* BB7 ....165 K1
Denby Cl *LEY/BBR* PR5 ....240 A8
Denebank *BISP* FY2 ....148 D6
Dene Bank Rd *ACC* BB5 ....247 J8
The Dene *BBNW* BB2 ....244 C3
  CLI BB7 ....191 G3
Deneway Av *BPOOLE* FY3 ....5 F1
Denford Av *LEY/BBR* PR5 ....285 K3
  LSTA FY8 ....231 G7
Denham La *CHLYE* PR6 ....287 J2
Denham Wy *FTWD* FY7 ....123 F1
Denholme *SKEL* WN8 ....364 B4
Denholme Gv *BISP* FY2 ....148 E6
Denis St *LANC* LA1 ....3 E3
Denmark Rd *CHTN/BK* PR9 ....302 C1
  LSTA FY8 ....231 K6
Denmark St *LANC* LA1 ....2 A4
Dennis St *MCMB* * LA4 ....41 H7
Denny Av *LANC* LA1 ....2 B1
Denny Beck La *HGHB* LA2 ....44 A5
Denshaw *SKEL* WN8 ....364 B4
Denstone Av *BISP* FY2 ....148 D7
Dentdale Cl *BBNW* BB2 ....266 E4
Denton Gv *WGNW/BIL/O* WN5 ....365 K3
Denton St *BWCK/EAR* BB18 ......118 E8
Dent Rw *BLY* BB11 ....10 C4
Dent St *COL* BB8 ....171 F8
Denville Av *CLV/TH* FY5 ....149 F3
Denville Rd *BBNW* BB2 ....8 B4
  PRES PR1 ....240 A2
Depot Rd *BPOOLE* FY3 ....176 E2
  NWD/KWIPK L33 ....367 G7
Derbe Rd *LSTA* FY8 ....231 F6
Derby Cl *DWN* BB3 ....291 K6
Derby Crs *KIRK/FR/WA* PR4 ....182 D3
Derby Dr *RNFD/HAY* WA11 ....369 G6
Derby Hill Crs *ORM* L39 ....348 E6
Derby Hill Rd *ORM* L39 ....348 E6
Derby Pl *CHLYE* PR6 ....337 G3
Derby Rd *BPOOL* FY1 ....176 B4
  CHTN/BK PR9 ....301 J4
  CLV/TH FY5 ....122 C8
  FMBY L37 ....343 J2
  FUL/RIB PR2 ....213 G7
  GAR/LONG PR3 ....129 H4
  GAR/LONG PR3 ....188 A4
  KIRK/FR/WA PR4 ....208 E5
  LANC LA1 ....3 D2
  LSTA FY8 ....231 J7
  PLF/KEOS FY6 ....149 K7
  SKEL WN8 ....362 C3
Derbyshire Av *GAR/LONG* PR3 ....129 H3
Derbyshire Rw *BOL* * BL1 ....341 J8
Derby Sq *PRES* PR1 ....240 A3
Derby St *ACC* BB5 ....248 C5
  BBN BB1 ....9 E3
  BBN BB1 ....247 G2
  BLY BB11 ....10 C4
  CHLYE PR6 ....289 G3
  CLI BB7 ....165 K3
  COL BB8 ....171 H6
  LEY/BBR PR5 ....285 K1
  MCMB LA4 ....41 G6
  NLSN BB9 ....198 C3
  ORM L39 ....348 D6
  PRES PR1 ....7 E2
  RAMS BL0 ....319 K5
Derby St West *ORM* L39 ....348 C6
Derek Rd *CHLYE* PR6 ....287 G2
Derham St *BBNW* BB2 ....8 C6
Derry Rd *FUL/RIB* PR2 ....214 C8
Dertern La *CARN* LA5 ....33 G4
Derwent Av *BRFD/BLYE* BB10 ....225 J1
  CHTN/BK PR9 ....302 B2
  FMBY L37 ....355 H1
  FTWD FY7 ....122 D1
  MCMB LA4 ....41 J6
  PDHM/BLYW BB12 ....223 J1

Derwent Cl *BBN* BB1 ....246 D2
  COL BB8 ....172 A5
  KIRK/FR/WA PR4 ....234 E5
  NWD/KWIPK L33 ....366 B7
  PLF/KEOS FY6 ....98 B5
Derwent Crs *CLI* BB7 ....165 C4
Derwent Dr *GAR/LONG* PR3 ....187 K6
  KIRK/FR/WA PR4 ....234 E5
Derwent Pl *CLV/TH* FY5 ....148 D3
  PLF/KEOS FY6 ....177 K2
Derwent Rd *CHLY/EC* PR7 ....311 F6
  LANC LA1 ....3 F2
  LSTA FY8 ....231 G1
  WGNW/BIL/O WN5 ....365 H3
Derwent St *DWN* * BB3 ....291 H1
Derwentwater Pl *PRES* * PR1 ....239 H1
Deva Cl *NWD/KWIPK* L33 ....366 C4
Dever Av *LEY/BBR* PR5 ....285 F2
De Vitre St *LANC* LA1 ....3 E3
Devona Av *BPOOLS* FY4 ....205 H2
Devon Av *ACC* BB5 ....247 F6
  FTWD FY7 ....96 E8
Devon Cl *LEY/BBR* PR5 ....240 B8
Devon Crs *RAW/HAS* BB4 ....295 H3
Devon Farm Wy *FMBY* L37 ....344 B8
Devon Gv *PDHM/BLYW* BB12 .....224 C4
Devon Pl *ACC* * BB5 ....247 J6
  LANC LA1 ....55 G7
Devonport Cl *LEY/BBR* PR5 ....240 C8
Devonport Rd *BBNW* * BB2 ....8 A4
Devonport Wy *CHLYE* PR6 ....311 J3
Devon Rd *BBN* BB1 ....246 B6
Devonshire Av *CLV/TH* FY5 ....149 H2
Devonshire Cl *NWD/KWIPK* L33 ..366 C7
Devonshire Ct
  CHLY/EC
  (off Devonshire Rd) PR7 ....311 G3
  GAR/LONG PR3 ....129 H3
Devonshire Dr *ACC* BB5 ....221 K8
Devonshire Ms *CLV/TH* FY5 ....149 H2
Devonshire Pl *PRES* PR1 ....240 C2
  BISP FY2 ....148 D8
Devonshire Rd *BBN* BB1 ....246 E2
  BPOOLE FY3 ....176 D4
  BRFD/BLYE BB10 ....11 D2
  CHLY/EC PR7 ....311 C4
  CHTN/BK PR9 ....302 C4
  FUL/RIB * PR2 ....213 J7
  HEY LA3 ....41 F8
  LSTA FY8 ....230 D4
Devonshire Sq *BPOOL* FY1 ....5 D2
  BPOOLE FY3 ....5 D2
Devonshire Square Ms
  BPOOLE (off Whitegate Dr) FY3 ...5 D2
Devonshire St *ACC* BB5 ....248 B4
  LANC LA1 ....3 D6
Devon St *BPOOLS* FY4 ....5 D6
  DWN BB3 ....291 K5
Dewberry Flds *SKEL* WN8 ....364 D4
Dew Forest *GAR/LONG* PR3 ......129 K7
Dewhirst Rd *WHIT* OL12 ....323 K8
Dewhirst Wy *WHIT* OL12 ....323 K7
Dewhurst Av *BPOOLS* FY4 ....204 E3
Dewhurst Cl *DWN* * BB3 ....291 K5
Dewhurst Clough Rd
  EDGW/EG BL7 ....341 H1
Dewhurst Ct *EDGW/EG* BL7 ......316 B8
Dewhurst Rd *GTH/LHO* BB6 ......219 H2
Dewhurst Rw *LEY/BBR* PR5 ......263 G4
Dewhurst St *BBN* BB1 ....9 E5
  COL BB8 ....171 H8
  DWN BB3 ....291 K5
  PRES PR1 ....240 A2
Deycroft Av *NWD/KWIPK* L33 ....366 E7
Diamond Jubilee Rd *BRSC* L40 ...306 C7
Dianne Rd *CLV/TH* FY5 ....149 K1
Dibbs Pocket *KIRK/FR/WA* PR4 ..235 H4
Dib Rd *KIRK/FR/WA* PR4 ....257 K5
Dicconson's La *ORM* L39 ....346 E8
Dicconson Ter *LSTA* FY8 ....232 E3
Dicconson Wy *ORM* * L39 ....348 E7
Dickens Av *BWCK/EAR* BB18 .....118 E8
Dickens Rd *CHLY/EC* PR7 ....335 J3
Dickens St *BBN* BB1 ....9 D6
Dicket's La *SKEL* WN8 ....362 A1
Dickie's La *BPOOLS* FY4 ....205 H4
Dickie's La South *BPOOLS* FY4 ..205 H5
Dickinson Cl *BBNW* BB2 ....8 A6
  FMBY L37 ....355 K1
Dickinson Rd *FMBY* L37 ....355 K1
Dickinson St *BBNW* BB2 ....8 B6
Dick La *CHLYE* PR6 ....288 C4
Dick's La *BRSC* L40 ....349 K7
Dickson Av *PRES* PR1 ....240 B1
Dickson Hey *KIRK/FR/WA* PR4 ...261 C3
Dickson Rd *BPOOL* FY1 ....4 B1

Dickson St *COL* BB8 ....17▮
  PDHM/BLYW BB12 ....22▮
  PRES * PR1 ....
Dickson St West *HOR/BR* BL6 ...33▮
Didsbury St *BBN* BB1 ....24▮
Digham Av *BISP* FY2 ....14▮
Digmoor Dr *SKEL* WN8 ....36▮
Digmoor Rd *SKEL* WN8 ....36▮
Dill Hall La *ACC* BB5 ....24▮
Dilworth Ct
  GAR/LONG (off Dilworth La) PR3 ...18▮
Dilworth La *GAR/LONG* PR3 ......18▮
Dimple Pk *EDGW/EG* BL7 ....31▮
Dimples La *GAR/LONG* PR3 ....12▮
Dinckley Gv *BPOOL* FY1 ....
Dinckley Sq *BBNW* BB2 ....24▮
Dinely St *ACC* BB5 ....24▮
Dingle Av *BPOOLE* FY3 ....17▮
  SKEL WN8 ....36▮
Dingle Cl *ORM* L39 ....36▮
Dingle Rd *SKEL* WN8 ....36▮
The Dingle *CHLYE* PR6 ....28▮
  FUL/RIB PR2 ....21▮
Dinmore Av *BPOOLE* FY3 ....17▮
Dinmore Pl *BPOOLE* FY3 ....17▮
Dinorwic Rd *STHP* PR8 ....30▮
Dirty Leech *WHIT* OL12 ....32▮
Disraeli St *BRFD/BLYE* BB10 .....22▮
Ditchfield *FMBY* L37 ....35▮
Division La *BPOOLS* FY4 ....20▮
Dixey St *HOR/BR* BL6 ....33▮
Dixon Av *WGNNW/ST* WN6 ....35▮
Dixon Dr *WGNNW/ST* WN6 ....35▮
Dixon Rd *GAR/LONG* PR3 ....18▮
Dixon's Farm Ms
  KIRK/FR/WA PR4 ....23▮
Dixons La *FUL/RIB* PR2 ....21▮
Dixon St *BBNW* BB2 ....▮
  HOR/BR BL6 ....33▮
  NLSN BB9 ....17▮
Dobbin Cl *RAW/HAS* BB4 ....29▮
Dobbin La *RAW/HAS* BB4 ....29▮
Dob Brow *CHLY/EC* PR7 ....31▮
Dobbs Dr *FMBY* L37 ....34▮
Dob La *KIRK/FR/WA* PR4 ....26▮
Dobs La *HGHB* LA2 ....6▮
Dobson Av *LSTA* FY8 ....23▮
Dobson Cl *WGNNW/ST* WN6 ......35▮
Dobson's La *PLF/KEOS* FY6 ....12▮
Dobson St *DWN* BB3 ....29▮
Dock Av *FTWD* FY7 ....12▮
Docker La *KKBYL* LA6 ....2▮
Dockinsall La *GAR/LONG* PR3 ....12▮
Dockray St *COL* BB8 ....17▮
Dock Rd *LSTA* FY8 ....23▮
Dock St *BBN* BB1 ....▮
  FTWD FY7 ....9▮
Doctor's Hl *HGHB* LA2 ....3▮
Doctor's La *CHLY/EC* PR7 ....30▮
  FMBY L37 ....35▮
  KIRK/FR/WA PR4 ....28▮
Doctors Rw *GAR/LONG* PR3 ....18▮
Dodd Wy *LEY/BBR* PR5 ....26▮
Dodgeons Cl *PLF/KEOS* FY6 ......17▮
Dodgson La *BWCK/EAR* BB18 ....14▮
Dodgson Pl *PRES* PR1 ....24▮
Dodgson Rd *PRES* PR1 ....24▮
Dodney Dr *FUL/RIB* PR2 ....23▮
Dodson Rd *BPOOLE* FY3 ....17▮
Dodworth Av *STHP* PR8 ....30▮
Doeford Br *CLI* BB7 ....13▮
Doeholme Rake *HGHB* LA2 ....8▮
Doe Meadow *SKEL* WN8 ....35▮
Dog Pits La *BCUP* OL13 ....27▮
Dole La *CHLY/EC* PR7 ....31▮
  CHLYE PR6 ....28▮
Doles La *KIRK/FR/WA* PR4 ....28▮
Dolly's La *CHTN/BK* PR9 ....30▮
Dollywood La *MTHPE* LA7 ....1▮
Dombey St *BBN* BB1 ....▮
Domingo Dr *NWD/KWIPK* L33 ....36▮
Dominica Av *DWN* BB3 ....26▮
Dominion Rd *BBNW* BB2 ....▮
Doncaster Rd *BPOOLE* FY3 ....20▮
Donnington Rd *LSTA* FY8 ....23▮
  PLF/KEOS FY6 ....14▮
Donshort Ms *NLSN* * BB9 ....19▮
Don St *LSTA* FY8 ....23▮
Doodstone Av *LEY/BBR* PR5 ......26▮
Doodstone Cl *LEY/BBR* PR5 ......26▮
Doodstone Nook *LEY/BBR* PR5 ..26▮
Dora St *RAMS* BL0 ....31▮
Dorchester Av *ACC* BB5 ....24▮
Dorchester Cl *BBN* BB1 ....▮
  CLV/TH FY5 ....14▮
Dorchester Dr *NWD/KWIPK* L33 ..36▮
Dorchester Gdns *HEY* LA3 ....5▮

HEY LA3 .....53 H1
Durham Dr ACC BB5.....247 K8
  BBN BB1.....219 H5
  RAMS BLO.....319 G8
Durham Gv GAR/LONG PR3.....129 H4
Durham Rd BBN BB1.....219 H4
  BPOOL FY1.....5 D2
  DWN BB3.....291 G1
Durham St ACC BB5.....248 C4
Durley Rd BPOOL FY1.....5 D5
D'urton La FUL/RIB PR2.....213 K2
  GAR/LONG PR3.....213 G2
Dutch Barn Cl CHLY/EC PR7.....311 F1
Dutton Rd BPOOLE FY3.....5 D1
Dutton St ACC BB5.....248 C5
Duty St BOL BL1.....341 J8
Duxbury Cl MGHL L31.....359 G8
  RNFD/HAY WA11.....369 F4
Duxbury Hall Rd CHLY/EC PR7.....311 H7
Duxbury St BWCK/EAR BB18.....146 C1
  DWN BB3.....291 K5
Dye House La LANC * LA1.....3 D3
Dyers La ORM L39.....348 C7
Dyer St KIRK/FR/WA PR4.....208 D6
Dyke Nook CLI BB7.....165 K5
Dykes La CARN LA5.....26 B1
Dymock La PRES * PR1.....240 B2
Dymock Rd North PRES * PR1.....240 B2
Dyneley Av BRFD/BLYE BB10.....226 D7
Dyneley Rd BBN BB1.....246 A4
Dyson St BBNW BB2.....268 A1

E

Eachill Gdns BBN BB1.....247 F3
Eachill Rd BBN BB1.....247 F2
Eager La MGHL L31.....358 D3
Eagle Brow Cl CLV/TH FY5.....123 H6
Eagle Crs RNFD/HAY WA11.....369 F5
The Eagles PLF/KEOS FY6.....150 A6
Eagle St ACC BB5.....248 D6
  ACC BB5.....270 E1
  BBN BB1.....246 A2
  NLSN BB9.....198 D2
Eagley Brook Wy BOL BL1.....341 K8
Eagley Brow EDGW/EG BL7.....341 K8
Eagley Rd BRFD/BLYE BB10.....198 A7
Eagley Wy EDGW/EG BL7.....341 K8
Ealing Gv CHLYE PR6.....287 K7
Eamont Av CHTN/BK PR9.....278 D6
Eamont Pl FTWD FY7.....122 D1
Eanam BBN BB1.....9 D4
Eanam Old Rd BBN BB1.....9 D4
Eanam Whf BBN BB1.....9 D4
Earby Rd BWCK/EAR BB18.....145 J3
Eardley Rd HEY LA3.....52 C3
Earlesdon Av DWN BB3.....291 F1
Earlham St BWCK/EAR BB18.....146 C1
Earl Av RAMS BLO.....319 H5
Earls Av LEY/BBR PR5.....263 K5
Earls Dr DWN BB3.....292 C2
Earl St ACC BB5.....247 K1
  BBN BB1.....8 C2
  BRFD/BLYE BB10.....11 D1
  BWCK/EAR BB18.....145 C1
  COL BB8.....171 H7
  GTH/LHO BB6.....221 F6
  LANC LA1.....3 D2
  NLSN BB9.....198 D2
  PRES * PR1.....7 D2
  RAMS BLO.....319 K5
Earlsway BPOOLE FY3.....177 K6
Earls Wy CHLY/EC PR7.....310 B1
Earlswood Av SKEL WN8.....364 A2
Earnsdale Av DWN BB3.....291 F1
Earnsdale Cl DWN BB3.....291 G1
Earnsdale Rd DWN BB3.....268 D8
Earnshaw Av WHIT OL12.....323 J8
Earnshaw Dr LEY/BBR PR5.....285 F2
Earnshaw Rd BCUP OL13.....275 J8
Earnshaw Rw BCUP OL13.....275 J8
Easby Cl FMBY L37.....356 A1
Easdale Av MCMB LA4.....42 A6
Easedale Cl CARN LA5.....43 F1
  PDHM/BLYW BB12.....224 D3
Easedale Dr STHP PR8.....325 H7
Easedale Wk NWD/KWIPK L33.....366 B6
Easington LANC LA1.....2 A1
Easington Crs BPOOLE FY3.....177 J3
East Av BWCK/EAR BB18.....145 F1
East Bank NLSN BB9.....170 B7
Eastbank Av BPOOLS FY4.....205 G4
East Bank Av RAW/HAS * BB4.....295 H4
East Bank Rd LSTA FY8.....230 E6
Eastbank St STHP PR8.....301 H5

East Beach LSTA FY8.....232 E8
East Boothroyden BPOOL * FY1.....176 B3
Eastbourne Cl FUL/RIB PR2.....212 B6
Eastbourne Rd BPOOLS FY4.....204 B5
  STHP PR8.....301 G8
East Cecil St LSTA FY8.....232 C8
East Cliff PRES PR1.....7 D4
East Cliffe LSTA FY8.....232 E8
East Cliff Rd PRES PR1.....7 D4
Eastcott Cl BBNW BB2.....268 D3
East Ct CLV/TH FY5.....122 C6
East Crs ACC BB5.....248 B3
Eastcroft NWD/KWIPK L33.....366 D6
East Dene SKEL WN8.....351 H1
East End St COL BB8.....171 G7
Eastern Av BRFD/BLYE BB10.....226 A2
Eastfield Dr CLI BB7.....139 K5
  KIRK/FR/WA PR4.....260 B2
Eastgate ACC BB5.....248 C5
  FUL/RIB PR2.....213 F6
  GAR/LONG PR3.....190 A7
  HEY LA3.....54 A1
  WHIT OL12.....323 G4
Eastgrove Av BOL BL1.....341 J5
Eastham Pl BLY BB11.....11 E3
Eastham St BRFD/BLYE BB10.....11 E4
  CLI BB7.....165 J2
  LANC LA1.....3 E4
  PRES PR1.....6 C1
East Holme LSTA FY8.....233 F7
East Lancashire Rd BBN BB1.....219 H8
Eastlands HEY LA3.....52 E4
  LEY/BBR PR5.....284 E4
East Leigh SKEL WN8.....363 K2
East Lodge Pl BRFD/BLYE * BB10.....252 C2
  ORM L39.....359 K2
Eastmoor Dr CLI BB7.....165 K4
East Mt WGNW/BIL/O WN5.....365 H5
Easton Cl FUL/RIB PR2.....214 B5
East Pde BWCK/EAR BB18.....145 F1
  RAW/HAS BB4.....275 H8
East Park Av BBN BB1.....8 B2
  DWN BB3.....291 H3
East Park Dr BPOOLE FY3.....5 F4
East Park Rd BBN BB1.....8 B2
Eastpines Dr CLV/TH FY5.....148 E3
East Rd BOL BL1.....341 J7
  FUL/RIB PR2.....213 J7
  LANC LA1.....3 E3
Eastside BPOOLS FY4.....205 F3
East Sq KIRK/FR/WA PR4.....260 A5
East St BBNW BB2.....266 E3
  BBNW BB2.....8 A6
  CHTN/BK PR9.....301 K4
  HEY LA3.....40 E7
  LEY/BBR PR5.....262 E8
  LEY/BBR PR5.....263 F1
  NLSN BB9.....198 B2
  NLSN BB9.....198 A6
  PDHM/BLYW BB12.....223 J2
  PDHM/BLYW BB12.....223 J7
  PRES PR1.....7 E2
  RAMS BLO.....295 K7
  RAW/HAS BB4.....275 G6
  RAW/HAS BB4.....295 G4
East Ter CHLYE PR6.....286 B7
East Topping St BPOOL FY1.....4 B2
East Vw BCUP OL13.....298 D1
  COL BB8.....200 C1
  KIRK/FR/WA (off Bunker St PR4.....235 G5
  LEY/BBR PR5.....240 A5
  PDHM/BLYW BB12.....222 D1
  PRES PR1.....7 E1
  RAMS BLO.....319 H2
  RAMS BLO.....319 J8
East View Ct LANC LA1.....42 D8
East Wk EDGW/EG BL7.....341 H1
East Wy CHLYE PR6.....311 H3
Eastway FUL/RIB PR2.....213 J3
  GAR/LONG PR3.....212 E3
  KIRK/FR/WA PR4.....234 C5
Eastwood Av BPOOLE FY3.....176 E3
  FTWD FY7.....97 F8
Eastwood Crs RAW/HAS BB4.....296 E1
Eastwood Rd LEY/BBR PR5.....285 H2
  TOD OL14.....255 H8
Eaton Av BPOOL FY1.....4 C6
Eaton Ct LSTA FY8.....231 F5
Eaton Pl KIRK/FR/WA PR4.....208 D5
Eaton Wy PLF/KEOS FY6.....178 A3
Eaves Av BLY BB11.....251 F1
Eavesdale SKEL WN8.....364 A3
Eaves Green La GAR/LONG PR3.....186 D3

Eaves Green Rd CHLY/EC PR7.....31
Eaves La CHLYE PR6.....31
  FUL/RIB PR2.....21
  KIRK/FR/WA PR4.....18
Eaves Rd LSTA FY8.....23
Eaves St BPOOL FY1.....17
Eaveswood Cl LEY/BBR PR5.....26
Ebony St BBN BB1.....
Ebony Wy NWD/KWIPK L33.....36
Ebor St BRFD/BLYE BB10.....22
Ecclesgate Rd BPOOLS FY4.....20
Eccleshill Gdns DWN BB3.....26
Eccleshill St PDHM/BLYW BB12.....22
Eccles Rd FMBY L37.....35
  WGNW/BIL/O WN5.....36
Eccles's La BRSC L40.....33
Eccles St ACC BB5.....24
  BBNW BB2.....26
  PRES* PR1.....24
  RAMS BLO.....31
Eccleston Rd BPOOL FY1.....
Eckersley Rd BOL BL1.....34
Eclipse St BBNW BB2.....26
Ecroyd Rd FUL/RIB * PR2.....23
Ecroyd St LEY/BBR PR5.....28
  NLSN BB9.....19
Edale Av RAW/HAS BB4.....29
Edale Cl LEY/BBR PR5.....28
Edale Ct PRES PR1.....
Eddington Rd LSTA FY8.....23
Eddleston Cl BPOOLE FY3.....17
Edelston Rd BPOOL FY1.....
Eden Av BOL BL1.....34
  CHTN/BK PR9.....27
  FTWD FY7.....12
  LSTA FY8.....23
  MCMB LA4.....4
  RAMS BLO.....31
  RNFD/HAY WA11.....31
Eden Cl NLSN BB9.....17
  NWD/KWIPK L33.....36
Eden Ct RAMS BLO.....31
Edenfield Av PLF/KEOS FY6.....17
Edenfield Cl STHP PR8.....30
Edenfield Rd ROCH OL11.....32
Eden Gdns GAR/LONG PR3.....18
Eden Gv BOL BL1.....34
  CARN LA5.....
Edenhurst Cl FMBY L37.....35
Edenhurst Dr FMBY L37.....35
Eden Mount Wy CARN LA5.....
Eden Pk BBNW BB2.....24
  LANC LA1.....
Edensor Ter DWN BB3.....29
Eden St ACC BB5.....24
  BBN BB1.....
  BOL BL1.....34
  BPOOL* FY1.....
  LEY/BBR PR5.....28
  RAMS BLO.....31
Edgar St West RAMS BLO.....31
Edgecott Cl HEY LA3.....
Edge End GTH/LHO BB6.....22
Edge End Av NLSN BB9.....19
Edge End La GTH/LHO BB6.....22
  NLSN BB9.....19
Edge End Rd GTH/LHO BB6.....22
Edgefield CHLY/EC PR7.....31
Edge Gate La CHLYE PR6.....28
Edge Hall Rd WGNW/BIL/O WN5.....36
Edgehill Cl FUL/RIB PR2.....21
Edgehill Crs LEY/BBR PR5.....28
Edgehill Dr FUL/RIB PR2.....21
Edge La BCUP OL13.....34
  BOL BL1.....34
  BWCK/EAR BB18.....31
  EDGW/EG BL7.....34
  RAW/HAS BB4.....29
Edgeley Ct PDHM/BLYW BB12.....1
Edgeside GTH/LHO BB6.....22
Edgeside La RAW/HAS BB4.....29
Edgeware Rd BBNW BB2.....
Edgeway Pl CLV/TH FY5.....14
Edgeway Rd BPOOLS FY4.....20
Edgewood CI WGNNW/ST WN6.....35
Edgeworth Gv BRFD/BLYE BB10.....1
Edge Yate La RAW/HAS BB4.....27
Edgley Dr ORM L39.....34
Edinburgh Cl LEY/BBR PR5.....28

burgh Dr ACC BB5 ....247 K8
burgh Pl FMBY L37 ....355 J2
Ford Rd CLI BB7 ....139 F7
BB7 ....165 F4
on St DWN BB3 ....291 H2
n St BBN BB1 ....9 E5
VCK/EAR BB18 ....119 F8
SN BB9 ....198 D3
ston St ACC BB5 ....247 K6
ondsen Pl FTWD FY7 ....123 F1
ondson's La SKP/WHF BD23 ......120 E2
onton Dr BBNW BB2 ....244 C3
onton Pl BISP FY2 ....148 E8
und Gennings Ct CLI BB7 ....140 D6
undson St ACC BB5 ....247 J5
NW BB2 ....8 A4
und St ACC BB5 ....248 B6
NW BB2 ....268 A4
*FD/BLYE BB10 ....225 K2
N BB3 ....291 K2
ES PR1 ....7 F2
ard Ct ACC * BB5 ....247 J5
ard Sq PRES PR1 ....7 E1
ard St ACC BB5 ....247 J5
C BB5 ....271 K2
N BB1 ....247 F2
UP OL13 ....275 K8
Y BB11 ....11 D3
POOL FY1 ....4 B2
VCK/EAR BB18 ....146 B1
LYE PR6 ....311 H4
V/TH FY5 ....123 H7
N BB3 ....291 J1
H/LHO BB6 ....221 G6
R/BR BL6 ....338 C8
NC LA1 ....3 E3
Y/BBR PR5 ....240 A6
Y/BBR PR5 ....263 H3
Y/BBR PR5 ....285 J3
TA FY8 ....231 F4
MB LA4 ....41 G6
SN BB9 ....198 D1
ES PR1 ....6 C2
W/HAS BB4 ....272 C5
W/HAS BB4 ....273 H3
HIT OL12 ....323 H1
ard VII Quay
L/RIB (off Navigation Wy) PR2 ....238 D3
ell Av BPOOLS FY4 ....204 D3
instowe Rd LSTA FY8 ....231 J5
n St PRES PR1 ....7 J2
ert St PRES PR1 ....7 E1
rton SKEL WN8 ....363 K3
ton Ct
L/RIB (off Egerton Rd) PR2 ....238 D2
rton Gv CHLY/EC PR7 ....311 F5
rton Ldg EDGW/EG BL7 ....341 J2
rton Rd BPOOL FY1 ....176 B4
GW/EG BL7 ....315 G7
L/RIB PR2 ....238 C2
Y/BBR PR5 ....285 H1
rton V EDGW/EG BL7 ....341 H1
r Cl CLV/TH FY5 ....122 D6
mont Av CLV/TH FY5 ....123 F6
forth La GAR/LONG PR3 ....130 C3
forth Rd MCMB LA4 ....41 H5
t Acre Av CLI * BB7 ....195 F3
t Acre La CARN LA5 ....17 F1
MBY L37 ....344 B5
n Dr PLF/KEOS FY6 ....177 K2
ne Av BPOOLS FY4 ....5 F6
w La FMBY L37 ....343 K8
w St CHLY/EC PR7 ....311 G4
o St PRES PR1 ....239 J1
rberry Cl CLV/TH FY5 ....123 F6
r Cl CHLYE PR6 ....287 G1
L/RIB PR2 ....214 B5
Y/BBR PR5 ....285 H1
RK/FR/WA PR4 ....234 C5
r St NLSN BB9 ....198 D1
rwood Av CLV/TH FY5 ....149 H4
n Gv HEY LA3 ....52 D4
n Rd BBN BB1 ....8 B3
ns Cft STHP PR8 ....325 K6
n St CHLYE PR6 ....311 H4
ES PR1 ....239 G1
vick St BRFD/BLYE BB10 ....226 A2
nor St BBN BB1 ....9 D4
SN BB9 ....198 D3
tricity St ACC BB5 ....248 B4
r Cl BBNW BB2 ....268 D2
a Crs BLY BB11 ....10 A5
n Pl BPOOLE FY3 ....177 G4
n St LANC LA1 ....3 E4
ES PR1 ....239 J1
h St PRES PR1 ....240 B3
abeth Av STHP PR8 ....326 A5

Elizabeth Cl BPOOLE FY3 ....177 K6
Elizabeth Ct PLF/KEOS FY6 ....149 K8
RAMS BL0 ....295 G8
Elizabeth Dr RAW/HAS BB4 ....295 G3
Elizabeth Sq PRES PR1 ....7 E1
Elizabeth St ACC BB5 ....247 K6
BBN BB1 ....9 D4
BLY BB11 ....11 D4
BPOOL FY1 ....4 C1
FTWD FY7 ....97 H6
NLSN BB9 ....198 B3
PDHM/BLYW BB12 ....223 J4
PRES PR1 ....7 D2
RAMS* BL0 ....295 K8
RAW/HAS BB4 ....274 C7
Eliza St BRFD/BLYE BB10 ....11 E4
RAMS BL0 ....319 K5
Elker La CLI BB7 ....192 C5
Elker Ms
   CLI (off Whalley Rd) BB7 ....192 D6
Elkfield Dr BPOOLE FY3 ....177 G2
Elkin Rd MCMB LA4 ....41 K6
Elland Pl BPOOL FY1 ....4 B6
Elland Rd NLSN BB9 ....198 A5
Ellel Hall Gdns HGHB LA2 ....67 F8
Ellen Ct PRES PR1 ....239 H1
Ellenshaw Cl DWN BB3 ....291 K4
Ellen St BOL BL1 ....341 G8
DWN BB3 ....291 J4
LEY/BBR PR5 ....263 H2
NLSN BB9 ....198 B3
PRES PR1 ....6 C1
Ellerbeck Av FUL/RIB PR2 ....214 C6
Ellerbeck Cl BRFD/BLYE BB10 .....226 C1
CLV/TH FY5 ....148 C1
Eller Brook Cl CHLYE PR6 ....337 F2
Ellerbrook Dr BRSC L40 ....331 F8
Ellerbrook Rd DWN BB3 ....291 K2
Ellerbrook Wy ORM L39 ....348 C5
Eller Gill La SKP/WHF BD23 ....121 G3
Ellerslie Rd FUL/RIB PR2 ....238 E1
Ellesmere Av CLV/TH FY5 ....149 K2
COL BB8 ....171 K6
Ellesmere Gv MCMB LA4 ....41 G8
Ellesmere Rd BPOOLS FY4 ....5 E6
DWN BB3 ....268 B8
MCMB LA4 ....41 F7
Elletson St PLF/KEOS FY6 ....149 K7
Elliot St BOL BL1 ....341 G8
Elliott Av DWN BB3 ....291 K5
Elliott Cl PRES PR1 ....239 C1
Elliott St BRFD/BLYE BB10 ....11 F4
PRES PR1 ....6 C1
Elliott Wk PRES PR1 ....6 C1
Ellis Dr MCMB LA4 ....42 A5
Ellisland BPOOLS FY4 ....205 J2
Ellison Fold ACC * BB5 ....221 J8
Ellison Fold Ter DWN BB3 ....292 A2
Ellison St ACC BB5 ....248 B5
BBN BB1 ....291 J1
Ellis Rd WGNNW/BIL/O WN5 ......371 F7
Ellis St BLY BB11 ....10 B4
BWCK/EAR BB18 ....145 F1
LANC LA1 ....43 F7
Ellwood Av HEY LA3 ....53 J1
Ellwood Gv HEY LA3 ....53 J1
Elm Av BPOOLE FY3 ....5 E2
FUL/RIB PR2 ....238 E1
HGHB LA2 ....67 F7
KIRK/FR/WA PR4 ....234 B5
PLF/KEOS FY6 ....149 K8
Elmbank Av CLV/TH FY5 ....148 C4
Elm Cl BBN BB1 ....247 F3
BWCK/EAR BB18 ....144 E2
BWCK/EAR BB18 ....145 J3
RAW/HAS BB4 ....272 C5
Elm Ct
   PLF/KEOS (off Elm Av) FY6 ....149 K8
Elmcroft La HTWN L38 ....356 A8
Elmdale Cl FMBY L37 ....355 H1
Elm Dr FMBY L37 ....355 H2
LEY/BBR PR5 ....263 J2
WGNW/BIL/O WN5 ....371 F6
Elmers Gn SKEL WN8 ....363 K2
Elmer's Green La SKEL WN8 ....351 J7
Elmers Wood Rd SKEL WN8 ....363 K1
Elmfield WGNNW/ST WN6 ....353 K5
Elmfield Dr LEY/BBR PR5 ....264 B5
Elmfield St ACC BB5 ....247 K4
BOL BL1 ....341 K8
Elm Gdns RNFD/HAY WA11 ....369 F5
Elm Gv CHLYE PR6 ....311 J1
DWN BB3 ....268 B8
FUL/RIB PR2 ....240 C1
KIRK/FR/WA PR4 ....209 F4
LEY/BBR PR5 ....263 G8

MCMB LA4 ....42 A4
SKEL* WN8 ....362 E2
Elmhurst Rd LSTA FY8 ....231 H3
Elmpark Ga WHIT OL12 ....323 F8
Elmpark Gv WHIT OL12 ....323 F8
Elmpark V WHIT OL12 ....323 F8
Elmpark Vw WHIT OL12 ....323 F8
Elmpark Wy WHIT OL12 ....323 F8
Elm Pl ORM L39 ....348 C7
Elmridge SKEL WN8 ....363 K3
Elmridge Crs BISP FY2 ....149 F8
Elm Rd BRSC L40 ....330 E8
KKBY L32 ....366 B8
STHP PR8 ....301 H7
Elms Av CLV/TH FY5 ....148 E1
LSTA FY8 ....232 A8
Elmsdale Cl LANC LA1 ....2 C1
Elms Dr KIRK/FR/WA PR4 ....207 K7
MCMB LA4 ....42 A5
Elmsfield Pk ORM L39 ....359 J5
Elmside Cl CLV/TH FY5 ....149 K1
Elmslack La CARN LA5 ....15 H7
Elmslack La CARN LA5 ....15 H7
Elmsley St PRES PR1 ....213 G8
Elms Rd MCMB LA4 ....42 A4
Elmstead SKEL WN8 ....363 K3
The Elms CHLYE PR6 ....287 F6
MCHL L31 ....359 F8
Elm St BBN BB1 ....9 E2
BCUP OL13 ....275 K8
BRFD/BLYE BB10 ....11 D1
COL BB8 ....171 J6
FTWD FY7 ....97 G7
GTH/LHO BB6 ....221 G7
NLSN BB9 ....198 C2
RAMS BL0 ....296 A8
RAMS* BL0 ....319 K5
RAW/HAS BB4 ....273 G8
WHIT OL12 ....323 H1
Elmswood Cl LSTA FY8 ....232 B7
Elmswood CHLY/EC PR7 ....311 F2
GAR/LONG PR3 ....188 A3
SKEL WN8 ....351 J8
Elmwood Av LEY/BBR PR5 ....285 G2
PLF/KEOS FY6 ....98 D7
Elmwood Cl ACC BB5 ....248 D5
Elmwood Ct KIRK/FR/WA PR4 .....207 H1
Elmwood Dr CLV/TH FY5 ....149 H2
PRES PR1 ....238 D7
Elmwood Gdns LANC LA1 ....67 G1
Elmwood St BLY * BB11 ....10 A4
Elnup Av WGNNW/ST WN6 ....353 K5
Elsby Av CLV/TH FY5 ....149 J3
Elsham Cl BOL BL1 ....341 J6
Elsie St RAMS * BL0 ....319 G7
Elsinore Cl FTWD FY7 ....97 F6
Elslack Br SKP/WHF BD23 ....121 F3
Elslack La SKP/WHF BD23 ....121 F3
Elson Rd FMBY L37 ....355 H2
Elston Av BPOOLE * FY3 ....177 G3
Elston Gn FUL/RIB PR2 ....215 J2
Elston La FUL/RIB PR2 ....215 J2
Elswick SKEL WN8 ....363 J3
Elswick Gdns BBNW BB2 ....217 K8
Elswick Ldg BBNW BB2 ....218 A8
Elswick Pl BPOOLS FY4 ....204 E6
LSTA FY8 ....231 H3
Elswick Rd CHTN/BK PR9 ....278 B7
FUL/RIB PR2 ....238 A2
LEY/BBR PR5 ....285 F3
Elswick St DWN BB3 ....291 K2
Elsworth CHLYE PR6 ....287 H1
Elsworth CHLY/EC PR7 ....355 G3
Elsworth Dr BOL BL1 ....341 K7
Elterwater Pl PLF/KEOS FY6 ....98 A6
LANC* LA1 ....3 E2
Elton Rd BBN BB1 ....269 J5
Elton St FUL/RIB PR2 ....6 A1
Elvaston Wy PLF/KEOS FY6 ....149 J6
Elvington Ct WGNNW/BIL/O WN5 ...365 K2
Ely Cl BBN BB1 ....219 H5
DWN BB3 ....292 A2
Ely Ms CHTN/BK PR9 ....302 C1
Embassy Cl BOL BL1 ....341 H6
Embsay Cl BOL BL1 ....341 H6
Emerald Av BBN BB1 ....245 H1
Emerald Cl CLV/TH FY5 ....149 F4
Emerald St BBN BB1 ....245 H2
BOL BL1 ....341 K8
Emerson Av BPOOLS FY4 ....204 D4
Emerson Cl HTWN L38 ....356 A7
Emerson Rd PRES PR1 ....240 B1
Emerson St LANC LA1 ....55 G7
Emesgate La CARN LA5 ....15 H8
Emily St BBN BB1 ....9 E3
BLY BB11 ....11 D5
LEY/BBR PR5 ....262 D3

Emmanuel Rd *CHTN/BK* PR9 ....**302** B1
Emmanuel St *FUL/RIB* PR2 ....**239** F1
Emma St *ACC* BB5 ....**247** K5
Emmaus Rd *HEY* LA3 ....**52** D5
Emmerdale Cl *ACC* BB5 ....**247** H6
Emmett St *HOR/BR* BL6 ....**338** D8
  PRES PR1 ....**7** D1
Emmott Ct *COL* BB8 ....**172** E5
Emmott La *COL* BB8 ....**172** D4
Emnie La *LEY/BBR* PR5 ....**284** E5
Empire Gv *BPOOLE* * FY3 ....**176** D4
Empire St *GTH/LHO* BB6 ....**221** H5
Empress Av *FUL/RIB* PR2 ....**213** G7
Empress Dr *BPOOLE* FY2 ....**176** B2
Empress St *ACC* BB5 ....**247** K5
  COL BB8 ....**171** J6
  *DWN** BB3 ....**268** C4
Empress Wy *CHLY/EC* PR7 ....**310** C1
Endcliffe Rd *MCMB* LA4 ....**41** J6
Endeavour St *FUL/RIB* PR2 ....**238** D4
Enderley Ct *CLV/TH* FY5 ....**149** J2
Ending Rake *WHIT* OL12 ....**323** G7
Endsleigh Gdns *BPOOLS* FY4 ....**204** D5
Endsleigh Gv *LANC* LA1 ....**42** C8
End St *COL* BB8 ....**171** F7
Enfield Cl *ACC* BB5 ....**248** D1
  CHLY/EC PR7 ....**308** E5
Enfield Rd *ACC* BB5 ....**248** D1
  BPOOL FY1 ....**176** C4
Engine La *FMBY* L37 ....**356** D4
England Av *BISP* FY2 ....**148** C7
Engledene *BOL* BL1 ....**341** H5
English Martyrs' Pl *PRES* PR1 ....**239** H1
Ennerdale Av *BBN* BB1 ....**246** A8
  FTWD FY7 ....**122** C2
  MCMB LA4 ....**41** K7
Ennerdale Cl *CLI* BB7 ....**165** G4
  FMBY L37 ....**343** H8
  GAR/LONG PR3 ....**80** C8
  LANC LA1 ....**3** F1
  LEY/BBR PR5 ....**285** J4
  NWD/KWIPK L33 ....**366** B5
  PLF/KEOS FY6 ....**98** B5
Ennerdale Cl *LEY/BBR* PR5 ....**240** C6
  ORM L39 ....**359** K1
Ennerdale Rd *BPOOLS* FY4 ....**205** J2
  BRFD/BLYE BB10 ....**226** C6
  CHLY/EC PR7 ....**310** E5
  CLI BB7 ....**165** G4
  FMBY L37 ....**343** H8
  GAR/LONG PR3 ....**187** K6
Ennismore St *BRFD/BLYE* BB10 ....**226** A2
Enoch Brow *BBNW* BB2 ....**266** D3
Enstone *SKEL* WN8 ....**363** K2
Enterprise Wy *COL* BB8 ....**170** D8
  FTWD FY7 ....**123** G5
Entwisle Av *ACC* BB5 ....**248** D5
Entwistle Hall La *EDGW/EG* BL7 ....**317** F3
Entwistle St *DWN* BB3 ....**291** J3
Ephraim St *PRES* PR1 ....**240** A4
Epping Cl *BISP* FY2 ....**148** E6
Epping Pl *CHLY/EC* PR6 ....**311** K5
Epsom Cl *CHLY/EC* PR6 ....**287** K7
Epsom Cft *CHLY/EC* PR6 ....**337** J4
Epsom Gv *NWD/KWIPK* L33 ....**366** E5
Epsom Rd *CLV/TH* FY5 ....**149** J5
Epsom Wy *ACC* BB5 ....**248** D6
Epworth St *DWN* BB3 ....**291** J3
Equity St *DWN* BB3 ....**291** J3
Erdington Rd *BPOOL* FY1 ....**4** B4
Erith Gv *BISP* FY2 ....**148** C6
Ermine St *BBNW* BB2 ....**268** D3
Ernest St *ACC* BB5 ....**247** J5
  BCUP OL13 ....**299** J3
  TOD OL14 ....**277** H2
Ernlouen Cl *BBNW* BB2 ....**267** H3
Erskine St *CHLY/EC* PR6 ....**311** J2
Escar St *BLY* BB11 ....**10** C4
Escott Gdns *BRFD/BLYE* * BB10 ....**11** D1
Esher Pond *FUL/RIB* PR2 ....**212** E5
Eshton Ter *CLI* BB7 ....**165** H4
Esk Av *FTWD* FY7 ....**122** D2
  RAMS BL0 ....**295** K6
Eskbank *SKEL* WN8 ....**363** J5
Eskbrook *SKEL* WN8 ....**363** J2
Eskdale *SKEL* WN8 ....**363** H3
Eskdale Av *FTWD* FY7 ....**122** D2
  ORM L39 ....**360** A1
Eskdale Cl *BPOOLS* FY4 ....**5** F6
  BRFD/BLYE BB10 ....**197** K7
  FMBY L37 ....**355** H1
  FUL/RIB PR2 ....**213** H1
Eskdale Crs *BBNW* BB2 ....**267** F3
Eskdale Dr *FMBY* L37 ....**355** H1
  KIRK/FR/WA PR4 ....**208** E4
Eskdale Gv *PLF/KEOS* FY6 ....**98** B5

Eskdale Pl *MCMB* LA4 ....**41** K7
Eskdale Rd *GAR/LONG* PR3 ....**187** K5
  LEY/BBR PR5 ....**285** K4
Eskew La *HGHB* LA2 ....**39** J5
Eskham Cl *KIRK/FR/WA* PR4 ....**208** C5
Eskrigge Cl *LANC* LA1 ....**42** E7
Eskrigge Ct
  LANC (off Beaumont Pl) LA1 ....**43** F7
Eskrigge La *HGHB* LA2 ....**36** E4
Esplanade *PLF/KEOS* FY6 ....**97** K6
  PRES PR1 ....**7** F5
  STHP PR8 ....**301** F4
The Esplanade *BBN* BB1 ....**246** D3
  FTWD FY7 ....**97** H6
Esp La *BWCK/EAR* BB18 ....**144** D2
Essex Av *PDHM/BLYW* BB12 ....**224** D4
Essex Cl *BBNW* BB2 ....**8** B6
Essex Pl *BISP* FY2 ....**177** F1
Essex Rd *BBN* BB1 ....**246** E2
  MCMB LA4 ....**42** B7
  STHP PR8 ....**326** C3
Essex St *ACC* BB5 ....**248** D5
  BWCK/EAR BB18 ....**145** F1
  COL BB8 ....**171** J7
  DWN BB3 ....**292** A2
  NLSN BB9 ....**198** C2
  PRES PR1 ....**7** E1
Essington Av *MCMB* LA4 ....**41** G7
Est Bank Rd *RAMS* BL0 ....**319** G8
Esther St *BBN* BB1 ....**246** A6
Ethel St *BWCK/EAR* BB18 ....**145** C1
  WHIT OL12 ....**323** H1
Ethersall Rd *NLSN* BB9 ....**198** C5
Eton Av *ACC* BB5 ....**248** C4
Eton Cl *PDHM/BLYW* BB12 ....**224** A5
Eton Pk *FUL/RIB* PR2 ....**214** A6
Eton Wy *WGNW/BIL/O* WN5 ....**365** H3
Ettrick Av *FTWD* FY7 ....**96** D3
Ettrick Cl *NWD/KWIPK* L33 ....**366** B5
Europa Wy *LANC* LA1 ....**2** A3
Euston Rd *MCMB* LA4 ....**41** H6
Euston St *PRES* PR1 ....**6** B3
Euxton Hall Gdns *CHLY/EC* PR7 ....**310** A1
Euxton La *CHLY/EC* PR7 ....**286** B7
Evans St *BLY* BB11 ....**10** C5
  FUL/RIB PR2 ....**6** B1
Evanstone Cl *HOR/BR* BL6 ....**338** D8
Evelyn Rd *DWN* BB3 ....**268** B6
Evelyn St *BRFD/BLYE* BB10 ....**225** J2
Evenwood *SKEL* WN8 ....**363** K2
Evenwood Ct
  SKEL (off Evenwood) WN8 ....**363** J2
Everard Cl *BRSC* L40 ....**328** C4
Everard Rd *STHP* PR8 ....**301** K7
Everdon Wd *NWD/KWIPK* L33 ....**366** C8
Everest Cl *LSTA* FY8 ....**231** G2
Everest Dr *BISP* FY2 ....**148** C5
Everest Rd *LSTA* FY8 ....**231** G1
Evergreen Av *LEY/BBR* PR5 ....**285** J4
Evergreen Cl *CHLY/EC* PR7 ....**311** F6
The Evergreens *BBNW* BB2 ....**267** G3
  FMBY L37 ....**343** H8
  KIRK/FR/WA PR4 ....**212** A7
Eversham Av *CHTN/BK* PR9 ....**279** J6
Eversholt Cl *PDHM/BLYW* BB12 ....**197** F4
Eversleigh Av *CLV/TH* FY5 ....**123** F8
Eversleigh St *PRES* PR1 ....**6** C1
Eversley St *SKEL* WN8 ....**363** K2
Everton Rd *BPOOLS* * FY4 ....**204** C5
  STHP PR8 ....**301** K7
Everton St *DWN* * BB3 ....**291** H2
Every St *BLY* BB11 ....**10** B4
  NLSN BB9 ....**198** A4
  *RAMS** BL0 ....**319** K5
Evesham Av *PRES* PR1 ....**262** B1
Evesham Cl *CLV/TH* FY5 ....**148** A1
  KIRK/FR/WA PR4 ....**260** D2
Evesham Rd *BPOOLE* FY3 ....**177** H3
  LSTA FY8 ....**231** G6
Evington *SKEL* WN8 ....**363** K2
Ewell Cl *CHLY/EC* PR6 ....**287** K7
Ewood *BBNW* BB2 ....**268** A5
Ewood La *RAW/HAS* BB4 ....**295** J4
Exchange St *ACC* BB5 ....**247** K6
  BPOOL FY1 ....**4** B1
  COL BB8 ....**171** J7
  DWN BB3 ....**291** J1
  RAMS BL0 ....**295** K8
Exe St *PRES* PR1 ....**239** K1
Exeter Av *LANC* LA1 ....**3** F5
Exeter Dr *CLV/TH* FY5 ....**149** G1
Exeter Pl *FUL/RIB* PR2 ....**238** A1
Exeter St *BBNW* BB2 ....**267** K1
  BPOOLS FY4 ....**4** C6
Exmoor Cl *CHTN/BK* PR9 ....**278** D5
Exmouth St *BLY* BB11 ....**11** D4

Exton St *NLSN* BB9 ....**19□**
Extwistle Rd *BRFD/BLYE* BB10 ....**22□**
Extwistle Sq *BRFD/BLYE* BB10 ....**22□**
Extwistle St *BRFD/BLYE* * BB10 ....**1□**
  NLSN BB9 ....**19□**
Eyes La *LEY/BBR* PR5 ....**28□**

F

Factory Brow *GAR/LONG* PR3 ....**1□**
  HOR/BR BL6 ....**33□**
Factory Hl *HOR/BR* BL6 ....**33□**
Factory La *CHLYE* PR6 ....**28□**
  PDHM/BLYW BB12 ....**2□**
  PRES PR1 ....**2□**
Factory St *RAMS* BL0 ....**31□**
Fairacres *WGNNW/ST* WN6 ....**35□**
Fairbairn Av *PDHM/BLYW* BB12 ....**22□**
Fairbank Gv *MCMB* LA4 ....**□**
Fairbank Wk *RAW/HAS* BB4 ....**27□**
Fairburn *SKEL* WN8 ....**35□**
Fairclough Rd *ACC* BB5 ....**□**
  CLV/TH FY5 ....**1□**
Fairfax Av *BISP* FY2 ....**1□**
Fairfax Cl *GAR/LONG* PR3 ....**1□**
Fairfax Pl *LEY/BBR* PR5 ....**2□**
Fairfax Rd *FUL/RIB* PR2 ....**2□**
Fairfield *GAR/LONG* PR3 ....**1□**
Fairfield Av *BPOOLE* FY3 ....**1□**
  PLF/KEOS FY6 ....**1□**
  RAW/HAS BB4 ....**2□**
Fairfield Cl *CARN* LA5 ....**□**
  CLI BB7 ....**1□**
  ORM L39 ....**3□**
Fairfield Ct *FTWD* FY7 ....**1□**
Fairfield Dr *BRFD/BLYE* BB10 ....**1□**
  CLI BB7 ....**1□**
  *FUL/RIB** PR2 ....**2□**
  ORM L39 ....**3□**
Fairfield Gv *HEY* LA3 ....**□**
Fairfield Rd *BPOOL* FY1 ....**17□**
  FUL/RIB PR2 ....**21□**
  HEY LA3 ....**□**
  LANC LA1 ....**□**
  LEY/BBR PR5 ....**28□**
  NLSN BB9 ....**19□**
  PLF/KEOS FY6 ....**1□**
  STHP PR8 ....**32□**
Fairfields *EDGW/EG* BL7 ....**34□**
Fairfields Dr *DWN* BB3 ....**26□**
Fairfield St *ACC* BB5 ....**24□**
  LEY/BBR PR5 ....**28□**
Fairgarth Dr *KKBYL* LA6 ....**□**
Fairham Av *PRES* * PR1 ....**26□**
Fairhaven *NWD/KWIPK* L33 ....**36□**
  SKEL WN8 ....**35□**
Fairhaven Av *FTWD* FY7 ....**12□**
Fairhaven Cl *CLV/TH* FY5 ....**14□**
Fairhaven La *LSTA* FY8 ....**23□**
Fairhaven Rd *BBNW* BB2 ....**□**
  BOL BL1 ....**34□**
  CHTN/BK PR9 ....**27□**
  LEY/BBR PR5 ....**28□**
  LSTA FY8 ....**23□**
  PRES PR1 ....**□**
Fairhaven Wy *MCMB* LA4 ....**□**
Fairheath Rd *HGHB* LA2 ....**□**
Fair Hl *RAW/HAS* BB4 ....**29□**
Fairholme Rd *BLY* BB11 ....**1□**
Fairholmes Cl *CLV/TH* FY5 ....**12□**
Fairholmes Wy *CLV/TH* FY5 ....**12□**
Fairhope Av *LANC* LA1 ....**□**
  MCMB LA4 ....**□**
Fair Hope Ct *BBNW* BB2 ....**□**
Fairhurst Av *WGNNW/ST* WN6 ....**33□**
Fairhurst's Dr *SKEL* WN8 ....**35□**
Fairhurst St *BPOOL* FY1 ....**□**
Fairlawne Cl *NWD/KWIPK* L33 ....**36□**
Fairlea Av *MCMB* LA4 ....**□**
Fairlie *SKEL* WN8 ....**35□**
Fairmont Dr *PLF/KEOS* FY6 ....**15□**
Fair Oak Cl *FUL/RIB* PR2 ....**21□**
Fairsnape Av *GAR/LONG* PR3 ....**18□**
Fairsnape Dr *GAR/LONG* PR3 ....**12□**
Fairsnape Rd *LSTA* FY8 ....**23□**
Fairstead *SKEL* WN8 ....**35□**
Fairview *RAW/HAS* BB4 ....**27□**
Fair Vw *WGNW/BIL/O* WN5 ....**37□**
Fairview Av *LSTA* FY8 ....**□**
Fair View Av *WGNW/BIL/O* WN5 ....**37□**
Fair View Cl *KIRK/FR/WA* PR4 ....**26□**
Fair View Crs *BCUP* OL13 ....**29□**
Fair View Rd *BLY* BB11 ....**1□**
Fair Wy *PLF/KEOS* FY6 ....**1□**
Fairway *BPOOLE* FY3 ....**1□**

.Y/EC PR7 ....311 G1
.TN/BR PR9 ....301 J1
.ND FY7 ....122 C2
.ES PR1 ....238 D5
.IT OL12 ....323 C4
.ray Gdns PLF/KEOS FY6 ....97 K6
.vay Rd BPOOLS FY4 ....204 E3
.vays FUL/RIB PR2 ....213 J5
.R/BR BL6 ....338 E8
.7A FY9 ....231 G5
.vays Av GAR/LONG PR3 ....184 E8
.vays Ct BBN BB1 ....219 H6
.BY L37 ....343 G6
.vays Dr BLY BB11 ....251 C1
.Fairways SKEL WN8 ....351 K8
.winds Av KIRK/FR/WA PR4 ....258 C7
.on Av DWN BB3 ....268 B8
.on Cl BBN BB1 ....8 B1
.on Dr PLF/KEOS FY6 ....177 H1
.on St PRES PR1 ....239 K1
.rk Av BISP FY2 ....148 C5
.and Av BPOOLS FY4 ....5 F5
.and St PRES PR1 ....6 C3
.arn Crs RAW/HAS BB4 ....296 C2
.arn Rd RAW/HAS BB4 ....296 D1
.Barn Rd RAW/HAS BB4 ....296 D1
.Kirk HGHB LA2 ....36 C1
.wfield NWD/KWIPK L33 ....366 C6
.wfield Cl KIRK/FR/WA PR4 ....208 C3
.wfield Dr PDHM/BLYW BB12 ....10 A1
.wfield Rd LSTA FY8 ....231 J5
.outh Av FTWD FY7 ....122 C3
.W/HAS BB4 ....295 J1
.mouth Rd BPOOL FY1 ....4 C5
.rone Av RAMS BLO 319 J7
.day Av CLI BB7 ....165 J5
.day Dr FUL/RIB PR2 ....214 A4
.day St PDHM/BLYW BB12 ....224 C4
.day Wy BISP FY2 ....149 F6
.F/KEOS FY6 ....149 F7
.lose Dr CARN LA5 ....14 E3
.ft LEY/BBR PR5 ....262 D2
.ham Dr CHTN/BK PR9 ....279 J6
.Fld PRES PR1 ....238 E8
.olme La BCUP OL13 ....298 B3
.ngdon Av BPOOLS FY4 ....204 E6
.ngton Av LEY/BBR PR5 ....285 F4
.ngton Ga LEY/BBR PR5 ....285 K1
.ngton Rd LEY/BBR PR5 ....262 C5
.a PRES PR1 ....261 K1
.eton Cr CARN LA5 ....25 J7
.eton Ct LANC LA1 ....43 F7
.eton Old Rd HGHB LA2 ....46 E1
.ey La SKEL WN8 ....352 C8
.n Av BCUP OL13 ....275 J7
.LYE PR6 ....337 C3
.n Cl CHTN/BK PR9 ....302 C3
.V/TH FY5 ....149 H1
.ndale Rd LANC LA1 ....3 F6
.nend Cl KIRK/FR/WA PR4 ....260 C3
.ner's Rw BBNW BB2 ....267 J4
.n House Cl BBN * BB1 ....246 A7
.LYE PR6 ....287 C5
.n Meadow Rd
.GNW/BIL/O WN5 ....365 C6
.Moor La LANC LA1 ....55 J3
.borough Rd BOL BL1 ....341 J5
.HP PR8 ....326 B3
.ell Pl BPOOLS FY4 ....204 D5
.ham Wy PLF/KEOS FY6 ....149 J6
.lea Dr MCMB LA4 ....42 A6
.Nook CHLYE PR6 ....287 F4
.aworth Gv NWD/KWIPK L33 ....366 C6
.aworth Rd CLV/TH FY5 ....149 J2
.er St NLSN BB9 ....198 A3
.ingdon Cl PRES PR1 ....240 D2
.ingdon La FUL/RIB PR2 ....240 D2
.ingdon La FUL/RIB PR2 ....214 D8
.ingdon Pl FUL/RIB PR2 ....240 D2
.ington Cl BLY BB11 ....224 E8
.ington Ct BLY BB11 ....224 D8
.ington Dr ORM L39 ....348 C5
.ington Pl BLY BB11 ....224 E8
.ington Rd BLY BB11 ....224 D8
.ington St CHLY/EC PR7 ....311 G3
.Farthings CHLY/EC PR7 ....310 D2
.kner Cl STHP PR8 ....325 J1
.kner Gdns STHP PR8 ....325 J5
.kner's La GAR/LONG PR3 ....103 H2
.ordale Rd COL BB8 ....172 A5
.cett SKEL WN8 ....351 H8
.cett Cl BBNW BB2 ....8 B6
.cett Rd MGHL L31 ....359 C4
.es Gv BPOOLS FY4 ....205 G1
.ackerley St FUL/RIB PR2 ....6 A1

Fazakerley St CHLY/EC PR7 ....311 G3
Fearnhead Av HOR/BR BL6 ....338 D6
Fearns Moss BCUP OL13 ....297 J2
Fecit La RAMS BLO 320 D3
Fecitt Brow BBN BB1 ....246 B7
Fecitt Rd BBNW BB2 ....244 D5
Federation St BWCK/EAR BB18 ....118 E8
Feilden Pl BBNW BB2 ....266 E3
Feilden St BBNW BB2 ....8 B1
Felgate Brow BPOOLE FY3 ....5 E2
Felix St BLY BB11 ....11 E2
Fell Brow GAR/LONG PR3 ....188 B5
Fell Cl LEY/BBR PR5 ....263 J3
Fellery St CHLY/EC PR7 ....311 G3
Fellgate HEY LA3 ....54 A1
Fell Rd CLI BB7 ....112 D8
 KKBYL LA6 ....12 C3
 MCMB LA4 ....42 B7
Fellside Vw HEY LA3 ....52 D4
Fellstone V CHLYE PR6 ....289 G2
Fellview CHTN/BK PR9 ....279 F5
Fell Vw BCUP OL13 ....275 K3
 BRFD/BLYE BB10 ....198 B8
 CHLYE PR6 ....311 J5
 CLI BB7 ....139 H4
 FUL/RIB PR2 ....215 G1
 GAR/LONG PR3 ....129 J3
 HGHB LA2 ....45 G6
Fell View Cl GAR/LONG PR3 ....129 J5
Fell Wy PLF/KEOS FY6 ....125 F4
Fellway Cl LEY/BBR PR5 ....263 F5
Felstead SKEL WN8 ....363 H1
Felstead St PRES PR1 ....240 B3
Feltons SKEL WN8 ....363 H1
Fenber Av BPOOLS FY4 ....204 C4
Fengrove KIRK/FR/WA PR4 ....260 B3
Fenham Carr La LANC LA1 ....55 J4
Feniscliffe Dr BBNW BB2 ....267 G1
Fennel Cl BISP FY2 ....149 F7
Fenney Ct SKEL WN8 ....363 J1
Fensway KIRK/FR/WA PR4 ....260 E1
Fenton Av BWCK/EAR BB18 ....119 F8
Fenton Rd BPOOL FY1 ....4 C1
 FUL/RIB PR2 ....214 A7
Fenton St LANC * LA1 ....2 C3
Fenwick St BLY BB11 ....224 E8
Ferguson Gdns WHIT OL12 ....323 K8
Ferguson Rd BPOOL FY1 ....5 E5
Ferguson St BBNW BB2 ....268 A4
Fermor Rd KIRK/FR/WA PR4 ....281 J7
 PRES PR1 ....240 C2
Fern Av ACC BB5 ....247 K8
 LANC LA1 ....3 E6
 NLSN BB9 ....198 C4
 RNFD/HAY WA11 ....368 E4
Fern Bank Av BWCK/EAR BB18 ....118 E8
Ferncliffe Dr HEY LA3 ....52 D1
Fern Cl LEY/BBR PR5 ....262 E3
 SKEL WN8 ....362 E2
Fern Ct FTWD FY7 ....122 C2
Ferndale BBN BB1 ....9 E3
 SKEL WN8 ....363 H1
Ferndale Av BPOOLS FY4 ....204 D4
Ferndale Cl CLV/TH FY5 ....149 J1
 LEY/BBR PR5 ....285 K4
Ferndale St BRFD/BLYE BB10 ....11 F1
Fern Gore Av ACC BB5 ....248 A8
Fern Gv BPOOL FY1 ....4 C4
Fernhill Av BCUP OL13 ....298 C3
Fernhill Cl BCUP OL13 ....298 C3
Fernhill Crs BCUP OL13 ....298 C3
Fernhill Dr BCUP OL13 ....298 B3
Fernhill Gv BCUP OL13 ....298 C2
Fern Hill La WHIT OL12 ....322 E7
Fernhill Pk BCUP OL13 ....298 C3
Fernhills EDGW/EG BL7 ....341 J1
Fernhill Wy BCUP OL13 ....298 C3
Fernhurst Av BPOOLS FY4 ....5 D6
Fernhurst Ga ORM L39 ....359 K1
Fernhurst St BBNW BB2 ....268 A3
Fern Isle Cl WHIT OL12 ....323 F5
Fernlea Av ACC BB5 ....248 A8
 BWCK/EAR BB18 ....145 F1
Fernlea Cl BBNW BB2 ....267 J3
Fernlea Dr ACC BB5 ....221 J7
Fern Lea St RAW/HAS BB4 ....297 F3
Fernleigh LEY/BBR PR5 ....284 C3
Fernleigh Cl BISP FY2 ....148 D6
Fernley Rd STHP PR8 ....301 G6
Fern Meadow CHLYE PR6 ....287 G1
Fern Rd BLY BB11 ....10 A5
The Ferns BCUP OL13 ....298 E2
 FUL/RIB PR2 ....238 E1
 LEY/BBR PR5 ....239 K8
Fernstone Cl HOR/BR BL6 ....338 C8

Fern St BCUP OL13 ....298 D1
 COL BB8 ....171 K5
 RAMS BLO 319 K5
 RAW/HAS BB4 ....297 H2
Fern Ter RAW/HAS * BB4 ....272 B8
Fernwood Av CLV/TH FY5 ....149 H4
Fernwood Cl LSTA FY8 ....232 A7
Fernyhalgh Ct FUL/RIB * PR2 ....214 B5
Fernyhalgh Gdns FUL/RIB PR2 ....214 B5
Fernyhalgh La FUL/RIB PR2 ....214 B3
Fernyhalgh Pl FUL/RIB PR2 ....214 B5
Ferny Knoll Rd RNFD/HAY WA11 ....363 F7
Ferrier Bank KIRK/FR/WA PR4 ....234 B6
Ferry Side La CHTN/BK PR9 ....278 E6
Festival Rd RNFD/HAY WA11 ....369 G6
Fewston Cl BOL BL1 ....341 J6
Fiddler's La CHLYE PR6 ....287 F1
 GAR/LONG PR3 ....133 J7
Fidler La LEY/BBR PR5 ....262 C5
Field Cl BRSC L40 ....331 F8
Fielden St BLY BB11 ....10 A4
 CHLYE PR6 ....311 J3
 LEY/BBR PR5 ....285 F2
Fieldfare Cl CLV/TH FY5 ....123 G6
 PRES PR1 ....239 G8
Fieldhouse Av CLV/TH FY5 ....149 K1
Fielding Crs BBNW BB2 ....267 H2
Fielding La ACC BB5 ....247 J8
 GTH/LHO BB6 ....221 F6
Fielding Pl CHLYE PR6 ....337 H3
Fielding Rd BISP FY2 ....176 D3
The Fieldings MGHL L31 ....358 D7
Fielding St BBN BB1 ....247 G2
Fieldlands STHP PR8 ....327 J1
Field Maple Dr FUL/RIB PR2 ....214 D7
Field Rd HEY LA3 ....52 B6
Fields End GTH/LHO BB6 ....220 A3
Fieldsend HEY LA3 ....52 E4
Fieldside Av CHLY/EC PR7 ....310 A3
Fieldside Cl LEY/BBR PR5 ....240 A8
Fields Rd RAW/HAS BB4 ....295 H2
The Fields CHLY/EC PR7 ....308 D4
Field St BBNW BB2 ....267 J1
 BPOOL FY1 ....4 C5
Fieldview SKEL WN8 ....364 C4
Field Wk ORM L39 ....349 F6
Fieldway LSTA FY8 ....230 E1
Fife Cl ACC BB5 ....248 A7
Fife St ACC BB5 ....248 A7
 NLSN BB9 ....198 A2
Fifth Av BPOOLS FY4 ....204 C4
 BRFD/BLYE BB10 ....197 K8
Fifth St BOL BL1 ....340 D7
Filbert Cl NWD/KWIPK L33 ....366 D5
Filberts Cl FUL/RIB PR2 ....212 E7
The Filberts FUL/RIB PR2 ....212 E8
File St CHLY/EC PR7 ....311 G4
Filey Pl BPOOL FY1 ....4 B1
 FUL/RIB PR2 ....212 C7
Filey Rd LSTA FY8 ....231 G2
Filton Gv HEY LA3 ....42 A8
Finch Av RNFD/HAY WA11 ....369 G6
Finch Cl BBN BB1 ....8 C3
Finches Cottages
 PRES (off Prospect Pl) PR1 ....6 C6
The Finches PLF/KEOS FY6 ....177 H1
Finch La KIRK/FR/WA PR4 ....212 A7
 WGNNW/ST WN6 ....352 D2
Finchley Rd BPOOL FY1 ....176 B3
Finch Mill Av WGNNW/ST WN6 ....353 F4
Finch St DWN * BB3 ....291 H1
Findon SKEL WN8 ....363 H2
Fine Jane's Wy CHTN/BK PR9 ....302 D3
Finnington La BBNW BB2 ....266 B5
Finsbury Av BPOOL FY1 ....5 D5
 LSTA FY8 ....231 H7
Finsbury Pl BBNW BB2 ....268 A4
Finsley Ga BLY BB11 ....11 D4
Finsley St BRFD/BLYE * BB10 ....198 C8
Firbank CHLY/EC PR7 ....310 A1
Firbank Av KIRK/FR/WA PR4 ....282 A4
Firbank Rd LANC LA1 ....3 E2
Firbeck SKEL WN8 ....363 J2
Fir Cl FTWD FY7 ....122 C1
Fircroft WGNNW/ST WN6 ....353 J1
Firfield Cl KIRK/FR/WA PR4 ....208 C6
Fir Gv BPOOL FY1 ....5 E5
 KIRK/FR/WA PR4 ....234 B5
Fir Grove Av BLY BB11 ....11 E5
Firs Cl FMBY L37 ....343 H6
Firs Crs FMBY L37 ....343 H6
Firshill Cl CLV/TH FY5 ....149 H3
Firs La ORM L39 ....347 G8
Firs Link FMBY L37 ....343 H7
First Av ACC BB5 ....248 C4
 BPOOLS FY4 ....204 C4
 CLI BB7 ....139 H4

FUL/RIB PR2.................................238 C1
KIRK/FR/WA PR4........................207 K7
KIRK/FR/WA PR4........................236 C7
PLF/KEOS (off Woodside Pk) FY6 ....124 E2
PLF/KEOS FY6.............................150 A8
Fir St BBN BB1..................................9 D2
BRFD/BLYE BB10..........................11 E4
NLSN BB9....................................198 D3
RAMS BL0....................................319 K4
RAW/HAS BB4.............................272 D8
STHP PR8....................................302 B5
First St BOL BL1.............................340 D7
Firswood CI LSTA FY8....................232 A7
Firswood Rd BRSC L40..................350 C7
Fir Tree Av FUL/RIB PR2................212 D7
Firtree CI CHLY/EC PR7.................311 G8
Fir Tree CI CARN LA5.......................33 F8
KIRK/FR/WA* PR4.......................259 K8
RNFD/HAY WA11.........................370 B4
SKEL WN8...................................363 K4
Fir Tree La ORM L39.....................359 J1
Fir Tree PI CLV/TH FY5.................149 F3
Fir Trees Av FUL/RIB PR2..............214 D7
KIRK/FR/WA PR4........................262 C2
Fir Trees Crs LEY/BBR PR5............262 D2
Firtrees Dr BBNW BB2...................267 G3
Fir Trees Gv PDHM/BLYW BB12......196 A6
Fir Trees La PDHM/BLYW BB12......196 A6
Fir Trees PI FUL/RIB PR2...............214 D7
Fir Trees Rd LEY/BBR PR5.............262 D2
Firwood SKEL WN8........................351 K8
Firwood La LEY/BBR PR5...............242 B6
Fisher Dr CHTN/BK PR9.................302 B4
WGNW/BIL/O WN5.....................365 G5
Fishergate PRES PR1........................7 D3
Fishergate Ct
  PRES (off Fishergate) PR1...............6 C3
Fishergate HI PRES PR1....................6 B4
Fishermans CI FMBY L37...............343 J5
Fisher's La BPOOLS FY4.................205 F6
Fisher St BPOOL FY1........................4 C1
Fish House La GAR/LONG PR3.......134 B3
Fish La BRSC L40..........................305 F8
Fishmoor Dr BBNW BB2.................268 C3
Fish Rake La RAW/HAS BB4...........296 A5
Fish St PRES PR1.............................7 D1
Fishwick La CHLYE PR6..................288 B2
Fishwick Pde PRES PR1.................240 B3
Fishwick Rd PRES PR1...................240 A3
Fishwick Vw PRES PR1...................240 B3
Fitchfield PRES PR1.......................262 C1
Fitzgerald St PRES PR1..................240 A2
Fitzroy Rd BISP FY2.......................148 D8
Fitzroy St PRES PR1.........................6 B3
Five Acres LEY/BBR PR5................262 B7
Five Ashes La HGHB LA2.................67 F4
Flag La CHLYE PR6........................311 K6
  LEY/BBR PR5.............................283 G6
  LEY/BBR PR5.............................285 F7
  PRES PR1...................................262 C2
Flag St BCUP OL13.......................298 C3
Flakefleet Av FTWD FY7................122 E2
Flamstead SKEL WN8....................363 J2
Flare Rd HEY LA3............................52 B5
Flash La BRSC L40........................306 C1
Flat La CARN LA5...........................17 F8
Flatman's La ORM L39...................358 A2
Flax CI RAW/HAS BB4...................295 G3
Flaxfield Rd FMBY L37..................344 A8
Flaxfield Wy KIRK/FR/WA PR4.......208 E6
Flax La BRSC L40..........................349 K1
Flax St RAMS BL0.........................319 C2
Flaxton SKEL WN8.......................363 J2
Fleetgreen LANC LA1......................42 E8
Fleet La HGHB LA2.........................37 F1
Fleet St BPOOL FY1.........................4 C3
  CHLY/EC PR7.............................311 G4
  GAR/LONG PR3..........................188 A4
  HOR/BR BL6...............................339 F8
  LSTA FY8....................................230 D4
  NLSN BB9...................................198 C1
  PRES PR1......................................7 D3
  WGNW/BIL/O WN5.....................365 G5
Fleet Street La GAR/LONG PR3......189 F5
Fleet Wk BLY BB11.........................11 D3
Fleetwood CI BBNW * BB2.............268 C2
  CHTN/BK PR9............................278 B8
Fleetwood Crs CHTN/BK PR9........279 J5
Fleetwood Dr CHTN/BK PR9..........279 J5
Fleetwood Gdns
  NWD/KWIPK L33.........................366 D6
Fleetwood Old Rd
  KIRK/FR/WA PR4........................180 C8
Fleetwood Rd BRFD/BLYE BB10....226 A1
  CHTN/BK PR9.............................301 J2
  CLV/TH FY5................................148 D3
  FTWD FY7..................................122 E1

PDHM/BLYW BB12......................223 K3
PLF/KEOS FY6.............................149 H5
PLF/KEOS FY6.............................151 K8
Fleetwood Rd North CLV/TH FY5...123 G6
Fleetwood Rd South CLV/TH FY5...149 H3
Fleetwood St FUL/RIB PR2................6 B1
  LEY/BBR PR5.............................285 K1
Fleming Sq BBNW * BB2...................8 C5
Flensburg Wy LEY/BBR PR5...........262 B5
Fletcher Av KIRK/FR/WA PR4.........282 A4
Fletcher Rd BBN * BB1..................246 E2
  PRES PR1......................................7 F2
Fletcher's Dr BRSC L40..................330 E7
Fletcher St NLSN BB9....................198 D4
Flett St FUL/RIB PR2........................6 A1
Flimby SKEL WN8.........................363 K2
Flimby CI BBNW BB2.....................268 C3
Flintoff Wy PRES PR1....................213 K8
Flintron Brow HGHB LA2.................70 E7
Flip Rd RAW/HAS BB4...................272 A8
Flordon SKEL WN8.......................363 K2
Florence Av BLY BB11....................224 E7
  BOL BL1....................................341 K7
  KIRK/FR/WA PR4........................234 B6
Florence PI BBN BB1........................9 E3
Florence St ACC BB5......................247 J5
  BBN BB1.......................................9 E3
  BLY BB11....................................224 E6
  BPOOLS FY4...............................205 G5
Flowerfield KIRK/FR/WA PR4.........212 A5
Flower Flds GAR/LONG PR3...........155 K1
Flower Scar Rd TOD OL14..............277 H5
Floyd Rd FUL/RIB * PR2.................214 C8
Floyer St PRES PR1..........................7 F1
Fluke Hall La GAR/LONG PR3...........99 H3
Fold Gdns WHIT OL12....................323 F8
Folds HOR/BR BL6.........................337 J8
Foldside KIRK/FR/WA PR4..............235 G4
Folds St PDHM/BLYW BB12............10 C1
The Fold SKP/WHF BD23................120 B5
Fold Vw EDGW/EG BL7..................341 J2
Folkestone CI CLV/TH FY5.............123 C6
  KIRK/FR/WA PR4........................234 C4
Folkestone Rd LSTA FY8................231 F5
  STHP PR8...................................302 A8
Folly La BWCK/EAR BB18...............144 D5
  LANC LA1.....................................42 D7
Fooden La CLI BB7.........................115 K4
Footeran La CARN LA5....................17 F8
Fordham CI STHP PR8....................302 A8
Ford La CARN LA5...........................15 K6
  GAR/LONG PR3..........................186 D7
Fordoe La WHIT OL12...................322 A7
Fordside Av ACC BB5.....................221 J7
Fordstone Av PLF/KEOS FY6............98 C7
Ford St BRFD/BLYE BB10..............225 K2
  LANC LA1......................................2 B2
  NLSN BB9...................................170 C7
Fordway Av BPOOLE FY3.................5 E1
Foregate FUL/RIB PR2...................213 C2
Foreside NLSN BB9........................170 C6
Forest Bank Rd RAW/HAS BB4.......273 H4
Forest Becks Brow CLI BB7..............92 C8
Forest CI LEY/BBR PR5..................240 A8
Forest Dr LSTA FY8.......................232 A7
  SKEL WN8...................................351 J8
  WGNW/ST WN6..........................353 J1
Forester Dr PDHM/BLYW BB12......197 F3
Forest Ga BPOOLE FY3....................5 D2
  HEY LA3.......................................54 A1
Forest Gv GAR/LONG PR3..............184 D3
Forest Holme CI RAW/HAS BB4......274 D4
Forest La NLSN BB9.......................197 K1
Forest Pk LANC LA1.........................2 A4
Forest Rd BOL BL1.........................341 F8
  STHP PR8...................................301 K5
Forest St BLY BB11..........................11 D3
  NLSN BB9...................................198 B2
  RAW/HAS BB4............................274 D4
Forest Wy FUL/RIB PR2.................213 H6
Forestway LEY/BBR PR5................285 H3
Forfar CI BLY BB11..........................10 A6
Forfar St BLY BB11..........................10 A6
  BOL BL1....................................341 F6
Forge CI BRSC L40.........................349 J7
Forge La GAR/LONG PR3................130 A3
Forge St BCUP OL13.....................298 D1
Forgewood CI HGHB LA2.................44 C5
Forgewood Dr HGHB LA2................44 B5
Formby Av FTWD FY7....................122 D4
Formby Br FMBY L37.....................355 J1
Formby CI BBNW BB2...................268 C3
Formby Crs KIRK/FR/WA PR4........260 A4
Formby Flds FMBY L37..................356 A1
Formby La ORM L39.....................359 G1

Formby PI FUL/RIB PR2...................2
Formby Rd FMBY L37......................3
  LSTA FY8.....................................2
Formby St FMBY L37.......................3
Forrester CI LEY/BBR PR5................2
Forrest St BBN BB1.........................2
Forshaw Av BPOOLE FY3................1
  LSTA FY8.....................................2
Forshaw CI FTWD FY7...................1
Forshaw Rd PRES PR1...................2
Fort Av GAR/LONG PR3..................1
Forton Rd FUL/RIB PR2...................2
Fort St ACC BB5............................2
  ACC* BB5....................................2
  BBN BB1......................................2
  CLI BB7..1
  PDHM/BLYW BB12......................2
Forty Acre La GAR/LONG PR3.........1
Foscote Rd NWD/KWIPK L33.........3
Fossdale Moss LEY/BBR PR5...........2
Fosse CI BBNW BB2.......................2
Foster Cft PRES PR1.......................2
Fosterfield PI CHLYE PR6...............3
Foster Rd BWCK/EAR BB18............1
  FMBY L37....................................3
Fosters CI CHTN/BK PR9................3
Fosters Green Rd SKEL WN8...........2
Foster St ACC BB5.........................2
  CHLYE PR6...................................3
Fothergill St COL BB8.....................1
Fouldrey Av PLF/KEOS FY6.............1
Foulds CI COL BB8.........................1
Foulds Rd COL BB8.........................1
Foul La STHP PR8...........................3
Foundry La HGHB LA2.....................4
Foundry St BBNW BB2....................
  BCUP OL13...................................
  BLY* BB11.....................................
  CHLY/EC* PR7..............................3
  RAW/HAS BB4.............................
Fountains Av BBN BB1.....................
  PDHM/BLYW BB12......................2
Fountains CI CHLY/EC PR7.............3
Fountain Sq NLSN BB9...................1
Fountain St ACC BB5......................2
  BWCK/EAR BB18..........................1
  COL BB8.......................................1
  DWN* BB3....................................2
  NLSN BB9.....................................1
Fountains Wy ACC BB5...................2
  FMBY L37.....................................3
Fouracre BBNW BB2.......................2
Four Acre La GAR/LONG PR3...........1
Fourfields LEY/BBR PR5..................2
Four La HGHB LA2...........................
Four Lane Ends LEY/BBR PR5..........2
Four Lanes End Rd BCUP OL13........2
Four Oaks Rd LEY/BBR PR5............2
Fourth Av BPOOLS FY4...................2
Fourth St BOL BL1..........................3
Fowler Av LEY/BBR PR5..................2
Fowler CI LEY/BBR PR5...................2
Fowler Height CI BBNW BB2...........2
Fowler Hill La GAR/LONG PR3.........1
Fowler La LEY/BBR PR5..................2
Fowler St FUL/RIB PR2....................2
Foxcote CHLY/EC PR7....................3
Foxcroft PDHM/BLYW BB12............1
Foxdale Av BPOOLE FY3.................1
Foxdale CI BCUP OL13...................2
  EDGW/EG BL7.............................3
  STHP PR8....................................3
Foxdale Gv PRES PR1.....................2
Foxdale PI LANC LA1.......................
Foxen Dole La PDHM/BLYW BB12....19
Foxes Ter
  GAR/LONG (off Garstang Rd) PR3....15
Foxfield Av MCMB LA4....................
Foxfield CI ACC BB5.......................2
Foxfield Gv WGNNW/ST WN6.........3
Foxfold SKEL WN8..........................
Foxglove CI KIRK/FR/WA PR4..........3
Foxglove Ct WHIT OL12..................3
Foxglove Dr CHLYE PR6.................2
Fox Gv HEY LA3.............................
Foxhall Rd BPOOL FY1...................
Foxhall Sq BPOOL FY1...................
Foxhill Bank Brow ACC BB5............2
Foxhill CI FMBY L37.......................3
Foxhill Dr RAW/HAS BB4................2
Foxhole Rd CHLY/EC PR7...............3
Foxholes Rd HOR/BR BL6...............3
  MCMB LA4....................................
Foxhouse St BBNW BB2.................2
Fox La LEY/BBR PR5......................2
  LEY/BBR PR5...............................2
Fox Lane Ends KIRK/FR/WA PR4......2

...stones Crs *BBNW* BB2 ....**267** H3
...stones La *BRFD/BLYE* BB10 ....**226** E8
...st *ACC* BB5 ....**248** B5
...* BB7 ....**165** J2
...HM/BLYW* BB12 ....**224** B5
...*ES* PR1 ....**7** D3
...well Cl *RAW/HAS* BB4 ....**295** J1
...vood Cha *ACC* BB5 ....**248** E3
...vood Cl *WGNW/BIL/O* WN5 ....**365** G6
...vood Dr *KIRK/FR/WA* PR4 ......**208** C6
...Foxwood *CHLY/EC* PR7 ....**335** G2
...ey Cl *STHP* PR8 ....**325** J7
...ces Pas *LANC* * LA1 ....**3** D3
...ces St *DWN* BB3 ....**291** H1
...ce St *ACC* BB5 ....**247** J5
...*NW* BB2 ....**8** B5
...cis Av *NLSN* BB9 ....**170** C6
...cis St *ACC* * BB5 ....**221** K8
...*NW* BB2 ....**267** J2
...*OOL* FY1 ....**4** B1
...*FD/BLYE* BB10 ....**225** J2
...*L* BB8 ....**171** F8
...*L/RIB* PR2 ....**6** A1
...klands *KIRK/FR/WA* PR4 ....**260** E3
...klands Dr *FUL/RIB* PR2 ....**214** D6
...klands Fold *KIRK/FR/WA* PR4...**260** B3
...klin Rd *BBNW* BB2 ....**244** D8
...klin St *CLI* BB7 ....**165** H4
...*NW* BB3 ....**291** J2
...*NC* LA1 ....**3** D6
...*HM/BLYW* * BB12 ....**224** E5
...k St *ACC* * BB5 ....**248** A2
...*VCK/EAR* BB18 ....**145** F1
...*ES* PR1 ....**7** D1
...er Av *PRES* PR1 ....**6** C6
...er St *ACC* BB5 ....**248** A7
...*FD/BLYE* BB10 ....**225** A7
...er Gv *BPOOLE* FY4 ....**4** B6
...kleton Dr *NWD/KWIPK* L33 ....**366** E6
...kleton Rd *CHTN/BK* PR9 ....**278** B4
...*RK/FR/WA* PR4 ....**209** F8
...kleton St *BBNW* BB2 ....**8** C5
...*OOL* FY1 ....**4** C3
...*TA* FY8 ....**232** E8
...erick Av *BBN* BB1 ....**9** F4
...erick St *ACC* BB5 ....**247** J7
...*8* **8** C6
...*OOLS* FY4 ....**204** D3
...LYE PR6 ....**311** J4
...*VN* BB3 ....**291** J1
...MS BL0 ....**319** H6
...ora Av *BPOOLE* FY3 ....**205** C1
...holds La *CLI* BB7 ....**138** D5
...holds Rd *WHIT* OL12 ....**299** J5
...La *RAW/HAS* BB4 ....**295** C5
...mantle Av *BPOOLE* FY4 ....**204** A3
...port Village
...*WD* (off Anchorage Rd) FY7 ....**97** H8
...Trade St *BLY* BB11 ....**10** C3
...ch Cl *BBNW* BB2 ....**244** D7
...ch Rd *BBNW* BB2 ....**244** C7
...chwood Av *LSTA* FY8 ....**232** D7
...*ES* PR1 ....**7** F4
...chwood Knoll *PRES* PR1............**7** F4
...chwood St *PRES* PR1 ....**7** E4
...nfield Rd *ACC* BB5 ....**221** J8
...nfield Rd *FMBY* L37 ....**343** J6
...nfields *FUL/RIB* PR2 ....**211** K8
...gate *PRES* PR1 ....**7** D2
...'s Moss Rd *HGHB* LA2 ....**56** D3
...'s Pas *LANC* LA1 ....**3** D3
...Friars *FUL/RIB* PR2 ....**213** C7
...St *LANC* LA1 ....**3** D3
...ry Cl *KIRK/FR/WA* PR4 ....**209** C7
...on Gv *BISP* FY2 ....**311** H3
...LYE PR6 ....**311** H1
...dhurst Rd *WHIT* OL12 ....**277** H2
...on Gv *BISP* FY2..........................**148** E5
...les Av *LEY/BBR* PR5 ....**264** D2
...La *BRSC* L40 ....**331** K8
...ne St *PRES* PR1 ....**240** B2
...m St *CHLEY* PR6 ....**311** J3
...rs Cl *PRES* PR1 ....**261** K2
...st *NLSN* BB9 ....**198** D3
...ord Av *FUL/RIB* PR2 ....**237** J2
...am St *NLSN* BB9 ....**198** D1
...rs Ter *BCUP* OL13 ....**298** C2
...Vw *BBNW* BB2 ....**267** J3
...Fulmars *PLF/KEOS* * FY6 ....**177** H1
...haw Rd *FUL/RIB* PR2 ....**238** D1
...ood Av *BPOOLE* FY3 ....**177** F3
...*RK/FR/WA* PR4 ....**281** K2
...HP PR8 ....**301** K7
...ood Dr *MCMB* LA4 ....**42** B6
...ood Hall La *FUL/RIB* PR2 ....**213** K7

Fulwood Hts *FUL/RIB* PR2 ....**214** A6
Fulwood Rw *FUL/RIB* PR2 ....**214** C6
Funchal Av *FMBY* L37 ....**355** H2
Furlong Crs *BPOOLE* FY3...........**177** G2
Furlong La *PLF/KEOS* FY6 ....**149** K7
Furness Av *BBN* BB1 ....**9** F1
  BPOOLE FY3.........................**177** G3
  FMBY L37 ....**343** K8
  FTWD FY7 ....**122** D2
  ORM L39 ....**348** C7
Furness Cl *CHLY/EC* PR7 ....**311** H6
  STHP PR8 ....**325** H8
Furness Dr *PLF/KEOS* FY6 ....**150** B8
Furnessford Rd *HGHB* LA2 ....**39** H8
Furness Rd *HEY* LA3.....................**52** D1
Furness St *BRFD/BLYE* BB10 .....**225** K2
Furnival Dr *BRSC* L40 ....**330** D7
Further Ends Rd
  KIRK/FR/WA PR4 ....**235** F5
Furthergate *BBN* BB1 ....**9** F4
Further La *BBNW* BB2 ....**242** E4
Fylde Av *LEY/BBR* PR5................**262** B7
Fylde Cl *CHTN/BK* PR9 ....**278** B7
  FUL/RIB PR2 ....**6** B1
  LSTA FY8 ....**231** K6
  PLF/KEOS FY6 ....**150** A7
  PRES PR1 ....**6** C2
Fylde School Cottages
  PLF/KEOS (off Normoss Rd) FY6...**177** J3
Fylde St *KIRK/FR/WA* PR4 ....**208** E7
  PRES PR1 ....**6** C2
Fylde View Cl *PLF/KEOS* FY6 .....**177** K1

G

Gabbot St *CHLY/EC* PR7 ....**337** F4
Gables Pl *MCMB* * LA4 ....**41** K6
The Gables *KIRK/FR/WA* PR4 .....**212** A7
Gadfield St *DWN* BB3 ....**291** K3
Gadsby St *BPOOL* FY1 ....**4** B5
Gage St *LANC* LA1 ....**3** D3
Gaghills Rd *RAW/HAS* BB4.........**297** G2
Gainsborough Av *BBNW* BB2 ....**8** A3
  BLY BB11...............................**10** B6
  LEY/BBR PR5 ....**262** D4
  MCMB LA4 ....**41** K5
Gainsborough Rd *BPOOL* FY1 ....**5** D3
  STHP PR8 ....**300** E8
Gaisgill Av *MCMB* LA4 ....**41** H8
Gales La *BRSC* L40 ....**307** G8
Gale St *WHIT* OL12 ....**323** K8
Galligreaves St *BBNW* BB2 ....**8** B6
Galligreaves Wy *BBNW* BB2 ....**8** A6
Gall La *TOD* OL14 ....**254** C8
Galloway Crs *BISP* FY2 ....**149** F6
Galloway Rd *FTWD* FY7 ....**97** F6
Gallowber La *KKBYL* LA6 ....**20** A2
Gallows La *GAR/LONG* PR3 ....**190** B7
Galston Cl *NWD/KWIPK* L33 ....**366** B5
Galway Av *BISP* FY2 ....**148** D8
Gamble Rd *CLV/TH* FY5 ....**123** H7
Gambleside Cl *RAW/HAS* BB4 ....**273** H2
Game St *GTH/LHO* BB6 ....**221** G6
Gamull La *FUL/RIB* PR2 ....**214** D6
Gandy La *WHIT* OL12 ....**323** G7
Gannow La *PDHM/BLYW* BB12 ...**224** D5
Gantley Av *WGNW/BIL/O* WN5 ...**365** F7
Gantley Crs *WGNW/BIL/O* WN5 ..**365** F8
Gantley Rd *WGNW/BIL/O* WN5....**365** F8
Ganton Cl *STHP* PR8.....................**302** A7
Ganton Ct *PRES* PR1 ....**238** C5
Garbett St *ACC* BB5 ....**248** A7
Garden Av *KIRK/FR/WA* PR4 ......**207** K7
Gardeners Ms *BPOOL* * FY1 ....**176** C4
Gardeners Rw *CLI* BB7 ....**195** F4
Gardeners Vw *NWD/KWIPK* L33...**366** D5
Garden Pl *KKBYL* LA6 ....**18** B6
Gardens Gv *MCMB* LA4 ....**41** G7
The Gardens *EDGW/EG* BL7 ....**317** J1
  EDGW/EG BL7 ....**341** K5
Garden St *ACC* BB5 ....**247** H8
  ACC BB5 ....**248** B4
  BBNW BB2 ....**8** A5
  BWCK/EAR * BB18 ....**145** F1
  CHLYE PR6 ....**289** J1
  COL BB8 ....**171** H7
  GTH/LHO BB6 ....**221** G7
  KIRK/FR/WA PR4 ....**208** E7
  LSTA * FY8 ....**230** E5
  NLSN * BB9 ....**197** K6
  NLSN BB9 ....**198** C3
  PDHM/BLYW BB12 ....**196** B6
  PDHM/BLYW BB12 ....**223** J2
  PRES PR1 ....**7** D3
  RAMS BL0 ....**319** J5

Garden Ter *BPOOLS* FY4 ....**4** B6
  CHLY/EC PR7 ....**311** G2
Garden Wk *CLV/TH* FY5 ....**122** D6
  FUL/RIB PR2 ....**238** D2
Gardiners Pl *SKEL* WN8 ....**362** E3
Gardner Rd *CARN* LA5 ....**25** K6
  FMBY L37 ....**344** A8
  HEY LA3 ....**40** E8
  LANC LA1 ....**3** D1
Gardner's La *GAR/LONG* PR3 .....**131** F8
Gardner St *PRES* PR1 ....**7** D2
Garfield Av *LANC* LA1 ....**2** B4
Garfield Dr *MCMB* LA4 ....**42** B7
Garfield St *ACC* BB5 ....**248** D6
  FTWD FY7 ....**97** H6
  TOD OL14 ....**277** H2
Garfield Ter *CHLYE* PR6 ....**311** H1
Garland Gv *FTWD* * FY7 ....**96** D8
Garlicks Cottages
  LSTA (off North Warton St) FY8....**232** E8
Garnet St *LANC* LA1 ....**3** E3
Garnett Gdns *ORM* L39 ....**348** B7
Garnett Pl *SKEL* WN8 ....**363** G4
Garnett Rd *CLI* BB7 ....**165** G4
Garnett St *BOL* BL1 ....**341** J8
  DWN BB3 ....**291** K2
  NLSN BB9 ....**198** B1
  RAMS BL0 ....**319** H5
Garrick Gv *BPOOLE* FY3..............**176** E4
Garrick Pde *STHP* PR8 ....**301** G5
Garrick St *NLSN* BB9....................**198** D1
Garrison Rd *FUL/RIB* PR2 ....**213** K8
Garsdale Av *BRFD/BLYE* BB10 ....**197** K7
Garsdale Cl *LEY/BBR* PR5 ....**240** C6
Garsdale Rd *FUL/RIB* PR2 ....**214** C7
Garsden Av *BBN* BB1 ....**269** H1
Garstang Cl *PLF/KEOS* FY6 ....**149** J8
Garstang New Rd *PLF/KEOS* FY6...**151** G8
Garstang Rd *CHTN/BK* PR9 ....**278** B7
  FUL/RIB PR2 ....**213** F3
  GAR/LONG PR3.....................**100** E8
  GAR/LONG PR3.....................**129** K7
  GAR/LONG PR3.....................**152** B6
  GAR/LONG PR3.....................**156** B8
  GAR/LONG PR3.....................**156** A2
  GAR/LONG PR3.....................**160** C1
  GAR/LONG PR3.....................**213** F3
  HGHB LA2 ....**102** D1
  PLF/KEOS FY6 ....**150** D8
Garstang Rd East
  PLF/KEOS FY6 ....**150** A8
Garstang Rd North
  KIRK/FR/WA PR4 ....**208** D4
Garstang Rd South
  KIRK/FR/WA PR4 ....**208** D5
Garstang Rd West *BPOOLE* FY3...**177** G2
  PLF/KEOS FY6 ....**177** J1
Garstang St *DWN* BB3 ....**291** J1
The Gars *HGHB* LA2 ....**38** A7
Garstone Cft *FUL/RIB* PR2 ....**212** E5
Garswood Av *RNFD/HAY* WA11 ...**369** G4
Garswood Cl *MGHL* L31 ....**359** G8
  PDHM/BLYW BB12 ....**225** H1
Garswood Crs *WGNW/BIL/O* WN5...**371** F7
Garswood Rd *WGNW/BIL/O* WN5...**371** G7
Garton Av *BPOOLS* FY4 ....**204** C5
Garwick Rd *BOL* BL1 ....**341** F8
Gas Field Rd *HEY* LA3 ....**64** D1
Gaskell Cl *CARN* LA5 ....**15** G8
Gaskell Crs *CLV/TH* FY5 ....**149** G1
Gaskell Rd *PRES* PR1 ....**6** C5
Gaskell St *CHLYE* PR6 ....**311** J3
Gas St *BCUP* OL13 ....**298** D1
  BLY BB11 ....**10** C3
  CHLY/EC PR7 ....**337** F5
  RAW/HAS BB4 ....**295** F2
Gas Ter *LEY/BBR* PR5 ....**285** K1
Gatefield Ct *BLY* BB11 ....**11** D5
Gategill Gv *WGNW/BIL/O* WN5 ...**371** F1
Gate House Br *HGHB* LA2 ....**68** D6
Gatesgarth Av *FUL/RIB* PR2 ....**213** H4
Gateside Dr *BPOOLE* FY3.............**177** F3
Gate St *BBN* BB1 ....**9** E4
Gateway Cl *CLV/TH* FY5 ....**149** K4
Gathurst Hall
  WGNNW/ST (off Gathurst La) WN6...**353** H6
Gathurst La *WGNNW/ST* WN6......**353** H6
Gathurst Rd *FUL/RIB* PR2 ....**238** C1
  WGNW/BIL/O WN5 ....**365** G2
Gaulter's La *PLF/KEOS* FY6 ....**98** E7
Gaw Hill La *ORM* L39 ....**347** J8
Gaw Hill Vw *ORM* L39 ....**347** K8
Gawthorpe Rd *PDHM/BLYW* BB12...**10** A2
Gawthorpe St *PDHM/BLYW* BB12...**223** J2
Gawthorpe Vw
  PDHM/BLYW * BB12 ....**196** B6
Gaydon Wy *CLV/TH* FY5 ....**148** E4

Gaylands La *BWCK/EAR* BB18............146 C1
Gaythorne Av *PRES* PR1 ....240 D2
Gaythorne St *BOL* BL1 ....341 K8
Geddes St *BBNW* BB2 ....267 C1
Geldof Dr *BPOOL* FY1 ....176 C3
Gencoyne Dr *BOL* BL1 ....341 H5
Gendre Rd *EDGW/EG* BL7 ....341 J3
General St *BPOOL* FY1 ....4 B1
Geneva Rd *FUL/RIB* PR2 ....214 A7
Genoa St *BLY* BB11 ....224 E7
Geoffrey St *CHLYE* PR6 ....311 H2
    PRES PR1 ....240 A2
    RAMS BL0 ....319 C7
George Av *BPOOLS* FY4 ....5 F6
    GTH/LHO BB6 ....221 F6
George Dr *STHP* PR8 ....326 A6
George La *PDHM/BLYW* BB12..............222 C1
George Rd *RAMS* BL0..............................319 H6
George's La *CHTN/BK* PR9 ....279 H3
    HOR/BR BL6 ....339 F4
George's Rd *PRES* PR1 ....7 D3
George's Rw *RAW/HAS* BB4 ....297 H3
George's Ter *WGNW/BIL/O* WN5 ....365 F6
George St *ACC* * BB5 ....221 K8
    ACC BB5 ....247 K7
    ACC BB5 ....247 J6
    BBN BB1 ....8 C5
    BBN BB1 ....247 F2
    BLY BB11 ....10 C4
    BPOOL FY1 ....4 C1
    BWCK/EAR BB18 ....146 B2
    CHLY/EC PR7 ....311 C4
    CLI BB7 ....165 H5
    CLI BB7 ....193 G6
    DWN * BB3 ....291 J1
    GAR/LONG PR3 ....188 A3
    GTH/LHO BB6 ....221 F6
    HOR/BR BL6 ....339 F8
    LANC LA1 ....3 D4
    LEY/BBR PR5 ....285 K1
    LSTA FY8 ....232 D8
    MCMB LA4 ....41 J6
    NLSN * BB9 ....198 B2
    PRES PR1 ....7 F3
    RAW/HAS * BB4 ....272 C8
    WHIT OL12 ....323 C3
Georgian St *BBNW* BB2 ....8 A5
Georgian Pl *FMBY* L37 ....355 J2
Gerald Ct *BLY* BB11 ....11 E5
German La *CHLY/EC* PR7 ....310 B3
Gerrard Pl *SKEL* WN8 ....363 F4
Gerrard Rd *WGNW/BIL/O* WN5 ....371 K7
Gerrard's Ter *PLF/KEOS* FY6 ....149 J7
Gerrard St *LANC* LA1 ....2 A4
    PRES PR1 ....6 B3
Gertrude St *NLSN* BB9 ....198 D1
Ghants La *PLF/KEOS* FY6.......................125 C8
Ghyll La *BWCK/EAR* BB18 ....119 J7
Ghyll Mdw *BWCK/EAR* BB18 ....119 H7
Gibbon Br *GAR/LONG* PR3 ....161 H2
Gib Field Rd *COL* BB8 ....170 E8
Gib Hey La *GAR/LONG* PR3 ....159 K4
Gib Hill La *RAW/HAS* BB4 ....273 J2
Gib Hill Rd *NLSN* BB9 ....199 F2
Gib La *BBNW* BB2 ....267 H4
    LEY/BBR PR5 ....242 C8
Gibraltar Rd *KIRK/FR/WA* PR4 ....179 G6
Gibraltar St *BBNW* BB2 ....244 D5
Gibson St *NLSN* * BB9 ....198 D1
Gidlow Av *CHLYE* PR6 ....337 C4
Gilbert Pl *SKEL* WN8 ....363 F4
Gilbertson Rd *CHLY/EC* PR7 ....336 E1
Gilbert St *BRFD/BLYE* BB10 ....226 C1
    CHLY/EC * PR7 ....311 C5
    RAMS BL0 ....319 J2
    RAW/HAS * BB4 ....297 F2
Gildabrook Rd *BPOOLS* FY4 ....204 D3
Gilderdale Ct *LSTA* FY8.........................232 E7
Gildow St *PRES* PR1 ....6 C2
Giles St *CLI* BB7 ....165 J4
    NLSN BB9 ....198 C2
Gilhouse Av *FUL/RIB* PR2 ....237 J2
Gill Av *WGNW/ST* WN6 ....353 K5
Gillcroft *CHLY/EC* PR7 ....308 D4
Giller Cl *PRES* PR1 ....262 B1
Giller Dr *PRES* PR1 ....262 B1
Giller Fold *PRES* PR1 ....262 C1
Gillett St *PRES* PR1 ....240 A2
Gillians La *BWCK/EAR* BB18 ....144 E2
Gillibrand Cl *PRES* PR1..........................261 K2
Gillibrands Rd *SKEL* WN8 ....363 H4
Gillibrand St *CHLY/EC* PR7 ....311 G4
    DWN BB3 ....268 C8
    LEY/BBR PR5 ....240 B6
Gillibrand Wks *CHLY/EC* PR7 ....311 C5
Gillies St *ACC* BB5 ....248 C5
    BBNW BB2 ....9 D6

Gillison Cl *KKBYL* LA6 ....29 K8
Gillisons Bungalows *LANC* * LA1 ....2 C4
Gill La *KIRK/FR/WA* PR4 ....260 B6
Gill Nook *KIRK/FR/WA* PR4 ....260 B6
Gillow Ct *LANC* LA1 ....3 D6
Gillow Pk *GAR/LONG* PR3 ....152 D5
Gillow Rd *KIRK/FR/WA* PR4 ....208 D4
Gills Cft *CLI* BB7 ....165 K5
Gill St *COL* BB8 ....171 F8
    NLSN BB9 ....198 A2
    PDHM/BLYW BB12 ....10 B3
Gilpin Cl *LANC* * LA1 ....2 A1
Gilsecroft Av *NWD/KWIPK* L33 ....366 E8
Gilstead Av *HEY* LA3 ....52 E3
Gin Bow *CHLY/EC* PR7 ....311 C4
Gin Croft La *RAMS* BL0 ....296 A8
Gingham Brow *HOR/BR* BL6 ....339 F7
Girvan Gv *BLY* BB11 ....10 A4
Gisburn Av *LSTA* FY8 ....231 J5
Gisburn Gv *BPOOLE* FY3 ....176 E4
    BRFD/BLYE BB10 ....226 B6
Gisburn Old Rd *CLI* BB7 ....143 K4
    NLSN BB9 ....144 C7
Gisburn Pl *BBNW* * BB2 ....244 D7
Gisburn Rd *BWCK/EAR* BB18 ....118 E8
    CLI BB7 ....115 H4
    FUL/RIB PR2 ....214 C7
    NLSN BB9 ....170 B4
Gisburn St *BBNW* BB2 ....8 A5
    BWCK/EAR BB18 ....119 F8
Gladden Pl *SKEL* WN8 ....362 E3
The Glades *LSTA* FY8 ....232 E7
The Glade *MCMB* LA4 ....42 A6
    WGNW/ST WN6 ....353 K5
Gladeway *CLV/TH* FY5 ....149 K4
Gladstone Crs *BCUP* OL13 ....298 E1
Gladstone Rd *CHTN/BK* PR9 ....302 B5
Gladstone St *BBN* BB1 ....9 F3
    BCUP OL13 ....298 E1
    BPOOLS FY4 ....4 C6
    GTH/LHO BB6 ....221 G6
    TOD OL14 ....277 C2
Gladstone Ter *BBNW* BB2 ....267 C2
    LANC LA1 ....3 E2
Gladstone Wy *CLV/TH* FY5 ....149 F2
Glaisdale Dr *STHP* PR8..........................302 B8
Glamis Dr *CHLY/EC* PR7 ....311 F3
    CHTN/BK PR9 ....278 D8
Glamis Rd *LEY/BBR* PR5 ....286 A3
Glamorgan Gv *PDHM/BLYW* BB12 ....224 C4
Glasson Cl *BBNW* BB2 ....268 C2
Glastonbury Av *BPOOL* FY1 ....5 E5
Glasven Rd *NWD/KWIPK* L33 ....366 D8
Glebe Cl *ACC* BB5 ....248 B6
    FUL/RIB PR2 ....213 H7
    KKBYL LA6 ....18 B5
Glebelands *KIRK/FR/WA* PR4 ....282 A6
Glebe La *CHTN/BK* PR9 ....279 J4
    KIRK/FR/WA PR4 ....209 C7
Glebe Pl *STHP* PR8 ....301 H4
Glebe Rd *SKEL* WN8 ....363 G4
Glebe St *BLY* BB11 ....11 D5
    GTH/LHO BB6 ....221 G6
The Glebe *LEY/BBR* PR5 ....284 D3
Gledstone Rd *SKP/WHF* BD23 ....119 G5
Gledstone Vw *BWCK/EAR* BB18 ....118 E8
Glenapp Av *BPOOLS* FY4 ....205 F5
Glenarden Av *CLV/TH* FY5 ....148 E3
Glenavon Dr *WHIT* OL12 ....323 H8
Glenborough Av *BCUP* OL13 ....298 A3
Glenbrook Cl *BBNW* BB2 ....267 J3
Glenburn Rd *SKEL* WN8 ....350 E7
Glencarron Cl *DWN* BB3 ....292 D3
    DWN BB3 ....292 C2
Glencoe Av *BPOOLS* FY4 ....177 G2
    DWN BB3 ....292 C2
Glencoyne Dr *CHTN/BK* PR9 ....278 D5
Glen Crs *BCUP* OL13 ....297 J3
Glencroft *CHLY/EC* PR7 ....285 K8
Glencross Pl *BPOOLS* FY4 ....204 E4
Glendale Av *LEY/BBR* PR5.....................263 F2
Glendale Cl *BISP* FY2 ....149 F6
    BLY BB11 ....11 D6
    LEY/BBR PR5 ....285 K4
    PLF/KEOS FY6 ....149 J8
Glendale Crs *LEY/BBR* PR5 ....263 F2
Glendale Dr *BBNW* BB2 ....244 A1
Glendale Gv *FUL/RIB* PR2 ....240 B1
Glendale Wy *FMBY* L37 ....355 K1
Glendene Pk *BBN* BB1 ....219 G6
Glendor Rd *BRFD/BLYE* BB10 ....226 C6
Glen Dr *WGNW/ST* WN6 ....353 C3
Gleneagles Av *DWN* BB3 ....292 C2
Gleneagles Ct *KIRK/FR/WA* PR4 ....209 F7
Gleneagles Dr *FUL/RIB* PR2 ....212 D4
    MCMB LA4 ....41 K6

    PRES PR1 ....23..
    STHP PR8 ....32..
Gleneagles Wy *RAMS* BL0.....................31..
Glen Eldon Rd *LSTA* FY8 ....23..
Glenfield Av *BISP* FY2 ....14..
Glenfield Pk
    NLSN (off Glenfield Rd) BB9 ....19..
Glenfield Rd *NLSN* BB9 ....19..
Glen Gdns *WHIT* OL12 ....32..
Glen Garth *BWCK/EAR* BB18 ....11..
Glengreave Av *BBN* BB1 ....9..
Glen Gv *FUL/RIB* PR2 ....21..
Glenholme Gdns *PLF/KEOS* FY6 ....17..
Glenluce Crs *BBN* BB1 ....24..
Glenluce Dr *PRES* PR1 ....24..
Glenmarsh Wy *FMBY* L37 ....34..
Glenmere Crs *CLV/TH* FY5 ....14..
Glenmore *CHLYE* PR6.............................28..
Glenmore Av *CLV/TH* FY5 ....14..
Glenmore Cl *ACC* BB5 ....27..
Glenpark Dr *CHTN/BK* PR9 ....27..
Glen Park Dr *KIRK/FR/WA* PR4 ....25..
Glen Rd *RAW/HAS* BB4 ....29..
Glenrose Ter *STHP* PR8 ....30..
Glenroy Av *COL* BB8 ....17..
Glenroyd Cl *BPOOLE* FY3......................
Glenroyd Dr *BRSC* L40 ....33..
Glenshiels Av *DWN* BB3 ....29..
Glenside *WGNW/ST* WN6 ....35..
Glen St *BCUP* OL13 ....29..
    BLY BB11 ....1..
    BPOOLE FY3 ....
    COL BB8 ....17..
    RAMS BL0 ....31..
The Glen *BBNW* BB2 ....26..
    FUL/RIB PR2 ....24..
    HGHB LA2 ....4..
    PLF/KEOS FY6 ....9..
Glentworth Rd West *MCMB* LA4 ....4..
Glen View Av *HEY* LA3 ....5..
Glenview Cl *FUL/RIB* PR2 ....21..
Glenview Ct *FUL/RIB* PR2 ....21..
Glen View Crs *HEY* LA3 ....5..
Glen View Dr *HEY* LA3 ....5..
Glen View Rd *BLY* BB11 ....25..
Glen View St *TOD* OL14 ....27..
Glen Wy *NLSN* BB9 ....19..
Glenway *NWD/KWIPK* L33 ....366..
    PRES PR1 ....
Glenwood St *BPOOLE* FY3 ....
Glentworth Rd East *MCMB* LA4 ....4..
Globe La *EDGW/EG* BL7 ....31..
Glossop Cl *BISP* FY2 ....14..
Gloucester Av *ACC* BB5 ....22..
    BPOOL FY1 ....
    CLV/TH FY5 ....122..
    LANC LA1 ....55..
    LEY/BBR PR5 ....263..
Gloucester Dr *HEY* LA3 ....40..
Gloucester Rd *BBN* BB1 ....246..
    BBN BB1 ....246..
    CHLY/EC PR7 ....311..
    LSTA FY8 ....231..
    STHP PR8 ....301..
Glover Cl *LEY/BBR* PR5 ....284..
Glover's Brow *KKBY* L32 ....366..
Glover's Ct *PRES* PR1 ....7..
Glover St *HOR/BR* BL6 ....338..
    PRES PR1 ....
Glynn St *ACC* BB5 ....247..
Godiva St *BRFD/BLYE* BB10 ....225..
Godley St *BLY* BB11 ....11..
Godwin Av *BPOOLE* FY3 ....5..
Goe La *KIRK/FR/WA* PR4 ....235..
Goitside *NLSN* * BB9 ....198..
Goit St *BBNW* BB2 ....267..
    RAW/HAS BB4 ....273..
Golbourne St *PRES* PR1 ....7..
Goldacre La *GTH/LHO* BB6 ....220..
Goldburn Cl *FUL/RIB* PR2 ....212..
Golden Hl *LEY/BBR* PR5 ....285..
Golden Hill La *LEY/BBR* PR5 ....285..
Golden Wy *PRES* PR1 ....6..
Goldfield Av *BRFD/BLYE* BB10 ....226..
Goldfinch St *PRES* PR1 ....236..
Goldhey St *BBN* * BB1 ....9..
Goldsboro Av *BPOOLE* FY3 ....5..
Goldstone Dr *CLV/TH* FY5 ....149..
Golf Rd *FMBY* L37 ....343..
Golf Vw *FUL/RIB* PR2 ....212..
Golgotha Rd *LANC* LA1 ....3..
Golgotha Village *LANC* LA1 ....3..
Gonder La *GAR/LONG* PR3.....................131..
Goodall Cl *BWCK/EAR* BB18 ....146..
Goodshaw Av *BBN* BB1 ....245..
    RAW/HAS BB4 ....273..

dshaw Av North
  W/HAS BB4 ....273 H1
dshaw Cl BBN BB1 ....245 C2
dshawfold Cl RAW/HAS BB4 ...273 H1
dshaw Fold Rd
  AW/HAS BB4 ....273 G1
dshaw La ACC BB5 ....272 D2
dshaw BB4 ....273 H3
d St PRES PR1 ....6 C3
dwood Av BISP FY2 ....176 D2
L/RIB PR2 ....213 H4
GHB LA2 ....43 F3
dwood Cl LANC LA1 ...55 H7
dwood Rd LANC LA1 ....55 H7
sebutts La CLI BB7 ....165 K4
se Cote Hl EDGW/EG BL7 ....341 J1
se Foot Cl LEY/BBR PR5 ....242 C4
se Foot La LEY/BBR PR5 ...242 C6
se Green Av CHLY/EC PR7 ....335 K2
se Green La COL BB8 ....200 B1
se Hill St BCUP OL13 ....275 J8
se House Rd DWN BB3 ....268 D7
seleach La PDHM/BLYW BB12 ...222 E3
snargh La GAR/LONG PR3 ...185 K4
VCK/EAR BB18 ....144 E1
lon Av ACC BB5 ....248 A7
TN/BK PR9 ....301 J2
GHL L31 ....358 C8
N/TH FY5 ....149 H1
lon Rd FTWD FY7 ....97 F8
TA FY8 ....231 J7
SN* BB9 ....198 B3
lonstoun Crs
  GNW/BIL/O WN5 ....365 H3
lonstoun Pl BBNW BB2 ....8 A6
N/TH FY5 ....149 C1
lon St ACC BB5 ....247 J6
C BB5 ....248 A1
UP OL13 ....275 J7
POOLS* FY4 ....4 B6
le Dr ORM L39 ....348 C8
es La FMBY L37 ....343 J6
VFD/HAY WA11 ....370 B5
VFD/HAY WA11 ....370 C6
st WGNW/BIL/O WN5 ....365 K5
ng St CHLY/EC PR7 ....311 H4
ole Gn BRFD/BLYE BB10 ....227 F6
ole Rd BRFD/BLYE BB10 ....227 G6
ole St BRFD/BLYE BB10 ....198 C8
rell Cl PDHM/BLYW BB12 ....197 F1
se Av CLV/TH FY5 ....122 E8
se Cl CHLYE PR6 ....287 J6
RK/FR/WA PR4 ....282 K5
sefield FMBY L37 ....344 A5
se Gv FUL/RIB PR2 ....214 A1
RK/FR/WA PR4 ....260 B2
W/HAS BB4 ....295 C3
se La KIRK/FR/WA PR4 ....281 C6
se Rd BBNW BB2 ....244 D6
POOLE FY3 ....5 D3
se St BBN BB1 ....9 F3
se Wy FMBY L37 ....343 G7
sewood LEY/BBR PR5 ....285 G2
sey La BRSC L40 ....332 E1
con St BPOOL FY1 ....4 C1
TN/BK PR9 ....302 B3
gh La LEY/BBR PR5 ....264 A6
ding Av LEY/BBR PR5 ....285 K2
ding St CHLY/EC PR7 ....311 H5
vans La CHLYE PR6 ....265 F3
ver Ct LEY/BBR PR5 ....285 F1
ver Gdns BRSC L40 ....331 F8
ver Gv KIRK/FR/WA PR4 ....260 B7
t Hey La WGNW/BIL/O WN5 ....371 G7
st LSTA FY8 ....231 F4
a La LANC LA1 ....55 J4
urn Rd FMBY L37 ....343 H4
camy Av KIRK/FR/WA * PR4 ....234 B6
se St HOR/BR BL6 ....338 D7

Gradwell St PRES PR1 ....6 C2
Grafton Av ACC BB5 ....248 E8
BRFD/BLYE BB10 ....197 K6
Grafton Ct CHLY/EC PR7 ....311 F6
DWN BB3 ....291 H1
Grafton Dr STHP PR8 ....325 G6
Grafton Pl HEY LA3 ....40 E2
Grafton Rd FUL/RIB PR2 ....214 D7
HEY LA3 ....40 E2
Grafton St BBNW BB2 ....268 A1
BPOOL FY1 ....176 C4
CHLY/EC PR7 ....337 F5
CLI BB7 ....165 K3
NLSN BB9 ....198 D2
PRES PR1 ....6 C4
Grafton Vis BCUP OL13 ....298 C2
Graham Av LEY/BBR PR5 ....263 F3
WGNNW/ST WN6 ....352 E1
Graham Rd GAR/LONG PR3 ....129 J1
Graham St LANC LA1 ....3 D5
MCMB* LA4 ....41 G6
PDHM/BLYW BB12 ....223 K4
PRES PR1 ....7 F1
Grampian Wy LSTA FY8 ....233 F6
Granby Av BPOOLE FY3 ....176 E3
Granby Cl CHTN/BK PR9 ....278 B8
Granby St PDHM/BLYW BB12 ....10 A3
Grand Manor Dr LSTA FY8 ....231 K4
Grane Pk RAW/HAS BB4 ....295 C1
Grane Rd RAW/HAS BB4 ....270 D8
Grane St RAW/HAS BB4 ....272 C8
Grange Av CHTN/BK PR9 ....302 A3
CLV/TH FY5 ....149 H1
FUL/RIB PR2 ....214 D7
GTH/LHO BB6 ....221 C5
NLSN BB9 ....170 D6
RAW/HAS BB4 ....273 J8
WGNW/BIL/O WN5 ....365 K4
Grange Cl ACC BB5 ....248 A8
GTH/LHO BB6 ....221 G5
PLF/KEOS FY6 ....98 B5
RAW/HAS* BB4 ....296 D1
Grange Crs RAW/HAS BB4 ....296 C1
Grange Dr CHLYE PR6 ....286 A7
LEY/BBR PR5 ....241 H7
Grangefield KIRK/FR/WA PR4 ....260 A2
Grange Gdns PLF/KEOS FY6 ....177 K1
Grange La ACC BB5 ....248 C6
FMBY L37 ....343 J6
KIRK/FR/WA PR4 ....235 K1
KIRK/FR/WA PR4 ....259 J2
PLF/KEOS FY6 ....124 C4
Grange Park La PRES PR1 ....238 C5
Grange Pl FUL/RIB PR2 ....214 D7
Grange Rd BBNW BB2 ....267 J1
BPOOLE FY3 ....176 E4
BRFD/BLYE BB10 ....252 E4
CHTN/BK PR9 ....302 A4
FTWD FY7 ....96 D8
FUL/RIB PR2 ....212 E8
HTWN L38 ....355 J5
KIRK/FR/WA PR4 ....180 C5
LEY/BBR PR5 ....285 F2
LSTA FY8 ....230 E4
PLF/KEOS FY6 ....151 F2
PLF/KEOS FY6 ....179 H1
RAW/HAS BB4 ....296 D1
WHIT OL12 ....323 H1
Grange St ACC BB5 ....221 J8
ACC* BB5 ....248 C6
BLY BB11 ....10 B4
BWCK/EAR BB18 ....118 E8
MCMB LA4 ....42 A4
Grange Ter RAW/HAS * BB4 ....273 H8
The Grange BBN BB1 ....219 H6
KIRK/FR/WA PR4 ....212 A6
Grange Vw CARN LA5 ....25 K8
The Granings KIRK/FR/WA PR4 ....211 K5
Grant Cl LANC LA1 ....2 E1
Grant Dr KIRK/FR/WA PR4 ....260 B6
Grantham Cl STHP PR8 ....326 C2
Grantham Rd BPOOL * FY1 ....176 C4
KIRK/FR/WA PR4 ....179 F5
NWD/KWIPK L33 ....366 C6
STHP PR8 ....326 C2
Grantham St BBNW BB2 ....267 J1
Granton Cl FMBY L37 ....343 J8
Grant Rd BBNW * BB2 ....244 D8
Grants La RAMS BL0 ....319 J5
Grant St ACC * BB5 ....248 A5
BLY BB11 ....10 B4
Granville Av KIRK/FR/WA PR4 ....281 J1
Granville Cl ORM L39 ....359 K2
Granville Gdns ACC BB5 ....248 D7
Granville Pk ORM L39 ....359 K3

Granville Pk West ORM L39 ....359 K3
Granville Rd ACC BB5 ....248 D8
BBNW BB2 ....244 D6
BPOOL FY1 ....5 D2
CHLYE PR6 ....311 J2
DWN BB3 ....291 H3
GTH/LHO BB6 ....221 H5
HEY LA3 ....40 D8
LANC LA1 ....42 D8
NLSN BB9 ....198 A5
STHP PR8 ....300 D8
Granville St BRFD/BLYE BB10 ....11 D1
BRFD/BLYE BB10 ....198 D8
CHLYE PR6 ....337 G4
COL BB8 ....171 J6
Grape La LEY/BBR PR5 ....307 J2
Grasmere Av BBN BB1 ....244 E2
CLV/TH FY5 ....149 H1
FTWD FY7 ....96 E7
LEY/BBR PR5 ....262 D8
PDHM/BLYW BB12 ....223 J1
SKEL WN8 ....364 D3
WGNW/BIL/O WN5 ....365 H3
Grasmere Cl ACC BB5 ....248 D3
CHLY/EC PR7 ....310 B2
FUL/RIB PR2 ....214 A7
LEY/BBR PR5 ....263 G1
NWD/KWIPK L33 ....366 B7
Grasmere Dr BBN BB1 ....246 E2
Grasmere Gv CHLYE PR6 ....287 F4
GAR/LONG PR3 ....187 K6
Grasmere Rd BPOOL FY1 ....4 C4
FMBY L37 ....343 H8
LANC LA1 ....3 E3
LSTA FY8 ....230 E2
MCMB LA4 ....41 K5
PLF/KEOS FY6 ....98 B5
RAW/HAS BB4 ....295 J3
Grasmere St BRFD/BLYE BB10 ....225 J1
Grasmere Ter BCUP OL13 ....275 J8
CHLY/EC PR7 ....311 F6
Grassington Dr BRFD/BLYE BB10 ....198 C8
Grassington Pl CLV/TH FY5 ....149 F3
Grassington Rd LSTA FY8 ....231 H4
Gratton Pl SKEL WN8 ....363 G3
Gravel La CHTN/BK PR9 ....279 H6
The Gravel KIRK/FR/WA PR4 ....304 D1
Grave-Yard La ORM L39 ....360 E4
Graving Dock Rd LSTA FY8 ....233 F7
Gravners Fld CLV/TH FY5 ....149 K1
Grayrigg Dr MCMB LA4 ....41 H7
Graysons Rd RNFD/HAY WA11 ....369 F3
Grays Pl HEY LA3 ....52 E1
Great Avenham St PRES PR1 ....7 E4
Great Bolton St PRES PR1 ....8 C6
Great Croft Cl BWCK/EAR BB18 ....118 E8
Great Eaves Rd RAMS BL0 ....319 J4
Great George St COL BB8 ....171 H7
PRES PR1 ....7 E1
Great Gill KIRK/FR/WA PR4 ....260 B6
Great Greens La LEY/BBR PR5 ....264 A6
Great Hanging Br LEY/BBR PR5 ....306 D3
Great Hanover St PRES PR1 ....7 E1
Great Hey KIRK/FR/WA PR4 ....282 D1
Great John St LANC LA1 ....3 D3
Great Lee WHIT OL12 ....323 H8
Great Meadow CHLY/EC PR7 ....310 E1
LEY/BBR PR5 ....262 D3
Great Shaw St PRES PR1 ....7 D2
Great Stones Cl EDGW/EG BL7 ....341 J1
Great Townley St PRES PR1 ....240 B3
Great Tunstead KIRK/FR/WA PR4 ....260 B4
Greave Cl RAW/HAS BB4 ....273 H7
Greave Clough Cl BCUP OL13 ....275 K8
Greave Clough Dr BCUP OL13 ....275 K8
Greave Rd BCUP OL13 ....276 A8
Greaves Cl CHTN/BK PR9 ....279 J6
WGNNW/ST WN6 ....353 H3
Greaves Dr LANC LA1 ....3 D5
Greaves Hall Av CHTN/BK PR9 ....279 J6
Greaves Meadow PRES PR1 ....262 B2
Greaves Rd LANC LA1 ....3 D5
Greaves St GTH/LHO BB6 ....221 G7
PRES PR1 ....7 E3
RAW/HAS BB4 ....295 F1
Greaves-Town La FUL/RIB PR2 ....237 K2
WGNS/IIMK WN3 ....365 K7
Grebe Cl BPOOLE FY3 ....177 H4
WGNS/IIMK WN3 ....365 K7
Grebe Whf LANC LA1 ....3 E2
Greenacre BRSC L40 ....349 J7
DWN BB3 ....268 C5
Green Acre GAR/LONG PR3 ....186 B5
Greenacre Cl RAMS BL0 ....320 A4
Greenacre Ct LANC LA1 ....55 H8
Greenacre Pk CARN LA5 ....42 E1
Greenacre Rd HGHB LA2 ....42 E1
Green Acres KIRK/FR/WA PR4 ....235 G4

Greenacres EDGW/EG BL7 ....**317** J5
  FUL/RIB PR2 ....**212** D4
  PDHM/BLYW BB12 ....**222** D1
Greenacres Av KIRK/FR/WA PR4 ....**208** E7
Greenacres Dr GAR/LONG PR3 ....**129** K5
The Greenacres KIRK/FR/WA PR4 ....**260** E1
Greenacre St CLI BB7 ....**165** J4
Green Av BPOOLS FY4 ....**204** C5
Green Bank BCUP OL13 ....**298** B3
  BWCK/EAR BB18 ....**119** H7
Greenbank ORM L39 ....**360** A1
  PLF/KEOS FY6 ....**150** A8
Greenbank Av MGHL L31 ....**358** E8
  PRES PR1 ....**239** F1
  WGNW/BIL/O WN5 ....**365** F8
Greenbank Dr PDHM/BLYW BB12 ....**197** G3
  STHP PR8 ....**326** A1
Greenbank Pk RAW/HAS BB4 ....**296** D1
Greenbank Rd BBN BB1 ....**9** F3
  PRES PR1 ....**6** C6
Greenbanks BISP FY2 ....**149** F8
Greenbank St PRES PR1 ....**6** C1
  RAW/HAS BB4 ....**296** D1
Greenbank Ter DWN BB3 ....**268** C5
Greenberfield La
  BWCK/EAR BB18 ....**119** F7
Greenbooth Rd WHIT OL12 ....**322** B8
Greenbriar CI BPOOLE FY3 ....**177** F2
Greenbrook CI PDHM/BLYW BB12 ....**224** B5
Greenbrook Rd
  PDHM/BLYW BB12 ....**224** B5
Greencliffe La BRFD/BLYE BB10 ....**252** E5
Green CI BLY BB11 ....**251** G1
Green Close Pk BBNW BB2 ....**267** K1
Greencroft PRES PR1 ....**239** F8
Greendale Av RAW/HAS BB4 ....**297** G2
Greendale CI BRFD/BLYE BB10 ....**252** E4
  FTWD FY7 ....**122** C1
Greendale Ms FUL/RIB PR2 ....**238** A1
Green Dick's La GAR/LONG PR3 ....**99** G6
Green Dr CLI BB7 ....**166** A1
  CLV/TH FY5 ....**122** C7
  FUL/RIB PR2 ....**213** G4
  GAR/LONG PR3 ....**184** D3
  LEY/BBR PR5 ....**263** F2
  LSTA FY8 ....**232** C6
  PLF/KEOS FY6 ....**178** A3
  PRES PR1 ....**238** D6
Green End BBNW BB2 ....**242** E4
Green End Av BWCK/EAR BB18 ....**146** B1
Green End CI BCUP * OL13 ....**275** K8
Green End Rd BWCK/EAR BB18 ....**146** B2
Greenfield Av CLI BB7 ....**140** D6
  CLI* BB7 ....**165** G3
  SKEL WN8 ....**351** H1
Greenfield Dr LEY/BBR PR5 ....**262** D3
Greenfield Rd BRFD/BLYE BB10 ....**226** B7
  CHLYE PR6 ....**311** J3
  CHLYE PR6 ....**337** D3
  CLV/TH FY5 ....**148** E3
  COL BB8 ....**170** E7
  FTWD FY7 ....**123** F1
  STHP PR8 ....**328** A2
Greenfields HGHB LA2 ....**45** G5
Greenfields Crs KIRK/FR/WA PR4 ....**208** C5
  LANC LA1 ....**3** E3
  RAW/HAS BB4 ....**272** C8
  RAW/HAS BB4 ....**273** H8
Greenfield Ter TOD OL14 ....**277** F2
Greenfield Vw DWN BB3 ....**268** D4
  WGNW/BIL/O WN5 ....**371** F7
Greenfield Wy FUL/RIB PR2 ....**212** D6
Greenfinch CI BPOOLE FY3 ....**177** H5
Greenfold Cottages
  RAW/HAS (off Goodshaw La) BB4 ....**273** J2
Greenfold Dr RAW/HAS BB4 ....**273** H1
Greenfoot La HGHB LA2 ....**39** K3
Greenford CI WGNW/BIL/O WN5 ....**365** F8
Greenford Rd STHP PR8 ....**325** J7
Green Ga FUL/RIB PR2 ....**212** E8
  KIRK/FR/WA PR4 ....**260** D2
Greengate CI PDHM/BLYW BB12 ....**10** A2
Greengate La GAR/LONG PR3 ....**33** J3
Greenhalgh La CHLYE PR6 ....**337** H3
  KIRK/FR/WA PR4 ....**180** A7
Greenhall CI GAR/LONG PR3 ....**129** K5
Greenham Av NWD/KWIPK L33 ....**366** D5
Greenhead Av BBN BB1 ....**9** F1
Greenhead La PDHM/BLYW BB12 ....**197** F5
Green Hey KIRK/FR/WA PR4 ....**259** K8
  LSTA FY8 ....**233** F2
Greenhey WGNW/BIL/O WN5 ....**365** J4

Greenhey PI SKEL WN8 ....**363** F3
Greenhill GTH/LHO BB6 ....**221** F6
Greenhill Av KIRK/FR/WA PR4 ....**208** E5
Greenhill Crs WGNW/BIL/O WN5 ....**371** H6
Green Hill La HGHB LA2 ....**34** M1
  HWTH BD22 ....**174** D2
Greenhill PI BPOOL FY1 ....**4** C1
Green Hill Rd BCUP OL13 ....**298** E2
Greenholme Av MCMB LA4 ....**41** H8
Green Howarth Vw ACC BB5 ....**248** A8
Greenhurst CI BBNW * BB2 ....**8** B5
Greenings La CHTN/BK PR9 ....**304** A3
Greenland La CHLYE PR6 ....**337** K6
Greenland Rd HBR HX7 ....**255** J5
Greenlands Crs FUL/RIB PR2 ....**214** C8
Green La BBNW BB2 ....**267** H2
  BRSC L40 ....**331** F7
  BRSC L40 ....**332** C4
  BRSC L40 ....**351** F5
  CHLY/EC PR7 ....**336** A4
  CHTN/BK PR9 ....**280** A7
  CLI BB7 ....**140** A2
  CLI BB7 ....**141** G5
  FMBY L37 ....**343** K5
  GAR/LONG PR3 ....**129** C3
  GAR/LONG PR3 ....**134** E8
  GAR/LONG PR3 ....**156** E8
  GAR/LONG PR3 ....**188** B3
  HEY LA3 ....**53** H1
  HGHB LA2 ....**43** G6
  HGHB LA2 ....**44** D3
  HGHB LA2 ....**67** H5
  HOR/BR BL6 ....**338** D6
  KIRK/FR/WA PR4 ....**182** D5
  KIRK/FR/WA PR4 ....**235** F5
  KIRK/FR/WA PR4 ....**261** K2
  KIRK/FR/WA PR4 ....**281** C7
  KIRK/FR/WA PR4 ....**305** H2
  LANC LA1 ....**43** H7
  LEY/BBR PR5 ....**241** K5
  LEY/BBR PR5 ....**242** C5
  LEY/BBR PR5 ....**262** B4
  LEY/BBR PR5 ....**265** B3
  LEY/BBR PR5 ....**283** J4
  ORM L39 ....**348** C5
  PDHM/BLYW BB12 ....**223** J3
  PLF/KEOS FY6 ....**124** E1
  RNFD/HAY WN4 ....**369** C6
  SKP/WHF BD23 ....**118** A2
  WGNW/BIL/O WN5 ....**365** F8
Green Lane Av ORM * L39 ....**348** C5
Green La East GAR/LONG PR3 ....**129** J2
Green La West GAR/LONG PR3 ....**129** H2
  KIRK/FR/WA PR4 ....**234** E6
Greenlea CI WGNW/BIL/O WN5 ....**365** F6
Greenlea Dr MCMB LA4 ....**41** K6
Greenloon's Dr FMBY L37 ....**343** C8
Greenloon's Wk FMBY L37 ....**355** C1
Greenmead CI KIRK/FR/WA PR4 ....**212** A6
Green Meadow COL BB8 ....**200** B1
Green Meadow La PLF/KEOS FY6 ....**150** D3
Green Moor La GAR/LONG PR3 ....**189** H4
Greenmount Av CLV/TH FY5 ....**123** C8
  KIRK/FR/WA PR4 ....**208** E5
Greenmount Dr TOT/BURYW BL8 ....**319** F8
Green Nook La GAR/LONG PR3 ....**187** K5
Green Oak PI CLV/TH FY5 ....**149** F3
Greenock CI BLY * BB11 ....**10** A5
Greenock St BLY BB11 ....**10** A5
Green Pk CLI BB7 ....**193** C6
Green PI LEY/BBR PR5 ....**263** K5
Green Ridge CI NLSN BB9 ....**198** B6
Green Rd COL BB8 ....**171** C7
Greens Arms Rd EDGW/EG BL7 ....**316** A4
Greenset CI LANC LA1 ....**42** E7
Greenside CHLY/EC PR7 ....**286** A8
  GAR/LONG PR3 ....**190** A3
Greenside Av BBNW BB2 ....**267** H3
  FUL/RIB PR2 ....**237** J2
Greenside CI NWD/KWIPK L33 ....**366** E5
  TOT/BURYW BL8 ....**318** B8
Greenside Gdns LEY/BBR PR5 ....**284** C4
Greens La BCUP OL13 ....**275** K8
  BCUP OL13 ....**298** B3
  MGHL L31 ....**358** E2
  PLF/KEOS FY6 ....**125** H4
  RAW/HAS BB4 ....**295** H4
Greenslate Ct WGNW/BIL/O WN5 ....**365** F8
Greenslate Rd WGNW/BIL/O WN5 ......**365** C8
Greensnook La BCUP OL13 ....**275** K8
Greensnook Ter BCUP OL13 ....**275** K8
The Greens WHIT OL12 ....**323** C2
Greenstone Av HOR/BR BL6 ....**338** C8
Green St ACC BB5 ....**270** B1
  BRFD/BLYE BB10 ....**225** D3
  BWCK/EAR BB18 ....**145** F1

CHLY/EC PR7 ....**3?**
CHLYE PR6 ....**3**
DWN BB3 ....**2**
GTH/LHO BB6 ....**2?**
LANC LA1 ....
LSTA FY8 ....**2?**
MCMB LA4 ....
PDHM/BLYW BB12 ....**2?**
RAMS* BL0 ....
RAW/HAS BB4 ....**2**
Green St East DWN BB3 ....**2?**
Greensward CI WGNNW/ST WN6 ....**3?**
Greensway GAR/LONG PR3 ....**1?**
The Green CARN LA5 ....**1**
  CARN LA5 ....
  CHLY/EC PR7 ....**3?**
  CHLYE PR6 ....**3**
  COL BB8 ....**1**
  DWN* BB3 ....**2**
  FUL/RIB PR2 ....**2**
  GAR/LONG PR3 ....**1**
  KIRK/FR/WA PR4 ....**2**
  KIRK/FR/WA PR4 ....**2**
  SKEL WN8 ....**3?**
  WGNW/BIL/O WN5 ....**3?**
Greenthorn Crs FUL/RIB PR2 ....**2?**
Greenthorne CI EDGW/EG BL7 ....**3**
Greenvale WGNNW/ST WN6 ....**3?**
Green Wk BWCK/EAR BB18 ....**1?**
  STHP PR8 ....**3?**
Green Wy BPOOLS FY4 ....**2?**
Greenway CHLY/EC PR7 ....**3?**
  FUL/RIB PR2 ....**2**
  GAR/LONG PR3 ....**1?**
  HOR/BR BL6 ....**3?**
  PRES PR1 ....**2?**
Greenway Av SKEL WN8 ....**3?**
Greenway CI SKEL WN8 ....**3?**
Greenways KIRK/FR/WA PR4 ....**2?**
  KKBYL LA6 ....**3**
  LSTA FY8 ....**2?**
  WGNW/BIL/O WN5 ....**3?**
Greenway St DWN BB3 ....**2?**
Greenwich Dr LSTA FY8 ....**2?**
Greenwood LEY/BBR PR5 ....**2?**
Greenwood Av BPOOL FY1 ....**2**
  CARN LA5 ....
Greenwood CI LSTA FY8 ....**2?**
  ORM L39 ....**3?**
Greenwood Crs CARN LA5 ....
Greenwood Dr CARN LA5 ....
Greenwood St LEY/BBR PR5 ....**2?**
  PRES PR1 ....**2?**
Greenwood V BOL BL1 ....**3?**
Greenwood V South BOL * BL1 ....**3?**
Greetby HI ORM L39 ....**3?**
Greetby PI SKEL WN8 ....**3?**
Gregareth CI LANC LA1 ....
Gregory Av BISP FY2 ....**1?**
Gregory Fold RAW/HAS BB4 ....**2?**
Gregory La ORM L39 ....**3?**
Gregory Meadow GAR/LONG PR3 ....**1?**
Gregory PI LSTA FY8 ....**2?**
Gregory's Ct LANC LA1 ....
Gregson CI BPOOLS FY4 ....**2?**
Gregson Dr FTWD FY7 ....**1?**
Gregson La BBNW BB2 ....
  LEY/BBR PR5 ....**2?**
Gregson Rd LANC LA1 ....
Gregson's Av FMBY L37 ....**3?**
Gregson St DWN * BB3 ....**2?**
  LSTA FY8 ....**2?**
Gregson Wy FUL/RIB PR2 ....**2?**
Grenfell Av BPOOLE FY3 ....**1?**
Grenville Av LEY/BBR PR5 ....**2?**
  LSTA FY8 ....**2?**
Gresham Rd CLV/TH FY5 ....**1?**
Gresham St BOL BL1 ....**3?**
  RAW/HAS BB4 ....**2?**
Gresley Av HOR/BR BL6 ....**3?**
Gresley Ct LANC LA1 ....
Gresley PI BISP FY2 ....**1?**
Gressingham Dr LANC LA1 ....
Greta PI FTWD FY7 ....**1?**
  LANC LA1 ....
Gretdale Av LSTA FY8 ....**2?**
Gretna Crs CLV/TH FY5 ....**1?**
Gretna Rd BBN BB1 ....**2?**
Gretna Wk BBN BB1 ....**2?**
Greyfriars Av FUL/RIB PR2 ....**2?**
Greyfriars Crs FUL/RIB PR2 ....**2?**
Greyfriars Dr PRES PR1 ....**2?**
Greyfriars Rd STHP PR8 ....**2?**
Grey Heights Vw CHLYE PR6 ....**3?**
Greyhound Bridge Rd LANC LA1 ....
Greystock Av FUL/RIB PR2 ....**2?**
Greystock CI LEY/BBR PR5 ....**2?**

stoke Av *BBNW* BB2 ....267 F3
stoke Dr *BOL* BL1 ....341 H5
stoke Pl *BPOOLS* FY4 ....204 B6
stokes *ORM* L39 ....360 H1
stones Dr *PDHM/BLYW* BB12 ......197 F3
t St *BRFD/BLYE* BB10 ....11 D1
SN BB9 ....198 B1
thwaite Ct *LANC* LA1 ....2 B5
rson St *BOL* BL1 ....341 J8
in Cl *ACC* BB5 ....249 F2
Y BB11 ....224 D6
in St *BBNW* BB2 ....244 D8
iths Dr *CHTN/BK* PR9 ....302 B3
eford La *CHLYE* PR6 ....337 K5
R/BR BL6 ....337 J6
eshaw La *HGHB* LA2 ....55 K1
ne St *CHLY/EC* PR7 ....311 H5
WN BB3 ....291 H1
AMS BL0 ....319 G7
adlestone Hirst *COL* BB8 ....171 G8
adleton Brow *CLI* BB7 ....140 B4
adleton Cl *BPOOLE* FY3 ....177 H3
adleton Gv *BRFD/BLYE* BB10 .....226 B7
adleton Rd *BBNW* BB2 ....8 A5
LI BB7 ....139 K5
agley Rd *MCMB* LA4 ....41 J8
astead Cl *STHP* PR8 ....326 E2
edale Cl *BBN* BB1 ....269 F1
edale Cl *FMBY* L37 ....343 J8
edale Pl *CHLY/EC* PR7 ....311 F6
edale Rd *GAR/LONG* PR3 ....129 H4
LF/KEOS FY6 ....149 J8
edale Br *HGHB* LA2 ....70 D8
edale Cl *ACC* BB5 ....247 J1
UL/RIB PR2 ....240 D1
edale Ct
LV/TH (off Patterdale Av) *PR6* ...123 H8
edale Crs *FUL/RIB* PR2 ....240 E1
edale Pl *FUL/RIB* PR2 ....240 E1
EY LA3 ....52 E3
edale Rd *BPOOLS* FY4 ....205 J2
ANC LA1 ....3 E1
svenor Ct *CARN* LA5 ....300 E8
svenor Cl *CARN* LA5 ....33 J2
svenor Gdns *STHP* PR8 ....301 F8
svenor Pl *CARN* LA5 ....33 J2
UL/RIB PR2 ....238 D1
THP PR8 ....301 F8
svenor Rd *CARN* LA5 ....33 K2
HLY/EC PR7 ....310 E5
EY LA3 ....40 D8
THP PR8 ....300 E7
svenor St *BPOOL* FY1 ....4 C1
OL BB8 ....171 K6
STA FY8 ....232 E8
PDHM/BLYW BB12 ....10 C2
PRES PR1 ....7 F3
ove Av *CHLYE* PR6 ....337 G4
KIRK/FR/WA PR4 ....260 A3
ove Ct *ACC* BB5 ....247 G8
ove Crs *CHLYE* PR6 ....337 G4
ove La *PDHM/BLYW* BB12 ....224 A2
ove Pk *CHTN/BK* PR9 ....302 A6
ORM L39 ....348 D4
ove Rd *LEY/BBR* PR5 ....240 A5
SKEL WN8 ....364 D3
St *ACC* BB5 ....247 G8
ACC BB5 ....248 A5
ove St *BBNW* BB2 ....268 B1
BCUP OL13 ....275 K8
BLY BB11 ....10 A4
BWCK/EAR BB18 ....146 B1
LEY/BBR PR5 ....263 J3
LEY/BBR PR5 ....285 F3
LSTA FY8 ....231 F4
MCMB LA4 ....41 F7
NLSN BB9 ....170 B8
NLSN BB9 ....198 C3
STHP PR8 ....301 C6
ove Ter *STHP* PR8 ....301 C6
e Grove *CARN* LA5 ....33 H2
CHLYE PR6 ....311 G1
CLI BB7 ....165 K2

CLI BB7 ....193 G6
CLV/TH FY5 ....122 E8
ORM L39 ....360 A4
PDHM/BLYW* BB12 ....224 D5
PRES PR1 ....238 D7
WGNNW/ST WN6 ....352 E1
Grovewood *STHP* PR8 ....300 E7
Grovewood Dr *WGNNW/ST* WN6 ..353 C4
Grundy Cl *STHP* PR8 ....302 A6
Grundy Ms *BPOOLS* FY4 ....204 C4
Grundy's La *CHLY/EC* PR7 ....336 C2
Grundy St *LEY/BBR* PR5 ....285 J1
Gubberford La *GAR/LONG* PR3 ...103 J8
Guide La *PDHM/BLYW* BB12 ....196 C4
Guide Rd *KIRK/FR/WA* PR4 ....258 B3
Guide Sq *BBN* BB1 ....268 E3
Guildford Av *BISP* FY2 ....148 C5
CHLYE PR6 ....287 K7
Guildford Rd *PRES* PR1 ....7 E4
STHP PR8 ....326 C3
Guildford Wy *PLF/KEOS* FY6 ....149 J8
Guild Hall Ar
PRES (off Lancaster Rd) PR1 ....7 E3
Guildhall St *PRES* PR1 ....7 D3
Guild Rw *PRES* PR1 ....7 E3
Guild Wy *PRES* PR1 ....6 B3
Guilford St *NLSN* BB9 ....197 K6
Guinea Hall La *CHTN/BK* PR9 ......279 J6
Gulf La *GAR/LONG* PR3 ....101 F4
HGHB LA2 ....102 A2
Gummers Howe Wk *CARN* LA5 ....34 A3
Gurney St *BBNW* BB2 ....244 D8
Gutter La *RAMS* BL0 ....319 H4
Guy St *PDHM/BLYW* BB12 ....223 J2
Guysyke *COL* BB8 ....171 G7
Gynn Av *BPOOL* FY1 ....176 B3

H

Habergham Dr
PDHM/BLYW BB12 ....224 B3
Habergham St *PDHM/BLYW* BB12 ..223 J2
Hackensall Rd *PLF/KEOS* FY6 ....98 A7
Hacking Cl *GTH/LHO* BB6 ....220 B1
Hacking Dr *GAR/LONG* PR3 ....187 F2
Hacking St *DWN* BB3 ....291 H2
NLSN BB9 ....198 D1
Hacklands Av *FUL/RIB* PR2 ....237 H2
Haddings La *PDHM/BLYW* BB12 ...196 C2
Haddon Pl *FUL/RIB* PR2 ....213 F8
Haddon Rd *BISP* FY2 ....148 C6
Hadlee Ter *LANC* LA1 ....2 B2
Hadleigh Rd *PLF/KEOS* FY6 ....149 J5
Hadrian St *HEY* LA3 ....42 A8
Hadstock Av *FMBY* L37 ....355 H2
Hagg La *GAR/LONG* PR3 ....153 G3
Hagg St *COL* BB8 ....171 G7
Haig Av *FUL/RIB* * PR2 ....239 F1
KIRK/FR/WA PR4 ....282 A4
LANC LA1 ....2 B3
LEY/BBR PR5 ....285 H2
STHP PR8 ....302 A6
Haigh Cl *CHLY/EC* PR7 ....310 E4
Haigh Crs *CHLY/EC* PR7 ....310 E4
MGHL L31 ....358 E2
Haigh Hall Rd *RAMS* BL0 ....319 H7
Haighton Ct *FUL/RIB* PR2 ....213 J4
Haighton Dr *FUL/RIB* PR2 ....214 C5
Haighton Green La *FUL/RIB* PR2 ..214 C1
Haig Rd *BPOOL* FY1 ....4 B6
Hail St *RAMS* * BL0 ....319 H7
Hala Crs *LANC* LA1 ....55 G8
Hala Gv *LANC* LA1 ....55 G8
Hala Hl *LANC* LA1 ....55 H8
Hala Rd *LANC* LA1 ....55 G8
Hala Sq *LANC* LA1 ....55 G8
Haldane Rd *BRFD/BLYE* * BB10 ...225 K1
Halden Rd *HEY* LA3 ....40 E8
Hale Carr Gv *HEY* LA3 ....52 E2
Hale Carr La *HEY* LA3 ....52 E2
Hales Rushes Rd *GAR/LONG* PR3 ..126 A7
Hale St *BLY* BB11 ....11 D5
Half Acre *LEY/BBR* PR5 ....262 D6
Halford Pl *CLV/TH* FY5 ....148 E4
Halfpenny La *CHLY/EC* PR7 ....308 D8
GAR/LONG PR3 ....187 K4
Halifax Rd *BRFD/BLYE* BB10 ....228 B3
NLSN BB9 ....198 A6
STHP PR8 ....325 J6
Halifax St *BPOOLE* FY3 ....5 F4
Hallam Crs *NLSN* BB9 ....198 E3
Hallam La *HEY* LA3 ....64 E1
Hallam Rd *NLSN* BB9 ....198 D2
Hallam St *ACC* BB5 ....248 A2
Hall Av *BPOOLS* FY4 ....4 C6

Hallbridge Gdns *SKEL* WN8 ....364 D3
Hall Brow Cl *BRSC* L40 ....349 F7
Hall Carr La *KIRK/FR/WA* PR4 .....259 H4
Hall Carr Rd *RAW/HAS* BB4 ....296 B2
Hall Cl *HEY* LA3 ....65 H3
HGHB LA2 ....45 F5
RAW/HAS BB4 ....273 H5
Hall Coppice *EDGW/EG* BL7 ....353 K5
The Hall Coppice *EDGW/EG* BL7 ..341 H2
Hall Cft *KIRK/FR/WA* PR4 ....260 E1
Hallcroft *SKEL* WN8 ....363 J1
Hall Dr *HEY* LA3 ....64 E1
HGHB LA2 ....45 F5
MCMB LA4 ....42 A7
Halley Rd *DWN* BB3 ....268 B8
Hallfield Rd *GTH/LHO* BB6 ....221 H5
Hall Fold *WHIT* OL12 ....323 G3
Hall Garth Gdns *KKBYL* LA6 ....34 E2
Hall Ga *CHLY/EC* PR7 ....310 E2
Halgate HI *CLI* BB7 ....112 A3
Hall Gate La *PLF/KEOS* FY6 ....124 E3
Hall Gn *SKEL* WN8 ....364 D4
Hall Green Cl *SKEL* WN8 ....364 D4
Hall Green La *CHLY/EC* PR7 ....308 C8
Hall Gv *HEY* LA3 ....64 E1
Hall HI *CLI* BB7 ....136 C1
Halliwell La *CHLYE* PR6 ....287 G7
Halliwell Pl *CHLY/EC* * PR7 ....311 G4
Halliwell Rd *BOL* BL1 ....341 G8
Halliwell St *ACC* BB5 ....271 K1
CHLY/EC PR7 ....311 G4
Hall La *BRSC* L40 ....307 K8
BRSC L40 ....332 C4
BRSC L40 ....350 A4
GAR/LONG PR3 ....153 F6
GAR/LONG PR3 ....154 E5
HOR/BR BL6 ....338 C1
HTWN L38 ....357 F7
KIRK/FR/WA PR4 ....259 J4
LEY/BBR PR5 ....285 H1
MGHL L31 ....358 E4
NWD/KWIPK L33 ....366 D5
ORM L39 ....361 J7
WGNNW/ST WN6 ....352 E1
WCNW/BIL/O WN5 ....365 H7
Hall Mdw *COL* BB8 ....172 B8
Hallmoor Cl *ORM* L39 ....360 B1
Hall Nook *ORM* L39 ....196 B6
Hall Pk *LANC* LA1 ....55 H7
Hall Park Av *BRFD/BLYE* BB10 ....226 D7
Hall Park Dr *LSTA* FY8 ....231 K5
Hall Rd *BRSC* L40 ....328 E4
COL BB8 ....172 B8
FUL/RIB PR2 ....213 G6
PRES PR1 ....239 G8
Hallsall Dr *MCMB* LA4 ....42 B5
Halls Sq
CHLYE (off Town La) PR6 ....287 J5
Hall St *BBNW* BB2 ....268 B1
BCUP OL13 ....275 J8
BLY BB11 ....11 D3
BRFD/BLYE BB10 ....226 E6
CHTN/BK PR9 ....301 J4
CLI BB7 ....165 J4
COL BB8 ....171 H7
FUL/RIB PR2 ....6 A1
MCMB LA4 ....41 H6
RAW/HAS BB4 ....273 H8
WHIT OL12 ....323 F3
Hallwell St *BRFD/BLYE* BB10 ....11 D1
Hallwood Cl *BRFD/BLYE* BB10 ....197 K7
Hallwood Rd *CHLY/EC* PR7 ....310 E6
Halmote Av *PDHM/BLYW* BB12 ...196 B6
Halsall Buildings *CHTN/BK* PR9 ..301 J3
Halsall Hall Dr *ORM* L39 ....346 D2
Halsall La *FMBY* L37 ....343 K7
ORM L39 ....347 F5
ORM L39 ....348 B5
Halsall Manor Ct *ORM* L39 ....346 D2
Halsall Rd *ORM* L39 ....346 E1
STHP PR8 ....326 C3
Halsbury St *PRES* PR1 ....7 E4
Halstead Cl *NLSN* BB9 ....170 B7
Halstead La *NLSN* BB9 ....170 B7
Halstead Rd *FUL/RIB* PR2 ....214 B6
Halstead St *BLY* * BB11 ....10 C4
BRFD/BLYE BB10 ....226 E5
Halton Av *CLV/TH* FY5 ....122 E7
LEY/BBR PR5 ....286 E1
Halton Cha *BRSC* L40 ....349 J7
Halton Ct *MCMB* LA4 ....41 H8
Halton Gdns *BPOOLS* FY4 ....205 F3
Halton Pl *FUL/RIB* PR2 ....214 D7
GAR/LONG PR3 ....188 B3
Halton Rd *KKBYL* LA6 ....34 A7
LANC LA1 ....43 G8
MGHL L31 ....359 F8

Halton St *KIRK/FR/WA* PR4 ....179 G5
Hambleton Dr *PRES* PR1 ....262 B1
Hambleton St *PDHM/BLYW* BB12 ....223 K3
Hambleton Vw
   PDHM/BLYW BB12 ....222 D2
Hambleton Cl *KIRK/FR/WA* PR4 ......260 A2
Hameldon Ap *BLY* BB11 ....10 A4
Hameldon Av *ACC* BB5 ....271 K1
Hameldon Cl *BLY* BB11 ....223 J8
Hameldon Rd *BLY* BB11 ....249 J1
   RAW/HAS BB4 ....273 H1
Hameldon Vw *GTH/LHO* BB6 ....221 H6
Hamer Av *BBN* BB1 ....246 B6
   RAW/HAS BB4 ....273 H2
Hamer Rd *FUL/RIB* PR2 ....213 F8
Hamer St *DWN* BB3 ....291 J3
   RAW/HAS BB4 ....296 C1
Hamerswood Dr *GAR/LONG* PR3 ....155 K1
Hamilton Cl *LSTA* FY8 ....233 F1
Hamilton Ct *LSTA* FY8 ....233 F7
Hamilton Dr *LANC* LA1 ....42 C8
Hamilton Gv *FUL/RIB* PR2 ....214 C7
Hamilton Rd *CHLY/EC* PR7 ....311 F4
   COL BB8 ....198 E1
   FUL/RIB PR2 ....214 B8
   MCMB LA4 ....42 C5
   NLSN BB9 ....198 A2
Hamilton St *BBNW* BB2 ....8 B6
   BOL BL1 ....341 J7
Hamlet Cl *BBNW* BB2 ....8 A6
Hamlet Rd *FTWD* FY7 ....96 E7
The Hamlet *CHLY/EC* * PR7 ....337 F2
   LSTA FY8 ....231 F1
Hammerton Gn *BCUP* OL13 ....275 K8
Hammerton Hall La *LANC* LA1 ....42 D7
Hammerton Pl *BPOOLE* FY3 ....177 G3
Hammerton St *BCUP* OL13 ....275 J7
   BLY BB11 ....10 C4
Hammond Av *BCUP* OL13 ....298 B3
Hammond Ct *PRES* PR1 ....6 C1
Hammond Dr *PDHM/BLYW* BB12 ....222 B1
Hammond Rd *NWD/KWIPK* L33 ......367 G8
Hammond's Rw *PRES* * PR1 ....7 E3
   *PRES** PR1 ....239 C1
Hampden Av *DWN* BB3 ....291 K4
Hampden Rd *LEY/BBR* PR5 ....285 J1
Hampden St *BLY* BB11 ....11 E5
Hampsfell Dr *MCMB* LA4 ....41 H8
Hampshire Av *BBN* BB1 ....219 J4
Hampshire Pl *BPOOLS* FY4 ....205 F5
Hampshire Rd *BBN* BB1 ....246 B2
   LEY/BBR PR5 ....240 B8
Hampson Av *LEY/BBR* PR5 ....286 B2
Hampson Gv *PLF/KEOS* FY6 ....98 C7
Hampson La *HGHB* LA2 ....80 C7
Hampson St *HOR/BR* BL6 ....338 D7
Hampstead Cl *LSTA* FY8 ....232 A5
Hampstead Ms *BPOOL* * FY1 ....176 C4
Hampstead Rd *FUL/RIB* PR2 ....240 B1
Hampton Cl *CHLY/EC* PR7 ....311 F3
Hampton Ct *LSTA* FY8 ....231 J3
Hampton Pl *CLV/TH* FY5 ....122 E8
Hampton Rd *BPOOLS* FY4 ....204 B3
   FMBY L37 ....355 J2
   HEY LA3 ....40 E8
   STHP PR8 ....301 H7
Hampton St *FUL/RIB* PR2 ....238 E1
Hanbury St *FUL/RIB* * PR2 ....6 A1
Hancock St *BBNW* BB2 ....8 A6
The Handbridge *FUL/RIB* PR2 ....213 G6
Handel St *BOL* BL1 ....341 H6
Hand La *CHLY/EC* PR7 ....308 B6
Handley Rd *BPOOL* FY1 ....4 C1
Handsworth Ct *BPOOL* FY1 ....176 C4
Handsworth Rd *BPOOL* FY1 ....176 C4
Hanging Green La *HGHB* LA2 ....42 E2
Hangington Clough Br *HGHB* LA2 ....84 B2
Hanley Cl *PLF/KEOS* FY6 ....124 C4
Hannah St *ACC* BB5 ....248 B6
   BCUP OL13 ....275 K8
   DWN BB3 ....291 J2
Hanover Crs *BISP* FY2 ....148 C5
Hanover St *COL* BB8 ....171 H5
   MCMB LA4 ....41 H6
   PRES PR1 ....7 D1
Hanson St *BBN* * BB1 ....247 G2
   GTH/LHO BB6 ....221 G7
Hanstock *WGNW/BIL/O* WN5 ....365 G6
Hants La *ORM* L39 ....348 G5
Happy Mount Ct *MCMB* LA4 ....42 B4
Happy Mount Dr *MCMB* LA4 ....42 A4
Hapton Rd *PDHM/BLYW* BB12 ....223 J4
Hapton St *CLV/TH* FY5 ....123 H7
   PDHM/BLYW BB12 ....223 K3
Hapton Wy *RAW/HAS* BB4 ....273 H1
Harbour Av *KIRK/FR/WA* PR4 ....234 C5

Harbour Cl *FTWD* FY7 ....123 F1
Harbour La *CHLYE* PR6 ....288 D4
   EDGW/EG BL7 ....317 H6
   KIRK/FR/WA PR4 ....234 C4
Harbour Wy *FTWD* FY7 ....97 H8
Harbury Av *STHP* PR8 ....325 G7
Harcourt Rd *ACC* BB5 ....248 D8
   BBNW BB2 ....8 A3
   BPOOLS FY4 ....204 D3
   LANC LA1 ....42 E8
Harcourt St *BCUP* OL13 ....275 J8
   BLY BB11 ....10 A4
   PRES PR1 ....6 C1
Hardacre La *CHLYE* PR6 ....287 F6
   CLI BB7 ....117 F8
Hardacre St *ORM* L39 ....348 D5
Hardcastle Rd *FUL/RIB* PR2 ....213 G8
Hardhorn Rd *PLF/KEOS* FY6 ....149 K8
Hardhorn Wy *PLF/KEOS* FY6 ....177 K1
Harding Rd *BRSC* L40 ....330 D7
Harding St *CHLYE* PR6 ....337 H3
Hard Knott Ri *CARN* * LA5 ....34 A3
Hardlands Av *MCMB* LA4 ....42 B7
Hardman Av *RAW/HAS* BB4 ....296 C2
Hardman Cl *BBN* BB1 ....246 C7
   RAW/HAS BB4 ....297 H4
Hardman Dr *RAW/HAS* BB4 ....297 H4
Hardmans La *EDGW/EG* BL7 ....341 K3
Hardman's La *EDGW/EG* BL7 ....341 K3
Hardman St *BBNW* BB2 ....8 A6
   BPOOL FY1 ....4 C1
Hardman Wy *DWN* BB3 ....291 J2
Hardsough La *RAMS* BL0 ....295 J6
Hardwicke St *PRES* PR1 ....7 E2
Hardy Av *NLSN* BB9 ....197 K5
Hardy Cl *NLSN* * BB9 ....198 C3
Hardy Dr *CHLY/EC* PR7 ....310 E4
Hardy St *BBN* BB1 ....245 H2
   NLSN BB9 ....197 K5
Harebell Cl *BBNW* BB2 ....266 E3
   FMBY L37 ....355 K2
   WHIT L37 ....323 H8
Hare Clough Cl *BBNW* BB2 ....9 D6
Hareden Brook Cl *BBN* BB1 ....9 D6
Hareden Cl *LEY/BBR* PR5 ....263 J3
Hareden Rd *FUL/RIB* PR2 ....240 D7
Harefield Ri *PDHM/BLYW* BB12 ....10 A1
Hareholme La *RAW/HAS* BB4 ....297 F2
Hares La *STHP* PR8 ....328 B2
Harestone Av *CHLY/EC* PR7 ....310 E6
Harewood Av *BPOOLE* FY3 ....177 G2
   HEY LA3 ....52 E1
   LANC LA1 ....55 G8
   PDHM/BLYW BB12 ....222 E1
   STHP PR8 ....325 J5
Harewood Cl *PLF/KEOS* FY6 ....149 J6
Harewood Rd *PRES* PR1 ....239 K1
Hargate Rd *CLV/TH* FY5 ....149 J1
Hargher St *BLY* BB11 ....10 A4
Hargreaves Av *LEY/BBR* PR5 ....285 K3
Hargreaves Ct *CLI* BB7 ....165 G4
   FUL/RIB PR2 ....212 B7
   RAW/HAS BB4 ....274 C5
Hargreaves Dr *RAW/HAS* BB4 ....296 B1
Hargreaves Fold La
   RAW/HAS BB4 ....274 C4
Hargreaves La *BBNW* BB2 ....8 C6
Hargreaves Rd *ACC* BB5 ....247 F7
Hargreaves St *ACC* BB5 ....248 C6
   BLY BB11 ....10 C3
   BRFD/BLYE BB10 ....198 D8
   CLV/TH FY5 ....123 H8
   COL BB8 ....171 F7
   DWN BB3 ....292 D2
   NLSN BB9 ....198 A3
   RAW/HAS BB4 ....272 C8
   RAW/HAS BB4 ....274 B6
   STHP PR8 ....301 J5
Hargrove Av *PDHM/BLYW* BB12 ......10 A1
   PDHM/BLYW BB12 ....223 J2
Harington Cl *FMBY* L37 ....343 H8
Harington Gn *FMBY* L37 ....343 H8
Harington Rd *FMBY* L37 ....343 G7
Harland St *FUL/RIB* PR2 ....213 F8
Harlech Av *BPOOL* FY1 ....5 D6
Harlech Cl *RAW/HAS* BB4 ....295 H2
Harlech Dr *ACC* BB5 ....247 G7
   LEY/BBR PR5 ....285 K2
Harleston Rd *NWD/KWIPK* L33 ......366 E8
Harley Rd *BPOOLE* FY3 ....5 E3
Harley St *PDHM/BLYW* BB12 ....224 E5
Harley Wd *TOD* OL14 ....277 K3
Harling Bank *KKBYL* LA6 ....21 C5
Harling Rd *PRES* PR1 ....240 B2
Harling St *PDHM/BLYW* BB12 ....224 D5
Harold Av *BLY* BB11 ....224 E7
   BPOOLS FY4 ....205 G5

Harold St *BLY* BB11 1
   COL * BB8 17
Harold Ter *LEY/BBR* PR5 26
Harperley *CHLY/EC* PR7 31
Harper's La *CHLY/EC* PR7 31
   PDHM/BLYW BB12 19
Harper St *BWCK/EAR* BB18 14
Harridge Av *WHIT* OL12 32
Harridge La *BRSC* L40 34
Harridge St *WHIT* OL12 32
The Harridge *WHIT* OL12 32
Harrier Dr *BBN* BB1 1
Harriet St *BLY* BB11 1
Harrington Av *BPOOLS* FY4 20
Harrington Rd *CHLY/EC* PR7 3
   HEY LA3 2
Harrington St *ACC* BB5 24
Harris Av *BPOOL* FY1 ....
Harris Ct *CLI* * BB7 16
Harrison Av *CLV/TH* FY5 14
   HOR/BR BL6 33
Harrison Dr *COL* BB8 17
   RNFD/HAY WA11 3
Harrison La *KIRK/FR/WA* PR4 26
Harrison Rd *CHLY/EC* PR7 3
   CHLY/EC PR7 33
   FUL/RIB PR2 2
Harrison St *BBNW* BB2 29
   BCUP OL13 29
   BPOOL FY1 ....
   BRFD/BLYE BB10 22
   BWCK/EAR BB18 14
   HOR/BR BL6 33
   RAMS BL0 31
   TOD * OL14 27
Harris Rd *WGNNW/ST* WN6 35
Harris St *FTWD* FY7 ....
   PRES PR1 ....
Harrock La *BRSC* L40 33
   WGNNW/ST WN6 33
Harrock Rd *LEY/BBR* PR5 28
Harrock Vw
   CHLY/EC (off Barmskin La) PR7 33
Harrod Dr *STHP* PR8 30
Harrogate Crs *BRFD/BLYE* BB10 22
Harrogate Rd *LSTA* FY8 23
Harrogate Wy *CHTN/BK* PR9 27
Harrop Pl *FUL/RIB* PR2 21
Harrow Av *ACC* BB5 24
   FTWD FY7 ....
Harrow Cl *PDHM/BLYW* BB12 22
   WGNW/BIL/O WN5 36
Harrowdale Pk *HGHB* LA2 0
Harrow Dr *BBN* BB1 ....
Harrow Gv *MCMB* LA4 4
Harrow Pl *BPOOLS* FY4 20
   LSTA FY8 20
Harrowside *BPOOLS* FY4 20
Harrowside West *BPOOLS* FY4 20
Harrow Stiles La *BCUP* OL13 27
Harrow St *ACC* BB5 24
Harry Potts Wy *BRFD/BLYE* BB10 1
Harry St *NLSN* BB9 1
Harsnips *SKEL* WN8 36
Hartford Av *BPOOL* FY1 ....
Hartington Rd *CHLYE* PR6 28
   DWN * BB3 26
   PRES PR1 ....
Hartington St *BBN* * BB1 24
   LANC LA1 ....
   *NLSN** BB9 19
Hartland Av *CHTN/BK* PR9 27
Hartlands Cl *BRFD/BLYE* BB10 19
Hartlet St *GTH/LHO* * BB6 22
Hartley Av *ACC* BB5 24
Hartley Crs *STHP* PR8 32
Hartley Gv *WGNW/BIL/O* WN5 36
Hartley Rd *STHP* PR8 32
Hartleys Ter *COL* BB8 1
Hartley St *ACC* BB5 24
   BLY * BB11 24
   BWCK/EAR BB18 1
   COL BB8 1
   NLSN BB9 1
   WGNW/BIL/O WN5 1
Hartmann St *ACC* BB5 24
Hartshead *SKEL* WN8 36
Hart's La *SKEL* WN8 36
Hart St *BBN* BB1 ....
   BLY BB11 1
   STHP PR8 30
Hart Street Br *CHTN/BK* PR9 30
Hartwood Gn *CHLYE* PR6 28
Hartwood Rd *CHTN/BK* PR9 30
Harvest Dr *CHLYE* PR6 28
Harvey St *ACC* BB5 24

...L BL1....................................341 H8
...SN BB9..................................198 C2
...ington Dr STHP PR8..................325 C6
...rich Rd LSTA FY8.....................231 F2
...vin Cl WHIT OL12.....................323 H8
...wood Av LSTA FY8....................230 E3
...wood Cl PLF/KEOS FY6..............124 C4
...wood Ga BBN BB1..........................9 E3
...wood La GTH/LHO BB6...............221 J5
...wood New Rd GTH/LHO BB6......221 J5
...wood Rd BBN BB1.......................220 B7
...RN BB1.......................................246 E1
...wood's La DWN BB3....................292 B3
...sett Cl STBN BB9............................9 E2
...VN BB3.......................................291 G1
...am Ct BRFD/BLYE BB10.............225 J2
...emere Av BPOOLE FY3.....................5 E4
...ingden Old Rd BBN BB1.............246 C8
...W/HAS BB4................................296 A1
...ingden Rd BBN BB1....................269 F2
...BW/HAS BB4..............................268 D1
...NW/HAS BB4...............................295 K2
...ow Pl BPOOLE FY3....................177 F4
...sall Dr KIRK/FR/WA PR4............180 E2
...tings Av BISP FY2......................148 E6
...RK/FR/WA PR4..........................234 C4
...tings Cl BBN BB1......................246 A7
...tings Pl LSTA FY8......................149 J2
...V/TH FY5....................................149 J3
...field Av FTWD FY7....................122 C1
...CMB LA4......................................42 B5
...field Cl CLV/TH FY5..................149 J1
...field Gdns FTWD FY7................122 C1
...field Ms FTWD FY7......................97 F8
...field Rd ACC BB5.......................248 C3
...UL/RIB PR2.................................214 C8
...THP PR8......................................325 J5
...field Wk FTWD FY7...................122 C1
...haway BPOOLE FY4....................204 E3
haway Fold
...OT/BURYW * BL8.......................319 G8
...ANC LA1..3 D6
...EY/BBR PR5................................285 K1
...THP PR8......................................326 A2
...ton Lee Av BBN BB1..................219 H8
...ty Brow Rd HGHB LA2..................42 D5
...field Av FTWD FY7....................122 C1
...CMB LA4......................................42 E8
...field Cl CLV/TH FY5..................149 J1
...field Gdns FTWD FY7................122 C1
...field Ms FTWD FY7......................97 F8
...field Rd ACC BB5.......................248 C3
...UL/RIB PR2.................................214 C8
...THP PR8......................................325 J5
...field Wk FTWD FY7...................122 C1
...haway BPOOLE FY4....................204 E3
...DHM/BLYW BB12........................223 K4
...haway Rd FTWD FY7.....................96 E7
...ANC LA1.......................................42 E8
...velock Cl BBNW BB2.......................8 B6
...velock Rd LEY/BBR PR5..............263 H4
...PRES PR1..6 C5
...'elock St ACC BB5.......................247 H8
...'BNW BB2....................................267 K1
...POOL FY1...4 B3
...ANC LA1..3 E5
...'DHM/BLYW BB12........................223 J2
...'DHM/BLYW BB12........................224 D5
...PRES PR1.....................................239 G1
...enbrook Gv
...OT/BURYW * BL8........................319 G8
...wen Brow ORM L39.....................360 A3
...wen Rd LSTA FY8........................232 D8
...wen St BRFD/BLYE BB10.............11 F4
...verbreaks Pl LANC LA1...................2 C5
...verbreaks Rd LANC LA1...................2 C6
...verholt Cl COL BB8....................171 G4
...verthwaite Av HEY LA3.................52 D4
...rre Pk BWCK/EAR BB18..............145 H6
...warden Av MCMB LA4..................41 J6
...warden Rd PRES PR1...................240 C2
...warden St BOL BL1.....................341 J7
...LSN BB9.......................................198 C4
...wes Dr COL BB8.........................171 K5
...wes Side La BPOOLE FY4................5 E6
...wesside St CHTN/BK PR9............301 J4
...wes Ter BRFD/BLYE BB10...........225 K1
...weswater Av CHLY/EC PR7.........311 F5
...weswater Cl NWD/KWIPK L33....366 B6
...weswater Pl MCMB LA4................42 A7
...weswater Rd ACC BB5.................248 D2
...wick Cl NWD/KWIPK L33............366 B5
...wkhurst Av FUL/RIB PR2.............213 F5
...wkhurst Crs FUL/RIB PR2............213 F5
...wkhurst Rd PRES PR1......................6 C6

PRES PR1......................................239 K1
Hawking Pl BISP FY2....................149 F6
Hawkins Cl PRES PR1.........................6 C1
Hawkins St BBNW BB2...................267 J1
PRES PR1..6 C1
Hawksbury Dr PRES PR1...............262 A1
Hawksclough SKEL WN8................363 J1
Hawks Gv RAW/HAS BB4...............296 C2
Hawkshaw Av DWN BB3................268 B8
Hawkshaw Bank Rd BBN BB1............8 B1
Hawkshaw La TOT/BURYW BL8....318 B5
Hawkshead PRES PR1....................239 G8
Hawkshead Av CHLY/EC PR7........310 B2
Hawkshead Dr MCMB LA4...............41 J8
Hawkshead Rd FUL/RIB PR2.........214 C6
PLF/KEOS FY6................................98 B5
Hawkshead St BBNW BB2.............244 D7
CHTN/BK PR9................................301 J3
Hawkshead Ter BPOOLS FY4.........205 K3
Hawksheath Cl EDGW/EG BL7......341 J2
Hawkstone Cl ACC BB5..................249 F2
CLV/TH FY5...................................149 K3
Hawk St BLY BB11...........................11 D3
Hawkswood CHLY/EC PR7.............308 D5
Hawkswood Gdns NLSN BB9.........197 J7
Hawksworth Av HEY * LA3..............52 D1
Hawksworth Cl FMBY L37.............344 A5
Hawksworth Dr FMBY L37.............344 A5
Hawksworth Gv HEY LA3................52 D2
Hawksworth Rd ACC BB5..............248 B5
Hawley St COL BB8.......................171 H5
COL BB8..172 C6
Haworth Av ACC * BB5..................248 D8
RAW/HAS BB4...............................296 B1
Haworth Dr BCUP OL13................298 B1
Haworth St ACC BB5.....................247 J7
ACC* BB5.......................................248 B2
BBN BB1..246 E2
EDGW/EG BL7..............................317 H6
Haworth to Hebden Bridge Wk
HBR HX7.......................................203 G8
Haws Av CARN LA5...........................33 K2
Hawshaw Rd HWTH BD22.............147 K6
Haws Hi CARN LA5...........................33 K2
Hawthorn Av ACC BB5...................247 J7
DWN BB3......................................292 A1
FTWD FY7......................................122 E3
HGHB LA2.......................................45 H6
WGNW/BIL/O WN5......................365 H5
Hawthorn Bank
ACC (off Burnley Rd) BB5............222 A3
Hawthorn Cl GTH/LHO BB6..........220 B3
HGHB LA2.......................................45 H6
KIRK/FR/WA PR4..........................208 C5
KIRK/FR/WA PR4..........................261 H4
LEY/BBR* PR5..............................285 G2
WGNW/BIL/O WN5......................371 F6
Hawthorn Crs FUL/RIB PR2...........237 K2
SKEL WN8.....................................362 E2
Hawthorn Dr BWCK/EAR BB18.....118 E6
GAR/LONG PR3.............................129 G4
KIRK/FR/WA PR4..........................209 K8
LEY/BBR PR5.................................241 G8
Hawthorn Gv CHLY/EC PR6...........264 A8
NLSN BB9......................................197 K2
NLSN* BB9....................................199 F3
Hawthorne Crs FMBY L37..............356 A1
Hawthorne Dr BWCK/EAR BB18....119 F8
Hawthorne Gv CHTN/BK PR9.........302 B4
NLSN* BB9....................................170 B8
PLF/KEOS FY6...............................149 G8
Hawthorne Mdw RAW/HAS BB4....273 H2
Hawthorne Pl CLI BB7...................165 J2
Hawthorne Rd BLY BB11..................10 B5
CLV/TH FY5...................................149 H3
Hawthorne St BBN BB1.....................9 D1
Hawthorn Rd BCUP OL13..............298 D5
CARN LA5..33 G5
FUL/RIB PR2.................................240 C1
MCMB LA4.......................................42 B7
The Hawthorns BBN BB1...............219 G5
CHLY/EC PR7................................308 D4
FUL/RIB PR2.................................213 H5
GAR/LONG PR3.............................156 C6
SKEL WN8.....................................351 G2
Haydock Av LEY/BBR PR5..............285 J3
Haydock Gv HEY LA3.......................52 D2
Haydock Rd LANC LA1.....................55 H8
Haydocks La KIRK/FR/WA PR4......211 K6
Haydock St BBN BB1.....................245 G2
BRFD/BLYE BB10..........................226 A2
LEY/BBR* PR5..............................263 H1
Haydon Av LEY/BBR PR5...............262 D4
Hayfell Av MCMB LA4......................41 J8
Hayfell Crs HGHB LA2......................42 D2
Hayfell Gv HGHB LA2......................42 D2

Hayfield BBNW BB2......................244 C4
Hayfield Av BISP FY2....................176 E1
LEY/BBR PR5.................................264 D2
PLF/KEOS FY6...............................150 A8
Hayfield Cl LEY/BBR PR5..............264 D2
Hayfield Rd ORM L39....................348 C4
Hayfields BWCK/EAR BB18...........145 J3
Hayhurst Cl CLI * BB7...................193 G5
Hayhurst Rd CLI BB7.....................193 G5
Hayhurst St CLI BB7......................165 K4
Hayling Pl FUL/RIB PR2.................212 C7
Haylot Dr HGHB LA2........................44 B4
Haylot Sq LANC * LA1........................3 E3
Haymarket LSTA FY8.....................231 H5
Haysworth St PRES PR1.................239 H1
Haywood Cl ACC * BB5..................248 B3
FUL/RIB PR2.................................213 J3
Haywood Rd ACC BB5....................248 B3
Hazel Av ACC BB5..........................247 K1
DWN BB3.......................................268 E8
FTWD FY7......................................125 F3
KKBY L32.......................................366 A8
LEY/BBR PR5.................................263 K2
Hazel Bank BBNW BB2........................8 A3
HEY LA3...52 D4
Hazelbank Gdns
FMBY (off Freshfield Rd) L37.......343 J6
Hazel Cl BBNW BB2...........................8 A5
LEY/BBR PR5.................................263 J2
PRES PR1......................................238 D8
Hazel Coppice FUL/RIB PR2..........212 A8
Hazeldene Rd FTWD FY7..............122 C1
Hazel Gv ACC BB5.........................248 A1
BBN BB1..246 C6
BCUP OL13....................................276 A8
BPOOLE * FY3...................................5 E2
CHLYE PR6.....................................287 G8
CLI BB7..165 G4
FUL/RIB PR2.................................214 B7
GAR/LONG PR3.............................188 B3
KIRK/FR/WA PR4..........................281 K3
LANC LA1...2 B2
LEY/BBR PR5.................................263 J2
RAW/HAS BB4...............................273 G7
STHP PR8......................................302 A4
Hazelhead La GAR/LONG PR3.......130 A1
Hazelhurst Cl RAMS BL0...............319 H7
Hazelhurst Dr GAR/LONG PR3......129 G4
Hazelhurst Rd FUL/RIB PR2..........240 E1
Hazel La SKEL WN8.......................351 H7
Hazelmere Rd FUL/RIB PR2..........213 F3
FUL/RIB PR2.................................238 C2
Hazel Mt EDGW/EG BL7...............341 J1
Hazelmount Av CARN LA5...............25 K8
Hazelmount Crs CARN LA5..............25 K8
Hazelmount Dr CARN LA5...............25 K8
The Hazels BBN BB1.....................219 G5
CHLY/EC PR7................................335 J5
Hazel St ACC BB5..........................272 B3
RAMS BL0......................................319 G7
Hazelwood CARN LA5......................15 H8
Hazelwood Av BRSC L40...............330 E7
Hazelwood Cl BBN BB1.................245 J2
LEY/BBR PR5.................................285 G2
Hazelwood Dr KIRK/FR/WA PR4....258 C7
MCMB LA4.......................................42 B5
Hazelwood Gdns LANC LA1.............67 G1
Hazelwood Rd NLSN BB9..............198 E3
Hazlehurst Cl FMBY L37................355 G1
Hazlewood Cl CLV/TH FY5............149 G1
Headbolt La NWD/KWIPK L33.......366 C7
STHP PR8......................................326 C7
Head Dyke La PLF/KEOS FY6..........99 H8
Headen Av WGNW/BIL/O WN5.....365 K6
Headfort Cl BISP FY2.....................176 D1
Headingley Cl ACC BB5.................249 F2
Headley Rd LEY/BBR PR5..............285 G2
Headroomgate Back Rd
LSTA * FY8.....................................231 F3
Headroomgate Rd LSTA FY8..........231 F3
Heads La BWCK/EAR BB18............146 B5
Heald Brow BWCK/EAR BB18........118 E6
Heald Cl BCUP OL13......................275 K3
WHIT OL12....................................323 G8
Heald Dr WHIT OL12.....................323 G8
Heald House Rd LEY/BBR PR5.......286 A4
Heald La BCUP OL13.....................275 K4
Heald Rd PDHM/BLYW BB12.........225 J1
Healds St BPOOLE * FY3...............176 D4
CHLYE PR6.....................................311 J3
Healdwood Cl PDHM/BLYW BB12..197 H8
Healdwood Dr PDHM/BLYW BB12..197 H8
Healey Av WHIT OL12....................323 H7
Healey Ct BLY BB11.........................10 C4
Healey Gv WHIT OL12...................323 G6
Healey La WHIT OL12....................323 J8
Healey Mt BLY BB11........................10 C4

Healey Rw *BLY* BB11 ....**10** C5
Healey St *BPOOLE* FY3 ....**5** D1
Healey Wood Rd *BLY* BB11 ....**10** C5
Heaning Av *ACC* BB5 ....**248** D4
  BBN BB1 ....**246** B7
Heanor Dr *STHP* PR8 ....**302** B8
Heapey Fold La *CHLYE* PR6 ....**312** C3
Heapey Rd *CHLYE* PR6 ....**288** A8
Heap St *BRFD/BLYE* BB10 ....**225** K2
  BRFD/BLYE BB10 ....**226** E5
  NLSN* BB9 ....**197** J6
  RAW/HAS BB4 ....**273** H3
Heapworth Av *RAMS* BL0 ....**319** H5
Heartwood Cl *BBNW* BB2 ....**244** C3
Heathbourne Rd *BCUP* OL13 ....**297** K3
Heather Bank *BLY* BB11 ....**224** E7
  RAW/HAS BB4 ....**296** B2
Heather Brow *BWCK/EAR* BB18 ....**146** D1
Heather Cl *BRSC* L40 ....**330** E7
  CHLYE PR6 ....**311** J3
  CLV/TH FY5 ....**149** H2
  FMBY L37 ....**344** B6
  HOR/BR BL6 ....**338** D7
  NLSN BB9 ....**198** A7
  RAW/HAS BB4 ....**295** G3
  STHP PR8 ....**344** D1
Heatherfield *BOL* BL1 ....**341** H6
  EDGW/EG BL7 ....**317** J3
Heather Gv *FUL/RIB* PR2 ....**214** C8
Heatherlands *WHIT* OL12 ....**299** H7
Heatherlea Cl *SKEL* WN8 ....**364** E4
Heather Lea Dr *CHLYE* PR6 ....**289** F3
Heatherlea Rd *PDHM/BLYW* BB12 ...**197** F3
Heatherleigh *FUL/RIB* PR2 ....**214** C6
Heatherleigh *LEY/BBR* PR5 ....**285** F1
Heatherleigh Gdns *DWN* BB3 ....**268** A5
Heatherside Rd *RAMS* BL0 ....**319** H4
The Heathers *LEY/BBR* PR5 ....**264** B7
Heatherway *FUL/RIB* PR2 ....**214** C6
Heatherways *FMBY* L37 ....**344** A5
Heathey La *STHP* PR8 ....**327** H3
Heathfield *CHLYE* PR6 ....**337** F2
Heathfield Av *BCUP* OL13 ....**298** A5
Heathfield Cl *FMBY* L37 ....**344** A5
Heathfield Dr *FUL/RIB* PR2 ....**214** C7
  NWD/KWIPK L33 ....**366** C6
Heathfield Pk *BBNW* BB2 ....**244** B5
Heathfield Rd *BCUP* OL13 ....**298** A3
  FTWD FY7 ....**122** E1
  STHP PR8 ....**326** A6
Heathfoot Av *HEY* LA3 ....**52** C5
Heathgate *PDHM/BLYW* BB12 ....**197** F3
  SKEL WN8 ....**363** J1
Heath Gv *HEY* LA3 ....**52** C5
Heath Hill Dr *BCUP* OL13 ....**298** A3
Heathrow St *CHLY/EC* PR7 ....**310** E4
Heath St *BRFD/BLYE* BB10 ....**11** E1
Heathway *FUL/RIB* PR2 ....**213** H5
Heathway Av *BPOOLE* FY3 ....**5** E1
Heathy La *ORM* L39 ....**345** G3
Heatley Cl *BBNW* BB2 ....**8** B6
Heatley St *PRES* PR1 ....**7** D3
Heaton Bottom Rd *HEY* LA3 ....**53** J5
Heaton Cl *BRSC* L40 ....**330** D7
  HEY LA3 ....**42** A8
  LEY/BBR PR5 ....**240** B7
  PLF/KEOS FY6 ....**149** J6
  SKEL WN8 ....**364** C4
Heaton Mount Av *FUL/RIB* PR2 .....**213** H4
Heaton Pl *PRES* PR1 ....**240** C2
Heaton Rd *LANC* LA1 ....**3** D6
  LSTA FY8 ....**231** G4
Heatons Bridge Rd *BRSC* L40 ....**329** H7
Heaton St *BBNW* BB2 ....**8** C5
  LEY/BBR PR5 ....**285** G1
Heaviley Gv *HOR/BR* BL6 ....**338** C6
Hebden Av *BPOOL* FY1 ....**5** D6
Heber Dr *SKP/WHF* BD23 ....**120** A1
Heber St *BLY* BB11 ....**250** D7
Hebrew Rd *BRFD/BLYE* BB10 ....**11** D1
Hebrew Sq *BRFD/BLYE** BB10 ....**11** D1
Heckenhurst Av *BRFD/BLYE* BB10 ...**226** D5
Hector Rd *DWN* BB3 ....**268** B6
Hedge Rw *KIRK/FR/WA** PR4 ....**207** K8
Hedge Rows *WHIT* OL12 ....**323** G1
Hedgerows *LEY/BBR* PR5 ....**284** C3
The Hedgerow *BBNW* BB2 ....**244** C3
Heeley Rd *LSTA* FY8 ....**230** D3
Height Barn La *BCUP* OL13 ....**298** E3
Height La *GAR/LONG* PR3 ....**159** J4
Heightside Av *RAW/HAS* BB4 ....**297** G1
Height Side La *RAW/HAS* BB4 ....**273** J4
Heights Rd *NLSN* BB9 ....**198** B5
Helena St *BRFD/BLYE* BB10 ....**11** E4
Helen Bank Dr *RNFD/HAY* WA11 ...**369** D3
Helen's Cl *BPOOLS* FY4 ....**204** E5
Helks Brow *HGHB* LA2 ....**49** J7

Hellifield *FUL/RIB* PR2 ....**213** G4
Hellifield Rd *CLI* BB7 ....**115** K2
Helm Cl *BLY* BB11 ....**251** F1
Helmn Wy *NLSN* BB9 ....**170** D8
Helmsdale *SKEL* WN8 ....**363** J1
Helmsdale Cl *RAMS* BL0 ....**319** G8
Helmsdale Rd *BPOOLS* FY4 ....**205** F4
  NLSN BB9 ....**198** E2
Helmshore Rd *RAMS* BL0 ....**295** G8
  RAW/HAS BB4 ....**295** G6
Helmside Av *MCMB* LA4 ....**41** J8
Helmsley Gn *LEY/BBR* PR5 ....**285** K1
Helsby Gdns *BOL* BL1 ....**341** K7
Helston Cl *BLY* BB11 ....**224** D7
  CHTN/BK PR9 ....**278** D6
Helton Cl *NLSN* BB9 ....**170** B7
Helvellyn Dr *PDHM/BLYW* BB12 ...**224** E3
Helvellyn Rd *WGNW/BIL/O* WN5 ....**365** K4
Hemingway *BPOOLS* FY4 ....**204** D3
Hempshaw Av *RAW/HAS* BB4 ....**273** H1
Hemp St *BCUP* OL13 ....**298** D2
Henderson Dr *RNFD/HAY* WA11 ....**369** C3
Henderson Rd *FTWD* FY7 ....**123** F1
  KIRK/FR/WA PR4 ....**179** C6
Henderson St *PRES* PR1 ....**213** G8
Hendon Pl *FUL/RIB* PR2 ....**238** A1
Hendon Rd *NLSN* BB9 ....**198** D3
Hendry La *BBNW* BB2 ....**268** A3
Henley Av *CLV/TH* FY5 ....**148** D1
Henley Cl *BPOOLE** FY3 ....**176** E2
Henley Dr *CHTN/BK* PR9 ....**302** A2
Henley Ms
  HEY (off Gloucester Dr) LA3 ....**40** E8
Hennel La *LEY/BBR* PR5 ....**240** A7
Henrietta St *BBNW* BB2 ....**8** A4
  BCUP OL13 ....**298** D1
  PRES PR1 ....**7** F2
Henry St *ACC* BB5 ....**247** K5
  ACC BB5 ....**248** A2
  BBN BB1 ....**247** F2
  BPOOL FY1 ....**4** C5
  COL BB8 ....**171** G7
  LANC LA1 ....**3** D4
  LSTA FY8 ....**232** C8
  NLSN* BB9 ....**198** B2
  RAMS BL0 ....**319** K4
  RAW/HAS BB4 ....**296** B1
Henry Whalley St *BBNW* BB2 ....**267** H1
Henson Av *BPOOLS* FY4 ....**204** E5
Henthorne St *BPOOL* FY1 ....**4** C3
Henthorn Rd *CLI* BB7 ....**165** G5
Henwick Hall Av *RAMS* BL0 ....**319** H7
Herbert St *BBNW* BB2 ....**268** A1
  BCUP OL13 ....**298** B3
  BLY BB11 ....**10** B4
  HOR/BR BL6 ....**338** C6
  LEY/BBR PR5 ....**285** J1
  PDHM/BLYW BB12 ....**223** K4
  PRES PR1 ....**7** F1
Hereford Av *BPOOLE* FY3 ....**5** E4
  GAR/LONG PR3 ....**129** H3
  PDHM/BLYW BB12 ....**224** D4
Hereford Cl *ACC* BB5 ....**248** B4
Hereford Dr *CLI* BB7 ....**165** K4
Hereford Gv *KIRK/FR/WA* PR4 ....**211** K6
Hereford Rd *BBN* BB1 ....**246** B6
  CHTN/BK PR9 ....**302** B4
  NLSN BB9 ....**198** E1
Hereford St *NLSN* BB9 ....**198** A3
Herevale Hall Dr *RAMS** BL0 ....**319** H7
Heriot Cl *CLV/TH* FY5 ....**149** H3
Heritage Wy *CLV/TH* FY5 ....**149** F2
  KIRK/FR/WA PR4 ....**282** A6
Herkomer Av *BLY* BB11 ....**251** G1
Herlebeck Ri *LANC* LA1 ....**3** F1
Hermitage Cl *WGNNW/ST* WN6 ....**353** G4
Hermitage St *BBN* BB1 ....**247** G2
The Hermitage *CLV/TH* FY5 ....**149** F1
Hermitage Wy *LSTA* FY8 ....**231** K5
Hermon Rd *CLV/TH* FY5 ....**148** E2
Hermon St *PRES* PR1 ....**240** A2
Hern Av *LEY/BBR* PR5 ....**262** D3
Heron Cl *BBN* BB1 ....**8** B1
  CLV/TH FY5 ....**123** F6
Heron Ct *BLY* BB11 ....**224** D5
Heron Dr *MCMB* LA4 ....**41** J8
Heron Gv *RNFD/HAY* WA11 ....**369** H6
Heronsyke *LANC* LA1 ....**42** E7
Heron Wy *ACC* BB5 ....**247** J8
  BPOOLS FY4 ....**177** H4
  KIRK/FR/WA PR4 ....**235** F1
Herring Arm Rd *FTWD* FY7 ....**123** G1
Herschel Av *PDHM/BLYW* BB12 .....**224** E3
Herschell St *BBNW* BB2 ....**267** J2
  PRES PR1 ....**7** E4
Hertford St *BBNW* BB2 ....**267** K1
Hesketh Av *BISP* FY2 ....**148** B7

  BOL BL1 ....**3**
  CHTN/BK PR9 ....**2**
Hesketh Cl *PRES* PR1 ....**2**
Hesketh Ct *GTH/LHO* BB6 ....**2**
Hesketh Dr *BRSC* L40 ....**3**
  CHTN/BK PR9 ....**3**
  WGNNW/ST WN6 ....**3**
Hesketh Gn *BRSC* L40 ....**3**
Hesketh La *GAR/LONG* PR3 ....**1**
  KIRK/FR/WA PR4 ....**2**
Hesketh Pl *FTWD* FY7 ....
Hesketh Rd *BRSC* L40 ....**3**
  CHTN/BK PR9 ....**3**
  FUL/RIB PR2 ....**3**
  GAR/LONG PR3 ....**18**
  HEY LA3 ....
  LSTA FY8 ....**23**
Hesketh St *FUL/RIB* PR2 ....**22**
  GTH/LHO BB6 ....**22**
Heskin Cl *MGHL* L31 ....**35**
Heskin La *ORM* L39 ....**34**
Hesse St *DWN** BB3 ....**29**
Hest Bank La *HGHB* LA2 ....
Hest Bank Rd *MCMB* LA4 ....
Hester Cl *HTWN* L38 ....**35**
Hestham Av *MCMB* LA4 ....
Hestham Crs *MCMB* LA4 ....
Hestham Dr *MCMB* LA4 ....
Hestham Pde *MCMB* LA4 ....
Hetherington Pl *BISP* FY2 ....**17**
Hetton Lea *NLSN* BB9 ....**17**
Heversham *SKEL* WN8 ....**36**
Heversham Av *FUL/RIB* PR2 ....**21**
Heversham Cl *LANC* LA1 ....
  MCMB LA4 ....
Hewitt St *LEY/BBR* PR5 ....
Hewlett St *CHLY/EC* PR7 ....**33**
Hexham Av *CLV/TH* FY5 ....**12**
Hexham Cl *ACC* BB5 ....**24**
Hexham Rd *MCMB* LA4 ....
Hey Bottom La *WHIT* OL12 ....**52**
Heycrofts Vw *RAMS* BL0 ....**29**
Heydon Cl *FMBY* L37 ....**35**
Hey End *KIRK/FR/WA* PR4 ....**26**
Heyes Av *RNFD/HAY* WA11 ....**36**
Heyescroft *ORM* L39 ....**35**
Heyes Gv *RNFD/HAY* WA11 ....**36**
Heyes Rd *WGNW/BIL/O* WN5 ....**36**
Heyes St *SKEL* WN8 ....**35**
The Heyes *CHLYE* PR6 ....**28**
Heyfold Gdns *DWN* BB3 ....**26**
Hey Head *RAW/HAS** BB4 ....**29**
Heyhead St *NLSN* BB9 ....**19**
Heyhouses La *LSTA* FY8 ....**23**
Heyhurst Rd *BBNW* BB2 ....
Heymoor Av *GTH/LHO* BB6 ....**22**
Heys *ACC* BB5 ....**24**
Heys Cl *BBNW* BB2 ....**26**
  RAW/HAS BB4 ....**29**
Heys Ct *ACC* BB5 ....**24**
  BBNW BB2 ....**26**
Heysham Av *HEY* LA3 ....**52**
Heysham Crs *BBNW* BB2 ....**26**
Heysham Hall Dr *HEY* LA3 ....**52**
Heysham Hall Gv *HEY* LA3 ....**52**
Heysham Mossgate Rd *HEY* LA3 ....**52**
Heysham Pk *HEY* LA3 ....**52**
Heysham Rd *CHTN/BK* PR9 ....**30**
  HEY LA3 ....
  WGNW/BIL/O WN5 ....**36**
Heysham St *PRES* PR1 ....
Heys La *ACC* BB5 ....**247**
  BBNW BB2 ....**267**
  DWN BB3 ....**291**
  DWN BB3 ....**291**
  PDHM/BLYW BB12 ....**168**
Heys St *BCUP* OL13 ....**298**
  CLV/TH FY5 ....**123**
  GTH/LHO BB6 ....**221**
  RAW/HAS BB4 ....**272**
  RAW/HAS BB4 ....**296**
The Heys *CHLY/EC* PR7 ....**335**
  SKEL WN8 ....**332**
Hey St *NLSN* BB9 ....**198**
Heywood Cl *FMBY* L37 ....**343**
Heywood Rd *FUL/RIB* PR2 ....**238**
Heywood's Hollow *BOL* BL1 ....**341**
Heywood St *GTH/LHO* BB6 ....**221**
Heyworth Av *BBNW* BB2 ....**267**
Hibson Rd *NLSN* BB9 ....**198**
Hibson St *NLSN* BB9 ....**198**
Hic-Bibi La *CHLY/EC* PR7 ....**335**
Hickson Av *MGHL* L31 ....**358**
Hick's Ter *BBN* BB1 ....**247**
Hidings Court La *MCMB* LA4 ....**41**
Hiers House La *COL* BB8 ....**171**
Higgin's La *BRSC* L40 ....**330**

in St *BRFD/BLYE* BB10	**11**	E4
FD/BLYE BB10	**227**	F6
*L BB8	**171**	G6
am Gv *BPOOLE* FY3	**5**	F5
am Hall Rd		
DHM/BLYW BB12	**196**	B6
am Rd *PDHM/BLYW* BB12	**195**	J8
am Side Rd *KIRK/FR/WA* PR4	**182**	B5
am St *PDHM/BLYW* BB12	**223**	K2
abank *BBN* BB1	**245**	H2
Bank *CHLYE* PR6	**288**	A8
DGW/EG BL7	**341**	K4
abank Av *WHIT* OL12	**205**	G3
Banks *MGHL* L31	**358**	E8
Barn La *WHIT* OL12	**299**	G8
abury Av *BPOOLE* FY3	**176**	E3
WD FY7	**96**	E8
abury Ga *KIRK/FR/WA* PR4	**180**	E1
abury Pl *BBN* BB1	**8**	C3
abury Rd *LSTA* FY8	**230**	D2
abury Rd East *LSTA* FY8	**230**	E2
abury Rd West *LSTA* FY8	**230**	D2
Cl *PDHM/BLYW* BB12	**224**	A5
Cop *CHLYE* PR6	**264**	E7
cote La *MTHPE* LA7	**16**	C1
Ct *MCMB* LA4	**42**	B6
croft *BISP* FY2	**148**	E6
croft Wy *WHIT* OL12	**323**	K7
ncross Av *PLF/KEOS* FY6	**177**	K3
ncross Hl *PLF/KEOS* FY6	**177**	K3
ncross Rd *PLF/KEOS* FY6	**177**	K3
her Antley St *ACC* BB5	**248**	B5
her Audley St *BBN* BB1	**9**	D4
her Bank Rd *FUL/RIB* PR2	**213**	H8
her Bank *CHLYE* PR6	**289**	G2
her Barn *HOR/BR* BL6	**339**	H4
her Barn St *BBN* BB1	**9**	D4
her Booths La *RAW/HAS* BB4	**273**	H2
her Cswy *NLSN* BB9	**170**	B8
her Commons La *BBNW* BB2	**217**	J7
her Cft *PRES* PR1	**261**	K1
her Croft Cottages		
WN (off Higher Croft Rd) BB3	**268**	C3
her Croft Rd *DWN* BB3	**268**	C3
her Cross Rw *BCUP* * OL13	**275**	J8
her Dunscar *EDGW/EG* BL7	**341**	J2
her Eanam *BBN* BB1	**9**	E4
her Fenisowles La		
BNW BB2	**266**	C3
her Fld *GTH/LHO* BB6	**220**	A3
her Firs Dr *ACC* BB5	**222**	A8
her Fold La *RAMS* BL0	**320**	A4
her Furlong *KIRK/FR/WA* PR4	**260**	B5
her Gate Rd *ACC* BB5	**249**	F2
her Gn *PLF/KEOS* FY6	**149**	K8
her Greenfield *FUL/RIB* PR2	**212**	D6
her House Cl *BBNW* BB2	**267**	J4
her House La *CHLYE* PR6	**288**	A8
her La *BWCK/EAR* BB18	**145**	F4
AR/LONG PR3	**104**	B6
RK/FR/WA PR4	**305**	G1
AW/HAS BB4	**272**	C7
NFD/HAY WA11	**369**	G5
KEL WN8	**351**	H2
KEL WN8	**364**	E4
her Lawrence St *DWN* * BB3	**291**	H1
her London Ter *DWN* BB3	**291**	K1
her Meadow *LEY/BBR* PR5	**286**	C2
her Mill St *RAW/HAS* BB4	**273**	H8
her Moor Rd *BPOOLE* FY3	**177**	G1
her Moss La *FMBY* L37	**345**	G8
her Park Rd *BWCK/EAR* BB18	**145**	G3
her Peel St *ACC* BB5	**247**	H8
her Perry St *DWN* BB3	**291**	K1
her Ramsgreave Rd *BBN* BB1	**218**	E8
her Reedley Rd *NLSN* BB9	**198**	A7
her Ridings *EDGW/EG* BL7	**341**	J3
her Rd *GAR/LONG* PR3	**188**	B3
her Saxifield *BRFD/BLYE* BB10	**198**	C8
her South St *DWN* * BB3	**291**	K2
her Syke *HGHB* LA2	**71**	H7
her Tentre *BLY* BB11	**11**	E4
her Vw *SKEL* WN8	**364**	E5
her Walton Rd *LEY/BBR* PR5	**240**	C7
her Witton Rd *BBNW* BB2	**244**	D7
hfield *BCUP* OL13	**298**	C1
HLYE PR6	**289**	F3
TH/LHO BB6	**221**	F6
WD/KWIPK L33	**366**	D5
hfield Av *BRFD/BLYE* BB10	**197**	K8
OL BB8	**171**	J2
UL/RIB PR2	**214**	A7
IRK/FR/WA PR4	**182**	C3
EY/BBR PR5	**263**	F8
EY/BBR PR5	**263**	F2
VGNNW/ST WN6	**353**	J5
hfield Cl *ACC* BB5	**247**	K8
CHLYE PR6	**337**	G4
KIRK/FR/WA PR4	**236**	C2
KIRK/FR/WA PR4	**282**	A6
Highfield Cl *RAW/HAS* BB4	**295**	G1
Highfield Crs *MCMB* LA4	**41**	F7
NLSN BB9	**170**	C8
Highfield Dr *FUL/RIB* PR2	**213**	G3
GAR/LONG PR3	**188**	B5
HGHB LA2	**42**	D2
KIRK/FR/WA PR4	**260**	A5
PRES PR1	**262**	A1
RNFD/HAY WA11	**370**	A7
Highfield Gdns *BBNW* BB2	**268**	B1
Highfield Gv *LEY/BBR* PR5	**263**	F2
Highfield La *BRSC* L40	**329**	C4
Highfield Ms *DWN* BB3	**291**	K3
Highfield Pk *RAW/HAS* BB4	**295**	G1
Highfield Rd *BBN* BB1	**246**	E2
BBNW BB2	**8**	C6
BPOOLS FY4	**204**	C5
BWCK/EAR BB18	**146**	B1
CARN LA5	**34**	A3
CHLYE PR6	**337**	G4
CHTN/BK PR9	**278**	D8
CLI BB7	**165**	J4
DWN BB3	**291**	K2
LEY/BBR PR5	**307**	J1
ORM L39	**348**	C5
RAMS BL0	**295**	K8
RAW/HAS BB4	**297**	F2
Highfield Rd North *CHLY/EC* PR7	**311**	G1
CHLYE PR6	**337**	G3
Highfield Rd South *CHLY/EC* PR7	**311**	G2
Highfield St *DWN* BB3	**291**	K3
High Fold *BWCK/EAR* BB18	**146**	A5
Highgale Gdns *LEY/BBR* PR5	**263**	F4
High Ga *FTWD* FY7	**96**	D8
Highgate *BPOOLS* FY4	**204**	D6
GAR/LONG PR3	**186**	B5
NLSN BB9	**198**	B4
PRES PR1	**238**	D6
Highgate Av *FUL/RIB* PR2	**213**	G3
Highgate Cl *KIRK/FR/WA* PR4	**213**	H7
KIRK/FR/WA PR4	**209**	K8
Highgate Crs *WGNNW/ST* WN6	**353**	C4
High Gate La *PLF/KEOS* FY6	**124**	C6
Highgate La *KIRK/FR/WA* PR4	**234**	C5
WHIT OL12	**323**	G5
Highgate Pl *LSTA* FY8	**231**	K5
Highgate Rd *MGHL* L31	**359**	F8
SKEL WN8	**364**	D4
High Gn *LEY/BBR* PR5	**285**	H2
Highgrove Av *CHLY/EC* PR7	**309**	H7
Highgrove Ct *BOL* BL1	**341**	K8
MCMB LA4	**41**	G7
Highgrove Ct *LEY/BBR* PR5	**284**	B3
High Houses		
BOL (off Belmont Rd) BL1	**341**	H5
High Knott Rd *CARN* LA5	**15**	F2
Highland Av *PRES* PR1	**238**	D7
Highland Brow *HGHB* LA2	**67**	G6
High La *BRSC* L40	**348**	E3
BWCK/EAR BB18	**145**	G7
HWTH BD22	**174**	D2
ORM L39	**361**	G3
High Meadow *LEY/BBR* PR5	**263**	F1
Highmeadow *SKEL* WN8	**364**	C4
Highmoor *NLSN* BB9	**198**	D5
High Moor La *WGNNW/ST* WN6	**333**	J7
Highmoor Pk *CLI* BB7	**165**	K4
High Moss *ORM* L39	**348**	C8
High Park Pl *CHTN/BK* PR9	**302**	C5
High Park Rd *CHTN/BK* PR9	**302**	C5
High Peak Rd *WHIT* OL12	**323**	G5
Highrigg Dr *GAR/LONG* PR3	**213**	H2
High Rd *HGHB* LA2	**44**	A5
HGHB LA2	**49**	K2
Highsands Av *BRSC* L40	**306**	A8
Highsted Gv *NWD/KWIPK* L33	**366**	C6
High St *ACC* BB5	**247**	K8
BBN BB1	**8**	C4
BBN BB1	**247**	F2
BPOOL FY1	**4**	B1
BRSC L40	**332**	D2
CHLY/EC PR7	**311**	G3
CLI BB7	**165**	F3
COL BB8	**171**	J6
DWN BB3	**291**	J2
EDGW/EG BL7	**314**	E6
EDGW/EG BL7	**317**	G7
FTWD FY7	**97**	H7
GAR/LONG PR3	**153**	F6
HOR/BR BL6	**338**	D7
KIRK/FR/WA PR4	**180**	D2
LANC LA1	**2**	C4
*NLSN** BB9	**197**	K6
*NLSN** BB9	**198**	B4
PDHM/BLYW BB12	**223**	K2
PRES PR1	**7**	E2
RAW/HAS BB4	**272**	C7
SKEL WN8	**362**	D3
Hightown Rd *RAW/HAS* BB4	**274**	B7
High View St *BOL* BL1	**341**	J6
Highways Av *CHLY/EC* PR7	**310**	B2
Highwood Ct *NWD/KWIPK* L33	**366**	C7
Higson St *BBNW* BB2	**8**	B4
Hilary Av *BISP* FY2	**148**	C6
Hilary St *BRFD/BLYE* BB10	**225**	J2
Hilbre Cl *CHTN/BK* PR9	**302**	A2
Hilderstone La *CARN* LA5	**17**	J6
Hildrop Rd *NLSN* BB9	**198**	D2
Hillam La *HGHB* LA2	**78**	E5
Hillbank Cl *BOL* BL1	**341**	G8
Hillbrook Rd *LEY/BBR* PR5	**285**	H1
Hill Cl *WGNNW/ST* WN6	**353**	G4
Hill Cot Rd *BOL* BL1	**341**	K6
Hill Crs *KIRK/FR/WA* PR4	**236**	A1
Hill Crest *BCUP* OL13	**298**	B2
Hillcrest *SKEL* WN8	**363**	H4
Hill Crest Av *BRFD/BLYE* BB10	**226**	D7
FUL/RIB PR2	**213**	G3
GAR/LONG PR3	**188**	A4
Hillcrest Av *CARN* LA5	**33**	C6
FUL/RIB PR2	**212**	C7
Hillcrest Cl *KIRK/FR/WA* PR4	**282**	A3
Hillcrest Cft *GAR/LONG* PR3	**188**	A4
Hillcrest Dr *BRSC* L40	**328**	D3
GAR/LONG PR3	**188**	A4
KIRK/FR/WA PR4	**282**	A3
MTHPE LA7	**16**	D1
Hillcrest Rd *BBNW* BB2	**267**	C3
BPOOLS FY4	**204**	B7
GTH/LHO BB6	**220**	A3
ORM L39	**348**	C5
Hillcroft *FUL/RIB* PR2	**212**	E4
Hilldean *SKEL* WN8	**364**	E3
Hill End La *HWTH* BD22	**174**	A1
RAW/HAS BB4	**296**	E2
Hill House Fold La		
WGNNW/ST WN6	**334**	A6
Hill House La *CHLYE* PR6	**265**	F3
WGNNW/ST WN6	**334**	A6
Hill Houses *DWN* BB3	**291**	J3
Hillingdon Rd *BRFD/BLYE* BB10	**198**	B8
Hillingdon Rd North		
BRFD/BLYE BB10	**198**	A7
Hillkirk Dr *WHIT* OL12	**323**	G8
Hill La *CHLYE* PR6	**287**	F2
COL BB8	**172**	B5
HOR/BR BL6	**337**	H8
KKBYL LA6	**34**	B7
Hillmount Av *HEY* LA3	**52**	D3
Hillock Cl *BRSC* L40	**328**	E4
Hillock La *BRSC* L40	**328**	E4
KIRK/FR/WA PR4	**234**	B4
SKEL WN8	**351**	J5
The Hillocks *LEY/BBR* PR5	**307**	H1
Hillpark Av *FUL/RIB* PR2	**213**	F7
LEY/BBR PR5	**264**	C2
Hill Pl *NLSN* BB9	**198**	B5
Hill Ri *RAMS* BL0	**319**	G2
RAW/HAS BB4	**295**	J2
Hill Rise Vw *ORM* L39	**359**	J2
Hill Rd *LANC* LA1	**43**	F8
LEY/BBR PR5	**286**	A2
PRES PR1	**6**	A5
Hill Rd South *PRES* PR1	**238**	E8
Hillsborough Av *NLSN* BB9	**198**	B6
Hills Ct *LANC* LA1	**3**	D1
Hillsea Av *HEY* LA3	**52**	D3
Hillside *BLY* BB11	**10**	A6
Hillside Av *BBN* BB1	**246**	B7
BRFD/BLYE BB10	**198**	A7
FUL/RIB PR2	**213**	F7
HOR/BR BL6	**338**	C7
KIRK/FR/WA PR4	**209**	G6
LEY/BBR PR5	**262**	C4
ORM L39	**348**	B7
PLF/KEOS FY6	**98**	D7
SKEL WN8	**333**	F6
Hillside Cl *BLY* BB11	**10**	A6
BPOOLE FY3	**5**	E1
CHLY/EC PR7	**310**	A2
CLI BB7	**165**	J5
CLV/TH FY5	**149**	K3
GTH/LHO BB6	**221**	G5
NLSN BB9	**198**	A6
WGNW/BIL/O WN5	**371**	F6
Hillside Crs *BCUP* OL13	**275**	J4
CHLYE PR6	**287**	G3
HOR/BR BL6	**338**	E7
Hillside Dr *CLI* BB7	**139**	J5
PLF/KEOS FY6	**124**	E4

RAW/HAS BB4 ....**297** G1
Hillside Gdns *DWN* BB3 ....**291** J3
Hillside Rd *HGHB* LA2 ....**39** K3
  PRES PR1 ....**240** A5
  RAMS BL0 ....**319** G6
  RAW/HAS BB4 ....**295** J1
  STHP PR8 ....**326** A2
Hillside Vw *NLSN* BB9 ....**198** A6
Hillside Wk *BBN* BB1 ....**246** A7
  WHIT OL12 ....**323** H7
Hillside Wy *WHIT* OL12 ....**323** G2
The Hills *FUL/RIB* PR2 ....**215** F4
Hillstone Av *WHIT* OL12 ....**323** G7
Hill St *ACC* BB5 ....**247** H6
  ACC BB5 ....**248** C6
  ACC* BB5 ....**248** A2
  BBN BB1 ....**9** F4
  BPOOLS FY4 ....**204** B3
  BURY BL9 ....**319** J8
  BWCK/EAR BB18 ....**145** F1
  CHTN/BK PR9 ....**301** H3
  COL BB8 ....**171** H7
  NLSN BB9 ....**197** K6
  PDHM/BLYW BB12 ....**197** H5
  PDHM/BLYW BB12 ....**223** H5
  PRES PR1 ....**7** D2
  RAW/HAS BB4 ....**273** H3
Hillsview Rd *STHP* PR8 ....**325** J7
Hill Top *KIRK/FR/WA* PR4 ....**261** H5
  NLSN BB9 ....**170** B7
Hill Top Cl *KIRK/FR/WA* PR4 ....**235** H4
Hilltop Dr *RAW/HAS* BB4 ....**295** J4
Hill Top La *BWCK/EAR* BB18 ....**146** A1
  CHLYE PR6 ....**287** H3
Hilltop Wk *LM* L39 ....**348** A8
Hill Vw *BBN* BB1 ....**8** C1
  RAW/HAS BB4 ....**296** B2
Hill View Dr *CHLY/EC* PR7 ....**335** H3
Hill View Rd *GAR/LONG* PR3 ....**129** J2
Hillview Rd *BOL ** BL1 ....**341** J7
  KIRK/FR/WA PR4 ....**208** E5
Hill Wk *LEY/BBR* PR5 ....**285** J1
Hilly Cft *EDGW/EG* BL7 ....**341** K3
Hillylaid Rd *CLV/TH* FY5 ....**149** J1
Hilmont Ter *BBN* BB1 ....**9** D2
Hilstone La *BISP* FY2 ....**176** D2
Hilton Av *BPOOLS* FY4 ....**4** B6
  HOR/BR BL6 ....**338** C8
  LSTA FY8 ....**231** J5
Hilton Rd *DWN* BB3 ....**291** K3
Hilton's Brow *CHLYE* PR6 ....**265** C3
Hilton St *DWN* BB3 ....**291** J3
Hindburn Cl *CARN* LA5 ....**34** B1
Hindburn Pl *LANC ** LA1 ....**2** C1
Hinde St *LANC* LA1 ....**3** E2
Hindle Fold La *GTH/LHO* BB6 ....**221** G5
Hindle St *ACC* BB5 ....**248** B5
  BCUP OL13 ....**298** A3
  DWN BB3 ....**291** C1
Hindley Cl *FUL/RIB* PR2 ....**214** A4
Hindley Ct *NLSN* BB9 ....**198** A2
Hindley St *CHLY/EC* PR7 ....**311** F5
Hind's Head Av *WGNNW/ST* WN6 ...**334** D5
Hind St *BRFD/BLYE* BB10 ....**225** K1
  PRES PR1 ....**6** C4
Hinton St *BRFD/BLYE* BB10 ....**11** E4
Hippings Wy *CLI* BB7 ....**165** J1
Hirst St *BLY* BB11 ....**11** E5
  PDHM/BLYW BB12 ....**223** J2
  TOD* OL14 ....**277** G2
Hoarstones Av
  PDHM/BLYW BB12 ....**197** F4
Hobart Dr *NWD/KWIPK* L33 ....**366** C5
Hobart Pl *CLV/TH* FY5 ....**149** F3
Hobart St *BLY* BB11 ....**11** E4
Hobbs La *GAR/LONG* PR3 ....**131** H7
Hobcross La *BRSC* L40 ....**350** A2
Hob Gn *BBNW* BB2 ....**244** B1
Hob La *EDGW/EG* BL7 ....**317** G4
Hobson's La *KKBYL* LA6 ....**27** H7
Hobson St *RAW/HAS* BB4 ....**273** G7
Hockley Pl *BPOOLE* FY3 ....**177** F4
Hodder Av *BPOOL* FY1 ....**5** D6
  CHLY/EC PR7 ....**311** F6
  FTWD FY7 ....**122** D1
  LANC LA1 ....**42** B1
Hodder Bridge Cottages
  CLI (off Chipping Rd) BB7 ....**163** K4
Hodder Brook *FUL/RIB* PR2 ....**214** E8
Hodder Cl *LEY/BBR* PR5 ....**263** J3
Hodder Dr *CLI* BB7 ....**139** H4
Hodder Gv *CLI* BB7 ....**165** G4
  DWN BB3 ....**268** B7
Hodder Pl *BBN* BB1 ....**9** D3
  LANC LA1 ....**3** F6
  LSTA FY8 ....**231** H4
Hodder St *ACC* BB5 ....**248** D5

BBN* BB1 ....**8** C3
  BRFD/BLYE BB10 ....**198** A8
  GAR/LONG* PR3 ....**188** B4
Hodder Wy *PLF/KEOS* FY6 ....**177** K1
Hoddlesden Rd *DWN* BB3 ....**292** C2
Hodge Brow *CHLYE* PR6 ....**313** F7
Hodge St *STHP* PR8 ....**301** H4
Hodgson Av *KIRK/FR/WA* PR4 ......**234** E5
Hodgson Pl *PLF/KEOS* FY6 ....**177** K1
Hodgson Rd *BPOOL* FY1 ....**176** B2
Hodgson St *ACC* BB5 ....**247** J7
  DWN BB3 ....**291** K2
Hodson St *LEY/BBR* PR5 ....**263** H2
  STHP PR8 ....**301** J5
Hogarth Av *BLY* BB11 ....**10** B6
Hogarth Crs
  KIRK/FR/WA
  (off Roseacre Rd) PR4 ....**181** K7
Hoggs Hill La *FMBY* L37 ....**355** J3
Hogg's La *CHLYE* PR6 ....**311** K6
Hoghton Av *BCUP* OL13 ....**298** E2
Hoghton Cl *LANC* LA1 ....**2** B5
  LSTA FY8 ....**231** F1
Hoghton Gv *CHTN/BK* PR9 ....**301** J3
Hoghton La *LEY/BBR* PR5 ....**241** H8
Hoghton Rd *GAR/LONG* PR3 ....**188** B4
  LEY/BBR PR5 ....**285** F2
Hoghton St *CHTN/BK* PR9 ....**301** H4
  LEY/BBR PR5 ....**262** D3
Hoghton Vw *PRES* PR1 ....**240** A4
Holbeck Av *BPOOLS* FY4 ....**205** F3
  MCMB LA4 ....**42** B7
  WHIT OL12 ....**323** H7
Holbeck St *BRFD/BLYE* BB10 ....**11** D1
Holborn Dr *ORM* L39 ....**348** A8
Holborn Hl *ORM* L39 ....**348** A8
Holcombe Dr *BRFD/BLYE* BB10 ......**11** E3
Holcombe Gv *CHLYE* PR6 ....**311** J2
Holcombe Lee *RAMS* BL0 ....**319** C8
Holcombe Old Rd
  TOT/BURYW BL8 ....**319** F8
Holcombe Rd *BISP* FY2 ....**176** E2
  RAW/HAS BB4 ....**295** F3
  TOT/BURYW BL8 ....**319** F8
Holcroft Pl *LSTA* FY8 ....**232** B7
Holden Av *BOL* BL1 ....**341** J5
  RAMS BL0 ....**319** G6
Holden Cl *NLSN* BB9 ....**198** A2
Holden Fold *DWN* BB3 ....**268** E8
Holden La *CLI* BB7 ....**91** G6
Holden Rd *BRFD/BLYE* BB10 ....**197** K8
  NLSN BB9 ....**197** J6
Holden St *ACC ** BB5 ....**248** B6
  BBN BB1 ....**269** J5
  BBNW* BB2 ....**8** A5
  BLY* BB11 ....**10** C3
  CHLY/EC PR7 ....**337** F4
  CLI BB7 ....**165** K3
Holden Wy *LANC ** LA1 ....**3** D6
Holden Wood Dr *RAW/HAS* BB4 ....**295** F2
Hole House La *CLI* BB7 ....**77** H6
Hole House St *BBN* BB1 ....**246** A6
Holgate *BPOOLS* FY4 ....**205** F4
Holgate Dr *RAW/BIL/O* WN5 ....**365** C6
Holgate St *BRFD/BLYE* BB10 ....**198** D8
  GTH/LHO BB6 ....**221** G6
Holker Cl *LANC* LA1 ....**2** B5
  LEY/BBR PR5 ....**241** J8
Holker La *LEY/BBR* PR5 ....**284** C7
Holker St *COL* BB8 ....**171** F7
  DWN BB3 ....**291** K3
Holland Av *LEY/BBR* PR5 ....**263** H1
  RAW/HAS BB4 ....**273** G7
Holland Ct *SKEL* WN8 ....**369** K1
Holland House Rd *LEY/BBR* PR5 ...**240** C8
Holland Moss *SKEL* WN8 ....**363** G6
Holland Pl *NLSN* BB9 ....**198** C1
Holland Rd *FUL/RIB* PR2 ....**6** A1
Holland's La *SKEL* WN8 ....**362** A1
Holland St *ACC* BB5 ....**247** K5
  BBN BB1 ....**8** B3
  BOL BL1 ....**341** K7
  PDHM/BLYW* BB12 ....**223** H3
Hollies Cl *BBNW* BB2 ....**267** G3
  GAR/LONG PR3 ....**155** K1
Hollies Rd *BBN* BB1 ....**219** J4
Hollin Bridge St *BBNW* BB2 ....**267** K1
Hollinghurst Rd *NWD/KWIPK* L33 ...**366** D6
Hollingreave Rd *BLY* BB11 ....**11** D5
Hollings *KIRK/FR/WA* PR4 ....**261** G4
Hollington St *COL* BB8 ....**172** B6
Hollinhead Crs *FUL/RIB* PR2 ....**212** D7
Hollin Hey Cl *WGNW/BIL/O* WN5 ...**371** F8
Hollin Hey Rd *BOL* BL1 ....**340** C8
Hollin Hl *BLY* BB11 ....**11** E6
Hollinhurst Av *PRES* PR1 ....**6** A4

Hollinhurst Brow *HGHB* LA2 ....**5**
Hollin La *CHLYE* PR6 ....**31**
  RAW/HAS BB4 ....**27**
Hollin Mill St *NLSN* BB9 ....**19**
Hollins Av *BRFD/BLYE* BB10 ....**22**
Hollins Cl *ACC* BB5 ....**24**
  LEY/BBR PR5 ....**24**
Hollins Gv *FUL/RIB* PR2 ....**21**
Hollins Grove St *DWN* BB3 ....**26**
Hollinshead St *CHLY/EC* PR7 ....**31**
Hollinshead Ter *DWN* BB3 ....**29**
Hollins La *ACC* BB5 ....**24**
  CARN LA5 ....**3**
  CARN LA5 ....**1**
  GAR/LONG PR3 ....**1C**
  LEY/BBR PR5 ....**28**
  RAMS BL0 ....**32**
Hollins Rd *BWCK/EAR* BB18 ....**14**
  DWN BB3 ....**26**
  NLSN BB9 ....**19**
  PRES PR1 ....**21**
Hollin St *BBNW* BB2 ....**26**
Hollin Wy *RAW/HAS* BB4 ....**27**
Hollinwood Dr *RAW/HAS* BB4 ....**27**
Holloworld La *BRSC* L40 ....**33**
Holloworth La *KIRK/FR/WA* PR4 ...**18**
Hollowhead Av *BBN* BB1 ....**21**
Hollowhead Cl *BBN* BB1 ....**21**
Hollowrane *KKBYL* LA6 ....**1**
Holly Av *RAW/HAS* BB4 ....**29**
Hollybank Cl *FUL/RIB* PR2 ....**21**
Hollybrook Rd *STHP* PR8 ....**3C**
Holly Cl *BRSC* L40 ....**34**
  CHLYE PR6 ....**28**
  CLV/TH FY5 ....**12**
  SKEL WN8 ....**36**
Holly Crs *CHLY/EC* PR7 ....**31**
  RNFD/HAY WA11 ....**36**
Holly Fold La *RNFD/HAY* WA11 .....**36**
  KIRK/FR/WA PR4 ....**28**
Holly Gv *GAR/LONG* PR3 ....**18**
  KIRK/FR/WA PR4 ....**28**
Holly La *BRSC* L40 ....**3C**
  ORM L39 ....**34**
  SKEL WN8 ....**36**
Holly Ms *LSTA* FY8 ....**23**
Holly Mill Crs *BOL* BL1 ....**34**
Holly Pl *LEY/BBR* PR5 ....**26**
Holly Rd *BPOOL* FY1 ....**17**
  CLV/TH FY5 ....**12**
Holly St *ACC* BB5 ....**24**
  BBN BB1 ....**3**
  BOL BL1 ....**34**
  BRFD/BLYE BB10 ....**1**
  NLSN BB9 ....**19**
  RAMS BL0 ....**31**
Holly Ter *BBN* BB1 ....**9**
Holly Tree Cl *DWN* BB3 ....**29**
Holly Tree Wy *BBNW* BB2 ....**26**
Hollywood Av *BPOOLE* FY3 ....**9**
  PRES PR1 ....**23**
Hollywood Gv *FTWD* FY7 ....**9**
Holman St *PRES* PR1 ....**24**
Holmbrook Cl *BBNW* BB2 ....**26**
Holmby St *BRFD/BLYE* BB10 ....**22**
Holmdale Av *CHTN/BK* PR9 ....**27**
Holme Av *FTWD* FY7 ....**12**
Holme Bank *RAW/HAS* BB4 ....**29**
Holme Cl *BWCK/EAR* BB18 ....**14**
Holme Crs *COL* BB8 ....**17**
Holme End *PDHM/BLYW* BB12 ......**19**
Holmefield *KKBYL* LA6 ....**1**
Holmefield Av *CLV/TH* FY5 ....**14**
Holmefield Cl *CLV/TH* FY5 ....**14**
Holmefield Rd *LSTA* FY8 ....**23**
  PLF/KEOS FY6 ....**9**
Holmehead Br *CLI* BB7 ....**8**
Holme Hl *CLI* BB7 ....**16**
Holme House Rd *TOD* OL14 ....**27**
Holme La *HGHB* LA2 ....**4**
  RAW/HAS BB4 ....**29**
Holme Lea *ACC* BB5 ....**22**
Holme Rd *ACC* BB5 ....**22**
  LEY/BBR PR5 ....**26**
  PDHM/BLYW BB12 ....**1C**
  PRES PR1 ....**2**
Holmes Cottages
  BOL (off Temple Rd) BL1 ....**34**
Holmes Crs *PRES* PR1 ....**21**
Holmes Dr *BCUP* OL13 ....**27**
Holme Slack La *PRES* PR1 ....**21**
Holmes La *BCUP* OL13 ....**27**
Holmes Meadow *LEY/BBR* PR5 .....**28**
Holmes Rd *CLV/TH* FY5 ....**12**
Holmes St *BLY* BB11 ....**1**
  PDHM/BLYW BB12 ....**22**
  RAW/HAS BB4 ....**27**

AW/HAS BB4 .... 274 D4
nes Ter RAW/HAS BB4 .... 273 G6
Holmes Ter RAW/HAS BB4 .... 273 C6
nestrand Av BLY BB11 .... 224 C7
ne St ACC BB5 .... 248 B5
CUP OL13 .... 298 B3
JL BB8 .... 172 B6
WN BB3 .... 291 J3
SN BB9 .... 198 B1
JD OL14 .... 277 K4
neswood KIRK/FR/WA PR4 .... 208 E6
neswood Crs GAR/LONG PR3 ...... 184 D4
neswood Pk RAW/HAS BB4 .... 296 A3
neswood Rd
RK/FR/WA PR4 .... 305 H5
nfield Crs FUL/RIB PR2 .... 237 K2
nfield Pk FMBY L37 .... 343 H7
nfield Rd BISP FY2 .... 176 B2
JL/RIB PR2 .... 213 J7
nrook Rd PRES PR1 .... 7 F1
nsley St BRFD/BLYE BB10 .... 11 E4
nwood Cl FMBY L37 .... 343 H8
nwood Dr FMBY L37 .... 343 H7
nwood Gdns FMBY L37 .... 343 H7
sands Cl FUL/RIB PR2 .... 214 C5
stein Av WHIT OL12 .... 323 H7
stein St PRES PR1 .... 7 E2
: Av WGNW/BIL/O WN5 .... 371 F7
: Brow LEY/BBR PR5 .... 285 J5
: Coppice ORM L39 .... 359 J4
: Crs WGNW/BIL/O WN5 .... 371 F7
: La CLYE PR6 .... 264 C8
: Mill Rd RAW/HAS BB4 .... 297 H3
sts La PLF/KEOS FY6 .... 150 B8
: Sq NLSN BB9 .... 170 C6
: St BBN BB1 .... 247 G1
AMS BL0 .... 319 A5
AW/HAS BB4 .... 297 G2
GNW/BIL/O WN5 .... 365 F6
WHIT OL12 .... 323 C2
: St West RAMS BL0 .... 319 H6
yoake Av BISP FY2 .... 176 E2
yoake St PDHM/BLYW BB12 .... 224 C5
JD OL14 .... 277 F2
necare Av CLI BB7 .... 195 F3
ne Farm Cl HGHB LA2 .... 38 A7
ne Rd GAR/LONG PR3 .... 129 J3
ner Av KIRK/FR/WA PR4 .... 281 K4
ner St BLY BB11 .... 224 E6
nestead LEY/BBR PR5 .... 264 C1
nestead Cl LEY/BBR PR5 .... 285 F2
nestead Dr FTWD FY7 .... 122 E2
: Homestead
STA (off Henry St) FY8 .... 232 C8
nestead Wy FTWD FY7 .... 122 E2
newood Av MCMB LA4 .... 42 B5
nfray Av HEY LA3 .... 42 A8
nfray Gv HEY LA3 .... 42 A8
ney Hole BBNW BB2 .... 268 B1
ney Holme La
RFD/BLYE BB10 .... 252 D4
ney Moor Dr CLV/TH FY5 .... 123 G7
neypot La PLF/KEOS FY6 .... 151 F7
neysuckle Cl CHLYE PR6 .... 287 K5
neysuckle Pl BISP FY2 .... 149 F5
neysuckle Wy WHIT OL12 .... 323 H8
neywood Cl TOT/BURYW BL8 .... 319 G8
nister Av BPOOLE FY3 .... 5 E5
nister Cl FTWD FY7 .... 96 D8
nister Rd BRFD/BLYE BB10 .... 197 K8
ANC LA1 .... 3 F1
VGNW/BIL/O WN5 .... 365 K5
nister Sq LSTA FY8 .... 231 F1
niton Av BBNW BB2 .... 267 K3
niton Wy KIRK/FR/WA PR4 .... 212 B5
od House St BLY * BB11 .... 10 B5
od St ACC BB5 .... 248 C4
le La CHTN/BK PR9 .... 279 J5
AR/LONG PR3 .... 128 B6
ols La GAR/LONG PR3 .... 99 J6
pe Cl CLV/TH FY5 .... 123 H7
pe Crs WGNW/BIL/O WN5 .... 353 J5
pe Island SKEL WN8 .... 363 F3
pe La GAR/LONG PR3 .... 160 D6
pe Sq CHTN/BK PR9 .... 301 J4
pe St ACC BB5 .... 248 B6
BNW BB2 .... 8 B4
CUP OL13 .... 275 J7
RFD/BLYE BB10 .... 226 E5
HLY/EC PR7 .... 311 G2
HLYE PR6 .... 337 H4
HTN/BK PR9 .... 301 J4
WN BB3 .... 291 H2
TH/LHO BB6 .... 221 G7
OR/BR BL6 .... 338 D7
ANC LA1 .... 3 E4
STA FY8 .... 231 G4

MCMB LA4 .... 41 J7
NLSN BB9 .... 197 K6
NLSN BB9 .... 198 B4
PDHM/BLYW * BB12 .... 223 K3
PRES PR1 .... 7 D2
RAMS BL0 .... 319 H6
RAW/HAS BB4 .... 295 H1
RAW/HAS BB4 .... 296 E2
Hope St North HOR/BR BL6 .... 338 D6
Hope Ter BBNW BB2 .... 8 A3
Hopkinson St COL * BB8 .... 172 B8
Hopton Rd BPOOL FY1 .... 4 B5
Hopwood Av HOR/BR BL6 .... 338 E7
Hopwood Crs RNFD/HAY WA11 .. 369 C6
Hopwood St ACC BB5 .... 248 A7
BLY BB11 .... 10 B3
LEY/BBR PR5 .... 263 J4
PRES PR1 .... 7 E2
Horace St PDHM/BLYW * BB12 ... 10 A3
Horden Bank BBNW BB2 .... 267 F4
Horden Vw BBNW BB2 .... 266 E4
Hordley St PDHM/BLYW BB12 .... 224 C5
Hornbeam Cl PRES PR1 .... 238 D8
Hornby Av FTWD FY7 .... 122 D3
FUL/RIB PR2 .... 214 C7
Hornby Bank HGHB LA2 .... 37 H4
Hornby Cl BBNW BB2 .... 8 A5
KIRK/FR/WA PR4 .... 209 F7
LANC LA1 .... 42 E7
Hornby Cft LEY/BBR PR5 .... 284 D4
Hornby Dr KIRK/FR/WA PR4 ...... 209 H8
LANC LA1 .... 55 C7
Hornby Hall Cl HGHB LA2 .... 37 G5
Hornby La GAR/LONG PR3 .... 153 K8
Hornby St BPOOL FY1 .... 4 C3
CHLYE PR6 .... 311 J5
CHTN/BK PR9 .... 278 C7
GAR/LONG PR3 .... 188 B3
HGHB LA2 .... 38 A7
HGHB LA2 .... 45 C5
HGHB LA2 .... 48 A8
LSTA FY8 .... 230 E6
Hornby's La GAR/LONG PR3 .... 125 J6
Hornby St ACC BB5 .... 247 J8
BLY BB11 .... 11 D4
Hornby Ter MCMB LA4 .... 41 J5
Hornchurch Dr CHLY/EC PR7 .... 310 E3
Horncliffe Cl RAW/HAS BB4 .... 296 A3
Horncliffe Rd BPOOLS FY4 .... 204 B5
Horncliffe Vw RAW/HAS BB4 ..... 295 H3
Horne St ACC BB5 .... 248 C4
Horning Crs BRFD/BLYE BB10 .... 226 B1
Hornsea Cl FUL/RIB PR2 .... 212 C7
Hornsey Av LSTA FY8 .... 204 B7
Horns La GAR/LONG PR3 .... 186 D2
Horridge Fold EDGW/EG BL7 ..... 316 C8
Horrobin La CHLYE PR6 .... 337 J3
Horrocks Fold Av BOL LA1 .... 341 H5
Horrocksford Wy LANC LA1 .... 2 B5
Horrocks Rd EDGW/EG BL7 .... 317 H4
Horsebridge Rd BPOOLE FY3 .... 177 H3
Horsefield Av WHIT OL12 .... 323 C5
Horse Market KKBYL LA6 .... 21 H1
Horse Park La GAR/LONG PR3 ... 100 E6
Horsfall Av LSTA FY8 .... 232 C8
Horsfall Cl ACC BB5 .... 248 B5
Horsfield Cl COL BB8 .... 171 K6
Horton Av BOL BL1 .... 341 J5
BRFD/BLYE BB10 .... 197 K8
Hoscar Moss Rd BRSC L40 .... 331 J8
Hosta Cl NWD/KWIPK L33 .... 366 B6
Hosticle La KKBYL LA6 .... 20 E5
Hothersall La GAR/LONG PR3 .... 188 D8
Hough Clough La GAR/LONG PR3 159 J2
Hough La EDGW/EG BL7 .... 341 K4
LEY/BBR PR5 .... 285 J2
Houghton Av BPOOLS FY4 .... 204 D3
Houghton Cl PRES PR1 .... 239 F8
Houghton Ct HGHB LA2 .... 44 A4
Houghton Rd PRES PR1 .... 238 E8
Houghton's La SKEL WN8 .... 363 J2
Houghtons St CHLYE PR6 .... 311 H5
Houghton St CHLYE PR6 .... 351 C8
Houldsworth Rd FUL/RIB PR2 .... 213 C8
Houseman Pl BPOOLS FY4 .... 204 E4
Hove Av FTWD FY7 .... 122 C3
Hove Rd LSTA FY8 .... 231 F5
Howard Cl ACC BB5 .... 247 K6
LSTA FY8 .... 230 E2
Howard Dr KIRK/FR/WA PR4 ...... 281 K4
Howard Ms CARN LA5 .... 33 J2
Howard Rd CHLY/EC PR7 .... 311 J2
Howards La WGNW/BIL/O WN5 . 365 H4
Howard St BBN BB1 .... 246 E2
BLY BB11 .... 10 A4
BPOOL FY1 .... 4 C1

NLSN* BB9 .... 198 A3
Howarth Av ACC BB5 .... 247 K4
Howarth Cl BLY BB11 .... 11 D6
Howarth Crs PLF/KEOS FY6 .... 150 A8
Howarth Fold
EDGW/EG (off Blackburn Rd) BL7 316 B8
Howarth Rd FUL/RIB PR2 .... 212 E8
Howarth's St RAW/HAS BB4 .... 274 C3
Howe Av BPOOLS FY4 .... 204 E3
Howe Cft CLI BB7 .... 165 K3
Howe Gv CHLY/EC PR7 .... 310 E4
Howe Wk BLY BB11 .... 11 D3
Howgill Av LANC LA1 .... 43 G7
Howgill Cl NLSN BB9 .... 198 D5
Howgill La CLI BB7 .... 143 H2
The Howgills FUL/RIB PR2 .... 213 J4
Howgill Wy LSTA FY8 .... 233 F6
Howick Cross La PRES PR1 .... 237 K5
Howick Moor La PRES PR1 .... 238 B8
Howick Park Av PRES PR1 .... 238 B7
Howick Park Cl PRES PR1 .... 238 B7
Howick Park Dr PRES PR1 .... 238 B7
Howorth Rd BLY BB11 .... 11 D5
Howsin St BRFD/BLYE BB10 .... 225 J2
Hoylake Cl FUL/RIB PR2 .... 212 D5
Hoyle Av LSTA FY8 .... 231 F1
Hoyles La KIRK/FR/WA PR4 .... 211 J6
Hoyle St ACC BB5 .... 272 B3
BCUP OL13 .... 298 C3
WHIT OL12 .... 299 H8
Hozier St BBN BB1 .... 246 A6
Hubert Pl LANC LA1 .... 2 B3
Hubie St PDHM/BLYW BB12 .... 10 C2
Huck La LSTA FY8 .... 233 G4
Hud Hey Rd RAW/HAS BB4 .... 272 B5
Hud Rake RAW/HAS BB4 .... 272 C6
Hudson Cl BBNW BB2 .... 244 D3
Hudson Ct LEY/BBR PR5 .... 264 B3
Hudson Rd BPOOL FY1 .... 5 D5
Hudson St ACC BB5 .... 248 C7
BLY BB11 .... 10 A4
NLSN* BB9 .... 197 K6
PRES PR1 .... 7 E3
TOD OL14 .... 277 H2
Hufling Ct BLY BB11 .... 11 E5
Hufling La BLY BB11 .... 11 E5
Hugh Barn La KIRK/FR/WA PR4 . 261 F4
Hughes Av HOR/BR BL6 .... 338 C7
Hughes Gv BISP FY2 .... 176 E2
Hughes St BLY BB11 .... 11 D4
Hugh La LEY/BBR PR5 .... 262 A8
Hugh Rake RAW/HAS BB4 .... 273 G5
Hullet Cl WGNNW/ST WN6 .... 353 C3
Hull Rd BPOOL FY1 .... 4 B3
Hull St BLY * BB11 .... 11 E4
FUL/RIB PR2 .... 6 A1
Hulme Av CLV/TH FY5 .... 149 J1
Hulme St STHP PR8 .... 301 G4
Hulton Dr NLSN BB9 .... 198 C5
Humber Av BPOOLE * FY3 .... 176 E3
Humber St GAR/LONG PR3 .... 188 A4
Humblescough La
GAR/LONG PR3 .... 128 D5
Humphrey St NLSN BB9 .... 197 K5
Hundred End La KIRK/FR/WA PR4 280 D1
Hungerford Rd LSTA FY8 .... 231 F6
Hunniball Ct FUL/RIB PR2 .... 238 E1
Hunslet St BLY BB11 .... 11 E3
NLSN BB9 .... 198 D4
Hunter Av KIRK/FR/WA PR4 .... 282 A5
Hunter Rd KIRK/FR/WA PR4 .... 235 F1
Hunters Cha WGNW/BIL/O WN5 371 G2
Hunters Dr PDHM/BLYW BB12 .... 10 A2
Hunters Fold KIRK/FR/WA PR4 .. 260 B6
Hunters Ga LANC LA1 .... 2 C6
Hunters Gn TOT/BURYW BL8 ..... 319 F8
Hunter's La KIRK/FR/WA PR4 ..... 281 F8
Hunters Ldg BBNW BB2 .... 267 C3
LEY/BBR PR5 .... 240 B8
Hunters Rd LEY/BBR PR5 .... 286 B2
Huntingdon Ct
CHTN/BK (off Manor Rd) PR9 ... 302 C1
Huntingdon Gv MGHL L31 .... 358 E7
Huntingdon Hall Rd GAR/LONG PR3 162 B8
Huntingdon Rd CLV/TH FY5 .... 148 C2
Hunting Hill Rd CARN LA5 .... 33 H2
Huntington Dr DWN BB3 .... 291 H4
Huntley Av BPOOLE FY3 .... 176 E4
Huntley Cl MCMB LA4 .... 42 A6
Huntley La LEY/BBR PR5 .... 242 D1
Huntroyde Av PDHM/BLYW BB12 223 H3
Huntroyde Cl PDHM/BLYW BB12 10 A2
Hunts Fld CHLYE PR6 .... 287 C1
Huntsman Cha
KIRK/FR/WA (off Treales Rd) PR4 209 K5
Hunt St PRES PR1 .... 6 B2
Hurlston Av SKEL * WN8 .... 363 J3

Hurlston Dr *ORM* L39....................**348** C4
Hurlston La *BRSC* L40....................**347** K2
Hurn Gv *CHLY/EC* PR7....................**310** E4
Hurst Brook *CHLY/EC* PR7....................**335** K2
Hurstead St *ACC* BB5....................**271** K2
Hurst Gn *BRSC* L40....................**332** E1
Hurst La *RAW/HAS* BB4....................**273** J8
Hurstleigh Dr *HEY* LA3....................**52** E1
Hurstleigh Hts *CLV/TH* FY5....................**150** A1
Hurstmere Av *BPOOLS* FY4....................**204** E3
Hurst Pk *PRES* PR1....................**6** A6
Hurst's La *ORM* L39....................**366** E1
Hurstway *FUL/RIB* PR2....................**213** F4
Hurstway Cl *FUL/RIB* PR2....................**213** F4
Hurstwood *BOL* BL1....................**341** H6
Hurstwood Av *BBNW* BB2....................**267** H2
  BRFD/BLYE BB10....................**226** B6
Hurstwood Gdns *NLSN* BB9....................**198** B7
Hurstwood La *BRFD/BLYE* BB10....................**227** F7
Hurtley St *BRFD/BLYE* BB10....................**11** D1
Hutch Bank Rd *RAW/HAS* BB4....................**295** F1
Hutchinson Ct *DWN* BB3....................**291** H2
Hutchinson St *BBNW* * BB2....................**8** C6
Hut La *CHLYE* PR6....................**312** B6
Huttock End La *BCUP* OL13....................**298** B3
Hutton Cl *KKBYL* LA6....................**18** B5
Hutton Ct *SKEL* WN8....................**362** D2
Hutton Dr *BRFD/BLYE* BB12....................**10** B2
Hutton Gv *MCMB* LA4....................**41** G7
Hutton Rd *SKEL* WN8....................**362** D2
Hutton St *BBN* BB1....................**9** E4
  WGN WN1....................**336** A8
Hutton Wy *LANC* LA1....................**2** B2
  ORM L39....................**348** C6
Huyton Rd *CHLY/EC* PR7....................**337** G5
Hyacinth Cl *RAW/HAS* BB4....................**295** F3
Hyatt Crs *WCNNW/ST* WN6....................**335** G8
Hyde Rd *BPOOL* FY1....................**4** B5
  MCMB LA4....................**42** B7
Hyde's Brow *RNFD/HAY* WA11....................**369** G3
Hyndburn Br *GTH/LHO* BB6....................**221** K6
Hyndburn Dr *DWN* BB3....................**268** A7
Hyndburn Rd *ACC* BB5....................**247** K5
  GTH/LHO BB6....................**221** J6
Hyndburn St *ACC* BB5....................**247** K5
Hyning Rd *CARN* LA5....................**26** A3
The Hynings *GTH/LHO* BB6....................**221** F5
Hythe Cl *BBN* BB1....................**246** A7
  STHP PR8....................**302** A8

Ibbison Ct *BPOOL* FY1....................**4** C4
Icconhurst Cl *ACC* BB5....................**271** J1
Ice St *BBN* BB1....................**8** C2
Iddesleigh Rd *PRES* * PR1....................**240** C2
Iddon Ct *BPOOL* FY1....................**4** C1
Idlewood Pl *CLV/TH* FY5....................**149** F3
Idonia St *BOL* BL1....................**341** H8
Idstone Cl *BBNW* BB2....................**268** D3
Ightenhill Park La
  PDHM/BLYW BB12....................**224** D1
Ightenhill Park Ms
  PDHM/BLYW BB12....................**224** E1
Ightenhill St *PDHM/BLYW* BB12....................**223** J2
Ighten Rd *PDHM/BLYW* BB12....................**224** E3
Ilford Rd *BPOOLS* FY4....................**5** E6
Ilkley Av *CHTN/BK* PR9....................**278** C5
  LSTA FY8....................**231** J5
Ilkley Gv *CLV/TH* FY5....................**148** D3
The Illawalla *CLV/TH* FY5....................**150** A5
Illingworth Rd *PRES* PR1....................**240** C2
Illston Ms
  NLSN (off Cambridge St) BB9....................**197** K6
Ilway *LEY/BBR* PR5....................**240** E1
Imperial St *BPOOL* FY1....................**176** B4
Imperial Yd
  BPOOL (off Back Eaves St) FY1....................**176** B4
Ince Crs *FMBY* L37....................**343** H8
Ince La *CHLY/EC* PR7....................**308** E6
Inch Fld *BRFD/BLYE* BB10....................**227** F5
Inchfield *SKEL* WN8....................**363** H1
India St *ACC* BB5....................**247** K5
  DWN BB3....................**291** K3
Industrial Pl *BCUP* OL13....................**298** D1
Industrial St *BCUP* OL13....................**298** E1
  RAMS BL0....................**319** J2
Industry St *DWN* BB3....................**291** K1
  WHIT OL12....................**323** H1
Infant St *ACC* BB5....................**248** C5
Infirmary Rd *BBNW* BB2....................**268** A1
Infirmary Cl *BBNW* * BB2....................**268** A1
Infirmary St *BBNW* BB2....................**268** B1

Ing Dene Av *COL* BB8....................**171** F7
Ing Dene Cl *COL* BB8....................**171** F7
Ingham St *NLSN* BB9....................**170** B8
Ingleborough Dr
  BWCK/EAR BB18....................**144** E1
Ingleborough Rd *LANC* LA1....................**42** C8
Ingleborough Vw *CARN* LA5....................**34** A3
Ingleborough Wy *LEY/BBR* PR5....................**286** A1
Ingleby Cl *CLV/TH* FY5....................**123** F6
Ingle Cl *CHLYE* PR6....................**311** H2
Ingle Head *FUL/RIB* PR2....................**213** F5
Inglehurst Rd *BLY* BB11....................**224** D6
Inglemere Ct *CARN* LA5....................**15** F1
Inglemere Dr *CARN* LA5....................**15** G2
Inglemere Gdns *CARN* LA5....................**15** G2
Ingle Nook *BRFD/BLYE* BB10....................**226** D7
Inglenook Cl *CLV/TH* FY5....................**149** F2
Ingleton Av *BISP* FY2....................**149** F7
Ingleton Cl *ACC* BB5....................**248** D6
Ingleton Dr *LANC* LA1....................**55** G7
Ingleton Rd *FUL/RIB* PR2....................**214** C7
  STHP PR8....................**302** A8
Ingleway *CLV/TH* FY5....................**122** E8
Ingleway Av *BPOOLE* FY3....................**5** E1
Inglewhite *SKEL* WN8....................**363** G1
Inglewhite Fold
  PDHM/BLYW BB12....................**223** K4
Inglewhite Rd *GAR/LONG* PR3....................**158** A7
Inglewood Cl *FTWD* FY7....................**122** C2
  KIRK/FR/WA PR4....................**234** B5
Inglewood Gv *BISP* FY2....................**148** E6
Ingol Gv *PLF/KEOS* FY6....................**150** E1
Ingol La *PLF/KEOS* FY6....................**151** F1
Ingot St *PRES* PR1....................**6** B2
Ingram *SKEL* WN8....................**363** H2
Ings Av *BWCK/EAR* BB18....................**119** F8
Ingthorpe Av *BISP* FY2....................**148** D6
Inkerman Rd *KIRK/FR/WA* PR4....................**179** G5
Inkerman St *BBN* BB1....................**8** C3
  BCUP OL13....................**298** E1
  FUL/RIB PR2....................**212** E8
  PDHM/BLYW * BB12....................**223** J3
Inner Prom *LSTA* FY8....................**231** J8
Inskip *SKEL* WN8....................**363** G1
Inskip Pl *BPOOLS* FY4....................**204** E6
  LSTA FY8....................**231** G3
Inskip Rd *CHTN/BK* PR9....................**278** C7
  FUL/RIB PR2....................**238** A2
  KIRK/FR/WA PR4....................**182** A7
  LEY/BBR PR5....................**285** F1
Inskip St *PDHM/BLYW* BB12....................**223** J3
Institute St *PDHM/BLYW* BB12....................**223** K3
Intack La *BBNW* BB2....................**243** H1
Intack Rd *KIRK/FR/WA* PR4....................**260** C3
Intake Crs *COL* BB8....................**171** K5
Intake La *ORM* L39....................**358** A3
  ORM L39....................**362** A7
Inverness Rd *DWN* BB3....................**291** H3
Inver Rd *BISP* FY2....................**148** D8
Inward Dr *WCNNW/ST* WN6....................**353** J6
Ipswich Pl *CLV/TH* FY5....................**148** C1
Ipswich Rd *FUL/RIB* PR2....................**240** B1
Irene Pl *BBNW* BB2....................**244** D6
Irene St *RAMS* BL0....................**319** H5
Irlam St *BOL* BL1....................**341** J8
Irma St *BOL* BL1....................**341** K8
Irongate *LEY/BBR* PR5....................**263** F3
Ironside Cl *FUL/RIB* PR2....................**213** K7
Iron St *CHTN/BK* PR9....................**302** A3
Irvin Av *CHTN/BK* PR9....................**278** E6
Irvine Cl *NLSN* * BB9....................**198** D1
Irving Cl *BISP* FY2....................**149** F6
Irving Pl *BBNW* BB2....................**244** D6
Irving St *CHTN/BK* PR9....................**301** H2
Irvin St *PRES* PR1....................**7** F1
Irwell *SKEL* WN8....................**351** G8
Irwell Rd *WGNW/BIL/O* WN5....................**365** H4
Irwell St *BCUP* OL13....................**298** D1
  GAR/LONG PR3....................**188** B3
  PDHM/BLYW BB12....................**224** C5
  RAMS BL0....................**319** J5
Irwell Ter *BCUP* OL13....................**275** J8
Irwell Vale Rd *RAW/HAS* BB4....................**295** J5
Irwell Valley Wy *BCUP* OL13....................**275** J6
  RAMS BL0....................**319** J7
  RAW/HAS BB4....................**295** K4
Isabella St *GAR/LONG* PR3....................**188** A3
Isa St *RAMS* BL0....................**319** G7
Isherwood Fold *EDGW/EG* BL7....................**317** H4
Isherwood St *BBNW* BB2....................**268** A2
  PRES PR1....................**240** A2
Island La *GAR/LONG* PR3....................**127** J1
Islay Rd *LSTA* FY8....................**231** K5
Isle of Man *BBN* BB1....................**219** G7
Isle of Man St *RAW/HAS* BB4....................**274** C4

Isleworth Dr *CHLY/EC* PR7....................**31**
Islington *BBNW* BB2....................
Islington Cl *BRFD/BLYE* BB10....................**19**
Ivan St *BRFD/BLYE* BB10....................**22**
Ivegate *COL* BB8....................**17**
Ivinson Rd *DWN* BB3....................**29**
Ivory Dr *NWD/KWIPK* L33....................**36**
Ivory St *PDHM/BLYW* BB12....................**22**
Ivy Av *BPOOLS* FY4....................**20**
  RAW/HAS BB4....................**27**
Ivy Bank *FUL/RIB* PR2....................**21**
Ivy Bank Rd *BOL* BL1....................**34**
Ivybridge *SKEL* WN8....................**36**
Ivy Cl *LEY/BBR* PR5....................**28**
Ivydale *SKEL* WN8....................**36**
Ivy St *BBNW* BB2....................**26**
  BRFD/BLYE BB10....................**22**
  NLSN BB9....................**19**
  RAW/HAS BB4....................**29**
  STHP PR8....................**30**
Ivy Ter *DWN* BB3....................**29**

J

Jack Anderton Br *GAR/LONG* PR3 ....**13**
Jacks Key Dr *DWN* BB3....................**29**
Jacksmere La *BRSC* L40....................**32**
Jackson Cl *LANC* LA1....................
  ORM L39....................**34**
Jackson Heights Rd *BBN* BB1....................**27**
Jackson Rd *CHLY/EC* * PR7....................**31**
  LEY/BBR PR5....................**28**
Jackson's Banks Rd *BBNW* BB2....................**21**
Jackson's Common La *BRSC* L40....................**34**
Jackson's La *BRSC* L40....................**33**
Jackson St *ACC* * BB5....................**24**
  BPOOLE FY3....................**17**
  BRFD/BLYE * BB10....................**1**
  CHLY/EC PR7....................**31**
  LEY/BBR PR5....................**26**
Jacob's La *KIRK/FR/WA* PR4....................**20**
Jacob St *ACC* BB5....................**24**
Jacson St *PRES* PR1....................
Jade Cl *NWD/KWIPK* L33....................**36**
Jagoe Rd *BWCK/EAR* BB18....................**14**
James Av *BPOOLS* FY4....................
  GTH/LHO BB6....................**22**
Jameson Rd *FTWD* FY7....................**12**
Jameson St *BPOOL* FY1....................
James Pl *CHLY/EC* PR7....................**33**
James St *ACC* BB5....................**22**
  ACC BB5....................**24**
  ACC BB5....................**24**
  BBN BB1....................
  BBN * BB1....................**24**
  BBN BB1....................**26**
  BCUP * OL13....................**29**
  BRFD/BLYE BB10....................**22**
  BWCK/EAR BB18....................**14**
  BWCK/EAR BB18....................**14**
  BWCK/EAR BB18....................**14**
  COL * BB8....................**17**
  DWN BB3....................**29**
  EDGW/EG BL7....................**31**
  GTH/LHO BB6....................**22**
  HOR/BR BL6....................**33**
  LANC * LA1....................
  LEY/BBR PR5....................**26**
  MCMB LA4....................**4**
  PRES PR1....................
  RAW/HAS BB4....................**29**
  WHIT OL12....................**32**
James St West *DWN* BB3....................**29**
Jane La *KIRK/FR/WA* PR4....................**18**
  LEY/BBR PR5....................**26**
Jane's Brook Rd *STHP* PR8....................**30**
Jane St *WHIT* OL12....................**29**
Janice Dr *FUL/RIB* PR2....................**21**
Jannat Cl *ACC* * BB5....................**24**
Jarrett Rd *NWD/KWIPK* L33....................**36**
Jasmine Rd *PRES* PR1....................**23**
Jasper St *BBN* BB1....................**24**
Jedburgh Dr *NWD/KWIPK* L33....................**36**
Jefferson Cl *LANC* LA1....................
Jefferson Wy *WHIT* OL12....................**32**
Jeffrey Av *GAR/LONG* PR3....................**18**
Jeffrey Hill Cl *FUL/RIB* PR2....................**21**
Jeffrey Sq *BPOOL* FY1....................**5**
Jellicoe Cl *LSTA* FY8....................**23**
Jem Ga *CLV/TH* FY5....................**14**
Jemmett St *PRES* PR1....................**21**
Jenkinson St *BPOOLS* FY4....................**20**
  CHLYE PR6....................**28**
Jenny Nook *HEY* LA3....................**5**
Jenny St *NLSN* BB9....................**19**

sen Cl *LANC* LA1 ....2 C5
sen Dr *BPOOLS* FY4 ....206 C5
p Hl *BWCK/EAR* BB18 ....145 F1
ps Av *GAR/LONG* PR3 ....184 D3
ps La *GAR/LONG* PR3 ....184 D3
son St *DWN* BB3 ....291 J3
son Wy *BPOOLS* FY4 ....205 F3
sey Av *BISP* FY2 ....176 E1
sey St *BBNW* BB2 ....267 J2
vis Cl *LSTA* FY8 ....230 D2
mond Av *BPOOLS* FY4 ....204 B4
mond Gv *MCMB* LA4 ....41 K8
mond Rd *BOL* BL1 ....341 F7
sel St *BBNW* BB2 ....267 J1
son Wy *CARN* LA5 ....33 J2
ington Wy *HEY* LA3 ....52 E4
y La *PDHM/BLYW* BB12 ....169 F8
ling La *KKBYL* LA6 ....21 H1
ling St *COL* * BB8 ....171 F8
key St *BLY* BB11 ....224 E6
Connolly Wy *RAW/HAS* BB4 ....297 C3
La *GAR/LONG* PR3 ....155 K2
nny Bank Cl *RAW/HAS* BB4 ....296 E1
DHM/BLYW BB12 ....223 J2
ANC LA1 ....2 A4
nson Cl *CARN* LA5 ....33 J2
nson New Rd *DWN* BB3 ....269 H8
nson Rd *BPOOLS* FY4 ....5 F5
WN BB3 ....269 F7
nson's Meanygate
IRK/FR/WA PR4 ....281 G2
nson St *CHTN/BK* PR9 ....301 H3
/CGNW/BIL/O WN5 ....365 K5
nspool *FUL/RIB* PR2 ....212 E5
nston Cl *BBNW* BB2 ....8 A4
nston St *BBNW* BB2 ....8 A4
n St *ACC* BB5 ....221 K8
CC BB5 ....247 H8
CC BB5 ....247 J4
POOL* FY1 ....4 B5
HLY/EC* PR7 ....335 J2
LV/TH FY5 ....123 H7
OL BB8 ....171 H7
WN BB3 ....291 H1
GHB LA2 ....67 G8
EY/BBR PR5 ....263 H2
EY/BBR PR5 ....285 J2
LSN BB9 ....170 C2
LSN BB9 ....197 K5
AW/HAS BB4 ....297 H2
HIT OL12 ....323 H1
nsville Av *BPOOLS* FY4 ....204 E4
n William St *PRES* * PR1 ....240 A3
ners Aly *GTH/LHO* * BB6 ....221 C6
ner's Rw *BBN* BB1 ....8 C6
y Tar La *CHLY/EC* PR7 ....336 A4
athan Cl *RAW/HAS* BB4 ....295 G3
es St *HOR/BR* BL6 ....338 D7
es's Yd *KKBYL* LA6 ....18 A6
eph St *DWN* BB3 ....291 J2
LSN BB9 ....198 B1
ce Av *BPOOLS* FY3 ....5 F5
St *RAMS* BL0 ....319 H5
ilee Av *FUL/RIB* PR2 ....237 K2
RM L39 ....348 D5
LF/KEOS FY6 ....98 C7
/CGNW/BIL/O WN5 ....365 K7
ilee Cl *RAW/HAS* BB4 ....295 G2
ilee Dr *CLV/TH* FY5 ....122 C8
KEL WN8 ....362 E3
ilee La *BPOOLS* FY4 ....205 H5
ilee La North *BPOOLS* FY4 ....205 G4
ilee Rd *ACC* BB5 ....247 K4
MBY L37 ....355 H2
EY/BBR PR5 ....262 D4
AW/HAS BB4 ....295 G2
ilee St *ACC* BB5 ....247 J7
CC* BB5 ....248 A2
BN BB1 ....8 C5
RFD/BLYE BB10 ....198 D8
WN BB3 ....291 J2
DHM/BLYW* BB12 ....222 D1
ilee Ter *KIRK/FR/WA* PR4 ....235 G4
IRK/FR/WA
off Preston Old Rd) PR4 ....236 C2
ilee Wy *LSTA* FY8 ....231 J1
d Holmes La *GAR/LONG* PR3 ....160 D5
eland *CHLY/EC* PR7 ....310 A1
e St *NLSN* BB9 ....198 B3
ge Flds *COL* BB8 ....171 H5
ith St *WHIT* OL12 ....323 G8
a St *HOR/BR* BL6 ....338 D7
nps La *TOD* OL14 ....277 K2
ction La *BRSC* L40 ....330 E7

BRSC L40 ....331 F8
Junction Rd *PRES* PR1 ....6 B3
RNFD/HAY WA11 ....368 B3
Junction St *BLY* BB11 ....10 B3
DWN BB3 ....291 K4
NLSN BB9 ....170 D8
NLSN BB9 ....197 K5
PDHM/BLYW* BB12 ....10 A2
June Av *BPOOLS* FY4 ....205 G2
June St *BBN* BB1 ....9 E5
June's Wk *KIRK/FR/WA* PR4 ....260 A6
Juniper Cl *PLF/KEOS* FY6 ....98 C6
Juniper Cft *CHLYE* PR6 ....286 E2
Juniper St *BBN* BB1 ....9 E2
Juno St *NLSN* BB9 ....198 D1
Jutland St *PRES* PR1 ....7 E1

K

Kairnryan Cl *BISP* FY2 ....149 F5
Kale Gv *NWD/KWIPK* L33 ....366 E6
Kaley La *CLI* BB7 ....140 E6
Kane St *FUL/RIB* PR2 ....6 A1
Kateholm *BCUP* OL13 ....275 K4
Kate St *RAMS* * BL0 ....319 H5
Kay Brow *RAMS* BL0 ....319 J5
Kay Gdns *BLY* BB11 ....11 E4
Kay St *ACC* BB5 ....247 H7
BBNW BB2 ....8 C6
BPOOL FY1 ....4 B5
BURY BL9 ....319 J8
CLI BB7 ....165 H4
DWN BB3 ....291 K2
EDGW/EG BL7 ....317 C7
PDHM/BLYW* BB12 ....223 K2
PRES PR1 ....6 C3
RAW/HAS BB4 ....296 C1
Kayswell Rd *MCMB* LA4 ....42 B6
Kearsley Av *KIRK/FR/WA* PR4 ....282 A5
Keasden Av *BPOOLS* FY4 ....204 D4
Keating Ct *FTWD* FY7 ....97 F8
Keats Av *CARN* LA5 ....33 G6
KIRK/FR/WA PR4 ....234 C5
WGNW/BIL/O WN5 ....371 G5
Keats Cl *ACC* BB5 ....271 K1
CHLY/EC* PR7 ....309 F6
CLV/TH FY5 ....149 G1
COL BB8 ....171 G5
Keats Fold *PDHM/BLYW* BB12 ....224 B4
Keats Ter *STHP* PR8 ....302 B5
Keats Wy *KIRK/FR/WA* PR4 ....211 K7
Kebs Rd *HBR* HX7 ....255 H8
Keele Cl *CLV/TH* FY5 ....149 G1
Keele Wk *BBN* BB1 ....9 E5
Keeper's Hey *CLV/TH* FY5 ....123 G7
Keeper's La *GAR/LONG* PR3 ....130 B1
Keer Bank *LANC* LA1 ....2 A1
Keer Holme La *KKBYL* LA6 ....27 J5
Keighley Av *COL* BB8 ....171 H5
Keighley Rd *BWCK/EAR* BB18 ....145 H3
Keirby Wk *BLY* BB11 ....11 D3
Keith Gv *CLV/TH* FY5 ....148 D5
Keith St *PDHM/BLYW* BB12 ....224 E5
Kelbrook Dr *BLY* BB11 ....10 B6
Kelbrook Rd *BWCK/EAR* BB18 ....145 H3
Kellet Acre *LEY/BBR* PR5 ....262 D4
Kellet Av *LEY/BBR* PR5 ....286 B2
Kellet La *CARN* LA5 ....33 K7
HGHB LA2 ....43 H6
KKBYL LA6 ....26 E5
LEY/BBR PR5 ....264 A5
Kellet Lane Br *KKBYL* LA6 ....26 D8
Kellet Rd *CARN* LA5 ....34 A2
CARN LA5 ....34 C3
Kellett St *CHLY/EC* * PR7 ....311 C3
EDGW/EG BL7 ....341 K5
Kelmarsh Rd *BPOOLS* FY3 ....205 H1
Kelsall Av *BBN* BB1 ....9 F1
Kelsey St *LANC* LA1 ....2 C3
Kelso Av *CLV/TH* FY5 ....148 C2
Kelso Cl *NWD/KWIPK* L33 ....366 B5
Kelsons Av *CLV/TH* FY5 ....149 J1
Kelswick Dr *NLSN* BB9 ....198 D5
Kelverdale Rd *CLV/TH* FY5 ....149 F3
Kelvin Gv *DWN* BB3 ....291 H2
Kelvin St *DWN* BB3 ....291 H2
Kem Mill La *CHLYE* PR6 ....287 F3
Kemp Ct *BBN* BB1 ....9 E5
Kemple Vw *CLI* BB7 ....165 G5
Kemp St *FTWD* FY7 ....97 H6
Kempton Av *BPOOLS* FY3 ....5 E4
Kempton Park Fold *STHP* PR8 ....302 B3
Kempton Ri *BBN* BB1 ....9 D6
Kempton Rd *LANC* LA1 ....55 H7
Kenbury Cl *NWD/KWIPK* L33 ....366 E7

Kenbury Rd *NWD/KWIPK* L33 ....366 E7
Kendal Av *BPOOLE* FY3 ....177 F2
CLV/TH FY5 ....122 D7
NLSN BB9 ....170 B7
Kendal Cl *RNFD/HAY* WA11 ....369 F1
Kendal Dr *MCMB* LA4 ....42 B7
RNFD/HAY WA11 ....369 F2
Kendal Rd *KKBYL* LA6 ....21 F1
LSTA FY8 ....230 D2
Kendal Rw *BBN* BB1 ....269 J5
Kendal St *BBN* BB1 ....8 C3
CLI BB7 ....165 K2
NLSN BB9 ....198 B2
PRES PR1 ....6 C2
Kendal Wy *STHP* PR8 ....325 H8
Kenilworth Av *FTWD* FY7 ....96 E8
Kenilworth Cl *PDHM/BLYW* BB12 ......224 A3
Kenilworth Dr *BWCK/EAR* BB18 ....146 A3
CLI BB7 ....165 G5
Kenilworth Gdns *BPOOLS* FY4 ....204 B4
Kenilworth Pl *LANC* LA1 ....3 E6
Kenilworth Rd *HEY* LA3 ....53 H1
LSTA FY8 ....231 F5
STHP PR8 ....325 J7
Kenlis Rd *GAR/LONG* PR3 ....130 B7
Kenmure Pl *PRES* PR1 ....239 H1
Kennedy Cl *LANC* LA1 ....2 B5
Kennelwood Av *NWD/KWIPK* L33 .....366 D8
Kennet Dr *FUL/RIB* PR2 ....213 H5
Kennett Dr *LEY/BBR* PR5 ....285 K1
Kennington Rd *FUL/RIB* PR2 ....213 J7
Kensington Av *PRES* PR1 ....238 D5
Kensington Dr *HOR/BR* BL6 ....338 E8
Kensington Pl *BLY* BB11 ....10 A5
Kensington Rd *BPOOLE* FY3 ....5 D3
CHLY/EC PR7 ....311 F4
CHTN/BK PR9 ....301 J4
CLV/TH FY5 ....122 D3
FMBY L37 ....355 J2
LANC LA1 ....3 D6
LEY/BBR* PR5 ....240 B8
MCMB* LA4 ....41 H6
Kensington St *NLSN* BB9 ....198 A4
FMBY L37 ....355 J2
LEY/BBR* PR5 ....263 G1
Kent Av *CLV/TH* FY5 ....122 E7
FMBY L37 ....356 A2
LEY/BBR* PR5 ....240 B8
Kent Cl *NLSN* BB9 ....170 B7
Kent Dr *BBN* BB1 ....246 C7
LEY/BBR PR5 ....286 B1
Kentmere Av *LEY/BBR* PR5 ....262 D8
LEY/BBR PR5 ....263 G1
Kentmere Cl *PDHM/BLYW* BB12 ....224 D3
Kentmere Dr *BBNW* BB2 ....267 F3
BPOOLS FY4 ....205 J2
KIRK/FR/WA PR4 ....260 C3
Kentmere Gv *MCMB* LA4 ....41 K7
Kentmere Rd *LANC* LA1 ....3 E2
Kenton Cl *FMBY* L37 ....343 K5
Kent Rd *BPOOL* FY1 ....4 B4
FMBY L37 ....356 A2
STHP PR8 ....301 G7
Kent's Cl *KIRK/FR/WA* PR4 ....208 C4
Kent St *BBN* BB1 ....9 D5
FTWD FY7 ....97 H6
LANC LA1 ....3 D1
PDHM/BLYW BB12 ....10 C2
PRES PR1 ....239 H1
Kent Wk *RAW/HAS* BB4 ....295 C3
Kent Wy *LANC* LA1 ....42 B8
Kenway *RNFD/HAY* WA11 ....369 G5
Kenwood Av *MCMB* LA4 ....41 G7
Kenwood Rd *BOL* BL1 ....341 F8
Kenworthys Flats *CHTN/BK* PR9 ....301 H3
Kenworthy St *BBN* BB1 ....9 D3
Kenwyn Av *BPOOLE* FY3 ....5 E4
Kenyon Cl *NWD/KWIPK* L33 ....366 D5
Kenyon La *CHLYE* PR6 ....287 K4
Kenyon Rd *MCMB* LA4 ....42 B6
NLSN BB9 ....197 J4
Kenyon's La *FMBY* L37 ....344 A8
MGHL L31 ....359 F7
Kenyon St *ACC* BB5 ....248 B5
BBN BB1 ....246 A5
BCUP OL13 ....299 F3
RAMS BL0 ....319 J4
RAW/HAS BB4 ....273 H8
Keppel Pl *BLY* BB11 ....10 B4
Kepple La *GAR/LONG* PR3 ....129 G5
Kerenhappuch St *RAMS* BL0 ....319 H6
Kerfoot's La *SKEL* WN8 ....362 C3
Kermoor Av *BOL* BL1 ....341 J5
Kerr Pl *PRES* PR1 ....6 B2
Kershaw Cl *RAW/HAS* BB4 ....273 H4
Kershaw St *ACC* BB5 ....247 J5
BCUP* OL13 ....298 D7
CHLYE PR6 ....311 J3
WGNW/BIL/O WN5 ....365 K5

Kerslake Wy HTWN L38 .....355 K7
Kerslea Av PLF/KEOS FY6 .....177 K3
Kerton Rw
  STHP (off Bickerton Rd) PR8 .....301 F7
Keston Gv BPOOLS FY4 .....204 C6
Kestor La GAR/LONG PR3 .....188 A4
Kestral Pk SKEL WN8 .....351 J7
Kestrel CI BBN BB1 .....8 B1
  CHLYE PR6 .....288 A8
  CLV/TH FY5 .....123 F6
Kestrel Ms SKEL WN8 .....351 J7
Keswick Av ACC BB5 .....248 D2
  STHP PR8 .....325 J8
Keswick CI LANC LA1 .....3 F2
Keswick Dr BBNW BB2 .....267 F3
Keswick Gv HEY LA3 .....52 C6
  PLF/KEOS FY6 .....98 B6
Keswick Rd BPOOL FY1 .....4 C4
  BRFD/BLYE BB10 .....225 J1
  LANC LA1 .....3 F2
  LSTA FY8 .....230 E3
Keswick Wk LANC LA1 .....3 F2
Keswick Wy RNFD/HAY WA11 .....369 F1
Kettering Rd STHP PR8 .....325 H6
Kevin Av PLF/KEOS FY6 .....150 B6
Kevin Gv HEY LA3 .....65 H2
Kew Gdns LEY/BBR PR5 .....262 E8
  PRES PR1 .....238 D5
Kew Gv CLV/TH FY5 .....148 D2
Kew Rd FMBY L37 .....355 H2
  STHP PR8 .....301 G8
Keynsham Gv PDHM/BLYW BB12 .....10 A2
Key Vw DWN BB3 .....292 A6
Khyber St COL BB8 .....171 G7
Kibble Crs BRFD/BLYE BB10 .....198 A8
Kibble Gv NLSN BB9 .....198 D1
Kibboth Crew RAMS BL0 .....319 H4
Kidbrooke Av BPOOLS FY4 .....204 B5
Kidder St BBNW BB2 .....268 A3
Kiddlington CI LEY/BBR PR5 .....263 F3
Kiddrow La PDHM/BLYW BB12 .....224 C5
Kidsgrove FUL/RIB PR2 .....212 B6
Kielder Ct LSTA FY8 .....232 E7
Kielder Dr PDHM/BLYW BB12 .....10 A2
Kilbane St FTWD FY7 .....123 F2
Kilburn Dr WGNNW/ST WN6 .....353 J4
Kilburn Rd SKEL WN8 .....364 E6
Kilcrash La GAR/LONG PR3 .....128 C4
Kildare Av CLV/TH FY5 .....123 G7
Kildare Rd BISP FY2 .....148 D8
Kilgrimol Gdns LSTA FY8 .....230 C3
Kilkerran CI CHLYE PR6 .....311 H3
Killer St RAMS * BL0 .....319 J5
Killiard La BBNW BB2 .....244 A7
Killingbeck CI BRSC L40 .....330 D7
Killington St BRFD/BLYE BB10 .....226 A1
Kilmory PI BISP FY2 .....149 F6
Kilmuir CI FUL/RIB * PR2 .....214 A6
Kilnbank Av MCMB LA4 .....41 G6
Kiln Bank La WHIT OL12 .....323 G1
Kiln CI CLI BB7 .....166 A1
Kiln Cft CHLYE PR6 .....263 K8
Kiln Fld EDGW/EG BL7 .....341 H6
Kilngate LEY/BBR PR5 .....240 A8
Kiln HI PDHM/BLYW BB12 .....196 B5
Kilnhouse La LSTA FY8 .....231 F2
Kiln House Wy ACC BB5 .....248 A8
Kiln La CLI BB7 .....94 A7
  CLI BB7 .....116 A8
  HCHB LA2 .....37 K6
  PLF/KEOS FY6 .....150 D1
  SKEL WN8 .....362 E1
The Kilns BLY BB11 .....11 E6
Kiln St NLSN BB9 .....198 B3
  RAMS BL0 .....319 H6
Kilruddery Rd PRES PR1 .....6 B5
Kilsby CI LEY/BBR PR5 .....240 C3
Kilshaw St PRES PR1 .....7 D1
Kilworth Height FUL/RIB PR2 .....212 E6
Kimberley Av BPOOLS FY4 .....204 D6
Kimberley CI BRFD/BLYE BB10 .....198 D8
Kimberley Rd BOL BL1 .....341 J6
  FUL/RIB PR2 .....238 E1
Kimberley St BCUP * OL13 .....297 L4
  BRFD/BLYE BB10 .....198 C8
  CHLY/EC PR7 .....335 J2
Kimberly CI KIRK/FR/WA PR4 .....235 F5
Kime St PDHM/BLYW BB12 .....224 C5
Kincardine Av BPOOLS FY4 .....205 G5
Kincrag PI BISP FY2 .....149 F5
Kincraig Rd BISP FY2 .....149 F7
King Edward Av BISP FY2 .....176 B2
King Edward St ACC BB5 .....247 G8
  LSTA FY8 .....231 G7
Kingfisher Bank BLY BB11 .....224 D7
Kingfisher CI BBN BB1 .....8 C1
  NWD/KWIPK L33 .....366 C5

Kingfisher Ct CHTN/BK PR9 .....301 K3
Kingfisher Dr PLF/KEOS FY6.....177 H1
Kingfisher Pk SKEL WN8 .....351 J2
Kingfisher St PRES PR1 .....239 K1
King George Av BISP FY2 .....176 B2
Kingham CI CLI BB7 .....165 J3
Kingsacre GAR/LONG PR3 .....129 G8
Kings Ar LANC * LA1 .....2 C3
Kings Av RAW/HAS BB4 .....296 C2
King's Bridge CI BBNW BB2 .....267 J2
Kingsbridge CI PRES PR1 .....262 B2
King's Bridge St BBNW BB2 .....267 J2
Kingsbury CI STHP PR8 .....325 G7
Kingsbury Ct SKEL WN8 .....351 J7
King's Cswy NLSN BB9 .....198 B6
Kings CI BPOOLE FY3 .....178 A6
  CARN LA5 .....15 G2
  FMBY L37 .....355 J1
  PLF/KEOS FY6 .....150 A8
Kingscote Dr BPOOLE FY3 .....5 E1
Kings Ct LEY/BBR PR5 .....285 J2
King's Crs HEY LA3 .....40 E8
  LEY/BBR PR5 .....285 J2
King's Cft LEY/BBR PR5.....240 B6
Kingsdale Av BRFD/BLYE BB10 .....197 K8
  FUL/RIB PR2 .....214 B6
  HEY LA3 .....52 D2
Kingsdale CI LEY/BBR PR5 .....240 C6
  LEY/BBR PR5 .....285 K5
Kingsdale Rd LANC LA1 .....2 B4
Kings Dr DWN BB3 .....292 C2
  FUL/RIB PR2 .....213 F6
  PDHM/BLYW BB12 .....224 A5
Kingsfold Dr PRES PR1 .....261 K1
Kingshaven Dr PRES PR1 .....262 B2
Kings Hey Dr CHTN/BK PR9 .....302 B2
King's Hwy ACC BB5 .....249 F3
  ACC BB5 .....249 H7
  ACC BB5 .....272 C3
Kingshotte Gdns NLSN BB9 .....170 A8
Kingsland Gv BLY BB11 .....11 E5
  BPOOL FY1 .....5 D4
Kingsland Rd BLY BB11 .....11 E6
Kingslea CHLY/EC PR7 .....337 F3
Kingsley Av PDHM/BLYW BB12 .....224 A4
  COL BB8 .....172 D5
  KIRK/FR/WA PR4 .....212 A5
Kingsley Dr CHLY/EC PR7 .....310 E2
Kingsley Rd BPOOLE FY3 .....205 H1
Kingsley St NLSN BB9 .....198 D1
Kingsmead BBN BB1 .....246 B7
  CHLY/EC PR7 .....311 G6
Kings Meadow STHP PR8 .....325 K8
Kingsmede BPOOLS FY4 .....204 E5
Kingsmere Av LSTA FY8 .....231 F2
Kingsmill Av CLI BB7 .....192 E3
King's Moss La RNFD/HAY WA11 .....370 A4
Kingsmuir Av FUL/RIB * PR2 .....214 B7
Kingsmuir CI HEY LA3 .....52 C4
King's Rd ACC BB5 .....248 B3
  BBNW BB2 .....267 J3
  CLV/TH FY5 .....148 C1
  FMBY L37 .....355 J1
  LSTA FY8 .....230 E6
King's Sq BPOOL * FY1 .....4 C2
Kingston Av ACC BB5 .....248 A7
  BPOOLS FY4 .....204 C6
Kingston CI PLF/KEOS FY6 .....98 B5
Kingston Crs CHTN/BK PR9 .....278 C6
  RAW/HAS BB4 .....295 F4
Kingston Dr LSTA FY8 .....231 K5
Kingston PI DWN BB3 .....268 B4
King St ACC * BB5 .....247 K1
  ACC BB5 .....248 B5
  BBNW BB2 .....8 B1
  BCUP OL13 .....298 D1
  BPOOL FY1 .....4 C2
  BRFD/BLYE BB10 .....198 D8
  CARN LA5 .....33 K2
  CHLY/EC PR7 .....311 H5
  CLI BB7 .....165 J3
  CLI BB7 .....193 G7
  COL BB8 .....171 J6
  EDGW/EG BL7 .....341 K3
  FTWD FY7 .....97 G7
  GAR/LONG PR3.....188 B4
  GTH/LHO BB6 .....221 G6
  HOR/BR BL6 .....338 C2
  LANC LA1 .....3 D3
  LEY/BBR PR5 .....262 E4
  LEY/BBR PR5 .....285 J2
  MCMB LA4 .....41 H6
  NLSN BB9 .....197 J6

  PDHM/BLYW BB12 22
  RAMS BL0 319
  RAW/HAS BB4 272
  RAW/HAS BB4 29
  STHP PR8 30
  WHIT OL12 299
King's Wk CLV/TH FY5 122
Kingsway ACC BB5 248
  ACC BB5 249
  BLY BB11 1
  BLY BB11 223
  BPOOLS FY4 204
  CHLY/EC PR7 310
  CLV/TH FY5.....148
  DWN BB3 268
  FUL/RIB PR2 238
  GTH/LHO BB6 221
  HEY LA3 52
  LANC LA1 3
  LEY/BBR PR5 263
  LEY/BBR PR5 285
  LSTA FY8 231
  PRES PR1 238
  STHP PR8 30
Kingsway Av GAR/LONG PR3 184
Kingsway West PRES PR1 238
Kingswood CHLY/EC PR7 311
Kingswood CI LSTA FY8 232
Kingswood Ct NWD/KWIPK L33 366
Kingswood Rd LEY/BBR PR5 285
Kingswood St PRES PR1 6
King William St BBN BB1 8
  BBNW* BB2 8
Kinloch Wy ORM L39 348
Kinnerton PI CLV/TH FY5 149
Kinnical La MTHPE LA7 17
Kinross CI BBN BB1 9
Kinross Crs BPOOLS FY4 205
Kinross St BLY BB11 10
Kinross Wk BBN BB1 9
Kintbury Rd LSTA FY8 231
Kintour Rd LSTA FY8 232
Kintyre CI BPOOLS FY4 205
Kintyre Wy HEY LA3 52
Kipling Dr BPOOLE FY3 205
Kipling PI GTH/LHO BB6 221
Kirby Dr KIRK/FR/WA PR4 235
Kirby Rd BBNW BB2 268
  BPOOL FY1 197
  NLSN BB9 197
Kirk Av CLI BB7 165
Kirkbeck CI HGHB LA2 45
Kirkby Av CLV/TH FY5 122
  LEY/BBR PR5 286
Kirkby Lonsdale Rd HGHB LA2 44
Kirkby Lonsdale Rd KKBYL LA6 34
Kirkby Rw KKBY L32 366
Kirkdale Av LSTA FY8 231
  RAW/HAS BB4 297
Kirkdale CI DWN BB3 292
Kirkdale Gdns SKEL * WN8 364
Kirkdale Rd GTH/LHO BB6 220
Kirkdene Av COL BB8 171
Kirkes Rd LANC LA1 3
Kirkfell Dr PDHM/BLYW BB12.....224
Kirkfield GAR/LONG PR3 134
Kirkgate BLY BB11 11
  KIRK/FR/WA PR4 209
Kirkgate La KKBYL LA6 26
Kirkham Av BPOOL FY1 5
Kirkham By-Pass
  KIRK/FR/WA PR4 209
Kirkham CI LEY/BBR PR5 285
Kirkham Rd CHTN/BK PR9 278
  KIRK/FR/WA PR4 207
  KIRK/FR/WA PR4 209
  KIRK/FR/WA PR4 235
Kirkham St PRES PR1 6
Kirk Head KIRK/FR/WA PR4 282
Kirkhill Av RAW/HAS BB4 272
Kirk Hill Rd RAW/HAS BB4 272
Kirklake Bank FMBY L37 355
Kirklake Rd FMBY L37 355
Kirklands GAR/LONG PR3 134
  HGHB LA2 42
Kirklands Rd KKBYL LA6 34
Kirklees STHP PR8 326
Kirkmoor CI CLI BB7 165
Kirkmoor Rd CLI BB7 165
Kirk Rd ACC BB5 247
Kirkstall Av BPOOL * FY1 5
  PDHM/BLYW BB12 222
Kirkstall CI CHLY/EC PR7 311
Kirkstall Dr BWCK/EAR BB18 119
  CHLY/EC PR7 311
  FMBY L37 356
Kirkstall Rd CHLY/EC PR7 31

THP PR8.................................326 B1
stone Av *BBNW* BB2..........267 F3
TWD FY7................................122 D2
stone Dr *CLV/TH* FY5.........148 C5
CMB LA4..................................41 K6
stone Rd *LSTA* FY8..............230 D2
: Vw *RAW/HAS* BB4............297 J2
on Crs *LSTA* FY8.................231 J5
on Pl *CLV/TH* FY5...............148 E2
son Wood Rd *TOD* OL14.....277 K3
iwake Cl *CLV/TH* FY5..........149 D2
iwake Rd *CHLYE* PR6.........288 A8
lingborne Brow *LEY/BBR* PR5....240 E8
ygill La *KKBYL* LA6..............21 F2
y La *BPOOLS* FY4..............205 H7
cks La *WHIT* OL12...............322 E6
aresboro Av *BPOOLE* * FY3........5 F4
aresborough Rd *PLF/KEOS* FY6..149 K6
ebworth Cl *CHLYE* PR6........287 G1
ghton Av *BBNW* BB2..............8 A1
ghtsbrdige Cl
RK/FR/WA* PR4.....................208 C5
OL BB8...................................171 F6
ghtsbridge Dr *BPOOLS* FY4....204 D5
ghtsbridge Cl *LSTA* FY8.....231 K5
ghtsbridge Wk
WD/KWIPK* L33....................366 B5
ghtscliffe Crs
CNNW/ST* WN6....................353 F5
ghts Cl *CLV/TH* FY5............149 F2
cting Row La *GAR/LONG* PR3....125 J8
b Hall Gdns *CHTN/BK* PR9........278 B8
b Hall La *CHTN/BK* PR9.....278 B8
ll La *KIRK/FR/WA* PR4........260 A7
Knoll *FMBY* L37...................42 E3
st Acre *KIRK/FR/WA* PR4....261 H3
tt La *CLI* BB7......................117 K1
EY/BBR* PR5........................240 C6
tt Hill St *WHIT* OL12..........299 J5
tts Brow *EDGW/EG* BL7....317 K7
tts Dr *COL* BB8...................171 C8
tts La *COL* BB8...................171 C7
DHM/BLYW* BB12................224 C5
KP/WHF* BD23.......................91 J4
tts Mt *COL* BB8...................171 C8
tts Rd *TOD* OL14...............277 J3
tt St *DWN* BB3....................291 J2
owe Hall La *LANC* LA1.........55 H8
owl Cl *RAMS* BL0...............319 J7
owle Av *BISP* FY2...............176 C2
LV/TH* FY5...........................148 E2
THP PR8.................................325 J5
owle Green Rd *GAR/LONG* PR3....188 C5
owle La *DWN* BB3...............268 D8
owlesly Rd *DWN* BB3.........291 K5
owles Brow *CLI* BB7...........163 K8
owles Rd *LSTA* FY8............230 E4
owle St *BBN* BB1................247 F2
HLY/EC* PR7..........................311 G5
RES* PR1..............................240 B3
- Knowle *BISP* FY2.............176 C1
owly Av *HEY* LA3..................52 C3
owly Crs *HEY* * LA3.............52 D3
owly Dr *HEY* LA3..................52 D3
owly Gv *HEY* LA3..................52 C3
owly St *HEY* LA3..................52 C3
owsley Av *BPOOLS* FY4.........5 E4
EY/BBR* PR5........................263 F7
owsley Cl *LANC* LA1..............2 B5
owsley Crs *CLV/TH* FY5.....149 J1
IRK/FR/WA* PR4....................207 G2
WHIT* OL12...........................299 J5
owsley Dr *LEY/BBR* PR5....264 C1
owsley Ga *FTWD* FY7...........96 D7
owsley La *CHLYE* PR6........312 D7
DGW/EG* BL7......................293 J7
owsley Park Wy *RAW/HAS* BB4....295 H3
owsley Rd *BBN* BB1...........219 H6
HTN/BK* PR9........................301 H2
EY/BBR* PR5........................286 A3
RM L39..................................348 D7
AW/HAS* BB4......................295 H1
owsley Rd West *BBN* BB1....219 G5
owsley St *COL* * BB8..........171 F5
RES* PR1..................................7 E3
owsley Vw *RNFD/HAY* WA11....368 E3
ox Gv *BPOOL* FY1..................5 D4
uck Knowles Dr *CLI* BB7....165 J1
utsford Rd *BPOOLE* FY3....205 H1
utsford Wk *MGHL* L31........359 F7

Korea Rd *FUL/RIB* PR2........213 K6
Kumara Crs *BPOOLS* FY4....205 H2
Kyan St *BRFD/BLYE* BB10....225 K1
Kylemore Av *BISP* FY2........176 D1
Kyston Cl *BPOOL* FY1..........176 D4

L

Laburnum Av *LEY/BBR* PR5....262 E3
LSTA* FY8.............................232 D6
Laburnum Cl *BLY* BB11..........10 A1
PRES* PR1............................214 A8
Laburnum Cottages
GAR/LONG* (off Taylors La) PR3....100 C6
Laburnum Crs *KKBY* L32....366 B5
Laburnum Dr *ACC* BB5........247 K8
FUL/RIB* PR2.......................213 F3
SKEL* WN8............................362 D2
Laburnum Gv *BRSC* L40......330 E5
LANC LA1...................................2 B3
STHP PR8..............................302 B4
Laburnum Pk *CARN* LA5........33 J3
Laburnum Rd *BBN* BB1...........9 E1
CHLYE* PR6..........................287 H8
LANC* LA1...............................3 D1
Laburnum St *BPOOL* FY3....176 D4
RAW/HAS* BB4......................272 B8
Lachman Rd *COL* BB8..........172 B8
Lacy Av *PRES* PR1...............262 B1
Ladbrooke Gv *BLY* BB11......251 G1
Lade End *HEY* LA3.................52 C3
Ladies Rw
KIRK/FR/WA*
(off Roseacre Rd) PR4..........181 K7
Ladies Wk *LANC* LA1...............3 E1
Lady Alice's Dr *BRSC* L40....349 J3
Lady Bower La *PLF/KEOS* FY6....177 H1
Lady Crosse Dr *CHLYE* PR6....287 G5
Lady Green Cl *HTWN* * L38....356 E8
Lady Green La *HTWN* L38....356 D7
Lady Hey Crs *FUL/RIB* PR2....237 J2
Ladyman St *PRES* * PR1...........6 C3
Lady Pl *LEY/BBR* PR5..........240 C7
Ladysmith Rd *FUL/RIB* PR2....238 E1
Lady St *PRES* PR1....................7 D2
Lady's Wk *BRSC* L40............349 J3
Lady Well Dr *FUL/RIB* PR2....214 A4
Ladywell St *PRES* PR1.............6 C1
Lafford La *SKEL* WN8...........352 E8
Lagonda Dr *BPOOLS* FY4....206 B5
Laidley's Wk *FTWD* FY7.........96 E1
Laithbutts La *KKBYL* LA6......34 B6
Laithe St *BLY* BB11................10 C5
COL BB8................................171 G7
Lake Av *MCMB* LA4................41 F8
Lake Gv *MCMB* LA4................41 F7
Lakeland Cl *CLI* BB7............192 B8
GAR/LONG* PR3.....................80 C8
Lakeland Gdns *CHLY/EC* PR7....310 E6
Lakeland Wy *PDHM/BLYW* BB12....224 D3
Lakenheath Cl *BOL* BL1.......341 K5
Lakenheath Dr *BOL* BL1......341 K5
Lake Rd *HEY* LA3...................41 F8
LSTA* FY8..............................231 J8
Lake Rd North *LSTA* FY8......231 J8
Lakes Dr *WGNW/BIL/O* WN5....365 G5
Lakeside Av *WGNW/BIL/O* WN5....365 G8
Lakeside Ct *RNFD/HAY* WA11....369 G5
STHP* (off Promenade) PR8....301 H3
Lakeside Gdns *RNFD/HAY* WA11....369 G5
Lake Vw *EDGW/EG* BL7.......314 E6
Lake View Rd *COL* BB8.........171 H4
Lakeway *BPOOLE* FY3.............5 F1
Lakewood Av *CLV/TH* FY5....148 D2
Lamaleach Dr *KIRK/FR/WA* PR4....234 E5
Lamberhead
WGNW/BIL/O* WN5..............365 K5
Lambert Cl *FUL/RIB* PR2......214 C8
Lambert Rd *FUL/RIB* PR2.....214 C8
LANC LA1.................................42 E8
Lambert St *COL* BB8............200 C1
Lambeth Cl *BBN* BB1...............9 E5
HOR/BR* BL6........................339 F7
Lambeth St *BBN* BB1...............9 E4
COL BB8................................172 B8
Lambing Clough La *CLI* BB7....191 G4
Lambourne *SKEL* WN8.........351 H1
Lambridge Cl *MGHL* LA4........41 H8
Lambshear La *MGHL* L31.....358 C7
Lambs Hill Cl *CLV/TH* FY5....149 K2
Lamb's La *GAR/LONG* PR3.....99 J7
Lambs Rd *CLV/TH* FY5.........149 K3
Lambton Gates *RAW/HAS* BB4....296 E1
Lambton St *WGNW/BIL/O* WN5....365 K6
Lamlash Rd *BBN* BB1...........246 B7

Lammack Rd *BBN* BB1.............8 A1
Lanark Av *BISP* FY2..............148 C5
Lanark St *BLY* BB11................10 A5
Lancambe Ct *LANC* LA1.........54 B1
Lancashire St *MCMB* LA4......40 E7
Lancaster Av *ACC* BB5..........248 A4
CLV/TH* AV...........................149 J1
GAR/LONG* PR3.....................153 G6
LEY/BBR* PR5.......................286 C2
LSTA* FY8.............................231 F7
RAMS BL0.............................319 G7
RAW/HAS* BB4......................295 G3
Lancaster Cl *CHLYE* PR6......337 H4
GAR/LONG* PR3....................153 G6
PLF/KEOS* FY6......................98 B6
STHP PR8..............................300 E7
Lancaster Crs *SKEL* WN8.....362 E2
Lancaster Dr *ACC* BB5..........221 K8
CHLYE* PR6..........................288 E3
CHTN/BK* PR9......................279 G6
CLI BB7.................................165 G3
PDHM/BLYW* BB12..............223 K5
Lancaster Ga *CHTN/BK* PR9....279 H6
FTWD FY7...............................96 D8
LANC* (off St Nicholas Arcades) LA1....3 D3
Lancastergate *LEY/BBR* PR5....285 H3
Lancaster Ga *NLSN* BB9.......198 A4
Lancaster La *LEY/BBR* PR5....286 D2
SKEL* WN8............................332 E8
Lancaster Pl *BBNW* BB2......244 D6
CHLYE* PR6...........................337 G3
Lancaster Rd *BPOOLE* FY3....205 G1
CARN LA5...............................33 H4
FMBY L37.............................355 J2
GAR/LONG* PR3....................129 J2
GAR/LONG* PR3....................152 E4
HEY LA3...................................65 H2
HGHB LA2................................45 F5
HGHB LA2................................71 H5
MCMB LA4..............................41 J6
PLF/KEOS* FY6......................98 E8
PRES* PR1................................7 E2
STHP PR8..............................300 E7
Lancaster Rd North *PRES* PR1....7 D1
Lancaster St *ACC* BB5..........247 G8
BBNW* BB2.............................8 A5
CHLY/EC* PR7.......................335 K2
COL BB8................................171 H6
Lanchester Ct *LEY/BBR* PR5....285 F5
Lancia Crs *BPOOLS* FY4.......206 C5
Lancing Pl *BBNW* BB2...........8 A6
Landcrest Cl *KIRK/FR/WA* PR4....235 F1
Land End La *BCUP* OL13.......298 E2
Land Ga *WHIT* OL12..............299 J6
Landing La *CLI* BB7...............113 K4
Land La *CHTN/BK* PR9..........278 E1
KIRK/FR/WA* PR4..................260 E5
Landseer Av *BISP* FY2..........148 C7
Landseer Cl *BLY* BB11...........10 B6
Landseer St *PRES* PR1.........240 E2
Landsmoor Dr *KIRK/FR/WA* PR4....260 B2
Lane Bottom *BWCK/EAR* BB18....144 E4
Lanedale *KIRK/FR/WA* PR4....260 E2
Lane End La *BCUP* OL13.......298 E2
Lane End Rd *BCUP* OL13.......298 E3
Lanefield Dr *CLV/TH* FY5......122 D7
Lane Foote Brow *HGHB* LA2....50 C4
Lane Head La *BCUP* OL13.....275 J8
Lane House Cl *BBNW* * BB2....267 J3
Lane House La *COL* BB8........200 C1
Laneshaw Cl *DWN* BB3........268 B7
Laneside *ACC* BB5...............222 D5
Laneside Av *ACC* BB5..........248 B5
PDHM/BLYW* BB12..............196 B5
Laneside Rd *RAW/HAS* BB4....295 H1
The Lane *HEY* LA3.................64 E6
Langcliffe Rd *FUL/RIB* PR2....214 C1
Langdale *HGHB* LA2...............45 G6
Langdale Av *CLI* BB7............165 G4
FMBY L37..............................343 H8
KIRK/FR/WA* PR4.................258 C2
LEY/BBR* PR5........................283 H8
RAW/HAS* BB4......................296 A1
Langdale Cl *ACC* BB5...........248 D2
BBNW* BB2..........................267 E3
CLV/TH* FY5.........................149 H1
FMBY L37.............................355 H1
KIRK/FR/WA* PR4.................234 E5
LEY/BBR* PR5........................263 G2
Langdale Crs *FUL/RIB* PR2....214 C8
WGNW/BIL/O* WN5..............365 K3
Langdale Dr *BRSC* L40.........330 E7
Langdale Gdns *STHP* PR8....326 B2
Langdale Gv *CHLYE* PR6......287 F4
Langdale Pl *BPOOLS* FY4......205 J2
LANC LA1..................................3 E1
Langdale Ri *COL* BB8............171 K5

Langdale Rd BBNW BB2 ....266 E4
  BPOOLS FY4 ....205 H2
  CARN LA5 ....34 A3
  FUL/RIB PR2 ....214 C8
  GAR/LONG PR3 ....187 K5
  LANC LA1 ....3 E1
  LEY/BBR PR5 ....285 K5
  LSTA FY8 ....230 D3
  MCMB LA4 ....41 J6
  PDHM/BLYW BB12 ....223 J1
  WGNW/BIL/O WN5 ....365 K4
Langden Br CLI BB7 ....110 C4
Langden Brook Ms LANC LA1 ....54 B1
Langden Brook Sq BBN BB1 ....9 E6
Langden Crs LEY/BBR PR5 ....263 J4
Langden Dr FUL/RIB PR2 ....214 E8
Langden Fold FUL/RIB PR2 ....215 H2
Langdon Wy BISP FY2 ....176 E1
Langfield BRFD/BLYE BB10 ....227 F5
Langfield Av BPOOLS FY4 ....204 C6
Langfield Cl FUL/RIB PR2 ....213 H3
Langford St ACC BB5 ....271 K2
Langham Av ACC BB5 ....248 B3
Langham Rd BBN BB1 ....8 B2
Langham St PDHM/BLYW BB12 .....224 D5
Langholm Cl LEY/BBR PR5 ....285 F2
Langholme St NLSN BB9 ....198 A2
Langholme Rd PRES PR1 ....238 C7
Langholme St NLSN BB9 ....198 C5
Langho St BBNW BB2 ....267 K2
Langley La GAR/LONG PR3 ....185 H5
Langley Pl BRSC L40 ....330 B7
Langley Rd BRSC L40 ....330 B7
  LANC LA1 ....3 E4
Langport Cl FUL/RIB PR2 ....213 H3
Langridge Wy MCMB LA4 ....41 H8
Langroyd Rd COL BB8 ....171 J5
Langshaw Dr CLI BB7 ....165 J5
Langshaw La HGHB LA2 ....67 K6
Langstone Cl HOR/BR BL6 ....338 D8
Lang St ACC BB5 ....248 A5
  BPOOL FY1 ....4 C1
Langthwaite Rd HGHB LA2 ....56 A6
Langton Brow CHLY/EC PR7 ....309 F6
  GAR/LONG PR3 ....188 B4
Langton Cl CHLY/EC PR7 ....309 F6
  LANC LA1 ....43 G7
  LEY/BBR PR5 ....285 J4
Langton Rd KIRK/FR/WA PR4 ....208 E6
  NWD/KWIPK L33 ....366 D6
Langton St PRES PR1 ....6 B3
Langtree SKEL WN8 ....351 H8
Langtree La KIRK/FR/WA PR4 ....180 D1
  WGNNW/ST WN6 ....335 H8
Langwood FTWD FY7 ....122 H1
Langwood La RNFD/HAY WA11 ......369 J2
Langwyth Rd BRFD/BLYE BB10 ......226 C6
Lansborough Cl LEY/BBR PR5 ....284 D3
Lansbury Pl NLSN BB9 ....198 A5
Lansbury St WGNW/BIL/O WN5 ....365 J5
Lansdowne Cl BLY BB11 ....10 B5
Lansdowne Gv MCMB LA4 ....42 A4
Lansdowne Pl BPOOL FY1 ....4 B1
Lansdowne Rd KIRK/FR/WA PR4 ....208 D4
  LSTA FY8 ....231 K6
  MCMB LA4 ....42 A4
  STHP PR8 ....302 A5
Lansdowne St BBNW BB2 ....244 D8
Lansdown Hl FUL/RIB PR2 ....212 E4
Lansil Wy LANC LA1 ....43 G8
The Lanterns PLF/KEOS FY6 ....149 K1
Lapford Crs NWD/KWIPK L33 ....366 E7
Lappet Gv KIRK/FR/WA PR4 ....212 A6
The Lapwings PLF/KEOS FY6 ....177 H1
Larbreck Av BPOOLE FY3 ....176 E4
  KIRK/FR/WA PR4 ....180 D2
Larbreck Rd BPOOLE FY3 ....176 E4
Larch ACC BB5 ....247 K8
  CHLYE PR6 ....311 J1
Larch Cl BBNW BB2 ....267 G8
  KIRK/FR/WA PR4 ....234 E6
  PLF/KEOS FY6 ....98 C6
  RAW/HAS BB4 ....296 B3
  SKEL WN8 ....362 E2
  WGNW/BIL/O WN5 ....371 F6
Larch Dr CHLYE PR6 ....288 E4
Larches Av FUL/RIB PR2 ....238 B2
Larches La FUL/RIB PR2 ....238 B2
The Larches BBN BB1 ....9 D2
Larchgate FUL/RIB PR2 ....214 A4
Larch Ga LEY/BBR PR5 ....264 D1
Larch Gv GAR/LONG PR3 ....129 J3
  LANC LA1 ....2 B2
  LEY/BBR PR5 ....263 J2
Larch St NLSN BB9 ....198 D3
  PDHM/BLYW* BB12 ....224 E4
  STHP PR8 ....302 A6
Larch Wy FMBY L37 ....343 H7
Larchway GAR/LONG PR3 ....188 B3
Larchwood FUL/RIB PR2 ....238 A2
  LANC LA1 ....55 H7
  PRES* PR1 ....238 D7
Larchwood Cl LSTA FY8 ....232 B7
Larchwood Crs LEY/BBR PR5 ....285 G2
Largs Rd BBN BB1 ....269 F1
Lark Av PRES PR1 ....6 C6
Lark Ct FTWD FY7 ....122 D2
Larkfield CHLY/EC PR7 ....308 D5
Larkfield La CHTN/BK PR9 ....278 C8
Lark Hl BBN BB1 ....9 D3
Larkhill Av BRFD/BLYE BB10 ....198 A6
Larkhill Gv HTWN L38 ....355 K8
Larkhill La FMBY L37 ....343 G7
Larkhill Rd PRES PR1 ....7 F3
Larkhill St BPOOL* FY1 ....4 C1
  PRES PR1 ....7 F3
Larkholme Av FTWD FY7 ....122 C2
Larkholme La FTWD FY7 ....122 C2
Larkholme Pde FTWD FY7 ....122 D2
Larkspur Cl BBNW BB2 ....266 E3
  STHP PR8 ....301 K5
Lark St COL BB8 ....171 J5
  DWN BB3 ....291 K6
  PDHM/BLYW BB12 ....224 E4
Latham Av BPOOLE FY3 ....5 H8
  ORM L39 ....348 E6
Latham Crs KIRK/FR/WA PR4 ....282 A5
Latham La WGNW/BIL/O WN5 ....365 J3
Latham Rd HOR/BR BL6 ....337 D8
Latham St BRFD/BLYE BB10 ....225 K2
  PRES PR1 ....7 E4
Lathom Av MCMB LA4 ....41 K7
  SKEL WN8 ....332 D8
Lathom Dr BRSC L40 ....330 E7
Lathom Dr MGHL L31 ....359 G8
  RNFD/HAY WA11 ....369 F4
Lathom Gv MCMB LA4 ....41 K7
Lathom La BRSC L40 ....349 G4
Lathom Rd CHTN/BK PR9 ....301 J2
  ORM L39 ....361 K4
Lathom Wy GAR/LONG PR3 ....129 K5
Latimer Cl WGNW/BIL/O* WN5 ....365 H4
Latimer Dr KIRK/FR/WA PR4 ....261 G3
Lauder Cl NWD/KWIPK L33 ....366 B5
Lauderdale Av CLV/TH FY5 ....148 D2
Lauderdale Rd FUL/RIB PR2 ....214 D7
Lauderdale St PRES PR1 ....6 C4
Laund Ga PDHM/BLYW BB12 ....197 J3
Laund Gv ACC BB5 ....248 D8
Laund Hey Vw RAW/HAS BB4 ....295 H2
Laund La CHLYE PR6 ....265 K6
  RAW/HAS BB4 ....272 D8
Laund Rd ACC BB5 ....271 J1
Laundry Rd North BPOOLS FY4 .....205 G5
Laund St RAW/HAS BB4 ....273 G7
The Laund LEY/BBR PR5 ....284 C2
Laurel Av BPOOL FY1 ....5 E5
  BRSC L40 ....330 E5
  CHLY/EC PR7 ....285 K8
  DWN BB3 ....291 K1
  FTWD FY7 ....123 F3
  LSTA FY8 ....232 B7
Laurel Bank LANC* LA1 ....2 B4
Laurel Bank Av FUL/RIB PR2 ....212 E8
Laurel Dr CLV/TH FY5 ....149 H3
  SKEL WN8 ....362 E1
Laurel Gv CHTN/BK PR9 ....302 A4
The Laurels CHLY/EC PR7 ....310 D8
Laurel St BCUP OL13 ....275 J8
  BLY* BB11 ....11 E5
  PRES PR1 ....7 E3
Laureston Av HEY LA3 ....52 D5
Laurier Av BPOOLS FY4 ....204 C5
Laurier Rd BRFD/BLYE BB10 ....197 K8
Lauriston Cl BPOOLS FY4 ....205 G5
Lavender Cl FUL/RIB PR2 ....214 A5
Lavender Gv CHLY/EC PR7 ....311 G6
Lavender Hl RAW/HAS BB4 ....296 B2
Laverick Rd HGHB LA2 ....44 C2
Laverton Rd LSTA FY8 ....231 F6
Lawley Rd BBNW BB2 ....244 C6
Lawns Av SKEL WN8 ....364 E6
The Lawns CHTN/BK PR9 ....302 B1
Lawn St BRFD/BLYE BB10 ....11 D1
Lawnswood Av LANC LA1 ....55 G8
  PLF/KEOS FY6 ....177 H1
Lawnswood Crs BPOOLS FY3 ....205 J1
Lawnswood Dr HEY LA3 ....53 H1
Lawn Tennis St BPOOLS FY4 ....204 D5
Lawnwood Av CHLY/EC PR7 ....310 E6

Lawrence Av BLY BB11 22
  LEY/BBR PR5 26
  LSTA FY8 23
  PDHM/BLYW BB12 22
  PRES PR1 ....
Lawrence Dr CARN LA5 1
Lawrence La CHLY/EC PR7 30
Lawrence Rd CHLY/EC PR7 31
  PRES PR1 23
Lawrence Rw
  FTWD FY7 (off Birch St) 9
Lawrence St BBNW BB2 ....
  BPOOLS* FY4 ....
  FUL/RIB PR2 21
  PDHM/BLYW BB12 22
  RAW/HAS BB4 27
Lawrie Av RAMS BL0 31
Lawson Cl LANC LA1 5
Lawson Gdns HGHB LA2 4
Lawson Pl HGHB LA2 4
Lawson Rd BPOOLE FY3 17
  HOR/BR BL6 33
  LSTA FY8 23
Lawsons Ct CLV/TH FY5 14
Lawsons Rd CLV/TH FY5 14
Lawson St BOL BL1 34
  CHLYE PR6 31
  CHTN/BK PR9 30
  PRES PR1 ....
  RAW/HAS BB4 27
Law St RAW/HAS BB4 29
  TOD OL14 27
Lawton Cl CHLYE PR6 28
Laxey Gv PRES PR1 21
Laxey Rd BBNW BB2 26
Laycock Ga BPOOLS FY3 ....
Layton Rd BPOOLE FY3 ....
  FUL/RIB PR2 23
Lazenby Av FTWD FY7 12
Lea Bank RAW/HAS BB4 29
Leach Crs LSTA FY8 23
Leaches Rd RAMS BL0 31
Leachfield Rd HGHB LA2 6
Leach La LSTA FY8 23
Leach Pl LEY/BBR PR5 26
Leach St BBNW BB2 26
  COL BB8 17
Leach Vls
  KIRK/FR/WA
  (off Preston Rd) PR4 18
Lea Crs ORM L39 34
Leacroft DWN BB3 26
Leadale FUL/RIB PR2 23
Leadale Gn LEY/BBR PR5 28
Leadale Rd LEY/BBR PR5 28
Lea Dr BBNW BB2 26
Leaford Av BPOOLE FY3 17
Leafy Cl LEY/BBR PR5 28
Leagram Crs FUL/RIB PR2 21
Lea La HEY LA3 5
  HGHB LA2 3
  KIRK/FR/WA PR4 23
Leamington Av BRFD/BLYE BB10 ...22
Leamington Rd BBNW BB2 24
  BPOOL FY1 ....
  LSTA FY8 23
  MCMB LA4 4
  STHP PR8 32
Leamington St NLSN BB9 19
Leander Av PLF/KEOS FY6 17
Leapers Vw KKBYL LA6 3
Lea Rd CHLYE PR6 2
  KIRK/FR/WA PR4 28
Leathercote GAR/LONG PR3 12
Leaverholme Cl BRFD/BLYE BB10 ...25
Leaver St PDHM/BLYW BB12 22
Leavesley Rd BPOOL FY1 17
Lea Way Cl CLV/TH FY5 14
Lebanon St BRFD/BLYE BB10 1
Leckhampton Rd BPOOL FY1 17
Leckonby St GAR/LONG PR3 15
Ledburn SKEL WN8 35
Ledbury Rd BPOOLE FY3 17
Ledson Gv ORM L39 35
Lee Br HGHB LA2 7
Lee Brook Cl RAW/HAS BB4 27
Leebrook Rd RAW/HAS BB4 27
Leeds Cl BBN BB1 ....
Leeds Rd BPOOL FY1 ....
  NLSN BB9 19
Lee Green St BRFD/BLYE BB10 1
Lee Gv BRFD/BLYE BB10 22
Leehouse Dr PLF/KEOS FY6 17
Leek St PRES PR1 24
Lee La BBN BB1 ....
  BRSC L40 33
  EDGW/EG BL7 31

OR/BR BL6 ....338 C7
Rd BCUP OL13 ....298 C4
POOLS FY4 ....205 H3
LSN BB9 ....198 D1
sands CI FUL/RIB PR2 ....214 B6
s Ct
WN (off Ribble Av) BB3 ....268 B7
EY LA3 ....52 C4
s La SKEL WN8 ....351 J3
SKEL WN8 ....352 C4
son Av CHLY/EC PR7 ....310 B3
s Rd CHLYE PR6 ....337 H3
's St BCUP OL13 ....299 C3
Lees BRFD/BLYE BB10 ....252 E4
St ACC BB5 ....248 D1
CUP OL13 ....298 D1
RFD/BLYE BB10 ....11 D1
AR/LONG PR3 ....187 K4
LSN BB9 ....170 B8
swood SKEL WN8 ....351 H8
t Rd PDHM/BLYW BB12 ....196 H6
ward CI DWN BB3 ....268 C5
ward Rd FUL/RIB PR2 ....238 B3
h La KIRK/FR/WA PR4 ....280 E7
cester Av CLV/TH FY5 ....122 D8
AR/LONG PR3 ....129 H4
cester Ga CLV/TH FY5 ....122 E8
cester Rd BBN BB1 ....246 A6
POOL FY1 ....5 D2
RES PR1 ....7 D1
cester St CHTN/BK PR9 ....301 H2
ster Rd LANC LA1 ....3 E6
nster Rd LANC LA1 ....3 E6
ghton Av FTWD FY7 ....96 D8
gh Pk BLY BB11 ....223 J8
gh Rw CHLY/EC PR7 ....311 C4
ghton Av FTWD FY7 ....96 D8
ghton CI MTHPE LA4 ....16 C1
ghton Dr LANC LA1 ....2 B4
THPE LA7 ....16 C1
ghton St PRES PR1 ....6 C2
nster Rd LANC LA1 ....3 E8
monious St ACC BB5 ....248 C7
ches Fold COL BB8 ....171 H8
ches Rd COL BB8 ....171 H8
ch Rd RAW/HAS BB4 ....297 F3
ch St RAW/HAS BB4 ....297 H3
del CI FMBY L37 ....343 J8
non St CHLY/EC PR7 ....311 C4
nox St BPOOLS FY4 ....204 D4
nox Ga BPOOLS FY4 ....204 D4
nox Rd TOD OL14 ....277 F2
nox St BRFD/BLYE BB10 ....226 E5
RES PR1 ....7 E3
ton Av PRES PR1 ....343 H7
tworth Av BISP FY2 ....148 D6
tworth Dr LANC LA1 ....55 C7
Case Ct PRES PR1 ....240 A3
nard St BWCK/EAR BB18 ....145 F1
LSN BB9 ....198 D3
pold Gv BPOOL FY1 ....4 B2
pold Rd BBNW BB2 ....244 D5
pold St COL BB8 ....171 F7
GNW/BIL/O WN5 ....365 K6
pold Wy BBNW BB2 ....268 D3
ley Rd STHP PR8 ....302 A4
ie Av CLV/TH FY5 ....149 J1
GHB LA2 ....45 G6
chworth CI CHLY/EC PR7 ....311 F5
chworth Wks CHLY/EC PR7 ....311 F5
hbridge Rd STHP PR8 ....301 K6
tia St HOR/BR BL6 ....338 C8
ant St PDHM/BLYW BB12 ....223 J4
en Av FTWD FY7 ....96 D8
en Gv DWN BB3 ....268 B7
ens CI BBNW BB2 ....268 C3
HTN/BK PR9 ....279 J6
ANC LA1 ....2 B4
LF/KEOS FY6 ....177 K3
ens Dr HEY LA3 ....52 E1
EY/BBR PR5 ....286 E1
LF/KEOS FY6 ....177 K2
ensgarth Av FUL/RIB PR2 ....213 H5
ens Gv BPOOL FY1 ....4 C5
ens St PRES PR1 ....240 B2
er St BLY BB11 ....11 E5
ens Wy CARN LA5 ....15 H8
er House La LEY/BBR PR5 ....286 A1
er Park Av HOR/BR BL6.....................338 C6
er St BPOOLE FY3 ....5 E3
AMS BL0 ....319 J5
AW/HAS BB4 ....296 D1
ine Av BPOOLS FY4 ....205 G2
vis CI CHLY/EC PR7 ....336 E5
vis St GTH/LHO BB6 ....221 H6

Lewtas St BPOOL FY1 ....4 B1
Lewth Farm KIRK/FR/WA PR4 ....183 G5
Lewth La KIRK/FR/WA PR4 ....183 F5
Lexington Wy NWD/KWIPK L33 ......366 B5
Lex St PRES PR1 ....240 A3
Lexton Dr CHTN/BK PR9 ....278 D8
Leybourne Av STHP PR8 ....326 A5
Leyburn Av BISP FY2 ....148 C6
  FTWD FY7 ....122 E1
Leyburn CI ACC BB5 ....248 E6
  FUL/RIB PR2 ....214 C6
Leyburn Rd BBNW BB2 ....267 J4
  LANC LA1 ....43 F8
Ley Ct LANC LA1 ....2 B3
Leyfield CI PRES PR1 ....262 A1
Leyfield CI BPOOLE FY3 ....177 G2
Leyfield Rd LEY/BBR PR5 ....285 H2
  ORM L39 ....348 D6
Leyland Rd BLY BB11 ....11 E3
  CHTN/BK PR9 ....301 J2
  PRES PR1 ....6 A4
  RNFD/HAY WA11 ....369 F5
  STHP PR8 ....301 J2
Leyland St ACC BB5 ....247 K6
Leyland Wy LEY/BBR PR5 ....286 A2
Leys Rd BISP FY2 ....176 D2
Leys CI KIRK/FR/WA PR4 ....180 E2
Leyster St MCMB LA4 ....41 J6
Ley St ACC BB5 ....271 K1
Leyton Av LEY/BBR PR5 ....285 H5
Libby La GAR/LONG PR3 ....100 A5
Library Rd CHLYE PR6 ....264 A7
Library St ACC BB5 ....247 J5
  CHLY/EC PR7 ....311 G4
  PRES* PR1 ....7 E3
Lichen CI CHLY/EC PR7 ....310 B7
Lichfield Av MCMB LA4 ....41 K5
Lichfield Rd BPOOL FY1 ....176 C3
  CHLY/EC PR7 ....311 F5
  FUL/RIB PR2 ....238 B1
Liddesdale Rd NLSN BB9 ....199 F1
Liddington CI BBNW BB2 ....268 D3
Liddington Hall Dr RAMS BL0 ....319 H7
Lidgate CI NWD/KWIPK L33 ....366 C6
Lidget Av FUL/RIB PR2 ....237 J2
Liege Rd LEY/BBR PR5 ....285 J3
Lifeboat Rd FMBY L37 ....354 C1
Lightbounds Rd BOL BL1 ....340 D8
Lightbown Av BPOOLE FY3 ....5 E4
Lightbown St DWN BB3 ....268 D8
Lightburne Av LSTA FY8 ....231 F6
Lightfoot CI GAR/LONG PR3 ....213 F3
Lightfoot Green La
  KIRK/FR/WA PR4 ....212 D3
Lightfoot La FUL/RIB PR2 ....212 D4
  KIRK/FR/WA PR4 ....212 B4
Lighthorne Dr STHP PR8 ....325 G7
Lighthurst Av CHLY/EC PR7 ....311 G5
Lighthurst La CHLY/EC PR7 ....311 G5
Lightwood Av BPOOLS FY4 ....204 C3
  LSTA FY8 ....231 K8
Lilac Av BPOOL FY1 ....5 D5
  CHLYE PR6 ....289 H1
  LSTA FY8 ....232 D6
  PRES PR1 ....262 C1
  STHP PR8 ....344 D1
Lilac CI KIRK/FR/WA PR4 ....234 B6
Lilac Gv CLI BB7 ....165 G4
  DWN BB3 ....268 B3
  PRES PR1 ....214 A8
  SKEL WN8 ....362 E2
  WGNW/BIL/O WN5 ....371 F7
Lilac Rd BBN BB1 ....9 E1
Lilac St COL BB8 ....171 K5
Lilac Ter BCUP OL13 ....298 B3
Lilburn CI RAMS BL0 ....319 J7
Lilford CI KIRK/FR/WA PR4 ....282 A6
Lilford Rd BBN BB1 ....8 B5
Lily Gv LANC LA1 ....3 E6
  PRES PR1 ....214 A8
Lily St BCUP OL13 ....298 D1
  BPOOL FY1 ....4 C2
  DWN BB3 ....291 K2
  NLSN BB9 ....198 D5
  TOD OL14 ....277 K3
Lima Rd LSTA FY8 ....231 D5
Limbrick BBN BB1 ....8 C3
  BBNW BB2 ....8 C4
Limbrick Rd CHLYE PR6 ....311 J4
Lime Av ACC BB5 ....270 C1
  HGHB LA2 ....67 G7
  KIRK/FR/WA PR4 ....208 D1
Limebrest Av CLV/TH FY5 ....149 K3
Lime Cha GAR/LONG PR3 ....212 E3

Limechase CI BPOOLS FY4 ....205 G5
Lime CI PRES PR1 ....238 C7
Limefield BBNW BB2 ....8 A4
Limefield Av CLI BB7 ....193 G6
  NLSN BB9 ....198 A5
Limefield CI BOL BL1 ....340 E7
Limefield Dr SKEL WN8 ....364 A4
Limefield Rd BOL BL1 ....341 F7
Limefield St ACC BB5 ....248 D6
Lime Gv BISP FY2 ....176 E1
  CHLY/EC PR7 ....311 G6
  CLV/TH FY5 ....149 J2
  FUL/RIB PR2 ....238 B1
  GAR/LONG PR3 ....129 H3
  GAR/LONG PR3 ....188 A3
  LANC LA1 ....2 B2
  LSTA FY8 ....230 D3
  PLF/KEOS FY6 ....178 A1
  RAMS BL0 ....319 K4
  RNFD/HAY WA11 ....369 F5
  SKEL WN8 ....362 E2
Limekiln La SKP/WHF BD23 ....94 E2
Limerick Rd BISP FY2 ....148 D8
Lime Rd ACC BB5 ....248 B4
  RAW/HAS BB4 ....272 D8
Limers Ga TOD OL14 ....276 E8
  WHIT OL12 ....323 K6
Limers La GTH/LHO BB6 ....220 E5
Limes Av CHLY/EC PR7 ....286 A7
  DWN BB3 ....291 H3
  HEY LA3 ....40 E8
Limestone Link KKBYL LA6 ....18 D1
  MTHPE LA7 ....16 A1
Lime St BBN BB1 ....8 C3
  CLI BB7 ....165 K2
  COL BB8 ....171 J5
  GTH/LHO BB6 ....221 G5
  NLSN BB9 ....198 A3
  STHP PR8 ....302 A5
Lime Tree Gv RAW/HAS BB4 ....273 H7
Lime Tree Wy FMBY L37 ....355 G1
Lime Vale Rd RNFD/HAY WA11 ....370 E8
Limewood CI ACC BB5 ....248 D5
Limey La BLY BB11 ....251 G5
Limont Rd STHP PR8 ....325 K6
Linacre La HTWN L38 ....357 C3
Linadale Av CLV/TH FY5 ....149 H1
Linaker Dr ORM L39 ....346 D3
Linaker St STHP PR8 ....301 H6
Lina St ACC BB5 ....247 K5
Linby St BRFD/BLYE BB10 ....11 E4
Lincoln Av CLV/TH FY5 ....122 E8
  FTWD FY7 ....96 E8
Lincoln Cha FUL/RIB PR2 ....237 J2
Lincoln CI BBN BB1 ....9 F5
  MCMB LA4 ....41 K8
Lincoln PI RAW/HAS BB4 ....272 B8
Lincoln Rd BBN BB1 ....9 F5
  BPOOL FY1 ....4 C2
  BWCK/EAR BB18 ....146 B1
  LANC LA1 ....2 C4
  STHP PR8 ....326 C2
Lincoln St BLY BB11 ....11 D5
  PRES PR1 ....7 F1
  TOD OL14 ....277 G2
Lincoln Wk
  PRES (off Lincoln St) PR1 ....7 F1
Lincoln Wy CLI BB7 ....166 A2
  GAR/LONG PR3 ....129 H4
Lindadale Av ACC BB5 ....248 A8
Lindadale CI ACC BB5 ....248 A8
Lindale Av FUL/RIB PR2 ....215 J2
Lindale CI CARN LA5 ....15 G1
Lindale Crs BRFD/BLYE BB10 ....225 J1
Lindale Rd FUL/RIB PR2 ....213 J7
  GAR/LONG PR3 ....187 K6
Lindbeck Rd BPOOLS FY4 ....205 J2
Lindel La PLF/KEOS FY6 ....124 D1
Lindel Rd FTWD FY7 ....122 E1
Linden Av BBN BB1 ....8 B3
  CLV/TH FY5 ....123 F8
  RAMS BL0 ....319 K5
  WGNW/BIL/O WN5 ....365 G5
Linden CI CLV/TH FY5 ....149 F1
  LEY/BBR PR5 ....262 E2
  NLSN BB9 ....197 K2
  RAMS BL0 ....319 K1
Linden Dr CLI BB7 ....165 K4
  LEY/BBR PR5 ....262 E2
Linden Fold KIRK/FR/WA PR4 ....180 E2
Linden Gn CLV/TH FY5 ....123 F8
Linden Gv CHLYE PR6 ....287 H8
  FUL/RIB PR2 ....214 C8
  GAR/LONG PR3 ....129 J3
  RNFD/HAY WA11 ....370 E6
  WGNW/BIL/O WN5 ....365 G5
Linden Lea BBNW BB2 ....267 G3

RAW/HAS BB4	296	B3
Linden Ms LSTA FY8	231	F1
Linden Pl BISP FY2	148	E8
Linden Rd BWCK/EAR BB18	146	A2
COL BB8	171	H6
Lindens SKEL WN8	351	H7
Lindeth Cl CARN LA5	24	C1
KKBYL LA6	34	B5
Lindeth Gdns LANC LA1	43	F8
Lindeth Rd CARN LA5	24	C1
Lindholme SKEL WN8	351	J8
Lindisfarne Cl PDHM/BLYW BB12	10	B2
Lindle Av KIRK/FR/WA PR4	261	F1
Lindle Cl KIRK/FR/WA PR4	261	F1
Lindle Crs KIRK/FR/WA PR4	261	F1
Lindle La KIRK/FR/WA PR4	261	F1
Lindley Av WGNW/BIL/O WN5	364	E6
Lindley Dr SKEL WN8	332	E8
Lindley St BBNW BB2	267	J1
LEY/BBR PR5	262	E3
Lindon Park Rd RAW/HAS BB4	295	J4
Lindow Cl LANC * LA1	3	D4
Lindow Sq LANC * LA1	2	C3
Lindow St LANC LA1	3	D4
Lindred Rd NLSN BB9	197	J4
Lindsay Av BPOOLE FY3	5	E4
LEY/BBR PR5	285	K2
LSTA FY8	231	H5
PLF/KEOS FY6	177	K1
Lindsay Ct HEY LA3	53	J1
LSTA (off New Rd) FY8	204	B7
Lindsay Pk BRFD/BLYE BB10	226	D6
Lindsay St BLY BB11	11	D3
Linedread La NLSN BB9	197	K4
Lineholme Av TOD OL14	277	K4
Lines St MCMB LA4	41	H6
Line St BCUP OL13	298	B3
Linfield Ter BPOOLS FY4	204	D5
Lingart La GAR/LONG PR3	130	A2
Lingdales FMBY L37	344	B5
Lingfield Av CLI BB7	165	J5
Lingfield Cl LANC LA1	55	H8
Lingfield Rd FTWD FY7	122	E2
Lingfield Wy BBNW BB2	266	E3
Lingmoor Dr PDHM/BLYW BB12	224	C3
Lingmoor Rd LANC LA1	3	F2
Lingwell Cl CHLYE PR6	287	C6
Links Av CHTN/BK PR9	302	A1
Links Fld FUL/RIB PR2	212	E8
Links Ga CLV/TH FY5	149	K4
FUL/RIB PR2	212	E8
LSTA FY8	231	C5
Linkside Av NLSN BB9	199	F3
Links Rd BBNW BB2	266	D3
BPOOL FY1	176	C2
LSTA FY8	230	E6
PLF/KEOS FY6	97	K6
PRES PR1	238	D5
The Links CLV/TH FY5	122	C8
Links Vw LSTA FY8	231	D8
Linnet Cl BPOOLE FY3	5	F5
Linnet La LSTA FY8	232	K4
Linnet St PRES PR1	239	K1
Linnet Wy NWD/KWIPK L33	366	C4
Linslade St NWD/KWIPK L33	366	D7
Linslade Crs NWD/KWIPK L33	366	D7
Linton Av HEY LA3	52	D2
Linton Dr BLY BB11	10	A6
Linton Gdns NLSN BB9	170	A8
Linton Gv PRES PR1	238	D6
Linton St FUL/RIB PR2	213	F8
Lion Ct ACC BB5	247	J5
Lionel St PDHM/BLYW BB12	224	E5
Lion St ACC BB5	247	J4
Liptrott Rd CHLY/EC PR7	310	E6
Lisbon Dr BLY BB11	10	B4
DWN BB3	292	A2
Lister Gv HEY LA3	52	D3
Lister St ACC BB5	248	A5
BBNW BB2	8	C6
Lister Well Rd BWCK/EAR BB18	144	E6
Little Acre CLV/TH FY5	149	K3
KIRK/FR/WA PR4	260	B3
Little Banks Cl LEY/BBR * PR5	264	A5
Little Carr La CHLY/EC PR7	311	H6
Little Cl PRES PR1	238	E8
Littledale Av HEY LA3	52	E3
Littledale Rd HGHB LA2	45	J6
Little Fell La HGHB LA2	56	B7
Little Fell Rd HGHB LA2	56	B5
Little Hey La FMBY L37	344	B7
Little La CHTN/BK PR9	302	D2
GAR/LONG PR3	188	A4
Little Meadow La BRSC L40	306	D7
Little Mdw EDGW/EG * BL7	341	K4

Little Moor CLI BB7	165	J5
Little Moor Clough EDGW/EG BL7	341	J4
Littlemoor Rd CLI BB7	165	J5
Little Moor Vw CLI BB7	165	J5
Little Poulton La PLF/KEOS FY6	150	B8
Little Queen St COL * BB8	171	G7
Little Stones Rd EDGW/EG BL7	341	J1
Little St ACC BB5	248	A5
Little Toms La BRFD/BLYE BB10	198	B8
Little Tongues La PLF/KEOS FY6	98	D7
Little Twining KIRK/FR/WA PR4	260	B4
Littondale Gdn BBNW * BB2	266	C4
Liverpool Rd STHP PR8	325	K7
Liverpool New Rd		
KIRK/FR/WA PR4	260	A7
Liverpool Old Rd		
KIRK/FR/WA PR4	282	C2
KIRK/FR/WA PR4	306	A1
STHP PR8	344	C2
Liverpool Rd BPOOL FY1	5	D2
BRSC L40	306	B5
FMBY L37	356	A1
KIRK/FR/WA PR4	238	A8
KIRK/FR/WA PR4	282	A7
MGHL L31	359	F7
ORM L39	359	K1
ORM L39	360	D7
PDHM/BLYW BB12	224	C5
PRES PR1	6	A5
SKEL WN8	362	D3
STHP PR8	344	C1
Liverpool Rd North BRSC L40	330	E7
Liverpool Rd South BRSC L40	330	D8
Livesey Branch Rd BBNW BB2	266	E3
Livesey Hall Cl BBNW BB2	267	F2
Livesey St BBN BB1	246	E1
BBN BB1	247	F1
LSTA FY8	232	C8
PDHM/BLYW BB12	223	J8
PRES PR1	7	F3
Livesley's La FMBY L37	357	F1
Livet Av BPOOLS FY4	204	D4
Livingstone Av ACC BB5	248	B3
BBNW BB2	244	D7
BPOOL FY1	4	C3
Livingstone St NLSN BB9	197	K6
Lloyd Cl LANC LA1	2	B2
NLSN BB9	198	C3
Lloyd's Av MCMB LA4	41	G7
Lloyd St DWN BB3	268	C8
WHIT OL12	323	C2
Lobden Crs WHIT OL12	323	H4
Lochinch Cl BPOOLS FY4	205	C5
Loch St WGNW/BIL/O WN5	365	K5
Locka La KKBYL LA6	28	B5
LANC LA1	42	E7
Lock Br CLI BB7	76	C2
Lockerbie Av CLV/TH FY5	148	D3
Lockfield Dr BWCK/EAR BB18	119	C7
Lock Ga RAW/HAS BB4	295	J2
Lockhart Rd PRES PR1	239	H1
Lockhurst Av CLV/TH FY5	149	F3
Lock La KIRK/FR/WA PR4	306	B1
Lockside BBNW BB2	268	A1
Lockside Rd FUL/RIB PR2	238	B3
Lock St ACC * BB5	247	J7
Lockwood Av PLF/KEOS FY6	149	K4
Lockyer Av PDHM/BLYW BB12	224	D5
Lodge Bank CHLYE PR6	289	F4
Lodge Cl CLV/TH FY5	148	C4
KIRK/FR/WA PR4	235	F5
KKBYL LA6	17	K1
LEY/BBR PR5	263	J2
Lodge Ct BPOOLE FY3	177	K6
Lodge La BCUP OL13	298	D2
HGHB LA2	38	D7
KIRK/FR/WA PR4	181	F2
KIRK/FR/WA PR4	233	H6
KIRK/FR/WA PR4	236	D3
LEY/BBR PR5	262	B5
PLF/KEOS FY6	179	F1
RNFD/HAY WA11	368	C2
Lodge Mill La RAMS BL0	320	C2
Lodge Pk		
GAR/LONG		
(off Catterall Gates La) PR3	129	K8
Lodge Rd GAR/LONG PR3	156	C2
WGNW/BIL/O WN5	365	G7
Lodges Gv MCMB LA4	42	A5
Lodgeside ACC BB5	221	K8
Lodge St ACC BB5	248	C5
LANC LA1	3	D3
PRES PR1	6	C2
RAMS BL0	319	J5
Lodge Ter ACC BB5	247	J6
The Lodge GTH/LHO BB6	221	F6

Lodge Vw GAR/LONG * PR3	18?	
KIRK/FR/WA PR4	26?	
The Lodgings FUL/RIB PR2	21?	
Lodore Rd BPOOLS FY4	20?	
Loen Crs BOL BL1	34?	
Loftos Av BPOOLS FY4	20?	
Logan St BOL BL1	34?	
Logwood St BBN BB1	8?	
Lois Pl BBNW BB2	8?	
Lomas La RAW/HAS BB4	29?	
Lomax St GTH/LHO BB6	22?	
Lomeshaye Rd NLSN BB9	19?	
Lomeshaye Wy NLSN BB9	19?	
Lomond Av BPOOLE FY3	5?	
LSTA FY8	23?	
Londonderry Rd HEY LA3	52?	
London Fids WGNW/BIL/O WN5	37?	
London La STHP PR8	32?	
London Rd BBN BB1	8?	
BPOOLE FY3	7?	
PRES PR1	7?	
London Sq STHP * PR8	30?	
London St FTWD FY7	90?	
STHP PR8	32?	
London Ter DWN BB3	29?	
London Wk BBN BB1	8?	
London Wy LEY/BBR PR5	24?	
Longacre CHTN/BK PR9	27?	
Long Acre LEY/BBR PR5	26?	
Long Acre Cl CARN * LA5	33?	
Long Acre Pl LSTA FY8	23?	
Long Acres Dr WHIT OL12	32?	
Longacres La WHIT OL12	32?	
Long Bank La SKP/WHF BD23	9?	
Long Barn Brow LEY/BBR PR5	26?	
Longber La KKBYL LA6	3?	
Longbrook WCNNW/ST WN6	35?	
Longbrook Av LEY/BBR PR5	26?	
Long Butts PRES PR1	26?	
Long Cswy CLI BB7	11?	
The Long Cswy BRFD/BLYE BB10	25?	
Longcliffe Dr STHP PR8	32?	
Long Cl CLI BB7	16?	
LEY/BBR PR5	28?	
Long Copse CHLY/EC PR7	31?	
Long Cft GAR/LONG PR3	18?	
KIRK/FR/WA PR4	26?	
Long Croft Meadow		
CHLY/EC PR7	31?	
Long Dales La KKBYL LA6	3?	
Longfield FMBY L37	34?	
FUL/RIB PR2	21?	
PRES PR1	23?	
Longfield Av CHLY/EC PR7	33?	
PLF/KEOS FY6	14?	
Longfield Ct BWCK/EAR BB18	14?	
Longfield Dr CARN LA5	3?	
Longfield Mnr CHLY/EC PR7	31?	
Longfield Pl PLF/KEOS FY6	14?	
Longford Av BISP FY2	14?	
Longford Rd STHP PR8	32?	
Long Gn BWCK/EAR BB18	14?	
Longhey SKEL WN8	35?	
Long Hey La DWN BB3	29?	
Long Heys La SKEL WN8	35?	
Long Heys or Back La SKEL WN8	35?	
Long Hill End HWTH BD22	17?	
Longhirst Cl BOL BL1	34?	
Longholme Rd RAW/HAS BB4	29?	
Longhouse La PLF/KEOS FY6	17?	
Long Ing La BWCK/EAR BB18	11?	
Longlands Av HEY LA3	5?	
Longlands Crs HEY LA3	5?	
Longlands La HEY LA3	5?	
Longlands Rd LANC LA1	4?	
Long La BBNW BB2	26?	
CHLYE PR6	31?	
CHTN/BK PR9	27?	
COL BB8	17?	
DWN BB3	26?	
GAR/LONG PR3	10?	
GAR/LONG PR3	13?	
HGHB LA2	3?	
HGHB LA2	6?	
HGHB LA2	8?	
ORM L39	34?	
SKEL WN8	36?	
Long Level KKBYL LA6	2?	
Longley Cl FUL/RIB PR2	21?	
Long Lover La CLI BB7	14?	
Long Marsh La LANC LA1	2?	
Long Meadow BBNW BB2	24?	
CHLY/EC PR7	31?	
COL * BB8	17?	
KIRK/FR/WA PR4	20?	
KIRK/FR/WA PR4	26?	
Longmeadow La CLV/TH FY5	12?	

*Y LA3 ....52 D5
Meanygate *CHTN/BK* PR9..........303 H3
meanygate *LEY/BBR* PR5 ....261 J8
mere Crs *CARN* LA5 ....33 J3
mire Wy *MCMB* LA4 ....41 G6
moor La *GAR/LONG* PR3 ....128 E5
Moss *LEY/BBR* PR5 ....284 C3
Moss La *KIRK/FR/WA* PR4 ....261 F5
ridge Av *BPOOLS* FY4 ....204 E6
ridge Heath
 RFD/BLYE BB10 ....198 B3
ridge Rd *CLI* BB7 ....190 E3
L/RIB PR2 ....214 D7
R/LONG PR3 ....188 A1
ridge Road Elm Brow
 R/LONG PR3 ....160 C7
Royd Rd *BWCK/EAR* BB18 ....146 B2
sands La *FUL/RIB* PR2 ....214 A6
shaw Av *WGNW/BIL/O* WN5 ...371 G3
shaw La *BRSC* L40 ....306 A6
GNW/BIL/O WN5 ....371 G2
shaw Common
 GNW/BIL/O WN5 ....371 G3
shaw Ford Rd *BOL* BL1..............340 D6
shaw La *BBNW* BB2......................268 A1
shaw Old Rd
 GNW/BIL/O WN5 ....371 G2
shaw La *BBNW* BB2......................268 A2
sight Av *ACC* BB5.........................249 F3
I BB7 ....165 K2
sight Rd *BBNW* BB2.....................217 J8
ston By-Pass
 RK/FR/WA PR4 ....260 A7
ston Cl *BBN* BB1 ....246 A6
ston Dr *FMBY* L37 ....344 A5
CMB LA4 ....42 A7
ston Rd *FMBY* FY1...........................4 C2
DHM/BLYW BB12 ....10 A1
ston St *BBN* BB1 ....9 F4
LYE PR6 ....311 J3
gway *BPOOLS* FY4 ....205 F3
Wham La *KIRK/FR/WA* PR4 ......283 J2
jworth Av *BRFD/BLYE* BB10 .....226 B5
LY/EC PR7 ....335 K1
OR/BR BL6 ....337 J8
jworth Clough *EDGW/EG* BL7 ...341 H1
jworth La *BOL* BL1 ....341 H3
jworth Rd *CLI* BB7 ....193 F7
DGW/EG BL7 ....316 A8
OR/BR BL6 ....338 C7
jworth Rd North
 DGW/EG BL7 ....315 G6
jworth St *CHLY/EC* PR7 ....311 F5
Y/BBR PR5 ....263 H1
RES PR1 ....240 A2
sdale Cha
Y/BBR (off Croston Rd) PR5 ......262 D3
sdale Cl *LEY/BBR* PR5 ....285 J5
sdale Crs *FTWD* FY7 ....96 E8
sdale Dr *LEY/BBR* PR5................283 H8
sdale Gv *MCMB* LA4......................42 A7
MBY L37 ....343 J8
GHB LA2 ....42 D2
CMB LA4 ....42 A7
RES PR1 ....240 A2
THP PR8 ....301 K7
sdale St *ACC* BB5 ....247 K5
LSN BB9 ....198 D2
Av *BCUP* OL13 ....298 A3
d's Av *LEY/BBR* PR5 ....262 E4
d's Close Rd *HGHB* LA2 ....50 E6
ds Cft *CHLYE* PR6 ....286 E1
Sefton Wy *FMBY* L37 ....356 D1
sgate Dr *BRSC* L40 ....330 E8
sgate La *BRSC* L40 ....349 F1
d's La *GAR/LONG* PR3 ....188 D5
RES PR1 ....262 B2
d's Lot Rd *KKBYL* LA6 ....35 H2
some Rd *HEY* LA3 ....52 E1
Sq *BBN* BB1 ....8 C4
St *ACC* BB5 ....247 J7
N BB1 ....247 F2
NW BB2 ....8 C4
UP OL13 ....298 C1
OOL FY1 ....4 B1
SC L40 ....330 E6

CHLY/EC PR7 ....308 E6
CHLYE PR6 ....311 H4
CHTN/BK PR9 ....301 H3
COL BB8 ....171 G6
DWN BB3 ....291 J1
FTWD FY7 ....97 G7
GTH/LHO BB6 ....221 G7
HOR/BR BL6 ....338 D7
LANC LA1 ....3 D2
LSTA FY8 ....230 D4
MCMB LA4 ....41 H5
NLSN BB9 ....197 J6
PRES PR1 ....7 E2
RAW/HAS BB4 ....273 C4
RAW/HAS BB4 ....296 C1
STHP PR8 ....301 G4
Lord St Boulevards *STHP* PR8 ..301 H4
Lord Street Ml *BBNW* BB2 ....8 C4
Lord St West *BBNW* * BB2 ....8 C4
 STHP PR8 ....301 F5
Lord's Wk *PRES* PR1 ....7 E2
Lorne Rd *BISP* FY2 ....176 D1
Lorne St *CHLY/EC* PR7 ....311 G4
 DWN BB3 ....291 H1
 LSTA FY8 ....232 E7
Lorraine Av *FUL/RIB* PR2 ....213 G8
Lorton Cl *FUL/RIB* PR2 ....213 H5
DHM/BLYW BB12 ....224 D3
Lostherdale Cl *BRFD/BLYE* BB10 ...198 B8
Lothian Av *FTWD* FY7 ....96 D8
Lothian Pl *BISP* FY2 ....148 E6
Lottice La *BBN* BB1 ....269 J2
Lotus Dr *BPOOLS* FY4.................206 C5
Loughlin Dr *NWD/KWIPK* L33 ...366 D6
Loughrigg Cl *PDHM/BLYW* BB12 ...224 D3
Loughrigg Ter *BPOOLS* FY4........205 J2
Louise St *BPOOL* FY1 ....4 B4
Louis Pollard Crs *GTH/LHO* BB6 ...221 H5
Louis St *RAMS* BL0 ....295 K6
Loupsfell Dr *MCMB* LA4................41 J7
Lourdes Av *LEY/BBR* PR5 ....262 D2
Louvaine Av *BOL* BL1 ....340 D7
Louvain St *BWCK/EAR* BB18 .....118 E3
Lovat Rd *PRES* PR1 ....239 H1
Love Clough Rd *RAW/HAS* BB4 ...273 G1
Lovely Hall La *BBN* BB1 ....219 F3
Low Bank Rd *PDHM/BLYW* BB12 ...224 D5
Lowcroft *KIRK/FR/WA* PR4 ....184 D8
 SKEL WN8 ....351 J8
Lowcross Rd *PLF/KEOS* FY6 .....178 A1
Lower Alt Rd *HTWN* L38 ....355 K7
Lower Antley St *ACC* BB5 ....247 K6
Lower Ashworth Cl *BBNW* BB2 ....8 A5
Lower Audley St *BBN* BB1 ....8 C5
Lower Bank Rd *FUL/RIB* PR2 .....213 H8
Lower Bank St *CHLYE* PR6 ....289 C3
Lower Barnes St *ACC* BB5 ....221 J5
Lower Barn St *DWN* BB3 ....292 A4
Lower Burgh Wy *CHLY/EC* PR7 ...310 E7
Lower Carr La *HTWN* L38 ....357 H4
Lower Chapel La *CLI* BB7 ....140 D3
Lower Clough St *NLSN* BB9 ....198 A1
Lower Clowes Rd *RAW/HAS* BB4 ...296 A3
Lower Cockcroft *BBNW* BB2 ....8 C4
Lower Copthurst
 CHLYE (off Copthurst La) PR6 ...287 J3
Lower Copthurst La *CHLYE* PR6...287 J4
Lower Cribden Av *RAW/HAS* BB4 ...296 A1
Lower Croft St *BWCK/EAR* BB18 ...146 B1
Lower Cross St *DWN* BB3 ....291 J2
Lower East Av *BWCK/EAR* BB18 ...119 F8
Lower Eccleshill Rd *DWN* BB3 ...268 D6
Lowerfield *GTH/LHO* BB6 ....219 K3
Lower Fld *LEY/BBR* PR5 ....262 C5
Lowerfields *PDHM/BLYW* BB12 ...224 B5
Lowerfold *GTH/LHO* BB6 ....221 G5
Lowerfold Cl *WHIT* OL12 ....323 G7
Lowerfold Crs *WHIT* OL12 ....323 G7
Lowerfold Dr *WHIT* OL12 ....323 G7
Lowerfold Rd *GTH/LHO* BB6 ......221 G5
Lowerfold Wy *WHIT* OL12 ....323 G7
Lowergate *CLI* BB7 ....165 J3
Lower Gate Rd *ACC* BB5 ....249 F1
Lower Gn *PLF/KEOS* FY6 ....150 A4
Lower Greenfield *FUL/RIB* PR2 ...212 D6
Lower Hazel La *BBNW* BB2 ....8 A5
Lower Hey *KIRK/FR/WA* PR4.......260 B2
Lower Hill Dr *CHLYE* PR6 ....337 G2

Lower Hollin Bank St *BBNW* BB2 ...268 A1
Lowerhouse Crs
 PDHM/BLYW BB12 ....224 C5
Lower House Gn *RAW/HAS* BB4 ...274 C3
Lowerhouse La
 PDHM/BLYW BB12 ....224 C5
Lower House Rd *LEY/BBR* PR5 ...285 F3
Lower Laithe Dr *NLSN* BB9 ....170 A8
Lower La *GAR/LONG* PR3 ....188 B4
 KIRK/FR/WA PR4 ....235 F1
 RAW/HAS BB4 ....272 C7
Lower Lune St *FTWD* FY7 ....97 H6
Lower Lyndon Av
 WGNNW/ST WN6 ....353 J5
Lower Manor La
 PDHM/BLYW BB12 ....225 H1
Lower Marlands *EDGW/EG* BL7 ...341 K3
Lower Md *EDGW/EG* BL7 ....341 K2
Lower Mead Dr
 PDHM/BLYW BB12 ....225 H1
Lower Meadow *EDGW/EG* BL7 ...317 H5
Lower North Av *BWCK/EAR* BB18 ...145 F1
Lower Park St *BWCK/EAR* BB18 ...145 G2
Lower Parrock Rd *NLSN* BB9 .....198 A2
Lower Philips Rd *BBN* BB1 ....9 F1
Lower Prom *STHP* PR8 ....301 G4
Lower Ridge Cl *BRFD/BLYE* BB10 ...11 E3
Lower Rd *RAMS* BL0 ....319 K3
Lower Rosegrove La
 PDHM/BLYW BB12 ....224 B6
Lower School St *COL* BB8 ....171 H7
Lower Tentre *BLY* BB11 ....11 E4
Lower Timber Hill La *BLY* BB11 ....11 D6
Lower Tong *EDGW/EG* BL7 ....341 K4
Lower Wk *CLV/TH* FY5 ....148 C3
Lower West Av *BWCK/EAR* BB18 ...145 F1
Lower Wilworth *BBN* BB1 ....245 G2
Lowesby Cl *LEY/BBR* PR5 ....240 C8
Lowes Gn *FMBY* L37 ....344 B8
Lowe's La *SKEL* WN8 ....350 E3
Loweswater Cl *ACC* BB5 ....248 E3
Loweswater Crs
 PDHM/BLYW BB12 ....224 D3
Loweswater Dr *MCMB* LA4............41 K7
Loweswater Wy *NWD/KWIPK* L33 ...366 B7
Lowesway *BPOOLS* FY4...............205 F3
 CLV/TH FY5 ....123 H8
Lowe Vw *RAW/HAS* BB4 ....297 H2
Lowfield Cl *KIRK/FR/WA* PR4 .....235 K1
Lowfield Rd *BPOOLS* FY4 ....205 F4
Low Fold *BWCK/EAR* BB18 ....146 A5
Lowgill La *HGHB* LA2 ....50 A4
Low Gn *LEY/BBR* PR5 ....285 H2
Lowick Cl *LEY/BBR* PR5 ....241 J7
Lowick Dr *PLF/KEOS* FY6.............177 K2
Lowlands Rd *CARN* LA5 ....33 G5
 MCMB LA4 ....41 J6
Lowland Wy *BISP* FY2 ....149 F5
Low La *KKBYL* LA6 ....22 D5
 MCMB LA4 ....42 B6
Low Moor La *BWCK/EAR* BB18 ...145 F2
Low Moor Rd *BISP* FY2 ....148 E2
Lowood Gv *FUL/RIB* PR2 ....237 K2
Lowood Pl *BBNW* BB2 ....244 C5
Lowrey Ter *BPOOL* FY1 ....4 B5
Low Rd *HEY* LA3 ....64 E1
 HGHB LA2 ....44 A5
Lowry Cl *LEY/BBR* PR5 ....262 D4
Lowry Hill La *BRSC* L40 ....350 B1
Lowstern Cl *EDGW/EG* BL7 ....341 J2
Lowther Av *BISP* FY2 ....176 B1
 HEY LA3 ....42 A8
Lowther Crs *LEY/BBR* PR5 ....285 F1
Lowther Dr *LEY/BBR* PR5 ....285 F1
Lowther La *COL* BB8 ....171 H2
Lowther Pl *BBN* BB1 ....9 E1
Lowther Rd *FTWD* FY7 ....97 F7
 LANC LA1 ....3 F2
Lowther St *FUL/RIB* PR2 ....6 A1
 NLSN BB9 ....198 A3
Lowther Ter *LSTA* FY8 ....232 C8
Lowthian St *PRES* * PR1 ....7 D2
Lowthorpe Crs *PRES* PR1 ....239 K1
Lowthorpe Rd *PRES* PR1 ....239 K1
Lowthwaite Dr *NLSN* BB9 ....198 C5
Lowton Rd *LSTA* FY8 ....231 G3
Loxham Gdns *BPOOLS* FY4 ....204 D5
Loxley Gn *FUL/RIB* PR2 ....214 A5
Loxley Pl *CLV/TH* FY5 ....148 E4
Loxley Pl East *CLV/TH* FY5 ....148 E4
Loxley Rd *STHP* PR8 ....301 K7
Lubbock St *PDHM/BLYW* BB12....224 D5
Lucas Av *CHLY/EC* PR7 ....310 E3
Lucas La *CHLYE* PR6 ....287 G5
Lucerne Rd *FUL/RIB* PR2 ....214 A7
Lucy St *LANC* LA1 ....3 D3
 MCMB LA4 ....41 H5

NLSN BB9 ......**170** B8
Ludlow *SKEL* WN8 ......**351** J7
Ludlow Dr *ORM* L39 ......**348** B4
Ludlow Gv *BISP* FY2 ......**177** F1
Ludlow St *WGNNW/ST* WN6 ......**335** G8
Luke St *BCUP* OL13 ......**298** A3
Lulworth Av *FUL/RIB* FY3 ......**205** G1
  FUL/RIB PR2 ......**239** F1
Lulworth Pl *LEY/BBR* PR5 ......**263** G1
Lulworth Rd *FUL/RIB* * PR2 ......**213** J1
  STHP PR8 ......**301** F7
Lumb Carr Av *RAMS* BL0 ......**319** G7
Lumb Carr Rd *RAMS* BL0 ......**319** G7
Lumb Holes La *RAW/HAS* BB4 ......**297** G4
Lumb La *HWTH* BD22 ......**174** C2
  RAW/HAS BB4 ......**274** C7
Lumb Scar *BCUP* OL13 ......**298** D1
Lumwood *BOL* BL1 ......**341** F8
Lunds La *KIRK/FR/WA* PR4 ......**282** D2
Lund St *BBNW* BB2 ......**244** D7
  PRES PR1 ......**7** D2
Lune Cl *KIRK/FR/WA* PR4 ......**209** F6
  KKBYL LA6 ......**21** H1
Lunedale Av *BPOOL* FY1 ......**4** C6
Lune Dr *LANC* LA1 ......**42** B8
  LEY/BBR PR5 ......**286** C1
Lunefield Dr *KKBYL* LA6 ......**21** H2
Lune Gv *BPOOL* FY1 ......**4** C4
Lune Rd *FTWD* FY7 ......**97** F7
  LANC LA1 ......**2** B2
Lunesdale Cl *LSTA* FY8 ......**231** J4
Lunesdale Ct *HGHB* LA2 ......**37** G7
  LANC LA1 ......**42** D8
Lunesdale Dr *GAR/LONG* PR3 ......**80** C8
Lunesdale Rd *KIRK/FR/WA* PR4 ......**208** E6
Lunesdale Vw *HGHB* LA2 ......**44** B4
Lune St *COL* BB8 ......**171** K4
  GAR/LONG PR3 ......**188** B3
  LANC LA1 ......**3** D2
  PDHM/BLYW BB12 ......**223** K3
  PRES PR1 ......**7** D3
Lune Ter *LANC* LA1 ......**3** D2
Lune Valley Ramble *HGHB* LA2 ......**37** F2
  HGHB LA2 ......**44** D5
  KKBYL LA6 ......**30** E1
  LANC LA1 ......**3** D2
Lune Vw *PLF/KEOS* FY6 ......**98** A6
Lupin Cl *ACC* BB5 ......**248** A4
  CHLYE PR6 ......**287** F6
Lupin Rd *ACC* BB5 ......**248** B4
Lupton Dr *NLSN* BB9 ......**170** B7
Lupton Pl *LANC* LA1 ......**42** D8
Lupton St *CHLY/EC* PR7 ......**311** G5
Lutner St *BLY* BB11 ......**11** D4
Luton Rd *CLV/TH* FY5 ......**148** D2
  FUL/RIB PR2 ......**238** A1
Lutwidge Av *PRES* PR1 ......**240** A2
Lyceum Av *BPOOLE* FY3 ......**5** D3
Lychfield *LEY/BBR* PR5 ......**263** H4
Lyddesdale Av *CLV/TH* FY5 ......**148** D2
Lydd Gv *CHLY/EC* PR7 ......**310** E4
Lydgate *BRFD/BLYE* BB10 ......**226** C1
  CHLY/EC PR7 ......**310** E2
Lydia St *ACC* BB5 ......**248** B7
Lydiate La *CHLY/EC* PR7 ......**308** D2
  GAR/LONG PR3 ......**156** E4
  LEY/BBR PR5 ......**263** F7
Lydiate Station Rd *MGHL* L31 ......**358** A6
Lydric Av *LEY/BBR* PR5 ......**264** D1
Lyelake La *BRSC* L40 ......**361** K2
Lyme Gv *PLF/KEOS* FY6 ......**98** A6
Lymm Av *LANC* LA1 ......**42** C8
Lynbridge Cl *WGNNW/BIL/O* WN5 ......**365** G6
Lyncroft Crs *BPOOLE* FY3 ......**176** B4
Lyndale *SKEL* WN8 ......**351** H7
Lyndale Av *BBN* BB1 ......**219** J4
  LEY/BBR PR5 ......**263** F2
  RAW/HAS BB4 ......**295** H1
Lyndale Cl *BBN* * BB1 ......**219** J4
  LEY/BBR PR5 ......**285** K5
  RAW/HAS BB4 ......**273** H4
Lyndale Gv *LEY/BBR* PR5 ......**263** F1
Lyndale Rd *BLY* BB11 ......**223** J8
Lynden Av *MCMB* LA4 ......**42** A7
Lyndeth Cl *FUL/RIB* PR2 ......**214** C5
Lyndhurst *SKEL* WN8 ......**351** H7
Lyndhurst Av *BBN* BB1 ......**246** C6
Lyndhurst Dr *FUL/RIB* PR2 ......**238** A1
Lyndhurst Gv *GTH/LHO* BB6 ......**221** J5
Lyndhurst Rd *BBNW* BB2 ......**268** B5
  BRFD/BLYE BB10 ......**11** F4
  DWN BB3 ......**268** B8
  STHP PR8 ......**326** C1
Lyndon Av *GTH/LHO* BB6 ......**221** J5
  WGNNW/ST WN6 ......**353** K4
Lyndon Ct *GTH/LHO* BB6 ......**221** J5

Lynfield Rd *GTH/LHO* BB6 ......**221** J5
Lynn Gv *BPOOL* FY1 ......**176** B4
Lynn Pl *FUL/RIB* * PR2 ......**240** B1
Lynslack Ter *CARN* LA5 ......**15** G3
Lynthorpe Rd *BBNW* BB2 ......**268** B1
  NLSN BB9 ......**198** E2
Lynton Av *BPOOLS* FY4 ......**204** D3
  LEY/BBR PR5 ......**286** A3
Lynton Ct *FTWD* FY7 ......**122** C3
Lynton Dr *STHP* PR8 ......**326** A2
Lynton Rd *ACC* BB5 ......**247** K7
  STHP PR8 ......**326** A3
Lynwood Av *ACC* BB5 ......**221** K7
  BPOOLE FY3 ......**176** E3
  DWN BB3 ......**268** B8
  FUL/RIB PR2 ......**215** G2
  ORM L39 ......**348** A8
Lynwood Cl *ACC* BB5 ......**221** K7
  COL BB8 ......**171** H4
  DWN BB3 ......**268** B8
  SKEL WN8 ......**363** K4
Lynwood Dr *PLF/KEOS* FY6 ......**124** E4
Lynwood End *ORM* * L39 ......**348** A8
Lynwood Rd *ACC* BB5 ......**248** E1
  BBNW BB2 ......**244** D5
Lyons La *CHLY/EC* PR7 ......**311** H4
  CHLYE PR6 ......**311** H4
Lyons La South *CHLY/EC* PR7 ......**311** H4
Lyons Rd *STHP* PR8 ......**301** G6
Lythall Av *LSTA* FY8 ......**233** F7
Lytham Ct *KKBY* L32 ......**366** A7
Lytham Rd *BBNW* BB2 ......**268** C3
  BPOOL FY1 ......**4** B5
  BPOOLS FY4 ......**204** B4
  BRFD/BLYE BB10 ......**226** A1
  CHTN/BK PR9 ......**278** C1
  FUL/RIB PR2 ......**212** E8
  KIRK/FR/WA PR4 ......**233** H7
  LSTA FY8 ......**233** F2
Lytham St *CHLYE* PR6 ......**311** J4
  WHIT OL12 ......**323** J8
Lythcoe Av *FUL/RIB* PR2 ......**212** E7
Lythe Fell Av *HGHB* LA2 ......**44** B4
Lythe Fell Rd *HGHB* LA2 ......**51** F8
Lythe La *HGHB* LA2 ......**50** D8
Lyth Rd *LANC* LA1 ......**3** F1
Lytles Cl *FMBY* L37 ......**356** A1
Lytton St *PDHM/BLYW* BB12 ......**224** B4

M

Mabel St *COL* BB8 ......**171** K6
Maberry Cl *WGNNW/ST* WN6 ......**353** F4
MacAulay St *BLY* BB11 ......**224** E6
MacAuley Av *BPOOLS* FY4 ......**204** E3
MacBeth Rd *FTWD* FY7 ......**96** E7
MacDonald St *WGNW/BIL/O* WN5 ......**365** K5
MacKay Cft *CHLYE* PR6 ......**311** H3
MacKenzie Gv *BOL* BL1 ......**341** H7
MacKenzie Cl *BOL* BL1 ......**341** H7
MacKenzie Cl *CHLYE* PR6 ......**311** H3
Maclaren Cl *BPOOLE* FY3 ......**177** K6
Macleod St *NLSN* BB9 ......**198** B3
Maddy St *PRES* PR1 ......**6** B2
Maden Fold *BCUP* OL13 ......**298** A1
Maden St *ACC* BB5 ......**247** J5
Maden Wy *BCUP* OL13 ......**298** D1
Madingley Ct
  CHTN/BK
  (off Cambridge Rd) PR9 ......**302** B1
Madison St *BISP* FY2 ......**148** B6
  CARN LA5 ......**42** E1
Maesbrook Cl *CHTN/BK* PR9 ......**279** K6
Mafeking Rd *FUL/RIB* PR2 ......**238** E1
Magdalen Av *CLV/TH* FY5 ......**148** D2
Maggots Nook Rd
  RNFD/HAY WA11 ......**369** G2
Maghull La *MGHL* L31 ......**366** A2
Magnolia Cl *FUL/RIB* PR2 ......**214** A5
Magnolia Dr *LEY/BBR* PR5 ......**286** C1
Magnolia Rd *PRES* PR1 ......**238** D8
Magpie Cl *BLY* BB11 ......**224** E6
Maida V *CLV/TH* FY5 ......**148** D3
Maiden St *RAW/HAS* BB4 ......**272** C5
Main Av *HEY* LA3 ......**52** D8
Main Cl *HEY* LA3 ......**65** H3
Main Dr *PLF/KEOS* FY6 ......**150** A8
Main Rd *HGHB* LA2 ......**43** F2
  HGHB LA2 ......**67** C8
  KKBYL LA6 ......**34** A6
Mains La *BRSC* L40 ......**332** D5
  PLF/KEOS FY6 ......**150** B6
Main Sprit Weind *PRES* PR1 ......**7** E3
Main St *BWCK/EAR* BB18 ......**146** A5
  CARN LA5 ......**25** J6

CLI BB7 ......**1**?
CLI BB7 ......**1**?
CLI BB7 ......**1**?
HEY LA3 ......?
HEY LA3 ......?
HGHB LA2 ......?
HGHB LA2 ......?
HGHB LA2 ......?
HGHB LA2 ......?
KKBYL LA6 ......?
KKBYL LA6 ......?
LANC LA1 ......?
WGNW/BIL/O WN5 ......**5**
Mainway *LANC* LA1 ......
Mainway Ct
  LEY/BBR (off Edward St) PR5 ......**2**?
Mairscough La *ORM* L39 ......**3**?
Maitland Av *CLV/TH* FY5 ......**1**?
Maitland Cl *PRES* PR1 ......**2**?
Maitland Pl *RAW/HAS* BB4 ......**2**?
Maitland St *BCUP* OL13 ......**2**?
  PRES PR1 ......**2**?
Major St *ACC* BB5 ......**2**?
  RAMS BL0 ......**3**?
  RAW/HAS BB4 ......**2**?
Makinson La *HOR/BR* BL6 ......**3**?
Malcolm Pl *FTWD* FY7 ......?
Malcolm St *PRES* PR1 ......**2**?
Malden St *LEY/BBR* PR5 ......**2**?
Maldern Av *PLF/KEOS* FY6 ......**1**?
Maldon Pl *FUL/RIB* * PR2 ......**2**?
Malham Av *ACC* BB5 ......**2**?
  BPOOLS FY4 ......**2**?
Malham Cl *LANC* LA1 ......?
  STHP PR8 ......**3**?
Malham Pl *FUL/RIB* PR2 ......**2**?
Malham Rd *BRFD/BLYE* BB10 ......**1**?
Malham Wend *NLSN* BB9 ......**1**?
Maliff Rd *BRFD/BLYE* BB10 ......**2**?
Malkin Cl *NLSN* BB9 ......**1**?
Malkin La *CLI* BB7 ......?
Mallard Cl *CLV/TH* FY5 ......**1**?
  HEY LA3 ......?
  LEY/BBR PR5 ......**2**?
  ORM L39 ......**3**?
Mallard Ct *BPOOLE* FY3 ......**1**?
  LANC LA1 ......?
Mallard Dr *HOR/BR* BL6 ......**3**?
Mallards Wk *LEY/BBR* PR5 ......**2**?
Mallee Av *CHTN/BK* PR9 ......**2**?
Mallee Crs *CHTN/BK* PR9 ......**2**?
Malley La *KIRK/FR/WA* PR4 ......**1**?
Mallison St *BOL* BL1 ......**3**?
Mallom Av *CHLY/EC* PR7 ......**2**?
Mallory Av *MGHL* L31 ......**3**?
Mallowdale *CLV/TH* FY5 ......**1**?
Mallowdale Av *HEY* LA3 ......?
Mallowdale Rd *LANC* LA1 ......
Mallow Wk *HEY* LA3 ......
The Mall *BLY* BB11 ......?
  FUL/RIB PR2 ......**2**?
  LSTA FY8 ......**2**?
Maltby Pl *BPOOLS* * FY4 ......?
Malthouse Ct *FUL/RIB* PR2 ......
Malthouse Wy *PRES* PR1 ......**2**?
The Maltings *CLV/TH* FY5 ......**1**?
  KIRK/FR/WA PR4 ......**2**?
Malt Kiln Brow *GAR/LONG* PR3 ......**1**?
Malt Kiln Gv *GAR/LONG* PR3 ......**1**?
Maltkiln La *BRSC* L40 ......**3**?
  ORM L39 ......**3**?
The Maltings *KKBYL* LA6 ......?
Malton Dr *LEY/BBR* PR5 ......**2**?
Malt St *ACC* BB5 ......**2**?
Malvern Av *ACC* BB5 ......**2**?
  BBNW BB2 ......**2**?
  BPOOL FY1 ......?
  LANC LA1 ......?
  PDHM/BLYW BB12 ......**2**?
  PLF/KEOS FY6 ......**1**?
  PRES PR1 ......?
Malvern Cl *HOR/BR* BL6 ......**3**?
  KKBY L32 ......**3**?
  LEY/BBR PR5 ......**2**?
Malvern Ct
  NLSN (off Smith St) BB9 ......**1**?
  NLSN BB9 ......**1**?
  PRES PR1 ......?
Malvern St *PRES* PR1 ......?
  WGNNW/ST WN6 ......**3**?
Malvern Wy *RAW/HAS* BB4 ......**2**?
Manby Cl *LEY/BBR* PR5 ......**2**?
Manchester Rd *ACC* BB5 ......**2**?
  BLY BB11 ......?
  BLY BB11 ......**2**?
  BPOOLE FY3 ......?

...CK/EAR BB18 ....145 F3
...TN/BK PR9 ....301 J4
...SN BB9 ....198 B3
...HM/BLYW BB12 ....223 J7
...ES PR1 ....7 E3
...MS BL0 ....320 A6
...W/HAS BB4 ....295 H1
cknols St NLSN BB9 ....198 D4
deville Rd STHP PR8 ....325 H6
della Ct BBN BB1 ....8 C3
field SKEL WN8 ....351 G8
ion Av MGHL L31 ....358 D6
ion Cl MGHL L31 ....358 D6
itoba Cl BBNW BB2 ....244 D3
ley Ter BOL * BL1 ....341 J7
ner Sutton St BBN BB1 ....9 D4
HP PR8 ....302 A5
or Av BRSC L40 ....349 H1
L/RIB PR2 ....213 K7
R/LONG PR3 ....189 K8
HB LA2 ....42 E3
ES PR1 ....238 D7
or Brook ACC BB5 ....248 C5
or Cl HGHB LA2 ....42 E3
Y/BBR PR5 ....241 K8
or Ct FUL/RIB PR2 ....212 D4
or Ctyd HEY LA3 ....52 B3
or Crs BRSC L40 ....349 H1
HB LA2 ....43 F3
orcroft KIRK/FR/WA PR4 ....260 A3
or Dr BRSC L40 ....349 H1
V/TH FY5 ....122 D8
HB LA2 ....42 E3
RK/FR/WA PR4 ....209 C7
or Flds CLI BB7 ....193 G6
or Gdns BRSC L40 ....349 H1
or Gv HEY LA3 ....53 F1
ES PR1 ....238 C7
EL WN8 ....363 F2
GNW/BIL/O WN5 ....365 K3
or House Cl LEY/BBR PR5 ....284 D3
or House Crs PRES PR1 ....213 K8
or House Dr SKEL WN8 ....364 A8
or House La PRES PR1 ....213 K8
ES PR1 ....238 D7
or Ldg FMBY L37 ....343 J7
or Pk PRES PR1 ....214 A8
or Pl ACC BB5 ....247 K4
or Rd BBNW BB2 ....244 D6
OOL FY1 ....5 D3
SC L40 ....349 H1
LYE PR6 ....264 A8
TN/BK PR9 ....302 C1
* BB7 ....165 H4
BB7 ....193 G6
N BB8 ....171 J4
VN BB3 ....291 H3
WD FY7 ....96 E6
R/LONG PR3 ....129 J2
HB LA2 ....43 F3
R/BR BL1 ....339 F7
RK/FR/WA PR4 ....182 C3
RK/FR/WA PR4 ....207 K7
HM/BLYW BB12 ....224 D6
GNNW/ST WN6 ....353 H5
or St ACC BB5 ....248 D4
CUP OL13 ....298 D2
SN BB9 ....198 D4
MS BL0 ....319 H4
or Wy KIRK/FR/WA PR4 ....207 K8
or Wd FTWD FY7 ....96 E7
se Av WGNNW/ST WN6 ....334 D5
sergh St BRFD/BLYE * BB10 ....226 A1
sfield Crs NLSN BB9 ....198 A5
sfield Dr LEY/BBR PR5 ....241 J8
sfield Gv NLSN BB9 ....198 A5
sion St South ACC * BB5 ....248 D5
ston Gv CHLY/EC PR7 ....310 E4
x Jane's La CHTN/BK PR9 ....278 C7
xman Rd BBNW BB2 ....268 C2
le Av BPOOLE FY3 ....5 D2
SC L40 ....330 E7
LYE PR6 ....289 F4
V/TH FY5 ....149 J3
WD* FY7 ....123 F3
EY LA3 ....40 E8
W/HAS BB4 ....272 D8
le Bank BRFD/BLYE BB10 ....11 F2
lebank FUL/RIB PR2 ....237 J2
le Cl BBN BB1 ....219 G5
BB7 ....193 H5
BY L37 ....355 C2
RK/FR/WA PR4 ....235 K1

WGNW/BIL/O WN5 ....371 F6
Maple Crs BBN BB9 ....247 F3
Maple Dr ACC BB5 ....247 K8
LEY/BBR PR5 ....263 J2
PLF/KEOS FY6 ....177 K1
Maple Gv CHLYE PR6 ....287 H8
FUL/RIB BB4 ....214 E7
FUL/RIB BB4 ....215 H2
KIRK/FR/WA PR4 ....234 B5
LANC LA1 ....2 A3
PRES PR1 ....238 D7
RAMS BL0 ....319 K6
Maple Rd GAR/LONG PR3 ....129 J3
The Maples LEY/BBR PR5 ....284 B5
Maple St ACC BB5 ....247 K2
BBN BB1 ....9 E2
BBN BB1 ....247 F2
GTH/LHO BB6 ....221 H6
STHP PR8 ....301 K5
Maplewood SKEL WN8 ....351 G7
Maplewood Av PLF/KEOS FY6 ....98 C6
Maplewood Cl LEY/BBR PR5 ....285 G3
LSTA FY8 ....232 B7
Maplewood Dr CLV/TH FY5 ....148 C3
Maplewood Gdns LANC LA1 ....67 G1
Marabou Dr DWN BB3 ....268 A8
Marathon Pl LEY/BBR PR5 ....261 K8
Marble St ACC BB5 ....247 J6
Marchbank Rd SKEL WN8 ....362 D2
March St PDHM/BLYW BB12 ....10 C1
Marchwood Rd BPOOLE FY3 ....177 H3
Marcroft Av BPOOLS FY4 ....204 E4
Mardale Av BPOOLS FY4 ....205 J2
MCMB LA4 ....41 K6
Mardale Cl STHP PR8 ....325 H7
Mardale Crs LEY/BBR PR5 ....285 K4
Mardale Rd GAR/LONG PR3 ....187 K6
LANC LA1 ....3 E2
PRES PR1 ....240 E2
Maresfield Rd PRES PR1 ....6 B5
Marewood CHLY/EC PR7 ....311 F1
Margaret Rd PRES PR1 ....6 C1
Margaret St ACC BB5 ....270 B1
BBN BB1 ....246 E5
BRFD/BLYE* BB10 ....11 D1
PRES PR1 ....7 E2
RAW/HAS BB4 ....273 G7
Margate Av BPOOLS FY4 ....204 E5
Margate Rd FUL/RIB PR2 ....212 C7
LSTA FY8 ....231 F3
Marians Dr ORM L39 ....348 C3
Maria Sq EDGW/EG BL7 ....314 E7
Maria St DWN BB3 ....291 K5
Maricourt Av BBN BB1 ....246 B6
Marilyn Av LEY/BBR PR5 ....262 E3
Marina Av BPOOL * FY1 ....5 D5
BPOOLE FY3 ....177 K3
Marina Cl LEY/BBR PR5 ....262 D2
Marina Dr FUL/RIB PR2 ....213 G4
LEY/BBR PR5 ....262 D2
Marina Gv LEY/BBR PR5 ....262 D2
Marina Ms FTWD FY7 ....97 H8
Marina Rd FMBY L37 ....355 K2
Marine Av BLY BB11 ....224 E7
Marine Dr CHTN/BK PR9 ....278 A6
HGHB LA2 ....42 C3
LSTA FY8 ....231 J8
STHP PR8 ....300 E5
Marine Gate Man
CHTN/BK (off Seabank Rd) PR9 ....301 H3
Marine Pde FTWD FY7 ....122 C2
STHP PR8 ....301 G3
Marine Rd Central MCMB LA4 ....41 G6
Marine Rd East MCMB LA4 ....41 K5
Marine Rd West HEY LA3 ....40 E7
MCMB LA4 ....41 F7
Mariners Cl FTWD FY7 ....122 C2
Mariners Wy FUL/RIB PR2 ....238 C3
Marion Cl CLV/TH FY5 ....149 K3
Maritime St FTWD FY7 ....123 F1
Maritime Wy FUL/RIB PR2 ....238 B4
Mark Cl PRES PR1 ....262 C2
Market Hall LANC LA1 ....3 D3
PRES (off Market St) PR1 ....7 D2
Market Pl CHLY/EC PR7 ....337 G4
COL BB8 ....171 J6
GAR/LONG PR3 ....129 J4
GAR/LONG PR3 ....188 B4
PLF/KEOS FY6 ....149 K8
RAMS BL0 ....319 J5
Market Prom BLY BB11 ....11 D3
Market Sq BLY BB11 ....10 C3
KKBYL LA6 ....21 H1
LSTA FY8 ....232 B2
NLSN BB9 ....198 B3
Market St ACC BB5 ....247 J6
BCUP OL13 ....298 D1

BCUP OL13 ....299 H4
BPOOL FY1 ....4 B2
CARN LA5 ....33 K1
CHLY/EC PR7 ....311 G3
CHLY/EC PR7 ....337 G5
COL BB8 ....171 H6
DWN BB3 ....291 J2
KIRK/FR/WA PR4 ....208 C5
KKBYL LA6 ....21 H1
LANC LA1 ....3 D3
MCMB LA4 ....41 G6
PLF/KEOS FY6 ....150 E1
PRES PR1 ....7 D2
RAMS BL0 ....295 K7
RAW/HAS BB4 ....297 H3
STHP PR8 ....301 G4
WHIT OL12 ....323 G3
Market Street La BBNW BB2 ....8 C5
Market St West PRES PR1 ....7 D2
Market Wy BBN * BB1 ....8 C4
Markham Dr STHP PR8 ....327 G1
Markham Rd BBNW BB2 ....244 D8
Marklands Rd HOR/BR BL6 ....339 G6
Markland St PRES PR1 ....6 C3
RAMS* BL0 ....319 J5
Mark Rd HTWN L38 ....355 K7
Markross St RAW/HAS BB4 ....296 C1
Mark's Av LEY/BBR PR5 ....262 B6
Mark St BCUP OL13 ....298 A3
BRFD/BLYE BB10 ....225 K2
Marland SKEL WN8 ....351 G7
Marl Av PRES PR1 ....238 D7
Marlboro Rd BPOOLE FY3 ....5 D3
Marlborough SKEL WN8 ....351 G7
Marlborough Av CLV/TH FY5 ....122 C6
KIRK/FR/WA PR4 ....234 B5
MGHL L31 ....359 F8
Marlborough Cl RAMS BL0 ....319 J8
Marlborough Dr FUL/RIB PR2 ....213 F3
LEY/BBR PR5 ....240 A7
Marlborough Rd ACC BB5 ....248 B3
CHTN/BK PR9 ....301 J4
HEY LA3 ....40 E8
LSTA FY8 ....230 E2
Marlborough St BLY BB11 ....11 D5
CHLYE PR6 ....311 J2
Marl Cop LEY/BBR PR5 ....283 G5
Marl Cft PRES PR1 ....262 A1
Marled Hey EDGW/EG BL7 ....317 H6
Marles Ct BRFD/BLYE BB10 ....11 E1
Marlfield KIRK/FR/WA PR4 ....260 A7
Marlfield Cl FUL/RIB PR2 ....212 B5
Marl Gv WGNNW/BIL/O WN5 ....365 F7
Marl Hill Crs FUL/RIB PR2 ....240 E1
Marl Hill La AIRE BD20 ....147 H4
Marlhill Rd BPOOLE FY3 ....177 G3
Marl Pits RAW/HAS BB4 ....273 J8
Marl Pl
ACC (off Whinney Hill Rd) BB5 ....248 D2
Marl Rd NWD/KWIPK L33 ....367 G8
Marlton Rd BBNW BB2 ....268 A2
Marlton Wy LANC LA1 ....2 C5
Marple Cl WGNNW/ST WN6 ....353 J1
Marquis Cl DWN BB3 ....268 C4
Marquis Dr KIRK/FR/WA PR4 ....235 G4
Marquis St KIRK/FR/WA PR4 ....208 D6
Marron Cl LEY/BBR PR5 ....285 G2
Marsden Cl CHLY/EC PR7 ....308 D4
Marsden Ct BRFD/BLYE BB10 ....198 A8
Marsden Crs NLSN BB9 ....198 E3
Marsden Dr NLSN BB9 ....198 E3
Marsden Gv NLSN BB9 ....198 A6
Marsden Hall Rd NLSN BB9 ....198 E3
Marsden Hall Rd North NLSN BB9 ....198 E2
Marsden Height Cl NLSN BB9 ....198 C6
Marsden Ml
NLSN (off Brunswick St) BB9 ....198 D5
Marsden Rd BPOOLS FY4 ....204 D3
BRFD/BLYE BB10 ....198 A8
CHTN/BK PR9 ....302 A4
Marsden St ACC BB5 ....248 B7
BBNW BB2 ....267 J1
KIRK/FR/WA PR4 ....209 F6
Marsett Pl FUL/RIB PR2 ....214 C3
Marshall Av ACC BB5 ....248 E1
Marshall Gv FUL/RIB PR2 ....212 C7
Marshallsay HEY LA3 ....356 A1
Marshall's Brow PRES PR1 ....239 G8
Marshall's Cl MGHL L31 ....358 E7
PRES PR1 ....6 C6
Marsham Cl GAR/LONG * PR3 ....129 K5
Marsham Gv DWN BB3 ....292 A2

/BBR PR5 ....285 J2
HM/BLYW BB12 ....223 J2
ES PR1 ....7 E2
low V DWN BB3 ....268 B5
... low Vw CLI BB7 ....165 C3
HB LA2 ....46 E1
K/FR/WA PR4 ....207 H4
P PR8 ....301 K1
low Wy BCUP OL13 ....298 C1
CK/EAR BB18 ....119 H7
LY/EC PR7 ....335 H3
GW/EG BL7 ....317 H5
R/LONG PR3 ....129 J1
ds Rd FUL/RIB PR2 ....238 D2
dup Ct HEY LA3 ....53 G1
dway BPOOLS FY4 ....5 F6
LYE PR6 ....264 A8
K/FR/WA PR4 ....281 J1
ES PR1 ....238 C6
MS BL0 ....319 J2
EL WN8 ....351 C7
dway LS HOR/BR BL6 ....339 F8
gles La GAR/LONG PR3 ....152 C8
house La CHLY/EC PR7 ....311 G3
rigg La KKBYL LA6 ....19 J6
nwood Av BPOOLS FY4 ....205 H4
nygate LEY/BBR PR5 ....263 H3
ley Brook Fold CLI BB7 ....165 K4
ley Rd FUL/RIB PR2 ....214 C7
ley St CLI BB7 ....165 J4
ley Syke CLI BB7 ....165 K3
ch Rd PRES PR1 ....6 B5
Mede HEY/FR/WA PR4 ....235 F1
na Cl ACC * BB5 ....248 B6
lar Cl KIRK/FR/WA PR4 ....208 C5
lar Ct KIRK/FR/WA * PR4 ....208 E5
ar Ga KIRK/FR/WA PR4 ....208 E5
ar La KIRK/FR/WA PR4 ....180 C7
ock Av FTWD FY7 ....96 C6
tway FUL/RIB PR2 ....215 H5
way Av FTWD FY7 ....122 D5
way LEY/BBR PR5 ....262 E2
way Dr HOR/BR BL6 ....339 F8
ting House La LANC * LA1 ....2 C3
s Cft BBNW BB2 ....244 C6
s Rd BBNW BB2 ....244 A5
a Rd FUL/RIB PR2 ....214 C8
ert Av FUL/RIB PR2 ....212 D8
ourne Av CLV/TH FY5 ....149 F4
WD FY7 ....122 D3
ourne CI HOR/BR BL6 ....338 E8
ourne Gv HOR/BR BL6 ....338 E8
ourne Rd LANC LA1 ....3 E3
 sta St ACC * BB5 ....247 H8
C BB5 ....248 A2
N* BB3 ....291 K5
HM/BLYW BB12 ....223 K4
ES PR1 ....7 D2
W/HAS BB4 ....297 H4
reck SKEL WN8 ....351 G7
ion Gra HEY LA3 ....52 E3
ion Rd HEY LA3 ....52 D4
reth Cl FMBY L37 ....355 G2
ord Cl CHLYE PR6 ....287 J8
ord Dr WGNW/BIL/O WN5 ....365 F8
a Cl RAW/HAS BB4 ....296 B1
sta St DWN BB3 ....291 K3
ng Cl
LYE (off Bolton Rd) PR6 ....337 C2
ng Ct MCMB LA4 ....41 G8
ng Dr KKBY L32 ....366 C8
ng Ms
R/LONG
f Archery Gdns) PR3 ....129 K2
ng Rd CHTN/BK PR9 ....302 A3
HB LA2 ....37 G4
ings PRES PR1 ....240 A5
ings Av WGNW/BIL/O * WN5 ....371 G2
ings Fold PRES * PR1 ....240 A5
ing's La LSTA FY8 ....231 C2
ing St PRES PR1 ....7 D2
ings Wd LSTA FY8 ....231 G2
ing Wy KKBY L32 ....366 C8
ishaw La HEY LA3 ....53 K2
or Brow BBNW BB2 ....217 J8
or CI BLY BB11 ....10 A6
or Ct GAR/LONG PR3 ....188 B4
or La BBNW BB2 ....244 A1
or PI PRES * PR1 ....7 F3
or Rd HEY/FR/WA PR4 ....208 E6
Y/BBR PR5 ....285 F1
ose Av ACC BB5 ....247 K8
LY BB11 ....10 A5
POOLE FY3 ....177 F3
HTN/BK PR9 ....278 D6

FUL/RIB PR2 ....214 A6
MCMB LA4 ....41 J6
Melrose Gdns LEY/BBR PR5 ....307 J1
Melrose Rd NWD/KWIPK L33 ....366 B5
Melrose St DWN BB3 ....291 H1
LANC LA1 ....3 E4
Melrose Wy CHLY/EC PR7 ....311 H5
Melton Gv LSTA FY8 ....232 A8
Melton PI CLV/TH FY5 ....148 C3
LEY/BBR PR5 ....285 K1
Melville Dr BBNW BB2 ....8 B7
Melville Gdns DWN BB3 ....291 J3
Melville Rd BISP FY2 ....148 C7
HEY* LA3 ....52 C6
Melville St BRFD/BLYE BB10 ....226 A2
DWN BB3 ....291 J3
Memory Cl KIRK/FR/WA PR4 ....235 F4
Menai Dr FUL/RIB PR2 ....213 F4
Mendip Cl HOR/BR BL6 ....338 E6
LSTA FY8 ....233 F6
Mendip Rd LEY/BBR PR5 ....286 F3
Menivale Cl CHTN/BK PR9 ....278 C5
Meols Cl FMBY L37 ....355 J1
Meols Cop Rd STHP PR8 ....302 B6
Meolsgate Av KIRK/FR/WA PR4 ....282 A4
Mercer Ct CHLY/EC PR7 ....337 F2
Mercer Crs RAW/HAS BB4 ....295 C3
Mercer Dr GTH/LHO BB6 ....221 J5
Mercer Rd LEY/BBR PR5 ....262 D2
Mercer's La ORM L39 ....361 F7
Mercer St ACC BB5 ....221 K8
GTH/LHO BB6 ....221 H6
PDHM/BLYW BB12 ....224 B4
PRES PR1 ....240 A3

Merchants House
BBN (off Merchants Quay) BB1 ....9 D5
Merchants Landing BBN BB1 ....9 D6
Merchants Quay BBN BB1 ....9 D6
Merclesden St NLSN BB9 ....199 F2
Mere Av BRSC L40 ....330 E5
FTWD FY7 ....122 D2
Merebrook Gv NWD/KWIPK L33 ....366 D6
Mere Brow La KIRK/FR/WA PR4 ....304 E1
Mere Ct GAR/LONG PR3 ....184 E8
SKEL WN8 ....363 F1
Mere Ct BLY BB11 ....224 D7
Meredith St NLSN BB9 ....198 C4
Merefell Rd CARN LA5 ....33 G5
Merefield CHLY/EC PR7 ....310 E2
Mere Fold CHLY/EC PR7 ....310 B8
Merefold HOR/BR BL6 ....338 B8
Mereland Cl WCNW/BIL/O WN5 ....365 G5
Mereland Rd BPOOLE FY3 ....205 G1
Mere La BRSC L40 ....305 H8
CHTN/BK PR9 ....279 J8
KIRK/FR/WA PR4 ....304 E4
Mere Park Ct BPOOLE FY3 ....177 G8
Merepark Dr CHTN/BK PR9 ....278 D7
Mere Rd BPOOLE FY3 ....5 D2
FMBY L37 ....355 H1
Mereside Cl KIRK/FR/WA PR4 ....260 A4
Meres Wy STHP PR8 ....326 D1
Merewood SKEL WN8 ....351 G7
Meriden St STHP PR8 ....325 H4
Merlecrest Dr KIRK/FR/WA PR4 ....282 A3
Merlewood Av CHTN/BK PR9 ....278 D8
Merlewood Av RAMS BL0 ....296 A4
Merlin Cl CHLYE PR6 ....288 A3
Merlin Dr ACC BB5 ....247 H8
Merlin Gv LEY/BBR PR5 ....285 F4
Merlin Rd BBNW BB2 ....244 D5
Merlyn Rd CLV/TH FY5 ....148 B2
Merrick Av PRES PR1 ....240 D3
Merryburn Cl FUL/RIB PR2 ....213 J7
Merry Trees La KIRK/FR/WA PR4 ....212 A6
Merscar La BRSC L40 ....329 H5
Mersey Av BCUP OL13 ....298 E2
FUL/RIB PR2 ....6 A2
GAR/LONG PR3 ....188 A4
PDHM/BLYW BB12 ....224 C5
Merton Av FUL/RIB PR2 ....215 H5
Merton Gv CHLYE PR6 ....287 J3
Merton Rd WGNS/IIMK WN3 ....365 K7
Merton St NLSN * BB9 ....198 B2
PDHM/BLYW* BB12 ....10 C2
Messenger St NLSN BB9 ....198 D4
Meta St BBNW BB2 ....268 B1
Metcalf Dr ACC BB5 ....222 D5
Metcalfe St PDHM/BLYW BB12 ....224 D6
Mete St PRES PR1 ....240 B3
Methuen Av FUL/RIB PR2 ....213 G5
LEY/BBR PR5 ....241 J8

Methuen Cl LEY/BBR PR5 ....241 J8
Methuen Dr LEY/BBR PR5 ....241 K8
Metropolitan Dr BPOOLE FY3 ....205 H1
Mettle Cote BCUP OL13 ....298 E2
Mewith La HGHB LA2 ....39 J7
The Mews MCMB LA4 ....42 A6
PDHM/BLYW
(off Chapel Wk) BB12 ....223 J3
STHP PR8 ....301 G6
Mexford Av BISP FY2 ....176 D2
Meyler Av BPOOLE FY3 ....176 E3
Michael Pl MCMB LA4 ....41 K6
Michaels Cl FMBY L37 ....343 J8
Michael's La ORM L39 ....326 E8
Michaelson Av MCMB LA4 ....42 A7
Michael Wife La RAMS BL0 ....296 A8
Mickering La ORM L39 ....360 A5
Mickleden Av FUL/RIB PR2 ....213 H4
Mickleden Rd BPOOLS FY4 ....205 J2
Micklegate CLV/TH FY5 ....148 C4
Micklehurst Crs BLY BB11 ....251 F1
Mickleton Dr STHP PR8 ....325 G6
Middlecot Cl WCNW/BIL/O WN5 ....365 G6
Middlefield LEY/BBR PR5 ....284 C3
Middleforth Gn PRES PR1 ....6 C6
Middlegate HEY LA3 ....54 A1
Middlegate Gn RAW/HAS BB4 ....273 H2
Middle Hey KIRK/FR/WA PR4 ....282 E1
Middle HI WHIT OL12 ....323 K7
Middle Holly Rd GAR/LONG PR3 ....103 J3
Middle Meanygate
KIRK/FR/WA PR4 ....281 G4
Middle Moss La FMBY L37 ....345 F8
Middlesex Av PDHM/BLYW BB12 ....224 C4
Middle St BPOOL FY1 ....4 B4
COL BB8 ....171 G7
LANC LA1 ....3 D5
WHIT OL12 ....323 G2
Middleton Av FTWD FY7 ....122 D2
Middleton Dr NLSN BB9 ....170 C5
Middleton Rd HEY LA3 ....52 C6
Middleton Wy HEY LA3 ....52 C4
Middle Turn EDGW/EG BL7 ....317 H4
Middle Withins La HTWN L38 ....357 F4
Middlewood SKEL WN8 ....351 G7
Middlewood Cl CHLY/EC PR7 ....308 E5
ORM L39 ....360 A4
Middlewood Dr ORM L39 ....360 A4
Middlewood Rd ORM L39 ....360 A4
Midfield GTH/LHO BB6 ....220 A3
Midford Dr BOL BL1 ....341 J4
Midge Hall La CHTN/BK PR9 ....329 G1
KIRK/FR/WA PR4 ....261 G7
Midgeland Rd BPOOLS FY4 ....205 G4
Midgeland Ter
BPOOLS (off School Rd) FY4 ....205 J6
Midgery La FUL/RIB PR2 ....213 J3
Midgley St COL BB8 ....171 J7
Midhurst Dr STHP PR8 ....325 H7
Midland St ACC BB5 ....248 C6
NLSN BB9 ....198 C2
Midsummer St BBNW BB2 ....8 A4
Milbanke Av KIRK/FR/WA PR4 ....208 E5
Milbeck Cl GAR/LONG PR3 ....187 K6
Milbourne St BPOOL FY1 ....4 C2
Milbrook Cl BLY BB11 ....224 D6
Milbrook Crs KKBY L32 ....366 B8
Milbrook Dr KKBY L32 ....366 C8
Milburn Av CLV/TH FY5 ....123 F6
Mildred Cl CLV/TH FY5 ....123 G8
Mile End Cl COL BB8 ....171 H2
Mile End Rd BBNW BB2 ....244 D5
Mile Rd PLF/KEOS FY6 ....179 H2
Miles Av BCUP OL13 ....298 B3
Miles La WGNNW/ST WN6 ....353 G4
Miles St PRES PR1 ....239 H1
Mile Stone Meadow CHLYE PR6 ....286 B7
Milestone Pl
HGHB (off Fell Vw) LA2 ....45 G6
Miles Wk PRES PR1 ....239 G1
Miletas Pl LSTA FY8 ....231 J8
Milford Av BISP FY2 ....176 D2
Milford Cl FMBY L37 ....355 G2
GAR/LONG PR3 ....155 K1
Milford St COL BB8 ....171 G7
Milford Ter
CLV/TH (off Heys St) FY5 ....123 H8
Milking La DWN BB3 ....268 D5
Milking Stile La LANC LA1 ....2 B3
Milk St RAMS * BL0 ....319 H6
Millar Barn La RAW/HAS BB4 ....297 H3
Millar's Pace CHTN/BK PR9 ....278 D6
Millbank FUL/RIB PR2 ....212 E8
Mill Bank WGNNW/ST WN6 ....353 F4
Millbank Brow BRSC L40 ....331 F8
Millbank La MGHL L31 ....359 H8
Millbrook PDHM/BLYW BB12 ....197 G3

MS BL0 ...319 K1
'croft Crs FUL/RIB PR2 ...214 B8
' Dr SKEL WN8 ...363 K4
' Edge CLI BB7 ...193 F5
e Dr PDHM/BLYW BB12 ...196 B6
end CLI BB7 ...165 K4
'end Cottages
H/LHO (off Ribchester Rd) BB6 ...191 J7
e St BPOOLS FY4 ...4 B6
' BB8 ...171 G6
SN BB9 ...198 D4
HM/BLYW BB12 ...224 B4
ES PR1 ...240 A4
e Tree Dr BPOOLS FY4 ...205 G3
' Fld CLI BB7 ...193 F5
K/FR/WA PR4 ...261 G4
field EDGW/EG BL7 ...317 H5
'D/KWIPK L33 ...366 D6
field Av ACC BB5 ...249 F3
N BB1 ...219 C8
OOLE FY3 ...5 E1
'/KEOS FY6 ...149 H6
field Cl ACC BB5 ...222 B8
/RIB PR2 ...213 G3
ES PR1 ...238 C8
field Dr ACC BB5 ...222 B8
/RIB PR2 ...214 C8
A FY8 ...232 C7
field La BRSC L40 ...329 F8
field Rd LEY/BBR PR5 ...284 E3
fields CHLYE PR6 ...311 J2
'/KEOS FY6 ...149 F7
fields Av FUL/RIB PR2 ...213 G3
field Wy ACC BB5 ...222 B8
Ga LANC LA1 ...3 E3
gate ACC BB5 ...271 G1
OOLS FY4 ...205 F5
/RIB PR2 ...213 H6
M L39 ...348 C7
gate Rd BWCK/EAR BB18...144 E2
gate St BBNW BB2 ...267 K2
' Hall La KIRK/FR/WA PR4 ...209 K7
' Hall St PRES PR1 ...239 G1
head Gdns KIRK/FR/WA PR4 ...234 C4
head St COL BB8 ...171 G6
hen Pl CLV/TH FY5 ...149 F2
hey Crs LEY/BBR PR5 ...263 K3
ES PR1 ...238 D6
hey Dr PRES PR1...238 D6
house Av ACC BB5 ...248 A7
houses HTWN L38 ...355 K8
house St ACC BB5 ...248 A7
' BB11 ...224 E6
OOL FY1 ...176 B4
ings Cl BBNW BB2 ...268 A1
Moorings CHLYE PR6 ...311 J3
HL L31 ...358 D7
HM/BLYW BB12 ...10 B2
land Av BBNW BB2 ...266 E4
CK/EAR BB18 ...146 C2
BB7 ...165 K5
N BB3 ...291 F1
/RIB PR2 ...214 B6
'/KEOS FY6 ...150 A7
IT OL12 ...323 C5
land Cl NLSN BB9 ...170 D5
land Ct
'/KEOS (off Moorland Rd) FY6 ...150 A7
land Crs CLI BB7 ...165 K4
/RIB PR2 ...214 B7
IT OL12 ...323 C4
land Dr HOR/BR BL6 ...339 H8
N BB9 ...198 B9
land Gdns PLF/KEOS FY6 ...150 A7
land Ga CHLYE PR6 ...311 G6
land Ri RAW/HAS BB4 ...272 D8
land Rd BBNW BB2 ...267 K8
' BB11 ...10 B6
BB7 ...165 K1
I/LHO BB6 ...220 A2
A FY8 ...231 G4
'/KEOS FY6 ...150 A7
lands Gv HEY LA3 ...40 E8
lands Ter BCUP OL13 ...298 E2
loorlands BCUP OL13 ...275 K3
land Vw
N (off Exchange St) BB3 ...268 C8
N BB9 ...198 D5
La BWCK/EAR BB18 ...145 G5
BB7 ...113 F8
BB7 ...165 J4
BB7 ...193 F5
BB7 ...193 K4
BB7 ...220 D2
N BB3 ...268 D8
HB LA2 ...47 J1

HTWN L38 ...356 D8
KIRK/FR/WA PR4 ...260 E2
LANC LA1...3 E3
PDHM/BLYW BB12 ...223 J2
PRES PR1 ...7 D2
RAW/HAS BB4 ...271 K5
SKP/WHF BD23 ...121 J5
STHP PR8 ...344 C1
Moor Park Av BISP FY2 ...148 E8
PRES PR1 ...239 J1
Moor Park Ct
PRES (off St Georges Rd) PR1 ...239 H1
Moor Platt Cl HOR/BR BL6 ...339 H8
Moor Rd CHLY/EC PR7 ...310 E6
CHLYE PR6 ...312 E4
LEY/BBR PR5 ...283 J8
RAW/HAS BB4 ...295 G6
TOT/BURYW BL8 ...319 G5
WGNW/BIL/O WN5 ...365 G5
Moorside KIRK/FR/WA PR4 ...181 H8
Moorside Av BBN BB1 ...246 A7
FUL/RIB PR2 ...214 D8
HOR/BR BL6 ...338 E7
NLSN BB9 ...198 B7
Moorside Cl KKBYL LA6 ...30 A8
Moorside Crs BCUP OL13 ...275 K7
Moorside Dr PRES PR1 ...238 D8
Moor Side La CLI BB7 ...193 K3
RAMS BL0 ...320 C1
Moorside La KIRK/FR/WA PR4 ...183 J7
Moorside Rd HGHB LA2 ...45 J6
EDGW/EG BL7 ...317 H2
Moor St ACC BB5 ...221 K8
KIRK/FR/WA PR4 ...208 E6
ORM L39 ...348 D6
Moorsview RAMS BL0 ...319 H5
Moorthorpe Cl DWN BB3 ...291 J5
Moor Vw BCUP OL13 ...275 K7
BCUP (off Stackstead) OL13 ...297 K4
Moorview Cl BRFD/BLYE BB10 ...226 C1
Moorview Ct BPOOLS * FY4 ...205 F4
Moorway PLF/KEOS FY6 ...150 B7
Moor Wy TOT/BURYW BL8 ...318 B8
Moray Cl RAMS BL0 ...319 G7
Morecambe Rd BBNW BB2 ...268 C2
LANC LA1...2 A1
Morecambe St East MCMB LA4 ...41 H5
Morecambe St West MCMB * LA4 ...41 H6
Moresby Av BPOOLE FY3 ...177 H4
Moreton Dr BPOOLE FY3...177 K6
PLF/KEOS FY6 ...177 K1
Moreton Gn HEY LA3 ...52 D4
Moreton St ACC BB5 ...248 B5
Morewood Dr KKBYL LA6 ...18 B5
Morland Av KIRK/FR/WA PR4 ...208 D4
LEY/BBR PR5 ...262 D4
Morley Av BBNW BB2 ...267 H2
CHTN/BK PR9 ...302 A3
LANC LA1...42 E8
Morley Cl LANC LA1 ...42 E8
Morley Rd BPOOLS FY4 ...204 E3
CHTN/BK PR9 ...302 A3
LANC LA1...42 E8
Morley St BLY BB11 ...11 E5
PDHM/BLYW BB12 ...223 J3
Morningside LANC LA1 ...3 D4
Mornington Rd CHLYE PR6 ...337 H3
CHTN/BK PR9 ...301 H4
LSTA FY8 ...233 G7
PRES* PR1 ...238 D6
PRES PR1 ...240 D2
Morris Cl LEY/BBR PR5 ...285 J3
Morris Ct FUL/RIB * PR2 ...240 B1
Morris Crs FUL/RIB PR2 ...240 B1
Morris Hey ORM L39 ...328 B8
Morris La ORM L39 ...328 B8
Morrison St CHLYE PR6 ...311 H1
Morris Rd CHLYE * PR6 ...311 J2
FUL/RIB PR2 ...240 B1
SKEL WN8 ...364 C4
Morse St BRFD/BLYE BB10 ...11 F4
Morston Dr BISP FY2 ...176 E1
Mortimer Gv HEY LA3 ...52 E3
Morton St BBN BB1 ...8 C4
Mort St HOR/BR BL6 ...338 D7
Morven Gv STHP PR8 ...302 A4
Moscow Mill St ACC BB5 ...247 J6
Mosedale Dr PDHM/BLYW BB12 ...224 D3
Moseley Av BWCK/EAR BB18 ...145 K2
Moseley Rd BLY BB11 ...11 D6
Mosley St BBNW BB2 ...268 B1
BWCK/EAR BB18 ...145 F1
LEY/BBR PR5 ...285 J2
NLSN BB9 ...198 B3
PRES PR1 ...240 A3
STHP PR8 ...301 H7
Mosman Pl NLSN BB9 ...170 A8
Moss Acre Rd PRES PR1 ...239 G8
Moss Av FUL/RIB PR2 ...238 C1

WGNW/BIL/O WN5 ...365 F8
Mossbank BBN * BB1 ...9 E3
Moss Bank CHLY/EC PR7 ...335 J2
ORM L39 ...360 B3
Moss Bank Cl BOL BL1 ...341 H7
Moss Bank Pk
BOL (off Moss Bank Wy) BL1 ...340 D8
Moss Bank Rd BPOOLS FY4 ...205 F3
Moss Bank Wy BOL BL1 ...341 H8
Mossborough Hall La
RNFD/HAY WA11 ...368 C8
Mossborough Rd
RNFD/HAY WA11 ...369 F6
Mossbourne Rd PLF/KEOS FY6 ...177 J1
Moss Bridge La BRSC L40 ...350 C1
Moss Bridge Pk LEY/BBR PR5 ...262 E3
Mossbrook Dr KIRK/FR/WA PR4 ...212 A6
Moss Brow RNFD/HAY WA11 ...368 E4
Moss Cl CHLYE PR6 ...311 J3
RAW/HAS BB4 ...295 G3
Mossdale BBN BB1 ...9 E3
Mossdale Rd NWD/KWIPK L33 ...366 D6
Moss Delph La ORM L39 ...359 K1
Moss Dr HOR/BR BL6 ...339 H8
Moss Edge La GAR/LONG PR3 ...126 A4
LSTA FY8 ...205 G8
Moss End La HWTH BD22 ...174 A1
Moss End Wy NWD/KWIPK L33 ...367 H8
Mossfield Cl LEY/BBR PR5 ...262 E3
Mossfield Rd CHLYE PR6 ...311 J3
Moss Fold Rd DWN BB3 ...268 B6
Moss Ga BBN BB1 ...9 E3
Mossgiel Av STHP PR8 ...325 H6
Moss Hall La LSTA FY8 ...232 A3
Moss Hall Rd ACC BB5 ...248 B3
Moss Hey KIRK/FR/WA PR4...280 E8
Mosshill Cl MGHL L31 ...358 E8
Moss House La BPOOLS FY4 ...206 C4
GAR/LONG PR3...100 D7
KIRK/FR/WA PR4 ...206 D4
KIRK/FR/WA PR4 ...283 F1
PLF/KEOS FY6 ...124 E2
Moss House Rd BPOOLS FY4 ...205 G5
KIRK/FR/WA PR4 ...212 D1
Mosslands LEY/BBR PR5 ...285 F2
Moss La BBN BB1 ...246 D7
BOL BL1...340 E8
BRSC L40...331 F5
CARN LA5 ...16 A7
CARN LA5 ...17 H2
CHLY/EC PR7 ...335 J2
CHLYE PR6 ...287 H6
CHTN/BK PR9 ...280 A5
CHTN/BK PR9 ...302 D3
FMBY L37 ...344 C7
GAR/LONG PR3...129 H4
GAR/LONG PR3...154 B3
GAR/LONG PR3...161 F2
GAR/LONG PR3...183 K1
HGHB LA2 ...78 D2
HTWN L38 ...356 B6
KIRK/FR/WA PR4 ...154 B8
KIRK/FR/WA PR4 ...182 E7
KIRK/FR/WA PR4 ...260 C7
KIRK/FR/WA PR4 ...261 F4
KIRK/FR/WA PR4 ...280 E3
LEY/BBR PR5 ...261 K6
LEY/BBR PR5 ...262 E3
LEY/BBR PR5 ...284 B5
LEY/BBR PR5 ...286 A1
LEY/BBR PR5 ...307 G3
MCMB LA4 ...41 G7
MGHL L31 ...359 F6
NWD/KWIPK L33 ...366 D3
NWD/KWIPK L33 ...367 F8
ORM L39 ...367 K1
PLF/KEOS FY6 ...151 F2
RNFD/HAY WA11 ...370 A6
SKEL WN8 ...363 F5
WGNNW/ST WN6 ...334 A7
Moss La East KIRK/FR/WA PR4...210 A3
Moss Lane Vw SKEL WN8 ...363 F5
Moss La West KIRK/FR/WA PR4 ...209 J4
Moss Lea BOL BL1...341 H7
Mosslea Dr GAR/LONG PR3 ...184 D3
Moss Nook BRSC L40 ...330 E5
ORM* L39 ...360 A1
Moss Nook La RNFD/HAY WA11 ...368 E5
Mossom La CLV/TH FY5 ...148 C4
Moss Pl LANC LA1 ...43 G7
Moss Rd HEY LA3 ...53 H4
STHP PR8 ...326 E1
WGNW/BIL/O WN5 ...365 F8
Moss Side BWCK/EAR BB18...145 G1
FMBY L37 ...344 B7
Moss Side La GAR/LONG PR3 ...125 K4
GAR/LONG PR3...153 J6

KIRK/FR/WA PR4 ....**233** H1
KIRK/FR/WA PR4 ....**280** D8
PLF/KEOS FY6 ....**125** F1
Moss Side St WHIT OL12 ....**299** J6
Moss Side Wy LEY/BBR PR5 ....**284** D8
Moss St BBN BB1 ....**9** E3
CLI BB7 ....**165** H3
GTH/LHO BB6 ....**221** C2
LEY/BBR PR5 ....**262** E3
PRES PR1 ....**7** D5
WCNW/BIL/O* WN5 ....**365** K5
Moss Ter WCNW/BIL/O WN5 .....**365** K6
Moss Vw STHP PR8 ....**326** A6
Moss Wy BPOOLS * FY4 ....**205** F4
Mossway KIRK/FR/WA PR4 ....**261** C5
Mossy Lea Fold WGNNW/ST WN6 ...**334** D8
Mossy Lea Rd WGNNW/ST WN6 .....**334** C5
Mostyn St DWN BB3 ....**268** B7
Motherwell Crs STHP PR8 ....**302** B8
Mottram Cl CHLYE PR6 ....**287** C5
Mottram St HOR/BR BL6 ....**338** D7
Moulden Brow BBNW BB2 ....**266** C4
Moulding Cl BBNW BB2 ....**244** D7
Mounsey Rd LEY/BBR PR5 ....**263** J3
Mountain Ash WHIT OL12 ....**323** F8
Mountain Ash Cl WHIT OL12 ....**323** F8
Mountain La ACC BB5 ....**248** C7
Mountain Rd CHLY/EC PR7 ....**335** J3
Mount Av LANC LA1 ....**43** F8
MCMB LA4 ....**42** A4
RAW/HAS BB4 ....**297** H3
Mountbatten Cl FUL/RIB PR2 .....**238** D4
Mountbatten Cl CHLY/EC PR7 .....**310** E5
Mount Cl KKBY L32 ....**366** A7
Mount Crs BRFD/BLYE BB10 ....**252** E3
KKBY L32 ....**366** A7
WGNW/BIL/O WN5 ....**365** H5
Mount Gdns MCMB LA4 ....**42** A4
Mount House La FMBY L37 ....**344** B6
Mount House Cl FMBY L37 ....**344** B6
Mount La BRFD/BLYE BB10 ....**252** C3
TOD OL14 ....**254** C8
Mount Pleasant BBN BB1 ....**9** D4
CARN LA5 ....**15** H3
CHLYE PR6 ....**287** G3
CHLYE PR6 ....**289** G3
CHLYE PR6 ....**337** G3
RAW/HAS BB4 ....**296** A1
Mount Pleasant La CARN LA5 ....**33** H7
Mount Pleasant St ACC * BB5 .....**247** J7
BLY BB11 ....**10** C4
TOD OL14 ....**277** F2
Mount Rd BLY BB11 ....**10** C5
FTWD FY7 ....**97** G6
Mount St ACC BB5 ....**248** B7
ACC BB5 ....**248** A1
BPOOL FY1 ....**4** D1
CHTN/BK PR9 ....**301** K4
FTWD FY7 ....**97** G7
GTH/LHO BB6 ....**221** G5
NLSN BB9 ....**170** D1
NLSN BB9 ....**197** K6
PRES PR1 ....**7** D3
RAMS BL0 ....**319** H4
RAW/HAS BB4 ....**296** A1
Mount Ter CHTN/BK PR9 ....**301** K4
RAW/HAS BB4 ....**296** C1
The Mount BBNW BB2 ....**8** A3
SKEL* WN8 ....**363** H3
Mount Vw
COL (off Hill Top) BB8 ....**171** G1
Mountwood SKEL WN8 ....**351** G7
Mowbray Av BBNW BB2 ....**268** C7
Mowbray Dr BPOOLE FY3 ....**176** E2
KKBY L32 ....**18** A6
Mowbray Rd FTWD FY7 ....**96** E7
Mowbray Ct KIRK/FR/WA PR4 .....**208** E5
Mowbreck La KIRK/FR/WA PR4 ...**208** D4
Mowbrick La HGHB LA2 ....**42** D2
Muirfield PRES PR1 ....**238** C5
Muirfield Cl FUL/RIB PR2 ....**212** D5
Muirfield Dr STHP PR8 ....**325** J7
Mulberry Av PRES PR1 ....**238** C8
Mulberry Cl KIRK/FR/WA PR4 ....**236** C2
NWD/KWIPK L33 ....**366** D5
Mulberry Ms BISP FY2 ....**149** F4
Mulberry St BBN BB1 ....**9** F4
Mulberry Wk BBN BB1 ....**9** F5
Mulgrave Av FUL/RIB PR2 ....**238** C5
Mullion Cl STHP PR8 ....**278** D6
Muncaster Dr RNFD/HAY WA11 ...**369** G4
Muncaster Rd PRES PR1 ....**239** H1
Munro Av WGNW/BIL/O WN5 .....**365** D5
Munro Cls FUL/RIB PR2 ....**214** C8
Munster Av BISP FY2 ....**148** D8
Murchison Gv CLV/TH FY5 ....**148** E3
Murdock Av FUL/RIB PR2 ....**239** F1

Murdock St BBNW * BB2 ....**244** D7
Murray Av ACC BB5 ....**262** B6
Murray St BRFD/BLYE BB10 ....**225** K2
LEY/BBR PR5 ....**285** K2
PRES PR1 ....**6** C1
Musbury Crs RAW/HAS BB4 ....**296** B2
Musbury Rd RAW/HAS BB4 ....**294** E4
Musden Av RAW/HAS BB4 ....**295** G4
Museum St BBN * BB1 ....**8** C4
Myerscough Av BPOOLS FY4 ......**205** F6
LSTA FY8 ....**230** D3
Myerscough Hall Dr
GAR/LONG PR3 ....**156** A6
Myerscough Planks
GAR/LONG PR3 ....**156** C8
Myerscough Smithy Rd
BBNW BB2 ....**216** E7
Myers St BRFD/BLYE BB10 ....**11** D1
BWCK/EAR BB18 ....**145** F2
Myndon St LANC LA1 ....**43** F8
Myra Av MCMB LA4 ....**41** J7
Myra Rd LSTA FY8 ....**231** H7
Myrescough Smithy Rd
BBNW BB2 ....**217** H8
Myrrh St BOL BL1 ....**341** J8
Myrtle Av BLY BB11 ....**10** A5
BPOOLE FY3 ....**5** D2
CLV/TH FY5 ....**123** F6
PLF/KEOS FY6 ....**150** A6
Myrtle Bank Rd BBNW * BB2 ......**267** K3
BCUP OL13 ....**275** J8
Myrtle Dr KIRK/FR/WA PR4 ....**209** G7
Myrtle Gv BRFD/BLYE BB10 ....**226** D7
HEY LA3 ....**40** E8
RAW/HAS BB4 ....**295** G2
STHP PR8 ....**302** A5
WCNW/BIL/O* WN5 ....**371** F7
Mythop Av LSTA FY8 ....**232** B1
Mythop Cl LSTA FY8 ....**232** D7
Mythop Pl FUL/RIB PR2 ....**238** B2
Mythop Rd BPOOLE FY3 ....**205** K1
KIRK/FR/WA PR4 ....**207** G1
LSTA FY8 ....**232** E7
Mytton Rd BOL BL1 ....**341** F8
Mytton St PDHM/BLYW BB12 ....**223** K3
Mytton Vw CLI BB7 ....**165** C4

N

Naarian Ct BBN BB1 ....**9** D2
Nabbs Fold TOT/BURYW BL8 ......**319** F8
Nab La ACC BB5 ....**247** F7
BBNW BB2 ....**8** B4
Nab Rd CHLYE PR6 ....**311** J2
Nab's Head La LEY/BBR PR5 ....**242** H6
Nairn Av SKEL WN8 ....**351** H6
Nairn Cl BPOOLS FY4 ....**205** G4
Nairne St BLY BB11 ....**10** A4
Nancy St DWN BB3 ....**291** J2
Nansen Rd BBNW BB2 ....**267** J1
FTWD FY7 ....**97** H7
Nantwich Av WHIT OL12 ....**323** K8
Napier Av BPOOLS FY4 ....**204** D5
KIRK/FR/WA PR4 ....**281** K3
Napier Cl LSTA FY8 ....**230** E2
Napier St ACC BB5 ....**248** C6
NLSN BB9 ....**198** C5
Napier Ter STHP PR8 ....**301** C6
Naples Av BLY * BB11 ....**10** A5
Naples Rd DWN BB3 ....**292** A2
Naptha La LEY/BBR PR5 ....**261** K5
Narcissus Av RAW/HAS BB4 ......**295** F3
Nares Rd BBNW BB2 ....**244** D8
Nares St FUL/RIB PR2 ....**6** A1
Narrow Croft La ORM L39 ....**359** K6
Narrow La LEY/BBR PR5 ....**284** B1
ORM L39 ....**359** K2
Narrow La (Clieves Hills)
ORM L39 ....**347** F4
Narrow Moss La BRSC L40 ....**348** B1
Narvik Av BLY BB11 ....**224** D7
Nasmyth St HOR/BR BL6 ....**338** E8
Nateby Av BPOOLS FY4 ....**204** E6
Nateby Cl GAR/LONG PR3 ....**187** K3
LSTA FY8 ....**231** H4
Nateby Crossing La
GAR/LONG PR3 ....**129** G3
Nateby Hall La GAR/LONG PR3 ...**129** F2
Nateby Pl FUL/RIB PR2 ....**238** B2
Nathan Gv NWD/KWIPK L33 ......**366** D7
Nave Cl DWN BB3 ....**292** A2
Navena Av FTWD FY7 ....**122** D1
Navigation Wy BBN BB1 ....**9** D6
FUL/RIB PR2 ....**238** C4
Naylorfarm Av WGNNW/ST WN6 ...**353** H6

Naylor's Ter EDGW/EG BL7 ....**3**
Naze La KIRK/FR/WA PR4 ....**2**
Naze La East KIRK/FR/WA PR4 .....**2**
Naze Rd RAW/HAS BB4 ....**2**
Naze View Av RAW/HAS BB4 ....**2**
Neales Fold CHTN/BK PR9 ....**2**
Neapsands Cl FUL/RIB PR2 ....**2**
Neargates CHLY/EC PR7 ....**3**
Neath Cl BBN BB1 ....
Neddy Hl KKBY L6 ....
Neddy La CLI BB7 ....**1**
Nedens Gv MGHL L31 ....**3**
Nedens La MGHL L31 ....**3**
Ned's La GAR/LONG PR3 ....
PLF/KEOS FY6 ....**1**
Needham Av MCMB LA4 ....
Needham Ri MCMB LA4 ....
Needham Wy SKEL WN8 ....**3**
Nell Carrs RAMS BL0 ....**3**
Nell La LEY/BBR PR5 ....**2**
Nell's La ORM L39 ....**3**
Nell St BOL BL1 ....
Nelson Av LEY/BBR PR5 ....**2**
Nelson Crs FUL/RIB PR2 ....**2**
Nelson Dr FUL/RIB PR2 ....
Nelson Gdns KIRK/FR/WA PR4 ...**1**
Nelson Rd BPOOL FY1 ....
BRFD/BLYE BB10 ....**1**
CHLY/EC PR7 ....**2**
FTWD FY7 ....
Nelson Sq BLY BB11 ....
Nelson St ACC BB5 ....**2**
BCUP OL13 ....
CLI BB7 ....
DWN BB3 ....**2**
GTH/LHO* BB6 ....**2**
HOR/BR BL6 ....**3**
KIRK/FR/WA PR4 ....**2**
LANC LA1 ....
LEY/BBR PR5 ....**2**
LSTA FY8 ....**2**
MCMB* LA4 ....
STHP PR8 ....**3**
Nelson Ter PRES PR1 ....
Nelson Wy FUL/RIB PR2 ....**2**
Nene Cl LEY/BBR PR5 ....**2**
Neps La CLI BB7 ....
Neptune St BLY BB11 ....
Nesswood Av BPOOLS FY4 ....**2**
Neston Av BOL BL1 ....**3**
Neston St PRES PR1 ....**2**
Nether Beck KKBYL LA6 ....
Netherby St BLY BB11 ....
Netherfield Cl PDHM/BLYW BB12 ...
Netherfield Rd NLSN BB9 ....**1**
Netherheys Cl COL BB8 ....**1**
Nether Kellet Rd KKBYL LA6 ....
Netherlands Rd MCMB LA4 ....
Netherley Rd CHLY/EC PR7 ....**3**
Nethertown Cl CLI BB7 ....**1**
Netherwood Rd
BRFD/BLYE BB10 ....
Netherwood St
BRFD/BLYE* BB10 ....**2**
Nethway Av BPOOLE FY3 ....
Netley Av WHIT OL12 ....**3**
Neverstitch Cl SKEL* WN8 ....**3**
Neverstitch Rd SKEL WN8 ....**3**
Nevett St PRES PR1 ....**2**
Neville Av CLV/TH FY5 ....
Neville Dr CLV/TH FY5 ....**2**
Neville St GAR/LONG PR3 ....**1**
Nevill St STHP PR8 ....**2**
Nevis Gv BOL BL1 ....**3**
Nevy Fold Av HOR/BR BL6 ....**3**
New Acres CARN LA5 ....**3**
SKEL WN8 ....**3**
Newark Pl FUL/RIB PR2 ....**2**
Newark Rd WHIT OL12 ....**2**
Newark Sq WHIT OL12 ....**2**
Newark St ACC BB5 ....**2**
Newarth La KIRK/FR/WA PR4 ......**2**
New Bank Rd BBNW BB2 ....**2**
New Barn RAW/HAS BB4 ....**2**
New Barn Ct BBNW BB2 ....**2**
New Barn La RAW/HAS BB4 ....**2**
New Barns Cl CARN LA5 ....
New Barns Rd CARN LA5 ....
New Bath St COL BB8 ....**1**
Newbigging Av RAW/HAS BB4 ....**2**
New Bonny St BPOOL FY1 ....
New Br GAR/LONG PR3 ....**1**
New Briggs Fold EDGW/EG BL7 ...**3**
New Brook Houses
PRES (off New Hall La) PR1 ....**2**
New Brown St NLSN* BB9 ....**1**
New Brunswick St HOR/BR BL6 ...**1**

Newmarket Av *LANC* LA1 ....55 H7
New Market St *CHLY/EC* PR7 ....311 G3
CLI BB7 ....165 J3
COL BB8 ....171 H6
Newmarket St *MCMB* LA4 ....41 K5
New Meadow La *FMBY* L37 ....356 E3
New Miles La *WGNNW/ST* WN6 ....353 H5
New Mill St *BBN* BB1 ....9 D3
CHLY/EC PR7 ....308 E5
New Moss La *CHLYE* PR6 ....287 G6
New Oxford St *COL* BB8 ....171 J6
New Park St *BBNW* BB2 ....8 B4
Newport St *NLSN* BB9 ....198 C2
New Preston MI
PRES (off New Hall La) PR1 ....7 F2
New Quay Rd *LANC* LA1 ....54 B3
New Rd *BLY* BB11 ....251 J1
BRSC L40 ....306 B7
BWCK/EAR BB18 ....146 B1
CARN LA5 ....25 F3
CHLY/EC PR7 ....310 D8
CHLYE PR6 ....337 K3
CLV/TH FY5 ....149 J4
FMBY L37 ....344 A6
KKBYL LA6 ....21 G1
LANC LA1 ....3 D3
LEY/BBR PR5 ....262 E2
LEY/BBR PR5 ....307 H4
LSTA FY8 ....204 B7
PLF/KEOS FY6 ....124 C7
RAW/HAS BB4 ....297 H1
TOD OL14 ....254 C6
WHIT OL12 ....323 F2
New Rough Hey *FUL/RIB* PR2 ....212 B5
New Rw *COL* BB8 ....172 C7
New Row Cottages
GAR/LONG (off Clitheroe Rd) PR3 .....189 K2
Newry St *BOL* BL1 ....341 H8
New Scotland Rd *NLSN* BB9 ....198 C2
Newsham Hall La
KIRK/FR/WA PR4 ....184 A8
Newsham PI *LANC* LA1 ....3 E5
Newsham Rd *LANC* LA1 ....3 E5
Newsham St *FUL/RIB* * PR2 ....6 B1
News La *RNFD/HAY* WA11 ....362 E3
Newsome St *LEY/BBR* PR5 ....285 J2
New Springs
BOL (off Smithills Dean Rd) BL1 ....341 F8
New St *BRSC* L40 ....332 E1
CARN LA5 ....33 K1
CHLY/EC PR7 ....308 E5
CHLYE PR6 ....289 F3
COL BB8 ....171 F8
HGHB LA2 ....44 A4
HGHB LA2 ....45 J5
LANC LA1 ....3 D3
MCMB LA4 ....41 G6
NLSN BB9 ....198 D2
ORM L39 ....346 D2
PDHM/BLYW* BB12 ....223 H3
RAW/HAS BB4 ....272 C8
WGNW/BIL/O WN5 ....365 K6
New Taylor Fold
BRFD/BLYE * BB10 ....198 D8
Newton Av *PLF/KEOS* FY6 ....177 J1
PRES PR1 ....240 D3
Newton CI *KIRK/FR/WA* PR4 ....235 G5
LEY/BBR PR5 ....284 D3
Newton Ct *FUL/RIB* PR2 ....238 D2
BPOOLE FY3 ....5 E2
BRFD/BLYE BB10 ....252 D4
SKEL WN8 ....351 H6
Newton Dr East *BPOOLE* FY3 ....177 H4
New Tong Fld *EDGW/EG* BL7 ....341 K4
Newton Gv *CLV/TH* FY5 ....149 H4
Newton PI *BPOOLE* FY3 ....177 G4
Newton Rd *FUL/RIB* PR2 ....238 D2
WGNW/BIL/O WN5 ....371 H5
Newton St *ACC* * BB5 ....247 F6
BBN BB1 ....9 F4
CHTN/BK PR9 ....302 C4
CLI BB7 ....165 H4
DWN BB3 ....291 K1
PDHM/BLYW* BB12 ....224 B4
PRES PR1 ....7 F2
Newtown *BWCK/EAR* BB18 ....145 F1
Newtown St *COL* BB8 ....171 J7
New Wy *ORM* L39 ....367 F1
WHIT OL12 ....323 G2
New Wellington CI *BBNW* BB2 ....267 K2
New Wellington St *BBNW* BB2 ....267 K2
Nib La *PRES* PR1 ....262 B3
Nicholas St *BLY* BB11 ....11 D4
BRFD/BLYE BB10 ....198 C8

Newmarket Av *LANC* LA1 ....55 H7

COL BB8 ....171 G7
DWN BB3 ....291 H2
Nicholl St *BRFD/BLYE* BB10 ....11 D1
Nicholson Crs *MCMB* LA4 ....41 K6
Nichol St *CHLY/EC* * PR7 ....311 G2
Nickey La *BBNW* BB2 ....244 B1
Nick Hilton's La *CHLYE* PR6 ....312 D8
Nickleton Brow *CHLYE* PR6 ....337 J1
Nicksons La *PLF/KEOS* FY6 ....98 D7
Nickson' Weind *GAR/LONG* PR3 ....129 J4
Nicola CI *BCUP* OL13 ....275 K4
Nicola St *EDGW/EG* BL7 ....341 J3
Nightfield La *BBNW* BB2 ....217 F5
Nightingale Crs *BLY* * BB11 ....224 E6
Nightingale Dr *PLF/KEOS* FY6 ....177 H1
Nightingale Rd *HOR/BR* BL6 ....337 J8
Nightingale St *CHLYE* PR6 ....337 G3
Nile St *LANC* LA1 ....3 D3
NLSN* BB9 ....198 B2
Nimes St *PRES* PR1 ....240 B3
Nine Elms *FUL/RIB* PR2 ....212 E5
Nineteen Acre La *CARN* LA5 ....17 G7
Nipe La *SKEL* WN8 ....363 H6
Nithside *BPOOLS* FY4 ....205 J2
Niton CI *RAW/HAS* * BB4 ....295 J2
Nixon La *LEY/BBR* PR5 ....284 B3
Nixons Ct *LEY/BBR* PR5 ....284 B3
Nixons La *SKEL* WN8 ....363 K4
STHP PR8 ....326 A4
Noble St *BBN* BB1 ....247 F2
DWN BB3 ....291 J3
GTH/LHO BB6 ....221 G7
Noblett Ct *FTWD* FY7 ....123 F1
Noblett St *BBN* * BB1 ....9 D4
Noel Ga *ORM* L39 ....359 K2
Noel Rd *LANC* LA1 ....42 E8
Noel Sq *FUL/RIB* * PR2 ....240 C2
Noggarth Rd *PDHM/BLYW* BB12 ....197 F3
Nolan St *STHP* PR8 ....301 J6
Nook Crs *FUL/RIB* PR2 ....215 G2
Nook Farm Av *WHIT* OL12 ....323 K8
Nook Fld *GAR/LONG* PR3 ....186 B5
Nookfield *LEY/BBR* PR5 ....284 C2
Nookfield CI *LSTA* FY8 ....232 C7
Nook Gld *FUL/RIB* PR2 ....215 G2
Nooklands *FUL/RIB* PR2 ....213 G7
Nook La *ACC* BB5 ....270 A1
BBNW BB2 ....267 G2
BRSC L40 ....308 A6
GAR/LONG PR3 ....129 G8
LEY/BBR PR5 ....263 G5
Nook Ter *BBNW* BB2 ....267 H2
The Nook *BPOOLE* FY3 ....177 K6
CARN LA5 ....33 G7
WGNNW/ST WN6 ....353 G4
Noor St *PRES* PR1 ....7 E1
Nora St *NLSN* BB9 ....170 B8
Norbreck CI *BBNW* BB2 ....268 C3
Norbreck Dr *FUL/RIB* PR2 ....238 A2
Norbreck Rd *BISP* FY2 ....148 C5
Norburn Crs *FMBY* L37 ....355 K1
Norbury Av *WGNW/BIL/O* WN5 ....371 F5
Norbury CI *CHTN/BK* PR9 ....278 E6
Norbury Gv *BOL* BL1 ....341 K7
Norcliffe Rd *BISP* FY2 ....148 C6
Norcross Brow *CHLYE* PR6 ....289 G3
Norcross La *CLV/TH* FY5 ....149 G4
Norcross PI *FUL/RIB* PR2 ....238 B2
Norfolk Av *BISP* FY2 ....148 B8
CLV/TH FY5 ....122 E8
HEY LA3 ....40 E8
PDHM/BLYW BB12 ....223 K5
PDHM/BLYW BB12 ....224 D4
Norfolk CI *ACC* BB5 ....221 K8
LEY/BBR PR5 ....285 G4
Norfolk Gv *ACC* BB5 ....248 A4
STHP PR8 ....326 B2
Norfolk Rd *BPOOLE* FY3 ....205 G1
LEY/BBR PR5 ....240 B7
LSTA FY8 ....232 D6
PRES PR1 ....7 E1
STHP PR8 ....326 B2
WGNW/BIL/O WN5 ....371 G2
Norfolk St *ACC* BB5 ....248 C4
BBN BB1 ....246 E2
BBNW BB2 ....267 K1
COL BB8 ....171 J6
DWN BB3 ....291 K2
LANC LA1 ....3 D1
NLSN BB9 ....198 B3
Norham CI *PDHM/BLYW* BB12 ....10 D7
Norkeed Rd *CLV/TH* FY5 ....148 C4
Norland Dr *HEY* LA3 ....52 D3
Norley Rd *WGNW/BIL/O* WN5 ....365 K4
Normanby St *WGNW/BIL/O* WN5 ....365 K5
Norman CI *CLV/TH* FY5 ....149 F2
Normandie Av *BISP* FY2 ....148 D8

Normandy Rd KIRK/FR/WA PR4......**184** D8
Normanhurst ORM L39 ......**348** E7
Norman Rd ACC BB5 ......**247** C6
Norman St BBNW BB2......**8** A6
  BRFD/BLYE BB10......**11** D2
Normoss Av BPOOLE FY3 ......**177** G4
Normoss Rd BPOOLE FY3 ......**177** H4
Norris House Dr L39 ......**360** A3
Norris St CHLY/EC PR7......**311** G5
  DWN BB3......**291** K2
  FUL/RIB PR2......**213** F8
  PRES PR1......**239** F1
Norris Wy FMBY L37 ......**344** B8
North Albert St FTWD FY7 ......**97** H6
North Albion St FTWD FY7 ......**97** G7
Northall KIRK/FR/WA PR4......**282** C1
Northam CI CHTN/BK PR9......**278** C6
North Av BPOOLE FY3 ......**176** D4
  BWCK/EAR BB18......**145** F1
North Bank Av BBN BB1......**245** G2
Northbrook Rd LEY/BBR PR5......**285** G1
North Church St FTWD FY7 ......**97** H6
Northcliffe GTH/LHO BB6......**221** F5
North Cliff St PRES PR1......**6** C4
North Clifton St LSTA FY8 ......**232** D8
Northcote Rd GTH/LHO BB6......**192** A8
  PRES PR1......**6** B3
Northcote St DWN BB3......**291** K5
  LEY/BBR PR5......**285** J2
North Ct CLV/TH FY5......**122** D6
North Crs LSTA FY8 ......**230** E5
Northdene SKEL WN8......**351** H1
North Dr CLV/TH FY5......**148** E3
  KIRK/FR/WA PR4......**182** C2
  KIRK/FR/WA PR4......**208** D5
Northdunes HTWN L38 ......**355** K7
Northenden Rd CHLY/EC PR7 ......**335** J2
Northern Av KIRK/FR/WA PR4 ......**282** D1
Northfield SKEL WN8......**351** H7
Northfield CI NWD/KWIPK L33 ......**366** E7
Northfield Rd ACC BB5 ......**272** B3
  BBN BB1......**8** C2
Northfleet Av FTWD FY7 ......**122** E1
Northgate BBNW BB2......**8** C4
  BISP FY2......**148** C7
  GAR/LONG PR3......**186** B5
  HEY LA3......**41** K8
  LEY/BBR PR5......**285** K1
  WHIT OL12......**323** G4
Northgate Dr CHLYE PR6......**311** J1
North Gv LEY/BBR PR5......**263** F3
North Highfield FUL/RIB PR2......**214** C5
North Houses La LSTA FY8 ......**231** K2
Northland Rd BOL BL1......**341** K5
Northlands FUL/RIB PR2......**213** G8
  LEY/BBR PR5......**284** E4
Northleach Av PRES PR1......**262** C5
North Leach Dr STHP PR8......**325** G6
North Meadowside
  KIRK/FR/WA PR4......**260** B6
North Moor La ORM L39 ......**347** H3
North Moss La FMBY L37......**344** D4
North Mount Rd KKBY L32......**366** A7
North Pde BWCK/EAR BB18 ......**119** F8
North Park Av NLSN BB9......**198** C3
North Park Dr BPOOLE FY3 ......**5** E2
North Park Rd KKBY L32......**366** A7
North Perimeter Rd
  NWD/KWIPK L33 ......**367** H7
North Pier
  BPOOL (off Promenade) FY1......**4** B2
North Prom LSTA FY8 ......**230** C4
North Ribble St LEY/BBR PR5......**240** A5
North Rd BBN BB1......**246** A8
  CARN LA5......**34** A1
  CHTN/BK PR9......**278** D7
  KKBYL LA6......**17** K1
  LANC LA1......**3** D3
  LEY/BBR PR5......**282** E5
  PRES PR1......**7** E1
  RAW/HAS BB4......**296** E1
Northside CHLY/EC PR7......**286** A8
North Sq BPOOLE FY3 ......**5** D1
  CLV/TH FY5......**122** C6
North St BRFD/BLYE BB10 ......**198** D8
  BRFD/BLYE BB10......**225** J2
  BWCK/EAR BB18......**145** F2
  CHLYE PR6......**311** G1
  CHTN/BK PR9......**301** J3
  CLI BB7......**165** K2
  COL BB8......**171** H5
  FTWD FY7......**97** H6
  MCMB LA4......**41** H6
  NLSN BB9......**198** B2
  PDHM/BLYW BB12......**223** J2

PDHM/BLYW BB12 ......**223** J6
PRES PR1......**7** D2
RAMS BLO......**319** J1
RAW/HAS BB4......**274** D3
RAW/HAS BB4......**295** J2
RAW/HAS BB4......**296** C1
RAW/HAS BB4......**297** D2
WHIT OL12......**323** C2
North Syke Av FUL/RIB PR2 ......**237** H2
Northumberland Av BISP FY2 ......**176** B2
  CLV/TH FY5......**122** E7
Northumberland St CHLY/EC PR7 ...**311** H4
  MCMB LA4......**41** G6
North V CHLYE PR6......**337** F2
North Valley Rd COL BB8......**171** G6
North Vw KIRK/FR/WA PR4......**208** D6
  LEY/BBR PR5......**285** H3
North View CI GAR/LONG * PR3 ......**153** C6
North Warton St LSTA FY8 ......**232** E8
Northway FTWD FY7 ......**122** D1
  FUL/RIB PR2......**213** F5
  GAR/LONG PR3......**184** E8
  MGHL L31......**359** C7
  SKEL WN8......**363** H2
Northwood CI LSTA FY8 ......**232** A7
  PDHM/BLYW BB12......**10** A1
Northwoody PLF/KEOS FY6......**177** K1
Norton Av HEY LA3......**40** D8
Norton Dr HEY LA3......**52** E1
Norton Gv HEY LA3......**52** D1
Norton PI HEY LA3......**52** D1
Norton Rd GAR/LONG PR3......**129** J1
  HEY LA3......**52** D1
  WHIT OL12......**323** H4
Norton St BOL BL1......**341** K8
  PDHM/BLYW BB12......**223** J7
Norwich PI BISP FY2......**148** D6
  PRES PR1......**7** E3
Norwood Av BBNW BB2......**268** B1
  BPOOLE FY3......**176** D3
  CHTN/BK PR9......**302** A3
  KIRK/FR/WA PR4......**281** K1
  NLSN BB9......**198** D1
Norwood CI CHLYE PR6......**337** G3
Norwood Crs CHTN/BK PR9......**302** A3
Norwood Dr MCMB LA4......**42** B7
Norwood Gv RNFD/HAY WA11 ......**369** C5
Norwood Rd LSTA FY8 ......**230** E5
  STHP PR8......**302** B4
Notre Dame Gdns BBN BB1......**9** D3
Nottingham Rd PRES PR1......**7** E1
Nottingham St BBN BB1......**9** E5
Novak PI MCMB LA4......**42** B7
Nova Scotia Whf
  BBNW (off Bolton Rd) BB2......**268** A1
Nowell Gv PDHM/BLYW BB12......**222** D1
Nowell St GTH/LHO * BB6......**221** C6
Noyna Av COL BB8......**171** J2
Noyna Vw COL BB8......**171** J4
Nun's St LANC LA1......**3** E3
The Nurseries FMBY L37......**356** A1
Nursery Av ORM L39 ......**348** E5
Nursery CI CHLY/EC PR7......**310** E7
  LEY/BBR PR5......**285** H3
Nursery Dr FMBY L37......**355** K1
  KIRK/FR/WA PR4......**281** K2
Nursery La KIRK/FR/WA PR4......**261** J2
Nursery Rd MGHL L31......**358** E7
Nuthall Rd STHP PR8......**302** A8
Nuttall CI RAMS BLO......**319** J6
  HOR/BR BL6......**338** C8
Nuttall Hall Rd RAMS BLO......**319** K7
Nuttall La RAMS BLO......**319** H6
Nuttall Rd BPOOL FY1......**5** D6
  RAMS BLO......**319** K7
Nuttall St ACC BB5......**248** C4
  BBNW BB2......**268** A3
  BCUP OL13......**276** A8
  BLY BB11......**11** E5
Nutter Crs PDHM/BLYW BB12......**196** B6
Nutter Rd ACC BB5......**248** C4
  CLV/TH FY5......**148** D1
  PRES PR1......**6** C3

O

Oak Av ACC BB5......**272** B3
  BPOOLS FY4......**204** D3
  CHLY/EC PR7......**286** B8
  CLV/TH FY5......**149** J3
  GAR/LONG PR3......**188** A4
  HGHB LA2......**67** F7
  KIRK/FR/WA PR4......**208** E7
  MCMB LA4......**42** B5

ORM L39 ......**3**...
PRES PR1......**2**...
Oakbank Dr BOL BL1......**3**...
Oak CI BBN BB1......**2**...
  CLI BB7......**1**
  WHIT OL12......**2**
Oak Crs SKEL WN8......**3**
Oak Cft CHLYE PR6......**2**
Oakdene Av ACC BB5......**2**
Oak Dr CHLYE PR6......**2**
  HGHB LA2......**2**
  KIRK/FR/WA PR4......**2**
Oaken Bank BRFD/BLYE BB10......**1**
Oaken CI BCUP OL13 ......**2**
Oakenclough Rd BCUP OL13 ......**2**
Oakeneaves Av BLY BB11 ......**2**
Oakengate FUL/RIB PR2 ......**2**
Oakenhead St PRES * PR1 ......**2**
Oakenhead Wood Old Rd
  RAW/HAS BB4......**2**
Oakenhurst Rd BBNW BB2......**2**
Oakenshaw Av WHIT OL12 ......**2**
Oakenshaw Vw WHIT OL12 ......**2**
Oakfield FUL/RIB PR2 ......**2**
  FUL/RIB PR2......**2**
Oakfield Av ACC BB5 ......**2**
  ACC BB5......**1**
  BWCK/EAR BB18......**1**
Oakfield Crs ACC BB5 ......**2**
Oakfield Dr FMBY L37 ......**3**
  LEY/BBR PR5......**3**
Oakfield Rd BBNW BB2......**2**
Oakford CI CHTN/BK PR9 ......**2**
Oakgate CI KIRK/FR/WA PR4 ......**2**
Oak Gates EDGW/EG BL7......**2**
Oak Gn ORM L39......**2**
Oakgrove BPOOLS FY4 ......**2**
Oak Gv DWN BB3......**2**
  GAR/LONG (off Bridge St) PR3 ......**1**
  KIRK/FR/WA PR4......**2**
Oakham Ct
  CHTN/BK (off Alexandra Rd) PR9 ......**3**
  PRES PR1......**2**
Oak Hill CI ACC BB5......**2**
Oakhill Cottage La MCHL L31......**3**
Oakhill Dr MGHL L31......**3**
Oakhurst Av ACC BB5......**2**
Oakland Av CLV/TH FY5......**1**
Oakland Gln PRES PR1......**2**
Oaklands Av KIRK/FR/WA PR4 ......**2**
  NLSN BB9......**1**
Oaklands Ct LANC LA1......**2**
Oaklands Dr PRES PR1......**2**
  RAW/HAS BB4......**2**
Oaklands Gv FUL/RIB PR2......**2**
Oaklands Rd RAMS BLO......**2**
Oaklands Ter BBN BB1......**2**
Oakland St LEY/BBR PR5......**2**
  NLSN BB9......**2**
Oak La ACC BB5......**2**
  KIRK/FR/WA PR4......**2**
Oaklea WGNNW/ST WN6......**3**
Oakleaf CI GAR/LONG PR3......**2**
Oakleaf Wy BPOOLS FY4 ......**2**
Oaklee Gv NWD/KWIPK L33 ......**3**
Oakleigh SKEL WN8 ......**3**
Oakley Av WGNW/BIL/O WN5 ......**3**
Oakley Rd HEY LA3......**2**
  RAW/HAS BB4......**2**
Oakley St RAW/HAS BB4 ......**2**
Oakmere CHLYE PR6......**2**
Oakmere Av CHLYE PR6......**2**
Oakmere CI DWN BB3......**2**
Oakmoor Av BISP FY2 ......**2**
Oak Rdg CLI BB7......**2**
Oakridge CI FUL/RIB PR2 ......**2**
Oak Rd GAR/LONG PR3 ......**2**
Oaks Brow BBN BB1 ......**2**
Oakshott PI LEY/BBR PR5......**2**
The Oaks CHLY/EC PR7 ......**3**
  GAR/LONG PR3......**2**
  LEY/BBR PR5......**2**
  PLF/KEOS FY6......**2**
Oak St ACC * BB5 ......**2**
  ACC BB5......**2**
  ACC BB5......**2**
  BBN BB1......**2**
  BLY BB11......**2**
  COL BB8......**1**
  FTWD FY7......**2**
  GTH/LHO BB6......**2**
  NLSN BB9......**1**
  NLSN BB9......**2**
  PDHM/BLYW BB12......**2**
  PRES PR1......**2**
  RAMS* BLO......**3**
  STHP PR8......**2**

...IT OL12		299 H7
...Ter		
...L (off Keighley Rd) BB8		172 E5
...ree Av FUL/RIB PR2		212 C4
...Y/BBR PR5		263 C7
...Tree CI FUL/RIB PR2		212 C7
...Tree Ct SKEL WN8		351 K8
...Vw LEY/BBR PR5		285 C1
...IT OL12		299 H6
...ville Rd HEY LA3		52 C6
...way GAR/LONG PR3		188 A3
...wood Av BBN BB1		245 J2
...HP PR8		240 A7
...TA FY8		232 A7
...HP PR8		325 K5
...GNNW/ST WN6		353 H6
...wood CI BPOOLS FY4		205 F7
...FD/BLYE BB10		198 B8
...WN8		149 K1
...wood Dr FUL/RIB PR2		213 F3
...HP PR8		326 A6
...wood Gdns LANC LA1		67 G1
...wood Gv CARN LA5		43 F1
...wood Rd ACC BB5		248 D8
...V/TH FY5		311 F5
...wood Vw CHLY/EC PR7		311 F7
...worth Av FUL/RIB PR2		214 D6
...worth CI NWD/KWIPK L33		366 C7
...worth Dr BOL BL1		341 H6
...s CI BRSC L40		306 B8
...St PDHM/BLYW BB12		223 J4
...n Ct FUL/RIB PR2		215 H2
...n Crs PRES PR1		214 B8
...n Dr BBN BB1		246 A8
...n Gv BOL BL1		341 J6
...n PI BISP FY2		148 E5
...n St BOL * BL1		341 H8
...RFD/BLYE BB10		226 A3
...ervatory Rd BBNW BB2		268 D1
...an Bvd		
...POOLS (off Promenade) FY4		204 A4
...an Wy CLV/TH FY5		122 C7
...fellows Ter RAW/HAS BB4		274 C8
...Botanic La CHTN/BK PR9		302 C2
...rton St HOR/BR BL6		338 C8
...Acre HTWN L38		355 K8
...Back La CLI BB7		193 K4
...Bank La BBN BB1		268 D1
...BNW BB2		268 C1
...Bank St BBNW * BB2		8 C5
...Boundary Wy ORM L39		348 B2
...Bridge La PLF/KEOS FY6		150 D4
...Bridge Wy CHLYE PR6		311 F5
...Buckley La GAR/LONG PR3		189 K4
...bury PI CLV/TH FY5		149 F3
...Chapel Ct		
...HLYE (off Railway Rd) PR6		337 G4
...Clitheroe Rd GAR/LONG PR3		188 E2
...Cock Yd PRES PR1		7 E3
...Colliers Rw		
...OL (off Colliers Row Rd) BL1		340 C6
...Cft FUL/RIB PR2		213 F3
...Dawber's La CHLY/EC PR7		309 K2
...Eagley Ms BOL BL1		341 K5
...Engine La SKEL WN8		362 C1
...e Stoneheath Ct CHLYE PR6		312 B7
...RES PR1		262 B7
...WN BB3		268 B8
...field Av BISP FY2		148 C7
...field Carr La PLF/KEOS FY6		178 A2
...field CI PLF/KEOS FY6		178 A2
...field Crs PLF/KEOS FY6		150 A8
...field Rd LEY/BBR PR5		263 K4
...Fold WGNNW/BIL/O WN5		365 K4
...Gates Dr RAMS * BL0		319 J5
...Ground St RAMS * BL0		319 J5
...Hall CI LEY/BBR PR5		263 H3
...MCMB LA4		42 D7
...NLSN BB9		169 J6
...Hall Dr ACC BB5		249 F2
...EY/BBR PR5		263 H3
...Hall Rd RNFD/HAY WA11		369 G5
...Hall La BBNW BB2		266 D1
...HLY/EC PR7		309 K5
...Hall Sq BRFD/BLYE BB10		226 E6
...Hall St BRFD/BLYE BB10		11 D1
...thams La BOL BL1		341 H6
...tham St BLY BB11		10 C5
...MCMB* LA4		41 H5
...Hey Cft PRES * PR1		262 A1
...House La BPOOLS FY4		205 J4
...Kiln BOL BL1		298 B3
...Lancaster La FUL/RIB PR2		6 B1
...Lancaster Rd GAR/LONG PR3		155 H1
...La BRSC L40		333 F3

BWCK/EAR BB18		120 B8
BWCK/EAR BB18		145 K7
BWCK/EAR BB18		146 B1
FMBY L37		343 K5
HWTH BD22		174 E1
HWTH BD22		203 H4
MGHL L31		359 G7
ORM L39		346 A8
RNFD/HAY WA11		369 F4
SKP/WHF BD23		121 H1
WGNNW/ST WN6		353 K5
WHIT OL12		299 J5
Old Langho Rd GTH/LHO BB6		191 K8
Old Laund St PDHM/BLYW BB12		197 G3
Old Links CI CHTN/BK PR9		302 D3
Old Lord's Crs HOR/BR BL6		338 D6
Old Lostock La LEY/BBR PR5		263 H4
Old Meadow La PLF/KEOS FY6		150 B5
Old Meadow La BPOOLE FY3		5 E4
Old Meadows Rd BCUP OL13		275 J6
Old Mill CI KIRK/FR/WA PR4		260 A6
Old Mill Dr COL BB8		171 K7
Old Mill HI ORM L39		348 B8
Old Mill La FMBY L37		343 K7
Old Millstones PRES PR1		6 B3
Old Mill St BBN BB1		9 D3
Old Moor Rd HGHB LA2		38 D5
Old Moss La ORM L39		345 J6
Old Oak Gdns PRES PR1		262 D1
Old Orch FUL/RIB PR2		213 F6
Old Park La CHTN/BK PR9		302 C1
Old Parsonage La		
PDHM/BLYW BB12		223 H3
Old Pepper La WGNNW/ST WN6		353 K1
Old Prescot CI MGHL L31		366 A1
Old Quarry La EDGW/EG BL7		341 K2
Old Rake HOR/BR BL6		339 F5
Old Rectory Gn ORM L39		359 J4
Old Riggs Yd		
KKBYL (off Main St) LA6		18 B6
Old Rd BOL BL1		341 J8
SKP/WHF BD23		120 B5
Old Roman Rd PDHM/BLYW BB12		194 B8
Old Rw KIRK/FR/WA PR4		209 F7
Old School CI LEY/BBR PR5		284 C3
Old School La CHLY/EC PR7		286 B8
CHLY/EC PR7		336 E6
DWN BB3		290 B1
LEY/BBR PR5		263 F5
Old School Ms BCUP OL13		298 A3
RAW/HAS (off Clegg St) BB4		272 C8
Old Station CI FUL/RIB PR2		215 H2
Old Station Ct CLI BB7		165 J3
Old Stone Brow BWCK/EAR BB18		146 A7
Old Stone Trough La		
BWCK/EAR BB18		146 A6
Old St RAW/HAS BB4		297 G2
Old Swan St EDGW/EG * BL7		341 J1
Old Tom's La GAR/LONG PR3		125 J3
PLF/KEOS FY6		125 J3
Old Town CI SKEL WN8		362 D3
Old Town La FMBY L37		343 J7
Old Town Wy SKEL WN8		362 D3
Old Vicarage PRES PR1		7 E2
Old Vicarage Rd HOR/BR BL6		339 H8
Old Will's La HOR/BR BL6		338 D5
Olivant St PDHM/BLYW BB12		224 E4
Olive CI CHLYE PR6		287 G6
Olive Gv BPOOLE FY3		5 E4
KIRK/FR/WA PR4		234 B5
SKEL WN8		362 C2
STHP PR8		302 A4
Olive La DWN BB3		291 K1
Old Rd LANC LA1		3 D1
Oliver's PI FUL/RIB PR2		213 J3
Oliver St BCUP OL13		298 A3
Olive St BCUP OL13		298 C3
Ollerton Fold		
CHLYE (off Ollerton La) PR6		265 J7
Ollerton La CHLYE PR6		265 K8
Ollerton Rd LSTA FY8		231 K6
Ollerton St BOL BL1		341 K5
CHLYE PR6		337 G3
Ollerton Ter		
CHLYE (off Chorley Rd) PR6		265 K8
Olympia St BRFD/BLYE BB10		11 F4
Onchan Dr BCUP OL13		299 F7
Onchan Rd BBNW BB2		268 B2
Onslow Crs STHP PR8		326 C1
Onslow Rd BPOOLE FY3		176 E4
Ontario CI BBNW BB2		244 C3
Oozebooth Ter BBN BB1		8 B2
Oozehead La BBNW BB2		244 D1
Openshaw Dr BBN BB1		8 C1
Oporto CI BLY BB11		10 B4
Orama MI		
WHIT (off Hall St) OL12		323 G3

Oram Rd LEY/BBR PR5		264 E3
Orange St ACC BB5		248 B4
Orchard Av BOL BL1		341 K8
BPOOLS FY4		204 C5
CARN LA5		33 G5
KIRK/FR/WA PR4		261 H4
PLF/KEOS FY6		178 A2
Orchard Br BLY BB11		10 C3
Orchard CI CHLY/EC PR7		286 B7
CLV/TH FY5		123 H7
DWN BB3		268 A5
FUL/RIB PR2		212 C6
HGHB LA2		43 F3
KIRK/FR/WA PR4		207 K8
KIRK/FR/WA PR4		234 C5
KIRK/FR/WA PR4		258 E8
WGNNW/ST WN6		353 J4
Orchard Cft LEY/BBR PR5		262 D3
Orchard Dr ACC BB5		247 K6
CHLYE PR6		287 G6
FTWD FY7		122 E2
Orchard La KIRK/FR/WA PR4		260 A3
LANC LA1		2 B4
STHP PR8		325 K7
Orchard Rd CARN LA5		15 G1
LSTA FY8		230 E5
The Orchards PLF/KEOS FY6		149 H6
WGNW/BIL/O WN5		365 G6
Orchard St GTH/LHO BB6		221 G7
LEY/BBR PR5		285 K2
PRES* PR1		7 D2
The Orchard KIRK/FR/WA PR4		209 J5
KIRK/FR/WA PR4		212 A2
KIRK/FR/WA PR4		234 C5
LEY/BBR PR5		283 J8
ORM L39		348 B6
Orchard Vw ORM L39		360 B2
Orchard Yd		
KKBYL (off Duke St) LA6		17 K1
Ord Av BPOOLS FY4		5 F5
Orders La KIRK/FR/WA PR4		208 E7
Ordnance St BBN BB1		9 E4
Ord Rd FUL/RIB PR2		238 E1
Oregon Av BPOOLE FY3		176 B3
Oriole CI BBN BB1		9 D3
Orion Buildings		
CLV/TH (off Crescent West) FY5		148 D1
Orkney CI BBN BB1		246 A8
Orkney Rd BPOOL FY1		4 C5
Ormerod Rd BRFD/BLYE BB10		11 E2
Ormerod St ACC BB5		248 A7
BLY* BB11		11 D4
BRFD/BLYE BB10		226 E6
CLV/TH FY5		123 H8
COL BB8		171 G7
NLSN* BB9		198 D3
RAW/HAS BB4		272 C4
RAW/HAS BB4		296 C1
Orme St BPOOL FY1		4 C4
Ormond Av BPOOL FY1		176 B3
BRSC L40		349 H7
Ormont Av CLV/TH FY5		148 E5
Ormskirk Old Rd ORM L39		361 K4
Ormskirk Rd ORM L39		361 G2
PRES PR1		7 E2
RNFD/HAY WA11		368 D2
SKEL WN8		362 C2
SKEL WN8		363 H3
Ormston Av HOR/BR BL6		338 D6
Orms Wy FMBY L37		343 J8
Ornatus St BOL * BL1		341 K6
Orpen Av BLY BB11		10 C5
Orrell CI LEY/BBR PR5		285 F2
Orrell Gdns WGNNW/BIL/O WN5		365 G4
Orrell Hall CI WGNW/BIL/O WN5		365 K4
Orrell Hill La HTWN L38		356 C7
Orrell La BRSC L40		330 D6
Orrell Ms		
BRSC (off Orrell La) L40		330 E6
Orrell Rd WGNW/BIL/O WN5		365 G4
Orrest Rd PRES PR1		240 E2
Orton Ct NLSN BB9		170 B7
Orwell CI FMBY L37		355 G2
Osbaldeston La BBNW BB2		217 K5
Osbert Cft KIRK/FR/WA PR4		260 B2
Osborne Av CLV/TH FY5		148 E1
Osborne Dr CHLYE PR6		287 G1
Osborne Gv CLV/TH FY5		122 D6
MCMB LA4		41 G8
Osborne Rd BBNW BB2		244 D5
CLV/TH FY5		122 D6
FMBY L37		355 J2
HEY LA3		41 F8
LEY/BBR PR5		240 B8
LSTA FY8		231 F6
STHP PR8		325 H5

Osborne St PRES PR1 ......6 C3
Osborne Ter BCUP OL13 ......298 B3
  DWN BB3 ......291 G1
  PDHM/BLYW BB12 ......197 F1
  RAW/HAS BB4 ......274 B7
Osbourne Rd BPOOLS FY4 ......204 B3
Oscar St BPOOLE FY3 ......5 F5
Oslo Rd BLY BB11 ......224 D6
Osprey Cl BBN BB1 ......8 B1
  CHLYE PR6 ......288 A8
Oswald Rd FUL/RIB PR2 ......6 A1
  LSTA FY8 ......233 F7
Oswald St ACC BB5 ......247 G8
  ACC BB5 ......248 D5
  BBN BB1 ......8 C3
  BBN BB1 ......247 G1
  PDHM/BLYW BB12 ......10 C1
Otley Rd LSTA FY8 ......231 H4
Ottawa Cl BBNW BB2 ......244 C3
Otterburn Cl BPOOLE FY3 ......177 H2
Otterburn Gv BRFD/BLYE BB10 ......226 B5
Otterburn Rd BBNW BB2 ......267 K4
Otters Cl FUL/RIB PR2 ......240 D1
Ottershaw Gdns BBN BB1 ......8 C1
Ottery Cl CHTN/BK PR9 ......278 C6
Otway Cl PRES PR1 ......239 G1
Oulton Cl MGHL L31 ......358 D7
Ousby Av HEY LA3 ......53 H1
Ousby Rd HEY LA3 ......53 H1
Ouseburn Rd BBNW BB2 ......267 K3
Outer Prom FTWD FY7 ......96 D6
Out La LEY/BBR PR5 ......307 H1
Outlet La MGHL L31 ......366 C2
Outram La BBN BB1 ......245 G2
Outram Wy LEY/BBR PR5 ......263 H3
Outterside St CHLY/EC PR7 ......337 C5
Outwood Gv BOL BL1 ......341 J6
Outwood Rd BOL BL1 ......11 E5
The Oval WGNNW/ST WN6 ......353 H6
Ovangle Rd LANC LA1 ......54 B1
Overdale Gv BPOOLE FY3 ......177 G2
Overdell Dr WHIT OL12 ......323 G8
Overshores Rd EDGW/EG BL7 ......316 E4
Overton Rd FUL/RIB PR2 ......238 A3
Over Town La WHIT OL12 ......321 J8
Ovington Dr STHP PR8 ......302 A8
Owen Av LANC L39 ......348 D5
Owen Ct ACC BB5 ......221 K8
Owen Rd LANC LA1 ......3 D1
Owen's La ORM L39 ......358 A1
Owens St CHLYE * PR6 ......311 J4
Owen St ACC BB5 ......248 B4
  PDHM/BLYW BB12 ......224 C6
  PRES PR1 ......7 F2
Owlet Hall Rd DWN BB3 ......291 G1
Owtram St PRES PR1 ......240 A3
Oxcliffe Av HEY LA3 ......52 D2
Oxcliffe Gv HEY LA3 ......52 D2
Oxcliffe Rd HEY LA3 ......52 E2
Oxendale Rd CLV/TH FY5 ......149 K1
Oxenholme Av CLV/TH FY5 ......122 D7
Oxenhurst Rd BPOOLE FY3 ......177 G3
Oxford Av ACC BB5 ......222 A8
Oxford Cl BBN BB1 ......9 D4
  PDHM/BLYW BB12 ......223 K5
Oxford Ct STHP PR8 ......301 F7
Oxford Dr BBN BB1 ......246 C7
  KIRK/FR/WA PR4 ......209 G7
Oxford Gdns STHP PR8 ......300 E7
Oxford Pl BLY BB11 ......11 E4
  LANC LA1 ......42 E8
Oxford Rd BLY BB11 ......11 E4
  BPOOL FY1 ......5 D2
  CLV/TH FY5 ......122 E8
  FTWD FY7 ......96 E8
  FUL/RIB PR2 ......213 F7
  LEY/BBR PR5 ......263 J5
  LSTA FY8 ......230 E4
  NLSN BB9 ......198 E1
  SKEL WN8 ......362 C2
  STHP PR8 ......300 E1
  WGNW/BIL/O WN5 ......365 H4
Oxford St ACC * BB5 ......248 B5
  CHLY/EC PR7 ......311 G4
  CHLY/EC PR7 ......337 K5
  COL BB8 ......171 J6
  DWN BB3 ......268 C7
  LANC LA1 ......42 E8
  MCMB LA4 ......41 H5
  NLSN BB9 ......197 K6
  PRES PR1 ......7 E3
Oxford Wy FTWD FY7 ......96 E8
Ox Hey ACC BB5 ......221 K7
Ox Hey Av FUL/RIB * PR2 ......237 J2
Oxhey Cl BRFD/BLYE BB10 ......226 D5

Oxheys St PRES PR1 ......239 F1
Oxhill Pl CLV/TH FY5 ......148 E4
Oxhouse Rd WGNW/BIL/O WN5 ......364 E7
Oxley Cl KIRK/FR/WA PR4 ......208 D6
Oxley Rd PRES PR1 ......240 B2
Oxley Rd North PRES * PR1 ......240 B2
Ox St RAMS BLO 319 H6
Oystercatcher Ga LSTA FY8 ......232 A4

P

Paa La CLI BB7 ......94 B6
Packet La CARN LA5 ......33 G7
Pad Cote La HWTH BD22 ......174 C3
Paddington Av GAR/LONG PR3 ......154 C4
Paddock Av LEY/BBR PR5 ......284 C3
Paddock Dr BPOOLE FY3 ......205 J1
Paddock Rd SKEL WN8 ......363 J6
Paddock St ACC * BB5 ......247 J7
The Paddock BBNW BB2 ......244 C3
  BRSC L40 ......306 C7
  CLI BB7 ......141 F2
  CLV/TH FY5 ......149 H3
  FMBY L37 ......344 A6
  FUL/RIB PR2 ......213 J5
  ORM L39 ......348 A3
  PLF/KEOS FY6 ......149 J6
  RAMS BLO 319 H4
  STHP PR8 ......325 H7
Padend Nook KIRK/FR/WA PR4 ......182 C1
Padgate Pl BLY BB11 ......224 D7
Padiham Rd CLI BB7 ......195 C5
  PDHM/BLYW BB12 ......10 A3
Padstow Cl CHTN/BK PR9 ......278 C6
Padway PRES PR1 ......262 A1
Page Ct FMBY L37 ......343 K8
Pagefield Crs CLI BB7 ......166 A4
Pages Ct LEY/BBR PR5 ......262 E4
Paignton Cl WGNW/BIL/O WN5 ......371 G3
Paignton Rd BBN BB1 ......8 B2
Painley Cl LSTA FY8 ......232 C7
Paisley St BLY BB11 ......10 A4
Palace Gdns PDHM/BLYW BB12 ......224 D4
Palace Rd STHP PR8 ......300 E6
Palace St PDHM/BLYW * BB12 ......224 E4
Palatine Av LANC LA1 ......3 E6
Palatine Cl BPOOLE FY3 ......177 J5
Palatine Rd BBNW BB2 ......8 A1
  BPOOL FY1 ......4 C3
  CLV/TH FY5 ......122 F7
  STHP PR8 ......301 F6
Palatine Sq BLY BB11 ......10 A1
Palatine St RAMS BLO 319 J5
Paley Rd PRES PR1 ......6 B3
Palfrey Cl PLF/KEOS FY6 ......149 H5
Pall Ml CHLY/EC PR7 ......311 G5
  HOR/BR (off Rivington La) BL6 ......338 C4
Palmaston Cl LANC LA1 ......2 C5
Palma St TOD OL14 ......277 G2
Palm Ct SKEL WN8 ......362 E1
Palm Dr PLF/KEOS FY6 ......149 H5
Palmer Av BPOOL FY1 ......4 C5
Palmer Gv MCMB LA4 ......42 A5
Palmer Rd BBN BB1 ......8 B3
Palmerston Cl RAMS BLO 319 H8
Palmerston Rd CHTN/BK PR9 ......302 B5
Palmerston St PDHM/BLYW BB12 ......223 K4
Palmer St BBN BB1 ......8 B3
Palm Gv STHP PR8 ......302 A5
Palm St BBN BB1 ......9 D2
  BLY BB11 ......10 A4
  BOL BL1 ......341 K8
Panorama Vw BWCK/EAR (off Dales View Pk) BB18 ......145 F4
Pansy St North ACC BB5 ......248 B4
Pansy St South ACC * BB5 ......248 B4
Paper Mill Rd EDGW/EG BL7 ......341 H4
The Parade CARN LA5 ......33 H2
Paradise Cl CHLYE PR6 ......287 F3
Paradise La BBNW BB2 ......8 B4
  FMBY L37 ......344 A6
  LEY/BBR PR5 ......284 D2
Paradise St ACC BB5 ......248 B6
  BBNW BB2 ......8 B5
  BLY BB11 ......10 C3
  CHLYE PR6 ......287 K8
  NLSN BB9 ......170 C6
  RAMS BLO 319 J5
  RAW/HAS BB4 ......297 H1
Paragon Wy LANC LA1 ......2 A3
Parbold Cl BPOOLE FY3 ......177 F2
  BRSC L40 ......330 E8
Parbold Hl SKEL WN8 ......351 K1

Parbrook La WGNNW/ST WN6 3
Pardoe Cl KIRK/FR/WA PR4 2
Paris BBN BB1 2
Parish St PDHM/BLYW BB12 2
Park Av BBN BB1 3
  BLY BB11 3
  BOL BL1 3
  BWCK/EAR BB18 3
  CHLY/EC PR7 3
  CHTN/BK PR9 3
  CLI BB7 1
  CLI BB7 3
  FMBY L37 3
  FTWD FY7 3
  GTH/LHO BB6 3
  KIRK/FR/WA PR4 2
  KIRK/FR/WA PR4 2
  LANC LA1 2
  LSTA FY8 2
  MGHL L31 3
  NLSN BB9 1
  ORM L39 3
  PRES PR1 2
  RAMS BLO 3
  RAW/HAS BB4 3
  WGNNW/ST WN6 3
  WGNW/BIL/O WN5 3
Park Bridge Rd BRFD/BLYE BB10 2
Park Cl FMBY L37 3
  PRES PR1 3
  SKEL WN8 3
Park Cottages BOL (off Smithills Dean Rd) BL1 3
Park Ct LANC LA1 3
Park Crs ACC BB5 2
  BBNW BB2 3
  CHTN/BK PR9 3
  MCMB LA4 3
  ORM L39 3
  RAW/HAS BB4 3
Parkdale Gdns DWN BB3 2
Park Dr FUL/RIB PR2 2
  NLSN BB9 1
  NLSN BB9 19
Parke Ms CHLYE PR6 16
Parker Av CLI BB7 16
Parker Crs ORM L39 34
Parker La BLY BB11 26
  KIRK/FR/WA PR4 ......2(
Parke Rd CHLYE PR6 26
Parkers Fold GAR/LONG PR3 19
Parker St ACC BB5 24
  ACC BB5 24
  BBN BB1 ......2(
  BLY BB11 1
  BPOOL* FY1 ......
  BRFD/BLYE* BB10 19
  BWCK/EAR BB18 11
  CHLY/EC PR7 31
  COL BB8 17
  FUL/RIB PR2 22
  LANC LA1 ......
  NLSN* BB9 19
Park Farm Cl KIRK/FR/WA PR4 ......2(
Park Farm Rd BBNW BB2 ......2(
Parkfield WGNNW/ST WN6 35
Parkfield Av FUL/RIB PR2 23
Parkfield Cl FUL/RIB PR2 23
  LEY/BBR PR5 28
  ORM L39 34
Parkfield Crs FUL/RIB PR2 23
Parkfield Dr LANC LA1 2
Parkgate GAR/LONG PR3 18
Parkgate Dr BOL BL1 34
  LEY/BBR PR5 28
Park Gate Rd BBN BB1 21
Park Hall Rd CHLY/EC PR7 30
Parkhead La GAR/LONG PR3 13
Park Hey Dr WGNNW/ST WN6 35
Park Hl BWCK/EAR BB18 14
Park Hill Ct GAR/LONG (off Park Hill Rd) PR3 12
Park Hill Rd GAR/LONG PR3 12
Park House La HGHB LA2 4
Parkin La TOD OL14 27
Parkinson La GAR/LONG PR3 16
Parkinson St BBNW BB2 26
  BLY BB11 1
  COL BB8 17
  RAW/HAS BB4 27
Parkinson Wy BPOOLS FY4 14
Parkland Cl CLV/TH FY5 14
Parkland Gv HEY LA3 5
Parklands CHTN/BK PR9 30
  RNFD/HAY WA11 36
  SKEL WN8 36
Parklands Av PRES PR1 23

ands Cl *PRES* PR1 ....238 C7
ands Dr *FUL/RIB* PR2 ....213 G3
ands Gv *FUL/RIB* PR2 ....213 G3
arklands *GAR/LONG* PR3 ......155 K1
and Vw *BLY* BB11 ....10 B6
La *ACC* BB5 ....247 J8
FD/BLYE BB10 ....198 A6
R/LONG PR3 ....103 F2
L/LHO BB6 ....221 H5
HB LA2 ....38 C4
HB LA2 ....45 F3
R/BR BL6 ....339 F8
TH BD22 ....174 B1
K/FR/WA PR4 ....208 C5
K/FR/WA PR4 ....305 F1
HL L31 ....359 G8
/KEOS FY6 ....98 C7
ES PR1 ....239 G8
Lee Rd *BBNW* BB2 ....268 B2
Link *ORM* L39 ....359 K2
Ms *CLI* BB7 ....117 F5
Mill Pl *PRES* PR1 ....7 J1
Pl *BBNW* BB2 ....266 E4
/BBR PR5 ....240 C7
ES PR1 ....7 E3
Rd *ACC* BB5 ....248 A5
V BB1 ....247 G2
VW BB2 ....8 C6
VW BB2 ....243 F2
JP OL13 ....298 D2
OOL FY1 ....4 C3
FD/BLYE BB10 ....252 C2
CK/EAR BB18 ....145 F2
RN LA5 ....15 J7
Y/EC PR7 ....311 G3
Y/EC PR7 ....335 J2
Y/EC PR7 ....336 E5
TN/BK PR9 ....301 K3
BB7 ....117 F5
/TH FY5 ....149 H3
V BB3 ....291 K5
3Y L32 ....355 J2
/RIB PR2 ....213 J7
L/LHO BB6 ....221 H5
K/FR/WA PR4 ....208 D7
3Y L32 ....366 A4
HM/BLYW BB12 ....223 J3
/KEOS FY6 ....150 A7
ES PR1 ....6 B6
V/HAS BB4 ....294 E3
V/HAS BB4 ....297 H2
/BURYW BL8 ....319 F8
NW/BIL/O WN5 ....365 J5
NW/BIL/O WN5 ....371 G2
Side *BWCK/EAR* BB18 ....146 A3
ide *FUL/RIB* PR2 ....237 K1
MB LA4 ....41 H8
ES PR1 ....213 K8
ide Av *CHLY/EC* PR7 ....311 G3
ide Crs *WCNW/BIL/O* WN5 ....365 H5
ide Dr *CARN* LA5 ....15 F2
YE PR6 ....287 F5
ide Dr South *CHLYE* PR6 ......287 F5
ide La *GAR/LONG* PR3 ....129 C3
ide Rd *LSTA* FY8 ....231 G4
V BB9 ....199 F3
O OL14 ....277 G2
Sq *LANC* LA1 ....3 E3
tone Av *CLV/TH* FY5 ....149 K3
/KEOS FY6 ....149 H6
St *ACC* BB5 ....248 C5
CK/EAR BB18 ....145 F2
Y/EC PR7 ....308 C5
Y/EC PR7 ....311 G3
BB7 ....165 J4
L/LHO BB6 ....221 H6
A FY8 ....232 D8
MB LA4 ....41 K5
N BB9 ....170 B7
V/HAS BB4 ....272 C8
V/HAS BB4 ....295 F4
St East *NLSN* BB9 ....170 C7
way *PLF/KEOS* FY6 ....97 K6
er *BBN* BB1 ....8 B2
horn Rd *FUL/RIB* PR2 ....237 H5
Vw *CARN* LA5 ....15 G2
HM/BLYW BB12 ....223 J3
ES PR1 ....6 B6
V/HAS BB4 ....297 H2
NW/BIL/O
Barton St) WN5 ....365 K6

Park View Av *FUL/RIB* * PR2 ...238 D1
Park View Cl *NLSN* BB9 ....197 K4
Park View Rd *LSTA* FY8 ....232 D7
Park Wall Rd *HTWN* L38 ....357 F8
Park Way *COL* BB8 ....171 G5
FMBY L37 ....355 K2
PRES PR1 ....6 B6
Parkway *BPOOLE* FY3 ....177 G5
WCNNW/ST WN6 ....353 J1
Parkwood Av *PDHM/BLYW* BB12 ...10 A2
Park Wood Dr *RAW/HAS* BB4 ...296 A1
Parkwood Rd *BBN* BB1 ....9 F5
Parliament St *BLY* BB11 ....11 D5
DWN* BB3 ....291 J2
HEY LA3 ....40 E7
LANC LA1 ....3 D2
SKEL WN8 ....364 E3
Parlick Av *GAR/LONG* PR3 ......188 B4
Parlick Rd *FUL/RIB* * PR2 ....240 E1
GAR/LONG PR3 ....129 G5
Parramatta St *RAW/HAS* BB4 ...296 C1
Parr Cottage Cl *CHLY/EC* PR7 ..308 E4
Parr La *CHLY/EC* PR7 ....308 D4
Parrock Cl *PRES* PR1 ....239 G8
Parrock Rd *NLSN* BB9 ....197 K1
Parrock St *BWCK/EAR* * BB18 ..145 F1
NLSN BB9 ....198 C3
RAW/HAS BB4 ....273 H4
Parrox Fold *PLF/KEOS* FY6 ......98 C6
Parrox La *KIRK/FR/WA* PR4 ....209 J8
Parr's La *ORM* L39 ....360 B5
Parsley Cl *BISP* FY2 ....149 F7
Parsonage Av *GAR/LONG* PR3 ..189 K8
Parsonage Brow *SKEL* WN8 ...364 B3
Parsonage Cl *HEY* LA3 ....53 J1
SKEL WN8 ....364 C4
Parsonage Dr *BRFD/BLYE* BB10 ...198 A6
Parsonage Gdns
KIRK/FR/WA PR4 ....282 A6
Parsonage La *GAR/LONG* PR3 ...160 C2
Parsonage Rd *BBN* BB1 ....219 H8
SKEL WN8 ....364 C4
Parsonage St *ACC* BB5 ....247 J6
COL BB8 ....171 G7
Parson La *CLI* BB7 ....165 J3
Parson's Brow *CHLY/EC* PR7 ..311 G4
RNFD/HAY WA11 ....368 E5
Parson's Bullough Rd *CHLYE* PR6 ...312 E6
Partridge Av *CLV/TH* FY5 ....123 F7
Partridge Dr *ACC* BB5 ....271 K2
Partridge Hl *PDHM/BLYW* BB12 ...223 K2
Partridge Hill St
PDHM/BLYW * BB12 ....223 K3
Part St *STHP* PR8 ....301 C6
Past La *CLI* BB7 ....114 A2
Pasture Cl *BLY* BB11 ....10 E5
BWCK/EAR BB18 ....119 C7
Pasture Dr *COL* BB8 ....171 H2
Pasture Field Cl *LEY/BBR* PR5 ...284 E3
Pasture Field *PLF/KEOS* FY6 ...149 H5
Pasturegate *BLY* BB11 ....10 A5
Pasturelands Dr *CLI* BB7 ....192 E8
Pasture La *CARN* LA5 ....32 E6
NLSN BB9 ....169 K6
RNFD/HAY WA11 ....369 G7
Pastures New *LEY/BBR* PR5 ...263 F3
The Pastures *BBNW* BB2 ....244 C3
CHTN/BK PR9 ....279 F6
FUL/RIB PR2 ....215 H2
Paterson St *BBNW* BB2 ....8 C6
Pathfinders Dr *LANC* LA1 ....54 E7
Patmos St *RAMS* BL0 ....319 K5
Paton St *WHIT* OL12 ....323 H8
Patrick Av *PDHM/BLYW* BB12 ...222 D1
Patrick Crs *RAW/HAS* BB4 ......296 C1
Patten St *BBN* BB1 ....246 A6
PRES PR1 ....7 D2
Patterdale Av *ACC* BB5 ....247 H6
BBN BB1 ....246 A8
BPOOLE FY3 ....5 F5
CLV/TH FY5 ....123 H8
FTWD FY7 ....122 D3
Patterdale Cl *BRFD/BLYE* BB10 ...198 A7
STHP PR8 ....325 H8
Patterdale Rd *LANC* LA1 ....3 E2
Pattison Cl *WHIT* OL12 ....323 C8
Paulhan St *BRFD/BLYE* BB10 ...225 K1
Paul's La *CHTN/BK* PR9 ....278 B8
PLF/KEOS FY6 ....150 E1
Pavey Cl *BPOOLS* FY4 ....205 F3
Pavilion Vw *LEY/BBR* PR5 ....307 G1
Paxton Pl *SKEL* WN8 ....363 H7
Paxton St *ACC* BB5 ....248 B5
Paynter Cl *ACC* BB5 ....248 A1
Paythorne Av *BRFD/BLYE* BB10 ...226 B6
Paythorne Br *CLI* BB7 ....94 B8
Paythorne Cl *BPOOLE* FY3 .....177 H2

Peabody St *DWN* BB3 ....291 J1
Peace St *BLY* * BB11 ....10 A4
Peachtree Cl *FUL/RIB* PR2 ......214 B5
Peacock Crs *HGHB* LA2 ....42 E2
Peacock Hall Rd *LEY/BBR* PR5 ...285 F4
Peacock Hill Cl *FUL/RIB* PR2 ...215 F4
Peacock La *HGHB* LA2 ....42 E2
Peahall La *GAR/LONG* PR3 ......100 E7
Pearfield *LEY/BBR* PR5 ....285 J1
Pearl Av *BISP* FY2 ....176 E2
Pearl St *ACC* BB5 ....247 K6
BBN BB1 ....245 H2
Pear Pl *TOD* OL14 ....277 F2
Pearson St *BBNW* BB2 ....8 B5
Pear Tree Av *CHLY/EC* PR7 ....310 D8
Pear Tree Cl *LEY/BBR* * PR5 ...263 H1
Pear Tree Crs *LEY/BBR* PR5 ...263 H1
Pear Tree Cft *KIRK/FR/WA* PR4 ...260 B3
Pear Tree La *CHLY/EC* PR7 .....286 C8
Pear Tree Rd *CHLYE* PR6 ....264 A8
Peartree St *LEY/BBR* * PR5 ....263 H1
Peart St *BRFD/BLYE* BB10 ......225 K1
Pechell St *FUL/RIB* PR2 ....6 A1
Pedder Av *HEY* LA3 ....65 G3
Pedder Dr *HEY* LA3 ....65 G3
Pedder Gv *HEY* LA3 ....65 H2
Pedder La *PLF/KEOS* FY6 ....150 D2
Pedder Rd *HEY* LA3 ....65 G2
Pedder's Gv *FUL/RIB* PR2 ......238 C3
Pedder's La *BPOOLS* FY4 ....204 D4
FUL/RIB PR2 ....238 C2
Pedder St *FUL/RIB* PR2 ....6 B2
MCMB LA4 ....41 H6
Pedders Wy *FUL/RIB* PR2 ......238 C3
Peebles Cl *NWD/KWIPK* L33 ...366 B5
Peebles Gv *BLY* BB11 ....10 A6
Peel Av *BPOOLE* FY3 ....176 D4
HEY LA3 ....52 C5
LANC LA1 ....3 D1
Peel Bank Rd *ACC* BB5 ....247 F7
Peel Brow *RAMS* BL0 ....319 K5
Peel Cl *BBNW* BB2 ....268 B3
Peel Dr *BCUP* OL13 ....299 F2
Peel Gdns *COL* BB8 ....171 G6
Peel Hall *PRES* PR1 ....7 F1
Peel Hl *BPOOLS* FY4 ....206 A4
Peel Hill Br *BPOOLS* FY4 ....206 C5
Peel Mt *BBN* BB1 ....246 C7
RAMS BL0 ....319 G7
Peel Mount Cl *BBN* BB1 ....246 D7
Peel Park Av *ACC* BB5 ....248 D4
CLI BB7 ....165 K4
Peel Park Cl *ACC* BB5 ....248 D4
CLI BB7 ....165 K4
Peel Pl *NLSN* BB9 ....170 C5
Peel Rd *BPOOLS* FY4 ....206 B6
COL BB8 ....171 F7
FTWD FY7 ....97 F8
SKEL WN8 ....364 A6
Peel St *ACC* BB5 ....247 H8
ACC BB5 ....248 C5
BBNW BB2 ....267 K1
CHLY/EC PR7 ....311 G4
CHLYE PR6 ....337 H3
CLI BB7 ....165 J4
PDHM/BLYW BB12 ....223 K3
RAW/HAS BB4 ....296 E1
STHP PR8 ....302 B5
Peel Wk *RAMS* BL0 ....319 H8
TOT/BURYW BL8 ....319 F6
Peers Clough Rd *RAW/HAS* BB4 ...274 C3
Peet Av *ORM* L39 ....348 B7
Peet's La *CHTN/BK* PR9 ....302 C2
Pegbank La *KKBYL* LA6 ....19 K3
Peg's La *LSTA* FY8 ....232 E3
Peg Wy *KIRK/FR/WA* PR4 ....234 D5
Pelham Av *BPOOLE* FY3 ....176 E3
Pelham St *BBN* BB1 ....9 E3
Pemberton Dr *MCMB* LA4 ....42 A6
Pemberton Pl *MCMB* LA4 ....42 A6
Pemberton Rd *WGNS/IIMK* WN3 ...371 G2
Pemberton St *BBN* BB1 ....245 G2
BOL* BL1 ....341 J7
Pembroke Av *BISP* FY2 ....148 B8
MCMB LA4 ....41 K5
Pembroke Cl *HOR/BR* BL6 ....338 C7
Pembroke Pl *CHLY/EC* PR7 .....311 F5
LEY/BBR PR5 ....285 J3
PRES PR1 ....7 E3
Pembroke Rd *LSTA* FY8 ....231 K8
Pembroke St *ACC* BB5 ....248 C5
BBNW BB2 ....8 B6
BRFD/BLYE BB10 ....225 K2
Pembury Av *PRES* PR1 ....239 G8
Pendle Av *ACC* BB5 ....221 K7
BCUP OL13 ....275 K7

CLI BB7 ....140 E6
Pendlebury St BOL BL1 ....341 K8
Pendle CI BCUP OL13 ....298 E1
   BPOOLE FY1 ....177 F2
Pendle Ct BOL BL1 ....341 H8
   GAR/LONG PR3 ....188 A5
   KIRK/FR/WA PR4 ....208 E5
Pendle Dr BBNW BB2 ....268 C1
   HOR/BR BL6 ....338 E6
   ORM L39 ....348 E5
Pendle Flds PDHM/BLYW BB12 ....197 F4
Pendle Hill CI FUL/RIB PR2 ....215 G4
Pendlehurst St BLY BB11 ....10 B5
Pendlemist Vw COL BB8 ....171 G8
Pendle PI LSTA FY8 ....232 E7
   SKEL WN8 ....363 K7
Pendle Rd CLI BB7 ....142 A8
   CLI BB7 ....165 K3
   CLI BB7 ....166 A4
   GTH/LHO BB6 ....221 J3
   LANC LA1 ....42 D8
   LEY/BBR PR5 ....286 B2
   NLSN BB9 ....197 J6
Pendleside CI CLI BB7 ....195 G4
Pendle St ACC BB5 ....248 A7
   BBN BB1 ....9 E4
   NLSN BB9 ....198 A1
   PDHM/BLYW BB12 ....223 K3
Pendle St East CLI BB7 ....195 F4
Pendle St West CLI BB7 ....195 F4
Pendleton Av ACC BB5 ....247 K7
   RAW/HAS BB4 ....273 H7
Pendleton Rd CLI BB7 ....194 D3
Pendle Vw
   ACC (off Burnley La) BB5 ....249 F1
   CLI BB7 ....139 H4
   GTH/LHO BB6 ....192 A5
Pendle Wy COL BB8 ....172 E6
   NLSN BB9 ....168 A7
   PDHM/BLYW BB12 ....10 A1
   SKP/WHF BD23 ....120 A6
Pengarth Rd HOR/BR BL6 ....338 E7
Penguin St PRES PR1 ....7 F1
Penhale CI HEY * LA3 ....52 C5
Penhale Ct HEY LA3 ....52 C5
Penhale Gdns HEY * LA3 ....52 C5
Penhill CI BISP FY2 ....176 D3
Penistone St PDHM/BLYW BB12 ....10 A3
Penketh PI SKEL WN8 ....363 J6
Pennine Av CHLY/EC PR7 ....310 B2
Pennine CI BPOOLE FY1 ....4 C3
   HOR/BR BL6 ....338 E6
Pennine Gdns NLSN BB9 ....198 A6
Pennine Gdns GAR/LONG PR3 ....129 G4
Pennine Gv PDHM/BLYW BB12 ....223 J1
Pennine PI SKEL WN8 ....363 H5
Pennine Rd BCUP OL13 ....298 C5
   CHLYE PR6 ....311 J2
   HOR/BR BL6 ....338 E6
The Pennines FUL/RIB PR2 ....213 J4
Pennine Vw GAR/LONG PR3 ....153 G6
   HGHB LA2 ....65 J7
   KIRK/FR/WA PR4 ....209 G6
   MCMB LA4 ....41 H7
Pennine Wy BWCK/EAR BB18 ....144 E1
   GAR/LONG PR3 ....153 G6
   HBR HX7 ....229 K8
   HWTH BD22 ....174 E8
   KKBY L32 ....366 A7
   NLSN BB9 ....198 A6
   PLF/KEOS FY6 ....125 F4
   SKP/WHF BD23 ....120 B2
Pennington Av ORM L39 ....348 C5
Penn St HOR/BR BL6 ....338 E6
Pennyfarthing La CLV/TH FY5 ....149 G1
Penny House La ACC BB5 ....248 C4
Pennystone Rd BISP FY2 ....148 B7
Penny Stone Rd HGHB LA2 ....44 A4
Penny St BBN BB1 ....8 C4
   LANC LA1 ....3 D4
   PRES PR1 ....7 E2
Penrhos St FTWD FY7 ....122 E2
Penrhyn Rd LANC LA1 ....2 A1
Penrith Av CLV/TH FY5 ....122 D7
   HEY LA3 ....52 D3
   STHP PR8 ....325 H8
Penrith Crs COL BB8 ....199 F1
Penrith Rd COL * BB8 ....170 E8
Penrod Wy HEY LA3 ....52 B6
Penrose Av BPOOLS FY4 ....5 F6
Penrose PI SKEL WN8 ....364 A7
Penshaw CI BBN BB1 ....245 G2
Penswick Av CLV/TH FY5 ....148 C3
Pentland Rd NWD/KWIPK L33 ....366 F2
Penwortham Ct PRES PR1 ....6 B6
Penwortham Hall Gdns
   PRES PR1 ....239 G8

Penwortham Wy PRES PR1 ....261 J1
Pen-y-Ghent Wy BWCK/EAR BB18 .....144 E1
Penzance St BBNW * BB2 ....267 J1
Peplow Rd HEY LA3 ....52 E3
Pepper La WGNNW/ST WN6 ....335 F8
Perch Pool La CHTN/BK PR9 ....303 H6
Percival St ACC BB5 ....247 K5
   BBN BB1 ....9 D2
   DWN BB3 ....268 C8
Percy Rd LANC LA1 ....3 D5
Percy St ACC BB5 ....247 F6
   ACC BB5 ....248 C5
   BBNW BB2 ....267 J1
   BPOOL FY1 ....176 C4
   CHLY/EC PR7 ....311 H4
   COL BB8 ....171 J5
   FTWD FY7 ....97 F7
   NLSN BB9 ....198 A4
   PRES PR1 ....7 E2
   RAMS* BL0 ....319 H6
   WHIT OL12 ....299 J5
Peregrine Dr DWN BB3 ....268 A8
Peregrine PI LEY/BBR PR5 ....285 F1
Peridot CI BBN BB1 ....245 H1
Peronne Crs BBN BB1 ....246 B6
Perpignan Wy
   LANC (off St Nicholas Arcades) LA1 ....3 D3
Perry St DWN BB3 ....291 J3
Pershore Gdns BPOOLE FY3 ....177 H3
Pershore Gv STHP PR8 ....325 G7
Pershore Rd LSTA FY8 ....231 H6
Persia St ACC BB5 ....247 K5
Perth CI CLV/TH FY5 ....149 F4
   NWD/KWIPK L33 ....366 B5
Perth St ACC BB5 ....248 A6
   BBNW BB2 ....8 A6
   BLY BB11 ....10 A4
   LANC LA1 ....3 E4
   NLSN BB9 ....198 D2
Peterfield Rd PRES * PR1 ....262 B1
Peter Martin St HOR/BR BL6 ....338 D7
Peters Av BRSC L40 ....330 E6
Petersbottom La HGHB LA2 ....50 E4
Peters Buildings
   BPOOLE (off Devonshire Rd) FY3 ....5 D1
Peters Rw
   BBN (off Holt St) BB1 ....247 G2
Peter St ACC BB5 ....248 A6
   BBN BB1 ....9 E3
   BPOOL FY1 ....4 C2
   CHLY/EC PR7 ....311 G3
   COL* BB8 ....171 J7
   LANC* LA1 ....3 D4
   NLSN* BB9 ....170 B7
   RAW/HAS BB4 ....296 C1
   WGNW/BIL/O WN5 ....365 K3
Petre Crs BBN BB1 ....247 F3
Petrel CI BBN BB1 ....8 B1
Petre Rd ACC BB5 ....247 J2
Petunia CI LEY/BBR PR5 ....286 C1
Petworth Rd STHP PR8 ....325 H5
Pharos PI FTWD FY7 ....97 H6
Pharos St FTWD FY7 ....97 H6
Pheasantford Gn BRFD/BLYE BB10 ...11 E1
Pheasantford St BRFD/BLYE BB10 ....11 E1
Pheasant Wood Dr CLV/TH FY5 ....123 F6
Philip Av KIRK/FR/WA PR4 ....209 F6
Philip Dr STHP PR8 ....326 A5
Philips Rd BBN BB1 ....9 D1
   BCUP OL13 ....275 K4
Philip St BWCK/EAR BB18 ....145 H7
   DWN BB3 ....291 K2
Phillip's CI FMBY L37 ....355 K1
Phillips La COL BB8 ....171 F7
   FMBY L37 ....355 K1
Phillip St BPOOLS FY4 ....5 F5
Phoenix Pk BBN BB1 ....246 B1
Phoenix St LANC LA1 ....3 D2
Phoenix Wy BLY BB11 ....224 E6
Picadilly WGNW/BIL/O WN5 ....371 G6
Piccadilly LANC LA1 ....55 F1
Piccadilly CI LANC LA1 ....55 F8
Piccadilly Rd BLY BB11 ....10 B4
Piccadilly Sq BLY BB11 ....10 B4
Piccadilly St RAW/HAS BB4 ....272 C8
Pickard CI BWCK/EAR BB18 ....119 H7
Pickard St LANC LA1 ....3 D5
Pickering CI LSTA FY8 ....231 H4
Pickering Fold BBN BB1 ....268 E4
The Pickerings RAW/HAS * BB4 ....263 F3
Pickering St NLSN * BB9 ....197 K6
Pickles Dr BRSC L40 ....330 D7
Pickles St PDHM/BLYW BB12 ....10 A2
Pickmere Av BPOOLS FY4 ....204 E3
Pickmere CI CLV/TH FY5 ....123 G7
Pickthorn CI LANC LA1 ....42 D7
Pickup Fold Rd DWN BB3 ....292 A4

Pickup Rd BBN BB1 2
Pickup St ACC BB5 2
   ACC BB5 2
   BBN BB1 2
   BCUP* OL13 2
Picton St BBNW * BB2 2
Pierce CI LANC LA1 2
   PDHM/BLYW BB12 2
Piercefield Rd FMBY L37 3
Piercy Rd RAW/HAS BB4 2
Pier La CARN LA5 2
Pierston Av BISP FY2 1
Pier St BPOOL FY1 ....
Pigot St WGNW/BIL/O WN5 ....
Pike Ct FTWD FY7 ....
Pikelaw PI SKEL WN8 ....
Pilgrim St NLSN BB9 ....
Pilkington Dr ACC BB5 ....
Pilkington Rd STHP PR8 ....
Pilkington St BBN BB1 3
   RAMS BL0 3
   RNFD/HAY WA11 3
Pilling Av ACC BB5 ....
   LSTA FY8 ....
Pilling CI CHLY/EC PR7 3
   CHTN/BK PR9 3
Pilling Crs BPOOLE FY3 1
Pilling Fld EDGW/EG BL7 3
Pilling La CHLY/EC PR7 3
   MGHL L31 ....
   PLF/KEOS FY6 3
Pilling PI SKEL WN8 3
Pilling St RAW/HAS BB4 3
   RAW/HAS BB4 3
Pilmuir Rd BBNW BB2 3
Pilot St ACC BB5 3
Pilsley CI WGNW/BIL/O WN5 3
Pimbo La SKEL WN8 3
Pimbo Rd RNFD/HAY WA11 3
   SKEL WN8 3
Pimlico Link Rd CLI BB7 1
Pimlico Rd CLI BB7 1
Pinch Clough Rd RAW/HAS BB4 2
Pincock Brow CHLY/EC PR7 3
Pincock St CHLY/EC PR7 3
Pinder CI CLI BB7 1
Pinder St NLSN BB9 1
Pine Av BPOOL FY1 1
   KIRK/FR/WA PR4 ....
   ORM L39 3
Pine CI BBN BB1 ....
   FUL/RIB* PR2 ....
   KKBY L32 ....
   SKEL WN8 ....
   SKEL WN8 ....
Pine Crs ACC BB5 ....
   PLF/KEOS FY6 ....
Pine Crest ORM L39 3
Pine DI RNFD/HAY WA11 3
Pine Dr ORM L39 3
Pine Gv CHLYE PR6 ....
   CHTN/BK PR9 ....
   GAR/LONG PR3 ....
   ORM L39 3
Pines CI LEY/BBR PR5 ....
The Pines LEY/BBR PR5 ....
Pine St BBN BB1 ....
   BLY BB11 ....
   DWN BB3 ....
   LANC LA1 ....
   MCMB* LA4 ....
   NLSN BB9 ....
Pine Vw WGNS/IIMK WN3 ....
Pine Wks FUL/RIB PR2 ....
Pineway FUL/RIB PR2 ....
Pine Wy KIRK/FR/WA PR4 ....
Pinewood BBNW BB2 ....
   SKEL WN8 ....
Pinewood Av BISP FY2 ....
   CARN LA5 ....
   CLV/TH FY5 ....
   FMBY L37 ....
   GAR/LONG PR3 ....
   HGHB LA2 ....
   MCMB LA4 ....
   PLF/KEOS FY6 ....
Pinewood CI FMBY L37 ....
   HGHB LA2 ....
   STHP PR8 ....
Pinewood Crs LEY/BBR PR5 ....
   LSTA FY8 ....
   WGNW/BIL/O WN5 ....
Pinewood Dr ACC BB5 ....
Pinewood Gdns NWD/KWIPK L33 ....
Pinfold KIRK/FR/WA PR4 ....
   NLSN BB9 ....

old Ct
VC (off Pinfold La) LA1 ....3 D1
old La BRSC L40 ....328 D8
R/LONG PR3 ....154 C7
R/LONG PR3 ....188 A7
2K/FR/WA PR4 ....182 C2
VC LA1 ....3 D1
HP PR8 ....325 G8
old La BRSC L40 ....363 K7
EL WN8 ....363 K7
old Pl NLSN BB9 ....199 F2
old St PRES PR1 ....240 B3
le Cft CHLYE PR6 ....286 E1
ot Rd WGNW/BIL/O WN5 ....371 G6
wood La NWD/KWIPK L33 ....366 E5
Pl BBNW BB2 ....244 D8
St PDHM/BLYW BB12 ....224 E5
acle Dr EDGW/EG BL7 ....341 H1
er La RAW/HAS BB4 ....273 F5
ers Cl RAMS BL0 ....319 H4
ail Cl LEY/BBR PR5 ....284 B2
eer St HOR/BR BL6 ....338 E7
eer St HOR/BR BL6 ....338 E7
r La HWTH BD22 ....175 F2
er Lea RAW/HAS BB4 ....297 H2
r's La KKBYL LA6 ....18 C2
in St BRSC L40 ....348 E1
LYE PR6 ....264 D7
mbe Cl BOL BL1 ....341 H4
ey Pl SKEL WN8 ....363 J6
a KKBYL LA6 ....20 E1
nan Cl FUL/RIB PR2 ....213 K4
nan Wy FUL/RIB PR2 ....213 K3
dale La BPOOLE FY3 ....205 G1
St CHTN/BK PR9 ....302 B5
VC LA1 ....3 D3
HM/BLYW* BB12 ....223 K3
ES PR1 ....6 C3
lle St DWN BB3 ....268 C8
moor Cl CLV/TH FY5 ....149 F4
Pl BBNW BB2 ....8 C6
e St BBN BB1 ....9 E1
UP OL13 ....275 J7
D OL14 ....277 K4
e Tree Cl BLY BB11 ....251 F1
e Tree Rd BBN * BB1 ....9 E2
tain Wk HEY LA3 ....53 H1
sant Gv CLV/TH FY5 ....149 H1
tation Av CARN LA5 ....15 F2
F/KEOS FY6 ....98 A6
tation Gv CARN LA5 ....15 H3
tation La HGHB LA2 ....82 E1
tation Rd ACC BB5 ....248 D5
NW BB2 ....267 J2
SC L40 ....330 E7
GW/EG BL7 ....317 K4
tation Sq ACC BB5 ....248 D5
tation St ACC BB5 ....248 C6
UP OL13 ....298 A3
FD/BLYE* BB10 ....11 D2
SN BB9 ....198 C2
W/HAS BB4 ....296 D1
t St ACC BB5 ....247 H8
L/RIB* PR2 ....6 A1
Cl ACC BB5 ....248 A6
en La MCMB LA4 ....41 J6
La WGN WN1 ....336 B8
s La BRSC L40 ....349 H1
St BPOOL FY1 ....4 C1
fair St EDGW/EG BL7 ....341 H1
sant Gv CLV/TH FY5 ....149 H1
sant Pl BLY BB11 ....10 C4
sant St BPOOL FY1 ....176 B4
A FY8 ....232 D8
sant Vw
OOLS (off School Rd) FY4 ....205 G7
VCK/EAR BB18 ....146 C2
LY/EC PR7 ....335 K1
LYE PR6 ....289 C2
N BB3 ....292 D2
W/HAS BB4 ....297 H2
sington Av GAR/LONG PR3 ....129 K5
sington Cl BBNW BB2 ....244 D7
OOLS FY4 ....205 G3
sington Gv BRFD/BLYE BB10 ....226 B6
La BBNW BB2 ....266 D3
sington Rd BBNW BB2 ....266 D1
sington St BBNW BB2 ....244 D7
Farm Av BBN BB1 ....8 C1
xgate Fold BBN BB1 ....245 F2
xgate Rd BBN BB1 ....8 B1
Pl PLF/KEOS FY6 ....149 H5
Rd ACC BB5 ....248 C5
na Rd PRES PR1 ....240 A3
La ORM L39 ....346 D5
Moss La STHP PR8 ....344 D2
Ploughlands FUL/RIB PR2 ....238 A2
gh La BRSC L40 ....350 A8

Plover Cl CLV/TH FY5 ....123 F6
Plover Dr HEY LA3 ....52 D6
Plover St PDHM/BLYW BB12 ....10 A5
PRES PR1 ....239 K1
Plovers Wy BPOOLE FY3 ....177 H5
Plover Vw PDHM/BLYW BB12 ....10 A5
Plox Brow KIRK/FR/WA PR4 ....282 A5
Plumbe St BLY BB11 ....11 D4
Plumpton Av BPOOLS FY4 ....205 F6
Plumpton Fld KIRK/FR/WA PR4 ....212 A1
Plumpton La KIRK/FR/WA PR4 ....207 G4
ORM L39 ....346 A1
Plumpton Rd FUL/RIB PR2 ....238 E1
Plumtree Cl FUL/RIB PR2 ....214 A5
Plunge Rd RAMS BL0 ....296 A8
Plungington Rd FUL/RIB PR2 ....213 G8
PRES PR1 ....239 G1
Plymouth Av CHLYE PR6 ....122 C3
Plymouth Gv CHLYE PR6 ....311 J3
Plymouth Rd BPOOLE FY3 ....176 E2
Poachers Wy CLV/TH FY5 ....123 G3
Pochard Pl CLV/TH FY5 ....149 F2
Pocklington Rd ACC BB5 ....271 J1
Poets' Ct PDHM/BLYW BB12 ....224 B4
Pointer Ct LANC LA1 ....3 D5
Pointer Gv HGHB LA2 ....44 B4
Poke St WGNW/BIL/O WN5 ....365 K5
Poland St ACC BB5 ....247 K6
Polefield FUL/RIB PR2 ....213 C4
Pole La DWN BB3 ....292 A4
Pole St PRES PR1 ....7 E2
Police St DWN BB3 ....291 J2
Pollard Pl LANC LA1 ....43 G7
Pollard St ACC BB5 ....248 C4
BLY BB11 ....10 A4
PRES PR1 ....6 C2
TOD OL14 ....277 K4
Pollux Ga LSTA FY8 ....231 J7
Polperro Dr KIRK/FR/WA PR4 ....234 E5
Pomfret St BBNW BB2 ....8 B6
BLY BB11 ....10 B3
Pompian Brow LEY/BBR PR5 ....282 E5
Ponden La HWTH BD22 ....203 J5
Pond Gdns PLF/KEOS FY6 ....149 H5
Pont St NLSN BB9 ....198 B4
Pool Ct FTWD FY7 ....122 C2
Poole Rd FUL/RIB PR2 ....213 J7
Poole St BBN BB1 ....246 A6
Pool Foot La PLF/KEOS FY6 ....151 F7
Poole Hey La STHP PR8 ....302 D8
Poolhill Cl CLV/TH FY5 ....148 E4
Pool House La FUL/RIB PR2 ....212 B6
Pool La KIRK/FR/WA PR4 ....234 E7
Poolside Wk CHTN/BK PR9 ....278 D4
Pool St CHTN/BK PR9 ....278 E7
Pope La FUL/RIB PR2 ....214 E8
KIRK/FR/WA PR4 ....261 J2
PRES PR1 ....261 K1
Pope Wk PRES PR1 ....239 F8
Poplar Av BOL BL1 ....341 K7
BPOOLE FY3 ....5 D2
CHLY/EC PR7 ....286 A7
GTH/LHO BB6 ....221 H5
KIRK/FR/WA PR4 ....208 E7
KIRK/FR/WA PR4 ....234 B5
KIRK/FR/WA PR4 ....260 C3
LEY/BBR PR5 ....263 J8
PLF/KEOS FY6 ....178 A1
Poplar Cl ACC BB5 ....247 K8
BBN BB1 ....247 F3
LEY/BBR PR5 ....263 J2
Poplar Dr GAR/LONG PR3 ....188 A3
KIRK/FR/WA PR4 ....234 D6
KKBY L32 ....366 B8
PRES PR1 ....6 A1
SKEL WN8 ....363 F2
Poplar Gv FUL/RIB PR2 ....214 E7
LEY/BBR PR5 ....263 J2
RAMS BL0 ....319 K6
The Poplars CHLY/EC PR7 ....337 F5
Poplar St BBN BB1 ....9 D3
CHLY/EC PR7 ....311 H5
NLSN BB9 ....198 D2
RAW/HAS BB4 ....272 C8
STHP PR8 ....302 A5
Poppy Av CHLYE PR6 ....311 H1
Poppyfield KIRK/FR/WA PR4 ....212 B5
Poppyfields KIRK/FR/WA PR4 ....258 C7
Poppy La ORM L39 ....361 F2
Porritt Wy RAMS BL0 ....319 J4
Portal Gv PDHM/BLYW BB12 ....224 D5
Porter Pl PRES PR1 ....7 E4
Porters Rw
PLF/KEOS (off Smithy La) FY6 ....124 E4
Porter St ACC BB5 ....247 K5
PRES PR1 ....7 F1
Porter St East KIRK/FR/WA PR4 ....208 D5

Porters Wood Cl
WGNW/BIL/O * WN5 ....365 K4
Portfield La CLI BB7 ....193 K8
Portfield Rd CLI BB7 ....193 J7
Portree Av BISP FY2 ....148 E5
Portland Dr HEY LA3 ....53 H1
Portland Rd BPOOL FY1 ....5 D3
GTH/LHO BB6 ....220 A3
Portland St ACC BB5 ....248 A5
BBNW BB2 ....8 A6
CHLY/EC PR7 ....311 H3
COL BB8 ....171 K6
DWN BB3 ....291 K5
LANC LA1 ....3 D4
NLSN BB9 ....170 B8
PRES PR1 ....6 B3
STHP PR8 ....301 G5
Portman St PRES PR1 ....7 F1
Portree Cl FUL/RIB PR2 ....214 A6
Portree Crs BBN BB1 ....246 B8
Port Royal Av LANC LA1 ....2 A4
Portsmouth Av BRFD/BLYE BB10 ......226 C1
Portsmouth Cl CLV/TH FY5 ....123 F7
Portsmouth Dr CHLYE PR6 ....311 J3
Portway BISP FY2 ....148 E5
Port Wy FUL/RIB PR2 ....6 A3
HEY LA3 ....52 B6
Postern Gate Rd HGHB LA2 ....56 C3
Post Horse La HGHB LA2 ....37 G6
Post La KIRK/FR/WA PR4 ....234 D5
Post Office Av CHTN/BK PR9 ....301 H4
DWN BB3 ....269 F8
Pot House La ACC BB5 ....270 D2
DWN BB3 ....269 F8
Potter La LEY/BBR PR5 ....241 G5
LEY/BBR PR5 ....241 J2
Potter Pl SKEL WN8 ....363 K6
Poulton Av ACC BB5 ....248 A3
LSTA FY8 ....231 G3
Poulton Crs LEY/BBR PR5 ....241 H8
Poulton Old Rd BPOOLE FY3 ....177 F2
Poulton Rd BPOOLE FY3 ....177 F3
CHTN/BK PR9 ....302 B4
FTWD FY7 ....96 E8
MCMB LA4 ....41 H6
PLF/KEOS FY6 ....149 J7
Poulton Sq MCMB LA4 ....41 H5
Poulton St FTWD FY7 ....97 G7
FUL/RIB PR2 ....6 A1
KIRK/FR/WA PR4 ....208 E6
Powder House La HGHB LA2 ....42 C6
Powderworks La MGHL L31 ....360 A8
Powell Av BPOOLS FY4 ....204 D3
Powell Dr WGNW/BIL/O WN5 ....371 F8
Powell St BLY BB11 ....10 B5
BWCK/EAR BB18 ....119 F8
DWN BB3 ....291 J1
Powis Dr KIRK/FR/WA PR4 ....282 A3
Powis Rd FUL/RIB PR2 ....238 C3
Powys Cl RAW/HAS BB4 ....295 H2
Poynter St PRES PR1 ....240 A7
Prairie Crs BRFD/BLYE BB10 ....197 K8
Pratt St BRFD/BLYE BB10 ....225 J2
Preesall Cl CHTN/BK PR9 ....278 B6
LSTA FY8 ....231 H4
Preesall Moss La PLF/KEOS FY6 ....125 F1
Preesall Rd FUL/RIB PR2 ....238 A2
Preese Gdns KIRK/FR/WA PR4 ....180 E2
Prelude Pk
KIRK/FR/WA
(off Liverpool Old Rd) PR4 ....260 A7
Premier Wy PLF/KEOS FY6 ....150 B8
Prenton Gdns CLV/TH FY5 ....149 F4
Prescot Gn ORM L39 ....348 B8
Prescot Pl BPOOLE FY3 ....205 G1
CLV/TH FY5 ....149 J1
Prescot Rd MGHL L31 ....366 A7
ORM L39 ....360 B7
Prescott Av BRSC L40 ....306 A8
Prescott Br BRSC L40 ....331 J5
Prescott La WGNW/BIL/O WN5 ....365 K3
Prescott Rd SKEL WN8 ....364 K7
Prescott St BRFD/BLYE BB10 ....11 E4
Press Rd LSTA * FY8 ....230 D3
Prestbury Av BPOOLS FY4 ....204 C6
STHP PR8 ....325 H6
Prestbury Dr HEY LA3 ....53 H1
Preston Lancaster New Rd
GAR/LONG PR3 ....129 G4
Preston Lancaster Old Rd
GAR/LONG PR3 ....129 K8
Preston Lancaster Rd
GAR/LONG PR3 ....103 H7
GAR/LONG PR3 ....156 B3
HGHB LA2 ....80 B1
Preston New Rd BBNW BB2 ....8 A4
BPOOLS FY4 ....206 C5
CHTN/BK PR9 ....278 C8

KIRK/FR/WA PR4 .....235 H4
LEY/BBR PR5 .....241 F2
PRES PR1 .....241 F2
Preston Nook CHLY/EC PR7 .....308 E6
Preston Old Rd BBNW BB2 .....266 C4
BPOOLE FY3 .....205 G1
KIRK/FR/WA PR4 .....235 G5
KIRK/FR/WA PR4 .....236 C2
Preston Rd CHLY/EC PR7 .....309 K8
CHLYE PR6 .....264 A8
CHTN/BK PR9 .....302 A3
FUL/RIB PR2 .....215 G2
GAR/LONG PR3 .....188 E4
GAR/LONG PR3 .....188 A8
KIRK/FR/WA PR4 .....182 A2
LEY/BBR PR5 .....285 K1
LSTA FY8 .....233 F8
Preston St CARN LA5 .....33 K1
CHLYE PR6 .....311 G1
DWN BB3 .....268 C8
FTWD FY7 .....97 H7
KIRK/FR/WA PR4 .....209 F6
Prestwich St BLY BB11 .....10 A5
Price Cl LANC LA1 .....42 E8
Price St BPOOLS * FY4 .....4 B6
Prickshaw La WHIT OL12 .....323 F5
Priestfield CLV/TH FY5 .....149 F4
Priestfield Av COL BB8 .....171 G6
Priesthouse Cl FMBY L37 .....344 A8
Priesthouse La FMBY L37 .....344 A8
Primet Br COL BB8 .....171 G7
Primet Hts COL BB8 .....171 F8
Primet Hl COL BB8 .....171 G7
Primet St COL BB8 .....171 G7
Primrose Bank BBN BB1 .....9 D3
BISP FY2 .....149 F5
Primrose Cl BBNW BB2 .....267 J1
CHTN/BK PR9 .....278 E5
FMBY L37 .....344 B6
KIRK/FR/WA PR4 .....258 D7
Primrose Ct
LANC (off Primrose St) LA1 .....3 E4
MCMB LA4 .....41 H6
Primrose Dr BBN BB1 .....9 D4
Primrose Gv PRES PR1 .....214 A8
Primrose Hl BBNW BB2 .....218 C8
PRES PR1 .....7 F3
Primrose La PRES PR1 .....214 A8
Primrose Rd CLI BB7 .....165 H5
PRES PR1 .....214 A8
Primrose St ACC BB5 .....248 A7
BOL* BL1 .....341 K7
BRFD/BLYE* BB10 .....226 A2
CHLYE PR6 .....311 H3
CLI BB7 .....165 H4
DWN BB3 .....291 K3
LANC LA1 .....3 E4
MCMB* LA4 .....41 H6
NLSN BB9 .....197 K6
NLSN BB9 .....198 C3
Primrose Ter BBNW BB2 .....267 J1
BPOOLS (off School Rd) FY4 .....205 G2
Primrose Wy PLF/KEOS FY6 .....149 H5
Primula Dr DWN BB3 .....268 C8
Primula St BOL BL1 .....341 K7
Prince Av CARN LA5 .....34 A2
Prince Charles Gdns STHP PR8 .....301 F6
Prince Lee Mdw DWN BB3 .....291 K3
Princes Ct PRES PR1 .....238 D5
Princes Crs MCMB LA4 .....42 A4
Prince's Dr FUL/RIB PR2 .....213 F5
Prince's Pk WGNNW/ST WN6 .....353 H7
Prince's Rd LEY/BBR PR5 .....240 C6
LSTA FY8 .....231 K7
PRES PR1 .....238 D5
Princess Alexandra Wy HEY LA3 .....52 B6
Princess Av CLI BB7 .....165 K2
KIRK/FR/WA PR4 .....208 D5
LANC LA1 .....3 D6
PLF/KEOS FY6 .....149 K8
Princess Ct BPOOL FY1 .....4 B4
Princess Dr BBNW BB2 .....266 E4
Princess Rd CHLYE PR6 .....337 H3
CLV/TH FY5 .....148 C1
Princess St ACC BB5 .....247 J5
BBNW BB2 .....267 K1
BCUP OL13 .....275 J8
BPOOL FY1 .....4 B4
CHLY/EC PR7 .....311 H5
CLI BB7 .....193 G6
COL BB8 .....171 G6
GTH/LHO BB6 .....221 H6
LEY/BBR PR5 .....262 E4
LEY/BBR PR5 .....285 K2
NLSN BB9 .....198 B4

PDHM/BLYW BB12 .....223 H3
PRES PR1 .....7 F3
Princes St BBN BB1 .....247 F2
BBNW BB2 .....8 B5
STHP PR8 .....301 C5
Princess Wy CHLY/EC PR7 .....310 B1
PDHM/BLYW BB12 .....10 C2
Prince St BCUP OL13 .....299 H4
BLY BB11 .....10 A1
DWN BB3 .....291 H2
RAMS BL0 .....319 J5
Princes Wy CLV/TH FY5 .....148 C2
FTWD FY7 .....122 C1
Princeway BPOOLS FY4 .....204 C4
Pringle St BBN BB1 .....9 D6
Pringle Wd GAR/LONG PR3 .....212 E1
Prinny Hill Rd RAW/HAS BB4 .....272 B8
Printers Fold PDHM/BLYW BB12 .....224 A4
Priorsgate HEY LA3 .....53 H1
Priors Wk CLI BB7 .....141 F2
Priorswood Pl SKEL WN8 .....364 B7
Priory Cl BRSC L40 .....330 D6
FMBY L37 .....356 B1
HEY LA3 .....53 J1
KIRK/FR/WA PR4 .....282 A5
LEY/BBR PR5 .....286 A1
PRES PR1 .....6 A4
RAW/HAS BB4 .....297 C2
WGNW/BIL/O WN5 .....365 K6
Priory Ct BBNW BB2 .....266 D1
BLY BB11 .....251 K1
BPOOL FY1 .....4 C2
Priory Crs PRES PR1 .....6 A4
Priory Dr DWN BB3 .....292 A3
Priory Gdns STHP PR8 .....301 F7
Priory Ga DWN BB3 .....292 A3
STHP PR8 .....301 G7
Priory Gv ORM L39 .....348 B7
Priory La HGHB LA2 .....37 C5
PRES PR1 .....6 A4
Priory Ms STHP PR8 .....301 F5
Priory Nook SKEL WN8 .....364 B7
Priory Pl DWN BB3 .....292 A3
Priory Rd SKEL WN8 .....364 B4
Priory St FUL/RIB PR2 .....6 B2
NLSN BB9 .....198 D2
Priory Wk LANC LA1 .....3 E3
Pritchard St BBNW BB2 .....268 B1
BLY BB11 .....10 B5
Private La RAW/HAS BB4 .....295 J3
Procter Moss Rd HGHB LA2 .....67 K2
Procter St BBNW BB2 .....9 D6
Proctor Cl NLSN BB9 .....198 D6
Proctor Fold
BBNW (off Osbaldeston La) BB2 .....217 K6
Proctor Rd FMBY L37 .....343 H3
Progress Av BBN * BB1 .....9 E2
Progress Rd NLSN BB9 .....170 D8
Progress St CHLYE PR6 .....311 J3
DWN BB3 .....291 K2
Progress Wy BPOOLS FY4 .....205 G6
Promenade BISP FY2 .....148 B7
BPOOL FY1 .....4 B4
BPOOLS FY4 .....204 B8
CLV/TH FY5 .....122 C6
CLV/TH FY5 .....148 C5
STHP PR8 .....301 C4
STHP PR8 .....325 H5
Promenade North CLV/TH FY5 .....122 C8
Promenade Rd FTWD FY7 .....97 C6
Promenade South CLV/TH FY5 .....148 C1
The Promenade CARN LA5 .....15 F1
Prospect Av DWN BB3 .....291 C1
HGHB LA2 .....42 E1
LEY/BBR PR5 .....262 E3
Prospect Ct GAR/LONG PR3 .....188 B5
Prospect Dr HGHB LA2 .....42 E2
Prospect Gv MCMB LA4 .....41 J7
Prospect Hl RAW/HAS BB4 .....295 C1
Prospect Pl FUL/RIB PR2 .....238 D7
PRES PR1 .....6 C6
SKEL WN8 .....364 B6
Prospect Rd RAW/HAS BB4 .....273 G8
Prospect St GTH/LHO BB6 .....221 G6
LANC LA1 .....3 E4
RAW/HAS BB4 .....297 A3
Prospect Ter CHLYE PR6 .....289 G3
NLSN* BB9 .....170 B7
Provence Av GTH/LHO BB6 .....192 A5
Providence St BBN BB1 .....9 E1
Prudy Hl PLF/KEOS FY6 .....149 K7
Pudding La TOD OL14 .....277 H1
Pudding Pie Nook La
GAR/LONG PR3 .....185 H7
Puddle House La PLF/KEOS FY6 .....178 B3
Pudsey Rd TOD OL14 .....277 G2

Pump House La LEY/BBR PR5 2
Pump St BBNW BB2 .....
BLY BB11 .....
CLI BB7 1
PRES PR1 .....
Punnell's La MGHL L31 3
Punstock Rd DWN BB3 2
Pyes Bridge La MTHPE LA7 .....
Pygon's Hill La MGHL L31 3

Quaile Holme Rd PLF/KEOS FY6 .....
Quaker Brook La LEY/BBR PR5 2
Quakerfields DWN BB3 2
Quaker La DWN BB3 2
Quarlton Dr TOT/BURYW BL8 3
Quarrybank CLV/TH FY5 1
Quarry Bank NWD/KWIPK L33 3
Quarry Bank St
PDHM/BLYW BB12 2
Quarry Cl NWD/KWIPK L33 3
Quarry Dl NWD/KWIPK L33 3
Quarry Dr ORM L39 3
Quarry Farm Ct CLI BB7 1
Quarry Gn NWD/KWIPK L33 3
Quarry Hey NWD/KWIPK L33 3
Quarry Mt ORM L39 3
Quarry Mount Ms LANC LA1 .....
Quarry Rd CHLYE PR6 2
CHLYE PR6 3
HGHB LA2 .....
LANC LA1 .....
Quarry St ACC BB5 2
BBN BB1 .....
BCUP OL13 2
PDHM/BLYW BB12 2
RAMS BL0 3
WHIT OL12 2
Quayle Av BPOOLS FY4 2
Quayside FTWD FY7 .....
The Quayside
FTWD (off Queens Ter) FY7 .....
Quebec Av BISP FY2 1
Quebec Rd BBNW BB2 2
Queen Anne St STHP PR8 3
Queen Elizabeth Ct MCMB * LA4 .....
Queen Elizabeth Crs ACC BB5 2
Queen Mary Av LSTA FY8 2
Queens Av FMBY L37 3
Queensberry Rd BLY BB11 .....
Queensborough Rd ACC BB5 2
Queensbury Cl BOL BL1 3
Queensbury Rd CLV/TH FY5 1
Queen's Cl PLF/KEOS FY6 1
Queenscourt Av PRES PR1 2
Queen's Crs KIRK/FR/WA PR4 2
Queens Cft FMBY L37 3
Queensdale Cl LEY/BBR PR5 2
Queen's Dr ACC BB5 2
BPOOLE FY3 1
CARN LA5 .....
FUL/RIB PR2 2
GAR/LONG PR3 1
MCMB LA4 .....
Queens Garth SKP/WHF BD23 1
Queensgate CHLY/EC PR7 2
NLSN BB9 1
Queens Gn ORM L39 3
Queen's Gv CHLY/EC PR7 3
Queen's Lancashire Wy BLY BB11 .....
Queen's Park Rd BBN BB1 .....
BRFD/BLYE BB10 .....
Queens Pl KIRK/FR/WA PR4 2
Queen's Prom BISP FY2 1
Queen Sq LANC LA1 .....
Queen's Rd ACC BB5 2
BBN BB1 .....
BRFD/BLYE BB10 .....
CHLY/EC PR7 3
CHTN/BK PR9 3
CLI BB7 1
DWN BB3 3
FMBY L37 3
FUL/RIB* PR2 2
LEY/BBR PR5 2
LSTA FY8 2
WGNW/BIL/O WN5 3
Queens Rd West ACC BB5 2
Queen's Sq PLF/KEOS FY6 1
Queen's Ter BBNW BB2 2
BCUP OL13 .....
FTWD FY7 .....
Queen St ACC BB5 2
ACC BB5 2

Red Barn Rd *WGNW/BIL/O* WN5 ......**370** D5
Red Br *BRSC* L40 ....**306** C1
Red Bridge La *CARN* LA5 ....**15** K7
Redbrow Wy *NWD/KWIPK* L33 ....**366** C7
Redcar Av *CLV/TH* FY5 ....**122** E6
  FUL/RIB PR2 ....**212** B7
Redcar Cl *STHP* PR8 ....**302** B8
Redcar Rd *BOL* BL1 ....**341** F7
  BPOOL FY1 ....**176** B3
  LANC LA1 ....**55** H8
Red Cat La *BRSC* L40 ....**330** C3
  RNFD/HAY WA11 ....**370** A7
Redcliffe Gdns *ORM* L39 ....**348** C8
Red Cross St *PRES* PR1 ....**6** C3
Red Delph La *RNFD/HAY* WA11 ....**368** D2
Redearth Rd *DWN* BB3 ....**291** J3
Redearth St *DWN* BB3 ....**291** J3
Rede Av *FTWD* FY7 ....**122** C1
Redeswood Av *CLV/TH* FY5 ....**148** D3
Red Fold *ORM* L39 ....**360** A1
Redgate *FMBY* L37 ....**356** A1
  ORM L39 ....**348** B7
Redgate Cl *BLY* BB11 ....**11** E6
Redgate Dr *FMBY* L37 ....**356** B1
Redhill *KIRK/FR/WA* PR4 ....**260** D2
Redhill Gv *CHLYE* PR6 ....**287** J8
Redhills Dr *STHP* PR8 ....**302** B8
Red Hills Rd *CARN* LA5 ....**15** F2
Red House La *CHLY/EC* PR7 ....**308** D5
Redisher Cft *TOT/BURYW* BL8 ....**319** F8
Redisher La *TOT/BURYW* BL8 ....**318** E8
Redlam *BBNW* BB2 ....**244** D8
Redlam Brow *BBNW* BB2 ....**244** D8
Red La *CHLY/EC* PR7 ....**309** G5
  COL BB8 ....**171** F4
Red Lees Av *BRFD/BLYE* BB10 ....**226** D7
Red Lees Rd *BRFD/BLYE* BB10 ....**226** D7
  BRFD/BLYE BB10 ....**252** E3
Red Lion St *BLY* BB11 ....**11** D4
  BWCK/EAR BB18 ....**146** C1
Red Lumb St *WHIT* OL12 ....**321** J7
Redman Rd *BRFD/BLYE* BB10...........**197** K7
Red Marsh Dr *CLV/TH* FY5 ....**123** J7
Redmayne Dr *CARN* LA5 ....**34** A1
Redmayne St *PRES* PR1 ....**240** B3
Redmoor Crs *NWD/KWIPK* L33 ......**366** C3
Redness Cl *NLSN* BB9 ....**198** C5
Red Rake *BBN* BB1 ....**8** A2
Redruth Dr *CARN* LA5 ....**33** J3
Redruth St *PDHM/BLYW* BB12 ....**10** A3
Red Sands *ORM* L39 ....**348** B8
Red Scar St *COL* * BB8 ....**171** G7
Red Spar Rd *BRFD/BLYE* BB10 ....**226** B1
Redstart Pl *CLV/TH* FY5 ....**149** F2
Redvers Rd *DWN* BB3 ....**268** B6
Redvers St *BRFD/BLYE* BB10 ....**225** K2
  LANC LA1 ....**2** B4
Redvers Ter *BPOOL* FY1 ....**176** B3
Redwald Cl *NWD/KWIPK* L33 ....**366** C5
Redwing Av *CLV/TH* FY5 ....**123** F7
Redwood Av *LEY/BBR* PR5 ....**285** G3
  MGHL L31 ....**358** E8
  WGNW/BIL/O WN5 ....**365** J5
Redwood Cl *BPOOLS* FY4 ....**204** C7
  WHIT OL12 ....**323** F8
Redwood Dr *GAR/LONG* PR3 ....**188** A3
  MCMB LA4 ....**42** A6
  ORM L39 ....**348** B7
  RAW/HAS BB4 ....**296** B3
Redwood Gdns *CLV/TH* FY5 ....**150** A1
Redwood Wy *NWD/KWIPK* L33 ......**366** C5
Redfield *BRFD/BLYE* BB10 ....**198** A1
  LEY/BBR PR5 ....**264** B7
Redfield Pl *LEY/BBR* PR5 ....**263** J4
Reedley Dr *BRFD/BLYE* BB10 ....**197** K7
Reedley Gv *BRFD/BLYE* BB10 ....**197** K8
Reedley Rd *BRFD/BLYE* BB10 ....**197** K7
Reedmace Wk *HEY* LA3 ....**53** H1
Reeds Brow *RNFD/HAY* WA11 ....**369** H3
Reeds Cl *RAW/HAS* BB4 ....**273** H5
Reedshaw La *HWTH* BD22 ....**174** B2
Reedsholme Cl *RAW/HAS* BB4 ....**273** H5
Reeds La *RAW/HAS* BB4 ....**273** H5
  RNFD/HAY WA11 ....**369** F8
The Reeds
  LANC (off Long Marsh La) LA1 ....**2** C2
  ORM L39 ....**348** B5
Reed St *BCUP* OL13 ....**275** K8
  BLY BB11 ....**11** D5
Reedy Acre Pl *LSTA* FY8 ....**232** B2
Reedyford Rd *NLSN* BB9 ....**198** C1
Reedymoor La *COL* BB8 ....**171** G2
Reeford Gv *CLI* BB7 ....**165** H4
Rees Pk *BRSC* L40 ....**331** F8

Reeval Cl *BWCK/EAR* BB18 ....**146** C1
Reeveswood *CHLY/EC* PR7 ....**308** D5
Regal Av *BPOOLS* FY4 ....**204** E5
Regal Ter
  LANC (off Clarendon Rd) LA1 ....**43** F8
Regan St *BOL* BL1 ....**341** H8
Regency Av *LEY/BBR* PR5 ....**263** G3
Regency Cl *KIRK/FR/WA* PR4 ....**208** C6
Regency Ct
  LANC (off Queen St) LA1 ....**3** D4
Regency Gdns *STHP* PR8 ....**300** D7
Regent Av *COL* BB8 ....**171** J5
  LSTA FY8 ....**231** K5
Regent Cl *STHP* PR8 ....**301** F7
Regent Ct *FUL/RIB* PR2 ....**213** G6
Regent Dr *FUL/RIB* PR2 ....**213** F7
Regent Gv *FUL/RIB* PR2 ....**213** G6
Regent Pk *FUL/RIB* PR2 ....**213** G5
Regent Park Av *HEY* LA3 ....**41** F8
Regent Park Gv *MCMB* LA4 ....**41** F7
Regent Pl *NLSN* BB9 ....**198** C1
Regent Rd *ACC* BB5 ....**247** K4
  BPOOL FY1 ....**4** C2
  CHLY/EC PR7 ....**311** F4
  LEY/BBR PR5 ....**240** F5
  *LEY/BBR** PR5 ....**285** H2
  MCMB LA4 ....**41** F7
  STHP PR8 ....**300** E2
Regent Rd East *BPOOL* * FY1 ....**4** C2
Regents Cl *BBNW* BB2 ....**266** D1
Regents Fld
  FMBY (off Victoria Rd) L37 ....**343** H6
Regents Wy *PLF/KEOS* FY6 ....**150** A3
Regent St *BBN* BB1 ....**8** C4
  BCUP OL13 ....**298** E1
  CHLY/EC PR7 ....**335** J2
  CLI BB7 ....**139** F7
  GAR/LONG PR3 ....**187** K4
  LANC LA1 ....**2** C4
  NLSN BB9 ....**197** K6
  NLSN BB9 ....**198** C2
  PRES PR1 ....**7** D4
  RAMS BL0 ....**319** C6
  RAW/HAS BB4 ....**272** B3
Regents Wy *CHLY/EC* PR7 ....**310** B1
Regentsway *LEY/BBR* PR5 ....**263** H3
Reginald St *COL* BB8 ....**171** J6
Reigate *CHLYE* PR6 ....**287** K8
Reiver Rd *LEY/BBR* PR5 ....**261** K8
Renacres La *ORM* L39 ....**327** G6
Rendel St *PDHM/BLYW* BB12 ....**224** E4
Rendsburg Wy
  LANC (off St Nicholas Arcades) LA1 ......**3** D3
Renfrey Cl *ORM* L39 ....**348** C3
Rennie Cl *GAR/LONG* PR3 ....**129** K5
Rennie Ct *LANC* LA1 ....**2** C6
Rennie St *BRFD/BLYE* BB10 ....**11** F1
Renshaw Dr *LEY/BBR* PR5 ....**263** H1
Renshaw St *BRFD/BLYE* BB10 ....**225** K2
Renwick Av *BPOOLS* FY4...................**204** D3
Repton Av *BPOOL* FY1 ....**176** C2
  MCMB LA4 ....**42** B7
Reservoir St *BLY* BB11 ....**10** C5
  DWN BB3 ....**291** H2
Reta Dr *CLV/TH* FY5 ....**123** G8
Revidge Rd *BBNW* BB2 ....**244** D5
Rewe Cl *BBNW* * BB2 ....**267** K3
Reynolds St *BLY* BB11 ....**10** B6
  LANC LA1 ....**2** C2
Rhoda St *NLSN* BB9 ....**198** D3
Rhoden Rd *ACC* BB5 ....**270** C1
  LEY/BBR PR5 ....**284** E2
Rhodes Av *BBN* BB1 ....**8** B1
  RAW/HAS BB4 ....**295** G4
Rhodesway *LEY/BBR* PR5 ....**264** D1
Rhyl Av *BBN* BB1 ....**8** C2
Rhyl St *FTWD* FY7 ....**97** H6
Ribble Av *BRFD/BLYE* BB10 ....**226** A1
  CHTN/BK PR9 ....**278** E7
  DWN BB3 ....**268** B7
  KIRK/FR/WA PR4 ....**234** E5
Ribble Bank *PRES* PR1 ....**238** D5
Ribble Cl *CHLYE* PR6 ....**289** G2
  KIRK/FR/WA PR4 ....**234** E5
  PRES PR1 ....**6** C6
Ribble Ct
  FUL/RIB (off Douglas St) PR2 ....**6** A1
  PRES PR1 ....**6** B4
Ribble Crs *KIRK/FR/WA* PR4 ....**209** F6
  *LEY/BBR** PR5 ....**240** A5
  WGNW/BIL/O WN5 ....**370** E8
Ribble Dr *CLI* BB7 ....**139** H4

KIRK/FR/WA PR4 ....**2**?
Ribble La *CLI* BB7 ....**1**?
Ribble Rd *BPOOL* FY1...
  FTWD FY7 ....**2**?
  LEY/BBR PR5 ....**2**?
  WGNNW/ST WN6 ....**3**?
Ribblesdale Av *ACC* BB5 ....**2**?
  BBN BB1 ....**2**?
  CLI BB7 ....**1**?
Ribblesdale Cl *BPOOLS* FY4 ....**2**?
  KIRK/FR/WA PR4 ....**2**?
Ribblesdale Ct *MCMB* * LA4 ....**4**?
Ribblesdale Dr *FUL/RIB* PR2 ....**2**?
  GAR/LONG PR3...........................**8**?
Ribblesdale Pl *BBNW* * BB2...
  BBNW (off Osbaldeston La) BB2 ......**2**?
  CHLY/EC PR7 ....**3**?
  NLSN BB9 ....**1**?
  PRES PR1
Ribblesdale Rd *GAR/LONG* PR3 ....**1**?
Ribblesdale St *BRFD/BLYE* BB10 ....**1**?
Ribblesdale Vw *CLI* BB7 ....**1**?
Ribble St *BBN* BB1...
  BCUP OL13 ....**2**?
  LSTA FY8 ....**2**?
  PRES PR1
Ribbleton Av *FUL/RIB* PR2 ....**2**?
Ribbleton Dr *ACC* BB5 ....**2**?
Ribbleton Hall Dr *FUL/RIB* PR2 ....**2**?
Ribbleton La *PRES* PR1...
Ribbleton Pl *PRES* * PR1...
Ribbleton St *PRES* PR1...
Ribble View Cl *KIRK/FR/WA* PR4 ......**2**?
Ribble Wy *CLI* BB7...
  CLI BB7 ....**1**?
  GAR/LONG PR3...........................**1**?
  GAR/LONG PR3...........................**1**?
  KIRK/FR/WA PR4 ....**2**?
  LEY/BBR PR5 ....**2**?
  PRES PR1...
  SKP/WHF BD23 ....**9**?
Ribby Av *KIRK/FR/WA* PR4 ....**2**?
Ribby Pl *BPOOLS* FY4...
  FUL/RIB PR2...............................**2**?
Ribby Rd *KIRK/FR/WA* PR4 ....**2**?
Ribchester Av *BPOOLE* FY3...............**2**?
  BRFD/BLYE BB10 ....**2**?
Ribchester Br *GAR/LONG* PR3 ....**1**?
Ribchester Rd *BBN* BB1 ....**2**?
  GAR/LONG PR3...........................**1**?
  LSTA FY8 ....**2**?
Ribchester Wy *NLSN* BB9 ....**1**?
Rice Gv *BPOOL* FY1...........................**1**?
Richardson Cl *KIRK/FR/WA* PR4 ....**2**?
Richardson St *BPOOL* * FY1...
Richards Rd *WGNNW/ST* WN6 ....**3**?
Richard's St *KIRK/FR/WA* PR4...........**2**?
Richard St *BBNW* BB2...
  BCUP OL13...
  BLY BB11...
  NLSN BB9 ....**1**?
  RAMS BL0 ....**3**?
Richards Wk *LANC* LA1...
Richards Wy *CLV/TH* FY5...................**1**?
  LSTA FY8 ....**2**?
Richmond Av *BRFD/BLYE* BB10 ....**2**?
  BRSC L40...................................**3**?
  CLV/TH FY5...............................**1**?
  KIRK/FR/WA PR4 ....**2**?
  LANC LA1 ....**4**?
  MCMB LA4 ....**4**?
  RAW/HAS BB4 ....**2**?
Richmond Cl *CHLYE* PR6 ....**2**?
Richmond Ct *CHLY/EC* PR7 ....**3**?
  LEY/BBR PR5 ....**2**?
Richmond Crs *BBN* BB1......................**2**?
Richmond Gv *MGHL* L31 ....**3**?
Richmond Hl *BBN* * BB1...
Richmond Hill La *GAR/LONG* PR3 ......**1**?
Richmond Hill St *ACC* BB5 ....**2**?
Richmond Ms *BRSC* L40.....................**3**?
Richmond Pk *DWN* BB3 ....**2**?
Richmond Rd *ACC* BB5 ....**2**?
  BPOOL FY1...................................**1**?
  BWCK/EAR BB18 ....**1**?
  CHLY/EC PR7 ....**3**?
  CHLYE PR6...................................**2**?
  LSTA FY8 ....**2**?
  NLSN BB9 ....**1**?
  STHP PR8...................................**3**?
Richmond St *ACC* BB5 ....**2**?
  BLY BB11...
  HOR/BR BL6................................**3**?
  PRES PR1...
Richmond Ter *BBN* * BB1...
  BBNW BB2...................................**1**?
  CLI BB7...

...WN BB3	291	J1
kard Rd NLSN BB9	198	C5
ding La CLI BB7	193	F6
dings Av BRFD/BLYE BB10	226	D5
dings La CLI BB7	193	C6
ehalgh La BRFD/BLYE BB10	199	K8
ehalgh St COL BB8	171	H8
ge Av BRFD/BLYE BB10	11	F2
ge CI CHTN/BK PR9	278	E7
ge Ct BRFD/BLYE BB10	11	F3
AR/LONG PR3	188	C3
jeford Gdns FUL/RIB PR2	213	F6
ge Av HEY LA3	52	D3
ge Sq LANC LA1	3	F2
ANC LA1	55	J1
DHM/BLYW BB12	169	H7
ge Rd BLY BB11	11	E3
HLYE PR6	311	J4
ge Rw BRFD/BLYE BB10	226	B3
ge Sq LANC LA1	3	F2
ge St LANC LA1	3	E2
geway GTH/LHO BB6	221	F5
LSN BB9	170	A8
ge Wy PRES PR1	6	C6
geway Av BBNW BB2	268	C3
geway Dr CLV/TH FY5	149	K3
GHL L31	359	F6
geways RAW/HAS BB4	295	J1
Ridgeway FTWD FY7	96	D8
LSN BB9	198	B4
gmont Dr HOR/BR BL6	339	H8
gwood Av BPOOLE FY3	5	E2
ng Barn St ACC BB5	247	K5
ing CI BWCK/EAR BB18	145	C1
ing Head La RAMS BL0	320	B3
ing La ORM L39	346	A7
Ridings CHLYE PR6	287	C5
HTN/BK PR9	278	C8
DHM/BLYW BB12	10	A1
ng St BLY BB11	10	B4
RES PR1	7	D1
THP PR8	301	H5
ey La BRSC L40	333	H1
EY/BBR PR5	283	K8
'ey Rd FUL/RIB PR2	238	E1
ey St BPOOLE FY3	5	D2
ield BOL BL1	341	F8
sling Dr NWD/KWIPK L33	366	B6
e St RAW/HAS BB4	295	H1
by CI KIRK/FR/WA PR4	235	C5
by Rd BPOOL FY1	4	B4
GHL L31	358	D8
bys House		
HLY/EC (off The Common) PR7	336	E5
by St COL BB8	171	G7
LSN BB9	198	B3
RES PR1	240	A2
by Wk		
HLY/EC (off High St) PR7	311	C3
g La HGHB LA2	56	E3
g St NLSN BB9	198	C3
y Av LSTA FY8	231	F7
y Green Switch Rd		
EY/BBR PR5	265	J4
y St ACC BB5	248	B7
CUP OL13	275	J6
LY* BB11	11	E5
WCK/EAR BB18	146	B1
ington Av ACC BB5	248	A8
RFD/BLYE BB10	226	B6
OL BB8	171	G7
ington La BBNW BB2	268	C1
ington La CLI BB7	141	J4
ington PI LSTA FY8	231	H5
LSN BB9	199	F2
mer Gn STHP PR8	328	B3
mer's Av FMBY L37	343	J5
THP PR8	301	H5
g Dyke Wy LSTA FY8	232	C7
gley Gv BOL BL1	341	J6
g Lows La WHIT OL12	323	K7
g O'Bells La BRSC L40	350	D4
gs Nook		
AW/HAS (off Burnley Rd) BB4	273	H1
gs St RAW/HAS BB4	273	H1
gstones La HGHB LA2	50	C4
gstones Crs NLSN BB9	199	F3
gtail Ct BRSC L40	330	B8
gtail St BRSC L40	330	B8
gtail Rd BRSC L40	330	B8
gton Av PLF/KEOS FY6	149	H5
gton La PLF/KEOS PR7	310	E1
LV/TH FY5	122	E7
g PRES PR1	7	E2

Ringwood Av RAMS BL0	319	G7
Ringwood CI ACC BB5	248	B2
LSTA FY8	232	A8
Ringwood Rd PRES PR1	240	A1
Ripley Ct		
LANC (off Princess Av) LA1	3	D5
Ripley Dr LSTA FY8	231	H5
Ripon Av LANC LA1	43	F7
Ripon CI CLV/TH FY5	122	E6
GAR/LONG PR3	153	G6
STHP PR8	302	B8
Ripon Hall Av RAMS BL0	319	H7
Ripon PI HEY LA3	52	C5
Ripon Rd ACC BB5	247	G6
BPOOL FY1	5	D3
LSTA FY8	231	K6
Ripon St BBN BB1	9	F5
NLSN BB9	198	B4
PRES PR1	239	G1
Ripon Ter PRES PR1	240	D2
Risedale Dr GAR/LONG PR3	188	B4
Risedale Gv BBNW BB2	267	H3
The Rise CARN LA5	33	H5
Rishton Rd ACC BB5	221	J8
BBN BB1	220	A6
Rishton St BPOOL FY1	4	B3
Rising Bridge Rd RAW/HAS BB4	272	A4
Ritherham Av CLV/TH FY5	122	D8
River CI FMBY L37	356	B2
River Dr PDHM/BLYW BB12	224	A3
River Hts LEY/BBR PR5	263	F3
River Lea Gdns CLI BB7	165	K2
Rivermead Ct GAR/LONG PR3	129	J2
Rivermead Dr GAR/LONG PR3	129	J3
Rivermeade STHP PR8	301	K7
River Pde PRES PR1	6	B4
River Rd CLV/TH FY5	150	A1
Riversdale CI NWD/KWIPK L33	366	C7
Riversedge Rd LEY/BBR PR5	284	E3
The Rivers Edge WHIT OL12	323	G3
Riversgate PRES PR1	97	F7
Riverside		
CARN (off Warton Rd) LA5	25	K8
HTWN L38	355	K7
LEY/BBR PR5	263	H4
Riverside Av LEY/BBR PR5	262	B7
Riverside Chalet Pk		
PLF/KEOS		
(off Occupation La) FY6	151	F7
Riverside CI HGHB LA2	44	A5
LEY/BBR PR5	262	B7
LEY/BBR PR5	307	G1
Riverside Cottages		
CHLYE (off Copthurst La) PR6	287	J3
Riverside Crs LEY/BBR PR5	307	G1
Riverside Dr PLF/KEOS FY6	150	D1
RAMS BL0	319	H8
Riverside Rd PRES PR1	6	C5
Riversleigh Av BPOOL FY1	176	C2
LSTA FY8	232	A8
Riversleigh CI BOL BL1	340	D8
Rivers St WCGNW/BIL/O WN5	365	G5
River St BBN BB1	9	D5
BCUP OL13	298	D2
COL BB8	171	H7
COL BB8	172	C8
DWN BB3	291	H1
LANC LA1	2	C2
PRES PR1	6	C3
RAMS BL0	319	J5
Rivers View Fold HGHB LA2	81	J4
Riversway BPOOLE FY3	5	F1
FUL/RIB PR2	238	B3
PLF/KEOS FY6	150	A6
Riversway Dr DWN BB3	268	C5
River Vw KIRK/FR/WA PR4	282	A3
River Wy NLSN BB9	170	B7
Riverway CI LEY/BBR PR5	263	F3
Rivington Av BISP FY2	148	C6
CHLYE PR6	337	G4
Rivington CI KIRK/FR/WA PR4	281	K3
PLF/KEOS FY6	149	K8
STHP PR8	301	G8
Rivington Dr BRSC L40	330	E8
SKEL WN8	364	E4
Rivington La CHLYE PR6	337	K4
HOR/BR BL6	338	B2
Rivington PI CHLY/EC PR7	335	H5
Rivington Rd CHLYE PR6	311	J2
EDGW/EG BL7	314	F7
HOR/BR BL6	314	B7
Rivington St BBN BB1	9	F5
Roach Rd LEY/BBR PR5	241	H5
Road La WHIT OL12	323	H7
Roberts St CHLY/EC PR7	311	G4
NLSN BB9	198	D3
RAW/HAS BB4	273	H8

Robert St ACC BB5	247	H8
ACC BB5	248	C4
BBNW BB2	8	C6
BWCK/EAR BB18	145	F1
COL BB8	171	J6
DWN BB3	291	H2
GTH/LHO* BB6	221	H6
LANC* LA1	3	D4
RAMS BL0	319	J2
RAW/HAS BB4	297	H1
Robin Bank Rd DWN BB3	291	J1
Robin CI CHLY/EC PR7	310	B8
Robin Hey LEY/BBR PR5	284	D2
Robin Hill Dr WGNNW/ST WN6	353	K1
Robin Hill La WGNNW/ST WN6	335	G8
Robin Hood La WGNNW/ST WN6	333	K8
Robin House La BRFD/BLYE BB10	199	G7
Robin La CLI BB7	142	E2
SKEL WN8	332	E6
Robin Rd RAMS BL0	319	H8
Robins CI PLF/KEOS FY6	149	G7
Robins La BISP FY2	149	F5
PLF/KEOS FY6	149	G7
RNFD/HAY WA11	370	B3
Robinson La PDHM/BLYW BB12	197	J7
Robinson St BBN BB1	9	E2
BRFD/BLYE BB10	225	J2
CLI BB7	140	E6
COL BB8	171	H2
FUL/RIB PR2	213	F8
HOR/BR BL6	338	D7
Robin St PRES PR1	240	B2
Robraine KKBYL LA6	21	H2
Robson St NLSN* BB9	197	K5
Robson Wy BPOOLE FY3	177	G1
Roby MI SKEL WN8	352	D8
Roby Well Wy WGNW/BIL/O WN5	371	F6
Rochdale Rd BCUP OL13	298	E2
RAMS BL0	320	D3
RAMS BL0	320	C2
Rochester Av CLV/TH FY5	123	F7
MCMB LA4	41	J8
Rochester CI BCUP OL13	275	K4
Rochester Dr BRFD/BLYE BB10	198	A8
Rochford Av CLV/TH FY5	148	E2
Rock Bridge Fold RAW/HAS BB4	274	B6
Rock Brow GAR/LONG PR3	161	H4
Rockburgh Crs KIRK/FR/WA PR4	260	B6
Rockcliffe Av BCUP OL13	298	C2
Rockcliffe CI BCUP OL13	298	C2
Rockcliffe Rd BCUP OL13	298	D2
Rockcliffe St BBNW BB2	268	B1
Rockfield St BBNW BB2	268	B1
Rock Fold		
EDGW/EG (off Cox Green Rd) BL7	341	K2
Rock Hall Rd RAW/HAS BB4	272	C8
Rockhaven Av HOR/BR BL6	338	E7
Rockingham Ct		
NWD/KWIPK * L33	366	D7
Rockingham Rd BISP FY2	148	D7
Rock La BLY BB11	11	E6
DWN BB3	267	H8
Rockliffe La BCUP OL13	298	E2
Rockliffe St RAW/HAS BB4	273	H6
Rock St ACC BB5	271	K1
CLI BB7	165	J3
CLV/TH FY5	123	H7
HOR/BR BL6	338	D2
RAMS BL0	320	A4
RAW/HAS BB4	272	C4
Rock Ter CARN LA5	15	G1
CLI (off Whalley Old Rd) BB7	220	E1
EDGW/EG BL7	341	K2
RAW/HAS BB4	273	H4
Rock Villa Rd CHLYE * PR6	287	G3
Rockville Av CLV/TH FY5	148	E3
Rockwood CI BRFD/BLYE BB10	198	C8
Roddlesworth La CHLYE PR6	290	A3
Rodhill La CLI BB7	114	B6
Rodmell CI EDGW/EG BL7	341	K4
Rodney Av LSTA FY8	230	E2
Rodney St BBNW BB2	8	A6
PRES PR1	7	D2
Rodwell Wk BPOOLE FY3	177	F3
Roe Br GAR/LONG PR3	155	G5
Roebuck CI BBNW BB2	8	B6
Roebuck St FUL/RIB PR2	238	C1
Roeburndale Crs HEY LA3	52	E3
Roeburndale Rd HGHB LA2	46	A8
Roeburn Dr LANC LA1	54	B1
Roeburn PI LANC * LA1	2	C1
Roedean Av MCMB LA4	42	B7
Roe Greave Rd ACC BB5	247	H8
Roehampton CI CLV/TH FY5	149	G2
Roe Hey Dr CHLY/EC PR7	335	K1
Roe La CHTN/BK PR9	302	A3
Roe Lee Pk BBN BB1	245	H1

Roe Park Ms *CHTN/BK* PR9 ....**301** K3
Rogerley Rd *LSTA* FY8 ....**232** C2
Rogersfield *GTH/LHO* BB6 ....**219** K3
Rolleston Rd *BBNW* BB2 ....**244** D7
Roman Crs *HGHB* LA2 ....**45** G6
Roman Rd *BBNW* BB2 ....**268** G2
  DWN BB3 ....**292** D7
  PRES PR1 ....**7** F3
Roman Wy *CLI* BB7 ....**165** K3
  CLV/TH FY5 ....**149** F2
  FUL/RIB PR4 ....**215** G5
  KIRK/FR/WA PR4 ....**209** G7
Rome Av *BLY* BB11 ....**224** E7
Romford Rd *PRES* PR1 ....**240** A1
Romford St *PDHM/BLYW* BB12 ....**224** E4
Romiley Dr *SKEL* WN8 ....**363** F1
Romney Av *BLY* BB11 ....**10** B6
  BPOOLS FY4 ....**4** C5
  FTWD FY7 ....**96** E8
  NLSN BB9 ....**170** B8
Romney St *NLSN* BB9 ....**198** B4
Romsey Av *FMBY* L37 ....**356** B1
Ronald St *BBN* BB1 ....**246** A6
  PDHM/BLYW BB12 ....**224** C6
Ronaldsway *PRES* PR1 ....**214** B8
Ronaldsway Cl *SKEL* WN8 ....**298** E2
Ronbury Cl *NLSN* * BB9 ....**198** A2
Roney St *BBNW* BB2 ....**8** A4
Ronwood *KIRK/FR/WA* PR4 ....**180** D2
Rookery Av *WGNNW/ST* WN6 ....**353** G3
Rookery Cl *CHLY/EC* PR7 ....**310** C5
  PRES PR1 ....**262** B1
Rookery Dr *PRES* PR1 ....**262** C1
  RNFD/HAY WA11 ....**369** G6
Rookery La *RNFD/HAY* WA11 ....**369** G6
Rookery Nook Vls
  BCUP (off Burnley Rd) OL13 ....**275** J7
Rookery Rd *BWCK/EAR* BB18 ....**145** G1
  CHTN/BK PR9 ....**302** E3
Rook Hill Rd *BCUP* OL13 ....**297** K3
Rook St *BWCK/EAR* BB18 ....**145** G1
  COL BB8 ....**171** H6
  NLSN BB9 ....**198** B2
  PRES PR1 ....**239** K1
  RAMS BL0 ....**319** J5
Rookwood *CHLY/EC* PR7 ....**308** D5
Rookwood Av *CHLY/EC* PR7 ....**311** C5
  CLV/TH FY5 ....**148** D3
Rooley Moor Rd *BCUP* OL13 ....**297** G5
  WHIT OL12 ....**297** K7
Rooley Vw *BCUP* OL13 ....**298** C2
Roosevelt Av *LANC* LA1 ....**2** B4
Root Hill Cottages
  CLI (off Whitewell Rd) BB7 ....**110** B3
Roots La *KIRK/FR/WA* PR4 ....**182** E8
Ropefield Wy *WHIT* OL12 ....**323** J8
Rope Wk *GAR/LONG* PR3 ....**129** J4
Rosary Av *BPOOLS* FY4 ....**5** E6
Roscoe Lowe Brow *CHLYE* PR6 ....**337** K4
Roseacre *BPOOLS* FY4 ....**204** C6
Roseacre Br *KIRK/FR/WA* PR4 ....**180** D2
Rose Acre La *CARN* LA5 ....**26** B1
Roseacre Pl *FUL/RIB* PR2 ....**238** A2
  LSTA FY8 ....**231** H3
Roseacre Rd *KIRK/FR/WA* PR4 ....**181** F4
  KIRK/FR/WA PR4 ....**181** J7
Rose Av *BLY* BB11 ....**10** B5
  BPOOL FY1 ....**5** D5
  FUL/RIB PR2 ....**212** E8
Rosebank *FUL/RIB* PR2 ....**237** J2
Rose Bank *RAW/HAS* BB4 ....**273** H8
Rosebank Av *BPOOLS* FY4 ....**204** C6
Rose Bank St *BCUP* OL13 ....**275** J8
Rosebay Av *BBNW* BB2 ....**266** E3
Rosebay St *FMBY* L37 ....**344** A8
Roseberry Av *KIRK/FR/WA* PR4 ....**212** A6
Roseberry Cl *RAMS* BL0 ....**319** J8
Roseberry Rd *TOD* OL14 ....**277** G2
Rosebery Av *BPOOLS* FY4 ....**204** B5
  LANC LA1 ....**3** E6
  LSTA FY8 ....**231** H7
  MCMB LA4 ....**41** J7
Rosebery St *BRFD/BLYE* BB10 ....**225** K1
  CHTN/BK PR9 ....**302** C5
Rose Cl *LEY/BBR* PR5 ....**286** C1
Rose Ct
  FTWD (off Lowther Rd) FY7 ....**123** F1
Rose Crs *SKEL* WN8 ....**362** F1
  STHP PR8 ....**344** C1
Rosecroft Cl *ORM* L39 ....**348** C5
Rosedale Av *BOL* BL1 ....**341** J6
  BPOOLE FY3 ....**205** C4
  HEY LA3 ....**52** E3
Rosedene
  HGHB (off Lancaster Rd) LA2 ....**43** F4
Rosedene Cl *KIRK/FR/WA* PR4 ....**212** A6

Rose Dr *RNFD/HAY* WA11 ....**369** G6
Rose Fold *PRES* PR1 ....**6** B6
Rose Gdns *KIRK/FR/WA* PR4 ....**258** D5
Rosegarth *HGHB* LA2 ....**43** F4
Rose Gv *HGHB* LA2 ....**67** F7
Rosegrove La *PDHM/BLYW* BB12 ....**224** D6
Rose Hill Av *BBN* BB1 ....**9** E5
Rosehill Av *BLY* BB11 ....**10** B5
  NLSN * BB9 ....**198** D3
Rosehill Dr *ORM* L39 ....**360** A1
Rosehill Mt *BLY* BB11 ....**10** B5
Rose Hill Rd *BBNW* BB2 ....**266** D2
Rosehill Rd *BLY* BB11 ....**10** C6
  COL BB8 ....**198** E1
Rose Hill St *BCUP* OL13 ....**298** D1
  DWN BB3 ....**291** K3
  RAW/HAS BB4 ....**273** H2
Roseland Av *NLSN* BB9 ....**198** A5
Roseland Cl *MGHL* L31 ....**358** D7
Rose La *PRES* PR1 ....**214** A8
Rose Lea *FUL/RIB* PR2 ....**214** B5
Roselea Dr *CHTN/BK* PR9 ....**278** E7
Roselyn Av *BPOOLS* FY4 ....**204** C6
Rosemary Av *BPOOLS* FY4 ....**204** C6
  CLV/TH FY5 ....**123** F8
Rosemary Ct *PRES* PR1 ....**261** K1
Rosemary La *FMBY* L37 ....**343** J8
  KIRK/FR/WA PR4 ....**211** C1
  LANC LA1 ....**3** D3
  ORM L39 ....**346** C6
Rosemeade Av *LEY/BBR* PR5 ....**262** E3
Rosemede Av *BPOOLE* FY3 ....**5** F5
Rosemount *BCUP* OL13 ....**275** K7
Rosemount Av *BLY* BB11 ....**98** C5
  PLF/KEOS FY6 ....**149** J8
Rosendale Cl *BCUP* OL13 ....**276** A8
Rosendale Crs *BCUP* OL13 ....**275** K8
Rose PI *ORM* L39 ....**360** B1
  RNFD/HAY WA11 ....**369** G6
Rose St *ACC* BB5 ....**248** B7
  BCUP OL13 ....**298** C1
  DWN BB3 ....**291** K2
  LEY/BBR PR5 ....**262** E8
  MCMB LA4 ....**41** H5
  PRES PR1 ....**7** E3
  RAW/HAS BB4 ....**297** C1
Rose Ter *FUL/RIB* PR2 ....**238** C2
Rose Vale St *RAW/HAS* BB4 ....**296** D1
Roseway *BPOOLS* FY4 ....**204** C6
  FUL/RIB PR2 ....**238** C2
  LSTA FY8 ....**231** H6
  NLSN BB9 ....**197** J4
  PLF/KEOS FY6 ....**149** J8
Rosewood *KIRK/FR/WA* PR4 ....**212** A6
Rosewood Av *BBN* BB1 ....**245** G2
  BLY BB11 ....**10** B6
  LEY/BBR PR5 ....**241** C8
  RAW/HAS BB4 ....**272** D8
Rosewood Cl *CLV/TH* FY5 ....**149** K2
  LSTA FY8 ....**232** A7
Rosewood Dr *LEY/BBR* PR5 ....**241** F8
Roshaw *FUL/RIB* PR2 ....**215** G2
Rosklyn Rd *CHLYE* PR6 ....**311** J4
Rosley St *COL* BB8 ....**172** B6
Rossall Cl *FTWD* FY7 ....**122** D3
  LEY/BBR PR5 ....**241** J7
  PDHM/BLYW BB12 ....**223** K5
Rossall Ct
  CLV/TH
  (off Promenade North) FY5 ....**122** C6
  FTWD (off Highbury Av) FY7 ....**96** E8
Rossall Dr *FUL/RIB* PR2 ....**212** E7
Rossall Gdns *CLV/TH* FY5 ....**122** D7
Rossall Ga *FTWD* FY7 ....**122** C3
Rossall Grange La *FTWD* FY7 ....**96** D8
Rossall La *FTWD* FY7 ....**122** E4
Rossall Rd *BPOOLE* FY3 ....**176** D4
  CHLYE PR6 ....**311** J2
  CLV/TH FY5 ....**122** D7
  FUL/RIB PR2 ....**212** E7
  LANC LA1 ....**2** A1
  LSTA FY8 ....**231** K7
Rossall St *FUL/RIB* PR2 ....**6** A1
Rossall Ter *BBNW* BB2 ....**268** D8
Ross *CI WGNW/BIL/O* WN5 ....**371** C6
Rossendale Av *BLY* BB11 ....**251** F1
  MCMB LA4 ....**41** J5
Rossendale Av North *CLV/TH* FY5 ....**149** H1
Rossendale Av South *CLV/TH* FY5 ....**149** H2
Rossendale Rd *BLY* BB11 ....**10** A6
  LSTA FY8 ....**231** G4
Rossendale Wy *BCUP* OL13 ....**276** A3
  RAW/HAS BB4 ....**294** C6
  RAW/HAS BB4 ....**296** E4
  TOT/BURYW BL8 ....**294** D7
  WHIT OL12 ....**322** D3

Rosser Ct *NLSN* BB9 ....**19**
Rossett Av *BPOOLS* FY4 ....**20**
Rossetti Av *BLY* BB11 ....**25**
Rossington Av *BISP* FY2 ....**148**
Rossini St *BOL* BL1 ....**34**
Rosslyn Av *PLF/KEOS* FY6 ....**9**
Rosslyn Crs *PLF/KEOS* FY6 ....**9**
Rosslyn Crs East *PLF/KEOS* FY6 ....**9**
Rossmoyne Rd *LANC* LA1 ....**5**
Ross St *DWN* BB3 ....**29**
  NLSN * BB9 ....**19**
Rostle Top Rd *BWCK/EAR* BB18 ....**14**
Rostrevor Cl *LEY/BBR* PR5 ....**28**
Rostron Crs *FMBY* L37 ....**35**
Rostron Rd *RAMS* BL0 ....**31**
Rothay Av *FTWD* FY7 ....**12**
Rothbury Pl *LSTA* FY8 ....**23**
Rotherwick Av *CHLY/EC* PR7 ....**31**
Rothesay Crs *HEY* LA3 ....**5**
Rothesay Rd *BBN* BB1 ....**26**
  HEY LA3 ....**5**
  NLSN BB9 ....**19**
Rothley Av *STHP* PR8 ....**32**
Rothwell Av *ACC* BB5 ....**24**
Rothwell Cl *ORM* L39 ....**34**
Rothwell Ct *LEY/BBR* PR5 ....**28**
Rothwell Crs *FUL/RIB* PR2 ....**21**
Rothwell Dr *FTWD* FY7 ....**9**
  ORM L39 ....**35**
  STHP PR8 ....**32**
Rothwell Rd *CHLYE* PR6 ....**33**
Rothwell St *RAMS* BL0 ....**31**
Rotten Rw *HGHB* LA2 ....**4**
  STHP PR8 ....**30**
Rough Hey Hy *FUL/RIB* PR2 ....**21**
Rough Hey Rd *FUL/RIB* PR2 ....**21**
Rough Heys La *BPOOLS* FY4 ....**20**
Rough Lea Rd *CLV/TH* FY5 ....**14**
Roughlee Gv *BRFD/BLYE* BB10 ....**22**
Rough Lee Rd *ACC* BB5 ....**24**
Roughlee St *NLSN* BB9 ....**19**
Roughwood Dr *NWD/KWIPK* L33 ....**36**
Round Acre *BBNW* BB2 ....**24**
  LEY/BBR PR5 ....**26**
Round Barn
  EDGW/EG (off Blackburn Rd) BL7 ....**29**
Roundell Rd *BWCK/EAR* BB18 ....**11**
Roundel St *BRFD/BLYE* * BB10 ....**22**
Roundhay *BPOOLS* FY4 ....**20**
Roundhill La *RAW/HAS* BB4 ....**27**
Round Hill Pl *BRFD/BLYE* * BB10 ....**25**
Roundhill Rd *ACC* BB5 ....**27**
Roundhill Vw *ACC* BB5 ....**27**
Round Meadow *LEY/BBR* PR5 ....**28**
Roundway *FTWD* FY7 ....**12**
Roundway Down *FUL/RIB* PR2 ....**21**
The Roundway *HTWN* L38 ....**35**
Roundwood Av *BRFD/BLYE* BB10 ....**19**
Rowan Av *ACC* BB5 ....**27**
  FUL/RIB PR2 ....**21**
Rowan Bank *HGHB* LA2 ....**4**
Rowan Cl *BBN* BB1 ....**24**
  BRSC L40 ....**33**
  GAR/LONG PR3 ....**12**
  PRES PR1 ....**23**
  WHIT OL12 ....**32**
Rowan Cft *CHLYE* PR6 ....**28**
Rowan Dr *KKBY* L32 ....**36**
Rowangate *FUL/RIB* PR2 ....**21**
Rowan Gv *BRFD/BLYE* BB10 ....**1**
  CHLYE PR6 ....**28**
Rowan La *SKEL* WN8 ....**35**
The Rowans *ORM* L39 ....**35**
  PLF/KEOS FY6 ....**17**
Rowan Tree Cl *ACC* * BB5 ....**24**
Rowberrow Cl *FUL/RIB* PR2 ....**21**
Rowen Pk *BBNW* BB2 ....**24**
Rowland Av *NLSN* BB9 ....**19**
Rowland Cl *CLV/TH* FY5 ....**14**
Rowland La *CLV/TH* FY5 ....**14**
Rowland St *ACC* * BB5 ....**24**
Rowley La *BRFD/BLYE* BB10 ....**22**
Rowntree Av *FTWD* FY7 ....**9**
Roworth Cl *LEY/BBR* PR5 ....**28**
Rowsley Rd *LSTA* FY8 ....**23**
The Row *CARN* LA5 ....**1**
Rowton Heath *FUL/RIB* PR2 ....**21**
Roxburgh Rd *BPOOLS* FY4 ....**20**
Royal Av *BPOOLE* FY3 ....**21**
  FUL/RIB PR2 ....**21**
  KIRK/FR/WA PR4 ....**20**
  LEY/BBR PR5 ....**28**
Royal Bank Rd *BPOOLE* FY3 ....**21**
Royal Cl *FMBY* L37 ....**35**
Royal Crs *FMBY* L37 ....**35**
Royal Fold *HEY* LA3 ....**5**

al Oak Av *BBN* BB1 ....245 G2
al Oak Meadow *HGHB* LA2...........37 C5
al Pl *LSTA* FY8 ....231 J3
al Rd *MCMB* LA4 ....41 J5
al Ter *STHP* * PR8..........................301 C4
al Troon Ct *KIRK/FR/WA* * PR4....208 E7
alty Av *KIRK/FR/WA* PR4...............261 H3
alty Gdns *KIRK/FR/WA* PR4...........261 H3
alty La *KIRK/FR/WA* PR4................261 H3
rden Crs *WGNW/BIL/O* WN5 ....371 C6
den Rd *WGNW/BIL/O* WN5 ....371 C6
rds Av *ACC* BB5 ....248 C7
EY LA3 ....52 D1
ds Gv *HEY* LA3 ....52 D2
ds Rd *BCUP* OL13 ....297 J4
ds St *ACC* BB5 ....248 C7
STA* FY8 ....230 E6
len Av *PLF/KEOS* FY6...................149 H6
le Rd *CHLY/EC* PR7 ....311 F3
DHM/BLYW* BB12 ....10 C2
rles Ct *CLV/TH* FY5 ....149 H1
rle St *BPOOL* * FY1 ....4 B6
nton Rd *HOR/BR* BL6 ....338 D5
rshaw Av *BBN* BB1 ....8 C1
rshaw Cl *BBN* BB1 ....8 C1
rston Rd *PLF/KEOS* FY6 ....150 B6
rton Dr *CHLYE* PR6 ....287 C6
by St *BBN* * BB1 ....245 H1
AMS BL0 ....319 J8
ddington Rd *STHP* PR8...................327 C1
lyard Dr *DWN* BB3 ....292 A3
lyard Pl *BPOOLE* * FY3..................177 F4
STA* FY8 ....230 E3
f La *ORM* L39 ....348 E7
ford Av *MGHL* L31 ....359 G8
ford Dr *CHTN/BK* PR9 ....279 H6
ford Park La *BRSC* L40 ....306 A6
ford Rd *BRSC* L40 ....332 B2
HTN/BK* PR9 ....278 E8
STA* FY8 ....231 J6
us St *PRES* PR1 ....240 A1
jby Av *ACC* BB5 ....248 C4
jby Dr *WGNW/BIL/O* WN5 ....365 H3
jby St *BPOOLS* FY4 ....5 D6
mley Rd *BLY* BB11 ....11 D5
mley's Fold *BLY* BB11 ....251 C1
acorn Av *BISP* FY2 ....177 F1
ndle Rd *FUL/RIB* PR2......................213 F8
anell Vis
POOLS (off Chapel Rd) FY4 ....205 G4
e Runnel *ORM* L39 ....346 D1
nymede Av *CLV/TH* FY5 ....148 D1
nshaw Av *WGNNW/ST* WN6 ....353 C3
nshaw La *CHLY/EC* PR7 ....285 J7
nshaw Hall La *CHLY/EC* PR7.........285 J7
nshaw La *CHLY/EC* PR7 ....309 F1
pert St *CARN* LA5 ....25 K8
*LSN BB9 ....198 A4
shbed Dr *RAW/HAS* BB4 ....273 H5
shes Farm La *ACC* BB5 ....247 C8
shey Cl *RAW/HAS* BB4 ....273 H5
shey Fld *EDGW/EG* BL7 ....341 K3
shford Gv *BOL* BL1 ....341 K7
shley Dr *HCHB* LA2 ....42 D2
shley Wy *HGHB* LA2 ....42 D2
shton Av *BWCK/EAR* BB18 ....146 B2
shton Cl *NLSN* BB9 ....199 F1
shton St *BCUP* OL13 ....298 C3
TH/LHO* BB6......................................221 F7
*LSN BB9 ....170 B8
shworth St East
RFD/BLYE* BB10 ....225 K2
shworth St West
RFD/BLYE* * BB10 ....225 K2
shy Fld *ACC* BB5 ....221 K6
shy Hey *LEY/BBR* PR5.....................262 D3
skin Av *ACC* BB5 ....247 C6
POOL FY1 ....4 B6
LV/TH FY5 ....123 C8
OL BB8 ....171 H5
LEY/BBR PR5 ....285 J1
skin Cl *DHM/BLYW* BB12 ....224 A4
skin Dr *KIRK/FR/WA* PR4 ....281 K5
skin Dr *KKBYL* LA6 ....21 H1
MCMB LA4 ....41 K5
skin Gv *BLY* BB11 ....223 J7
CARN LA5 ....33 C6
ANC* LA1 ....43 F8
skin Rd *KIRK/FR/WA* PR4 ....235 F5
RES PR1 ....7 F4
sland Av *BPOOLS* FY4 ....205 K2
sland Dr *LEY/BBR* PR5 ....241 J7
slands Gdns *MCMB* LA4 ....41 H7
ssell Av *CHTN/BK* PR9 ....302 C4
LV/TH FY5 ....148 D3

LEY/BBR* PR5 ....286 A3
PRES PR1 ....240 E3
Russell Ct *BLY* BB11 ....11 E5
Russell Dr *MCMB* LA4 ....42 C7
Russell Pl *GTH/LHO* BB6 ....221 F6
Russell Rd *CARN* LA5 ....34 A2
CHTN/BK PR9 ....302 C4
Russell Sq *CHLYE* PR6 ....311 H2
Russell Sq West *CHLYE* PR6 ....311 H2
Russell St *ACC* BB5 ....248 C6
BBNW BB2 ....8 C1
LANC LA1 ....3 D3
NLSN BB9 ....198 D3
Russell Ter *PDHM/BLYW* BB12 ......223 K4
Russel St *BCUP* OL13 ....275 J7
Russia St *ACC* BB5 ....247 K5
Rutherford Pl *BPOOLS* FY4............204 D2
Ruthin Cl *BBN* BB1 ....8 C2
Ruth St *WHIT* OL12 ....323 H2
Rutland Av *BBN* BB1 ....246 C7
CLV/TH FY5 ....122 E8
FTWD FY7 ....96 E8
KIRK/FR/WA PR4 ....235 G2
LANC LA1 ....3 E6
LEY/BBR* PR5 ....240 B8
PDHM/BLYW BB12 ....224 C5
PLF/KEOS FY6 ....149 J8
Rutland Cl *ACC* * BB5 ....221 K8
GAR/LONG PR3...................................129 H3
Rutland Ct *LSTA* FY8.......................231 K6
Rutland Crs *ORM* L39 ....348 B4
Rutland Pl *PDHM/BLYW* BB12 ....223 H4
Rutland Rd *LSTA* FY8 ....231 K6
STHP PR8 ....301 K6
Rutland St *ACC* BB5 ....247 K6
BBNW BB2 ....244 D8
COL BB8 ....171 K6
NLSN BB9 ....198 C2
PRES PR1 ....240 A3
Ryburn Av *BBNW* BB2 ....244 D5
BPOOLS FY4 ....5 E6
Ryburn Rd *ORM* L39 ....348 B7
Rycliffe St *PDHM/BLYW* BB12 ....223 J2
Rydal Av *BPOOL* FY1 ....4 C1
CLV/TH FY5 ....149 H2
DWN BB3 ....291 H2
FMBY L37 ....355 H1
FTWD FY7 ....96 E7
KIRK/FR/WA PR4 ....234 E5
LEY/BBR PR5 ....263 G2
PLF/KEOS FY6 ....149 K8
PRES PR1 ....238 C3
WGNW/BIL/O WN5 ....365 H4
Rydal Cl *ACC* BB5 ....248 C5
BRFD/BLYE BB10 ....198 A7
FUL/RIB PR2.......................................214 A7
HOR/BR BL6 ....337 J8
NWD/KWIPK L33 ....366 B7
PDHM/BLYW BB12 ....223 J2
Rydal Gv *HEY* LA3 ....52 D1
PLF/KEOS FY6 ....98 B5
Rydal Mt *BBN* BB1 ....269 J5
Rydal Pl *CHLY/EC* PR7 ....311 C5
COL BB8 ....172 A6
Rydal Rd *BBN* BB1 ....9 E2
CARN LA5 ....33 F7
HEY LA3 ....52 D1
LANC LA1 ....3 E3
LSTA FY8 ....230 E3
PLF/KEOS FY6 ....150 E1
PRES PR1 ....240 B1
RAW/HAS BB4 ....295 J3
Rydal St *BRFD/BLYE* BB10.............225 J1
Ryddingwood *PRES* PR1 ....238 D5
Ryde Cl *RAW/HAS* BB4 ....295 J2
Ryden Av *CLV/TH* FY5 ....122 D8
LEY/BBR PR5 ....286 A2
Ryden Rd *BBN* BB1 ....219 F5
Ryder Cl *ORM* L39 ....360 A3
Ryder Crs *ORM* L39 ....360 A2
STHP PR8 ....326 A3
The Rydinge *FMBY* L37 ....344 A5
Ryding's La *CHTN/BK* PR9..............280 B2
The Rydings *GTH/LHO* BB6 ....219 H3
Ryecroft Av *PLF/KEOS* FY6 ....150 E2
Ryecroft La *EDGW/EG* BL7 ....314 E6
Ryefield Cl *CHLYE* PR6 ....288 A3
Ryefield Av *PRES* PR1....................262 A1
RAW/HAS BB4 ....295 H1
Ryefield Av West *RAW/HAS* BB4 ...295 G1
Ryefield Ct
RAW/HAS
(off Ryefield Av West) BB4 ....295 G1
Ryefield Pl *RAW/HAS* BB4.............295 H1
Rye Gdns *BBNW* BB2 ....268 A3
Ryeheys Rd *LSTA* FY8....................230 D3
Ryelands Crs *FUL/RIB* PR2 ....238 A3

Ryelands Rd *LANC* LA1.....................2 B1
Rye Moss La *FMBY* L37 ....357 C3
Rye St *PRES* PR1 ....7 E1
Ryknild Wy *HEY* LA3........................42 B8
Ryland Av *PLF/KEOS* FY6..............149 J8
Rylands Rd *CHLY/EC* PR7 ....311 F4
Rylands St *BRFD/BLYE* BB10.........225 K2
Ryldon Pl *BPOOLS* FY4..................205 C1
Rylstone Dr *BWCK/EAR* BB18 ....144 E1
HEY LA3 ....52 D3
Rymers Gn *FMBY* L37 ....343 J7
Ryson Av *BPOOLS* FY4 ....5 F6

S

Sabden Pl *LSTA* FY8 ....231 J4
Sabden Rd *CLI* BB7 ....193 K7
PDHM/BLYW BB12 ....195 H5
PDHM/BLYW BB12 ....196 B5
Saccary La *BBN* BB1........................218 C7
Sackville St *BLY* BB11 ....10 C4
BPOOLS FY4 ....204 C4
BWCK/EAR BB18 ....144 E2
CHLYE PR6 ....311 J4
NLSN BB9 ....197 K6
NLSN BB9 ....198 D5
Saddleback Crs *WGNW/BIL/O* WN5...365 K4
Saddleback Rd *WGNW/BIL/O* WN5 ...365 K4
Saddler Nook La *KKBYL* LA6 ....20 D4
Sadler St *ACC* * BB5 ....247 J6
Saer Cl *FTWD* FY7 ....96 D8
Saffron Cl *NLSN* BB9 ....198 A2
Sagar Dr *KIRK/FR/WA* PR4 ....234 E5
Sagar Fold *ORM* L39 ....360 B3
Sagar Holme Ter *RAW/HAS* BB4....274 B6
Sagar La *TOD* OL14 ....277 J1
Sagar St *CHLY/EC* PR7 ....308 E5
NLSN BB9 ....198 C3
Sage Ct *PRES* PR1 ....261 K1
Sage La *PRES* PR1 ....213 K8
Sahara Fold *BBN* BB1 ....9 E2
St Aidan's Av *BBNW* BB2................267 K2
DWN BB3 ....291 K3
St Aidan's Cl *BBNW* BB2 ....267 K2
WGNW/BIL/O WN5 ....371 C5
St Aidans Pk *LEY/BBR* PR5 ....263 H1
St Albans Ct *BBN* BB1 ....9 D3
St Alban's Pl *CHLY/EC* PR7 ....311 H6
St Albans Rd *BBN* BB1...................246 E3
BPOOL FY1 ....5 D3
DWN BB3 ....268 B7
LSTA FY8 ....231 F4
MCMB LA4 ....42 B5
St Ambrose Ter *LEY/BBR* * PR5 ....285 K1
St Andrew's Av *CLV/TH* FY5 ....148 D1
FUL/RIB PR2.......................................238 C1
St Andrew's Cl *ACC* BB5.................247 H7
CHLYE PR6 ....286 B7
LEY/BBR PR5 ....285 J3
RAMS BL0 ....319 J6
St Andrews Gv *MCMB* LA4 ....41 K5
St Andrew's Pl *STHP* PR8...............301 H5
St Andrews Rd *GTH/LHO* BB6........192 D5
PRES* PR1 ....239 J1
St Andrew's Rd North *LSTA* FY8 ...230 D4
St Andrew's Rd South *LSTA* FY8 ...230 E5
St Andrew's St *BBN* BB1 ....8 B3
BRFD/BLYE* BB10 ....225 K2
St Andrew's Vw *NWD/KWIPK* L33...366 C6
St Andrews Wy *LEY/BBR* PR5 ....285 J3
St Anne's Av *MCMB* LA4 ....42 B5
St Annes Cl *ACC* * BB5 ....247 J6
BBN BB1 ....9 D6
FMBY L37 ....343 K5
HGHB LA2 ....45 J6
St Annes Ct
BPOOLS (off St Annes Rd) FY4 ....4 C6
WGNNW/ST WN6 ....353 H6
St Anne's Crs *RAW/HAS* BB4.........274 C8
St Anne's Dr *PDHM/BLYW* BB12....197 F4
WGNNW/ST WN6 ....353 J6
St Anne's Pth *FMBY* L37 ....343 K5
St Anne's Pl *LANC* * LA1 ....3 D3
St Annes Rd *BPOOLS* FY4 ....4 C6
CHLYE PR6 ....311 J4
CHTN/BK PR9 ....278 B7
FMBY L37 ....343 K5
GAR/LONG PR3...................................153 C6
HOR/BR BL6 ....338 C7
LEY/BBR PR5 ....286 A1
ORM L39 ....348 B7
St Anne's Rd East *LSTA* FY8 ....231 C3
St Anne's Rd West *LSTA* FY8..........230 E4
St Anne's St *PDHM/BLYW* BB12 ....223 J4
PRES PR1 ....239 J1

St Anne's Wy *PDHM/BLYW* BB12 ......**197** F4
St Ann's Sq *CLI* BB7 ....**165** F3
St Ann's St *BBNW* BB2 ....**8** C6
St Anthony's CI *FUL/RIB* PR2 ......**212** E7
St Anthony's Crs *FUL/RIB* PR2 ......**212** E7
St Anthony's Dr *FUL/RIB* PR2 ......**212** E7
St Anthony's PI *BPOOL* FY1 ....**176** D3
  KIRK/FR/WA PR4 ....**208** E7
St Anthony's Rd *PRES* * PR1 ....**239** J1
St Austell PI *CARN* LA5 ....**33** J3
St Austin's Dr *PRES* PR1..........................**7** E3
St Austin's Rd *PRES* PR1..........................**7** E3
St Barnabas' PI *PRES* * PR1 ....**7** E1
St Barnabas St *BBNW* BB2 ....**8** A4
  DWN * BB3....................................**291** K5
St Bede's Wy *BPOOL* FY1 ....**4** B6
St Bedes Av *ORM* L39....................**348** B8
St Bee's CI *BBNW* BB2 ....**268** C2
St Bernard Av *BPOOLE* FY3............**177** F4
St Bernard's Rd *PLF/KEOS* FY6........**98** A6
St Brides CI *HOR/BR* BL6................**338** D7
St Catherine CI *BPOOLE* FY3..........**177** H2
St Catherines CI *LEY/BBR* PR5........**286** A1
St Catherines Ct
  LANC (off Friar St) LA1 ....**3** D3
St Catherine's Dr *FUL/RIB* PR2......**212** E7
St Catherines Wy *LEY/BBR* PR5.......**263** F4
St Cecilia St *GTH/LHO* BB6............**221** H6
St Celia's Wy *MCMB* LA4 ....**42** A5
St Chad's Av *CLI* BB7 ....**140** D6
St Chads CI *PLF/KEOS* FY6............**177** K1
St Chad's Dr *LANC* LA1 ....**42** D8
St Chad's Rd *BPOOL* FY1 ....**4** B5
  PRES PR1 ....**240** A2
St Charles' Rd *BBN* * BB1 ....**246** E2
St Christines Av *LEY/BBR* PR5........**263** F7
St Christopher's Rd *PRES* * PR1......**239** J1
St Christopher's Wy *MCMB* LA4........**41** K5
St Clair Dr *CHTN/BK* PR9 ....**302** C2
St Clair Rd *TOT/BURYW* BL8..........**319** F8
St Clares Av *FUL/RIB* PR2..............**213** J5
St Clement CI *DWN* * BB3..............**268** B8
  FUL/RIB PR2................................**213** F8
  LSTA FY8....................................**232** C8
St Clement's Rd *CHTN/BK* PR9........**302** D1
  LEY/BBR PR5..............................**262** D2
  PRES * PR1 ....**239** J1
St Cuthbert CI *BRFD/BLYE* BB10 ....**225** K1
  CLV/TH FY5................................**148** D1
St David's Av *BBNW* BB2................**266** E2
  CLV/TH FY5................................**148** D3
St David's Gv *LSTA* FY8 ....**230** D3
St David's Rd *LEY/BBR* PR5............**286** A1
  PRES * PR1 ....**239** J1
St David's Rd North *LSTA* FY8........**230** D2
St David's Rd South *LSTA* FY8........**230** E5
St Edmund Hall CI *RAMS* BL0 ....**319** J7
St Edmund's Rd *BPOOLS* FY4................**5** E6
St Edmund's St *GTH/LHO* BB6........**221** H6
St Frances CI *BBN* * BB1 ....**9** D6
St Francis CI *FUL/RIB* PR2..............**213** J4
St Francis' Rd *BBNW* BB2 ....**267** H1
St Gabriel's Av *BBN* BB1................**219** H8
St George Ct *BPOOL* * FY1 ....**5** D1
St George's Av *BBNW* BB2..............**267** J2
  CLV/TH FY5................................**148** D3
  LSTA FY8....................................**230** E4
St Georges CI *COL* BB8..................**171** G8
St George's La *CLV/TH* * FY5..........**148** D1
  LSTA FY8....................................**230** D5
St George's PI *CHTN/BK* PR9..........**301** H4
St George's Quay *LANC* LA1 ....**2** B2
St George's Rd *BPOOLS* FY4..........**204** C5
  FMBY L37....................................**343** J7
  HTWN L38..................................**355** K6
  LSTA FY8....................................**230** D5
  NLSN BB9 ....**198** D4
  PRES PR1 ....**239** H1
St George's Sq *LSTA* FY8 ....**230** D4
St George's St *CHLY/EC* PR7..........**311** G4
St Georges Ter
  DWN (off Harwood St) BB3 ....**291** H2
  RAW/HAS (off Cowpe Rd) BB4 ....**297** J3
St Gerrard's Rd *LEY/BBR* PR5........**262** D2
St Giles St *PDHM/BLYW* BB12 ......**223** J2
St Gregory Rd *PRES* PR1 ....**239** K1
St Gregory's PI *CHLY/EC* PR7 ....**311** G6
St Helens CI *ACC* BB5 ....**247** K8
St Helen's Rd *CHLYE* PR6..............**287** C2
  HEY LA3..**65** H3
  ORM L39....................................**348** D7
  ORM L39....................................**348** D6

St Helier CI *BBNW* BB2..................**267** J3
St Helier's PI *GAR/LONG* PR3..........**184** C4
St Heliers Rd *BPOOL* FY1....................**4** C5
St Hilda's CI *CHLY/EC* PR7 ....**311** G7
St Hilda's Rd *LSTA* FY8..................**230** D4
St Hubert's Rd *GTH/LHO* BB6........**221** G7
St Hubert's St *GTH/LHO* BB6........**221** H6
St Ignatius' PI *PRES* * PR1 ....**7** E2
St Ives Av *BPOOL* FY1 ....**5** D4
  KIRK/FR/WA PR4 ....**234** E5
St Ives Crs *FUL/RIB* PR2................**212** C7
St Ives Rd *BBN* BB1 ....**246** B7
St James CI *ACC* BB5 ....**247** J1
  BRSC L40....................................**349** G8
  LEY/BBR PR5..............................**262** E5
  RAW/HAS * BB4..........................**272** C8
St James CI *BBN* BB1 ....**8** B2
St James' Crs *DWN* * BB3 ....**291** J1
St James Rd *ACC* BB5 ....**247** H4
  BBN BB1 ....**8** C2
  BPOOLS FY4..............................**204** C5
  WGNW/BIL/O WN5......................**365** F7
St James Rw *RAW/HAS* * BB4........**273** H8
St James's Av *BWCK/EAR* * BB18 ....**145** F1
St James's Gdns *LEY/BBR* PR5........**284** C3
St James's La *BLY* * BB11................**11** D3
St James's PI *BBN* BB1 ....**8** C2
  CHLYE PR6..................................**311** J4
St James's Rw *BLY* * BB11 ....**10** C3
St James's Sq *BLY* BB11..................**10** C3
  CLI BB7......................................**165** J4
St James's St *ACC* BB5..................**248** B6
  BBNW BB2..................................**267** K2
  BCUP OL13..................................**298** D1
  NLSN BB9 ....**197** K6
  RAW/HAS BB4............................**297** G3
  STHP PR8....................................**301** H6
St John Av *FTWD* FY7....................**122** D1
St Johns *BBN* BB1 ....**8** B3
St John's Av *CARN* LA5 ....**15** H8
  CLV/TH FY5................................**149** K2
  DWN BB3....................................**291** K3
  GAR/LONG PR3..........................**100** A6
  HEY LA3..**52** E1
  KIRK/FR/WA PR4 ....**208** D7
  PLF/KEOS FY6............................**150** A6
St John's CI *ACC* BB5 ....**271** K1
  CHLYE PR6..................................**287** F4
  PDHM/BLYW BB12 ....**222** C1
  RAW/HAS BB4............................**273** G4
St Johns Ct
  STHP (off Liverpool Rd) PR8 ......**325** K7
St John's Gn *LEY/BBR* PR5............**285** C2
St John's Gv *CARN* LA5 ....**15** H8
  HEY LA3..**52** D1
St Johns Ms *LANC* LA1 ....**3** D2
St John's PI *NLSN* BB9....................**198** E3
  PRES PR1 ....**7** E3
St John's Rd *HEY* LA3......................**52** D1
  LEY/BBR PR5..............................**240** B6
  PDHM/BLYW BB12 ....**223** J5
  PDHM/BLYW BB12 ....**224** E5
  STHP PR8....................................**326** B2
St John's St *DWN* BB3....................**291** K3
  GTH/LHO BB6............................**221** G7
  LSTA FY8....................................**232** E8
  RAW/HAS * BB4..........................**297** H3
St John's Ter *HEY* LA3......................**53** J1
St John St *BCUP* OL13....................**275** J8
  HOR/BR BL6................................**338** D7
  WGNW/BIL/O WN5......................**365** K5
St Josephs CI *BPOOLE* * FY3..............**5** E2
St Joseph's Ter *PRES* * PR1............**240** A2
St Judes Av *LEY/BBR* PR5..............**263** F7
  LEY/BBR PR5..............................**263** G2
St Katherines Dr *HOR/BR* BL6........**337** J8
St Lawrence Av *BBNW* BB2............**244** D3
St Lawrence's Av *GAR/LONG* PR3 ..**184** D3
St Lawrence St *GTH/LHO* BB6........**221** G6
St Leonard Ct *LANC* * LA1 ....**3** E2
St Leonard's Ga *LANC* LA1 ....**3** D3
St Leonard's Rd *BPOOLE* FY3............**5** F5
St Leonard's Rd East *LSTA* FY8......**230** E3
St Leonard's Rd West *LSTA* FY8......**230** D3
St Leonard's St
  PDHM/BLYW BB12 ....**223** J2
St Louis Av *BPOOLE* * FY3............**177** F4
St Luke Av *BPOOLE* * FY3..............**177** F4
St Lukes Ct
  LANC (off Fairfield Rd) LA1 ....**2** C3
St Luke's Dr *FMBY* L37..................**355** G1
  WGNW/BIL/O WN5......................**365** F7
St Luke's Gv *CHTN/BK* PR9............**302** A4
St Luke's PI *PRES* PR1..................**240** A1

St Luke's Rd *BPOOLS* FY4................**20**
  CHTN/BK PR9 ....**30**
St Margarets CI *FUL/RIB* PR2..........**21**
St Margarets Ct *BBN* BB1..................**8**
St Margaret's Gdns *BLY* BB11..........**22**
St Margaret's Rd *CARN* LA5 ....**3**
  LEY/BBR PR5................................**28**
  MCMB LA4 ....**6**
St Margarets Wy *BBN* BB1................**1**
St Mark's PI *BBNW* * BB2................**24**
  BPOOLS FY4................................**17**
St Mark's PI East *PRES* PR1............**7**
St Mark's PI West *PRES* * PR1 ....**7**
St Mark's Rd *BBNW* BB2 ....**24**
  PRES PR1 ....**7**
St Marlow Av *LEY/BBR* * PR5..........**26**
St Martins CI *PLF/KEOS* FY6............**14**
St Martin's Ct *CLV/TH* FY5..............**14**
St Martin's Dr *BBNW* BB2 ....**26**
St Martin's Rd *BPOOLS* FY4..........**20**
  LANC LA1..
  PRES * PR1 ....**23**
St Mary CI *BPOOLE* FY3..................**17**
St Mary's Av *BWCK/EAR* BB18 ......**11**
  LEY/BBR PR5................................**28**
  WGNW/BIL/O WN5......................**37**
St Marys Ct *ACC* BB5......................**27**
  BBNW (off Church La) BB2............**21**
  FTWD (off Dock St) FY7....................**9**
  PRES * PR1 ....
  RAW/HAS BB4..............................**29**
St Mary's Dr *GTH/LHO* BB6............**22**
St Mary's Gdns *BBNW* BB2............**24**
  STHP PR8....................................**32**
St Mary's Ga *BLY* * BB11....................**1**
  CHLY/EC PR7 ....**28**
St Mary's Pde *LANC* LA1....................
St Mary's Rd *GAR/LONG* PR3..........**15**
  HEY LA3..
  LEY/BBR PR5................................**26**
St Mary's St *CLI* BB7......................**16**
  NLSN BB9 ....**19**
  PRES PR1 ....
St Mary's St North *PRES* PR1..........
St Mary's Ter *RAW/HAS* BB4..........**29**
St Mary's Wy *RAW/HAS* BB4..........**29**
St Marys Wharf *BBNW* BB2..............
St Matthews Ct *BLY* BB11..................**1**
St Matthew St *BLY* BB11....................**1**
St Michael Rd *ORM* L39..................**35**
St Michael's CI *BBNW* BB2..............**26**
  CARN LA5 ....
  CHLY/EC PR7 ....**31**
  CHTN/BK PR9 ....**27**
St Michaels CI *BBN* BB1..................
  NLSN BB9 ....**19**
St Michael's Crs *CARN* LA5 ....
St Michael's Gv *MCMB* LA4 ....**4**
St Michael's La *CARN* LA5 ....
St Michaels Pk *ORM* L39................**35**
St Michael's PI *CARN* LA5................
  GAR/LONG PR3..........................**18**
St Michaels Rd *BISP* FY2..................
  GAR/LONG PR3..........................**15**
  KIRK/FR/WA PR4 ....**20**
  LEY/BBR PR5................................**26**
  PRES * PR1 ....
St Michael's St *BBN* BB1..................
St Mildred's Wy *HEY* LA3....................
St Monica's Wy *BPOOLS* FY4..........**20**
St Nicholas Arcades *LANC* * LA1......
St Nicholas' Av *CLI* BB7..................**19**
St Nicholas Crs *CARN* LA5 ....
St Nicholas Gv *KIRK/FR/WA* PR4 ....**20**
St Nicholas La *CARN* LA5 ....
St Nicholas Rd *ACC* * BB5 ....**24**
  BPOOLS FY4................................**24**
St Ogg's Rd *MCMB* LA4 ....**4**
St Oswald's CI *BBN* BB1..................**24**
  PRES PR1 ....**24**
St Oswald's Rd *BBN* BB1................**24**
St Oswald St *LANC* LA1 ....
St Patrick's CI *NWD/KWIPK* * L33....**36**
St Patricks Ct
  LSTA
  (off St Patricks Rd South) FY8..........**23**
St Patrick's Rd North *LSTA* FY8......**23**
St Patrick's Rd South *LSTA* FY8......**23**
St Patrick's Wk *HEY* LA3....................**5**
St Paul's Av *BBNW* BB2..................**23**
  LSTA FY8....................................**23**
  PRES * PR1 ....
St Paul's CI *CHLYE* PR6..................**33**

...] BB7 ...165 G3
EY/BBR PR5 ...262 C4
WD/KWIPK L33 ...366 B6
aul's Ct BLY * BB11 ...10 C4
aul's Dr HGHB LA2 ...45 J5
ANC LA1 ...3 D6
aul's Pas STHP * PR8 ...301 C5
POOL FY1 ...176 B3
ANC LA1 ...3 D6
aul's Rd BBN * BB1 ...246 E2
LSN BB9 ...198 B5
RES PR1 ...7 E2
aul's Sq PRES PR1 ...7 E2
aul's St ACC BB5 ...247 J7
BNW BB2 ...8 B4
LJ BB7 ...165 G3
AMS* BL0 ...319 J5
THP PR8 ...301 C5
aul's Ter CLI BB7 ...165 G3
eter's Av FMBY L37 ...343 H7
ieter's CI BBN BB1 ...219 F5
WN BB3 ...291 K3
MBY L37 ...343 H7
WD/KWIPK L33 ...366 B6
eters Ms LANC LA1 ...3 E3
eter's PI FTWD FY7 ...97 H6
eter Rd LANC LA1 ...3 E3
eter's Av LANC LA1 ...297 C1
THP PR8 ...301 C8
eter's Sq PRES PR1 ...6 C2
eter's St CHLYE PR6 ...311 J2
RES PR1 ...7 D2
eter St BBN BB1 ...246 E2
BNW BB2 ...8 C5
hilip's Rd PRES PR1 ...239 J1
hilip's St BBNW BB2 ...244 D8
LSN BB9 ...198 A3
hilip St BRFD/BLYE BB10 ...225 J2
aviour's CI LEY/BBR PR5 ...263 J4
ilas's Rd BBNW BB2 ...244 D6
tephen's Av BISP FY2 ...176 B1
tephen's Rd BBN BB1 ...9 E2
TWN L38 ...355 K7
IRK/FR/WA PR4 ...208 D7
RES PR1 ...239 J1
tephen's St BLY BB11 ...11 E5
tephen's Wy COL BB8 ...171 K6
eresa's Dr FUL/RIB PR2 ...148 D2
homas CI PLF/KEOS FY6 ...177 H2
homas More Wk LANC LA1 ...2 B3
homas' PI PRES * PR1 ...7 D1
homas Rd KIRK/FR/WA PR4 ...208 E7
STA FY8 ...231 F5
RES PR1 ...239 H1
homas's Ct
KEL (off Church St) WN8 ...364 E4
homas's Rd CHLY/EC PR7 ...311 F3
AW/HAS BB4 ...273 H4
homas St BBN BB1 ...9 F5
RES PR1 ...7 D1
incent Av BPOOL FY1 ...5 D4
incents CI FUL/RIB PR2 ...213 C6
incent's Wy STHP PR8 ...301 C5
alburga's Rd BPOOLE FY3 ...177 F3
alburge's CI PRES PR1 ...6 C2
alburges Gdns FUL/RIB PR2 ...6 B2
ilfred's Pk HGHB LA2 ...44 A4
ilfrid's Ter GAR/LONG PR3 ...188 A4
ilfrid St PRES PR1 ...7 D3
combe Av BISP FY2 ...176 E1
combe Dr CHTN/BK PR9 ...278 C6
combe Rd LSTA FY8 ...230 C3
em Ms HEY LA3 ...52 C3
erno St RAW/HAS BB4 ...272 C8
esbury CI BBN BB1 ...219 H1
ord BBN BB1 ...8 C4
ord Rd HGHB LA2 ...67 H2
THP PR8 ...325 J6
sbury PLF/KEOS FY6 ...98 A6
sbury Rd BPOOL FY1 ...5 D3
HLYE PR6 ...289 F5
WN BB3 ...268 B8
ANC LA1 ...2 B3
RES PR1 ...6 B3
sbury St CHLY/EC * PR7 ...311 H4
HTN/BK PR9 ...302 C5
TH/LHO BB6 ...221 H5
RES PR1 ...240 B2
owfields WGNW/BIL/O WN5 ...365 H6
y Barn Cottages
AW/HAS (off Holme La) BB4 ...296 A3
y's La CHTN/BK PR9 ...302 C1

Salmesbury Av BISP FY2 ...176 E1
Salmon St PRES PR1 ...240 A4
Salmsbury Hall CI RAMS BL0 ...319 H7
Salop Av BISP FY2 ...148 C3
Saltash Rd CLV/TH FY5 ...123 H6
Salt Ayre La LANC LA1 ...2 B2
Saltburn St PDHM/BLYW * BB12 ...224 D5
Saltcotes PI LSTA FY8 ...233 F7
Saltcotes Rd LSTA FY8 ...233 F7
Salter Fell Rd LANC LA1 ...2 B1
Salterford La BRFD/BLYE BB10 ...226 E8
Salterforth La BWCK/EAR BB18 ...145 H5
BWCK/EAR BB18 ...145 J2
Salterforth Rd BWCK/EAR BB18 ...146 A2
Salter St PRES PR1 ...7 D1
Salthill Rd CLI BB7 ...165 K2
Salthouse Av BPOOL * FY1 ...4 C4
Salt Marsh La PLF/KEOS FY6 ...150 D2
Salt Marsh La PLF/KEOS FY6 ...150 D1
Salt Pie La KKBYL LA6 ...21 H1
Salus St BRFD/BLYE BB10 ...226 A2
Salvia Wy NWD/KWIPK L33 ...366 B6
Salwick Av BISP FY2 ...148 D6
Salwick CI CHTN/BK PR9 ...278 B6
Salwick PI FUL/RIB PR2 ...238 A2
LSTA FY8 ...231 H3
Salwick Rd KIRK/FR/WA PR4 ...182 A7
Sambourn Fold STHP PR8 ...325 G6
Samuel St PRES PR1 ...240 B3
Sandbank Gdns WHIT OL12 ...323 G1
Sand Banks BOL BL1 ...341 K5
Sandbeds La HGHB LA2 ...36 C1
Sand Beds La RAMS BL0 ...296 B6
Sandbrook Gdns
WGNW/BIL/O WN5 ...365 F6
Sandbrook Rd STHP PR8 ...325 J8
STHP PR8 ...325 K6
WGNW/BIL/O WN5 ...364 E6
Sanderling CI CLV/TH FY5 ...149 F2
LSTA FY8 ...232 H3
Sanderling Rd NWD/KWIPK L33 ...366 B6
Sanders Gv MCMB LA4 ...41 G7
Sanderson La CHLY/EC PR7 ...333 J3
Sandersons Wy BPOOLS FY4 ...205 F3
Sandfield
CLV/TH (off Gaskell Crs) FY5 ...149 G1
Sandfield Pk ORM L39 ...360 H1
Sandfield Rd BCUP OL13 ...298 E1
Sandfield St LEY/BBR PR5 ...285 K2
Sandgate BPOOLS FY4 ...204 D6
CHLY/EC PR7 ...311 H6
LSTA FY8 ...230 C4
Sandham St CHLYE PR6 ...311 H3
Sandheys Dr CHTN/BK PR9 ...302 B2
Sandhills Av BPOOLS FY4 ...204 B6
Sandhills CI BWCK/EAR BB18 ...145 J3
Sandhill St BBN BB3 ...291 K6
Sandholme La GAR/LONG PR3 ...130 C6
Sandhurst Av BISP FY2 ...148 B6
LSTA FY8 ...230 E4
Sandhurst CI FMBY L37 ...355 G2
KIRK/FR/WA PR4 ...208 D6
Sandhurst St BLY BB11 ...11 E3
Sandhurst Wy MGHL L31 ...358 D6
Sandicroft Av PLF/KEOS FY6 ...150 E2
Sandicroft PI PLF/KEOS FY6 ...98 D7
Sandicroft Rd BPOOL FY1 ...176 C2
Sandilands Gv HTWN L38 ...355 K8
Sandiway Dr BRFD/BLYE BB10 ...198 D8
Sandiways CI CLV/TH FY5 ...149 J3
Sand La CARN LA5 ...25 H7
Sandlewood Gv NWD/KWIPK L33 ...366 D7
Sandon Gv RNFD/HAY WA11 ...369 G5
Sandon PI BPOOLS FY4 ...204 C7
Sandon Rd STHP PR8 ...326 B2
Sandon St BBNW BB2 ...8 A6
DWN BB3 ...291 K1
Sandon Ter BBNW BB2 ...8 A6
Sandown CI KIRK/FR/WA PR4 ...208 C6
Sandown Rd CLV/TH FY5 ...149 H2
LANC LA1 ...55 H8
RAW/HAS BB4 ...295 J1
Sandpiper CI BBN BB1 ...9 D3
Sandpiper Rd WGNS/IIMK WN3 ...365 K7
Sandpiper Sq BLY BB11 ...224 D6
Sandridge Av CHLY/EC PR7 ...311 F4
Sandridge PI BPOOLS FY4 ...204 B7
LSTA* FY8 ...204 D5
Sandringham Av CLV/TH FY5 ...149 H2
LEY/BBR PR5 ...286 A2
Sandringham CI CHLY/EC PR7 ...336 E5
KIRK/FR/WA PR4 ...282 K5
NLSN BB9 ...197 K2
NWD/KWIPK L33 ...366 C6
Sandringham Dr CHTN/BK PR9 ...301 H3

Sandringham Dr CHLYE PR6 ...288 E3
Sandringham Gv RAW/HAS BB4 ...295 G2
Sandringham Park Dr
KIRK/FR/WA PR4 ...261 G3
Sandringham Rd CHLY/EC PR7 ...308 E4
CHLY/EC PR7 ...311 F3
DWN BB3 ...268 B7
FMBY L37 ...355 J2
LEY/BBR PR5 ...240 B8
LSTA FY8 ...231 G6
MCMB LA4 ...41 F7
STHP PR8 ...300 E8
STHP PR8 ...325 J6
Sandringham Wy KIRK/FR/WA PR4 ...212 A5
Sandsdale Av FUL/RIB PR2 ...214 A6
Sandside Dr MCMB LA4 ...41 J8
Sandside Rd MTHPE LA7 ...15 J1
Sands Rd BBN BB1 ...247 F1
The Sands CLI BB7 ...193 F6
Sands Wy BPOOL FY1 ...4 C5
Sandwash CI RNFD/HAY WA11 ...369 H7
Sandwich CI BBN BB1 ...246 A7
Sandwick CI FUL/RIB PR2 ...213 G4
Sandybeds CI ACC BB5 ...271 J1
Sandybrook CI FUL/RIB PR2 ...214 C6
Sandy CI CLV/TH FY5 ...122 C8
Sandycroft FUL/RIB PR2 ...240 D1
Sandyfields KIRK/FR/WA PR4 ...212 A5
Sandyforth Av CLV/TH FY5 ...123 H8
Sandyforth La HWTH BD22 ...173 K1
KIRK/FR/WA PR4 ...212 C4
Sandygate BLY BB11 ...10 B3
Sandygate La GAR/LONG PR3 ...212 D1
Sandyhall La NLSN BB9 ...169 H8
Sandylands Prom HEY LA3 ...40 D8
Sandy La ACC BB5 ...248 E6
ACC BB5 ...248 C6
ACC BB5 ...249 G6
BBNW BB2 ...266 D1
BPOOLS FY4 ...205 G7
BRSC L40 ...305 J6
BRSC L40 ...306 A4
BRSC L40 ...332 B1
BRSC L40 ...349 H4
CHLY/EC PR7 ...336 E4
CHLYE PR6 ...264 C7
CHLYE PR6 ...265 C5
CHLYE PR6 ...288 B5
DWN BB3 ...268 B5
FTWD FY7 ...122 D4
GAR/LONG PR3 ...152 D2
HTWN L38 ...356 A8
KIRK/FR/WA PR4 ...211 K4
KIRK/FR/WA PR4 ...305 C5
LEY/BBR PR5 ...285 J3
MGHL L31 ...358 E6
NLSN BB9 ...198 B1
ORM L39 ...359 K5
PLF/KEOS FY6 ...98 D7
PLF/KEOS FY6 ...150 E7
SKEL WN8 ...351 F2
SKEL WN8 ...362 D2
WGNW/BIL/O WN5 ...365 F7
Sandy PI LEY/BBR PR5 ...285 J3
Sandy Wy BRSC L40 ...305 H7
Sanfield CI ORM L39 ...348 B5
Sangara Dr DWN BB3 ...268 C4
Sangness Dr STHP PR8 ...302 A8
Sansbury Crs NLSN BB9 ...198 E1
Santon CI KIRK/FR/WA PR4 ...208 E4
Sanvino Av STHP PR8 ...325 K6
Sapphire Dr NWD/KWIPK L33 ...366 C6
Sapphire St BBN BB1 ...245 H2
Sarah La LEY/BBR PR5 ...283 F5
Sarahs Fold PLF/KEOS FY6 ...124 E4
Sarah St BCUP OL13 ...299 G3
DWN BB3 ...291 K2
RAMS BL0 ...296 A8
Sarmatian Fold GAR/LONG PR3 ...189 K8
Sarscow La LEY/BBR PR5 ...308 A2
Saul's Dr CARN LA5 ...15 F3
Saul St PRES PR1 ...7 D2
Saunder Bank BLY BB11 ...10 C4
Saunder Height La RAW/HAS BB4 ...274 E8
Saunders CI RAW/HAS BB4 ...273 H4
Saunders' La KIRK/FR/WA PR4 ...260 E1
Saunders Ms CHLY/EC PR7 ...311 G8
Saunders Rd BBNW BB2 ...8 A4
Saunders St CHTN/BK PR9 ...301 H2
Savick Av FUL/RIB PR2 ...237 K2
Savick CI LEY/BBR PR5 ...263 J3
Savick Rd FUL/RIB PR2 ...213 F7
Savick Wy FUL/RIB PR2 ...212 B8
Saville Av PLF/KEOS FY6 ...149 H5
Saville Rd BPOOL FY1 ...4 C5
MGHL L31 ...358 E8
Saville St CHLY/EC PR7 ...311 G6

Savon Hook FMBY L37 ....**356** B2
Savoy Av HEY LA3 ....**41** J8
Savoy St ACC BB5 ....**247** K6
  PRES PR1 ....**6** C3
Sawdon Av STHP PR8 ....**302** A7
Sawley Av ACC BB5 ....**248** D4
  BPOOLS FY4 ....**204** D6
  LSTA FY8 ....**231** J5
  PDHM/BLYW BB12 ....**222** D2
Sawley Cl DWN BB3 ....**292** A3
Sawley Crs FUL/RIB PR2 ....**214** D8
Sawley Dr GTH/LHO BB6 ....**221** J6
Sawley Rd CLI BB7 ....**140** D3
Sawrey Ct ACC BB5 ....**221** J8
Sawthorpe Wk PLF/KEOS FY6 ....**149** G8
Saxby Av EDGW/EG BL7 ....**341** K3
Saxby Gv BPOOLS FY4 ....**5** F6
Saxifield St BRFD/BLYE BB10 ....**198** C8
Saxon Cl ACC BB5 ....**247** G6
  CLV/TH FY5 ....**149** H3
Saxon Hey FUL/RIB PR2 ....**212** E8
Saxon Rd STHP PR8 ....**301** F6
Saxon St BRFD/BLYE BB10 ....**11** D2
Saxon Wy NWD/KWIPK L33 ....**366** C5
Scafell Av MCMB LA4 ....**41** K6
Scafell Cl PDHM/BLYW BB12 ....**224** E3
Scafell Dr WGNW/BIL/O WN5 ....**365** K5
Scafell Rd LANC LA1 ....**3** E1
  LSTA FY8 ....**231** G1
Scaffold La HTWN L38 ....**356** C6
Scaitcliffe St ACC BB5 ....**248** B6
Scale Farm Rd LANC LA1 ....**2** A1
Scale Hall La KIRK/FR/WA PR4 ....**236** A1
  LANC LA1 ....**2** B1
Scant Rw
  HOR/BR (off Chorley Old Rd) BL6 ....**340** A8
Scarborough Rd BBNW BB2 ....**268** D2
  LSTA FY8 ....**231** G3
Scargill Rd HGHB LA2 ....**44** B3
  STHP PR8 ....**301** G4
Scarisbrick Av SKEL WN8 ....**351** J1
  STHP PR8 ....**301** G4
Scarisbrick Cl RAW/HAS BB4 ....**296** B1
Scarisbrick New Rd STHP PR8 ....**301** J6
Scarisbrick St CHTN/BK PR9 ....**301** H4
  ORM L39 ....**348** C5
Scarlet St CHLYE PR6 ....**311** J4
Scarlett St BLY BB11 ....**10** B4
Scarr La BBNW BB2 ....**244** C5
Scarsdale Av BPOOLS FY4 ....**204** C6
Scar St BBNW BB2 ....**244** D8
Scarth Hill La BRSC L40 ....**361** F1
  ORM L39 ....**360** C1
Scarth La PDHM/BLYW BB12 ....**223** H7
Scarth Pk SKEL WN8 ....**363** J4
Scar Top Rd HWTH BD22 ....**205** H4
Scawfell Cl PR7 ....**311** F6
Sceptre Wy LEY/BBR PR5 ....**264** A5
Schleswig St PRES PR1 ....**7** E2
Schleswig Wy LEY/BBR PR5 ....**284** E4
Schofield Av BPOOLE FY3 ....**177** H4
Schofield Cl RAW/HAS BB4 ....**296** B1
Schofield Rd RAW/HAS BB4 ....**296** B1
Schofield St DWN BB3 ....**291** H1
  RAW/HAS BB4 ....**297** G3
Schola Green La MCMB LA4 ....**41** H6
Scholars Gn FUL/RIB PR2 ....**237** J2
Scholefield Av NLSN BB9 ....**198** C6
Scholefield La NLSN BB9 ....**198** D6
Scholes Bank HOR/BR BL6 ....**338** C6
Scholes St DWN BB3 ....**291** H1
Scholey Head La
  BRFD/BLYE BB10 ....**252** B8
School Av FMBY L37 ....**343** K8
  WGNW/BIL/O WN5 ....**371** G6
School Brow CHLYE PR6 ....**287** F4
School Cl ORM * L39 ....**360** A2
  STHP PR8 ....**326** D1
School Ct RAMS BL0 ....**319** G2
School Dr WGNW/BIL/O WN5 ....**371** G6
School Fld LEY/BBR PR5 ....**264** A6
School Flds BWCK/EAR BB18 ....**120** B8
Schoolfold KIRK/FR/WA PR4 ....**258** C5
Schoolhouse Fold BLY BB11 ....**223** J8
School House Gn ORM L39 ....**348** D6
School House Gv BRSC * L40 ....**330** D6
School House La ACC BB5 ....**271** G1
Schoolhouse La HGHB LA2 ....**84** B4
School Houses
  SKEL (off Tawd Valley Pk) WN8 ....**363** H3
School La BBN BB1 ....**269** G3
  BLY BB11 ....**11** D3
  BRFD/BLYE BB10 ....**252** E2
  BRSC L40 ....**331** F6
  BRSC L40 ....**332** D2
  BRSC L40 ....**349** J8
  BWCK/EAR BB18 ....**146** B1

CHLY/EC PR7 ....**286** B8
CHLYE PR6 ....**266** A7
CHLYE PR6 ....**288** E3
CLI BB7 ....**77** C5
COL BB8 ....**172** E5
EDGW/EG BL7 ....**317** H3
FMBY L37 ....**343** K8
GAR/LONG PR3 ....**80** C3
GAR/LONG PR3 ....**100** A5
GAR/LONG PR3 ....**102** E6
GAR/LONG PR3 ....**152** D1
HGHB LA2 ....**38** A8
KIRK/FR/WA PR4 ....**182** C2
KIRK/FR/WA PR4 ....**183** H7
KIRK/FR/WA PR4 ....**209** F6
KIRK/FR/WA PR4 ....**235** K1
KIRK/FR/WA PR4 ....**260** B3
LEY/BBR PR5 ....**262** C4
LEY/BBR PR5 ....**263** J1
LEY/BBR PR5 ....**284** C2
LEY/BBR PR5 ....**285** H1
LSTA FY8 ....**232** C8
ORM L39 ....**346** B8
PDHM/BLYW BB12 ....**222** E2
PLF/KEOS FY6 ....**98** D8
SKEL WN8 ....**352** D8
SKEL WN8 ....**362** D2
SKEL WN8 ....**364** E4
School Nook BPOOLS FY4 ....**205** G7
CLV/TH FY5 ....**149** J3
HEY LA3 ....**52** C4
HTWN L38 ....**355** H7
School St ACC BB5 ....**248** B5
BBN BB1 ....**247** E2
BCUP OL13 ....**297** K3
BWCK/EAR* BB18 ....**146** A5
DWN BB3 ....**291** J2
EDGW/EG BL7 ....**341** K4
GTH/LHO BB6 ....**221** G7
HOR/BR BL6 ....**338** E8
KIRK/FR/WA PR4 ....**260** A6
LEY/BBR PR5 ....**240** D8
LEY/BBR PR5 ....**285** K1
NLSN BB9 ....**198** A3
PRES PR1 ....**6** C3
RAMS BL0 ....**319** H6
RAW/HAS BB4 ....**273** H3
RAW/HAS BB4 ....**274** C7
Schwartzman Dr CHTN/BK PR9 ....**279** J5
Scorton Av BPOOLE FY3 ....**177** F5
Scorton Hall Pk GAR/LONG PR3 ....**104** A5
Scotch Green La GAR/LONG PR3 ....**157** H3
Scotforth Ct
  LANC (off Lentworth Dr) LA1 ....**55** G8
Scotforth Rd HGHB LA2 ....**67** F3
  LANC LA1 ....**3** E6
  PRES PR1 ....**240** A3
Scotland Bank Ter BBNW BB2 ....**267** J3
Scotland Rd CARN LA5 ....**26** A8
  KKBYL LA6 ....**34** C2
  NLSN BB9 ....**198** B2
Scotswood Av BPOOLS FY4 ....**204** D5
Scott Av ACC BB5 ....**271** K1
  MCMB LA4 ....**41** F8
  PDHM/BLYW BB12 ....**222** E2
Scott Cl ACC BB5 ....**247** H6
  BPOOLS FY4 ....**205** F3
Scott Dr ORM L39 ....**348** D4
Scott Gv MCMB LA4 ....**41** G7
Scott Ms BPOOLS FY4 ....**205** F3
Scott Park Rd BLY BB11 ....**10** B5
Scott Rd HEY LA3 ....**41** F8
Scott's Ter BLY BB11 ....**10** A3
Scott St ACC BB5 ....**221** K8
  CHTN/BK PR9 ....**302** C4
  NLSN BB9 ....**198** B2
  PDHM/BLYW BB12 ....**224** B4
Scott's Wd FUL/RIB PR2 ....**212** E5
Scout Rd BOL BL1 ....**340** E5
  RAMS BL0 ....**320** C1
  RAW/HAS BB4 ....**274** B8
Scowcroft Dr MCMB LA4 ....**42** A6
Scow Croft La CHLYE PR6 ....**288** C7
Scriffen La HGHB LA2 ....**67** J3
Scudamore Crs BPOOLS FY4 ....**5** D6
Seabank Rd CHTN/BK PR9 ....**301** H3
  FTWD FY7 ....**97** C6
Seaborn Gv MCMB LA4 ....**41** K5
Seaborn Rd MCMB LA4 ....**41** K5
Seabourne Av BPOOLS FY4 ....**204** B4
Seabrook Dr CLV/TH FY5 ....**148** E3
Seacrest Av BPOOL FY1 ....**176** C3
Seacroft Crs CHTN/BK PR9 ....**278** D6
Seafield FMBY L37 ....**356** A1
Seafield Rd BPOOL FY1 ....**176** B3
  LSTA FY8 ....**232** B8

STHP PR8 ....**32** [...]
Seafore Cl MGHL L31 ....**35**[...] A8
Seaforth Rd BOL BL1 ....**34**[...]
Sealand Av FMBY L37 ....**35**[...]
Sealand Cl FMBY L37 ....**35**[...]
Seascale Cl BBNW BB2 ....**26**[...]
Seaside Wy BPOOL FY1 ....**[...]**
Seathwaite Av BPOOLS FY4 ....**20**[...]
  HEY LA3 ....**52**[...]
Seathwaite Crs NWD/KWIPK L33 ....**36**[...]
Seatoller Pl WGNW/BIL/O WN5 ....**36**[...]
Seaton Av CLV/TH FY5 ....**12**[...]
Seaton Crs LSTA FY8 ....**23**[...]
Seaton Pl SKEL WN8 ....**35**[...]
Seaton Wy CHTN/BK PR9 ....**27**[...]
Seattle Av BISP FY2 ....**14**[...]
Sea Vw KIRK/FR/WA PR4 ....**26**[...]
Sea View Cl HGHB * LA2 ....**4**[...]
Sea View Dr HGHB LA2 ....**4**[...]
Seaview Wy FTWD FY7 ....**9**[...]
Sea Wall FTWD FY7 ....**9**[...]
Seawell Av HEY LA3 ....**52**[...]
Seawell Gdns
  HEY (off Seawell Av) LA3 ....**5**[...]
Second Av ACC BB5 ....**248**[...]
  BPOOLS FY4 ....**20**[...]
  PLF/KEOS (off Woodside Pk) FY6 ....**12**[...]
Second St BOL BL1 ....**34**[...]
Sedbergh Av BPOOLS FY4 ....**5**[...]
Sedbergh Cl ACC BB5 ....**24**[...]
Sedberg St FUL/RIB PR2 ....**21**[...]
Sedburgh St BRFD/BLYE BB10 ....**22**[...]
Seddon Pl SKEL WN8 ....**35**[...]
Sedge Ct HEY * LA3 ....**5**[...]
Sedgefield Cl KIRK/FR/WA PR4 ....**25**[...]
Sedgefield Dr BOL BL1 ....**34**[...]
Sedgeley Ms KIRK/FR/WA PR4 ....**23**[...]
Sedgfield Cl BPOOLS FY4 ....**20**[...]
Sedgley Av KIRK/FR/WA PR4 ....**23**[...]
Sedgwick St PRES PR1 ....**[...]**
Sedum Gv NWD/KWIPK L33 ....**36**[...]
Sedwell Cl LSTA FY8 ....**23**[...]
Seedall Av CLI BB7 ....**16**[...]
Seedhill Ter NLSN * BB9 ....**19**[...]
Seedlee Rd LEY/BBR PR5 ....**26**[...]
Seed St BPOOL FY1 ....**[...]**
  PRES* PR1 ....**[...]**
Sefton Av BLY * BB11 ....**1**[...]
  PLF/KEOS FY6 ....**17**[...]
  WGNW/BIL/O WN5 ....**36**[...]
Sefton Cl ACC BB5 ....**22**[...]
  DWN BB3 ....**29**[...]
  KKBY L32 ....**36**[...]
  WGNW/BIL/O WN5 ....**36**[...]
Sefton Dr KKBY L32 ....**36**[...]
  LANC LA1 ....**[...]**
Sefton Fold Dr
  WGNW/BIL/O WN5 ....**37**[...]
Sefton Fold Gdns
  WGNW/BIL/O WN5 ....**37**[...]
Sefton Gdns ORM L39 ....**36**[...]
Sefton Rd FMBY L37 ....**35**[...]
  HEY LA3 ....**4**[...]
  LEY/BBR PR5 ....**24**[...]
  LSTA FY8 ....**23**[...]
  WGNW/BIL/O WN5 ....**36**[...]
Sefton St COL BB8 ....**17**[...]
  NLSN BB9 ....**19**[...]
  STHP PR8 ....**30**[...]
Sefton Ter BLY BB11 ....**1**[...]
Sefton Vw WGNW/BIL/O WN5 ....**36**[...]
Segar's La STHP PR8 ....**32**[...]
Segar St GTH/LHO * BB6 ....**22**[...]
  KIRK/FR/WA PR4 ....**20**[...]
Selborne St BBNW BB2 ....**24**[...]
  PRES PR1 ....**[...]**
Selbourne BWCK/EAR BB18 ....**14**[...]
Selbourne Rd BPOOL FY1 ....**[...]**
Selby Av BPOOLS FY4 ....**20**[...]
  CLV/TH FY5 ....**12**[...]
  LANC LA1 ....**4**[...]
Selby Cl ACC BB5 ....**24**[...]
Selby Dr FMBY L37 ....**35**[...]
Selby Pl SKEL WN8 ....**35**[...]
Selby Rd KIRK/FR/WA PR4 ....**20**[...]
Selby St COL BB8 ....**17**[...]
  NLSN BB9 ....**19**[...]
  PRES PR1 ....**[...]**
Seldon St COL * BB8 ....**17**[...]
  NLSN BB9 ....**19**[...]
Selkirk Cl BBN BB1 ....**[...]**
Selkirk Dr LEY/BBR PR5 ....**26**[...]
Selkirk Gv WGNW/BIL/O WN5 ....**36**[...]
Selkirk Rd BOL BL1 ....**34**[...]
Selkirk St BLY BB11 ....**1**[...]
Sellers St PRES PR1 ....**24**[...]
Selous Rd BBNW BB2 ....**24**[...]

ide Dr MCMB LA4.....................................41 H8
vorthy Rd STHP PR8..............................300 D8
or Av BPOOL5 FY4...................................5 F6
ors Dr CLV/TH FY5...............................123 F8
nton Dr ORM L39....................................348 D4
nton St LEY/BBR PR5...........................262 D3
enade Rd NWD/KWIPK L33.................366 D5
jeant St LEY/BBR PR5..........................263 J3
entine La BLY BB11................................10 C3
Serpentine La LSTA FY8......................232 C8
RM L39..360 B3
End Rd BBN BB1................................269 F2
le La CLI BB7..93 K4
le Pl LSTA FY8......................................231 J4
le Ter BRFD/BLYE BB10.......................226 A1
en Acres LEY/BBR PR5.........................264 B6
enoaks CHLY/EC PR7............................311 G7
enoaks Av STHP PR8............................325 H6
enoaks Dr CLV/TH FY5.........................149 F5
en Sands KIRK/FR/WA PR4...................260 A2
en Stars Rd LEY/BBR PR5....................284 E1
enth Av BPOOL5 FY4............................204 C4
en Trees Av BBN * BB1............................9 E1
ern Av FTWD FY7.................................122 D3
ern Cl WGNW/BIL/O WN5.....................371 F7
ern Ct LANC LA1....................................54 B1
ern Dr LEY/BBR PR5.............................263 G1
ern Hl FUL/RIB PR2..............................212 E3
ern Rd BPOOL5 FY4.............................204 B4
WD/KWIPK L33.....................................366 D5
ern St GAR/LONG PR3.........................188 A5
mour Av HEY LA3...................................52 D4
mour Ct PRES PR1...............................239 F1
mour Dr MGHL L31...............................359 C8
mour Gv HEY LA3..................................52 D4
mour St BOL BL1.................................341 K8
POOL FY1...4 C5
L/RIB PR2..212 E1
STA FY8...231 K6
mour St CHLYE PR6.............................311 H4
TWD FY7...97 F7
NC LA1...3 E3
cklady Rd NWD/KWIPK L33.................366 E7
ckleton St KIRK/FR/WA PR4.................235 F1
ckleton St BRFD/BLYE BB10..................11 E1
OD OL14...277 H2
dsworth Cl BBN BB1...........................246 A7
dsworth Rd BBN BB1..........................269 F2
dy La HGHB LA2....................................42 E3
Y/BBR PR5...263 H7
rttesbury Av BISP FY2.........................176 C3
Y BB11..10 C5
POOLE FY3..177 H5
V/TH FY5...122 C6
WN BB3...268 B8
TH/LHO BB6..221 J5
RK/FR/WA PR4......................................261 G3
RES PR1..238 D5
HP PR8..326 C3
tesbury Cl LSTA FY8...........................231 K6
tesbury La STHP PR8.........................326 C2
tesbury Pl CHLY/EC PR7.....................311 F3
NC LA1...55 F7
tesbury Rd STHP PR8.........................326 C3
tsbury Av NWD/KWIPK L33................366 B6
tsbury Rd WGNW/BIL/O WN5.............365 J3
keshaft St BBN BB1.................................9 E5
kespeare Av GTH/LHO BB6.................221 F7
kespeare Rd FTWD FY7.........................96 E7
NC LA1...42 D7
RES PR1..240 B2
kespeare St
DHM/BLYW BB12................................223 K4
HP PR8..301 H6
kespeare Ter CHLYE PR6....................311 H1
kespeare Wy BBNW BB2........................8 A6
lbourn Rd LSTA FY8............................231 G7
e St PDHM/BLYW BB12..........................10 A3
grove Fld FUL/RIB PR2........................212 E4
nnon St BPOOL FY1..................................4 B4
p Cl ACC BB5..248 B8
SN BB9..170 B7
p Ct FTWD FY7.....................................122 D2
p Ga WGNW/BIL/O WN5.......................365 K4
p Gv BRFD/BLYE BB10.........................197 J8
rd La PLF/KEOS FY6............................150 D3
rd Rd PLF/KEOS FY6............................150 D5
rman Rd LSTA FY8................................231 F2
roe Green La FUL/RIB PR2...................213 G4
roe Green Pk FUL/RIB PR2...................213 J6
roe Mount Av FUL/RIB PR2...................213 H4
row Gv FUL/RIB PR2................................5 D5
pe's Av LANC LA1...................................3 E6
ples Av BOL BL1...................................341 K5
ples Gn EDGW/EG BL7.........................317 H5
ples Hall Dr BOL BL1............................341 K5
ples Hall Fold BOL BL1.........................341 K6

Sharples Hall Ms BOL BL1....................341 K5
Sharples Pk BOL BL1.............................341 H7
Sharples St ACC BB5............................247 K6
    BBNW BB2..8 B6
Sharp St BRFD/BLYE BB10....................225 K1
    NLSN BB9..170 B8
Sharratts Pth CHLY/EC PR7..................310 C7
Shawbridge Ct CLI BB7.........................165 K3
Shaw Bridge St CLI BB7........................165 K3
Shaw Brook St BBN BB1........................246 E3
Shawbrook Cl CHLY/EC PR7..................286 A6
Shaw Brow CHLYE PR6..........................287 F4
Shawcliffe La GTH/LHO BB6..................220 E3
Shaw Cl BBNW BB2..................................8 A4
    ORM L39...327 H5
Shawclough Cl WHIT OL12....................323 H8
Shawclough Dr WHIT OL12....................323 G8
Shaw Clough Rd RAW/HAS BB4............274 C8
Shawclough Rd WHIT OL12...................323 G8
Shaw Clough St RAW/HAS * BB4...........274 C8
Shawclough Wy WHIT OL12...................323 G8
Shaw Crs FMBY L37...............................344 B7
Shawes Dr CHLYE PR6............................337 J4
Shawfield RAW/HAS BB4.......................296 B2
Shaw Hl CHLYE PR6................................287 F5
Shaw Hill Dr CHLYE PR6.........................287 F5
Shaw Hill St CHLY/EC PR7.....................311 G4
Shaw La KKBYL LA6...............................34 B7
    ORM L39..345 K5
    TOD OL14...254 B8
Shaw Rd BPOOL FY1..................................4 B6
    HOR/BR BL6..338 D6
Shaw's Av STHP PR8..............................326 C2
Shaws Garth ORM L39...........................327 H5
Shaw's La GAR/LONG PR3.......................99 J8
Shaw's Rd STHP PR8.............................326 C2
Shaw St BBNW BB2...................................8 A4
    COL BB8...171 G7
    LANC LA1...3 E3
    PRES* PR1..7 E2
    RAW/HAS BB4......................................272 C5
Shay La CLI BB7.......................................89 C5
    GAR/LONG PR3.....................................187 K6
Shays Dr CLI BB7...................................165 K5
The Shay CLV/TH FY5.............................149 F4
Shear Bank Cl BBN BB1.............................8 B3
Shear Bank Gdns BBN BB1.......................8 B3
Shear Bank Rd BBN BB1...........................8 B3
Shear Brow BBN BB1.................................8 B3
Shearwater Dr BBN BB1............................9 D3
Sheddon Gv BRFD/BLYE BB10...............226 C6
Shed St ACC BB5...................................247 H8
    COL BB8...171 G7
    WHIT OL12..323 H2
Sheep Gn RAW/HAS BB4.......................272 C8
Sheep Hey
    RAMS (off Leaches Rd) BL0.................319 G4
Sheep Hill Brow CHLYE PR6...................286 E1
Sheep Hill La CHLYE PR6.......................286 D1
Sheephill La KIRK/FR/WA PR4...............261 G4
Sheep House La HOR/BR BL6.................338 D1
Sheernest La KKBYL LA6..........................17 K2
Sheffield Dr FUL/RIB PR2.......................237 K1
Sheldon Ct PRES * PR1.............................7 D1
Shelfield La BRFD/BLYE BB10................199 J4
Shelfield Rd NLSN BB9...........................199 F2
Shelley Cl CARN LA5................................33 G6
    CHLY/EC PR7.......................................335 K3
Shelley Dr ACC BB5...............................271 K1
    CHLY/EC PR7.......................................309 F6
    ORM L39...348 B5
    WGNW/BIL/O WN5...............................365 J3
Shelley Gdns GTH/LHO BB6...................221 F7
Shelley Gv CLV/TH FY5..........................148 D3
    DWN BB3..292 A2
    STHP PR8..302 B4
Shelley Ms FUL/RIB PR2............................6 A1
Shelley Rd FUL/RIB PR2.........................238 E1
Shellfield Rd CHTN/BK PR9....................278 C3
Shellingford Cl WGNNW/ST WN6...........353 H1
Shelly Road Ml
    FUL/RIB (off Shelly Rd) PR2.................6 A1
Shelton Dr STHP PR8.............................325 G7
Shenley Wy CHTN/BK * PR9....................279 F5
Shenstone Rd BPOOLE FY3....................176 E4
Shepherd Rd LSTA FY8...........................231 G4
Shepherd Rd North LSTA FY8.................231 G3
Shepherd's Av GAR/LONG PR3...............129 K7
Shepherds Cl HOR/BR BL6.....................337 J8
Shepherd's Dr HOR/BR BL6....................339 J8
Shepherd's La ORM L39..........................347 F6
Shepherd St BCUP OL13.........................275 J8
    DWN BB3..291 J4
    LSTA FY8..232 D8
    PRES PR1..7 E3
Shepherds Wy CHLY/EC PR7..................311 H3

Sheppard St BPOOL FY1............................4 B2
Shepton Cl BOL BL1...............................341 H4
Sheraton Cl WGNW/BIL/O WN5..............365 K2
Sheraton Pk FUL/RIB PR2......................212 C5
    WGNW/BIL/O WN5...............................365 J3
Sherborne Rd ACC BB5..........................248 E8
    WGNW/BIL/O WN5...............................365 J3
Sherbourne Cl PLF/KEOS FY6................149 J6
Sherbourne Crs PRES PR1.....................213 K8
Sherbourne Rd BPOOL FY1....................176 B3
    PLF/KEOS* FY6....................................150 E1
Sherbourne St CHLYE PR6.....................311 H4
Sherburne Av KIRK/FR/WA PR4.............208 D6
Sherburn Rd PRES PR1..........................239 C8
Sherdley Rd LEY/BBR PR5......................262 E4
Sheridan Rd COL BB8............................172 D5
Sheridan St NLSN BB9...........................198 D1
Sheringham Av CLV/TH FY5...................148 D5
Sheringham Wy PLF/KEOS FY6..............150 A3
Sherrat St SKEL WN8.............................362 D2
Sherringham Rd STHP PR8.....................326 A1
Sherwood Av BPOOLE FY3......................176 E3
    ORM L39..360 A1
Sherwood Ct
    BPOOLE (off Sherwood Av) FY3............176 E3
    BRFD/BLYE BB10...................................11 F4
Sherwood Dr SKEL WN8..........................351 K8
Sherwood Pl CHLYE PR6........................311 H3
    CLV/TH FY5...149 F2
Sherwood Rd BBN BB1...............................9 F5
    LSTA FY8...231 J5
Sherwood St BOL BL1............................341 K8
Sherwood Wy ACC BB5..........................248 A2
Shetland Cl BBN BB1..............................219 H5
    BBN BB1...246 A8
Shetland Rd BPOOL FY1............................4 C5
Shevington Cswy LEY/BBR PR5..............307 G1
Shevington La WGNNW/ST WN6............353 K2
Shevington Moor
    WGNNW/ST WN6..................................353 J1
Shevington's La NWD/KWIPK L33...........366 C6
Shilton St RAMS BL0..............................319 H6
Shipley Cl BPOOLE FY3..........................177 H2
Shipley Rd LSTA FY8..............................231 H4
Shipper Bottom La RAMS BL0.................319 K6
Shirdley Crs STHP PR8...........................325 J8
Shire Bank Crs FUL/RIB PR2...................213 G5
Shireburn Av CLI BB7.............................165 G4
Shireburn Rd FMBY L37.........................343 G6
Shire La CLI BB7.....................................191 F3
Shireshead Crs LANC LA1........................67 G1
The Shires DWN BB3..............................268 A5
Shirewell Rd WGNW/BIL/O WN5.............365 G6
Shirley Crs BISP FY2...............................148 D5
Shirley Hts PLF/KEOS FY6......................149 K7
Shirley La KIRK/FR/WA PR4....................260 B2
Shop La ACC BB5...................................248 D6
    LEY/BBR PR5...241 F7
Shore Av BRFD/BLYE BB10.....................226 C1
Shore Cl CARN LA5...................................24 B1
Shorefield Mt EDGW/EG BL7..................341 J3
Shore Gn CARN LA5..................................24 B1
    CLV/TH FY5...123 F8
    TOD OL14..277 G1
Shore New Rd TOD OL14........................277 G1
Shore Rd CARN LA5...................................24 B1
    CLV/TH FY5...148 C3
    HEY LA3...52 B5
    KIRK/FR/WA PR4..................................257 K8
    STHP PR8..325 C5
Shoreswood BOL BL1.............................341 H6
The Shore CARN LA5................................32 E6
Shorey Bank BLY BB11.............................11 D2
Shorrock La BBNW BB2...........................267 J2
Shorrocks Av GAR/LONG PR3.................154 C3
Shorrock St DWN BB3............................291 J3
Shortbutts La KKBYL LA6..........................19 K2
Short Clough Cl RAW/HAS BB4...............273 H5
Short Clough La RAW/HAS BB4...............273 H5
Short Croft La FMBY L37.........................356 D2
Shorten Brook Dr ACC BB5.....................222 E5
Shorten Brook Wy ACC BB5....................222 E5
Shortlands Dr HEY LA3.............................52 C4
The Shortlands
    PDHM/BLYW BB12................................223 J1
Short La GAR/LONG PR3.........................185 H6
Shortridge Rd BPOOL5 FY4.....................205 F3
Short St BCUP OL13...............................297 K3
    COL BB8..171 H7
    WGNW/BIL/O WN5...............................365 K5
Shoxfield BRFD/BLYE BB10....................227 H5
Showley Rd BBN BB1..............................218 C6
Shrewsbury Cl KIRK/FR/WA PR4.............209 G6
Shrewsbury Dr CLV/TH FY5....................149 G1
    LANC LA1..3 F6
Shropshire Dr BBN BB1...........................219 H5
Shuttle Cl ACC BB5................................248 A5

Shuttleworth Md
PDHM/BLYW
(off Blackburn Rd) BB12 .....222 D2
Shuttleworth St PRES PR1 .....239 H1
Shuttleworth St BBN BB1 .....247 F1
  BRFD/BLYE* BB10 .....225 K1
  BWCK/EAR* BB18 .....146 B1
  PDHM/BLYW BB12 .....223 J3
Shuttling Fields La LEY/BBR PR5 .....264 A1
Sibbering Brow Preston Rd
  CHLY/EC PR7 .....310 A3
Sibsey St LANC LA1 .....2 C4
Siddows Av CLI BB7 .....165 G4
Sidebeet La BBN BB1 .....246 C3
Sidegarth La HGHB LA2 .....35 J5
Side La CLI BB7 .....142 E4
Sidgreaves La KIRK/FR/WA PR4 .....211 H6
Siding La RNFD/HAY WA11 .....368 D2
Siding Rd FTWD FY7 .....97 G8
Sidings Rd HEY LA3 .....64 D1
The Sidings BCUP OL13 .....298 E3
  CLI BB7 .....193 G5
  DWN BB3 .....291 K4
Siding St BCUP OL13 .....298 A3
Sidmouth Av RAW/HAS BB4 .....295 J1
Sidmouth Rd LSTA FY8 .....230 C2
Sidney Av BISP FY2 .....176 E1
  KIRK/FR/WA PR4 .....258 E8
Sidney Rd CHTN/BK PR9 .....302 B3
Sidney Ter LANC* LA1 .....3 E3
Silbury Cl BBNW BB2 .....268 C3
Silk Mill La GAR/LONG PR3 .....157 K8
Silloth Cl BBNW BB2 .....268 C2
Silly La HGHB LA2 .....50 D7
Silsden Cl BPOOLE FY3 .....177 H2
Silver Birch Wy MGHL L31 .....358 D6
Silverdale BISP FY2 .....148 E5
  KIRK/FR/WA PR4 .....258 E8
Silverdale Av FTWD FY7 .....122 C2
  HEY LA3 .....52 D5
Silverdale Cl ACC BB5 .....247 J1
  BBNW BB2 .....268 C3
  BRFD/BLYE BB10 .....197 K8
  LEY/BBR PR5 .....241 J7
  LEY/BBR PR5 .....285 K5
Silverdale Dr FUL/RIB PR2 .....214 B6
Silverdale Moss Rd CARN LA5 .....15 J4
Silverdale Rd CARN LA5 .....15 G2
  CARN LA5 .....16 E6
  CHLYE PR6 .....311 J4
  LSTA FY8 .....231 J4
  WGNW/BIL/O WN5 .....365 K3
Silverstone Gv MGHL L31 .....358 D6
Silver St KIRK/FR/WA PR4 .....236 D2
  RAMS BLO 319 J5
Silverthorne Dr CHTN/BK PR9 .....302 B2
Silverton Gv BOL BL1 .....341 K7
Silverwell St HOR/BR BL6 .....338 D7
Silverwood Av BPOOLS FY4 .....204 C3
Silverwood Cl LSTA FY8 .....232 A2
Silvester Rd CHLY/EC PR7 .....311 G5
Silvia Wy FTWD FY7 .....96 E7
Simmonds Wy NLSN BB9 .....197 K4
Simmons Av LEY/BBR PR5 .....239 K8
Simmons' St BBNW BB2 .....8 B4
Simonstone La
  PDHM/BLYW 222 E3
Simonstone Rd CLI BB7 .....195 F5
Simonswood La ORM L39 .....360 D8
Simpson Cl BWCK/EAR BB18 .....119 H8
Simpson St ACC BB5 .....247 H8
  BPOOLS FY4 .....204 B3
  PDHM/BLYW BB12 .....223 J7
  PRES PR1 .....7 D2
Sineacre La ORM L39 .....367 J2
Singleton Cl FUL/RIB PR2 .....213 H4
Singleton Av HOR/BR BL6 .....338 E6
  LSTA FY8 .....231 H4
  PDHM/BLYW BB12 .....222 D1
Singleton Cl FUL/RIB PR2 .....213 H4
Singleton Rd KIRK/FR/WA PR4 .....179 G5
Singleton Rw PRES PR1 .....7 D2
Singleton St BPOOL* FY1 .....4 B4
Sion Cl FUL/RIB PR2 .....214 D7
Sir Simon's Ar LANC* LA1 .....3 D3
Six Acre La KIRK/FR/WA PR4 .....260 D5
Sixfields CLV/TH FY5 .....149 F4
Sixth Av BPOOLS FY4 .....204 C4
Sizehouse St PRES PR1 .....7 D2
Sizergh Ct LANC LA1 .....2 B4
Sizergh Rd MCMB LA4 .....42 A6
Sizer St PRES PR1 .....7 D1
Size St WHIT OL12 .....323 H2
The Skaithe CLI BB7 .....89 H5
Skeffington Rd PRES PR1 .....239 K1
Skeleron La CLI BB7 .....142 D5
Skelmersdale Rd ORM L39 .....362 A4

Skelshaw Cl BBN* BB1 .....9 E6
Skelton St COL BB8 .....171 J6
Skelwith Rd BPOOLE FY3 .....205 H1
Skerton LANC LA1 .....3 D1
Skiddaw Cl PDHM/BLYW BB12 .....224 E2
Skiddaw Rd BPOOLS FY4 .....205 F3
  LANC LA1 .....3 E1
Skiddaw St BBN BB1 .....9 E4
Skip La KIRK/FR/WA PR4 .....237 H8
Skippool Av PLF/KEOS FY6 .....150 A6
Skippool Br PLF/KEOS FY6 .....150 B5
Skippool Rd CLV/TH FY5 .....150 A4
Skipton Av CHTN/BK PR9 .....278 C5
  PLF/KEOS FY6 .....149 J6
Skipton Cl BPOOLS FY4 .....5 F1
  LEY/BBR PR5 .....263 H1
Skipton New Rd COL BB8 .....171 J2
Skipton Old Rd COL BB8 .....171 J1
  COL BB8 .....172 D3
Skipton Rd BWCK/EAR BB18 .....120 B8
  BWCK/EAR BB18 .....145 F1
  COL BB8 .....171 J3
  COL BB8 .....172 B8
  LSTA FY8 .....231 H5
Skipton St MCMB* LA4 .....41 G6
Skitham La GAR/LONG PR3 .....126 E8
Skull House La WGNNW/ST WN6 .....353 F3
Skull House Ms WGNNW/ST WN6 .....352 E2
Skye Crs BBN BB1 .....246 B8
Slack PDHM/BLYW BB12 .....196 B5
Slackey La CHTN/BK PR9 .....278 E7
Slack Ga WHIT OL12 .....323 J3
Slack's La CHLYE PR6 .....337 J1
Slack La HGHB LA2 .....78 B2
Slape La KKBYL LA6 .....18 C4
Slate La SKEL WN8 .....362 C1
Slater Av COL BB8 .....171 H5
  HOR/BR BL6 .....338 C7
Slater La LEY/BBR PR5 .....284 D3
Slater Rd CLV/TH FY5 .....148 C1
Slater St BBNW BB2 .....267 K2
Slinger Rd CLV/TH FY5 .....122 C8
Sliven Clod Rd RAW/HAS BB4 .....273 F1
Sluice La BRSC L40 .....306 B8
Slyne Rd CARN LA5 .....33 G8
  LANC LA1 .....43 F7
  MCMB LA4 .....42 B7
Smalden La CLI BB7 .....114 A3
Smalley Cft PRES PR1 .....239 H8
Smalley St BLY BB11 .....11 E5
Smalley Wy BBNW BB2 .....268 B1
The Smallholdings
  MGHL (off Millbank La) L31 .....359 J8
Small La BRSC L40 .....329 J3
  ORM L39 .....347 H8
  ORM L39 .....348 D7
Small La North ORM L39 .....347 F1
Small La South ORM L39 .....346 E6
Smallshaw La BLY BB11 .....224 D6
Smallshaw Rd WHIT OL12 .....322 E1
Smallwood Hey Rd
  GAR/LONG PR3 .....99 K6
Smelt Mill Cottages
  CLI (off Trough Rd) BB7 .....109 H1
Smethurst Park Hall
  WGNW/BIL/O WN5 .....370 E1
Smethurst Rd WGNW/BIL/O WN5 .....370 E1
Smirthwaite St BLY* BB11 .....10 A4
Smith Av KIRK/FR/WA PR4 .....281 K2
  WGNW/BIL/O WN5 .....365 K3
Smith Cl FUL/RIB PR2 .....215 G2
Smith Cft LEY/BBR PR5 .....284 C3
Smithills Cl CHLYE PR6 .....311 J2
Smithills Croft Rd BOL BL1 .....340 E8
Smithills Dean Rd BOL BL1 .....340 E6
Smithills Hall Cl RAMS BLO 319 H7
Smith La EDGW/EG BL7 .....341 K3
Smith Rd CLV/TH FY5 .....148 D1
Smith's La KIRK/FR/WA PR4 .....306 A2
Smith St BRFD/BLYE BB10 .....227 F6
  BWCK/EAR BB18 .....144 E2
  CHLY/EC PR7 .....311 H5
  CHLYE PR6 .....287 G3
  COL BB8 .....171 G7
  KIRK/FR/WA PR4 .....208 D6

  LEY/BBR PR5 26
  NLSN BB9 198
  PDHM/BLYW BB12 1
  RAMS BLO 31
  SKEL WN8 56
Smithy Bridge St ACC BB5 24
  WGNNW/ST WN6 33
Smithy Cl CHLYE PR6 26
  FMBY L37 34
  GAR/LONG PR3 12
  PLF/KEOS FY6 12
Smithy Cft EDGW/EG BL7 34
Smithyfield Av BRFD/BLYE BB10 22
Smithy Fold KIRK/FR/WA * PR4 207
Smithy Gn FMBY L37 34
Smithy La BPOOLE FY3 17
  BRSC L40 32
  BRSC L40 33
  CHLYE PR6 26
  COL BB8 17
  GAR/LONG PR3 15
  HEY LA3 52
  KIRK/FR/WA PR4 28
  KIRK/FR/WA PR4 30
  LSTA FY8 23
  ORM L39 34
  ORM L39 35
  PLF/KEOS FY6 98
  PLF/KEOS FY6 12
Smithy Ms BPOOLE FY1 17
Smithy Rw CLI BB7 19
Smithy St LEY/BBR PR5 26
  RAMS* BLO 31
The Smithy
  CLI (off Station Rd) BB7 19
Snaefell Rd BBNW BB2 26
Snape Gn STHP PR8 32
Snape La CARN LA5 2
Snape Rake La GAR/LONG PR3 13
Snape St DWN BB3 26
Snapewood La GAR/LONG PR3 10
Snell Gv COL BB8 17
Sniddle Hill La DWN BB3 29
Snipe Cl BPOOLE FY3 17
  CLV/TH FY5 12
Snipewood CHLY/EC PR7 30
Snodworth Rd GTH/LHO BB6 22
Snowden St PDHM/BLYW BB12 22
Snowdon Av BBN BB1 .....
Snowdon Cl BPOOL FY1 .....
Snowdon Dr HOR/BR BL6 33
Snowdon Rd LSTA FY8 23
Snowdrop Cl LEY/BBR PR5 28
  RAW/HAS BB4 29
Snow Hl PRES PR1 .....
Snowhill La GAR/LONG PR3 10
Snowshill Crs CLV/TH FY5 14
Snow St BBN BB1 .....
Sod Hall La KIRK/FR/WA PR4 26
Sollam's Cl LEY/BBR PR5 26
Sollom La BRSC L40 30
Solway Av BBNW BB2 26
Solway Cl BISP FY2 14
  PRES PR1 23
Somersby Rd MCMB LA4 4
Somerford Cl PDHM/BLYW BB12 1
Somersby Dr EDGW/EG BL7 34
Somerset Av BBN BB1 21
  BPOOL FY1 .....
  CHLY/EC PR7 31
  CLI BB7 16
  DWN BB3 26
  LANC LA1 .....
Somerset Cl ACC BB5 24
Somerset Ct BPOOL FY1 .....
Somerset Dr STHP PR8 34
Somerset Gv ACC BB5 24
Somerset Pk FUL/RIB PR2 21
Somerset Pl NLSN BB9 19
Somerset Rd BBN BB1 24
  LEY/BBR PR5 28
  PRES PR1 .....
Somerset St BLY* BB11 .....
Somerset Wk RAW/HAS BB4 29
Somerville Sq BOL BL1 34
Somerville St BOL BL1 34
Sorrel Cl CLV/TH FY5 12
Sorrel Ct PRES PR1 26
Soudan St BRFD/BLYE * BB10 22
Soughbridge Ml
  BWCK/EAR (off Colne Rd) BB18 14
Sough La BBN BB1 26
  BWCK/EAR BB18 14
Sough Rd DWN BB3 29
Sourhall Ct TOD OL14 27
Sourhall Rd TOD OL14 27

th Av BWCK/EAR BB18 ....119 F8
HLY/EC PR7 ....311 H5
.V/TH FY5 ....122 C7
RK/FR/WA PR4 ....261 C3
CMB LA4 ....41 J6
thbank Av BPOOLS FY4 ....205 G4
thbank Rd STHP PR8 ....301 H4
thbourne Av PLF/KEOS FY6 ....177 J1
thbourne Rd BPOOLE FY3 ....5 F5
thbrook Rd LEY/BBR PR5 ....285 G2
thcliffe GTH/LHO BB6 ....221 F5
thcliffe Rd BRFD/BLYE BB12 ....224 E4
th Cliff St PRES PR1 ....6 C4
th Clifton St LSTA FY8 ....232 D8
thdene SKEL WN8 ....351 H1
thdown Dr CLV/TH FY5 ....149 K3
thdowns Rd CHLY/EC PR7 ....311 H6
th Dr FUL/RIB PR2 ....213 G3
RK/FR/WA PR4 ....182 C3
OHM/BLYW BB12 ....224 A3
GNNW/ST WN6 ....352 E1
ch End PRES PR1 ....6 C5
thern Av PDHM/BLYW BB12 ....224 D4
RES PR1 ....7 F4
thern Cl GAR/LONG PR3 ....188 K3
thern Pde PRES PR1 ....7 F4
thern Rd STHP PR8 ....301 H5
thern's La RNFD/HAY WA11 .....369 C5
thfield KIRK/FR/WA PR4 ....259 K8
thfield Dr BPOOLE FY3 ....177 J3
J BB7 ....139 K5
RK/FR/WA PR4 ....261 C4
thfield La BRFD/BLYE BB10 .....199 G3
OL BB8 ....199 H2
thfield Sq NLSN * BB9 ....198 D3
thfleet NLSN BB9 ....198 D4
thfleet Av FTWD FY7 ....122 E2
thfleet Pl FTWD FY7 ....122 E2
thfold Pl LSTA FY8 ....232 C7
thgate FTWD FY7 ....122 D3
JL/RIB PR2 ....213 F6
EY LA3 ....53 K1
RES PR1 ....7 D1
HIT OL12 ....323 F4
thgates CHLY/EC PR7 ....310 B8
th Gv FUL/RIB PR2 ....213 C3
AR/LONG PR3 ....184 D3
CMB LA4 ....41 J6
thgrove Av BOL BL1 ....341 J5
th Hey LSTA FY8 ....231 J5
th Holme LSTA FY8 ....232 D7
th King St BPOOL FY1 ....4 C2
thlands KIRK/FR/WA PR4 ....208 E7
thlands Av LEY/BBR PR5 ....262 E2
thlands Dr LEY/BBR PR5 ....284 E4
th Lawn BPOOL FY1 ....5 E5
th Meadow La PRES PR1 ....6 C4
th Meadow St PRES PR1 ....7 E2
th Moss Rd LSTA FY8 ....231 J4
th Pde CLV/TH FY5 ....148 C2
th Pk LSTA FY8 ....232 B7
th Park Dr BPOOLE FY3 ....5 F5
th Park Rd KKBY L32 ....366 A8
thport New Rd CHTN/BK PR9 ...279 K7
RK/FR/WA PR4 ....281 H7
thport Old Rd FMBY L37 ....344 C5
thport Rd CHLY/EC PR7 ....310 C3
MBY L37 ....344 A6
EY/BBR PR5 ....308 C1
GHL L31 ....358 C4
RM L39 ....346 C5
RM L39 ....348 B3
THP PR8 ....327 J1
thport Ter CHLYE PR6 ....311 J4
ANC LA1 ....3 C4
FY/BBR PR5 ....282 E6
CMB LA4 ....41 J6
th Shore St ACC BB5 ....247 J6
AW/HAS BB4 ....272 B8
thside CHLY/EC PR7 ....286 A8
th Sq BPOOLE FY3 ....5 D1
.V/TH FY5 ....122 C6
th Strd FTWD FY7 ....122 D4
th St ACC BB5 ....248 E3
CC BB5 ....248 C6
CUP OL13 ....298 E1
LY BB11 ....11 D3
WN BB3 ....291 J2
AR/LONG PR3 ....153 F6
STA FY8 ....233 F7
MS BL0 ....319 K5
/HAS BB4 ....273 H8

RAW/HAS BB4 ....295 J2
RAW/HAS BB4 ....297 G2
South Ter ORM L39 ....348 C7
South Valley Dr COL BB8 ....171 G8
South Vw EDGW/EG BL7 ....314 E6
KIRK/FR/WA PR4 ....208 E7
LEY/BBR (off School La) PR5 ......262 D4
NLSN BB9 ....198 B4
PDHM/BLYW (off Whins La) BB12 .194 E8
South View St TOD OL14 ....277 H2
South View Ter LEY/BBR PR5 ....285 J3
South Warton St LSTA FY8 ....232 E8
Southway FTWD FY7 ....122 D2
SKEL WN8 ....363 H3
South Westby St LSTA FY8 ....232 D8
Southwood Av FTWD FY7 ....96 B8
Southwood Cl LSTA FY8 ....232 A7
Southwood Dr ACC BB5 ....248 E8
Southworth Av BPOOLS FY4 .....204 E4
Southworth St BBNW BB2 ....268 A1
Southworth Wy CLV/TH FY5 .....122 C6
Sow Clough Rd BCUP OL13 ....298 B2
Sowerby Av BPOOLS FY4 ....204 D3
Sowerby Rd GAR/LONG PR3 ......154 E7
Sowerby St PDHM/BLYW BB12 ..223 J3
Sower Carr La PLF/KEOS FY6 ....125 F7
Spa Garth CLI BB7 ....165 K3
Spa La BRSC L40 ....350 B7
Spark La BRSC L40 ....306 B5
Spa Rd PRES PR1 ....6 B2
Sparrow Hl SKEL WN8 ....352 C1
Sparth Av ACC BB5 ....221 K8
Sparth Rd ACC BB5 ....221 K8
Spa St PDHM/BLYW BB12 ....10 B2
PDHM/BLYW BB12 ....223 K3
PRES PR1 ....6 B2
Speakmana Dr WGNNW/ST WN6 .352 E5
Speedwell Cl CLV/TH FY5 ....123 F6
Speedwell St BBNW BB2 ....267 J1
Speke St BBNW BB2 ....267 J1
Spenbrook Rd PDHM/BLYW BB12 .168 E8
Spen Brow HGHB LA2 ....39 J8
Spencer Ct BPOOL FY1 ....176 C4
Spencer Gv GTH/LHO BB6 ....221 F6
Spencer Pl
  CHTN/BK (off Ashley Rd) PR9 ....301 C1
Spencers Dr KIRK/FR/WA PR4 ...282 A3
Spencer's La ORM L39 ....326 D8
  SKEL WN8 ....363 H3
  WGNW/BIL/O WN5 ....365 F4
Spencer St ACC BB5 ....248 D5
  BRFD/BLYE BB10 ....225 J3
  RAMS BL0 ....319 H6
  RAW/HAS BB4 ....273 H4
Spendmore La CHLY/EC PR7 .....335 H3
Spen La KIRK/FR/WA PR4 ....209 J5
Spenleach La TOT/BURYW BL8 ..318 C7
Spen Pl BPOOLS FY4 ....205 F3
Spenser Cl BRFD/BLYE BB10 .....227 G7
Spenser St PDHM/BLYW BB12 ...223 K4
Spey Cl LEY/BBR PR5 ....285 C3
Speyside BPOOLS FY4 ....204 D4
Spindle Berry Ct ACC * BB5 ......248 C7
Spinners Dr LANC LA1 ....3 C3
Spinners Sq LEY/BBR * PR5 ....263 H4
Spinney Brow FUL/RIB PR2 ....214 B7
Spinney Cl CHLYE PR6 ....287 F5
  KIRK/FR/WA PR4 ....261 C3
  ORM L39 ....348 B8
Spinney La CARN LA5 ....15 H3
The Spinney BBNW BB2 ....244 C3
  CARN LA5 ....15 H3
  CHLYE PR6 ....311 C1
  CLV/TH FY5 ....149 F4
  FMBY L37 ....344 A6
  KIRK/FR/WA PR4 ....282 A4
  LANC LA1 ....3 F6
  PDHM/BLYW BB12 ....10 A1
  PLF/KEOS FY6 ....150 A7
  PRES PR1 ....238 B8
  RNFD/HAY WA11 ....369 F4
  WHIT OL12 ....323 H8
Spinning Av BBN BB1 ....269 G3
The Spinnings
  RAMS (off Waterside Rd) BL0 ......319 J8
Spires Cv KIRK/FR/WA PR4 ....212 A6
Spodden Fold WHIT OL12 ....323 C3
Spouthouse La ACC BB5 ....249 F2
Spout La HGHB LA2 ....30 D8
Spread Eagle St ACC BB5 ....247 F6
Spring Av GTH/LHO BB6 ....221 G5
Spring Bank CARN LA5 ....15 H8
  GAR/LONG PR3 ....129 C3
  PRES PR1 ....6 C3
Springbank Av CLV/TH FY5 ....149 J1
Springbank Gdns RAW/HAS BB4 .273 G1
Spring Bank Ter BBNW BB2 ......267 K1

Springbrook Av CLV/TH FY5 .....148 E3
Spring Cl NWD/KWIPK * L33 ......366 E6
  RAMS BL0 ....319 H5
  STHP PR8 ....301 G6
Spring Crs CHLYE PR6 ....287 J5
Springcroft LEY/BBR PR5 ....263 F8
Springdale Rd GTH/LHO BB6 .....220 A3
Springdale CARN LA5 ....15 C2
  NLSN BB9 ....170 B3
Spring Fld RNFD/HAY WA11 ....368 E1
Springfield Av ACC BB5 ....247 K7
  BBNW BB2 ....267 F2
  BCUP OL13 ....275 K8
  BWCK/EAR BB18 ....146 C2
  KIRK/FR/WA PR4 ....208 C6
Springfield Bank BLY BB11 ....11 D4
Springfield Cl BRSC L40 ....349 H1
  CLI BB7 ....193 H4
  FMBY L37 ....355 G1
Springfield Dr CLV/TH FY5 ....123 H7
  RAW/HAS BB4 ....297 G2
Springfield Gdns GAR/LONG PR3 .104 A5
  KKBYL LA6 ....34 B6
Springfield Rd BLY BB11 ....11 D5
  BOL BL1 ....341 J4
  BPOOL FY1 ....4 B1
  CHLY/EC* PR7 ....311 C3
  CHLY/EC PR7 ....335 J3
  CLI BB7 ....337 C3
  GTH/LHO BB6 ....221 F7
  LEY/BBR PR5 ....285 F4
  LSTA FY8 ....230 E5
  NLSN BB9 ....198 B5
  ORM L39 ....359 H6
  RAW/HAS BB4 ....273 J8
Springfield Rd North
  CHLY/EC * PR7 ....335 J2
Springfield St ACC BB5 ....247 H8
  BBNW BB2 ....244 D8
  DWN BB3 ....291 J3
  LANC LA1 ....3 D4
  MCMB LA4 ....41 F7
  PRES PR1 ....6 C1
Springfield Ter BBNW BB2 ....267 G2
Springfield Vw BLY BB11 ....250 E6
Spring Gdns ACC BB5 ....248 C6
  BCUP OL13 ....275 K8
  CLI (off Clitheroe Rd) BB7 ....139 G7
  DWN BB3 ....291 J3
  HOR/BR BL6 ....338 D7
  KIRK/FR/WA PR4 ....235 F3
  LEY/BBR PR5 ....285 H3
  LSTA FY8 ....231 F2
  PDHM/BLYW BB12 ....223 J2
  PRES PR1 ....262 C1
Spring Gardens Rd COL BB8 ......171 H7
Spring Gardens St RAW/HAS BB4 .297 H3
Spring Garden St LANC * LA1 ....3 D4
Spring Gv COL BB8 ....172 C5
Spring Hall ACC BB5 ....221 K6
Spring HI BBN BB1 ....8 C4
  KIRK/FR/WA PR4 ....235 H4
Springhill Av BCUP OL13 ....298 A4
Spring Hill Rd ACC BB5 ....247 K7
  BLY BB11 ....10 C5
Springhill Vls BCUP OL13 ....298 B3
Spring La BBNW BB2 ....244 D8
  COL BB8 ....171 H6
  LEY/BBR PR5 ....242 C7
  RAW/HAS BB4 ....272 C7
Spring Meadow LEY/BBR PR5 ....286 C1
Spring Mdw DWN BB3 ....292 B4
Spring Ms CHLYE PR6 ....287 J5
Springmount BWCK/EAR BB18 ..146 C2
Springmount Dr SKEL WN8 ....332 E6
Spring Pl WHIT OL12 ....299 H8
Springpool WGNS/IIMK WN3 .....371 K1
Spring Rd WGNW/BIL/O WN5 ....365 K2
Spring Rw
  COL (off Keighley Rd) BB8 ....172 C5
Springsands Cl FUL/RIB * PR2 ...214 C6
Spring Side WHIT OL12 ....299 H7
Springs Rd CHLYE PR6 ....311 H1
  GAR/LONG PR3 ....188 B3
Spring St ACC BB5 ....247 J7
  BBN BB1 ....247 F1
  BCUP* OL13 ....298 D2
  HOR/BR BL6 ....338 D7
  LEY/BBR PR5 ....285 K2
  NLSN BB9 ....198 A4
  RAMS BL0 ....319 K4
  RAMS BL0 ....319 H5
  RAW/HAS BB4 ....273 H3
  TOD OL14 ....277 H2
Springthorpe St DWN BB3 ....291 K5
Springvale ACC BB5 ....247 K7
Spring V GAR/LONG PR3 ....80 C8

er's La ACC BB5 ....247 J5
er St ACC BB5 ....248 A5
hendale Av LEY/BBR PR5 ....264 A3
hens Cv HEY LA3 ....65 H3
henson Dr
  HM/BLYW BB12 ....224 E4
henson St CHLYE PR6 ....311 H4
henson Wy FMBY L37 ....344 C8
hen St BBNW BB2 ....267 J1
*rA FY8 ....230 E4
enson Av LEY/BBR PR5 ....263 F8
enson St East ACC BB5 ....247 K6
enson St West ACC BB5 ....247 K7
*ard Av LANC LA1 ....3 F6
art Cl CARN LA5 ....15 G3
art St BBNW BB2 ....268 A3
*V BB11 ....11 E5
*ES PR1 ....6 B2
s Av KIRK/FR/WA PR4 ....260 D2
s Rd NWD/KWIPK L33 ....366 D5
Stiles ORM L39 ....348 C6
ng Cl CHLYE * PR6 ....311 J4
*BB7 ....165 G5
*/BBR PR5 ....286 A2
ng Ct BRFD/BLYE BB10 ....199 F7
ng Dr BBN BB1 ....9 D5
ng Rd BOL BL1 ....341 J6
*POOLE FY3 ....5 D1
*NC LA1 ....3 E4
ng St BBNW BB2 ....267 J2
kbridge Dr
  *HM/BLYW BB12 ....224 B2
kbridge Rd
  *HM/BLYW BB12 ....223 K3
kclough La BBNW BB2 ....266 E4
kdale Crs LEY/BBR PR5 ....263 J4
kdove Wy CLV/TH FY5 ....122 D8
kdove Wd CLV/TH FY5 ....122 E8
kholm St BLY BB11 ....224 D6
kley Crs ORM L39 ....361 J5
ks Cottages
  *R/BR (off Gingham Brow) BL6 ....339 F7
ks La CHLY/EC PR7 ....309 G8
SN BB9 ....143 H4
F/KEOS FY6 ....149 G7
ks Park Dr HOR/BR BL6 ....338 E8
ks Rd FUL/RIB PR2 ....6 A1
ks St PRES PR1 ....6 C2
kwood Cl BBNW BB2 ....244 C3
e Av BPOOL FY1 ....5 D5
es Hall Av LEY/BBR PR5 ....285 J3
ebarn Dr MGHL L31 ....358 E8
ebridge Cl LEY/BBR PR5 ....263 F3
e Bridge La ACC BB5 ....247 H8
ebridge Ter
  R/LAW (off Preston Rd) PR3 ....188 A4
echat Cl BPOOLE FY3 ....177 H5
e Cl RAMS BL0 ....319 G7
ecroft Rd LEY/BBR PR5 ....285 F4
e Cross Gdns GAR/LONG PR3 ....155 K1
e Edge Rd NLSN BB9 ....170 C5
efield KIRK/FR/WA PR4 ....260 A3
*ES PR1 ....6 C6
efold Av KIRK/FR/WA PR4 ....260 D2
e Hall La SKEL WN8 ....352 B7
egate Fold CHLYE PR6 ....337 H2
e Hall Av LEY/BBR PR5 ....285 K2
ehill Crs WHIT OL12 ....322 E8
e Hill Dr BBN BB1 ....245 J2
ehill Dr WHIT OL12 ....322 E8
ehill Rd WHIT OL12 ....322 E8
eholme Rd RAW/HAS BB4 ....273 H3
e House Fold
  *Y (off Dyneley La) BB11 ....252 C5
ehouse Gn CHLYE PR6 ....264 A8
eleigh Cl STHP PR8 ....325 J7
e Park Rd GAR/LONG PR3 ....184 E8
e Pits RAMS BL0 ....296 A8
e Row Head LANC LA1 ....55 J3
es Bank Rd EDGW/EG BL7 ....315 H6
es La GAR/LONG PR3 ....130 A8
*D OL14 ....277 K7
e St RAW/HAS BB4 ....295 F1
*AW/HAS BB4 ....297 H3
eway Rd CLV/TH FY5 ....148 E2
ewell LANC LA1 ....3 D3
ey Brow SKEL WN8 ....364 D1
ey Butts FUL/RIB PR2 ....237 K3
eycroft Rd HOR/BR BL6 ....339 F7
eycroft Rd HOR/BR BL6 ....339 F6
eycroft Dr CARN LA5 ....15 G2
eygate CLV/TH FY5 ....149 F2
ES PR1 ....7 E3
eygate La WGNNW/ST WN6 ....352 D1
ey Holt LEY/BBR PR5 ....286 C2

Stonehurst Av BRFD/BLYE BB10 ....226 B6
  CLV/TH FY5 ....149 K3
Stoneyhurst Height NLSN BB9 ....198 B7
Stoney La CHLY/EC PR7 ....336 E7
  COL BB8 ....171 J2
  HGHB LA2 ....67 H8
  KIRK/FR/WA PR4 ....235 F6
  LEY/BBR PR5 ....263 F5
  PLF/KEOS FY6 ....150 E1
Stoneyroyd WHIT * OL12 ....323 H1
Stoney St BLY BB11 ....11 E6
Stonor Rd CHLY/EC PR7 ....337 F4
Stony Bank CHLYE PR6 ....265 F6
Stony Bank Rd BWCK/EAR BB18 ....146 B1
Stonybutts BBNW BB2 ....8 C4
Stonycroft Av BPOOLS FY4 ....204 C6
Stony Croft Pl BPOOLS * FY4 ....204 C6
Stonygate La GAR/LONG PR3 ....189 J3
Stony Hill Av BPOOLS FY4 ....204 B5
Stonyhurst CHLY/EC PR7 ....311 G7
Stonyhurst Cl BBNW BB2 ....8 B5
  PDHM/BLYW BB12 ....223 K5
Stonyhurst Rd BBNW BB2 ....8 B5
Stony La GAR/LONG PR3 ....80 E8
  GAR/LONG PR3 ....80 A8
  SKEL WN8 ....333 C7
  TOD OL14 ....277 K2
Stoopes Hl BWCK/EAR BB18 ....146 C1
Stoops Fold BBNW BB2 ....218 A8
Stoops La CLI BB7 ....142 B3
Stoop St BLY BB11 ....224 E6
Stopes Brow DWN BB3 ....268 D4
Stopford Av BISP FY2 ....176 E1
Stopgate La NWD/KWIPK L33 ....366 E5
Stopper La CLI BB7 ....142 D4
Stopping Hey
  BBN (off Parsonage Rd) BB1 ....219 K6
Store St DWN BB3 ....268 D4
  HOR/BR BL6 ....338 E7
Storey Av LANC LA1 ....2 B3
Storey Home
  LANC (off Ashton Rd) LA1 ....2 C6
Stork Cl CLV/TH FY5 ....149 F2
Storrs La CARN LA5 ....16 A4
Storth Rd MTHPE LA7 ....15 K2
Stott St NLSN BB9 ....198 B3
Stour Ldg FUL/RIB PR2 ....212 E5
Stourton Rd STHP PR8 ....325 J7
Stourton St BBN BB1 ....246 E1
Stout St BBNW BB2 ....8 B5
Straight Up La CHTN/BK PR9 ....302 E3
Strait La HGHB LA2 ....83 H2
Straits ACC BB5 ....247 J7
Straits La PDHM/BLYW BB12 ....222 D1
Strand Rd PRES PR1 ....6 B1
Strand St West FUL/RIB * PR2 ....6 A2
The Strand BPOOL FY1 ....4 B2
  FTWD FY7 ....122 C3
  HOR/BR BL6 ....339 F8
Strange St BLY BB11 ....11 E5
Strang St RAMS BL0 ....319 J5
Stransdale Cl GAR/LONG PR3 ....129 G4
Stratfield Pl LEY/BBR PR5 ....285 K2
Stratford Cl LANC LA1 ....42 E8
  STHP PR8 ....325 G5
Stratford Dr FUL/RIB PR2 ....213 F7
Stratford Pl BPOOL FY1 ....5 E5
Stratford Rd CHLYE PR6 ....311 H3
  LSTA FY8 ....231 H5
Strathclyde Rd BBN BB1 ....9 E5
Strathdale BPOOLS FY4 ....205 F4
Strathmore Cl RAMS BL0 ....319 J8
Strathmore Gv CHLY/EC PR7 ....311 F4
Strathmore Rd FUL/RIB PR2 ....213 G7
Strathyre Cl BISP FY2 ....149 F6
Stratton Ct NLSN BB9 ....198 C5
Strawberry Bank BBNW BB2 ....8 B4
Street Br HGHB LA2 ....81 J1
Strellas La CARN LA5 ....43 J2
Stretford Cl NWD/KWIPK L33 ....366 C5
Stretton Av BPOOLS FY4 ....204 E3
  WGNW/BIL/O WN5 ....371 G6
Stretton Dr CHTN/BK PR9 ....302 B3
Strickens La GAR/LONG PR3 ....131 F3
Strickland Dr MCMB LA4 ....42 A6
Strickland's La PLF/KEOS FY6 ....125 F5
  PRES PR1 ....6 B6
Strike La KIRK/FR/WA PR4 ....235 F5
The Strine BRSC L40 ....306 A2
Strongstry Rd RAMS BL0 ....319 J5
Stronsay Pl BISP FY2 ....149 F5
Stroyan St BRFD/BLYE BB10 ....11 F4
Strutt St PRES PR1 ....7 F1
Stryands KIRK/FR/WA PR4 ....260 D2
Stuart Av BCUP OL13 ....298 B3
  MCMB LA4 ....41 K5

Stuart Cl FUL/RIB PR2 ....214 C8
Stuart Crs WGNW/BIL/O WN5 ....371 F6
Stuart Rd CLV/TH FY5 ....149 J1
  FUL/RIB PR2 ....214 C8
Stuart St ACC BB5 ....248 B4
  BWCK/EAR BB18 ....145 G1
Stubbins La CLI BB7 ....195 G4
  GAR/LONG PR3 ....156 A1
  RAMS BL0 ....319 J3
Stubbins St RAMS BL0 ....319 J2
Stubbins Vale Rd RAMS BL0 ....319 H2
Stubbylee La BCUP OL13 ....298 D3
Stub La BRSC L40 ....348 E1
Stubley Holme TOD OL14 ....277 F2
Stubley La TOD OL14 ....277 F2
Studfold CHLY/EC PR7 ....311 F1
Studholme Av PRES PR1 ....262 B1
Studholme Cl PRES PR1 ....262 B1
Studholme Crs PRES PR1 ....239 G8
Stump Cross La CLI BB7 ....116 A1
Stump Hall Rd PDHM/BLYW BB12 ....196 A4
Stump La CHLYE PR6 ....311 H3
Stunstead Rd COL BB8 ....172 C8
Sturgess Cl ORM L39 ....348 D4
Sturminster Cl PRES PR1 ....262 B1
Styan St FTWD FY7 ....97 G7
Stydd La GAR/LONG PR3 ....190 A7
Sudell Cl DWN BB3 ....292 A2
Sudell Cross BBNW BB2 ....8 B4
Sudell La MGHL L31 ....359 F5
Sudell Rd DWN BB3 ....291 K1
Sudellside St DWN BB3 ....291 K1
Suffolk Av PDHM/BLYW BB12 ....224 C5
Suffolk Rd BPOOLE FY3 ....205 G1
  PRES PR1 ....7 E1
  STHP PR8 ....326 C3
Suffolk St BBNW BB2 ....267 K1
Sugar Stubbs La CHTN/BK PR9 ....280 A7
Sugham La HEY LA3 ....52 D3
Sulby Cl STHP PR8 ....301 F8
Sulby Dr FUL/RIB PR2 ....214 D6
  LANC LA1 ....3 D5
Sulby Gv FUL/RIB PR2 ....214 E6
  MCMB LA4 ....42 A5
Sulby Rd BBNW BB2 ....268 B2
Sullivan Dr BBNW BB2 ....268 D2
Sullom Side La GAR/LONG PR3 ....130 E6
Sullom Vw GAR/LONG PR3 ....129 J5
Sultan St ACC BB5 ....248 C5
Sulyard St LANC * LA1 ....3 D3
Summerfield LEY/BBR PR5 ....262 C8
Summerfield Cl PRES PR1 ....262 D1
Summerfield Dr HGHB LA2 ....42 E4
Summerfields CHLY/EC PR7 ....335 K4
  LSTA FY8 ....230 C3
Summersgill Rd LANC LA1 ....2 B1
Summer St HOR/BR BL6 ....338 D7
  NLSN BB9 ....198 A4
  SKEL WN8 ....351 F7
Summer Trees Av FUL/RIB PR2 ....211 K8
Summerville BPOOLS FY4 ....204 C5
Summerville Av BPOOLE FY3 ....177 K6
Summerville Wk BBNW BB2 ....8 B4
Summerwood Cl BISP FY2 ....176 D1
Summerwood La ORM L39 ....346 C2
Summit Dr KIRK/FR/WA PR4 ....235 G5
The Summit
  BWCK/EAR
  (off Dales View Pk) BB18 ....145 F4
Sumner Av ORM L39 ....346 B7
Sumner Gv NWD/KWIPK L33 ....366 D6
Sumner Rd FMBY L37 ....343 K8
Sumner's La BRSC L40 ....307 G4
Sumner St BBNW BB2 ....8 C6
  LEY/BBR PR5 ....285 J2
Sumpter Cft PRES PR1 ....262 B1
Sunbury Av PRES PR1 ....239 F8
Sunbury Dr STHP PR8 ....325 H7
Suncliffe Rd NLSN BB9 ....198 B3
Sunderland Av CLV/TH FY5 ....122 E7
  PLF/KEOS FY6 ....151 F1
Sunderland Dr HEY LA3 ....53 G1
Sunderland St
  PDHM/BLYW BB12 ....224 D6
Sunfield Cl BPOOLS FY4 ....205 G4
Sunninghale Av RAW/HAS BB4 ....297 J2
Sunningdale Av CLV/TH FY5 ....149 K3
Sunningdale Av BPOOLS FY4 ....205 G1
  FTWD FY7 ....122 D4
  HGHB LA2 ....42 D2
Sunningdale Cl KIRK/FR/WA PR4 ....208 E7
Sunningdale Ct LSTA FY8 ....231 G5
Sunningdale Crs HGHB LA2 ....42 D3
Sunningdale Dr CLV/TH FY5 ....149 K3
Sunningdale Gdns
  BRFD/BLYE BB10 ....198 B8
  FMBY L37 ....343 J8

Sunningdale Pl *KIRK/FR/WA* PR4....182 C3
Sunny Bank
  BCUP (off Todmorden Rd) OL13 ...276 B6
  KIRK/FR/WA PR4 ....208 D6
Sunny Bank Av *BISP* FY2 ....148 C3
  KIRK/FR/WA PR4 ....236 A1
Sunny Bank Cl *RAW/HAS* BB4 ......295 G4
Sunnybank Dr *ACC* BB5 ....270 E1
Sunny Bank Rd *BBNW* BB2 ....268 A2
  RAW/HAS BB4 ....295 G5
Sunnybank Rd *CARN* LA5 ....33 C6
Sunnybank St *DWN* * BB3 ....291 J2
  RAW/HAS BB4 ....272 B8
Sunny Bank Ter *TOD* OL14 ....277 G2
Sunny Bower *Cl BBN* BB1 ....245 K2
Sunny Brow *CHLY/EC* PR7 ....336 A1
Sunny Dr *WGNW/BIL/O* WN5 ....365 H5
Sunnyfield Av *BRFD/BLYE* BB10...252 E3
  MCMB LA4 ....42 A5
Sunnyfield La *DWN* BB3 ....292 D3
Sunnyfields *ORM* L39 ....348 E6
Sunny Hi
  LANC (off Westbourne Rd) LA1 ...2 B4
Sunnyhill Cl *DWN* BB3 ....291 F1
Sunnyside Av *BPOOLS* FY4 ....204 D5
Sunnyside Cl *DWN* BB3 ....291 F1
Sunnyside La *DWN* BB3 ....291 F1
Sunnyhurst Rd *BBNW* BB2 ....8 B5
Sunny Lea St *RAW/HAS* BB4 ....273 G6
Sunnymead Av *BOL* BL1 ....341 K7
Sunnymead Dr *MGHL* L31 ....359 F8
Sunnymede V *TOT/BURYW* BL8 ...319 G8
Sunnymere Dr *DWN* BB3 ....291 G1
Sunny Rd *CHTN/BK* PR9 ....302 C1
Sunnyside *ORM* L39 ....360 A4
  STHP PR8 ....301 F8
Sunnyside Av *BBN* BB1 ....219 J4
  BBNW BB2 ....267 F2
  CLI BB7 ....193 F6
  GAR/LONG PR3.....................189 K8
  KIRK/FR/WA PR4 ....234 D5
Sunnyside Cl *KIRK/FR/WA* PR4 .....235 F4
  LANC LA1..................................2 C4
  RAW/HAS BB4 ....273 H5
Sunnyside La *LANC* LA1 ....2 C4
Sunset Cl *NWD/KWIPK* L33 ....366 E6
Sun St *ACC* BB5 ....247 J7
  CLI BB7 ....165 J4
  COL BB8 ....171 J6
  LANC LA1..................................3 D3
  NLSN BB9 ....198 A3
  RAMS BL0.............................319 H4
Sun Ter *TOD* * OL14 ....277 G2
Super St *ACC* BB5 ....221 J7
Surgeon's Ct *PRES* PR1 ....7 D3
Surrey Av *DWN* BB3 ....268 C8
  PDHM/BLYW BB12 ....224 D4
Surrey Rd *BBNW* BB2 ....246 B5
  NLSN BB9 ....198 A1
Surrey St *ACC* BB5 ....248 D5
  PRES PR1 ....240 A3
Sussex Cl *BBN* BB1 ....9 E5
  GAR/LONG PR3.....................129 H3
  RAW/HAS BB4 ....295 G3
Sussex Rd *BBN* BB1 ....246 D3
  BPOOLE FY3 ....5 E1
  CHTN/BK PR9 ....301 J4
  STHP PR8 ....302 A5
Sussex St *BLY* BB11 ....11 E5
  BWCK/EAR BB18 ....145 F1
  NLSN BB9 ....198 C2
  PRES PR1 ....7 E1
Sutch La *BRSC* L40 ....331 H7
Sutcliffe St *BCUP* OL13 ....299 G3
  BLY BB11................................10 C3
  BRFD/BLYE BB10 ....198 H4
  CHLY/EC PR7 ....311 H4
Sutherland Cl *BBN* BB1 ....219 J4
Sutherland Rd *BPOOL* FY1 ....176 C4
Sutherland St *COL* BB8 ....171 G7
Sutton Av *BRFD/BLYE* BB10 ....226 B1
  KIRK/FR/WA PR4 ....282 A3
Sutton Cl *ACC* BB5 ....249 F2
Sutton Gv *CHLYE* PR6 ....287 K7
Sutton La *CHLYE* PR6 ....337 G2
  KIRK/FR/WA PR4 ....281 K6
Sutton Pl *BPOOL* FY1 ....4 C5
Sutton Rd *FMBY* L37 ....355 J2
Sutton's La *FMBY* L37 ....344 E8
Sutton's St *BBNW* BB2 ....266 C3
Swainbank St *BLY* BB11 ....11 E4
Swaine St *NLSN* BB9 ....198 B3
Swainson St *BPOOL* * FY1 ....4 C1
  LSTA FY8 ....232 B8
Swallow Av *PRES* PR1 ....6 C6
Swallow Cl *CLV/TH* FY5 ....123 G7

NWD/KWIPK L33 ....366 C4
Swallow Ct *CHLYE* PR6 ....287 G2
Swallow Dr *BBN* BB1 ....8 C3
Swallow Fld *KIRK/FR/WA* PR4 ....259 K8
Swallowfields *BBN* BB1 ....8 B1
Swallowfold *FUL/RIB* PR2 ....215 H2
Swallow Pk *BLY* BB11 ....224 E6
Swallow Whf *LANC* LA1 ....3 E2
Swanage Av *BPOOLS* FY4 ....204 B5
Swanage Rd *BRFD/BLYE* BB10 .....226 A2
Swan Ctyd
  CLI (off Castle St) BB7 ....165 J3
Swan Delph *ORM* L39 ....360 A1
Swan Dr *CLV/TH* FY5 ....149 F2
Swan Farm Cl *DWN* BB3 ....268 C4
Swan La *ORM* L39 ....359 G5
Swanpool La *ORM* L39 ....360 A1
Swansea St *FUL/RIB* PR2 ....6 A1
Swansey La *CHLYE* PR6 ....287 F2
Swan St *BBNW* BB2 ....8 C6
  DWN BB3 ....291 K5
  PRES PR1 ....7 F2
Swan Yd *LANC* LA1 ....3 E4
Swarbrick Cl *BPOOL* FY1 ....176 D4
Swarbrick Ct *GAR/LONG* PR3 ......188 D4
Swarbrick St *KIRK/FR/WA* PR4 ....208 E7
Sweetloves Gv *BOL* BL1 ....341 J6
Sweetloves La *BOL* BL1 ....341 J6
Swift Cl *BBN* BB1 ....9 D4
Swilkin La *PLF/KEOS* FY6 ....125 C5
Swill Brook La *PRES* PR1 ....240 A5
Swinate Rd *CARN* LA5 ....15 H2
Swinburne Cl *ACC* BB5 ....271 K1
Swinburn Gv *WGNW/BIL/O* WN5 ...371 F2
Swinden Hall Rd *NLSN* BB9 ....198 C1
Swinden La *COL* BB8 ....198 E1
Swindon Av *BPOOLS* FY4 ....204 D3
Swindon St *BLY* BB11 ....10 A4
Swinglehurst Cottages
  GAR/LONG (off Garstang Rd) PR3 ...134 E8
Swinless St *BRFD/BLYE* BB10 ....225 K2
Swinshaw Cl *RAW/HAS* BB4 ....273 H1
Swiss St *ACC* BB5 ....247 K5
Swithemby St *HOR/BR* BL6 ....338 C7
Sword Meanygate
  KIRK/FR/WA PR4 ....281 F5
Swords Cross Cl *CHLY/EC* PR7 .....310 E6
Sycamore Av *BPOOLS* * FY4 ....205 F6
  CHLY/EC PR7 ....286 B8
  GAR/LONG PR3.....................129 H3
  PDHM/BLYW BB12 ....224 D4
Sycamore Cl *BBN* * BB1 ....9 D1
  BBN BB1 ....247 F3
  BRSC L40 ....332 E1
  FUL/RIB PR2 ....214 A5
  KIRK/FR/WA PR4 ....180 C2
  PDHM/BLYW BB12 ....224 E5
Sycamore Ct *CHLY/EC* PR7 ....311 F6
Sycamore Crs *ACC* BB5 ....221 K7
  HGHB LA2 ....45 H5
Sycamore Dr *PRES* PR1 ....239 G8
  SKEL WN8 ....362 C1
  WGNS/IIMK WN3 ....371 K1
Sycamore Gdns *COL* BB8 ....171 H2
  COL BB8 ....171 G5
  HEY LA3 ....52 C5
Sycamore Gv *ACC* BB5 ....248 E8
  DWN BB3 ....291 K1
  FMBY L37 ....355 G2
  LANC LA1..................................2 A3
Sycamore Ri *COL* BB8 ....171 H2
Sycamore Rd *BBN* BB1 ....9 D1
  CHLYE PR6 ....311 H1
  FUL/RIB PR2 ....240 C1
  GAR/LONG PR3.....................156 C5
  HGHB LA2 ....45 H5
Sycamore Wy *BWCK/EAR* BB18 ...144 E2
Syd Brook La *BRSC* L40 ....308 A5
Sydney Av *CLI* BB7 ....193 H6
Sydney St *ACC* BB5 ....248 C5
  ACC BB5 ....248 A2
  BLY BB11................................10 C3
  DWN BB3 ....291 K4
  DWN BB3 ....292 D2
  LSTA FY8 ....231 F5
Sykefield *NLSN* BB9 ....197 J6
Syke Hl *PRES* PR1 ....7 E3
Syke House La *GAR/LONG* PR3 .....158 C2
Sykelands Av *HGHB* LA2 ....44 B4
Sykelands Gv *HGHB* LA2 ....44 B4
Syke La *WHIT* OL12 ....323 K7
Syke Rd *WHIT* OL12 ....323 K7
Syke Side Dr *ACC* BB5 ....222 E5
Syke St *PRES* PR1 ....7 E3
  RAW/HAS BB4 ....295 K5
Sylvancroft *FUL/RIB* PR2 ....212 C6
Sylvan Dr *BLY* BB11 ....224 C7

Sylvan Gv *LEY/BBR* PR5 2
Sylvan Pl *HEY* LA3 ....
Sylvester St *LANC* LA1 ....
Symonds Rd *FUL/RIB* PR2 2

T

Tabby Nook *KIRK/FR/WA* PR4 3
Tabby's Nook *SKEL* WN8...................3
Taber La *KIRK/FR/WA* PR4 2
Tabor St *PDHM/BLYW* BB12 ....2.
Tadema Gv *BLY* BB11 ....2°
Tadlow Cl *FMBY* L37 35
Tag Cft *FUL/RIB* PR2 2
Tag Farm Ct *FUL/RIB* PR2 21
Tag La *FUL/RIB* PR2 21
  KIRK/FR/WA PR4 21
Talaton Cl *CHTN/BK* PR9 2
Talbot Av *ACC* BB5 24
Talbot Br *CLI* BB7 13
Talbot Cl *CLI* BB7 ....1€
  RAW/HAS BB4 29
Talbot Ct *BOL* BL1............................34
Talbot Dr *BRFD/BLYE* BB10 22
  CHLY/EC PR7 ....3°
  STHP PR8 ....3C
Talbot Rd *ACC* BB5 24
  BPOOLE FY3 17
  LEY/BBR PR5 28
  LSTA FY8 23
Talbot Rw
  CHLY/EC (off Balshaw La) PR7 ...31
Talbot St *BBN* BB1 24
  BLY BB11...................................1°
  BRFD/BLYE BB10 22
  CHLYE PR6 ....3°
  COL BB8 17
  FUL/RIB PR2 21
  GAR/LONG PR3........................13
  STHP PR8 ....3C
Talbot Ter *LSTA* FY8 23
Tamar Cl *LEY/BBR* PR5.........................2
Tamar St *PRES* PR1 24
The Tamneys *SKEL* WN8 ....3€
Tanfield Nook *SKEL* WN8.................35
Tanfields *SKEL* WN8 ....3€
Tanglewood *FUL/RIB* PR2 21
Tan Hill Dr *LANC* LA1............................€
Tan House Cl *SKEL* WN8...................33
Tanhouse La *CHLYE* PR6 ....2€
Tan House La *SKEL* WN8 35
Tanhouse Rd *SKEL* WN8 ....3€
Tanners Cft *RAMS* BL0......................31
Tannersmith La *CHLY/EC* PR7.........3€
Tanners St *RAMS* BL0........................31
Tanner St *BLY* BB11 1
Tanpits La *KKBYL* LA6 ....
Tanpits Rd *ACC* BB5 24
Tansley Av *CHLY/EC* PR7 33
Tansy La *GAR/LONG* PR3 8
Tanterton Hall Rd *FUL/RIB* PR2 21
Tanyard Ct *CHLY/EC* PR7 33
Tan Yard La *GAR/LONG* PR3 18
Tape St *RAMS* BL0.............................31
Tapestry St *BBNW* BB2 ....2€
Tarbert Crs *BBN* BB1 ....2€
Tarbet St *LANC* LA1...............................
Tarleswood *SKEL* WN8 ....3€
Tarleton Av *BLY* BB11 1
Tarleton Rd *CHTN/BK* PR9 ....3C
Tarleton St *BLY* BB11 1
Tarlscough La *BRSC* L40 33
Tarnacre La *GAR/LONG* PR3 15
Tarnacre Vw *GAR/LONG* PR3 12
Tarn Av *ACC* BB5 22
Tarnbeck Dr *BRSC* L40 ....3C
Tarnbrick Av *KIRK/FR/WA* PR4 23
Tarn Brook Cl *ACC* BB5 ....2€
Tarnbrook Cl *CARN* LA5 3
  CARN LA5 ....
Tarnbrook Cottages
  GAR/LONG (off Taylors La) PR3 ...1C
Tarnbrook Ct
  MCMB (off Euston Rd) LA4 ....
Tarnbrook Dr *BPOOLE* FY3 17
Tarnbrook Rd *HEY* LA3 ....
  LANC * LA1 ....
Tarn Brow *ORM* L39 ....3€
Tarn Cl *PRES* PR1 23
Tarn Ct *FTWD* FY7 12
Tarn Hows Cl *CHLY/EC* * PR7 31
Tarn La *KKBYL* LA6 ....
Tarn Rd *CLV/TH* FY5 ....1€
  FMBY L37 ....3€
Tarnside Rd *WGNW/BIL/O* WN5 ......3€

...syke Rd *LANC* LA1 ....2 B1
...way Av *CLV/TH* FY5 ....149 K3
...dale *KIRK/FR/WA* PR4 ....260 A2
...agon Dr *BISP* FY2 ....149 F7
...y Barn La *CLI* BB7 ....166 A8
...in Cl *BRFD/BLYE* BB10 ....198 D8
...TN/BK* PR9 ....279 F6
...er St *ACC* BB5 ....248 C5
...am Ct *FTWD* FY7 ....122 C2
...ock Cl *WGNW/BIL/O* WN5 ....371 G6
...ersall St *ACC* BB5 ....247 H7
...BNW* BB2 ....8 C5
...AW/HAS* BB4 ....272 C5
...on St *COL* BB8 ....171 F8
...nton Rd *BBNW* BB2 ....244 D6
...nton St *BPOOLS* FY4 ....5 D6
...RES* PR1 ....240 B2
...stock Pl *STHP* PR8 ....325 H5
...stock St *NLSN* BB9 ....198 D3
...d Rd *NLSN* BB9 ....363 J3
...bank Av *BPOOLS* FY4 ....204 D4
...or Av *ORM* L39 ....348 E6
...AW/HAS* BB4 ....297 H1
...or Cl *BBNW* BB2 ....8 A6
...or Ct *RAW/HAS* BB4 ....272 B8
...or La *GAR/LONG* PR3 ....42 B5
...ors Cl *PLF/KEOS* FY6 ....149 J6
...or's La *GAR/LONG* PR3 ....100 B5
...RK/FR/WA* PR4 ....281 H8
...or's Meanygate
...or St *BBNW* BB2 ....8 B6
...RFD/BLYE* BB10 ....11 D1
...WCK/EAR* BB18 ....144 E1
...ILY/EC* PR7 ....311 F6
...l BB7 ....165 K3
...WN* BB3 ....291 J3
...OR/BR* BL6 ....338 D8
...SN* BB9 ....197 K5
...RES* PR1 ....6 B4
...AW/HAS* BB4 ....272 D5
...AW/HAS* BB4 ....273 H8
...EL* WN8 ....362 C2
...HIT* OL12 ....323 H3
...or St West *ACC* * BB5 ....248 B5
...mouth Rd *BPOOLS* FY4 ....205 G5
...St *BLY* BB11 ....10 A4
...RES* PR1 ....6 B4
...wood Cl *PLF/KEOS* FY6 ....150 B7
...wood Rd *CLV/TH* FY5 ....123 G8
...Cl *BBN* BB1 ....8 B1
...V/TH* FY5 ....123 G7
...Y/BBR* PR5 ....285 F4
...RM* L39 ....360 A1
...GNS/IIMK* WN3 ....365 K7
...s La *LSTA* FY8 ....232 A5
...s La *SKEL* WN8 ....351 F3
...el Wk *HEY* LA3 ....53 H1
...ay Av *CLV/TH* FY5 ....122 D7
...RK/FR/WA* PR4 ....209 G6
...ay Ct *LANC* LA1 ....42 E7
...der Av *CHTN/BK* PR9 ....302 C4
...DHM/BLYW* BB12 ....224 D5
...aadore Av *BPOOLS* FY4 ....204 E4
...s Ct *FTWD* FY7 ....122 D1
...sdale *HGHB* LA2 ....67 G7
...sdale Av *BISP* FY2 ....176 D3
...s St *PRES* PR1 ....240 A1
...Gn *FUL/RIB* PR2 ....214 C5
...perance St *CHLYE* PR6 ....311 J3
...ple Cl *BBN* BB1 ....9 F5
...plecombe Dr *BOL* BL1 ....341 H6
...ple Ct *PRES* * PR1 ....7 D3
...ple Dr *BBN* BB1 ....9 F5
...L BL1 ....341 G8
...ple Flds
...ILYE* (off Heapey Rd) PR6 ....288 A8
...ple Rd *BOL* BL1 ....341 G8
...ple St *BLY* BB11 ....11 E4
...POOL* FY1 ....4 B2
...L BB8 ....171 J5
...SN* BB9 ....198 D3
...pleton Cl *DWN* BB3 ....291 J1
...ple Wy *CHLYE* PR6 ....287 H8
...oy Cl *BBN* BB1 ....8 C2
...oy Rd *PRES* PR1 ....7 E4
...ais St *BRFD/BLYE* BB10 ....11 D1
...yson Av *ACC* BB5 ....247 G5
...ILY/EC* PR7 ....311 G5
...V/TH* FY5 ....123 G8
...RK/FR/WA* PR4 ....234 B5
...TA* FY8 ....233 F7
...HM/BLYW* BB12 ....222 C1
...HM/BLYW* BB12 ....224 A1
...yson Cl *CARN* LA5 ....33 G6
...yson Dr *ORM* L39 ....348 B5

WGNW/BIL/O WN5 ....371 F2
Tennyson Gdns *KIRK/FR/WA* PR4 .....234 B5
Tennyson Pl *GTH/LHO* BB6 .....221 F7
LEY/BBR PR5 ....263 G1
Tennyson Rd *BPOOLE* FY3 ......177 F4
COL BB8 ....171 H6
FTWD FY7 ....97 G7
PRES PR1 ....240 B2
Tennyson St *BRFD/BLYE* * BB10 ....198 D8
PDHM/BLYW BB12 ....223 J7
Ten Rw *HGHB* LA2 ....65 J6
Tensing Av *BISP* FY2 ....148 D6
Tenterfield St *PRES* PR1 ....7 D2
RAW/HAS BB4 ....297 H3
Terance Rd *BPOOLS* FY4 ....204 E3
Tern Cl *NWD/KWIPK* L33 ....366 C4
Terrace St *PRES* PR1 ....240 A2
Terry St *NLSN* BB9 ....198 E1
Tetbury Cl *BBNW* BB2 ....267 F3
Teven St *LEY/BBR* PR5 ....263 H2
Teversham *SKEL* WN8 ....363 F1
Teviot Av *FTWD* FY7 ....96 D8
Tewkesbury *SKEL* * WN8 ....362 E1
Tewkesbury Av *BPOOLS* FY4 ...204 D6
Tewkesbury Cl *ACC* BB5 ....248 D8
Tewkesbury Dr *LSTA* FY8 ....233 F6
Tewksbury Dr *BBNW* BB2 ....267 J2
Thames Av *BRFD/BLYE* BB10 ...198 A8
Thames Dr *WGNW/BIL/O* WN5 .....365 H4
Thames Rd *BPOOLS* FY4 ....204 B4
Thames St *KIRK/FR/WA* PR4 ....235 K1
Thanet *SKEL* WN8 ....363 F1
Thanet Lee Cl *BRFD/BLYE* BB10 ....252 C1
Thealby Cl *SKEL* WN8 ....362 E1
Theatre St *PRES* PR1 ....7 D3
Thelma St *RAMS* BLO 319 H5
Thermdale Cl *GAR/LONG* * PR3 .....129 H4
Thetis Rd *LANC* LA1 ....2 A3
Thickwood Moss La
RNFD/HAY WA11 ....369 F6
Third Av *BPOOLS* FY4 ....204 A4
PLF/KEOS (off Woodside Pk) FY6 .....124 E2
Third St *BOL* BL1 ....340 D7
Thirlemere Av *FTWD* FY7 ....122 C3
COL BB8 ....171 K5
FMBY L37 ....356 A1
PDHM/BLYW BB12 ....223 J1
PLF/KEOS FY6 ....149 H7
RAW/HAS BB4 ....295 J3
SKEL WN8 ....364 D4
WGNW/BIL/O WN5 ....365 H4
Thirlmere Ct *ACC* BB5 ....248 D2
BBN BB1 ....9 D5
CHLYE PR6 ....337 H3
KIRK/FR/WA PR4 ....260 C3
PLF/KEOS FY6 ....98 D5
Thirlmere Dr *CHLYE* PR6 ....288 D1
DWN BB3 ....292 A1
GAR/LONG PR3 ....187 K6
MCMB LA4 ....41 H7
STHP PR8 ....325 H8
Thirlmere Gdns *MCMB* LA4 ....41 H7
Thirlmere Ms
HTWN (off Thirlmere Rd) L38 .....356 A7
Thirlmere Rd *BPOOLS* FY4 ....204 C3
BRFD/BLYE BB10 ....226 C6
CHLY/EC PR7 ....310 E5
HOR/BR BL6 ....337 J8
HTWN L38 ....356 A7
LANC LA1 ....3 F2
PRES PR1 ....240 D2
WGNW/BIL/O WN5 ....365 K4
Thirlmere Wk *NWD/KWIPK* L33 .....366 B7
Thirlspot Cl *BOL* BL1 ....341 J5
Thirsk *SKEL* WN8 ....362 E1
Thirsk Av *LSTA* FY8 ....231 H4
Thirsk Gv *BPOOL* FY1 ....5 D5
Thirsk Rd *LANC* LA1 ....55 H7
Thistle Break *HEY* LA3 ....52 D4
Thistle Cl *CHLYE* PR6 ....311 J3
CLV/TH FY5 ....125 F6
KIRK/FR/WA PR4 ....258 D7
Thistlecroft *FUL/RIB* PR2 ....212 C6
Thistlemount Av *RAW/HAS* BB4 .....297 H2
Thistle St *BCUP* OL13 ....298 D1
Thistleton Ms *CHTN/BK* PR9 ...301 J3
Thistleton Rd *FUL/RIB* PR2 ......238 A2
PLF/KEOS FY6 ....180 A2
Thomas Gv *MCMB* LA4 ....41 H6
Thomas St *ACC* * BB5 ....247 H8
BBNW BB2 ....8 B5
BLY BB11 ....11 D4
COL BB8 ....171 J5
NLSN * BB9 ....197 J6
NLSN BB9 ....198 C4

PRES PR1 ....7 F3
TOD OL14 ....277 H2
Thomas's Weind *GAR/LONG* PR3 .....129 J4
Thompson Av *ORM* L39 ....348 E6
Thompson St *BBNW* BB2 ....8 A5
DWN BB3 ....291 K4
HOR/BR BL6 ....338 C8
KIRK/FR/WA PR4 ....208 D5
PDHM/BLYW BB12 ....223 J3
PRES PR1 ....240 B1
Thonock Rd *MCMB* LA4 ....41 K8
Thorburn Dr *WHIT* OL12 ....323 F4
Thorn Bank *BCUP* OL13 ....298 E1
Thornbank *BPOOLE* FY3 ....177 H4
Thornbank Dr *GAR/LONG* PR3 ...129 K8
Thornbeck Av *HTWN* L38 ....355 K8
Thornber Ct *BRFD/BLYE* BB10 ...226 A2
Thornber Gv *BPOOL* FY1 ....5 D4
Thornber St *BBNW* BB2 ....267 K1
Thornbridge Av *BRSC* L40 ....330 E8
Thornbury *SKEL* WN8 ....363 F1
Thorncliffe Dr *DWN* BB3 ....292 B3
Thorncliffe Rd *BOL* BL1 ....341 J6
Thorn Crs *BCUP* OL13 ....298 E1
Thorn Dr *BCUP* OL13 ....298 E1
Thorne St *NLSN* BB9 ....198 E1
Thorney Bank St *BLY* BB11 ....10 C4
Thorneycroft Cl *PLF/KEOS* FY6 ....149 H6
Thorneyholme Rd *ACC* BB5 .....248 C4
Thorneylea *WHIT* OL12 ....323 H2
Thornfield *KIRK/FR/WA* PR4 .....259 K8
Thornfield Av *FUL/RIB* PR2 ....214 D8
GAR/LONG PR3 ....188 A3
RAW/HAS BB4 ....297 G2
Thorn Gdns *BCUP* * OL13 ....298 E1
Thorngate *PRES* PR1 ....238 D7
Thorngate Cl *PRES* PR1 ....238 D7
Thorn Gv *BPOOL* FY1 ....5 E5
COL BB8 ....171 K5
Thornham Dr *BOL* BL1 ....341 K5
Thornhill *ORM* L39 ....359 K2
Thornhill Av *BBN* BB1 ....246 E3
PLF/KEOS FY6 ....98 C6
Thorn Hill Cl *BBN* BB1 ....9 E4
Thornhill Cl *BPOOLS* FY4 ....205 F6
Thornhill Rd *CHLYE* PR6 ....311 H1
LEY/BBR PR5 ....284 E3
Thorn La *GAR/LONG* PR3 ....216 A1
Thornleigh Cl *CLV/TH* FY5 ....149 G1
Thornleigh Dr *KKBYL* LA6 ....18 B6
Thornley Av *BBN* BB1 ....246 A5
Thornley Pl *FUL/RIB* PR2 ....214 E8
Thornley Rd *FUL/RIB* PR2 ....214 E8
Thornpark Dr *FUL/RIB* PR2 ......237 K3
Thorns Av *BOL* BL1 ....341 H8
HGHB LA2 ....42 D2
Thorns Cl *BOL* BL1 ....341 H8
Thorns Rd *BOL* BL1 ....341 H8
Thorn St *BCUP* OL13 ....298 E1
BRFD/BLYE BB10 ....11 D1
CLI BB7 ....165 H3
CLI BB7 ....195 G4
GTH/LHO BB6 ....221 G5
PRES PR1 ....240 A1
RAMS BLO 319 J8
RAW/HAS BB4 ....273 G6
Thornton Av *FUL/RIB* PR2 ....212 D7
LSTA FY8 ....231 H3
MCMB LA4 ....41 J5
Thornton Cl *ACC* BB5 ....248 A3
BBNW BB2 ....268 C3
BRSC L40 ....306 C8
Thornton Crs *BRFD/BLYE* BB10 ...226 C6
MCMB LA4 ....41 J6
Thornton Dr *LEY/BBR* PR5 ......241 J8
LEY/BBR PR5 ....262 B7
Thornton Gv *CLV/TH* FY5 ....122 C7
Thornton Gv *MCMB* LA4 ....41 J6
Thornton Ms
CLV/TH (off Skippool Rd) FY5 .....150 A4
Thornton Rd *BRFD/BLYE* BB10 ...226 C6
CHTN/BK PR9 ....302 B4
MCMB LA4 ....41 J6
Thorntrees Av *FUL/RIB* PR2 .....237 K2
GAR/LONG PR3 ....184 D6
Thornway Av *CLV/TH* FY5 ....149 K3
Thornwood *SKEL* WN8 ....363 F1
Thornwood Cl *BBN* BB1 ....245 G2
LSTA FY8 ....232 A7
Thornydyke Av *BOL* BL1 ....341 J6
Thornylea *BBNW* BB2 ....268 A4
Thoroughgood Cl *BRSC* L40 .....349 H1
Thorough Wy *GAR/LONG* PR3 ...102 E4
Thorpe *SKEL* WN8 ....363 F1
Thorpe Av *MCMB* LA4 ....42 B7
Thorpe Cl *PRES* PR1 ....7 D1
Thorpe St *RAMS* * BLO 319 H6

Thorsby Cl EDGW/EG BL7 .....341 K3
Thrang Brow La CARN LA5 .....16 D6
Threagill La CARN LA5 .....26 B6
Threefields FUL/RIB PR2 .....212 C6
Three Nooks LEY/BBR PR5 .....264 B6
Three Oaks Cl BRSC L40 .....350 B1
Three Pools CHTN/BK PR9 .....278 E8
Three Tuns La FMBY L37 .....343 K8
Threlfall CHLY/EC PR7 .....310 D1
Threlfall Rd BPOOL FY1 .....5 D5
Threlfalls La CHTN/BK PR9 .....302 B1
Threlfall St FUL/RIB PR2 .....6 A1
Threlkeld Rd BOL BL1 .....341 H4
Threshers Ct GAR/LONG PR3 .....103 J1
Threshfield Av HEY LA3 .....52 D3
Thropps La KIRK/FR/WA PR4 .....260 D5
Throstle Gv HGHB LA2 .....42 E4
Throstle Nest La GAR/LONG PR3 .....102 C3
Throstle St BBNW BB2 .....8 A5
  NLSN* BB9 .....198 C2
Throstle Wk HGHB LA2 .....43 F3
Throstle Wy CLV/TH FY5 .....149 G5
Throup Pl NLSN BB9 .....198 C1
Thrum Fold WHIT OL12 .....323 H7
Thrum Hall La WHIT OL12 .....323 J8
Thrushgill Dr HGHB LA2 .....44 B4
Thurcroft Dr SKEL WN8 .....362 C1
Thurland St LANC LA4 .....41 G8
Thurnham Rd FUL/RIB PR2 .....238 A3
Thurnham St LANC LA1 .....3 D4
Thursby Av BPOOLS FY4 .....204 D5
Thursby Cl STHP PR8 .....325 H8
Thursby Pl NLSN* BB9 .....198 D5
Thursby Rd BRFD/BLYE BB10 .....226 A2
  NLSN BB9 .....198 D1
Thursby Sq BRFD/BLYE BB10 .....11 D1
Thursden Av BRFD/BLYE* BB10 .....198 D8
Thursden Pl NLSN BB9 .....199 F2
Thursfield Av BPOOLS FY4 .....204 E3
Thursfield Rd BRFD/BLYE BB10 .....11 E4
Thursgill Av MCMB LA4 .....41 J8
Thurston SKEL WN8 .....362 C1
Thurston Rd LEY/BBR PR5 .....285 J2
Thurston St BLY BB11 .....11 E3
Thwaite Brow La CARN LA5 .....33 H5
Thwaite La HGHB LA2 .....49 K1
Thwaites Av BBNW BB2 .....244 A1
Thwaites Rd ACC BB5 .....247 G3
Thwaites St ACC BB5 .....247 G8
Thyme Cl BISP FY2 .....149 F8
Tiber Av BLY BB11 .....224 E7
Tiber St PRES PR1 .....7 F3
Tibicar Dr East HEY LA3 .....52 D2
Tibicar Dr West HEY LA3 .....52 D2
Tib St RAMS* BLO 319 H6
Tideswell Av WGNW/BIL/O WN5 .....365 J2
Tilbury Gv WGNNW/ST WN6 .....353 F4
Tilcroft SKEL WN8 .....362 E1
Timber St ACC BB5 .....248 C6
  BCUP OL13 .....298 D2
  NLSN* BB9 .....197 K5
Timbrills Av CLI BB7 .....195 F3
Timms Cl FMBY L37 .....343 K6
Timms La FMBY L37 .....343 K6
Tincklers La BRSC L40 .....308 D5
Tinedale Vw PDHM/BLYW BB12 .....223 G4
Tinkerfield FUL/RIB PR2 .....213 C4
Tinker's La HGHB LA2 .....82 A5
Tinklers La CLI BB7 .....90 D6
Tinniswood FUL/RIB* PR2 .....238 D1
Tinsley Av STHP PR8 .....302 A8
Tinsley's La GAR/LONG PR3 .....126 B7
  STHP PR8 .....327 H2
Tintagel SKEL WN8 .....362 D1
Tintagell Cl BBNW BB2 .....266 D4
Tintern Av CHLY/EC PR7 .....311 H6
Tintern Cl ACC BB5 .....248 E8
  PDHM/BLYW BB12 .....222 D7
Tintern Crs BBN BB1 .....9 F1
Tintern Dr FMBY L37 .....356 B1
Tippet Cl BBNW BB2 .....268 D2
Titan Wy LEY/BBR PR5 .....284 D2
Tithebarn Ga PLF/KEOS FY6 .....149 K7
Tithebarn Hl HGHB LA2 .....65 J7
Tithe Barn La CHLYE PR6 .....288 A7
  GAR/LONG PR3 .....104 A6
  LEY/BBR PR5 .....285 H6
Tithebarn Pl PLF/KEOS FY6 .....149 K7
Tithebarn Rd STHP PR8 .....301 K5
Tithebarn St PLF/KEOS FY6 .....149 K7
  PRES PR1 .....7 E3
  SKEL* WN8 .....364 D4
Tiverton Av SKEL WN8 .....362 E1
Tiverton Cl FUL/RIB PR2 .....213 H3
Tiverton Dr BBNW BB2 .....267 K3
  BRFD/BLYE BB10 .....198 D8

Tockholes Rd CHLYE PR6 .....290 D7
  DWN BB3 .....267 J6
  DWN BB3 .....291 G1
Todd Carr Rd RAW/HAS BB4 .....297 H2
Todd Hall Rd RAW/HAS BB4 .....272 B8
Todd La North LEY/BBR PR5 .....263 F2
Todd La South LEY/BBR PR5 .....263 F3
Todd's La CHTN/BK PR9 .....279 J5
Todmorden Old Rd BCUP OL13 .....275 K7
Todmorden Rd BCUP OL13 .....275 K8
  BLY BB11 .....11 E6
  BRFD/BLYE BB10 .....198 E8
  LSTA FY8 .....230 D5
  TOD OL14 .....276 E7
Toll Bar Crs LANC LA1 .....55 F8
Tollgate PRES PR1 .....6 C1
Tollgate Rd BRSC L40 .....330 B8
Tolsey Dr KIRK/FR/WA PR4 .....260 E1
Tom Benson Wy FUL/RIB PR2 .....212 A8
Tom La HWTH BD22 .....147 J6
  RAW/HAS BB4 .....297 H1
Tomlinson Rd FUL/RIB PR2 .....238 E1
  HEY LA3 .....52 D5
  LEY/BBR PR5 .....262 C8
Tomlinson St HOR/BR BL6 .....338 D8
Tonacliffe Ter WHIT OL12 .....323 C4
Tonacliffe Wy WHIT OL12 .....323 C5
Tongbarn SKEL WN8 .....362 E1
Tong End WHIT OL12 .....323 C1
Tongfields EDGW/EG BL7 .....341 K3
Tong La BCUP OL13 .....275 K8
  WHIT OL12 .....323 C2
Tongues La GAR/LONG PR3 .....98 E5
Tonnacliffe Rd WHIT OL12 .....323 C6
Tontine Rd SKEL WN8 .....364 E5
Tontine St BBN BB1 .....8 C4
Toogood La WGNNW/ST WN6 .....334 B4
Tootell St CHLY/EC PR7 .....311 F5
Tootle La BRSC L40 .....305 K8
Tootle Rd GAR/LONG PR3 .....188 B3
Top o' th' Cft BBNW* BB2 .....268 A3
Top Acre KIRK/FR/WA PR4 .....260 D2
Top Acre Rd SKEL WN8 .....363 J4
Topaz St BBN BB2 .....245 H1
Top Barn La RAW/HAS BB4 .....297 F2
Top Delph ORM L39 .....348 E5
Top La COL BB8 .....172 C7
Top of Fawna Rd GAR/LONG PR3 .....189 K2
The Toppings GAR/LONG PR3 .....129 J5
Topping St BPOOL FY1 .....4 B2
Torcross Cl CHTN/BK PR9 .....278 C6
Tor End Rd RAW/HAS BB4 .....295 F5
Tormore Cl CHLYE PR6 .....288 A8
Toronto Av BISP FY2 .....148 E8
  FTWD FY7 .....122 D1
Toronto Rd BBNW BB2 .....8 A1
Torquay Av BPOOLE FY3 .....205 C1
  BRFD/BLYE BB10 .....226 A1
Torquay Dr WGNW/BIL/O WN5 .....371 C3
Torra Barn Cl EDGW/EG BL7 .....341 J1
Torrisholme Rd LANC LA1 .....42 C8
Torrisholme Sq MCMB* LA4 .....42 B7
Torside Gv PLF/KEOS FY6 .....149 H8
Torsway Av BPOOLE FY3 .....5 F1
Torver Cl PDHM/BLYW BB12 .....224 D3
Tor Vw RAW/HAS BB4 .....296 C2
Tor View Rd RAW/HAS BB4 .....295 J2
Totnes Cl PLF/KEOS FY6 .....149 J6
Totnes Dr CHTN/BK PR9 .....278 C6
Tottenham Rd DWN BB3 .....268 C5
Tottleworth Rd BBN BB1 .....221 C8
Toulmin Cl GAR/LONG PR3 .....155 K1
Tower Buildings
  CHTN/BK (off Leicester St) PR9 .....301 J3
  HOR/BR (off Chorley Old Rd) BL6 .....339 J8
Tower Cswy TOD OL14 .....277 G3
Tower Ct CLV/TH FY5 .....123 G7
Tower Ct EDGW/EG BL7 .....317 G7
  LANC LA1 .....3 D4
Tower End FMBY L37 .....343 G6
Tower Gn FUL/RIB PR2 .....213 H4
Tower Hl CLI BB7 .....165 K2
  ORM L39 .....348 E6
Tower Hill Rd SKEL WN8 .....364 C6
Tower La FUL/RIB PR2 .....213 J3
Tower Nook SKEL WN8 .....364 C6
Tower Rd BBNW BB2 .....267 F1
  DWN BB3 .....291 K3
Tower St ACC BB5 .....247 F6
  BCUP OL13 .....298 D1
  BPOOL* FY1 .....4 B2
  EDGW/EG BL7 .....317 G7
  TOD OL14 .....277 F2
Tower Vw DWN BB3 .....292 A2
  PRES PR1 .....6 A3
Town Brow CHLYE PR6 .....286 D1
Towneley Av ACC BB5 .....249 F1

Towneley Rd GAR/LONG PR3 18
Towneley Rd West
  GAR/LONG * PR3 18
Towneleyside BLY BB11 25
Towneley St BRFD/BLYE BB10 22
Town End CARN LA5 3
  CLI BB7 8
  CLV/TH (off Gaskell Crs) FY5 149
Townfield Av BRFD/BLYE BB10 22
Townfield Cl KIRK/FR/WA PR4 26
Townfield La HGHB LA2 4
Towngate CHLY/EC PR7 30
  COL BB8 17
  LEY/BBR PR5 28
Town Green La ORM L39 36
Town Hall St BBNW BB2 1
  GTH/LHO BB6 22
Town Hill Bank
  PDHM/BLYW BB12 22
Town House Rd NLSN BB9 199
Town La CHLY/EC PR7 33
  CHLY/EC PR7 33
  CHLYE PR6 33
  KIRK/FR/WA PR4 28
Town La (Kew) STHP PR8 30
Townlea Cl PRES PR1 23
Townley Av BPOOLS FY4 20
Townley Cl LANC LA1 .....
Townley La PRES PR1 23
Townley St BRFD/BLYE BB10 19
  CHLYE PR6 31
  COL BB8 17
  MCMB LA4 17
  NLSN BB9 19
Town Rd LEY/BBR PR5 30
Townsend St RAW/HAS BB4 27
  RAW/HAS BB4 29
Townsfield CARN LA5 1
Townsley St NLSN BB9 19
Townsway LEY/BBR PR5 26
Town Vw BBN BB1 .....
Town Wk BBN BB1 .....
Towpath Wk CARN LA5 3
Toxhead Cl HOR/BR BL6 33
Tracks La WGNW/BIL/O WN5 36
Trafalgar Cl FUL/RIB PR2 21
Trafalgar Rd BPOOL FY1 .....
  LANC LA1 .....
  STHP PR8 30
Trafalgar St BLY BB11 1
  CHLY/EC PR7 3
  LSTA FY8 23
Trafford St PRES * PR1 23
Tram La KKBYL LA6 2
Tramway La LEY/BBR PR5 26
Tranmere Av HEY LA3 5
Tranmere Crs HEY LA3 5
Tranmere Rd BPOOLS FY4 .....
Tranmoor KIRK/FR/WA PR4 26
Trap Hl FMBY L37 35
Trapp La PDHM/BLYW BB12 19
Trash La CLI BB7 14
  DWN BB3 29
Travellers Ct CLI BB7 11
Travers Pl FUL/RIB PR2 .....
Travis St BRFD/BLYE BB10 1
Trawden Cl ACC BB5 24
Trawden Crs FUL/RIB PR2 21
Trawden Rd COL BB8 17
Treales Rd KIRK/FR/WA PR4 20
Trecastle Rd NWD/KWIPK L33 36
Treen Cl CHTN/BK PR9 27
Treesdale Cl STHP PR8 30
Treetops Av TOT/BURYW BL8 31
Treetop Vls
  CHTN/BK (off St Annes Rd) PR9 27
Trefoil Cl CLV/TH FY5 12
Tremellen St ACC BB5 24
Trent Cl BRSC L40 33
  LANC LA1 3
Trent Rd BPOOLS FY4 20
  NLSN BB9 19
  WGNW/BIL/O WN5 37
Trent St GAR/LONG PR3 18
  LSTA FY8 23
Tresco Cl BBNW BB2 24
Tretower Wy CLV/TH FY5 14
Trevelyan Dr WGNW/BIL/O WN5 37
Treviot Cl NWD/KWIPK L33 36
Trevor Cl BBN BB1 .....
Trevor Rd BRSC L40 33
  STHP PR8 32
The Triangle ACC BB5 24
  FUL/RIB PR2 21
Tricklebanks
  GAR/LONG (off Catterall La) PR3 15
Trigg La CHLYE PR6 28

Vaughan St *NLSN* BB9 ....198 D4
Vauxhall St *BBNW* * BB2 ....244 D8
Veevers St *BLY* BB11 ....10 C3
  NLSN BB9 ....197 J5
  PDHM/BLYW BB12 ....223 K3
Velvet St *BBNW* * BB2 ....268 A3
Venables Av *COL* BB8 ....171 K5
Venice Av *BLY* BB11 ....224 E7
Venice St *BLY* BB11 ....10 A4
Ventnor Av *BOL* BL1 ....341 K8
Ventnor Pl *FUL/RIB* PR2 ....212 C7
Ventnor Rd *BPOOLS* FY4 ....204 B5
  CHLY/EC PR7 ....311 F5
  RAW/HAS BB4 ....295 J2
Venture Ct *ACC* BB5 ....222 D6
Venture Rd *FTWD* FY7 ....123 C5
Venture St *BCUP* OL13 ....275 K8
Verax St *BCUP* OL13 ....298 D2
Vermont Cl *NWD/KWIPK* L33 ...366 B5
Vermont Gv *CLV/TH* FY5 ....148 E3
Vernon Av *BPOOLE* FY3 ....5 E4
Vernon Crs *HGHB* LA2 ....67 G8
Vernon Rd *CHTN/BK* PR9 ....302 C3
  COL BB8 ....172 D5
  LSTA FY8 ....230 E2
Vernon St *BBNW* BB2 ....8 C5
  DWN BB3 ....291 K2
  NLSN BB9 ....198 C4
  PRES PR1 ....7 D1
Verona Av *BLY* BB11 ....224 E6
Veronica St *DWN* BB3 ....268 B7
Verulam Rd *CHTN/BK* PR9 ....278 D8
Vesta St *RAMS* BL0 ....319 H5
Vevey St *LEY/BBR* PR5 ....285 J3
Viaduct Rd *LEY/BBR* PR5 ....266 A1
Vicarage Av *CLV/TH* FY5 ....148 D1
  HGHB LA2 ....45 H6
  PDHM/BLYW BB12 ....223 H3
Vicarage Cl *CHLY/EC* PR7 ....286 B8
  CHLYE PR6 ....337 G3
  FMBY L37 ....343 J7
  FUL/RIB PR2 ....213 H7
  HEY LA3 ....53 J1
  KIRK/FR/WA PR4 ....207 K7
  KKBYL LA6 ....18 B5
  LSTA FY8 ....231 F4
  ORM L39 ....349 F8
Vicarage Dr *DWN* BB3 ....292 A3
Vicarage Fold *DWN* BB3 ....193 J4
Vicarage Gdns *BRSC* L40 ....330 D7
Vicarage La *ACC* BB5 ....271 K2
  BBN BB1 ....219 H5
  BPOOLS FY4 ....5 E6
  BRSC L40 ....349 H8
  CHTN/BK PR9 ....279 H4
  FUL/RIB PR2 ....213 H7
  GAR/LONG PR3 ....155 G1
  KIRK/FR/WA PR4 ....210 A8
  KKBYL LA6 ....18 B5
  KKBYL LA6 ....21 H1
  LEY/BBR PR5 ....241 J3
  WGNNW/ST WN6 ....353 J6
Vicarage Rd *BWCK/EAR* BB18 ...119 F8
  BWCK/EAR BB18 ....146 A5
  FMBY L37 ....343 H7
  PLF/KEOS FY6 ....149 K8
  WGNW/BIL/O WN5 ....365 F7
Vicarage St *CHLYE* PR6 ....311 H2
Vicarage Wk *ORM* L39 ....348 C6
Vicar La *KKBYL* LA6 ....29 K7
Vicarsfields Rd *LEY/BBR* PR5 ....285 J4
Vicar St *GTH/LHO* * BB6 ....221 G7
Victor Av *MCMB* LA4 ....42 A6
Victoria Av *ACC* BB5 ....271 J1
  BBNW BB2 ....267 F2
  CLI BB7 ....140 E6
  LANC LA1 ....3 D6
  NLSN BB9 ....197 K5
Victoria Bank
  DWN (off Robin Bank Rd) BB3 ...291 J1
Victoria Bridge Rd *STHP* PR8 ....301 J5
Victoria Ct *BBN* BB1 ....8 C4
  CLI BB7 ....140 D6
  GAR/LONG PR3 ....212 E1
  STHP PR8 ....301 F7
Victoria Dr *RAW/HAS* BB4 ....295 G1
Victoria Gdns *NLSN* BB9 ....198 A1
Victoria Gdn *PDHM/BLYW* BB12 ..222 D1
Victoria Ms *MCMB* LA4 ....41 J5
Victoria Pde *FUL/RIB* PR2 ....238 D2
  MCMB LA4 ....41 J5
  RAW/HAS BB4 ....297 G3
Victoria Pk *SKEL* WN8 ....362 G2
Victoria Park Av *FUL/RIB* PR2 ...237 K2
  LEY/BBR PR5 ....284 E4
Victoria Park Dr *FUL/RIB* PR2 ...237 K2
Victoria Pl *LANC* LA1 ....3 D4

Victoria Rd *BWCK/EAR* BB18 ....145 G1
  BWCK/EAR BB18 ....146 B1
  FMBY L37 ....343 F6
  FUL/RIB PR2 ....213 H8
  HOR/BR BL6 ....338 E8
  HTWN L38 ....356 E8
  KIRK/FR/WA PR4 ....208 D6
  LEY/BBR PR5 ....240 A5
  LSTA FY8 ....231 F6
  ORM L39 ....348 A8
  PDHM/BLYW BB12 ....224 A4
  PLF/KEOS FY6 ....150 A7
Victoria Rd East *CLV/TH* FY5 ....149 G2
Victoria Rd West *CLV/TH* FY5 ...148 C1
Victoria St *ACC* BB5 ....221 K8
  ACC BB5 ....247 H8
  ACC BB5 ....247 J5
  ACC BB5 ....247 K1
  ACC BB5 ....248 B6
  BBN BB1 ....8 C3
  BBN* BB1 ....8 C4
  BBN BB1 ....247 F2
  BCUP OL13 ....298 B3
  BLY BB11 ....10 C3
  BPOOL FY1 ....4 B2
  BRSC L40 ....330 E6
  BWCK/EAR BB18 ....146 B1
  CHLY/EC PR7 ....311 H4
  CHLYE PR6 ....288 A4
  CLI BB7 ....165 H4
  DWN BB3 ....291 J2
  FTWD FY7 ....97 H6
  GAR/LONG PR3 ....188 A4
  GTH/LHO BB6 ....221 H6
  LEY/BBR PR5 ....262 E3
  LSTA FY8 ....232 E8
  MCMB LA4 ....41 G6
  NLSN BB9 ....170 B8
  NLSN BB9 ....198 A3
  PRES PR1 ....6 C1
  RAMS BL0 ....319 H5
  RAW/HAS BB4 ....272 B5
  RAW/HAS BB4 ....296 E2
  RAW/HAS BB4 ....297 G3
  RNFD/HAY WA11 ....369 F4
  STHP PR8 ....301 H3
  TOD OL14 ....277 H2
  WHIT OL12 ....323 H1
Victoria Ter *CHLYE* PR6 ....311 H2
  HGHB LA2 ....65 K6
Victoria Wy *FMBY* L37 ....343 H6
  RAW/HAS BB4 ....296 E1
  STHP PR8 ....301 F4
Victory Av *CHTN/BK* PR9 ....302 C4
Victory Cl *NLSN* BB9 ....198 C3
Victory Rd *BPOOL* FY1 ....4 C1
Viewfield Ms
  BBNW (off Oozehead La) BB2 ...244 D6
View Rd *DWN* BB3 ....268 B6
Vihiers Cl *CLI* BB7 ....193 C5
Viking Pl *BRFD/BLYE* BB10 ....11 D2
Viking Wy *HEY* LA3 ....52 D6
Village Cl *SKEL* WN8 ....362 D3
Village Ct
  PLF/KEOS (off Hardhorn Rd) FY6 ...149 K8
Village Cft *CHLY/EC* PR7 ....286 A8
Village Dr *FUL/RIB* PR2 ....240 D1
Village Green La *FUL/RIB* PR2 ...212 B5
Village Wks
  PLF/KEOS (off Queensway) FY6 ...149 K8
Village Wy *BISP* FY2 ....148 D3
  HTWN L38 ....355 K7
  SKEL WN8 ....362 D3
The Villas *KIRK/FR/WA* PR4 ......212 A6
Villa Wy *GAR/LONG* PR3 ....129 J5
Villiers Ct *PRES* PR1 ....239 C1
Villiers St *BLY* BB11 ....224 E6
  PDHM/BLYW BB12 ....223 K4
  PRES* PR1 ....239 F1
Vincent Ct *BBNW* BB2 ....268 A3
Vincent Rd *NLSN* BB9 ....198 D3
Vincent St *BBNW* BB2 ....268 A3
  COL BB8 ....171 K6
  LANC LA1 ....3 E4
Vincit St *BRFD/BLYE* BB10 ....11 E1
The Vinery *KIRK/FR/WA* PR4 .....261 G3
Vine St *ACC* BB5 ....247 G8
  ACC BB5 ....248 A5
  CHLY/EC PR7 ....311 G2
  LANC LA1 ....3 D5
  PRES PR1 ....6 B3
  RAMS BL0 ....319 C7
Violet St *BRFD/BLYE* BB10 ....225 J2
Virginia Av *MGHL* L31 ....358 E3
Virginia Gv *MGHL* L31 ....359 F8
Virginia St *STHP* PR8 ....301 J5
Vivary Wy *COL* BB8 ....171 G6

Vivian Dr *STHP* PR8 32
Vulcan Rd *KIRK/FR/WA* PR4 23
Vulcan St *BLY* * BB11 1
  CHTN/BK PR9 30
  NLSN BB9 19

W

Wackersall Rd *COL* BB8 17
Waddington Av *BRFD/BLYE* BB10 ..22
Waddington Rd *ACC* BB5 24
  CLI BB7 13
  CLI BB7 16
  FUL/RIB PR2 26
  LSTA FY8 23
Waddington St *BWCK/EAR* BB18 ..14
  PDHM/BLYW BB12 22
Waddow Gn *CLI* BB7 16
Waddow Gv *CLI* BB7 13
Waddow Vw *CLI* BB7 13
Wade Brook Rd *LEY/BBR* PR5 28
Wades Cft *KIRK/FR/WA* PR4 23
Wade St *PDHM/BLYW* BB12 22
Wadham Rd *PRES* PR1 ....
Wagner St *BOL* BL1 34
Wagon Rd *HGHB* LA2 8
Waidshouse Cl *NLSN* BB9 19
Waidshouse Rd *NLSN* BB9 19
Waingap Crs *WHIT* OL12 32
Waingap Ri *WHIT* OL12 32
Waingap Vw *WHIT* OL12 32
Waingate *FUL/RIB* PR2 21
Waingate Cl *RAW/HAS* BB4 27
Waingate La *RAW/HAS* BB4 27
Waitholme La *CARN* LA5 1
Wakefield Av *MCMB* LA4 4
Wakefield Dr *LANC* LA1 ....
Wakefield Rd *BISP* FY2 14
Walden Rd *BBN* BB1 21
Waldon St *PRES* PR1 24
Walesby Pl *LSTA* FY8 23
Wales Rd *RAW/HAS* BB4 29
Walgarth Dr *CHLY/EC* PR7 31
Walkdale *KIRK/FR/WA* PR4 24
Walker Av *ACC* BB5 24
Walker Cl *FMBY* L37 35
Walker Fold Rd *BOL* BL1 34
Walker Gv *HEY* LA3 5
Walker La *FUL/RIB* PR2 21
Walker Pl *PRES* PR1 ....
Walker Rd *BBN* BB1 26
Walkers Hl *BPOOLS* FY4 20
Walker St *BBN* BB1.......................
  BPOOL FY1 ....
  CLI BB7 16
  PRES PR1 ....
Walker Wy *CLV/TH* FY5 12
Walk Mill Pl *BRFD/BLYE* BB10 ...25
The Walk *KIRK/FR/WA* PR4 25
  STHP PR8 30
Wallace Hartley Ms
  COL (off Lancaster St) BB8 17
Wallace La *GAR/LONG* PR3 8
Wallbank Dr *WHIT* OL12 32
Wallbrook Av *WGNNW/BIL/O* WN5 ..37
Wallcroft St *SKEL* WN8 36
The Walled Gdn *CHLYE* PR6 28
Wallend Rd *FUL/RIB* PR2 23
Waller Av *BISP* FY2 14
Waller Hl *COL* BB8 17
Walletts Rd *CHLY/EC* PR7 31
Walley St *BOL* BL1 34
Wallhurst Cl *BRFD/BLYE* BB10 ...22
Walling's La *CARN* LA5 ....
Wallpool Br *GAR/LONG* PR3 15
Wall Pool Br *GAR/LONG* PR3 15
Wallstreams La *BRFD/BLYE* BB10 ..22
Wall St *BPOOL* FY1 17
  RAW/HAS BB4 29
Wallsuches *HOR/BR* BL6 33
Walmer Ct *STHP* PR8 30
Walmer Gn *KIRK/FR/WA* PR4 26
Walmer Rd *LSTA* FY8 25
  STHP PR8 30
Walmesley Dr *RNFD/HAY* WA11 ..36
Walmsgate *BWCK/EAR* BB18 14
Walmsley Av *BBN* BB1 24
Walmsley Br *GAR/LONG* PR3 15
Walmsley Brow *CLI* BB7 29
Walmsley Cl *ACC* BB5 24
  GAR/LONG PR3 12
Walmsley St *BBN* BB1 24
  DWN BB3 29
  FTWD FY7 ....
  GTH/LHO BB6 2

...ney Pl BPOOLE FY3 ......177 G4
...nut Av RAW/HAS BB4 ......272 D8
...nut Cl PRES PR1 ......238 D8
...nut St BBN BB1 ......9 D2
...CUP OL13 ......275 K8
...DL BL1 ......341 K8
...HP PR8 ......301 J7
...oole Av BPOOLS FY4 ......204 B6
...oole St BBN BB1 ......9 D5
...o Ms CHTN/BK PR9 ......278 C8
...sden Gv BRFD/BLYE BB10 ......11 F3
...shaw La BRFD/BLYE BB10 ......226 B1
...sh St BBNW BB2 ......268 B1
...OR/BR BL6 ......338 D7
...ter Av LSTA FY8 ......231 G1
...ter St ACC BB5 ......247 H8
...'C BB5 ......248 A5
...'C BB5 ......248 E1
...BN BB1 ......9 E5
...WN* BB3 ......291 K6
...SN BB9 ......197 K6
...ham Av BPOOLS FY4 ......204 D6
...ham Ct HGHB* LA2 ......44 A4
...hew House La
...GNW/BIL/O WN5 ......365 K2
...con Av MCMB LA4 ......42 A6
...ES PR1 ......238 D8
...con Cl BCUP OL13 ......298 E2
...con Crs BBNW BB2 ......268 D2
...con Gn LEY/BBR PR5 ......240 A7
...con Gv MCMB LA4 ......42 B6
...con La NLSN BB9 ......198 D1
...con's Pde PRES PR1 ......6 C3
...con St ACC BB5 ......248 A2
...TN/BK PR9 ......301 J3
...LY/EC PR7 ......337 C5
...OL BB8 ......171 H7
...SN BB9 ......198 C2
...con Summit Rd LEY/BBR PR5 ......263 K5
...con Vw PRES PR1 ......240 B3
...verden Av BPOOLS FY4 ......204 D3
...verden Crs NLSN BB9 ......198 C3
...verden Rd BRFD/BLYE BB10 ......199 F7
...SN BB9 ......198 B6
...dales La KKBYL LA6 ......22 A1
...es Blades Rd BRSC L40 ......332 A7
...nishar La ORM L39 ......346 C6
...asbeck Av FTWD FY7 ......122 D1
...isfell Rd CLI BB7 ......165 H4
...nstead St PRES PR1 ......240 C3
...oreck Hill Rd BISP FY2 ......176 D2
...bury St PRES PR1 ......240 C2
...cock La BCUP OL13 ......276 A8
...d Av ACC BB5 ......247 G8
...V/TH FY5 ......122 D8
...MBY L37 ......355 H1
...de St NLSN BB9 ......198 C3
...d Green La GAR/LONG PR3 ......189 F3
...dle Ct CHLYE PR6 ......287 C5
...dle Dr CLV/TH FY5 ......123 F8
...dle St BCUP* OL13 ......298 B3
...dley's La PLF/KEOS FY6 ......124 C7
...dley Vw WGNW/BIL/O WN5 ......365 K6
...dlow La WGNW/BIL/O WN5 ......365 J3
...d's End PRES PR1 ......7 E3
...d St BLY BB11 ......10 B3
...POOL FY1 ......4 B6
...LYE PR1 ......311 J4
...GW/EG BL7 ......314 E6
...H/LHO BB6 ......221 G6
...RK/FR/WA PR4 ......208 E6
...Y/BBR PR5 ......262 E4
...eham Cl ACC BB5 ......248 B2
...eham Rd BPOOLS FY4 ......177 F2
...eham St BBN BB1 ......9 E2
...ehouse La COL BB8 ......171 H7
...ing Dr CLV/TH FY5 ......123 G8
...Warings CHLY/EC PR7 ......309 F7
...SN BB9 ......198 C5
...ley Av HEY LA3 ......42 A8
...ley Dr HEY LA3 ......42 A7
...ley Rd BISP FY2 ......176 D3
...POOL FY1 ......176 B3
...ley Wise La COL BB8 ......147 G8
...mden Av ACC BB5 ......248 E8
...mden Gdns BBN BB1 ......9 E2
...mer Rd PRES PR1 ......240 B2
...ner St ACC BB5 ......248 C5
...AW/HAS BB4 ......272 C8
...pers Moss Cl BRSC L40 ......331 F6
...per's Moss La BRSC L40 ......331 F5
...ren Av North FTWD FY7 ......97 F7
...ren Av South FTWD FY7 ......97 F7
...ren Cl HGHB LA2 ......42 E3
...ren Ct STHP PR8 ......300 E6

Warren Dr BCUP OL13 ......299 G3
CLV/TH FY5 ......148 D3
HGHB LA2 ......42 E3
NLSN BB9 ......170 A8
Warren Fold CLI BB7 ......191 H2
Warren Gn FMBY L37 ......343 H7
Warren Gv HEY LA3 ......52 C6
Warrenhouse Rd
NWD/KWIPK L33 ......366 E7
Warrenhurst Rd FTWD FY7 ......97 F8
Warren Rd CHTN/BK PR9 ......302 C3
HEY LA3 ......52 C5
Warrenside Cl BBN BB1 ......219 J7
Warren St FTWD FY7 ......97 H7
The Warren BBNW BB2 ......244 C4
FUL/RIB PR2 ......214 B5
Warrington St BBN BB1 ......9 E1
Warth La RAW/HAS BB4 ......297 F3
Warton Av HEY LA3 ......52 C5
Warton Pl CHLY/EC PR7 ......310 E3
Warton Rd CARN LA5 ......25 K8
Warton St LSTA FY8 ......232 E8
PRES PR1 ......6 C3
Wartonwood Vw CARN LA5 ......33 K2
Warwick Av ACC BB5 ......221 K8
ACC BB5 ......248 A4
CLV/TH FY5 ......122 C7
LANC LA1 ......3 E6
MCMB LA4 ......42 B5
Warwick Cl ACC BB5 ......247 K4
FUL/RIB PR2 ......213 G7
STHP PR8 ......301 H8
Warwick Dr BWCK/EAR BB18 ......145 H2
CLI BB7 ......165 K1
NLSN BB9 ......198 B6
PDHM/BLYW BB12 ......223 K4
Warwick Pl BPOOLE FY3 ......177 H3
Warwick Rd BPOOLE FY3 ......5 D1
CHLY/EC PR7 ......308 E4
LEY/BBR PR5 ......240 B7
LEY/BBR PR5 ......285 C4
LSTA FY8 ......231 F5
Warwick St ACC BB5 ......247 K4
BOL BL1 ......341 J7
CHLY/EC PR7 ......337 F5
GAR/LONG PR3 ......188 A3
NLSN BB9 ......198 C4
PRES PR1 ......7 D2
RAW/HAS BB4 ......272 C8
STHP PR8 ......301 H7
Wasdale Av BBN BB1 ......246 A8
Wasdale Cl LEY/BBR PR5 ......285 K5
PDHM/BLYW BB12 ......223 J2
Wasdale Gv GAR/LONG PR3 ......187 K6
Wasdale Rd BPOOLS FY4 ......205 G3
Washbrook Cl CLI BB7 ......193 H2
Washbrook Wy ORM L39 ......348 C7
Washburn Ct LANC LA1 ......54 B1
Washington Av BISP FY2 ......176 E1
Washington Cl LANC LA1 ......2 B4
Washington Ct BISP FY2 ......176 E1
Washington Dr NWD/KWIPK L33 ......366 B5
Washington La CHLY/EC PR7 ......310 C1
Washington St ACC BB5 ......248 C5
Waste La HGHB LA2 ......82 C6
Wastwater Dr MCMB LA4 ......42 A7
Watchyard La FMBY L37 ......344 A8
Waterbarn La BCUP* OL13 ......297 K3
Waterbarn St BRFD/BLYE BB10 ......225 K2
Waterdale BISP FY2 ......148 E6
Waterfield Av DWN BB3 ......291 K5
Waterfoot Av BPOOLE FY3 ......5 E1
STHP PR8 ......325 H8
Waterford Cl CHLYE PR6 ......337 G2
FUL/RIB PR2 ......214 A6
Waterford St NLSN BB9 ......198 D2
Waterfront
BBN (off Merchants Quay) BB1 ......9 D6
Waterhead Crs CLV/TH FY5 ......148 C5
Watering Pool La LEY/BBR PR5 ......262 C4
Water La CHTN/BK PR9 ......279 F6
FUL/RIB PR2 ......6 A2
RAMS BL0 ......319 K1
Waterloo Cl BBNW BB2 ......267 J3
Waterloo Rd BLY BB11 ......11 E5
BPOOLS FY4 ......4 C6
BWCK/EAR BB18 ......146 A5
CLI BB7 ......165 K3
FUL/RIB PR2 ......238 D1
STHP PR8 ......326 A2
Waterloo St ACC BB5 ......248 A2
CHLY/EC PR7 ......311 G2
Waterloo Ter FUL/RIB PR2 ......6 A1
Watermans Cl HOR/BR BL6 ......338 E7
Water Mdw BBNW BB2 ......268 A4
Watermede WGNW/BIL/O WN5 ......365 G8
Watermillock Gdns BOL BL1 ......341 K8

Waters Edge BBN BB1 ......9 D6
FUL/RIB PR2 ......212 B8
Waterside Cl GAR/LONG PR3 ......129 H4
Waterside Ms PDHM/BLYW BB12 ......223 J3
Waterside Rd COL BB8 ......171 H7
RAW/HAS BB4 ......295 G1
Waterslack Rd CARN LA5 ......15 K5
Waters Meeting Rd BOL BL1 ......341 K8
Waters Reach
LSTA (off Inner Prom) FY8 ......231 K8
Water St ACC BB5 ......248 C5
BRFD/BLYE BB10 ......227 F6
BWCK/EAR BB18 ......146 B1
CHLY/EC PR7 ......311 G3
CHLY/EC PR7 ......337 G5
CHLYE PR6 ......264 E6
EDGW/EG BL7 ......341 H1
GAR/LONG PR3 ......190 A8
GTH/LHO BB6 ......221 G6
GTH/LHO BB6 ......221 K6
LANC LA1 ......3 D2
LEY/BBR PR5 ......263 H1
NLSN BB9 ......198 C3
PDHM/BLYW BB12 ......223 J7
RAW/HAS BB4 ......273 H4
WHIT OL12 ......323 F3
Waterworks Rd ORM L39 ......348 E5
Watery Gate La KIRK/FR/WA PR4 ......181 H1
Watery La DWN BB3 ......291 K5
GAR/LONG PR3 ......130 A2
LANC LA1 ......42 D8
PRES PR1 ......240 B3
Watkin La LEY/BBR PR5 ......262 E4
Watkin Rd CHLYE PR6 ......287 F3
Watkins Cl BRFD/BLYE BB10 ......198 A7
Watling Cl BBNW BB2 ......268 D3
HEY LA3 ......42 A8
Watling Street Rd FUL/RIB PR2 ......213 G8
Watson Ct BPOOLS FY4 ......204 D4
Watson Gdns WHIT OL12 ......323 H8
Watson Rd BPOOLS FY4 ......204 B4
Watson St ACC BB5 ......247 J7
BBNW BB2 ......267 J1
Watts Cl NWD/KWIPK L33 ......366 E7
Watt St CLI BB7 ......195 F4
PDHM/BLYW BB12 ......224 E4
Wavell Av CHTN/BK PR9 ......302 D4
Wavell Cl ACC BB5 ......272 A1
CHTN/BK PR9 ......302 D4
Wavell St PDHM/BLYW BB12 ......224 E5
Waverledge Rd GTH/LHO BB6 ......221 F7
Waverledge St GTH/LHO BB6 ......221 G7
Waverley SKEL WN8 ......362 D2
Waverley Av BPOOL FY1 ......176 C3
FTWD FY7 ......96 D8
Waverley Cl NLSN BB9 ......198 B7
PDHM/BLYW BB12 ......222 D2
Waverley Dr KIRK/FR/WA PR4 ......261 G4
KIRK/FR/WA PR4 ......281 K5
Waverley Gdns FUL/RIB PR2 ......240 C1
Waverley Pl BBNW BB2 ......244 D6
Waverley Rd ACC BB5 ......248 E8
BBN BB1 ......219 G2
BBN BB1 ......246 C7
BOL BL1 ......341 J8
PRES PR1 ......240 B2
Waverley St BLY BB11 ......10 A3
STHP PR8 ......301 G4
Waxy La KIRK/FR/WA PR4 ......235 G4
Wayfarers Ar
STHP (off Lord St) PR8 ......301 H4
Way Ga CLV/TH FY5 ......122 D6
Wayman Rd BPOOLE FY3 ......5 D1
Wayoh Cft EDGW/EG BL7 ......317 H5
Wayside PLF/KEOS FY6 ......97 K6
The Weald KIRK/FR/WA PR4 ......211 K6
Weasel La DWN BB3 ......290 C1
Weatherhill Crs NLSN BB9 ......198 C6
Weaver Av BRSC L40 ......331 F6
NWD/KWIPK L33 ......366 D5
Weaver's Brow CHLYE PR6 ......312 A6
Weber St RAW/HAS BB4 ......297 F2
Webster Av BPOOLS FY4 ......204 E4
Webster Gv MCMB LA4 ......42 C5
Webster St FUL/RIB PR2 ......6 A1
Wedgewood Rd ACC BB5 ......249 F2
Weeton Av BPOOLS FY4 ......204 E6
CLV/TH FY5 ......122 D8
LSTA FY8 ......231 G3
Weeton Pl FUL/RIB PR2 ......238 A2
Weeton Rd KIRK/FR/WA PR4 ......207 H1
KIRK/FR/WA PR4 ......207 H4
PLF/KEOS FY6 ......179 G3
Weets Vw BWCK/EAR BB18 ......119 G8
The Weind GAR/LONG PR3 ......153 F6
Weirden Cl PRES PR1 ......261 K2

Weir La *BCUP* OL13.....................................275 J4
Weir St *BBNW* BB2..8 C5
Welbeck Av *BBN* BB1.......................................9 F1
   BPOOLS FY4...5 E6
   FTWD FY7..97 F7
Welbeck Rd *STHP* PR8...............................301 F7
Welbeck Ter *STHP* PR8...............................301 F7
Welbury Cl *BWCK/EAR* BB18.....................146 B1
Weld Av *CHLY/EC* PR7..................................311 G6
Weldbank La *CHLY/EC* PR7........................311 G6
Weldbank St *CHLY/EC* PR7........................311 G6
Weld Blundell Av *MGHL* L31......................358 D7
Weldon Dr *ORM* L39......................................348 D7
Weldon St *BLY* * BB11.....................................10 B4
Weld Pde *STHP* PR8.....................................301 F7
Weld Rd *STHP* PR8..300 E6
Welland Cl *BISP* FY2.....................................148 E7
Wellbrow Dr *GAR/LONG* PR3.....................188 B3
Wellcross Rd *SKEL* WN8..............................364 D5
Wellesley St *PDHM/BLYW* BB12................224 D5
Well Fld *ACC* BB5..248 A1
Wellfield *KIRK/FR/WA* PR4.........................260 A2
   RNFD/HAY WA11......................................369 G7
Wellfield Av *LEY/BBR* PR5..........................285 H2
Wellfield Dr *PDHM/BLYW* BB12................224 E3
Wellfield La *BRSC* L40.................................361 C3
Wellfield Rd *BBNW* BB2...............................244 D5
   LEY/BBR PR5..262 D4
   PRES PR1...6 B2
Well Fold *CLI* BB7..165 K3
Wellgate *CLI* BB7..165 K3
Well Head Rd *PDHM/BLYW* BB12.............196 C1
Wellhouse Rd *BWCK/EAR* BB18................145 F1
Wellhouse St *BWCK/EAR* BB18.................145 F1
Wellington Av *LEY/BBR* PR5......................285 K3
Wellington Ct *BLY* BB11................................11 E3
Wellington Ms *EDGW/EG* BL7...................317 H7
Wellington Pl *LEY/BBR* PR5.......................263 C1
Wellington Rd *BBNW* BB2.............................8 A6
   BPOOL FY1..4 B5
   EDGW/EG BL7..317 H7
   FUL/RIB PR2...238 D2
   LANC LA1...3 E6
Wellington St *ACC* BB5...............................247 K1
   ACC BB5..248 C6
   BBN BB1...8 B3
   BWCK/EAR BB18.....................................145 F1
   CHLY/EC PR7...311 G3
   GTH/LHO * BB6...221 G7
   KIRK/FR/WA PR4.....................................208 D6
   LSTA FY8..233 F2
   NLSN BB9..198 B3
   PRES PR1...6 B2
   STHP PR8...301 C5
Wellington Ter *MCMB* LA4...........................41 H6
Well La *CARN* LA5..17 F8
   CARN LA5..26 A6
   CHLYE PR6..289 F4
   GAR/LONG PR3.......................................152 B5
   KKBYL LA6..20 C1
   KKBYL LA6..22 A1
   ORM L39...346 A5
Wellogate Gdns *BPOOLS* FY4...................204 D5
Well Orch *LEY/BBR* PR5...............................264 A6
Wellow Pl *LSTA* FY8.....................................231 K6
Wells Av *WGNW/BIL/O* WN5......................371 F6
Wells Cl *CLV/TH* FY5....................................149 G1
   HEY LA3...53 H1
Wells Fold Cl *CHLYE* PR6............................287 G2
Wells St *PRES* PR1.......................................240 B2
   RAW/HAS BB4..272 C8
Well St *BBN* BB1..247 F1
   PDHM/BLYW BB12..................................223 H2
   RAW/HAS BB4..274 C8
Well St West *RAMS* * BL0............................319 H6
Well Ter *CLI* BB7...165 K2
Welsby Rd *LEY/BBR* PR5.............................285 F3
Welwyn Av *STHP* PR8...................................325 K5
Welwyn Pl *CLV/TH* FY5................................148 D2
Wembley Av *BPOOLE* FY3...........................176 E3
   PLF/KEOS FY6...150 A8
   PRES PR1..238 D6
Wembley Rd *CLV/TH* FY5............................123 H7
Wemyss Cl *HEY* * LA3....................................52 C4
Wendover Rd *PLF/KEOS* FY6.....................149 C5
Wenlock Cl *HOR/BR* BL6.............................338 E5
Wenning Pl *LANC* LA1.....................................2 C1
Wenning St *NLSN* BB9.................................198 D4
Wennington Rd *CHTN/BK* PR9...................302 B3
   HGHB LA2..38 A7
Wensley Av *FTWD* FY7.................................122 E2
Wensley Cl *BLY* BB11.....................................10 B6
Wensleydale Av *BPOOLE* FY3....................177 G4
Wensleydale Cl *CLV/TH* FY5......................149 K3
Wensley Dr *ACC* BB5...................................248 D5
   LANC LA1...43 F8

Wensley Pl *FUL/RIB* PR2.............................214 B7
Wensley Rd *BBNW* BB2...............................244 D7
Wentcliffe Dr *BWCK/EAR* BB18................146 B2
Wentworth Av *FTWD* FY7...........................122 D4
   KIRK/FR/WA PR4....................................182 C3
Wentworth Cl *PRES* PR1.............................238 C5
   STHP PR8...325 J7
Wentworth Crs *HEY* LA3...............................41 H8
Wentworth Dr *CHLYE* PR6..........................286 B7
   CLV/TH FY5..149 J3
   GAR/LONG PR3.......................................184 E8
Wentworth Ms *LSTA* FY8............................231 G5
Werneth Cl *PRES* PR1..................................262 C5
Wescoe Cl *WGNW/BIL/O* WN5..................365 C6
Wesham Hall Rd *KIRK/FR/WA* PR4..........208 E5
Wesley Dr *HEY* LA3..52 D4
Wesley Gv *PDHM/BLYW* BB12....................10 A2
Wesley Ms *BPOOLS* FY4.............................205 C4
Wesley Pl *BCUP* OL13.................................298 C2
Wesley St *ACC* BB5......................................247 K5
   BBN BB1...9 D2
   CLI BB7...195 F3
   LEY/BBR PR5..263 J3
   NLSN BB9..197 K5
   STHP PR8...301 H5
Wessex Cl *ACC* BB5.....................................248 E3
West Av *BWCK/EAR* BB18............................145 F1
   FUL/RIB PR2..212 C5
West Bank *CHLY/EC* PR7............................311 G3
Westbank Av *BPOOLS* FY4.........................205 C4
West Bank Av *LSTA* FY8..............................232 A8
Westboro Cl *HEY* LA3....................................52 D2
Westbourne Av *BLY* BB11.............................10 A6
   BPOOL FY1..4 C6
   KIRK/FR/WA PR4....................................207 K8
Westbourne Av South *BLY* BB11................10 A6
Westbourne Dr *LANC* LA1.............................2 B4
Westbourne Gdns *STHP* PR8...................300 E7
Westbourne Pl *LANC* LA1..............................2 B3
Westbourne Rd *CARN* LA5...........................25 J7
   CHLY/EC PR7...311 F5
   CLV/TH FY5..122 C6
   HEY LA3..64 E1
   LANC LA1...2 B4
   PLF/KEOS FY6...97 K6
   STHP PR8...300 D7
West Bradford Rd *CLI* BB7.........................139 F7
   CLI BB7..139 K7
Westbrook Crs *FUL/RIB* PR2.....................212 C7
Westbury Cl *BRFD/BLYE* BB10.................226 C1
   CLV/TH FY5..148 C4
Westbury Gdns *BBN* BB1...........................246 A7
Westby Av *BPOOLS* FY4..............................204 E6
Westby Pl *FUL/RIB* PR2...............................238 D2
Westby Rd *KIRK/FR/WA* PR4.....................207 C6
   LSTA FY8..230 E3
Westby St *LSTA* FY8.....................................232 C8
Westby Wy *PLF/KEOS* FY6..........................177 K1
West Cliff *PRES* PR1.......................................6 C4
Westcliffe *GTH/LHO* BB6.............................221 F5
West Cliffe *LSTA* FY8....................................232 E8
Westcliffe Dr *BPOOLE* FY3.........................176 E3
   HEY LA3..53 C1
Westcliffe Rd *BOL* BL1.................................341 K5
   STHP PR8...300 E6
West Cliff Ter *PRES* PR1................................6 C4
West Close Av *PDHM/BLYW* BB12............196 B6
West Close Rd *BWCK/EAR* BB18...............119 F8
Westcote St *DWN* BB3.................................291 K5
West Ct *CLV/TH* FY5.....................................122 C6
West Crs *ACC* BB5..248 B3
   GAR/LONG PR3.......................................184 B4
   LSTA FY8..230 E5
Westcroft *KIRK/FR/WA* PR4.......................259 K8
West Dene *SKEL* WN8.................................351 H4
West Dr *CLV/TH* FY5....................................122 D8
   KIRK/FR/WA PR4....................................182 C5
   KIRK/FR/WA PR4....................................208 C4
   LANC LA1...2 B1
   LEY/BBR PR5..263 G8
West End *GAR/LONG* PR3...........................152 E6
   PRES PR1..238 C5
Westend Av *CHLY/EC* PR7..........................335 H2
West End La *KIRK/FR/WA* PR4...................233 K5
West End Rd *MCMB* LA4................................41 G7
Westerdale Dr *CHTN/BK* PR9.....................279 K6
Westerlong Av *FUL/RIB* PR2......................237 F2
Western Av *BLY* BB11.....................................10 B5
Western Ct *BCUP* OL13................................297 K3
Western Dr *LEY/BBR* PR5............................285 F2
Western Rd *BCUP* OL13...............................298 A3
West Exchange St *COL* * BB8.....................171 H7
Westfield *LEY/BBR* PR5...............................262 D3
   NLSN BB9..198 B2
Westfield Av *BPOOLE* FY3..........................177 F2
   FTWD FY7..122 E1
   PDHM/BLYW BB12..................................222 D2

Westfield Dr *CARN* LA5..................................3
   CLI BB7...13
   FUL/RIB PR2...2
   KIRK/FR/WA PR4.......................................23
   LEY/BBR PR5...26
   LEY/BBR PR5...28
Westfield Gv *MCMB* LA4................................4
Westfield Rd *BPOOL* FY1...............................
West Field Rd *BWCK/EAR* BB18...............11
Westfields *LEY/BBR* PR5..............................30
West Ga *FTWD* FY7..
Westgate *BLY* BB11...
   BWCK/EAR BB18......................................14
   FUL/RIB PR2..21
   HEY LA3...
   LEY/BBR PR5...28
   PDHM/BLYW BB12......................................2
   SKEL WN8...36
   WHIT OL12..32
Westgate Av *HEY* LA3...................................32
Westgate Cl *WHIT* OL12..............................32
Westgate Dr *WGNW/BIL/O* WN5...............36
West Ing La *SKP/WHF* BD23.......................11
Westland Av *DWN* BB3.................................29
Westlands *LEY/BBR* PR5..............................26
Westlands Ct *CLV/TH* FY5...........................14
West La *CLI* BB7...14
   FMBY L37...34
Westleigh Ms
   KIRK/FR/WA (off Lea Rd) PR4................21
West Leigh Rd *BBN* BB1.................................
Westleigh Rd *FUL/RIB* PR2.........................23
West Meadow *FUL/RIB* PR2.......................21
Westminster Av *MCMB* LA4.........................4
Westminster Cl *ACC* BB5............................24
   HEY LA3..
   PDHM/BLYW BB12......................................22
Westminster Dr *STHP* PR8..........................32
Westminster Pl *CHLY/EC* PR7....................30
   KIRK/FR/WA PR4.......................................26
Westminster Rd *BOL* BL1.............................34
   BPOOL FY1...1
   CHLY/EC PR7...31
   DWN * BB3...26
Westmoor Gv *HEY* LA3....................................5
Westmoreland Rd *STHP* PR8......................30
Westmoreland St *NLSN* BB9.......................19
Westmorland Av *BPOOL* FY1........................
   CLV/TH FY5..12
Westmorland Cl *PRES* PR1..........................23
Westmorland St *BLY* BB11.............................1
West Moss La *LSTA* FY8................................23
West Mt *WGNW/BIL/O* WN5........................36
Weston Pl *BPOOL* FY1......................................
Weston St *FUL/RIB* PR2..................................
Westover Rd *CARN* LA5..................................2
Westover St *MCMB* LA4...................................4
West Paddock *LEY/BBR* PR5.......................28
West Park Av *FUL/RIB* PR2...........................23
West Park Dr *BPOOLE* FY3.............................
West Park La *FUL/RIB* PR2............................23
West Park Rd *BBNW* BB2..............................24
West Rd *FUL/RIB* PR2....................................21
   LANC LA1...
West Rosser Ct *NLSN* * BB9........................19
Westside *BPOOLS* FY4.................................20
West Sq *KIRK/FR/WA* PR4............................26
West Strd *PRES* PR1..
West St *BPOOL* FY1..
   BRFD/BLYE BB10..1
   CHLY/EC PR7...31
   COL BB8..17
   HEY LA3..
   LANC LA1...
   NLSN BB9..19
   PDHM/BLYW BB12......................................22
   RAMS * BL0...31
   RAW/HAS BB4..2
   STHP PR8...30
West Vw *ACC* BB5...24
   BBNW BB2..24
   BPOOL FY1...
   CHLYE PR6...26
   CLI BB7...16

CHB LA2 ....65 J6
OR/BR (off Wilderswood) BL6 ......339 C6
RK/FR/WA PR4 ....208 D4
RK/FR/WA PR4 ....260 B3
Y/BBR PR5 ....263 H4
RES PR1 ....240 A1
MS BL0 ....319 J1
AW/HAS BB4 ....272 C7
AW/HAS BB4 ....295 G4
WFD/HAY
F Ormskirk Rd) WA11 ....369 F5
KEL WN8 ....351 H1
t View Av BPOOL * FY1 ....4 B5
t View La BBNW BB2 ....244 D5
t View Rd MCMB LA4 ....41 G6
t View Ter FUL/RIB PR2 ....6 A2
OHM/BLYW BB12 ....223 J4
JL/RIB PR2 ....213 J7
TWN L38 ....355 K7
WD FY7 ....122 C4
tway BLY BB11 ....10 A3
JL/RIB PR2 ....213 J7
RK/FR/WA PR4 ....234 D5
twell Gv BPOOL FY1 ....4 C3
twell Pl BBNW BB2 ....244 D5
twell St DWN BB3 ....268 B7
TH/LHO* BB6 ....221 C6
twood Av BBN BB1 ....246 E2
POOLE FY3 ....5 E3
WD FY7 ....96 E8
LF/KEOS FY6 ....150 A8
twood Cl STHP PR8 ....302 A8
twood En BBN BB1 ....9 E3
twood Ms LSTA FY8 ....232 C8
twood Rd BBN BB1 ....9 F5
Y/BBR PR5 ....264 B7
Y/BBR PR5 ....285 J1
TA FY8 ....232 C8
OHM/BLYW BB12 ....224 E3
twood St ACC BB5 ....248 B4
herall St FUL/RIB PR2 ....6 B1
herby Av BPOOL FY4 ....204 B6
herfield Cl LANC LA1 ....43 G7
rmouth Rd BPOOLE FY3 ....5 F4
rthorne Dr BOL BL1 ....341 K7
alley Av BOL BL1 ....340 D8
WFD/HAY WA11 ....369 F5
alley Banks BBNW BB2 ....8 A5
alley Crs BPOOLE FY3 ....178 A6
WN BB3 ....291 K2
alley Dr FMBY L37 ....356 A1
RM L39 ....360 A4
AW/HAS BB4 ....273 H7
alley La BPOOLS FY4 ....205 C3
alley New Rd BBN BB1 ....9 D3
J BB7 ....192 D8
BNW BB2 ....217 J8
HLY/EC PR7 ....309 G7
J BB7 ....165 H7
J BB7 ....165 J4
J BB7 ....191 J2
J BB7 ....193 H3
TH/LHO BB6 ....220 B2
TH/LHO BB6 ....221 K6
ANC LA1 ....43 F7
Y/BBR PR5 ....242 B1
OHM/BLYW BB12 ....222 A2
MS BL0 ....320 A2
alleys Rd SKEL WN8 ....351 H7
alley St BBN BB1 ....8 C3
alley St BPOOL BB10 ....225 J2
HLY/EC* PR7 ....311 G4
J BB7 ....165 H3
Y/BBR PR5 ....263 J1
am Bottom La WHIT OL12 ....323 H7
am Brook St ACC BB5 ....247 F6
am Hey KIRK/FR/WA PR4 ....261 H4
am La KIRK/FR/WA PR4 ....260 D7
ams La HGHB LA2 ....80 E4
arf BRSC L40 ....328 D7
arfdale Av BRFD/BLYE BB10 ....197 K7
arfe Ct LANC LA1 ....54 B1
GHB LA2 ....67 H8
arfedale BPOOLS FY4 ....204 E4
JL/RIB PR2 ....214 C6
arfedale Cl BBNW BB2 ....266 E4
Y/BBR PR5 ....285 J5

Wharfedale Ct
PLF/KEOS (off Chester Av) FY6 ....149 J8
Wharfedale Rd LANC LA1 ....2 A3
Wharf St BBN BB1 ....9 D4
BBN BB1 ....247 F2
LSTA FY8 ....232 E8
Wharton Av CLV/TH FY5 ....149 K2
Whave's La CHLYE PR6 ....265 J6
Wheatacre SKEL WN8 ....362 E3
Wheatcroft Av
PDHM/BLYW BB12 ....197 F3
Wheatfield LEY/BBR PR5 ....284 C3
Wheatfield Cl CLV/TH FY5 ....149 F4
Wheatfield Ct LANC * LA1 ....2 C3
Wheatfield St BBN BB1 ....247 F1
LANC LA1 ....2 C3
Wheathead La NLSN BB9 ....169 J3
Wheatholme St RAW/HAS BB4 ....296 D1
Wheatlands Crs BPOOLE FY3 ....205 J1
Wheat La BRSC L40 ....331 G8
Wheatley Cl PDHM/BLYW BB12 ....10 A2
PDHM/BLYW BB12 ....197 F4
Wheatley Dr GAR/LONG PR3 ....188 B3
Wheatley Gv NLSN BB9 ....170 A8
Wheatley Lane Rd
PDHM/BLYW BB12 ....197 F4
Wheatsheaf Av GAR/LONG PR3 ......188 B4
Wheat St ACC BB5 ....248 A5
PDHM/BLYW BB12 ....223 J4
Wheel La GAR/LONG PR3 ....99 J5
Wheelton La LEY/BBR PR5 ....285 J1
Whernside BPOOLS FY4 ....205 F4
Whernside Cl BWCK/EAR BB18 ......144 E4
Whernside Crs FUL/RIB PR2 ....214 B6
Whernside Gv CARN LA5 ....34 B1
Whernside Rd LANC LA1 ....42 D8
Whernside Wy LEY/BBR PR5 ....286 A2
Whimberry Cl CHLYE PR6 ....311 J3
Whimbrel Dr CLV/TH FY5 ....123 J7
Whin Av CARN LA5 ....33 H5
Whinberry La RAW/HAS BB4 ....296 C2
Whin Dr CARN LA5 ....33 H5
Whinfell Dr LANC LA1 ....55 C8
Whinfield Av CHLYE PR6 ....311 H2
FTWD FY7 ....122 E1
Whinfield La FUL/RIB PR2 ....238 B1
Whinfield Pl BBNW BB2 ....244 C5
FUL/RIB PR2 ....238 B1
Whinfield St ACC BB5 ....248 A2
Whin Gv CARN LA5 ....33 H5
Whin La GAR/LONG PR3 ....151 J3
Whinney Brow GAR/LONG PR3 ....80 D8
Whinneyfield La KIRK/FR/WA PR4 ...212 A1
Whinney Heys Rd BPOOLE FY3 ......177 C5
Whinney Hill Quarry
ACC (off Whinney Hill Rd) BB5 ....248 C2
Whinney Hill Rd ACC BB5 ....248 B2
Whinney La BBNW BB2 ....8 A1
GTH/LHO BB6 ....220 B3
Whinny La CHLYE PR6 ....286 C8
CLI BB7 ....138 C6
PLF/KEOS FY6 ....98 A7
Whinnysty La HEY LA3 ....52 D2
Whinpark Av BPOOLS FY3 ....177 G5
Whinsands Cl FUL/RIB PR2 ....214 B6
Whins Av CLI BB7 ....194 E4
Whins La CHLYE PR6 ....288 A3
PDHM/BLYW BB12 ....222 C1
Whipp Av CLI BB7 ....165 H4
Whitaker Gn RAW/HAS BB4 ....296 A1
Whitaker St ACC BB5 ....248 B4
Whitbarrow Sq LANC LA1 ....3 E3
Whitburn Rd NWD/KWIPK L33 ....366 E7
Whitby Av CHTN/BK PR9 ....278 E5
FUL/RIB PR2 ....212 B6
Whitby Dr BBNW BB2 ....268 C2
Whitby Pl FUL/RIB PR2 ....212 B7
Whitby Rd LSTA FY8 ....231 G3
MCMB* LA4 ....41 J6
Whiteacre WGNNW/ST WN6 ....353 J1
Whiteacre La CLI BB7 ....193 H3
White Acre Rd ACC BB5 ....271 G2
White Ash La ACC BB5 ....247 H7
Whitebeam Cl CLV/TH FY5 ....123 F6
NWD/KWIPK L33 ....366 D5
PRES PR1 ....238 D7
Whitebeck La KKBYL LA6 ....27 F2
Whitebirk Dr BBN BB1 ....9 F1
Whitebirk Rd BBN BB1 ....246 B5
White Br BRSC L40 ....306 D7
White Bull St PDHM/BLYW * BB12 ..224 C5
White Carr La CLV/TH FY5 ....149 F4
GAR/LONG PR3 ....81 F8
KIRK/FR/WA PR4 ....209 G1
Whitecotes Dr LSTA FY8 ....233 F7
Whitecrest Av CLV/TH FY5 ....123 F7
Whitecroft Cl RAW/HAS BB4 ....295 H1

Whitecroft La BBNW BB2 ....244 A2
Whitecroft Mdw RAW/HAS BB4 ....295 H1
Whitecroft Vw ACC BB5 ....271 K1
White Cross St LANC LA1 ....3 D4
Whitefield La BRSC L40 ....306 C8
Whitefield Pl HEY LA3 ....53 J1
Whitefield Rd PRES PR1 ....238 C7
Whitefield Rd East PRES PR1 ....238 C7
Whitefield Rd West PRES PR1 ....238 C7
Whitefield St PDHM/BLYW BB12 .....223 J7
Whitefield Ter BLY BB11 ....11 D5
Whitefriar Cl FUL/RIB PR2 ....212 C6
Whitegate HEY LA3 ....53 K1
Whitegate Cl PDHM/BLYW BB12 .....224 A4
Whitegate Dr BOL BL1 ....341 K6
BPOOLE FY3 ....5 D3
White Gate Fold CHLY/EC PR7 ....310 C8
White Gv COL BB8 ....171 G5
Whitehalgh La GTH/LHO BB6 ....220 A3
Whitehall Av WGNNW/ST WN6 ....353 G3
Whitehall La BOL BL1 ....341 H5
CLI BB7 ....140 A2
HOR/BR BL6 ....337 K8
Whitehall Rd BBNW BB2 ....244 D4
DWN BB3 ....291 J6
Whitehall St DWN BB3 ....291 K6
NLSN BB9 ....198 D3
Whitehaven Cl BBNW BB2 ....268 D2
STHP PR8 ....325 H8
Whitehaven St BLY * BB11 ....10 B4
Whitehead Cl BPOOLE FY3 ....177 K6
Whitehead St BBNW BB2 ....8 A4
RAW/HAS BB4 ....273 H8
Whitehey Rd SKEL WN8 ....362 E3
White Hill Cl WHIT OL12 ....323 H7
White Hill La AIRE BD20 ....147 K2
Whitehill Rd BPOOLS FY4 ....205 K6
Whiteholme Dr PLF/KEOS FY6 ....149 H5
Whiteholme Pl FUL/RIB PR2 ....238 A2
Whiteholme Rd BISP FY2 ....149 F4
CLV/TH FY5 ....148 D3
White Horse Cl HOR/BR BL6 ....338 E6
White Horse La GAR/LONG PR3 ......184 B2
Whitehouse Av FMBY L37 ....344 A8
White House La BRSC L40 ....329 G2
GAR/LONG PR3 ....153 H7
Whitehouse La FMBY L37 ....344 A8
White Lea GAR/LONG PR3 ....129 J2
Whiteledge Rd SKEL WN8 ....363 H5
White Lee Av COL BB8 ....200 C1
White Lee La GAR/LONG PR3 ....158 A1
Whitelees Wy PLF/KEOS FY6 ....149 K8
Whiteley's La BRSC L40 ....361 G1
Whitelow Rd RAMS BL0 ....320 A6
White Lund Av HEY LA3 ....53 J1
White Lund Rd HEY LA3 ....53 J1
Whitely Gv NWD/KWIPK L33 ....366 E5
White Meadow FUL/RIB PR2 ....212 A8
Whitemoor Rd COL BB8 ....171 G1
Whitemoss Av BPOOLS FY3 ....177 H4
White Moss La PLF/KEOS FY6 ....125 G7
White Moss Rd SKEL WN8 ....362 C4
White Moss Rd South SKEL WN8 ....362 K4
Whitendale LANC LA1 ....2 A1
Whitendale Crs BBN BB1 ....9 D6
Whitendale Dr CARN LA5 ....43 F1
LEY/BBR PR5 ....263 J4
Whitepits La HGHB LA2 ....50 C7
Whiterails Dr ORM L39 ....348 B5
Whiterails Ms ORM L39 ....348 A5
Whiteray Rd LANC LA1 ....2 B1
White Rd BBNW BB2 ....244 D5
Whiteside St BPOOL FY1 ....4 C1
Whiteside Wy CLV/TH FY5 ....122 D8
Whitestock SKEL WN8 ....362 E3
White St COL BB8 ....171 F7
PDHM/BLYW BB12 ....224 D5
WGNW/BIL/O WN5 ....365 K5
Whitethorn Cl CHLYE PR6 ....286 C1
Whitethorne Ms CLV/TH FY5 ....149 H3
Whitethorn Ms LSTA FY8 ....231 G1
Whitethorn Sq FUL/RIB PR2 ....237 K2
White Walls Cl COL BB8 ....170 D8
Whitewalls Dr COL BB8 ....170 E8
Whitewell Cl GAR/LONG PR3 ....129 K8
Whitewell Dr CLI BB7 ....165 G4
Whitewell Pl BBN BB1 ....9 D3
Whitewell Rd ACC BB5 ....248 D3
Whitewood Cl LSTA FY8 ....232 A7
Whitley Av BPOOLS FY3 ....5 D2
CLV/TH FY5 ....122 E6
Whitley Rd SKEL WN8 ....365 F2
Whitmore Dr FUL/RIB PR2 ....240 E1
Whitmore Gv FUL/RIB PR2 ....240 E1
Whitmore Pl FUL/RIB PR2 ....240 D1
Whitsters Hollow BOL BL1 ....341 F8
Whitstone Dr SKEL WN8 ....363 K4

Whittaker Av *BPOOLE* FY3 ....176 D4
Whittaker Cl *PDHM/BLYW* BB12 ....224 D3
Whittakers La *CLI* BB7 ....139 K4
Whittaker St *BBNW* BB2 ....8 A4
Whittam Av *BPOOLS* FY4 ....5 E6
Whittam Crs *CLI* BB7 ....192 E5
Whittam Rd *CHLY/EC* PR7 ....311 F6
  CLI BB7 ....192 E5
Whittam St *BLY* BB11 ....10 C4
Whitters La *GAR/LONG* PR3 ....128 D1
Whittingham Dr *RAMS* BL0 ....319 J8
Whittingham La *FUL/RIB* PR2 ....215 F1
  GAR/LONG PR3 ....185 J6
Whittingham Rd *GAR/LONG* PR3 ....187 K4
Whittle Cl *CLI* BB7 ....165 K2
Whittle Dr *ORM* L39 ....348 C4
Whittle Gn *KIRK/FR/WA* PR4 ....184 A8
Whittle Hl *EDGW/EG* BL7 ....316 C8
  KIRK/FR/WA PR4 ....184 A8
Whittle La *WGNNW/ST* WN6 ....333 C6
Whittle Pk *CHLYE* PR6 ....287 F1
Whittles St *BCUP* OL13 ....299 F3
  WHIT OL12 ....299 H7
Whittle St *RAW/HAS* BB4 ....273 H8
Whittlewood Ct *NWD/KWIPK* L33 .....366 D2
Whittlewood Dr *ACC* BB5 ....248 B2
Whittycroft Av *NLSN* BB9 ....170 C5
Whittycroft Dr *NLSN* BB9 ....170 C5
Whitwell Av *BPOOLS* FY4 ....204 C6
Whitworth Ct *KIRK/FR/WA* * PR4 .....208 E7
Whitworth Dr *CHLY/EC* PR7 ....310 E5
Whitworth Rake *WHIT* OL12 ....323 H3
Whitworth Sq *WHIT* OL12 ....323 H3
Whitworth St *KIRK/FR/WA* PR4 ....208 D5
Whitworth Wy *BWCK/EAR* BB18 ....119 G7
Wholesome La *CHTN/BK* PR9 ....329 G1
  KIRK/FR/WA PR4 ....261 F5
Whowell Fold *BOL* BL1 ....341 G8
Whytha Rd *CLI* BB7 ....143 F5
Wickliffe St *NLSN* BB9 ....198 C2
Wicklow Av *LSTA* FY8 ....233 C6
Wicks Crs *FMBY* L37 ....343 G7
Wicks Gdns *FMBY* L37 ....343 J8
Wicks Gn *FMBY* L37 ....343 G8
Wicks Green Cl *FMBY* L37 ....343 G7
Wicks La *FMBY* L37 ....343 G8
Wickworth St *NLSN* BB9 ....198 D4
Widgeon Cl *CLV/TH* FY5 ....123 F7
Widow Hill Rd *BRFD/BLYE* BB10 ....226 B1
Wigan La *CHLY/EC* PR7 ....336 D4
Wigan Rd *CHLY/EC* PR7 ....286 A8
  CHLYE PR6 ....286 A5
  ORM L39 ....348 D6
  SKEL WN8 ....363 F3
  WGNNW/ST WN6 ....353 K6
  WGNW/BIL/O WN5 ....371 H4
Wiggins La *BRSC* L40 ....304 E6
Wight Moss Wy *STHP* PR8 ....301 K8
Wignalls Meadow *HTWN* L38 ....355 K8
Wignall St *PRES* * PR1 ....240 A2
Wigston Cl *STHP* PR8 ....325 H7
Wigton Av *LEY/BBR* PR5 ....285 F4
Wilbraham St *PRES* PR1 ....240 A2
Wilcove *SKEL* WN8 ....363 F2
Wilderswood Av *HOR/BR* BL6 ....338 E7
Wilderswood Cl *CHLYE* PR6 ....287 G1
Wilderswood Ct *HOR/BR* BL6............339 F7
Wilding's La *LSTA* FY8 ....231 H3
Wild La *BPOOLS* FY4 ....205 K6
Wildman St *BPOOLE* * FY3 ....176 D4
  PRES PR1 ....239 G1
Wildoaks Dr *CLV/TH* FY5 ....149 K3
Wilds Pl *RAMS* * BL0 ....319 H6
Wildwood Cl *RAMS* BL0 ....319 G7
Wilfield St *BLY* BB11 ....10 B3
Wilford St *BPOOLE* FY3 ....176 E4
Wilfred St *ACC* BB5 ....248 C7
Wilkie Av *BLY* BB11 ....251 E3
Wilkinson Av *BPOOLE* FY3 ....5 E3
Wilkinson Mt
  BWCK/EAR (off Water St) BB18.....146 B1
Wilkinson Rd *BOL* BL1 ....341 H6
Wilkinson St *BLY* BB11 ....250 D7
  LEY/BBR PR5 ....262 E3
  NLSN BB9 ....170 A8
  NLSN * BB9 ....198 C4
  PDHM/BLYW BB12 ....196 B6
  RAW/HAS BB4 ....272 C7
Wilkinson Wy *PLF/KEOS* FY6 ....98 B6
Wilkin Sq *CLI* BB7 ....165 J3
Willacy La *KIRK/FR/WA* PR4 ....182 E8
Willacy Pde *HEY* LA3 ....52 E2
Willard Av *WGNW/BIL/O* WN5 ....365 F8
Willaston Av *NLSN* BB9 ....170 C3
William Henry St *PRES* PR1 ....240 A3
William Herbert St *BBN* * BB1 ....9 D3
William Hopwood St *BBNW* BB1 ....9 E5

William Young Cl *PRES* * PR1 ....240 A1
Williams Av *HGHB* LA2 ....42 C5
Williams La *FUL/RIB* PR2 ....214 A4
Williamson Rd *LANC* LA1 ....3 E3
Williams Pl *NLSN* BB9 ....198 D3
Williams Rd *BRFD/BLYE* BB10 ....225 K2
William St *ACC* BB5 ....248 CA
  ACC BB5 ....248 A2
  BBNW BB2 ....268 B1
  BCUP OL13 ....299 G3
  BPOOLE FY3 ....176 E4
  BWCK/EAR BB18 ....146 B2
  COL BB8 ....171 J7
  DWN * BB3 ....291 J2
  HOR/BR BL6 ....338 C8
  LEY/BBR * PR5 ....262 D3
  NLSN BB9 ....197 K5
  NLSN BB9 ....198 C2
  RAMS BL0 ....319 J2
  WHIT OL12 ....323 G2
Willis St *BLY* BB11 ....10 B4
Willoughby Av *CLV/TH* FY5 ....148 D1
Willoughby St *BBN* BB1 ....8 C3
Willow Av *KKBY* L32 ....366 A8
  RAW/HAS BB4 ....273 H7
Willow Bank *DWN* BB3 ....291 J5
  GAR/LONG (off Garstang Rd) PR3 ..156 C6
Willowbank Av *BPOOLS* FY4.............204 E6
Willowbank Ct
  PLF/KEOS (off Blackpool Rd) FY6 ..149 H6
Willow Brook *ORM* L39 ....327 J5
Willowbrook Dr *WGNNW/ST* WN6 ....353 K4
Willow Cl *CHLYE* PR6 ....337 H3
  CLV/TH FY5 ....149 K2
  GAR/LONG PR3 ....80 C8
  KIRK/FR/WA PR4 ....234 E6
  LEY/BBR PR5 ....262 D3
  LEY/BBR PR5 ....264 D2
  NLSN BB9 ....197 K2
  PRES PR1 ....238 C7
Willow Coppice *FUL/RIB* PR2 ....212 A8
Willow Crs *BRSC* L40 ....331 F5
  FUL/RIB PR2 ....240 B1
  LEY/BBR PR5 ....263 G8
Willowcroft Dr *PLF/KEOS* FY6 ....150 D2
Willow-Dale *CLV/TH* FY5 ....149 K2
Willowdene *CLV/TH* FY5 ....148 E2
Willowdene Cl *EDGW/EG* BL7 ....341 K3
Willow Dr *CHLY/EC* PR7 ....310 B8
  CLI BB7 ....193 H3
  GAR/LONG PR3 ....129 J2
  KIRK/FR/WA PR4 ....208 A7
  KIRK/FR/WA PR4 ....234 E6
  PLF/KEOS FY6 ....177 K3
  SKEL WN8 ....362 E2
Willow End *BRSC* L40 ....331 F7
Willow Fld *CHLYE* PR6 ....264 B8
Willow Field Cha *LEY/BBR* * PR5 .....265 G1
Willowfield Rd *HEY* LA3 ....52 E4
Willow Gn *BRSC* L40 ....306 A8
  FUL/RIB PR2 ....238 C3
  ORM L39 ....348 D6
Willow Gv *BPOOLE* FY3 ....177 G2
  CHTN/BK PR9 ....302 A4
  CLI BB7 ....139 H4
  FMBY L37 ....343 K7
  GAR/LONG PR3 ....186 A5
  MCMB LA4 ....42 B5
  PLF/KEOS FY6 ....150 D1
Willow Grove Pk
  PLF/KEOS (off Sandy La) FY6...........98 C5
Willowhey *CHTN/BK* PR9 ....278 B8
Willow Hey *KIRK/FR/WA* PR4 ....281 K4
  SKEL WN8 ....363 F2
Willow La *LANC* LA1 ....2 A4
Willowmead Pk *LSTA* FY8 ....233 H1
Willow Mt *BBN* BB1 ....219 H8
Willow Pk *ACC* BB5 ....270 B1
Willow Pl *KIRK/FR/WA* PR4 ....180 D2
Willow Rd *CHLYE* PR6 ....311 J1
  LEY/BBR PR5 ....284 B5
Willow Rocks
  BWCK/EAR
  (off Dales View Pk) BB18 ....145 F4
Willows Av *CLV/TH* FY5 ....148 E2
  LSTA FY8 ....232 A8
Willows La *ACC* BB5 ....248 A6
  KIRK/FR/WA PR4 ....208 D6
Willows Park La *GAR/LONG* PR3 ....188 B3
The Willows *BBNW* BB2 ....217 J8
  BRSC L40 ....332 E1
  STHP (off Warwick St) PR8 ....301 J7
Willow St *ACC* BB5 ....221 J8
  ACC BB5 ....248 B5
  BBN BB1 ....9 E2
  DWN BB3 ....291 H2

FTWD FY7 9
GTH/LHO BB6 22
PDHM/BLYW BB12 1
RAW/HAS BB4 29
Willow Ter
  BPOOLE (off Staining Old Rd) FY3 ...17
Willow Tree Av *GAR/LONG* PR3 18
  RAW/HAS BB4 18
Willow Tree Crs *LEY/BBR* PR5 28
Willow Trees Dr *BBN* BB1 ....
Willow Wk *SKEL* WN8 35
Willow Wy *KIRK/FR/WA* PR4 26
Willshaw Rd *BISP* FY2 17
Willy La *HGHB* LA2 7
Wilmar Rd *LEY/BBR* PR5 28
Wilmcote Gv *STHP* PR8 32
Wilmore Cl *COL* BB8 17
Wilmot Rd *FUL/RIB* PR2 21
Wilmot St *BOL* BL1 34
Wilmslow Av *BOL* BL1 34
Wilpshire Banks *BBN* BB1 21
Wilpshire Rd *BBN* BB1 22
Wilson Cl *KIRK/FR/WA* PR4 28
Wilson Dr *KIRK/FR/WA* PR4 18
Wilson Gv *HEY* LA3 5
Wilson Sq *CLV/TH* FY5 14
Wilson St *BBNW* BB2 26
  CLI BB7 16
  COL BB8 17
  HOR/BR BL6 33
Wilton Cl *LANC* * LA1 4
Wilton Gv *PRES* PR1 23
Wilton Pde *BPOOL* FY1 17
Wilton Pl *LEY/BBR* * PR5 28
Wilton Rd *BOL* BL1 34
  WGNNW/ST WN6 35
Wilton St *BOL* BL1 34
  BRFD/BLYE BB10 22
  NLSN BB9 17
  NLSN BB9 19
Wiltshire Av *PDHM/BLYW* BB12 22
Wiltshire Dr *RAW/HAS* BB4 29
Wiltshire Ms *KIRK/FR/WA* PR4 21
Wilvere Dr *CLV/TH* FY5 14
Wilworth Crs *BBN* BB1 24
Wimberley Banks *BBN* BB1 ....
Wimberley Gdns *BBN* BB1 ....
Wimberley Pl *BBN* * BB1 ....
Wimberley St *BBN* BB1 ....
Wimbledon Av *CLV/TH* FY5 14
Wimborne Rd *WGNW/BIL/O* WN5 36
Wimbourne Pl *BPOOLS* FY4 20
Wimbrick Cl *ORM* L39 34
Wimbrick Crs *ORM* L39 34
Wincanton Dr *BOL* BL1 34
Winchcombe Rd *CLV/TH* FY5 14
Winchester Av *ACC* * BB5 24
  BPOOLS FY4 ....
  CHLY/EC PR7 ....
  LANC LA1 ....
  MCMB LA4 4
Winchester Cl *HEY* * LA3 5
  WGNW/BIL/O WN5 36
Winchester Dr *PLF/KEOS* FY6...........14
Winchester Rd
  PDHM/BLYW BB12 22
  WGNW/BIL/O WN5 37
Winchester St *BBN* BB1 ....
  PRES PR1 ....
Winckley Rd *ACC* BB5 24
  PRES PR1 ....
Winckley Sq *PRES* PR1 ....
Winder Garth *KKBYL* LA6 3
Winder La *GAR/LONG* PR3 10
Windermere Av *ACC* BB5 24
  BRFD/BLYE BB10 22
  CLI BB7 16
  COL BB8 17
  FTWD FY7 12
  LEY/BBR PR5 26
  MCMB LA4 4
Windermere Cl *BBN* BB1 ....
Windermere Crs *STHP* PR8 32
Windermere Dr *BBN* BB1 33
  CHLYE PR6 24
  DWN BB3 36
  NWD/KWIPK L33 26
  RAMS BL0 31
  RNFD/HAY WA11 36
Windermere Rd *BCUP* OL13 27
  BPOOLS FY4 20
  CARN LA5 3
  CARN LA5 3
  CHLYE* PR6 31
  FUL/RIB PR2 21
  HTWN L38 35
  LANC LA1 ....
  PDHM/BLYW BB12 22

RES PR1 ....240 E2
CNW/BIL/O WN5 ....365 H3
dermere Sq LSTA FY8 ....231 F1
dermere St BOL BL1 ....341 K8
dfield CI NWD/KWIPK L33 ....366 E5
dflower Dr LEY/BBR PR5 ....286 C1
RK/FR/WA PR4 ....282 E1
dgate KIRK/FR/WA PR4 ....282 A6
KEL WN8 ....363 F2
dham PI LANC LA1 ....42 C8
dholme LANC LA1 ....2 A1
dmill Av KIRK/FR/WA PR4 ....209 F7
RM L39 ....348 D6
dmill CI BPOOLE FY3 ....178 A6
WD/KWIPK* L33 ....366 C6
dmill Ct
ANC (off Claughton Dr) LA1 ....55 G8
dmill Hts SKEL WN8 ....364 C3
dmill La CHLYE PR6 ....265 C4
dmill PI BPOOLS FY4 ....205 F5
dmill Rd SKEL WN8 ....364 C3
dmill St LANC LA1 ....2 B2
dmill Vw KIRK/FR/WA PR4 ....208 B5
drows SKEL WN8 ....363 F2
Windrush WHIT OL12 ....323 C7
dsor Av ACC BB5 ....248 A3
POOLS FY4 ....204 B3
HLY/EC PR7 ....336 E5
LJ BB7 ....165 G4
LV/TH FY5 ....149 H1
JL/RIB PR2 ....212 D8
AR/LONG PR3 ....187 K4
IRK/FR/WA PR4 ....261 H2
ANC LA1 ....3 F6
CMB LA4 ....41 F8
RES PR1 ....238 E8
AW/HAS BB4 ....295 G2
AW/HAS BB4 ....297 G2
dsor CI BBN BB1 ....9 F6
RSC L40 ....330 E8
HLY/EC PR7 ....311 F4
dsor Dr CHLYE PR6 ....288 E3
DHM/BLYW BB12 ....222 D1
dsor Ct PLF/KEOS FY6 ....150 A8
THP CR8 ....300 E7
dsor Gdns GAR/LONG PR3 ....129 H4
dsor Gv MCMB LA4 ....41 G7
dsor PI BWCK/EAR BB18 ....119 H8
dsor Rd GAR/LONG PR3 ....246 C6
BNW BB3 ....244 D5
POOLE FY3 ....177 H4
HLY/EC PR7 ....308 E4
HLY/EC PR7 ....311 F4
HTN/BK PR9 ....301 K5
WN BB3 ....268 C8
MBY L37 ....355 J2
AR/LONG PR3 ....129 H4
TH/LHO BB6 ....221 H6
EY LA3 ....41 F8
EY/BBR PR5 ....240 B8
STA FY8 ....231 C6
KEL WN8 ....364 C3
CNW/BIL/O WN5 ....371 H6
dsor St ACC * BB5 ....248 C5
OL BB8 ....171 J6
LSN BB9 ....198 D4
DHM/BLYW BB12 ....224 E5
dsor Ter FTWD FY7 ....97 H6
dy Bank COL BB8 ....171 J6
dy Harbour Rd PLF/KEOS FY6 ......151 J7
THP CR8 ....326 A4
dy Strret GAR/LONG PR3 ....134 E8
dy Hill LANC LA1 ....3 D3
ewall La COL BB8 ....172 C6
gate Av CLV/TH FY5 ....148 D3
CMB LA4 ....41 J7
gate PI CLV/TH FY5 ....148 D3
gate Rd NWD/KWIPK L33 ....366 D7
gates PRES PR1 ....238 E8
gate Saul Rd LANC LA1 ....2 C4
ifred La ORM L39 ....359 K2
ifred St BPOOL FY1 ....4 B6
AMS BL0 ....319 H6
marleigh Rd FUL/RIB PR2 ....238 D2
ANC LA1 ....67 C1
marleigh St BBN BB1 ....246 A6
marleigh Wk BBN BB1 ....246 A7
amoss Dr NWD/KWIPK L33 ....366 C6
nipeg CI BBNW BB2 ....244 D3
nipeg PI BISP FY2 ....148 E3
scar Wk PLF/KEOS FY6 ....149 H8
asford Crs CLV/TH FY5 ....148 C3
aslow Av PLF/KEOS FY6 ....149 H6
aslow CI PRES PR1 ....262 B1

Winsor Av LEY/BBR PR5 ....285 K3
Winstanley Gv BPOOL FY1 ....4 C2
Winstanley Rd AIMK WN4 ....371 K4
SKEL WN8 ....363 F3
WGNW/BIL/O WN5 ....365 H8
Winster CI LEY/BBR PR5 ....241 J7
Winster Pk LANC LA1 ....2 A1
Winster PI BPOOLS FY4 ....205 K2
The Winsters SKEL WN8 ....363 F2
Winster Wk LANC LA1 ....2 A1
Winston Av CLV/TH FY5 ....149 F1
LSTA FY8 ....231 H5
Winston Crs STHP PR8 ....327 C1
Winston Rd BBN BB1 ....8 B2
Winterburn Rd BBNW BB2 ....267 K4
Winter Gap La AIRE BD20 ....147 J3
Winter Hey La HOR/BR BL6 ....338 D8
Winter Hill CI FUL/RIB PR2 ....215 C4
Winterley Dr ACC BB5 ....248 E2
Winter St BOL BL1 ....341 H8
Winterton Rd DWN BB3 ....291 J1
Winthorpe Av MCMB LA4 ....41 K7
Winton Av BPOOLS FY4 ....205 C2
FUL/RIB PR2 ....213 H5
Winton Rd BPOOLS FY4 ....205 C1
Wiseman St BLY BB11 ....10 B3
Wisteria Dr BBN BB1 ....268 E4
Wiswell CI BRFD/BLYE BB10 ....226 C1
RAW/HAS BB4 ....273 H7
Wiswell La CLI BB7 ....193 H5
Wiswell Shay CLI BB7 ....193 J4
Witham Rd SKEL WN8 ....362 D2
Withens Rd MGHL L31 ....359 F8
Witherslack CI MCMB LA4 ....41 H8
Withers St BBN BB1 ....9 D5
Within Gv ACC BB5 ....248 D3
Withington La CHLY/EC PR7 ....334 C1
Withins Fld HTWN L38 ....355 K8
Withins La HTWN L38 ....357 F4
Withnell Fold Old Rd CHLYE PR6 ..288 E2
Withnell Gv CHLYE PR6 ....311 J2
Withnell Rd BPOOLS FY4 ....204 B3
Withy Grove CI LEY/BBR PR5 ......263 J2
Withy Grove Crs LEY/BBR PR5 ....263 J2
Withy Grove Rd LEY/BBR PR5 ......263 J2
Withy Pde FUL/RIB PR2 ....213 G7
Withy Trees Av LEY/BBR PR5 ......263 J2
Withy Trees CI LEY/BBR PR5 ....263 J2
Witney Rd BBNW BB2 ....267 F3
Witton Av FTWD FY7 ....122 E2
Witton Gv FTWD FY7 ....122 E2
Witton Pde BBNW BB2 ....8 A6
Witton St PRES PR1 ....7 C5
Witton Wy RNFD/HAY WA11 ....369 C4
Witton Weavers Wy BBNW BB2 ..243 K7
DWN BB3 ....316 A1
Woborrow Rd HEY LA3 ....52 C4
Woburn CI ACC BB5 ....248 E8
Woburn Gn LEY/BBR PR5 ....285 K2
Woburn Rd BPOOL FY1 ....176 C3
The Wold CHLYE PR6 ....288 A8
Wolfenden Gn RAW/HAS BB4 ......297 H3
Wollaton Dr STHP PR8 ....302 B8
Wolseley CI LEY/BBR PR5 ....285 J3
Wolseley PI PRES PR1 ....7 F5
Wolseley Rd PRES PR1 ....6 C5
Wolseley St BBNW BB2 ....268 A2
LANC LA1 ....3 E3
Wolsey CI CLV/TH FY5 ....122 E8
Wolsley Rd BPOOL FY1 ....4 B6
FTWD FY7 ....97 F7
Wolverton SKEL WN8 ....363 F3
Wolverton Av BISP FY2 ....176 B1
Woodacre Rd FUL/RIB PR2 ....240 E1
Woodale Laithe NLSN BB9 ....170 A8
Wood Bank PRES PR1 ....238 E8
Woodbank Av DWN * BB3 ....291 C1
Woodberry CI NWD/KWIPK L33 ..366 D5
Woodbine Gdns
PDHM/BLYW BB12 ....224 D4
Woodbine Rd BBNW BB2 ....244 D5
PDHM/BLYW BB12 ....224 E5
Woodbine Ter TOD OL14 ....277 C2
Woodburn CI BBNW BB2 ....244 D5
Woodburn Dr BOL BL1 ....341 F8
Woodbury Av BBNW BB2 ....268 A2
PDHM/BLYW BB12 ....197 F4
Wood CI NLSN BB9 ....169 J6
Wood Clough Platts NLSN BB9 ....197 J6
Woodcock CI CLV/TH FY5 ....123 C6
Woodcock Fold CHLY/EC PR7 ......308 E4
Woodcock Hill Rd BBNW BB2 ......266 C3
Woodcote CI NWD/KWIPK L33 ....366 E7
Woodcourt Av BLY BB11 ....10 A6
Woodcrest BBN BB1 ....219 H6
Woodcroft SKEL WN8 ....363 F3

WGNNW/ST WN6 ....353 G5
Woodcroft Av RAW/HAS BB4 ....273 C6
Woodcroft CI PRES PR1 ....261 K1
Woodcroft St RAW/HAS BB4 ....273 C6
Wood End PDHM/BLYW BB12 ......197 H8
PRES PR1 ....261 K1
Wood End Rd CHLYE PR6 ....263 K8
Woodfall CHLY/EC PR7 ....311 F1
Woodfield LEY/BBR PR5 ....264 B5
Woodfield Av ACC BB5 ....248 D8
BPOOL* FY1 ....4 B5
Woodfield Rd BPOOL FY1 ....4 B5
CHLY/EC PR7 ....311 G2
CLV/TH FY5 ....149 K2
ORM L39 ....348 A8
Woodfield Vw CLI BB7 ....193 G7
Woodfold CI BBNW BB2 ....217 H8
Woodfold La GAR/LONG PR3 ....103 J6
Woodfold PI BBNW BB2 ....244 D6
Woodford Copse CHLY/EC PR7 ....310 D4
Woodford St CNW/BIL/O WN5 ....365 K5
Woodgate HEY LA3 ....54 A1
Woodgate Pk
HEY (off Middlegate) LA3 ....54 B1
Woodgates Rd BBNW BB2 ....244 B6
Wood Gn KIRK/FR/WA PR4 ....209 F4
LEY/BBR PR5 ....285 C1
Wood Green Dr CLV/TH FY5 ....149 F3
Woodgrove Rd BLY BB11 ....11 E6
Woodhall Crs LEY/BBR PR5 ....241 J7
Woodhall Gdns PLF/KEOS FY6 ....150 E1
Woodhart La CHLY/EC PR7 ....308 E6
Woodhead CI RAMS BL0 ....319 J7
RAW/HAS BB4 ....297 J1
Woodhead Rd PDHM/BLYW BB12 ..222 D1
Wood Hey Gv WHIT OL12 ....323 K7
Woodhey Rd RAMS BL0 ....319 C8
Woodhill Av MCMB LA4 ....41 C8
Woodhill CI MCMB LA4 ....41 C8
Woodhill La MCMB LA4 ....41 C7
Wood House La CLI BB7 ....89 F5
Woodhouse La WHIT OL12 ....322 H8
Woodhouse Rd CLV/TH FY5 ....150 A3
Woodhouse St BLY BB11 ....11 E5
Woodland Av BCUP OL13 ....275 J6
BRSC L40 ....328 D4
CLV/TH FY5 ....149 H1
Woodland CI KIRK/FR/WA PR4 ......207 K8
PLF/KEOS FY6 ....151 F1
Woodland Crs PLF/KEOS FY6 ......98 C5
Woodland Dr ACC BB5 ....221 K6
PLF/KEOS FY6 ....178 A2
Woodland Gv BPOOLE FY3 ....5 E3
EDGW/EG BL7 ....341 H1
PRES PR1 ....238 D6
Woodland Pk CLI BB7 ....193 H6
Woodland PI DWN BB3 ....268 C5
Woodland Rd WHIT OL12 ....323 C8
Woodlands Av BBNW BB2 ....267 F2
FUL/RIB PR2 ....240 C1
KIRK/FR/WA PR4 ....208 D6
LEY/BBR PR5 ....263 K1
PRES PR1 ....239 F8
Woodlands CI CHTN/BK PR9 ....301 K3
FMBY L37 ....355 H1
KIRK/FR/WA PR4 ....209 K8
ORM L39 ....348 E7
Woodlands Crs GAR/LONG PR3 ..184 D5
Woodlands Dr CARN LA5 ....15 H7
CLI BB7 ....139 H4
CLI BB7 ....193 G6
FUL/RIB PR2 ....213 G3
HEY LA3 ....52 E1
KIRK/FR/WA PR4 ....209 H4
KIRK/FR/WA PR4 ....234 A6
LEY/BBR PR5 ....285 H3
WGNNW/ST WN6 ....353 H7
Woodlands Gv DWN BB3 ....291 F1
FUL/RIB PR2 ....215 J2
HEY LA3 ....52 E1
PDHM/BLYW BB12 ....223 H3
Woodlands Meadow
CHLY/EC PR7 ....311 C8
Woodlands Rd FMBY L37 ....355 H1
LANC LA1 ....43 H7
LSTA FY8 ....231 K7
NLSN BB9 ....198 D3
RAMS BL0 ....319 K1
The Woodlands FUL/RIB PR2 ....238 A2
GTH/LHO BB6 ....192 A5
STHP PR8 ....325 J6
Woodlands Vw KKBYL LA6 ....34 E3
Woodlands Wy GAR/LONG PR3 ..184 D5
KIRK/FR/WA PR4 ....260 A3
Woodland Ter BCUP OL13 ....275 J6
Woodland Vw BCUP OL13 ....275 J7
CHLYE (off School La) PR6 ....289 F4

Y

rtree Cl CHLY/EC PR7 ....311 F8
v Tree Cl KIRK/FR/WA PR4 ....209 K8
v Tree Dr ACC BB5 ....247 G8
BNW BB2 ....244 B3
rtree Gv LEY/BBR PR5 ....262 D4
v Tree Gv RAW/HAS BB4 ....296 B3
v Tree Rd BPOOLE FY3 ....177 G2
RM L39 ....348 D5
v Tree Ter
  HIT (off Market St) OL12 ....299 J5
v Tree Vls
  HLY/EC (off Preston Rd) PR7 ....309 K8
k Av CLV/TH FY5 ....148 D1
WD FY7 ....96 E8
JL/RIB PR2 ....213 G7
AW/HAS BB4 ....295 G3
HP PR8 ....301 G6
k Cl ACC BB5 ....221 K8
CC* BB5 ....248 B4
MBY L37 ....343 K5
EY/BBR PR5 ....285 G2
k Crs BBN BB1 ....219 H8
k Dr GAR/LONG PR3 ....153 G6
RK/FR/WA PR4 ....235 F1
MS BLO 319 G8
k Flds BWCK/EAR BB18 ....145 F2

York Gdns STHP PR8 ....301 G6
York Gv GAR/LONG PR3 ....129 G4
York La GTH/LHO BB6 ....220 B3
York Mnr
  FMBY (off Three Tuns La) L37 ....343 K8
York Pl CHLYE PR6 ....337 G3
  MCMB LA4 ....41 H6
York Rd BBN BB1 ....220 A6
  BISP FY2 ....148 B7
  FMBY L37 ....343 K8
  LANC LA1 ....3 E6
  LSTA FY8 ....231 F6
  STHP PR8 ....301 F7
Yorkshire St ACC BB5 ....248 C7
  ACC BB5 ....248 E1
  BCUP OL13 ....275 J8
  BLY BB11 ....11 D3
  BPOOL FY1 ....4 B4
  NLSN BB9 ....198 C3
Yorkshire St West HEY LA3 ....40 E7
York St ACC* BB5 ....247 G8
  ACC BB5 ....247 J5
  ACC BB5 ....248 B4
  BBN* BB1 ....246 E2
  BBNW BB2 ....8 C6
  BPOOL FY1 ....4 B4

BWCK/EAR BB18 ....145 F2
CHLY/EC PR7 ....311 H4
CLI BB7 ....165 K2
COL BB8 ....171 J6
GTH/LHO BB6 ....221 H6
NLSN BB9 ....198 D3
RAW/HAS BB4 ....273 H4
York Ter BBNW BB2 ....266 E3
CHTN/BK PR9 ....301 J3
Young Av LEY/BBR PR5 ....286 A2
Young St BBNW BB2 ....267 J1
RAMS BLO 319 H5

Z

Zama St RAMS * BLO 319 G7
Zebudah St BBNW BB2 ....267 K1
Zetland St CHTN/BK PR9 ....301 K4
  PRES PR1 ....240 A4
Zion Rd BBN BB1 ....9 E1
Zion St BCUP OL13 ....275 K8
  COL BB8 ....171 H7

Index - featured places

ey Farm Caravan Park
  BRSC L40 ....349 G3
ey Gisburn Park
  Private Hospital
  CLI BB7 ....117 F3
ey Lakes Sports Centre
  WGNW/BIL/O WN5 ....365 F4
ey Lane Industrial Estate
  BRSC L40 ....349 G2
ey Road Clinic
  BPOOLS FY4 ....204 C5
Cinema
  LANC LA1 ....3 D3
aham Guest High School
  WGNW/BIL/O WN5 ....365 J5
rington Business Centre
  ACC BB5 ....248 B5
rington Cricket Club
  ACC BB5 ....248 C3
rington & District Golf Club
  ACC BB5 ....247 F5
rington & Rossendale College
  ACC BB5 ....248 B6
rington & Rossendale College
  ACC BB5 ....248 D6
rington & Rossendale College
  RAW/HAS BB4 ....296 B1
rington Stanley FC
  ACC BB5 ....248 B3
rington Victoria Hospital
  ACC BB5 ....248 B4
hurst Business Park
  CHLY/EC PR7 ....310 D2
hurst Park Industrial Estate
  CHLY/EC PR7 ....310 C3
ngton CP School
  CHLY/EC PR7 ....337 F4
ngton Cricket Club
  CHLY/EC PR7 ....337 G5
ngton Medical Centre
  CHLYE PR6 ....337 H3
niral Shopping Centre
  NLSN BB9 ....198 B3
lt Education Centre
  BBNW BB2 ....8 A4
scough Business Park
  WGNW/ST WN6 ....334 C5
sdale CE Primary School
  STHP PR8 ....325 K7
sdale Clinic
  STHP PR8 ....325 K8
sdale High School
  STHP PR8 ....325 J5
Business Park
  CHTN/BK PR9 ....302 C5
any High School
  CHLYE PR6 ....311 J6
ert Street Business Park
  HOR/BR BL6 ....338 D6
er Grange High School
  RAW/HAS BB4 ....273 H7

Alhambra Leisure Centre
  HEY LA3 ....40 E7
Al Islah School
  BBN BB1 ....9 E5
All Hallows RC High School
  PRES PR1 ....238 C8
Alliance Business Park
  ACC BB5 ....248 A6
All Saints CE Primary School
  ACC BB5 ....247 J1
All Saints CE Primary School
  CHLY/EC PR7 ....311 F6
All Saints CE Primary School
  WGNNW/ST WN6 ....352 E2
All Saints RC High School
  RAW/HAS BB4 ....295 K2
All Seasons Leisure Centre
  CHLY/EC PR7 ....311 H2
Alston Hall Residential College
  GAR/LONG PR3 ....216 B3
Alston Lane RC School
  GAR/LONG PR3 ....215 K1
Altham Business Park
  ACC BB5 ....223 F5
Altham Industrial Estate
  ACC BB5 ....222 E5
Altham St James CE
  Primary School
  ACC BB5 ....222 D5
AMF Bowling
  BLY BB11 ....11 D4
AMF Bowling
  BPOOL FY1 ....4 C4
AMS Trading Estate
  KIRK/FR/WA PR4 ....260 E4
Anchor Retail Park
  PDHM/BLYW BB12 ....11 D2
Anchorsholme Primary School
  CLV/TH FY5 ....148 E3
Ansdell CP School
  LSTA FY8 ....231 J6
Apollo 4 Cinema
  MCMB LA4 ....41 F6
Aqueduct Street Industrial Estate
  FUL/RIB PR2 ....6 B1
Archbishop Temple School
  FUL/RIB PR2 ....213 H6
Argyle Lawn Tennis Club
  CHTN/BK PR9 ....302 A1
Arkholme CE Primary School
  KKBYL LA6 ....29 G6
Arndale Shopping Centre
  ACC BB5 ....248 C5
Arndale Shopping Centre
  MCMB LA4 ....41 G6
Arnold Medical Centre
  BPOOLS FY4 ....204 D4
Arnold School
  BPOOLS FY4 ....204 C4
Arnside National CE School
  CARN LA5 ....15 G1

Artson Works
  BBNW BB2 ....267 H1
Ashleigh County School
  DWN BB3 ....291 J5
Ashton Health Centre
  FUL/RIB PR2 ....238 C2
Ashton & Lea Golf Club
  FUL/RIB PR2 ....237 J1
Ashton on Ribble High School
  FUL/RIB PR2 ....238 B1
Ashurst Health Centre
  SKEL WN8 ....351 H7
Asmall CP School
  ORM L39 ....348 B5
Astley Bridge Cricket Club
  BOL BL1 ....341 H7
Astley Hall Museum &
  Art Gallery
  CHLY/EC PR7 ....310 E2
Astley Park School
  CHLY/EC PR7 ....311 F3
Astra Business Centre
  FUL/RIB PR2 ....215 G5
Atherton Holme Works
  BCUP OL13 ....297 K3
Atkinson Art Gallery
  STHP PR8 ....301 H4
Atlanta Swimming
  STHP PR8 ....301 G7
Atlas Foundry Estate
  PRES PR1 ....6 C2
Atlas Works
  DWN BB3 ....291 K2
Audley Junior & Infant School
  BBN BB1 ....9 E6
Audley Sports Centre
  BBN BB1 ....9 E5
Aughton Christ Church CE
  Primary School
  ORM L39 ....348 A8
Aughton St Michaels CE School
  ORM L39 ....359 K2
Avondale County School
  DWN BB3 ....268 B8
Bacup FC
  BCUP OL13 ....275 J7
Bacup Golf Club
  BCUP OL13 ....298 C1
Bacup Leisure Hall
  BCUP OL13 ....275 J8
Bacup & Rawtenstall
  Grammar School
  RAW/HAS BB4 ....297 H3
Baines Endowed CE School
  BPOOLS FY4 ....5 F6
Baines Endowed CP School
  CLV/TH FY5 ....149 J3
Baines School
  PLF/KEOS FY6 ....177 K2
Balderstone CE Primary School
  BBNW BB2 ....217 G6

Balladen CP School
RAW/HAS BB4 .... 296 B3

Balmoral Works
BBNW BB2 .... 8 B6

Balshaws CE High School
LEY/BBR PR5 .... 285 K4

Bamber Bridge Clinic
LEY/BBR PR5 .... 263 J1

Bamber Bridge FC
LEY/BBR PR5 .... 263 G3

**Bamber Bridge Methodist
Primary School**
LEY/BBR PR5 .... 263 J3

**Bamber Bridge (Withy Park)
Leisure Centre**
LEY/BBR PR5 .... 263 J2

Bancroft Mill
BWCK/EAR BB18 .... 144 E3

Bank Hey School
BBNW BB2 .... 267 K4

Bank Lane Caravan Park
KIRK/FR/WA PR4 .... 234 B7

Banks Health Centre
CHTN/BK PR9 .... 279 H5

**Banks Methodist
Primary School**
CHTN/BK PR9 .... 279 K5

Bank View Industrial Estate
PLF/KEOS FY6 .... 150 E2

Barden High School
BRFD/BLYE BB10 .... 225 J1

Barden Junior School
BRFD/BLYE BB10 .... 225 J2

Barden Lane Athletics Track
BRFD/BLYE BB10 .... 225 J2

Barnfield Business Centre
NLSN BB9 .... 198 D5

Barnoldswick CE School
BWCK/EAR BB18 .... 145 F1

Barnoldswick Civic Centre
BWCK/EAR BB18 .... 145 F1

**Barrow Controlled
Primary School**
CLI BB7 .... 193 H1

Barrowford Clinic
NLSN BB9 .... 170 B8

Barrowford CP School
NLSN BB9 .... 170 B8

Barton CE School
GAR/LONG PR3 .... 184 D4

Bates Swimming Pool
PLF/KEOS FY6 .... 150 E1

Baxenden CE School
ACC BB5 .... 271 K2

Baxenden & District Golf Club
ACC BB5 .... 272 A1

BBC Radio Lancs
BBNW BB2 .... 8 C5

Beach Patrol HQ
BPOOL FY1 .... 176 B4

Beacon Fell View Holiday Park
GAR/LONG PR3 .... 188 C3

Beacon Park Public Golf Centre
SKEL WN8 .... 352 A8

Beardwood Hospital
BBNW BB2 .... 244 C5

Beardwood School
BBNW BB2 .... 244 C5

Beaumont College
LANC LA1 .... 42 E7

The Beeches Medical Centre
KIRK/FR/WA PR4 .... 260 B3

Beech Industrial Estate
BCUP OL13 .... 275 K8

Beech Tree School
LEY/BBR PR5 .... 264 A7

Beehive Industrial Estate
BPOOLS FY4 .... 205 H3

Belmont CP School
EDGW/EG BL7 .... 314 E6

Belmont School
RAW/HAS BB4 .... 296 A1

Belthorn CE Primary School
BBN BB1 .... 269 J5

**Belvedere & Caldervale
Sports Club**
BRFD/BLYE BB10 .... 197 K7

Benjamin Hargreaves CE School
ACC BB5 .... 248 D6

Bentgate School
RAW/HAS BB4 .... 295 K3

Bentham School Senior Girls
HGHB LA2 .... 39 K4

Berry Lane Medical Centre
GAR/LONG PR3 .... 188 A4

Best Business Centre
MCMB LA4 .... 41 H5

Bickerstaffe CE Junior School
ORM L39 .... 361 J6

Bigdale Medical Centre
NWD/KWIPK L33 .... 366 E8

**Billinge Chapel End
Parish Council**
WGNW/BIL/O WN5 .... 371 G6

Billinge Clinic
WGNW/BIL/O WN5 .... 371 F7

Billinge Hospital
WGNW/BIL/O WN5 .... 371 F1

**Billington & Langho St Leonards
CE Primary School**
GTH/LHO BB6 .... 192 C8

Birch Green CP School
SKEL WN8 .... 351 H8

Birchwood Medical Centre
FUL/RIB PR2 .... 238 D1

Birkdale High School
STHP PR8 .... 326 A4

Birkdale Primary School
STHP PR8 .... 301 H8

**Birkdale School for
Hearing Impaired Children**
STHP PR8 .... 300 E8

Birkdale Trading Estate
STHP PR8 .... 326 B1

Birleywood Health Centre
SKEL WN8 .... 363 K5

**Bishop David Sheppard
CE School**
CHTN/BK PR9 .... 302 D4

**Bishop Martins Junior &
Infant School**
SKEL WN8 .... 363 K5

Bishop Rawstone School
LEY/BBR PR5 .... 307 J1

**Bispham Endowed
Junior School**
BISP FY2 .... 148 D7

Bispham Hall Business Park
WGNW/BIL/O WN5 .... 370 E1

Bispham High School
BISP FY2 .... 176 E1

Blackamoor School
BBN BB1 .... 268 E3

Blackburn Arena
BBN BB1 .... 8 C6

Blackburn College
BBNW BB2 .... 8 A3

Blackburn Golf Club
BBNW BB2 .... 244 D4

**Blackburn Museum &
Art Gallery**
BBN BB1 .... 8 C4

Blackburn Ragged School
BBNW BB2 .... 8 B5

Blackburn RFC
BBN BB1 .... 245 F1

**Blackburn Rovers FC
(Ewood Park)**
BBNW BB2 .... 268 A3

Blackburn Royal Infirmary
BBNW BB2 .... 268 A1

Black Moss Special School
SKEL WN8 .... 362 D1

Blackpool & Flyde College
FTWD FY7 .... 122 E4

Blackpool Business Park
BPOOLS FY4 .... 204 E6

Blackpool Crematorium
BISP FY2 .... 149 F8

Blackpool Cricket Club
BPOOLE FY3 .... 5 E3

Blackpool FC (Bloomfield Road)
BPOOL FY1 .... 4 C5

Blackpool & Fylde College
BISP FY2 .... 148 E5

Blackpool & Fylde College
BPOOL FY1 .... 4 C3

Blackpool & Fylde College
LSTA FY8 .... 231 J6

Blackpool & Fylde College
PLF/KEOS FY6 .... 178 A1

Blackpool-Ice Drome
BPOOLS FY4 .... 204 B4

**Blackpool North Shore
Golf Club**
BISP FY2 .... 176 C1

Blackpool Pleasure Beach
BPOOLS FY4 204

**Blackpool Reform
Jewish Synagogue**
BPOOL FY1 4

Blackpool Rugby Club
CLV/TH FY5 148

The Blackpool Sixth Form College
BPOOLE FY3 177

Blackpool Tower
BPOOL FY1 176

Blackpool Wyre & Fylde
BPOOLE FY3 177

**Blackpool Wyre & Fylde
Community Health Services**
KIRK/FR/WA PR4 208

Blackpool Zoo Park
BPOOLE FY3 177

Bleasdale CE School
GAR/LONG PR3 132

Bleasdale House School
CARN LA5 15

**Blessed Sacrament RC
Primary School**
FUL/RIB PR2 214

Bloomfield Medical Centre
BPOOL FY1 4

Blowick Business Centre
CHTN/BK PR9 302

Bolton by Bowland CE School
CLI BB7 115

Bolton Holmes Farm
CARN LA5 33

**Bolton le Sands CE
Primary School**
CARN LA5 33

Bolton le Sands Cricket Club
CARN LA5 33

Bolton Old Links Golf Club
BOL BL1 340

Botanic Gardens Museum
CHTN/BK PR9 302

Bowerham School
LANC LA1 3

Bowland County High School
CLI BB7 140

Bowling Alley
LEY/BBR PR5 240

Brabins Endowed Primary School
GAR/LONG PR3 134

Bradley Primary School
NLSN BB9 198

Breck CP School
PLF/KEOS FY6 150

**Brennands Endowed
Primary School Slaidburn**
CLI BB7 89

Bretherton Endowed CE School
LEY/BBR PR5 283

Bridgebank Industrial Estate
HOR/BR BL6 338

**Bridge House Marina &
Caravan Park**
GAR/LONG PR3 129

Briercliffe Business Centre
BRFD/BLYE BB10 198

Briercliffe County Primary
BRFD/BLYE BB10 198

Briercliffe Shopping Centre
BRFD/BLYE BB10 225

Brierfield Health Centre
NLSN BB9 197

**Brindle St James CE
Primary School**
CHLYE PR6 264

Brinscall Public Baths
CHLYE PR6 289

**Britannia County
Primary School**
BCUP OL13 299

The British Lawnmower Museum
STHP PR8 301

**Broadfield County
Junior School**
LEY/BBR PR5 285

Broadfield School
ACC BB5 270

Broad Oak Industrial Estate
ACC BB5 248

Broadoaks Centre
LEY/BBR PR5 285

Broadway CP School
RAW/HAS BB4 295

~okfield CP School	*FUL/RIB* PR2	214	C6
~okfield CP School	*SKEL* WN8	362	D1
~okhouse Business Centre	*BBN* BB1	9	D3
~okhouse Primary School	*BBN* BB1	9	D2
~ok Lodge Primary School	*RNFD/HAY* WA11	369	F3
~okside Business Park	*RAW/HAS* BB4	273	G5
~ughton CE Primary School	*GAR/LONG* PR3	213	F2
~ughton High School	*GAR/LONG* PR3	212	E1
~ughton Mill Business Park	*SKP/WHF* BD23	121	H1
~ughton Park Private Hospital	*GAR/LONG* PR3	213	G2
~ownedge St Marys RC School	*LEY/BBR* PR5	263	J2
~nshaw CP School	*BRFD/BLYE* BB10	226	B7
~bbles Leisure Pool	*MCMB* LA4	41	F5
~ckshaw CP School	*CHLY/EC* PR7	310	E1
~pa Flyde Coast Hospital	*BPOOLE* FY3	177	F4
~rn Hall Industrial Estate	*FTWD* FY7	123	G5
~rnley Business Centre	*BLY* BB11	11	D3
~rnley Cemetery	*BLY* BB11	224	C7
~rnley College	*BLY* BB11	11	D2
~rnley College Higher Education Centre	*BLY* BB11	11	D2
~rnley County Court	*BLY* BB11	10	C4
~rnley Crematorium	*BLY* BB11	224	C7
~rnley Cricket Club Ltd	*BRFD/BLYE* BB10	11	E3
~rnley FC (Turf Moor)	*BRFD/BLYE* BB10	11	E3
~rnley General Hospital	*BRFD/BLYE* BB10	225	K1
~rnley Golf Club	*BLY* BB11	251	H1
~rnley Lawn Tennis Club	*BRFD/BLYE* BB10	11	E3
~rnley Road Medical Centre	*COL* BB8	171	F8
~rnley Sixth Form Centre	*PDHM/BLYW* BB12	224	B4
~rnley Wood CP School	*BLY* BB11	11	E5
~rnley Wood Health Centre	*BLY* BB11	11	E5
~rnley Youth Theatre	*BRFD/BLYE* BB10	11	F1
~rn Naze CP School	*CLV/TH* FY5	123	H8
~rscough Bridge Methodist School	*BRSC* L40	330	D6
~rscough County Primary School	*BRSC* L40	331	F6
~rscough Cricket Club	*BRSC* L40	331	F7
~rscough Health Centre	*BRSC* L40	330	E6
~rscough Industrial Estate	*BRSC* L40	330	B6
~rscough Priory High School	*BRSC* L40	330	D6
~rscough RC Primary School	*BRSC* L40	349	J1
~rscough Sports Centre	*BRSC* L40	330	E6
~rton Morewood CE Primary School	*KKBYL* LA6	18	B5
~rwains Sailing Club	*COL* BB8	171	G3
~derstones Hospital	*CLI* BB7	192	E4
Calder Vale School	*GAR/LONG* PR3	131	H2
Calder View School	*PDHM/BLYW* BB12	10	C1
Calder Works	*PDHM/BLYW* BB12	222	E4
Camelot Theme Park	*CHLY/EC* PR7	309	J7
Canning Road Industrial Estate	*CHTN/BK* PR9	302	C5
Cardinal Allen RC School	*FTWD* FY7	122	D3
Cardinal Newman College	*PRES* PR1	7	F3
Carleton Cemetery	*BISP* FY2	149	F7
Carleton CE Primary School	*PLF/KEOS* FY6	149	H6
Carleton Green CP School	*PLF/KEOS* FY6	149	H5
Carlton Lawn Tennis Club	*STHP* PR8	326	B1
Carnforth Cricket Club	*CARN* LA5	33	J2
Carnforth High School	*CARN* LA5	34	A2
Carr Head CP School	*PLF/KEOS* FY6	178	A1
Carr Hill High School	*KIRK/FR/WA* PR4	209	F7
Carrs Industrial Estate	*RAW/HAS* BB4	272	B7
Casterton County School	*BRFD/BLYE* BB10	198	A8
Catforth Primary School	*KIRK/FR/WA* PR4	183	G8
Cathedral	*BBN* BB1	8	C4
Cathedral of Saint Peter	*LANC* LA1	3	E3
Caton Primary School	*HGHB* LA2	45	G6
Cawthornes Endowed School	*HGHB* LA2	83	H2
Cedar House School	*KKBYL* LA6	21	G1
Cedars County Infant School	*BBN* BB1	9	D1
Central Lancaster High School	*LANC* LA1	3	F2
Centurion Industrial Estate	*LEY/BBR* PR5	262	E7
Century Works	*DWN* BB3	291	K1
Chandlers Business Park	*LEY/BBR* PR5	285	G1
Chapel End CP School	*WGNW/BIL/O* WN5	371	G7
Chapel Hill Trading Estate	*GAR/LONG* PR3	188	A5
Chapel Lane Business Park	*CHLY/EC* PR7	335	K3
Charles Saer County School	*FTWD* FY7	96	D8
Charnley Fold Industrial Estate	*LEY/BBR* PR5	240	D8
Charnock Richard CE Primary School	*CHLY/EC* PR7	310	B7
Charnock Richard Golf Club	*CHLY/EC* PR7	309	K7
Charter Walk Shopping Centre	*BLY* BB11	11	D3
Chatburn School	*CLI* BB7	140	D6
Chaucer CP School	*FTWD* FY7	97	G7
Cherry Tree Cricket Club	*BBNW* BB2	267	G2
Childrens Centre NHS Trust	*CHTN/BK* PR9	301	J3
Chingle Hall	*GAR/LONG* PR3	186	B7
Chorley AFC	*CHLY/EC* PR7	311	G5
Chorley Business & Technology Centre	*CHLYE* PR6	286	C7
Chorley Cricket Club	*CHLY/EC* PR7	311	F3
Chorley East Business Centre	*CHLYE* PR6	311	K4
Chorley Golf Club	*CHLYE* PR6	337	G1
Chorley Mayfield School	*CHLY/EC* PR7	311	G6
Chorley North Business Park	*CHLYE* PR6	287	H8
Chorley North Industrial Park	*CHLYE* PR6	311	H1
Chorley Retail Park	*CHLY/EC* PR7	311	G4
Chorley & South Ribble District General Hospital	*CHLY/EC* PR7	287	G8
Chorley West Business Park	*CHLY/EC* PR7	310	D3
Christ Church CE School	*COL* BB8	172	B6
Christ Church CE School	*HGHB* LA2	65	J7
Christ Church CE School	*LANC* LA1	3	F3
Christina Hartley Maternity Hospital	*STHP* PR8	301	K6
Christ the King High School	*PRES* PR1	7	F4
Christ the King Primary School	*BPOOLE* FY3	177	G4
Christ the King RC Primary School	*BLY* BB11	10	B6
Christ the King School	*STHP* PR8	326	D1
Chromolite Industrial Estate	*STHP* PR8	301	H6
Church Bridge Works	*ACC* BB5	247	J4
Churchtown County Junior & Infant School	*CHTN/BK* PR9	302	D1
Churchtown Medical Centre	*CHTN/BK* PR9	302	C1
Claremont Junior & Infant School	*BPOOL* FY1	176	C3
Clarence House School	*FMBY* L37	343	J5
Claughton Industrial Estate	*GAR/LONG* PR3	156	A2
Claughton Manor Brick Works	*HGHB* LA2	46	C1
Claylands Caravan Park	*GAR/LONG* PR3	103	K5
Clayton Brook County School	*LEY/BBR* PR5	264	A6
Clayton Business Park	*ACC* BB5	247	K1
Clayton Green Business Park	*LEY/BBR* PR5	264	A7
Clayton Green Sports Centre	*LEY/BBR* PR5	264	A7
Clayton-le-Moors Industrial Park	*ACC* BB5	247	J2
Clayton-le-Woods CE Primary School	*CHLYE* PR6	286	E1
Clayton Street Industrial Estate	*NLSN* BB9	198	B2
Cleveleys Health Centre	*CLV/TH* FY5	148	D1
Clifton CP School	*LSTA* FY8	231	J5
Clifton Retail Park	*BPOOLS* FY4	205	K3
Clitheroe Brookside County School	*CLI* BB7	165	K3
Clitheroe Castle	*CLI* BB7	165	J4
Clitheroe Cricket Club	*CLI* BB7	165	K1
Clitheroe Golf Club	*CLI* BB7	165	H8
Clitheroe Health Centre	*CLI* BB7	165	J2
Clitheroe Hospital	*CLI* BB7	166	A1
Clitheroe Royal Grammar School	*CLI* BB7	165	K2
Cliviger Holme CE Primary School	*BRFD/BLYE* BB10	253	F5
Clock Tower	*MCMB* LA4	41	G5

Cloughfold CP School
RAW/HAS BB4 .... 296 E1
Clough Fold Primary School
SKEL WN8 .... 363 J1
Coal Clough CP School
BLY BB11 .... 10 A4
Coates Lane Infant School
BWCK/EAR BB18 .... 119 H8
Cobbs Brow CP School
SKEL WN8 .... 351 G8
Cob Wall Works
BBN BB1 .... 9 E2
Cockerham Parochial School
HGHB LA2 .... 79 J7
Cocker Trading Estate
BPOOL FY1 .... 176 C4
College of Further Education
COL BB8 .... 171 G6
Collegiate High School
BPOOLE FY3 .... 177 G2
Colne Cricket Club
COL BB8 .... 172 A6
Colne Gibfield School
COL BB8 .... 199 F1
Colne Golf Club
COL BB8 .... 172 B4
Colne Health Centre
COL BB8 .... 171 H6
Colne Primet High School
COL BB8 .... 171 F8
Common Bank
Employment Area
CHLY/EC PR7 .... 310 D4
Common Bank Industrial Estate
CHLY/EC PR7 .... 310 D4
Concourse Shopping Centre
SKEL WN8 .... 363 H2
Constable Lee CE School
RAW/HAS BB4 .... 273 H7
Cop Lane CE Primary School
PRES PR1 .... 238 E8
Copper Works Wood
CHLY/EC PR7 .... 310 D4
Coppice School
LEY/BBR PR5 .... 263 J2
Coppull Community
Leisure Centre
CHLY/EC PR7 .... 335 J3
Coppull CP School
CHLY/EC PR7 .... 335 J2
Coppull Parish Church School
CHLY/EC PR7 .... 335 K2
Copse View Business Park
FTWD FY7 .... 123 F1
Corn Exchange
PRES PR1 .... 7 D2
Cornholme Junior &
Infant School
TOD OL14 .... 277 F2
Corpus Christi RC High School
FUL/RIB PR2 .... 213 G6
Corpus Christi RC Primary School
RNFD/HAY WA11 .... 369 F4
Cottage Museum
LANC LA1 .... 2 C3
Cottam CP School
KIRK/FR/WA PR4 .... 211 K6
Cottam Hall Brick Works
FUL/RIB PR2 .... 212 B8
Coupe Green CP School
LEY/BBR PR5 .... 241 J7
Courtyard Works
NWD/KWIPK L33 .... 367 G8
Cowling Brow Industrial Estate
CHLYE PR6 .... 311 J5
Crawford County School
SKEL WN8 .... 364 A8
Crawshawbooth CP School
RAW/HAS BB4 .... 273 H3
Creamery Industrial Estate
GAR/LONG PR3 .... 130 B6
The Crematorium
ACC BB5 .... 248 D3
Cribden House Special School
RAW/HAS BB4 .... 296 A2
Croasdale School of Dance
BLY BB11 .... 10 C4
Crookhey Hall Special School
HGHB LA2 .... 79 K8
Crossens CE Primary School
CHTN/BK PR9 .... 278 E6
Crossens Cricket Club
CHTN/BK PR9 .... 279 F7

Cross Hall High School
BRSC L40 .... 349 F6
Crosshill Special School
BBN BB1 .... 269 F1
Crossley House Industrial Estate
PRES PR1 .... 7 D6
Croston Medical Centre
LEY/BBR PR5 .... 283 J8
Croston Sports Club
LEY/BBR PR5 .... 307 H1
Crowland Street
Industrial Estate
CHTN/BK PR9 .... 302 B5
Crown Prosecution Service
BLY BB11 .... 10 C4
Crown Stage & Theatre
LEY/BBR PR5 .... 261 K8
Cuba Industrial Estate
RAMS BL0 .... 319 J3
Daisyfield Business Centre
BBN BB1 .... 9 E3
Daisyfield Primary School
BBN BB1 .... 9 E3
Daisyhill Industrial Estate
BBN BB1 .... 247 F2
Dallas Road CP School
LANC LA1 .... 2 C4
Dalweb Industrial Park
CHTN/BK PR9 .... 280 A8
Dance School
CLI BB7 .... 165 J3
Daneshouse Community
Health Centre
PDHM/BLYW BB12 .... 10 C1
Darwen Cricket Club
DWN BB3 .... 268 B7
Darwen Football & Social Club
DWN BB3 .... 268 C6
Darwen Golf Club
DWN BB3 .... 268 A8
Darwen Leisure Centre and Pool
DWN BB3 .... 291 H2
Darwen Market
DWN BB3 .... 291 J2
Darwen Moorland High School
DWN BB3 .... 268 E8
Darwen Tennis Club
DWN BB3 .... 291 G1
Darwen Vale High School
DWN BB3 .... 268 B6
Deakins Business Park
EDGW/EG BL7 .... 341 H1
Dean Wood Golf Club
SKEL WN8 .... 364 E3
Deepdale County Junior &
Infant School
PRES PR1 .... 239 K1
Deepdale Shopping Park
PRES PR1 .... 214 A8
Delphside Primary School
SKEL WN8 .... 363 H3
Dental Health Centre
PRES PR1 .... 213 K8
De Vere Blackpool
(Herons Reach Golf Course)
BPOOLE FY3 .... 177 H7
Devereux Preparatory School
NLSN BB9 .... 198 A3
Devonshire Junior School
BPOOLE FY3 .... 5 D1
Dewan Industrial Estate
RAW/HAS BB4 .... 295 H3
Dewhurst Industrial Estate
PRES PR1 .... 6 B1
Diamond Business Park
RNFD/HAY WA11 .... 369 H7
Docklands Medical Centre
FUL/RIB PR2 .... 6 A1
Dolphinholme CE School
HGHB LA2 .... 81 J3
Douglas Farm Riding School
SKEL WN8 .... 351 J2
Dover Lodge School of Equitation
LEY/BBR PR5 .... 265 H4
Downham School
CLI BB7 .... 141 H6
Dukes Playhouse
LANC LA1 .... 3 D3
Duke Street County
Infant School
CHLY/EC PR7 .... 311 G5
Dunkirk Hall Industrial Estate
LEY/BBR PR5 .... 284 E3

Dunscar Golf Club
EDGW/EG BL7 341
Dunscar Industrial Estate
EDGW/EG BL7 341
Duxbury Jubilee Park Golf Club
CHLY/EC PR7 311
Duxbury Park Golf Club
CHLY/EC PR7 311
Earby County Primary School
BWCK/EAR BB18 146
Earby Cricket Club
BWCK/EAR BB18 146
Earnshaw Bridge County
Infant School
LEY/BBR PR5 285
East Chorley Business Centre
CHLYE PR6 311
Eastcroft Park Primary School
NWD/KWIPK L33 366
Eastgate Retail Park
ACC BB5 248
East Gilbrands Industrial Estate
SKEL WN8 363
Eastham Hall Caravan Site
LSTA FY8 233
East Lancashire Cricket Club
BBNW BB2 8
Eccleston CP School
CHLY/EC PR7 308
Edenfield CE School
RAMS BL0 295
Edenfield Cricket Club
RAMS BL0 296
Edge End High School
NLSN BB9 198
Edge Hill University College
ORM L39 348
Edgeside School
RAW/HAS BB4 274
Edgworth Cricket Club
EDGW/EG BL7 317
Edisford CP School
CLI BB7 165
Egerton CP School
EDGW/EG BL7 316
Egerton Cricket Club
EDGW/EG BL7 316
Egerton & Dunscar
Health Centre
EDGW/EG BL7 341
Eldon Street CP School
PRES PR1 239
Ellel St Johns CE Primary School
HGHB LA2 67
Elmers Green CP School
SKEL WN8 363
Elmslie Girls School
BPOOLE FY3 5
Elswick Trading Park
KIRK/FR/WA PR4 180
Empire Theatre
BCUP OL13 298
Endowed Primary School
BRSC L40 333
English Martyrs Junior School
PRES PR1 6
Enterprise Works
CLI BB7 165
Eric Morecambe Statue
MCMB LA4 41
Ernest Street School
ACC BB5 247
Euro Trading Estate
BBN BB1 9
Euxton CE Primary School
CHLY/EC PR7 286
Euxton CP School
CHLY/EC PR7 285
Euxton Hall Hospital
CHLY/EC PR7 310
Fairhaven Golf Club
LSTA FY8 232
Farington Business Park
LEY/BBR PR5 285
Farington CP School
LEY/BBR PR5 262
Farington St Pauls CE School
LEY/BBR PR5 262
Farnborough Road
Junior School
STHP PR8 326
Fearns High School
RAW/HAS BB4 297

niscowles County
Infant School
BBNW BB2 .... 266 D3

niscowles Primary School
BBNW BB2 .... 266 E3

rnlea Hotel &
Leisure Complex
LSTA FY8 .... 230 D5

stival Market
MCMB LA4 .... 41 F6

hergate Shopping Centre
PRES PR1 .... 7 D3

hwick Hall Golf Club
PRES PR1 .... 240 D3

kefleet County Junior &
Infant School
FTWD FY7 .... 122 E1

etwood Cricket Club
FTWD FY7 .... 122 E3

etwood FC
FTWD FY7 .... 97 F8

etwood Golf Club
FTWD FY7 .... 96 D8

etwood Health Centre
FTWD FY7 .... 97 H7

etwood Hesketh High School
FTWD FY7 .... 96 E8

etwood Hosp
FTWD FY7 .... 97 H6

etwood Leisure Centre &
Swimming Pool
FTWD FY7 .... 97 G6

etwood Museum
FTWD FY7 .... 97 J6

rmby AFC
FMBY L37 .... 343 K8

rmby Business Park
FMBY L37 .... 344 B8

rmby Business Park
HTWN L38 .... 356 B5

rmby Cricket Club
FMBY L37 .... 343 K6

rmby Golf Club
FMBY L37 .... 343 H6

rmby Hall Golf Club
FMBY L37 .... 344 C3

rmby High Lower School
FMBY L37 .... 343 K7

rmby High School
FMBY L37 .... 343 J7

rmby Junior Sports Club
FMBY L37 .... 344 A6

rmby Ladies Golf Club
FMBY L37 .... 343 H6

rmby Lawn Tennis Club
FMBY L37 .... 343 K6

rte Posthouse Hotel
PRES PR1 .... 7 E2

rton CP School
GAR/LONG PR3 .... 80 C8

e Forward Industrial Estate
LEY/BBR PR5 .... 285 G1

eckleton CE School
KIRK/FR/WA PR4 .... 235 G4

eckleton Cricket Club
KIRK/FR/WA PR4 .... 235 F5

eeport Fleetwood
Outlet Village
FTWD FY7 .... 97 G8

enchwood CP School
PRES PR1 .... 7 F4

eshfield Primary School
FMBY L37 .... 344 A7

eshlea Private Clinic
FMBY L37 .... 355 H2

ends Meeting House
LANC LA1 .... 2 C3

ontierland
MCMB LA4 .... 41 F7

lwood & Cadley CP School
FUL/RIB PR2 .... 213 F7

lwood Hall Hospital
FUL/RIB PR2 .... 213 K5

lwood High School
FUL/RIB PR2 .... 213 F5

lwood Leisure Centre
FUL/RIB PR2 .... 213 F6

nland
STHP PR8 .... 301 G3

rthergate Industrial Park
BBN BB1 .... 9 E4

de Cricket Club
PLF/KEOS FY6 .... 150 A7

Fylde Road Industrial Estate
CHTN/BK PR9 .... 278 D7

Fylde Road Industrial Estate
PRES PR1 .... 6 B1

Fylde Rugby Club
LSTA FY8 .... 231 K6

Galgate Health Centre
HGHB LA2 .... 67 G7

Gannow Business Park
PDHM/BLYW BB12 .... 224 D5

Gannow Pool & Fitness Centre
PDHM/BLYW BB12 .... 224 D5

Garden Vale Business Centre
COL BB8 .... 171 F7

Garstang Country Hotel &
Golf Club
GAR/LONG PR3 .... 129 J7

Garstang CP School
GAR/LONG PR3 .... 129 J3

Garstang High School
GAR/LONG PR3 .... 129 K7

Garstang Leisure Centre
GAR/LONG PR3 .... 129 H3

Garswood United FC
AIMK WN4 .... 371 K6

Gathurst Golf Club
WGNNW/ST WN6 .... 353 H6

Gawthorpe County High School
PDHM/BLYW BB12 .... 224 A3

Gec Business Park
ACC BB5 .... 247 J2

General Hospital
RAW/HAS BB4 .... 295 J2

Ghousia Mosque
BBN BB1 .... 9 D5

Ghyll Golf Club
BWCK/EAR BB18 .... 119 J6

Gillibrand Primary School
CHLY/EC PR7 .... 311 F5

Gisburn Primary School
CLI BB7 .... 117 F5

Gisburn Road CP School
BWCK/EAR BB18 .... 145 F1

Glades Clinic
FUL/RIB PR2 .... 240 D1

Glasson Sailing Club
HGHB LA2 .... 65 J6

Glenburn High School
SKEL WN8 .... 363 G2

Glenfield Business Park
BBN BB1 .... 9 F2

Glenfield Park Industrial Estate
BBN BB1 .... 9 F1

Glenfield Park Industrial Estate
NLSN BB9 .... 198 E2

The Globe Centre
ACC BB5 .... 248 B6

Goosnargh Oliversons CE School
GAR/LONG PR3 .... 186 B5

Gothic Works
PDHM/BLYW BB12 .... 223 K2

Grand Cinema
CLI BB7 .... 165 K2

Grand Theatre
BPOOL FY1 .... 4 B2

Grange CP School
FUL/RIB PR2 .... 214 D7

Grange Park County
Infant School
BPOOLE FY3 .... 177 F4

Grange Park County
Junior School
BPOOLE FY3 .... 177 G4

Grange Park Health Centre
BPOOLE FY3 .... 177 G3

Grapevine Fitness &
Leisure Centre
BLY BB11 .... 10 C3

Great Arley Special School
CLV/TH FY5 .... 123 H8

Great Arley Swimming Pool
CLV/TH FY5 .... 123 H8

Great Eccleston Copp CE School
GAR/LONG PR3 .... 152 E8

Great Eccleston Health Centre
GAR/LONG PR3 .... 153 F6

Great Harwood Cricket Club
GTH/LHO BB6 .... 221 F4

Great Harwood Golf Club
GTH/LHO BB6 .... 221 K4

Great Harwood Primary School
GTH/LHO BB6 .... 221 F6

Great Wood CP School
MCMB LA4 .... 42 A6

Greenbank Business Park
BBN BB1 .... 246 A4

Greenbank High School
STHP PR8 .... 326 A2

Green Bank Industrial Estate
BBN BB1 .... 9 F3

Greenbank Industrial Estate
BBN BB1 .... 9 F3

Green Haworth Golf Club
ACC BB5 .... 271 G2

Greenlands CP School
FUL/RIB PR2 .... 214 C8

Greetby Hill CE Junior School
ORM L39 .... 348 D5

Gregson Lane Primary School
LEY/BBR PR5 .... 264 D2

Griffin Park CP School
BBNW BB2 .... 244 D8

Grimeford Industrial Estate
CHLYE PR6 .... 337 K5

Grimsargh St Michaels CE
Primary School
FUL/RIB PR2 .... 215 G2

Grimshaw Retail Park
BBN BB1 .... 8 C6

Grindleton CE School
CLI BB7 .... 140 C3

Grosvenor Park CP School
LANC LA1 .... 54 B1

Grove Park Industrial Estate
CHLY/EC PR7 .... 308 E6

Guild Community Healthcare
FUL/RIB PR2 .... 212 C5

Guild Community Healthcare
FUL/RIB PR2 .... 213 G8

Guild Community Healthcare
NHS Trust
PRES PR1 .... 240 A3

Guild Trading Estate
PRES PR1 .... 7 F1

Guys Industrial Estate
BRSC L40 .... 349 F1

Habergham High School
PDHM/BLYW BB12 .... 224 B4

Hall Green Clinic
SKEL WN8 .... 364 D4

Halliwell Industrial Estate
BOL BL1 .... 341 H8

Hall More Caravan Park
CARN LA5 .... 17 F4

Hall Park CP School
LSTA FY8 .... 232 B8

Hambleton County School
PLF/KEOS FY6 .... 151 F1

Hambleton Health Centre
PLF/KEOS FY6 .... 150 D1

Hannah Street School
ACC BB5 .... 248 B6

Hapton CE Methodist
Primary School
BLY BB11 .... 223 J7

Harbour Trading Estate
FTWD FY7 .... 123 F1

Hardmans Business Centre
RAW/HAS BB4 .... 296 A2

Hargher Clough Junior School
BLY BB11 .... 10 A4

Harris CP School
FUL/RIB PR2 .... 212 D4

Harris Museum & Art Gallery
PRES PR1 .... 7 E3

Harrison Trading Estate
PRES PR1 .... 240 A2

Haskayne CE School
ORM L39 .... 346 A8

Haslemere Industrial Estate
LEY/BBR PR5 .... 285 H1

Haslingden Baths
RAW/HAS BB4 .... 295 H1

Haslingden County
Primary School
RAW/HAS BB4 .... 295 H1

Haslingden Cricket Club
RAW/HAS BB4 .... 295 J3

Haslingden High School
RAW/HAS BB4 .... 295 H3

Haslingden Sports Centre
RAW/HAS BB4 .... 295 G2

Hawes Side Clinic
BPOOLS FY4 .... 204 E4

Hawes Side Primary School
BPOOLS FY4 .... 204 E4

Haworth Art Gallery
ACC BB5 .... 248 D8

Hawthorne Industrial Park
CLI BB7................................. **166** A2

Hazel Business Park
RNFD/HAY BB4.......................... **369** J7

Hazelhurst CP School
RAMS BL0.............................. **319** G7

Healey Primary School
WHIT OL12............................. **323** J8

Healey Wood Infant School
BLY BB11............................... **10** C5

Healey Wood Road
Industrial Estate
BLY BB11............................... **10** C4

Heasandford CP School
BRFD/BLYE BB10....................... **11** E1

Heasandford Industrial Estate
BRFD/BLYE BB10...................... **226** B3

Helmshore CP School
RAW/HAS BB4.......................... **295** G4

Helmshore Textile Museums
RAW/HAS BB4.......................... **295** F3

Henrietta Street Industrial Estate
BCUP OL13............................ **298** D1

Hesketh Centre (Hospital)
CHTN/BK PR9.......................... **301** J2

Hesketh Golf Club
CHTN/BK PR9.......................... **302** A1

Hesketh with Becconsall
All Saints CE School
KIRK/FR/WA PR4....................... **258** C7

Heskin FC
CHLY/EC PR7.......................... **309** F8

Heskin Pembertons
Primary School
CHLY/EC PR7.......................... **334** D1

Hewitt Business Park
WGNW/BIL/O WN5...................... **365** G7

Heyhouses Endowed CE
Infant School
LSTA FY8............................. **231** F4

Heyhouses Endowed CE
Junior School
LSTA FY8............................. **231** F3

Heysham Business Park
HEY LA3................................ **64** D1

Heysham County High School
HEY LA3................................ **53** F1

Heysham Cricket Club
HEY LA3................................ **52** C4

Heysham Golf Club
HEY LA3................................ **52** C7

Heysham Mossgate
County Primary School
HEY LA3................................ **52** D3

Heysham Nuclear Power Station
HEY LA3................................ **52** A7

Higher Walton CE Primary School
LEY/BBR PR5.......................... **241** F8

Higher Walton CE School
LEY/BBR PR5.......................... **241** F8

Highfield CP School
CHLYE PR6............................ **311** H3

Highfield Industrial Estate
CHLYE PR6............................ **311** G1

Highfield Industrial Estate
CLI BB7............................... **165** J3

Highfield Priory School
FUL/RIB PR2.......................... **214** D6

Highfield Works
BBNW BB2................................ **8** C6

Highfurlong Special School
BPOOLE FY3........................... **177** G1

High Lawn CP School
BOL BL1.............................. **341** J5

Hillside CP School
SKEL WN8............................. **363** K3

Hillside Golf Club
STHP PR8............................. **326** A2

Hillside Health Centre
SKEL WN8............................. **363** J2

Hippings Methodist School
ACC BB5.............................. **247** J8

HM Prison
KIRK/FR/WA PR4....................... **208** E8

Hodge Bank Business Park
NLSN BB9............................. **198** B1

Hodgson High School
PLF/KEOS FY6......................... **150** B8

Holcombe Brook Sports Club
TOT/BURYW BL8........................ **319** G8

Holcombe CE Primary School
TOT/BURYW BL8........................ **319** G5

Holder Station and Workshops
HEY LA3................................ **41** K8

Holgate CP School
WGNW/BIL/O WN5...................... **365** G6

Holgate's Caravan Park
CARN LA5................................ **15** G7

Holker Business Centre
COL BB8.............................. **171** F7

Holland Business Park
BRSC L40............................. **350** C7

Holland Moor CP School
SKEL WN8............................. **364** A4

Hollies Surgery
FMBY L37............................. **343** K8

The Hollins County High School
ACC BB5.............................. **271** J1

Hollywood Park Cinema
BLY BB11............................... **10** C5

Holme Mills Industrial Estate
KKBYL LA6............................. **17** K2

Holme Slack CP School
PRES PR1............................. **214** A8

Holmeswood Methodist School
KIRK/FR/WA PR4....................... **305** F5

Holy Angels Primary School
KKBY LA6............................. **366** B8

Holy Cross RC High School
CHLY/EC PR7.......................... **311** G7

Holy Family Primary School
KIRK/FR/WA PR4....................... **234** C5

Holy Family RC Primary School
BPOOL FY1............................ **176** C3

Holy Family RC Primary School
CHTN/BK PR9.......................... **302** A4

Holy Family RC Primary School
FUL/RIB PR2.......................... **212** B7

Holy Infant RC Primary School
BOL BL1.............................. **341** J7

Holy Souls RC School
BBN BB1............................... **245** G2

Holy Trinity CE Primary School
CHTN/BK PR9.......................... **301** J4

Holy Trinity CE Primary School
FMBY L37............................. **343** K8

Holy Trinity CE School
DWN BB3.............................. **291** J2

Holy Trinity RC Primary School
NLSN BB9............................. **198** A6

Holy Trinity Stacksteads CE
Primary School
BCUP OL13............................ **298** A3

Hoohill Industrial Estate
BPOOLE FY3........................... **176** E3

Hornby High School
HGHB LA2............................... **37** G5

Hornby Primary School
HGHB LA2............................... **37** G5

Horse & Bamboo Theatre
RAW/HAS BB4.......................... **297** F3

Horwich Leisure Centre
HOR/BR BL6........................... **338** E8

Horwich Parish CE School
HOR/BR BL6........................... **338** E7

Houghwood Golf Club
WGNW/BIL/O WN5...................... **370** D4

Howick Primary School
KIRK/FR/WA PR4....................... **238** B8

Hud Hey Industrial Estate
RAW/HAS BB4.......................... **272** C5

Hugh Business Park
BCUP OL13............................ **298** A3

Hulmes Bridge Business Centre
ORM L39.............................. **346** E1

Huncoat Business Park
ACC BB5.............................. **248** D2

Huncoat County School
ACC BB5.............................. **249** F1

Huncoat Industrial Estate
ACC BB5.............................. **248** C3

Hurlston Hall Country
Caravan Park
BRSC L40............................. **348** A1

Hurlston Hall Golf Club
BRSC L40............................. **348** A1

Hutton Grammar School
KIRK/FR/WA PR4....................... **260** E1

Hyndburn Park County School
ACC BB5.............................. **248** A5

Hyndburn Sports Centre
ACC BB5.............................. **247** K5

Ightenhill County School
PDHM/BLYW BB12...................... **224** E4

India Mill Business Centre
DWN BB3.............................. **291** J3

Indoor Bowls
BPOOL FY1.............................. **4** C1

Industrial Centre for the
Blind & Disabled
BPOOLS FY4........................... **205**

Ingol CP School
FUL/RIB PR2.......................... **212**

Ingol Golf Club
FUL/RIB PR2.......................... **212**

Ingol Pool House School
FUL/RIB PR2.......................... **212**

Inland Revenue Office
ACC BB5.............................. **248**

Intack County School
BBN BB1.............................. **246**

Islamic Community
Centre & Mosque
BPOOL FY1.............................. **4**

Island Business Centre
GAR/LONG PR3......................... **128**

Ivy Bank High School
PDHM/BLYW BB12...................... **224**

Jamea Al Kauthar
LANC LA1................................ **3**

J Nelson War Memorial
Sports Club
NLSN BB9............................. **198**

John Cross CE School
GAR/LONG PR3......................... **156**

Johnson Fold CP School
BOL BL1.............................. **340**

Jubilee Industrial Estate
PRES PR1.............................. **6**

Judge's Lodgings Town
House & Gillow Museum
LANC LA1................................ **2**

Junction 7 Business Park
ACC BB5.............................. **247**

Kaymar Industrial Estate
PRES PR1............................. **240**

Kelbrook Primary School
BWCK/EAR BB18........................ **146**

Kellet Road Industrial Estate
CARN LA5.............................. **34**

Kellets Trading Estate
PRES PR1.............................. **6**

The Kenneth Macrae
Medical Centre
RNFD/HAY WA11........................ **369**

Kensington Industrial Estate
CHTN/BK PR9.......................... **301**

Kenyon Business Centre
NLSN BB9............................. **197**

Kestrels Leisure Centre
BLY BB11............................. **251**

Kew Medical Centre
STHP PR8............................. **302**

Kew Retail Park
STHP PR8............................. **302**

Kew Woods CP School
STHP PR8............................. **302**

Kiddrow Health Centre
PDHM/BLYW BB12...................... **224**

Kincraig Primary &
Junior School
BISP FY2............................. **149**

King Edward School
LSTA FY8............................. **231**

Kingfold Medical Centre
PRES PR1............................. **238**

King Georges Hall
BBNW BB2................................ **8**

King George VI Sixth
Form College
STHP PR8............................. **302**

Kingsbury School
ORM L39.............................. **348**

Kingsfold Christian School
KIRK/FR/WA PR4....................... **281**

Kingsfold Primary School
PRES PR1............................. **262**

Kinsbury School
SKEL WN8............................. **362**

Kirkham Baths
KIRK/FR/WA PR4....................... **208**

Kirkham Grammar
Junior School
KIRK/FR/WA PR4....................... **208**

Kirkham Grammar School
KIRK/FR/WA PR4....................... **208**

Kirkham Health Centre
KIRK/FR/WA PR4....................... **208**

Kirkham Museum
KIRK/FR/WA PR4....................... **208**

Kirkham Trading Park
KIRK/FR/WA PR4....................... **209**

kham & Wesham CP School
KIRK/FR/WA PR4 .... **208** D6
eps Farm Holiday Park
CLV/TH FY5 .... **150** A1
ott End Golf Club
PLF/KEOS FY6 .... **97** J6
owsley Industrial Park
WWD/KWIPK L33 .... **367** H8
owsley Road
Industrial Estate
RAW/HAS BB4 .... **295** H2
lies Walk Industrial Estate
LANC LA1 .... **3** E1
nberhead Green
County Infants School
WGNW/BIL/O WN5 .... **365** J4
nberhead Green CP School
WGNW/BIL/O WN5 .... **365** K4
nberhead Industrial Estate
WGNW/BIL/O WN5 .... **365** K6
nmack County School
BBNW BB2 .... **244** E2
ncashire Area
Health Authority
BPOOL FY1 .... **5** D1
ncashire Area
Health Authority
BPOOLS FY4 .... **204** C6
ncashire College for
Adult Education
CHLY/EC PR7 .... **310** D3
ncashire College of
Agriculture
GAR/LONG PR3 .... **155** K6
ncashire County Council
LSTA FY8 .... **231** F3
ncashire County
Museum Service
PRES PR1 .... **7** F2
ncashire Enterprise
Business Park
LEY/BBR PR5 .... **262** C6
e Lancashire Priory Hospital
KIRK/FR/WA PR4 .... **211** H2
ncashire Schools ICT Centre
CHLY/EC PR7 .... **310** E3
ncaster Castle (HM Prison)
LANC LA1 .... **2** C3
ncaster City FC (Giant Axe)
LANC LA1 .... **2** B3
ncaster City Museum
LANC LA1 .... **3** D3
ncaster Cricket Club
LANC LA1 .... **2** B2
ncaster Girls Grammar School
LANC LA1 .... **2** C4
ncaster Golf Club (Ashton Hall)
HGHB LA2 .... **66** C4
e Lancaster & Lakeland
Nuffield Hospital
LANC LA1 .... **3** E5
ncaster Lane CP School
LEY/BBR PR5 .... **286** B2
ncaster Leisure Park
LANC LA1 .... **55** J5
ncaster Magistrates Court
LANC LA1 .... **3** D4
ncaster Maritime Museum
LANC LA1 .... **2** C2
ncaster Moor Hospital
LANC LA1 .... **55** K3
ncaster & Morecambe College
LANC LA1 .... **3** D4
ncaster & Morecambe College
MCMB LA4 .... **41** H6
ncaster Road CP School
MCMB LA4 .... **41** J7
ncaster Royal Grammar School
LANC LA1 .... **3** E3
ncaster University
LANC LA1 .... **2** C3
ncaster University Sports
Centre & Swimming Pool
LANC LA1 .... **67** G4
e Ends Trading Estate
FUL/RIB PR2 .... **238** E1
neshawbridge CP School
COL BB8 .... **172** D5
gdale Preparatory School
BISP FY2 .... **176** C2
nsil Golf Club
LANC LA1 .... **43** H7
nsil Industrial Estate
LANC LA1 .... **43** G8

Larkfield CP School
CHTN/BK PR9 .... **278** C8
Larkholme County
Secondary School
FTWD FY7 .... **122** D2
Larkholme CP School
FTWD FY7 .... **122** D3
Lathom High School
SKEL WN8 .... **351** F7
Lathom Park CE Primary School
BRSC L40 .... **350** A3
Layton Medical Centre
BPOOLE FY3 .... **177** F4
Layton Primary School
BPOOLE FY3 .... **177** F3
Leachfield Industrial Estate
GAR/LONG PR3 .... **129** J2
Lea CP School
FUL/RIB PR2 .... **237** K2
Lea Endowed School
KIRK/FR/WA PR4 .... **211** J7
Lea Town School
KIRK/FR/WA PR4 .... **211** F8
Leck CE School
KKBYL LA6 .... **22** D5
Leighton Hall
CARN LA5 .... **25** J2
Leisure Centre
BLY BB11 .... **11** D4
Leisure Lakes
CHTN/BK PR9 .... **304** B3
Leyland Golf Club
LEY/BBR PR5 .... **286** B3
Leyland Leisure Centre
LEY/BBR PR5 .... **285** H3
Leyland Methodist Junior &
Infant School
LEY/BBR PR5 .... **285** K2
Library
BPOOL FY1 .... **4** B6
Library & Arts Cen
SKEL WN8 .... **363** H2
Library & Grundy Art Gallery
BPOOL FY1 .... **4** A1
The Lido Pool
BPOOLS FY4 .... **4** B6
Lidun Park Industrial Estate
LSTA FY8 .... **233** G6
Lifeboat Station
MCMB LA4 .... **41** G5
Light Industrial Estate
KIRK/FR/WA PR4 .... **260** A6
Linaker County Primary School
STHP PR8 .... **301** H6
Lincoln Road Health Centre
STHP PR8 .... **326** C2
Lisieux Hall Hospital
CHLYE PR6 .... **286** E3
Little Digmoor CP School
SKEL WN8 .... **363** H5
Little Hoole CP School
KIRK/FR/WA PR4 .... **260** B6
Little Theatre
CHLY/EC PR7 .... **311** G3
Little Theatre
CHTN/BK PR9 .... **301** H4
Lobden Golf Club
WHIT OL12 .... **323** J4
Lomeshaye Business Village
NLSN BB9 .... **198** A3
Lomeshaye Industrial Estate
NLSN BB9 .... **197** K3
Long Ing Business Park
BWCK/EAR BB18 .... **145** G1
Longridge CE Primary School
GAR/LONG PR3 .... **188** A4
Longridge Gallery
GAR/LONG PR3 .... **188** A3
Longridge GM Primary School
GAR/LONG PR3 .... **187** K3
Longridge Golf Club
GAR/LONG PR3 .... **161** G7
Longridge Golf Club (Fell Barn)
GAR/LONG PR3 .... **189** F1
Longridge Health Centre
GAR/LONG PR3 .... **188** B4
Longridge High School &
Sports Centre
GAR/LONG PR3 .... **188** A5
Longsands CP School
FUL/RIB PR2 .... **214** B5
Longshaw County Junior School
BBNW BB2 .... **268** B2

Longshaw Junior & Infant School
BBNW BB2 .... **268** B3
Longton Business Park
KIRK/FR/WA PR4 .... **259** K7
Longton Health Centre
KIRK/FR/WA PR4 .... **260** B2
Longton School
KIRK/FR/WA PR4 .... **260** B3
Lordsgate Township CE
Primary School
BRSC L40 .... **330** E8
Lord Street CP School
HOR/BR BL6 .... **338** D7
Lostock Hall CP School
LEY/BBR PR5 .... **262** E2
Lostock Hall High School &
Sports Centre
LEY/BBR PR5 .... **263** F2
Lostock Hall Primary School
LEY/BBR PR5 .... **262** E3
Louis Tussauds Waxworks
BPOOL FY1 .... **4** A3
Low Bentham CP School
HGHB LA2 .... **39** K3
Lower Audley Industrial Estate
BBN BB1 .... **8** C5
Lowerhouse County
Junior School
PDHM/BLYW BB12 .... **224** C5
Lowerhouse Cricket Club
PDHM/BLYW BB12 .... **224** C5
Lune Industrial Estate
LANC LA1 .... **2** A3
Lydiate Primary School
MGHL L31 .... **358** E7
Lyne Riggs Estate
CARN LA5 .... **33** K2
Lytham CE Primary School
LSTA FY8 .... **232** D7
Lytham Community YMCA
Sports Centre
LSTA FY8 .... **232** E7
Lytham Cricket Club
LSTA FY8 .... **232** B8
Lytham Green Drive Golf Club
LSTA FY8 .... **232** D6
Lytham Hospital
LSTA FY8 .... **233** F8
Lytham Posey Bowl
LSTA FY8 .... **232** D8
Lytham St Anne's High School
LSTA FY8 .... **231** J6
Lytham St Anne's Sports &
Leisure Centre
LSTA FY8 .... **231** K6
Lytham Windmill
LSTA FY8 .... **232** E8
Madisons New Leisure Centre
KIRK/FR/WA PR4 .... **236** C2
Magneta Works
PDHM/BLYW BB12 .... **223** J6
Manchester Mill Industrial Estate
PRES PR1 .... **240** A3
Mandelay Health Centre
BOL BL1 .... **341** J5
Manor Beach CP School
CLV/TH FY5 .... **122** D8
Mansfield County
Secondary School
NLSN BB9 .... **197** K5
Marble Place Shopping Centre
STHP PR8 .... **301** H4
Mariclough Hampsfield
Camping Site
BPOOLS FY4 .... **206** B5
Marine Business Centre
LSTA FY8 .... **233** G7
Marine Gardens
FTWD FY7 .... **97** H6
Marine Hall
FTWD FY7 .... **97** G6
Marine Industrial Centre
LSTA FY8 .... **233** G7
Markazi Jamia Ghosia Mosque
NLSN BB9 .... **198** B2
Marketgate Shopping Centre
LANC LA1 .... **3** D3
Market Walk Shopping Centre
CHLY/EC PR7 .... **311** G3
Marl Pits Sports Centre
RAW/HAS BB4 .... **273** J8
Marsden County Infant School
NLSN BB9 .... **198** B4

Marsden County Junior School
NLSN BB9...................................... 198   B4

Marsden Hall
COL BB8... 199   G1

**Marsden Park Public
Golf Course**
NLSN BB9...................................... 199   F3

Marsh CP School
LANC LA1... 2   B3

Marsh House Industrial Estate
DWN BB3.. 292   A2

Marsh Mill Museum
CLV/TH FY5................................... 149   H1

Marton CP School
BPOOLS FY4.................................. 205   F4

Marton Medical Centre
BPOOLE FY3...................................... 5   E5

Marton Mere Holiday Village
BPOOLE FY3.................................. 177   J8

Masjid-Bilal Mosque
BBN BB1.. 9   D1

Masjid-e-Momineen Mosque
BBN BB1.. 9   E2

**Masjid-e-Raza
Randal Street Mosque**
BBN BB1.. 8   C3

**Masjid-e-Tauheedul
Islam Mosque**
BBN BB1.. 8   B3

Mawdesley CE School
BRSC L40...................................... 307   J8

Mayfield County School
LSTA FY8.. 230   E3

Mayflower Industrial Estate
FMBY L37...................................... 356   A2

**Meadowhead County
Infant School**
BBNW BB2..................................... 267   J2

**Meadowhead County
Junior School**
BBNW BB2..................................... 267   J3

Meadowville Works
CLI BB7... 193   F7

Melbreak Caravan Park
HEY LA3.. 64   D2

Melling with Wrayton CE School
KKBYL LA6...................................... 30   A8

Mellor St Mary CE Primary School
BBNW BB2..................................... 243   K1

Meols Cop High School
STHP PR8...................................... 302   B6

Meols Cop Retail Park
STHP PR8...................................... 302   B7

Mercer Hall Leisure Centre
GTH/LHO BB6................................. 221   G6

Mere Brow CE School
KIRK/FR/WA PR4............................ 304   D1

Merefield School
STHP PR8...................................... 325   H7

Mereside Junior & Infant School
BPOOLS FY4.................................. 205   H2

Methodist School
KIRK/FR/WA PR4............................ 260   A3

Metropolitan Business Park
BPOOLE FY3.................................. 205   H1

Middleforth CE School
PRES PR1...................................... 239   F8

Middleton Business Park
HEY LA3.. 52   E8

Millbrook Business Centre
RNFD/HAY WA11............................ 369   J8

Millbrook CP School
WGNNW/ST WN6............................ 353   K5

Millbrook Primary School
KKBY LA6....................................... 366   B8

Millfield High School
CLV/TH FY5.................................... 149   J4

Mill Lane Industrial Estate
CLI BB7... 117   F5

Mine Museum
BWCK/EAR BB18............................ 120   B8

Model Village
STHP PR8...................................... 301   G4

Mohamaddi Mosque
NLSN BB9...................................... 198   C3

Montgomery High School
BISP FY2.. 148   D6

Moorbrook School
FUL/RIB PR2.................................. 213   G8

Moor End CP School
ACC BB5.. 247   H8

Moorfield Industrial Estate
ACC BB5.. 222   B8

Moorhead County High School
ACC BB5.. 248   A3

Moorhey School
LEY/BBR PR5................................. 262   D2

Moorland School
CLI BB7... 165   J1

Moor Nook CP School
FUL/RIB PR2.................................. 214   E8

Moor Park High School
PRES PR1...................................... 239   J1

Moor Park Industrial Estate
BISP FY2.. 149   F7

Moor Park Junior & Infant School
BISP FY2.. 148   E8

Moor Park Swimming Pool
BISP FY2.. 148   D7

Moorside CP School
SKEL WN8...................................... 364   A4

Moorside School
LANC LA1... 55   H7

Morecambe Bay Primary School
MCMB LA4....................................... 41   H6

Morecambe Bay Yacht Club
MCMB LA4....................................... 41   H5

Morecambe County High School
MCMB LA4....................................... 41   J5

Morecambe Cricket Club
MCMB LA4....................................... 41   G7

Morecambe FC (Christie Park)
MCMB LA4....................................... 41   K7

Morecambe Golf Club
MCMB LA4....................................... 42   B4

Morecambe Road School
HEY LA3.. 42   A8

Morecambe Super Bowl
MCMB LA4....................................... 41   F6

Mossock Hall Golf Club
ORM L39.. 360   C7

Moss Side CP School
LEY/BBR PR5................................. 284   D2

Moss Side Industrial Estate
LEY/BBR PR5................................. 261   K8

Mosswood Caravan Park
HGHB LA2...................................... 102   C3

Mossy Lea CP School
WGNNW/ST WN6............................ 334   D5

Mount Carmel RC High School
ACC BB5.. 248   A7

Mount Carmel School
ORM L39.. 360   B1

Mount Pleasant County School
ACC BB5.. 248   A1

Much Hoole School
KIRK/FR/WA PR4............................ 282   C1

Myerscough College
GAR/LONG PR3.............................. 155   K7

Myrtle Bank Infant School
BLY BB11... 10   A5

**Mytton Fold Hotel &
Golf Complex**
GTH/LHO BB6................................. 220   C1

Nateby Primary School
GAR/LONG PR3.............................. 128   C5

National Football Museum
FUL/RIB PR2.................................. 239   K1

The Natural Health Centre
PRES PR1.. 7   E1

Natural Therapy Clinic
BPOOLE FY3.................................. 177   F4

Naze Lane Industrial Estate
KIRK/FR/WA PR4............................ 235   F6

Nelson Castercliff City School
NLSN BB9...................................... 198   E2

Nelson & Colne College
COL BB8.. 170   E6

Nelson & Colne College
NLSN BB9...................................... 198   A1

Nelson Cricket & Bowling Club
NLSN BB9...................................... 198   A2

Nelson FC
NLSN BB9...................................... 198   B2

Nelson Golf Club
NLSN BB9...................................... 198   D6

Nelson Health Centre
NLSN BB9...................................... 198   C2

Nether Kellet Primary School
KKBYL LA6....................................... 34   A7

Nether Kellet School
KKBYL LA6....................................... 34   A6

Network 65 Business Park
BLY BB11....................................... 224   A7

Newburgh CE School
SKEL WN8...................................... 351   G2

Newburgh Cricket Club
SKEL WN8...................................... 351

Newchurch CE School
RAW/HAS BB4................................ 297

**Newchurch in Pendle
St Mary CE School**
PDHM/BLYW BB12.......................... 168

New Hall Hey Business Park
RAW/HAS BB4................................ 296

New House Caravan Park
KKBYL LA6....................................... 22

New Line Industrial Estate
BCUP OL13.................................... 298

New Longton CE School
KIRK/FR/WA PR4............................ 261

New Mill Industrial Estate
LEY/BBR PR5................................. 263

New Parkside Farm Caravan Park
HGHB LA2.. 44

Newton Bluecoat School
KIRK/FR/WA PR4............................ 236

Nook Gallery
KKBYL LA6....................................... 21

Norbreck Primary School
CLV/TH FY5.................................... 148

Norden County High School
BBN BB1.. 246

Norley Hall Cricket Club
WGNW/BIL/O WN5.......................... 365

North Bolton Sixth Form College
BOL BL1... 341

Northcliffe School
GTH/LHO BB6................................. 221

Northern County School
BCUP OL13.................................... 275

Northfold CP School
CLV/TH FY5.................................... 122

**North Meols Community
Leisure Centre**
CHTN/BK PR9................................. 279

North Meols Lawn Tennis Club
CHTN/BK PR9................................. 302

North Mersey Business Centre
NWD/KWIPK L33............................ 367

North Quarry Business Park
WGNNW/ST WN6............................ 353

North Valley Retail Park
COL BB8... 171

Northway Primary School
MGHL L31....................................... 359

Norwood CP School
CHTN/BK PR9................................. 302

Nugent House School
WGNW/BIL/O WN5.......................... 371

Nye Bevan Swimming Pool
SKEL WN8...................................... 363

Oakfield House School
KIRK/FR/WA PR4............................ 210

Oakhill College
CLI BB7... 193

The Oaks CP School
BOL BL1... 341

Ocean Edge Caravan Park
HEY LA3.. 64

Old Barnabys School
DWN BB3....................................... 291

Old Brewery Trading Estate
PRES PR1.. 6

Old Hall Caravan Park
KKBYL LA6....................................... 27

Old Hall Farm Business Park
CHTN/BK PR9................................. 302

Old Hall Farm Business Park
CHTN/BK PR9................................. 302

Oldhams Lane CP School
BOL BL1... 341

Old Mill Hotel & Leisure Centre
RAMS BL0...................................... 319

Old Mill Industrial Estate
LEY/BBR PR5................................. 263

Old Mill Leisure Club
CHLYE PR6..................................... 311

Open Air Swimming Pool
MCMB LA4.. 41

Ormskirk Business Park
ORM L39.. 348

Ormskirk College
ORM L39.. 348

Ormskirk Cricket Club
ORM L39.. 348

**Ormskirk & District
General Hospital**
ORM L39.. 348

nskirk Golf Club
BRSC L40 .... 349 J4
nskirk Grammar School
ORM L39 .... 348 D7
nskirk Rugby Union FC
ORM L39 .... 348 C5
n Works
SKEL WN8 .... 362 C2
ell Clinic
WGNW/BIL/O WN5 .... 365 G4
ell Holgate Primary School
WGNW/BIL/O WN5 .... 365 C6
ell Newfold CP School
WGNW/BIL/O WN5 .... 365 F7
ell RUFC
WGNW/BIL/O WN5 .... 365 C6
ers Leisure Pool
GAR/LONG PR3 .... 213 G1
Lady & All Saints RC School
SKEL WN8 .... 351 J1
Lady of Assumption
RC School
BPOOLS FY4 .... 205 F6
Lady of Compassion RC Primary
School
FMBY L37 .... 344 A8
Lady of Lourdes RC School
CARN LA5 .... 34 A2
Lady of Perpetual Succour
RC School
BBNW BB2 .... 268 B3
Lady Queen of Peace RC
High School
SKEL WN8 .... 351 F7
Lady & St Edwards RC
Primary School
GAR/LONG PR3 .... 213 F3
Lady & St Huberts
RC School
GTH/LHO BB6 .... 221 H5
Lady & St John RC
High School
BBN BB1 .... 246 A8
Ladys High School
FUL/RIB PR2 .... 212 E6
Ladys High School
LANC LA1 .... 3 D2
Rawcliffe School
GAR/LONG PR3 .... 152 D1
erdale Primary School
NWD/KWIPK L33 .... 366 D7
r Wrye Sports Centre
PLF/KEOS FY6 .... 98 C6
r Wyre Medical Centre
PLF/KEOS FY6 .... 98 B6
ord Medical Centre
BPOOL FY1 .... 5 E5
ey Trading Estate
PRES PR1 .... 239 F1
iham County
Primary School
PDHM/BLYW BB12 .... 224 A3
iham Cricket Club
PDHM/BLYW BB12 .... 223 H2
iham FC
PDHM/BLYW BB12 .... 223 H3
iham Green CE
Primary School
PDHM/BLYW BB12 .... 223 J3
iham Town Hall
PDHM/BLYW BB12 .... 223 J3
ace Cinema
GAR/LONG PR3 .... 188 B4
agon Works
ACC BB5 .... 272 A3
bold Douglas CE
Primary School
SKEL WN8 .... 333 F8
Park CP School
COL BB8 .... 171 K6
k Crematorium
LSTA FY8 .... 232 B4
ker Street Industrial Estate
FUL/RIB PR2 .... 6 B1
k Hall Leisure Centre
CHLY/EC PR7 .... 309 J7
k High School
COL BB8 .... 171 K5
k Pool
ORM L39 .... 348 C6
k Road Industrial Estate
BCUP OL13 .... 298 D2
k School
BPOOLE FY3 .... 5 E3

Path Industrial Estate
DWN BB3 .... 268 E5
Pearlbrook Industrial Estate
HOR/BR BL6 .... 338 D8
Peel Bank Works
ACC BB5 .... 247 K4
Peel Brow County
Primary School
RAMS BL0 .... 319 K5
Peel Park CP School
ACC BB5 .... 248 D4
Pendle Business Centre
NLSN BB9 .... 198 C3
Pendle CP School
CLI BB7 .... 165 K2
Pendle Forest Sports Club
PDHM/BLYW BB12 .... 197 G3
Pendle Industrial Estate
NLSN BB9 .... 198 D4
Pendle Leisure Centre
COL BB8 .... 171 G7
Pendle Trading Estate
CLI BB7 .... 140 C8
Pendle View Medical Centre
NLSN BB9 .... 197 K5
Pendle Wavelengths
Swimming Pool
NLSN BB9 .... 198 C3
Penwortham Broad Oak
County School
PRES PR1 .... 261 K1
Penwortham County
Primary School
PRES PR1 .... 238 C6
Penwortham Cricket Club
PRES PR1 .... 6 C6
Penwortham Girls High School
PRES PR1 .... 6 A5
Penwortham Golf Club
PRES PR1 .... 238 D4
Penwortham Holme
Recreation Centre
PRES PR1 .... 6 B4
Penwortham Leisure Centre
PRES PR1 .... 238 C6
Penwortham Sports Club
PRES PR1 .... 6 C6
Peterhouse School
CHTN/BK PR9 .... 278 D8
Peterhouse School
STHP PR8 .... 301 K6
Phoenix Sporting &
Leisure Centre
CLV/TH FY5 .... 148 E4
Photogenic Gallery
CARN LA5 .... 15 F1
Pike View Medical Centre
HOR/BR BL6 .... 338 D7
Pilling St Johns CE School
GAR/LONG PR3 .... 100 A5
Pipers Height Caravan Park
BPOOLS FY4 .... 206 A5
Plantation Mill Industrial Estate
BCUP OL13 .... 298 D2
Platts Lane Industrial Estate
BRSC L40 .... 349 H1
Playhouse Theatre
PRES PR1 .... 7 D2
Plaza Shopping Arcade
MCMB LA4 .... 41 H6
Pleasington Crematorium
BBNW BB2 .... 243 K8
Pleasington Golf Club
BBNW BB2 .... 266 D2
Pleasure Island
LSTA FY8 .... 230 E6
Pleasureland
STHP PR8 .... 301 F4
Pleckgate High School
BBN BB1 .... 245 F2
Pontville School
ORM L39 .... 348 B8
Postal Delivery Office
SKEL WN8 .... 363 G3
Post Graduate Medical Centre
FUL/RIB PR2 .... 213 H7
Poulton CE School
PLF/KEOS FY6 .... 149 K8
Poulton Le Fylde Golf Club
PLF/KEOS FY6 .... 149 K6
Poulton le Sands CE
Primary School
MCMB LA4 .... 41 H5

Poulton Swimming &
Fitness Centre
PLF/KEOS FY6 .... 150 A6
Powderhouse Lane Crematorium
LANC LA1 .... 42 D7
Preesall Fleetwood Charity School
PLF/KEOS FY6 .... 98 D8
Preesall Mill Industrial Estate
PLF/KEOS FY6 .... 124 D1
Premier Business Park
BBN BB1 .... 9 F1
Premier Business Park
GTH/LHO BB6 .... 221 H5
Prestfield School
CHTN/BK PR9 .... 278 C8
Preston Bowl
PRES PR1 .... 239 F1
Preston College
FUL/RIB PR2 .... 213 H6
Preston College
PRES PR1 .... 7 D3
Preston College
PRES PR1 .... 239 H1
Preston College Park School
PRES PR1 .... 239 H1
Preston Crematorium
FUL/RIB PR2 .... 215 C6
Preston Cricket Club
PRES PR1 .... 6 C5
Preston Golf Club
FUL/RIB PR2 .... 213 K6
Preston Grasshoppers RFC
KIRK/FR/WA PR4 .... 212 D3
Preston Muslim Girls
Secondary School
PRES PR1 .... 7 F1
Preston North End FC (Deepdale)
PRES PR1 .... 239 K1
Preston Sports Arena
KIRK/FR/WA PR4 .... 212 A8
Preston Sports Club
PRES PR1 .... 6 C4
Primary School
LEY/BBR PR5 .... 262 D2
Primet Business Centre
COL BB8 .... 171 F7
Primetime Leisure Centre
BBN BB1 .... 246 E1
Primet Primary School
COL BB8 .... 171 F8
Primrose Bank Medical Centre
BBN BB1 .... 9 D3
Primrose Hill School
BRFD/BLYE BB10 .... 226 B1
Priory High School
PRES PR1 .... 238 C6
The Priory Pool
PRES PR1 .... 238 B6
Progress Business Park
KIRK/FR/WA PR4 .... 208 E7
Prospect House Medical Centre
WGNW/BIL/O WN5 .... 365 J5
Public Baths
BBN BB1 .... 9 D3
Queen Elizabeth School
KKBYL LA6 .... 21 G1
Queen Elizabeth's
Grammar School
BBNW BB2 .... 8 A3
Queen Mary School
LSTA FY8 .... 231 G7
Queens Drive Primary School
FUL/RIB PR2 .... 213 F6
Queens Park Hospital
BBNW BB2 .... 268 E1
Queens Retail Park
PRES PR1 .... 7 F2
Queen Street Mill
BRFD/BLYE BB10 .... 226 D1
Queensway Industrial Estate
LSTA FY8 .... 231 G1
Queen Victoria Hospital
MCMB LA4 .... 41 H6
Quernmore CE School
HGHB LA2 .... 56 D6
Railway Centre
STHP PR8 .... 301 J5
Railway Road Industrial Estate
DWN BB3 .... 291 J2
Rainford CE Primary School
RNFD/HAY WA11 .... 369 F5
Rainford Health Centre
RNFD/HAY WA11 .... 369 G5

Rainford High School
RNFD/HAY WA11.............. **369** G3
Rainford Industrial Estate
RNFD/HAY WA11.............. **369** J7
Ramsbottom Cottage Hospital
RAMS BL0 .... **319** J6
Ramsbottom Health Centre
RAMS BL0 .... **319** H4
Ramsbottom Swimming Pool
RAMS BL0 .... **319** J4
Ramsgreave Works
BBN BB1 .... **245** G1
Range High School
FMBY L37 .... **355** G3
Ravenscroft Primary School
NWD/KWIPK L33 .... **366** C6
Rawtenstall Cricket Club
RAW/HAS BB4 .... **296** D1
Raza Mosque
PRES PR1 .... **7** E1
Read Congregational School
PDHM/BLYW BB12 .... **222** D1
Read Cricket Club
PDHM/BLYW BB12 .... **222** D2
Read Hall Golf & Country Club
PDHM/BLYW BB12 .... **222** B1
The Redbrick Theatre
BBNW BB2 .... **268** A2
Redgate Primary School
FMBY L37 .... **356** A1
Redmarsh School
CLV/TH FY5 .... **123** H8
Red Rose Radio Station
PRES PR1 .... **7** E2
Red Scar Industrial Estate
FUL/RIB PR2 .... **215** F6
Reedley CP School
BRFD/BLYE BB10 .... **198** A7
Regent Caravan Park
HEY LA3 .... **53** F1
Renacres Hall Hospital
ORM L39 .... **327** K6
Revoe CP School
BPOOL FY1 .... **4** C4
Rhyddings County High School
ACC BB5 .... **247** J7
Rhyddings Works
ACC BB5 .... **247** J8
Ribble Business Park
BBN BB1 .... **9** F1
Ribblesdale CP School
CLI BB7 .... **165** J4
Ribblesdale Pool
CLI BB7 .... **165** F3
Ribbleton Avenue County
Infant School
PRES PR1 .... **240** A1
Ribbleton Avenue Methodist
Junior School
PRES PR1 .... **240** B1
Ribbleton Hall High School
FUL/RIB PR2 .... **214** D8
Ribbleton Hospital
FUL/RIB PR2 .... **240** D1
Ribble Village Health Centre
FUL/RIB PR2 .... **240** C1
Ribby School
KIRK/FR/WA PR4 .... **207** K7
Ribchester Hospital
GAR/LONG PR3 .... **189** F5
Ribchester Roman Museum
BBN BB1 .... **190** A8
Ribchester St Wilfreds
CE School
GAR/LONG PR3 .... **190** A8
Richard Thorntons
CE Primary School
KKBYL LA6 .... **31** K6
Richmond Industrial Estate
ACC BB5 .... **248** B6
Ridge CP School
LANC LA1 .... **3** E2
Ridge Lea Hospital
LANC LA1 .... **55** J2
Rimington Caravan Park
CLI BB7 .... **142** E1
Ringtail Industrial Estate
BRSC L40 .... **349** F1
Ripley St Thomas School
LANC LA1 .... **2** C5
Ripleys Believe It Or Not Museum
BPOOLS FY4 .... **204** A4
Rishton Cricket Club
BBN BB1 .... **246** E3

Rishton Golf Club
BBN BB1 .... **247** F3
Rishton Methodist School
BBN BB1 .... **247** F2
Riverside Business Centre
NLSN BB9 .... **198** C2
Riverside Caravan Park
HEY LA3 .... **53** K3
Riverside Industrial Estate
BBN BB1 .... **247** H1
Riverside Industrial Estate
DWN BB3 .... **268** C4
Riverside Industrial Park
GAR/LONG PR3 .... **129** H8
Riverside Medical Centre
LEY/BBR PR5 .... **240** B6
Rivington & Blackrod
High School
HOR/BR BL6 .... **338** D5
Rivington Primary School
HOR/BR BL6 .... **338** B2
RNIB Sunshine House School
STHP PR8........................ **300** E6
Roby Mill CE Primary School
SKEL WN8 .... **352** D8
Roebuck Street CP School
BBN BB1 .... **239** F1
Roefield Leisure Centre
CLI BB7 .... **165** F3
Roe Lee Industrial Estate
BBN BB1 .... **245** G2
Roe Lee Park County School
BBN BB1 .... **245** H1
Roman Road Industrial Estate
BBN BB1 .... **268** E4
Roman Road Leisure Centre
BBNW BB2...................... **268** C3
Roman Way Industrial Estate
FUL/RIB PR2 .... **215** G4
Roseacre CP School
BPOOLS FY4 .... **204** C6
Rosegrove Infant School
PDHM/BLYW BB12 .... **224** C5
Rosehill Business Park
CHTN/BK PR9 .... **301** K5
Rosehill County Infant School
BLY BB11 .... **10** C6
Rosehill County Junior School
BLY BB11 .... **10** C6
Rossall Hospital
FTWD FY7 .... **122** C3
Rossall School
FTWD FY7 .... **122** C5
Rossendale Golf Club
RAW/HAS BB4 .... **295** J4
Rossendale Museum
Whitaker Park
RAW/HAS BB4 .... **296** B1
Rossendale Road
Industrial Estate
BLY BB11 .... **224** D8
Rossendale United FC
RAW/HAS BB4 .... **297** G2
Roughlee Junior School
NLSN BB9........................ **169** H7
The Royal Birkdale Golf Club
STHP PR8........................ **325** K2
Royal Cross Primary School
FUL/RIB PR2 .... **238** A2
Royal Lancaster Infirmary
LANC LA1 .... **3** D4
Royal Lytham &
St Anne's Golf Club
LSTA FY8 .... **231** G5
Royal Preston Hospital
FUL/RIB PR2 .... **213** H5
Royal Umpire Caravan Park
LEY/BBR PR5 .... **308** A1
Royles Brook Primary School
CLV/TH FY5 .... **149** G1
Rufford CE School
BRSC L40 .... **306** B7
Ruffwood Community
Comprehensive School
NWD/KWIPK L33 .... **366** D8
Runshaw College
CHLY/EC PR7 .... **285** K5
Runshaw College
CHLY/EC PR7 .... **311** G4
The Ryan Medical Centre
LEY/BBR PR5 .... **263** H2
Ryelands CP School
LANC LA1 .... **2** B1

Sabden CP School
CLI BB7.......................... **195**
Sabden RC School
CLI BB7.......................... **195**
Sacred Heart RC Primary School
BBNW BB2...................... **244**
Sacred Heart RC Primary School
CHLYE PR6...................... **311**
Sacred Heart RC Primary School
COL BB8 .... **171**
Sacred Heart RC School
FUL/RIB PR2 .... **6**
Sacred Heart School
CLV/TH FY5 .... **123**
Sadler Street Industrial Estate
ACC BB5 .... **247**
St Aidans CE High School
PLF/KEOS FY6 .... **98**
St Aidans CE Primary School
WGNW/BIL/O WN5 .... **371**
St Aidans CE School
BBNW BB2...................... **267**
St Aidans School
LEY/BBR PR5 .... **263**
St Albans RC Primary School
BBN BB1 .... **9**
St Andrews CE Infant School
LEY/BBR PR5 .... **285**
St Andrews CE Primary School
ACC BB5 .... **247**
St Andrews CE Primary School
RAMS BL0 .... **319**
St Andrews CE School
BBNW BB2...................... **267**
St Andrews Cricket &
Bowling Club
BRFD/BLYE BB10 .... **226**
St Andrews Cricket Club
BRFD/BLYE BB10 .... **226**
St Andrews Primary School
FUL/RIB PR2 .... **238**
St Annes CE Primary School
RAW/HAS BB4 .... **297**
St Anne's College
Grammar School
LSTA FY8 .... **230**
St Anne's Cricket Club
LSTA FY8 .... **230**
St Anne's Old Links Golf Club
LSTA FY8 .... **230**
St Anne's Pier
LSTA FY8 .... **230**
St Annes RC Infant School
ACC BB5 .... **248**
St Annes RC Junior School
BBNW BB2...................... **8**
St Annes RC Primary School
ORM L39 .... **348**
St Annes School
KIRK/FR/WA PR4 .... **207**
St Annes School
LEY/BBR PR5 .... **285**
St Anne's Swimming Pool
LSTA FY8 .... **230**
St Anselms RC School
WHIT OL12...................... **323**
St Anthonys RC Junior School
BBN BB1 .... **246**
St Anthonys School
FUL/RIB PR2 .... **212**
St Augustines RC High School
CLI BB7.......................... **192**
St Augustines RC Primary School
PRES PR1........................ **7**
St Augustines RC School
PDHM/BLYW BB12 .... **224**
St Barnabas CE School
DWN BB3 .... **292**
St Barnabas & St Pauls CE School
BBNW BB2...................... **8**
St Bartholomews CE
Primary School
GTH/LHO BB6 .... **221**
St Bartholomews CE
Primary School
WHIT OL12...................... **323**
St Bartholomews CE School
BBNW BB2...................... **268**
St Bedes RC High School
BBNW BB2...................... **267**
St Bedes RC High School
LSTA FY8 .... **232**
St Bedes RC School
ORM L39 .... **348**

...ernadettes RC
...rimary School
...ISP FY2 .... 148 D6
...ernadettes RC
...rimary School
...VGNNW/ST WN6 .... 353 J5
...ernadettes RC School
...ANC LA1 .... 55 H7
...ernards RC Primary School
...UL/RIB PR2 .... 237 J2
...atherines CE
...rimary School
...OR/BR BL6 .... 338 D8
...ecilias RC High School
...AR/LONG PR3 .... 188 A5
...hads RC Primary School
...HLYE PR6 .... 287 K5
...harles RC School
...BN BB1 .... 246 E2
...hristophers CE High School
...CC BB5 .... 248 A3
...lares RC School
...UL/RIB PR2 .... 213 H5
...uthberts CE School
...WN BB3 .... 268 B8
...uthberts CE School
...RM L39 .... 346 D2
...uthberts Primary School
...POOLS FY4 .... 204 C3
...uthberts Sunday School
...RFD/BLYE BB10 .... 225 K1
...dmunds RC Junior School
...TWD FY7 .... 122 E3
...dmunds RC Primary School
...KEL WN8 .... 363 F2
...dwards RC School
...WN BB3 .... 268 B7
...rancis CE School
...BNW BB2 .... 267 F2
...rancis R C Primary School
...AR/LONG PR3 .... 186 E1
...abriels CE School
...BN BB1 .... 245 G1
...eorges High School
...POOLS FY4 .... 205 G2
...eorges Primary School
...HLY/EC PR7 .... 311 J6
...eorges Shopping Centre
...RES PR1 .... 7 D3
...errards School
...EY/BBR PR5 .... 262 E3
...regorys RC Junior School
...MCHL L31 .... 358 E7
...regorys RC Primary School
...RES PR1 .... 213 K8
...elens CE School
...EY LA3 .... 65 H2
...ildas RC Girls High School
...LY BB11 .... 10 A5
...natius Primary School
...RES PR1 .... 7 E2
...es Business Park
...BN BB1 .... 246 C7
...ames CE Primary School
...LI BB7 .... 165 J4
...ames CE Primary School
...WN BB3 .... 291 K1
...ames CE Primary School
...AW/HAS BB4 .... 272 B7
...ames CE School
...CC BB5 .... 247 K2
...ames CE School
...BNW BB2 .... 268 D3
...ames CE School
...RSC L40 .... 349 J7
...ames CE School
...HLYE PR6 .... 311 J4
...ames CE School
...EY/BBR PR5 .... 284 D3
...ames Clinic
...LY BB11 .... 10 C3
...ames Lanehead CE
...rimary School
...RFD/BLYE BB10 .... 226 B1
...ames RC Primary School
...KEL WN8 .... 351 H1
...ames RC Primary School
...VGNW/BIL/O WN5 .... 365 F7
...ames the Less RC
...rimary School
...AW/HAS BB4 .... 273 G8
...eromes RC Primary School
...MBY L37 .... 343 G8

St John Rigby College and
Sports Centre
WCNW/BIL/O WN5 .... 365 H1
St Johns CE County
Primary School
BRSC L40 .... 331 F6
St Johns CE Infant School
NLSN BB9 .... 199 F4
St Johns CE & Methodist
Primary School
CHLYE PR6 .... 288 B7
St Johns CE Primary School
ACC BB5 .... 248 C4
St Johns CE Primary School
BPOOL FY1 .... 4 C2
St Johns CE Primary School
NLSN BB9 .... 198 E3
St Johns CE School
GTH/LHO BB6 .... 221 G7
St Johns CE School
PDHM/BLYW BB12 .... 222 D1
St Johns CE School
WCNW/BIL/O WN5 .... 365 K5
St John's Market
BPOOL FY1 .... 4 C2
St John Southworth RC School
NLSN BB9 .... 198 B4
St Johns Primary School
PDHM/BLYW BB12 .... 196 C5
St Johns RC Infant School
BRFD/BLYE BB10 .... 225 K2
St Johns RC Junior School
BRFD/BLYE BB10 .... 198 A8
St Johns RC Primary School
EDGW/EG BL7 .... 341 K3
St Johns RC Primary School
PLF/KEOS FY6 .... 150 A6
St Johns RC Primary School
SKEL WN8 .... 363 J2
St Johns School
CHLY/EC PR7 .... 335 H5
St Johns School
RAMS BL0 .... 320 A3
St Johns Shopping Centre
PRES PR1 .... 7 E2
St John Stone RC
Primary School
STHP PR8 .... 344 D1
St John the Baptist School
PDHM/BLYW BB12 .... 223 J4
St John Vianney RC
Primary School
BPOOL FY1 .... 5 E5
St John with St Michael School
WHIT OL12 .... 299 J6
St Josephs Convent School
PDHM/BLYW BB12 .... 224 C3
St Josephs RC College
SKEL WN8 .... 364 D1
St Josephs RC Primary School
CHLYE PR6 .... 337 H4
St Josephs RC Primary School
KIRK/FR/WA PR4 .... 208 D4
St Josephs RC Primary School
PRES PR1 .... 240 A2
St Josephs RC Primary School
RAMS BL0 .... 319 H5
St Josephs RC School
CHLYE PR6 .... 311 H1
St Josephs RC School
CLI BB7 .... 191 H2
St Josephs RC School
DWN BB3 .... 291 J4
St Josephs RC School
WCNW/ST WN6 .... 334 E8
St Josephs School
BCUP OL13 .... 298 D3
St Josephs School
LANC LA1 .... 43 F8
St Kentigerns RC Primary School
BPOOL FY3 .... 5 D2
St Lawrence's CE Primary School
CHLY/EC PR7 .... 311 G2
St Leonards CE Primary School
LEY/BBR PR5 .... 240 A7
St Leonards CE Primary School
PDHM/BLYW BB12 .... 223 J2
St Lukes C E Primary School
FMBY L37 .... 355 H2
St Lukes RC Primary School
SKEL WN8 .... 364 A5
St Lukes & St Philips CE School
BBNW BB2 .... 8 A6

St Lukes School
LANC LA1 .... 43 F8
St Maria Goretti School
FUL/RIB PR2 .... 214 D6
St Maries RC School
NWD/KWIPK L33 .... 366 E8
St Marks RC Primary School
SKEL WN8 .... 364 A3
St Marks School
BRSC L40 .... 328 B3
St Martins College
LANC LA1 .... 3 E3
St Mary Magdalenes RC School
PDHM/BLYW BB12 .... 10 A1
St Mary Magdalenes CE School
ACC BB5 .... 248 B4
St Mary Magdalenes School
PRES PR1 .... 6 C6
St Marys CE Primary School
CHLY/EC PR7 .... 308 E5
St Marys CE Primary School
KKBYL LA6 .... 21 F1
St Marys CE School
RAW/HAS BB4 .... 273 G8
St Marys College
BBN BB1 .... 8 C2
St Marys Health Centre
PRES PR1 .... 238 D6
St Marys Primary School
KIRK/FR/WA PR4 .... 184 C6
St Marys Primary School
LEY/BBR PR5 .... 285 H2
St Marys Primary School
MCMB LA4 .... 41 J5
St Marys RC Primary School
RAW/HAS BB4 .... 295 J1
St Marys RC High School
BPOOL FY3 .... 177 F4
St Marys RC Primary School
BCUP OL13 .... 299 F1
St Marys RC Primary School
BRFD/BLYE BB10 .... 11 F3
St Marys RC Primary School
CHLY/EC PR7 .... 310 E4
St Marys RC Primary School
FTWD FY7 .... 97 G6
St Marys RC Primary School
GAR/LONG PR3 .... 134 E8
St Marys RC Primary School
WGNW/BIL/O WN5 .... 371 F7
St Marys RC School
ACC BB5 .... 247 K7
St Marys RC School
BBNW BB2 .... 9 D6
St Marys RC School
BBNW BB2 .... 217 K7
St Marys RC School
GAR/LONG PR3 .... 129 J5
St Marys RC School
GAR/LONG PR3 .... 153 F6
St Marys RC School
GTH/LHO BB6 .... 220 A2
St Marys RC School
LEY/BBR PR5 .... 285 G4
St Marys & St Benedicts
RC Primary School
LEY/BBR PR5 .... 263 H2
St Marys School
ACC BB5 .... 221 K8
St Marys School
CHLY/EC PR7 .... 286 A8
St Marys School
GAR/LONG PR3 .... 157 F2
St Matthews CE
Primary School
PRES PR1 .... 240 B3
St Matthews Primary School
BBN BB1 .... 9 D5
St Matthews RC
Primary School
SKEL WN8 .... 363 K4
St Michael & All Angels CE
Primary School
COL BB8 .... 171 J3
St Michaels CE High School
CHLY/EC PR7 .... 311 G1
St Michaels CE Primary School
SKEL WN8 .... 351 K6
St Michaels CE School
GAR/LONG PR3 .... 154 C5
St Michaels Primary School
KIRK/FR/WA PR4 .... 209 F6
St Michaels & St Johns RC School
CLI BB7 .... 165 J3

St Michael with St John CE Primary School
BBN BB1 .... 8 C3
St Nicholas Arcades
LANC LA1 .... 3 D3
St Nicholas CE School
ACC BB5 .... 247 K4
St Nicholas CE School
BPOOLS FY4 .... 205 G7
St Oswalds CE Primary School
BBN BB1 .... 246 C7
St Oswalds RC Primary School
CHLY/EC PR7 .... 335 G3
St Oswalds RC School
ACC BB5 .... 248 A8
St Patricks Primary School
CHTN/BK PR9 .... 302 C1
St Patricks CE School
HEY LA3 .... 52 E3
St Patricks School
LEY/BBR PR5 .... 240 C7
St Pauls CE Primary School
BOL BL1 .... 341 K8
St Pauls CE Primary School
DWN BB3 .... 292 D2
St Pauls CE Primary School
HGHB LA2 .... 45 J6
St Pauls CE School
ACC BB5 .... 247 J7
St Pauls CE School
CHLYE PR6 .... 337 G3
St Pauls CE School
RAMS BL0 .... 319 J4
St Pauls Medical Centre
BPOOL FY1 .... 176 B4
St Pauls Primary School
NLSN BB9 .... 198 B4
St Paul's RC Primary School
BRFD/BLYE BB10 .... 226 E3
St Pauls School
KIRK/FR/WA PR4 .... 234 C6
St Peter & St Pauls Primary School
NWD/KWIPK L33 .... 366 D6
St Peters CE Junior School
CHLYE PR6 .... 311 J1
St Peters CE Primary School
BLY BB11 .... 11 D3
St Peters CE Primary School
FMBY L37 .... 344 A6
St Peters CE Primary School
KIRK/FR/WA PR4 .... 182 B3
St Peters CE School
ACC BB5 .... 271 F1
St Peters CE School
DWN BB3 .... 291 K3
St Peters CE School
HEY LA3 .... 52 C4
St Peters Primary School
FUL/RIB PR2 .... 213 H4
St Peters RC High School
WGNNW/BIL/O WN5 .... 365 H4
St Peters RC Infant School
BBNW BB2 .... 267 J1
St Peters RC Junior School
BBNW BB2 .... 267 J1
St Peters RC School
LSTA FY8 .... 232 D8
St Peters RC School
LSTA FY8 .... 232 E6
St Peters RC School
RAW/HAS BB4 .... 297 G1
St Peters School
LANC LA1 .... 3 E4
St Peters Smithills Dean CE Primary School
BOL BL1 .... 341 F7
St Philips CE Junior School
NLSN BB9 .... 198 C3
St Phillips CE Primary School
STHP PR8 .... 301 J5
St Pius X Preparatory School
FUL/RIB PR2 .... 213 G6
St Richards RC Primary School
SKEL WN8 .... 362 D2
St Saviours CE Primary School
LEY/BBR PR5 .... 263 J4
St Silas CE School
BBNW BB2 .... 244 D5
St Stephens CE Infant School
BBN BB1 .... 9 F2
St Stephens CE Junior School
BBN BB1 .... 9 F2

St Stephens CE School
BLY BB11 .... 11 F5
St Stephens Primary School
CHTN/BK PR9 .... 279 J6
St Stephens School
CHTN/BK PR9 .... 279 H5
St Stephens School
PRES PR1 .... 6 C4
St Teresa's Primary School
PRES PR1 .... 238 C6
St Teresas RC Primary School
PRES PR1 .... 240 C3
St Teresas School
CLV/TH FY5 .... 148 D2
St Theodores RC School
BRFD/BLYE BB10 .... 11 E2
St Theresa's School
SKEL WN8 .... 364 D2
St Thomas CE Primary School
BBN BB1 .... 9 F4
St Thomas CE Primary School
LSTA FY8 .... 231 F5
St Thomas CE Primary School
MGHL L31 .... 359 F7
St Thomas School
GAR/LONG PR3 .... 129 H5
St Thomas's Primary School
NLSN BB9 .... 170 B8
St Thomas the Martyr CE Primary School
SKEL WN8 .... 364 D4
St Veronicas RC Primary School
RAW/HAS BB4 .... 295 H4
St Wilfreds CE School
HGHB LA2 .... 44 A4
St Wilfreds School
GAR/LONG PR3 .... 188 A3
St Wilfrids CE GM High School and Technology College
BBNW BB2 .... 8 B6
St Williams RC School
GAR/LONG PR3 .... 100 C7
St Wulstans RC School
FTWD FY7 .... 96 E8
Salesbury CE School
BBN BB1 .... 219 F5
Salmesbury Hall
LEY/BBR PR5 .... 242 E1
Salt Ayre Athletics Track
LANC LA1 .... 2 A2
Salterforth Primary School
BWCK/EAR BB18 .... 145 H3
Salthill Industrial Estate
CLI BB7 .... 166 A2
Samlesbury CE School
LEY/BBR PR5 .... 241 H2
Sandcastle Leisure Centre
BPOOLS FY4 .... 204 A3
Sandside Caravan & Camping Park
CARN LA5 .... 33 F6
Sandylands CP School
HEY LA3 .... 40 E8
Sandy Lane Clinic
LEY/BBR PR5 .... 285 J3
Sandy Lane Health Centre
SKEL WN8 .... 362 D2
Savick County Junior School
FUL/RIB PR2 .... 238 A1
Sawmill Industrial Estate
BPOOL FY1 .... 5 D1
Scarisbrick CP School
BRSC L40 .... 328 D8
Science Park
BBN BB1 .... 9 F3
Scorton CE School
GAR/LONG PR3 .... 104 A5
Scotforth CE Primary School
LANC LA1 .... 55 F7
Scotshaw Brook Industrial Estate
DWN BB3 .... 268 B4
Scoutbottom Industrial Estate
RAW/HAS BB4 .... 274 C8
Sealife Centre
BPOOL FY1 .... 4 A3
Sealife Centre
BPOOL FY1 .... 4 A4
Seedhill Athletics Stadium
NLSN BB9 .... 198 A1
Segar Street Mosque
GTH/LHO BB6 .... 221 G6
Selby Industrial Estate
KIRK/FR/WA PR4 .... 208 D5

Seven Stars CP Infants School
LEY/BBR PR5 285
Shadsworth County Infant School
BBN BB1 246
Shadsworth County Junior School
BBN BB1 269
Shadsworth Industrial Park
BBN BB1 269
Shadsworth Industrial Park
BBN BB1 269
Shadsworth Leisure Centre
BBN BB1 269
Shakespeare CP School
FTWD FY7 96
Sharneyford County School
BCUP OL13 276
Sharoe Green Hospital
FUL/RIB PR2 213
Shawclough CP School
WHIT OL12 323
Shawclough Trading Estate
WHIT OL12 323
Shaw Hall Caravan Park
BRSC L40 329
Shaw Hill Hotel Golf & Country Club
CHLYE PR6 287
Shay Lane Industrial Estate
GAR/LONG PR3 187
Shelley Road Works
FUL/RIB PR2 6
Sherburn School
PRES PR1 213
Sherwood County Primary School
FUL/RIB PR2 213
Shevington County High School
WGNNW/ST WN6 353
Shevington CP School
WGNNW/ST WN6 353
Shevington Vale CP School
WGNNW/ST WN6 353
Shopping Centre
BBN BB1 8
Shopping Parade
COL BB8 171
Shopping Precinct
LEY/BBR PR5 285
Shoreshird School
STHP PR8 325
Shorrocks Hill Country Club
FMBY L37 355
Silverdale CE School
CARN LA5 15
Silverdale Golf Club
CARN LA5 15
Simonstone Business Park
PDHM/BLYW BB12 223
Simonstone CE School
PDHM/BLYW BB12 223
Simonswood Industrial Park
NWD/KWIPK L33 367
Singleton CE School
PLF/KEOS FY6 179
Skelmersdale College
SKEL WN8 351
Skelmersdale College
SKEL WN8 363
Skelmersdale College (Westbank)
SKEL WN8 363
Skelmersdale Crow Orchard County Primary School
SKEL WN8 363
Skelmersdale Park CP School
SKEL WN8 362
Skelmersdale Sports Centre
SKEL WN8 363
Skelmersdale United FC
SKEL WN8 362
Skerton Community Primary School
LANC LA1 3
Skerton High School
LANC LA1 3
Skipton Road Business Park
BWCK/EAR BB18 119
Ski Rossendale
RAW/HAS BB4 273
Slaidburn Health Centre
CLI BB7 89

burn Industrial Estate
HTN/BK PR9 .... 278 C7
e with Hest CE School
GHB LA2 .... 42 E3
lshaw Industrial Estate
LY BB11 .... 224 E6
hills Hall Museum
OL BL1 .... 341 F7
hbank Tennis Club
HP PR8.. 302 A7
hlands High School
HLY/EC PR7 .... 310 E6
hport & Ainsdale Golf Club
HP PR8... 325 J5
hport & Birkdale
ricket Club
HP PR8.. 300 E8
hport Business Centre
HTN/BK PR9 .... 301 H4
hport Business Park
HP PR8.. 301 G8
hport College
HP PR8.. 301 J4
hport Crematorium
HP PR8.. 327 K1
hport FC
HP PR8... 302 A6
hport Flower Show Site
HP PR8... 301 F4
hport & Formby
strict General Hospital
HP PR8... 302 A7
hport & Formby Hospital
HTN/BK PR9 .... 301 H4
hport General Infirmary
HP PR8... 301 K6
hport Girls FC
HP PR8.. 302 B5
hport Municipal Golf Club
HTN/BK PR9 .... 301 J1
hport New Synagogue
HP PR8... 301 H5
hport Old Links Golf Club
HTN/BK PR9 .... 302 D3
hport Pier
HP PR8... 301 F2
hport RFC
HP PR8.. 326 A2
hport Sailing Club
HP PR8... 301 G2
hport Swimming Baths
HP PR8... 301 F4
hport Zoo &
onservation Trust
HP PR8... 301 F4
h Ribble Industrial Estate
EY/BBR PR5 .... 240 A6
h Ribble Museum &
xhibition Centre
EY/BBR PR5 .... 285 J3
a Farm Business Park
POOLS FY4 .... 205 J3
ynx Tennis Club
HP PR8... 302 A7
tualist Temple
BNW BB2 .... 8 B5
Sporting Edge Track
RM LA3 .... 348 E8
ngfield Industrial Estate
RES PR1... 6 C1
ngvale Business Park
WN BB3 .... 291 K5
res Gate Industrial Estate
POOLS FY4 .... 204 E6
ohn Fisher & Thomas More
C High School
OL BB8 .... 199 F1
ning CE School
POOLE FY3 .... 177 K6
ah CP Infant School
LV/TH FY5 .... 149 K2
ah CP Junior School
LV/TH FY5 .... 149 K2
hill Works
CC BB5 .... 247 G7
ley High School
HTN/BK PR9 .... 278 B7
ley Infant School
POOLE FY3 .... 205 H1
ley Junior School
POOLE FY3 .... 205 H1
ley Park Athletics Arena
POOLE FY3 .... 5 E3

Stanley Park Municipal
Golf Course
BPOOLE FY3 .... 5 E2
Stanley Park Sports Arena
BPOOLE FY3 .... 5 E3
Starkie Industrial Estate
FUL/RIB PR2 .... 239 F1
Station Road Industrial Estate
GTH/LHO BB6 .... 221 J6
Steamtown Railway Museum
CARN LA5....................................... 33 J1
Stocks Park Special School
HOR/BR BL6 .... 338 E8
Stonefold CE School
ACC BB5 .... 272 B4
Stoneholme Industrial Estate
RAW/HAS BB4 .... 273 G3
Stoneyholme CP School
PDHM/BLYW BB12 .... 10 C1
Stonyhurst College
CLI BB7 .... 163 J8
Strike Lane County School
KIRK/FR/WA PR4 .... 235 G3
Stubbins CP School
RAMS BL0 .... 319 K2
Stutelea Hotel & Leisure Club
CHTN/BK PR9 .... 301 J2
Sudell County School
DWN BB3 .... 291 K2
Summersales Industrial Estate
WGNS/IIMK WN3 .... 365 K7
Summit Works
BLY BB11 .... 251 G1
Sunnybank Industrial Estate
PLF/KEOS FY6 .... 151 F2
Sunny Bank Preparatory School
BLY BB11 .... 10 B5
Sunnycliff Retail Park
HEY LA3... 53 K2
Sunnymede School
STHP PR8.................................... 301 F5
Superbowl Leisure Parcs
BPOOL FY1 .... 4 A2
Swimming Pool
LEY/BBR PR5 .... 285 H3
Swimsafe Swimming Pool
PDHM/BLYW BB12 .... 224 C6
Sycamore Trading Estate
BPOOLS FY4 .... 205 F7
Talbot Road Industrial Centre
LEY/BBR PR5 .... 285 F1
Tardygate Trading Estate
LEY/BBR PR5 .... 262 D3
Tarleton CE Primary School
KIRK/FR/WA PR4 .... 282 A6
Tarleton CP School
KIRK/FR/WA PR4 .... 281 F7
Tarleton High School
KIRK/FR/WA PR4 .... 282 A4
Tatham Fells School
HGHB LA2 .... 50 A4
Tauheedul Islam Girls
High School
BBN BB1 .... 8 B3
Taylor Holme Industrial Estate
BCUP OL13 .... 297 J3
Taylors Industrial Estate
GAR/LONG PR3 .... 100 C6
Tennis Centre
LEY/BBR PR5 .... 263 G4
Thames Road Primary School
BPOOLS FY4 .... 204 B4
Theatre & Floral Hall
STHP PR8.................................... 301 G3
Thompson Street
Industrial Estate
BBNW BB2 .... 8 B5
Thorneyholme RC School
CLI BB7 .... 110 B5
Thornleigh Salesian College
BOL BL1 .... 341 H7
Thornton Cleveleys Cricket Club
CLV/TH FY5 .... 150 B5
Thornton Cleveleys RUFC
CLV/TH FY5 .... 149 G1
Thornton In Craven CP School
SKP/WHF BD23 .... 120 B5
Three Point Business Park
RAW/HAS BB4 .... 295 F1
Three Worlds Business Centre
LSTA FY8 .... 233 F7
Tockholes CE Primary School
DWN BB3..................................... 267 H8

Todmorden Road
County School
BLY BB11 .... 11 E4
Toll Bar Business Park
BCUP OL13 .... 298 A3
Toll Bar Business Park
BCUP OL13 .... 298 C3
Tonacliffe School
WHIT OL12 .... 323 G5
Torrisholme CP School
MCMB LA4..................................... 42 B6
Tower Dene Preparatory School
CHTN/BK PR9 .... 302 B1
Tower Hill Health Centre
NWD/KWIPK L33......................... 366 D6
Tower Shopping Centre
BPOOL FY1 .... 4 B2
Tower World
BPOOL FY1 .... 176 A6
Towneley Golf Club
BLY BB11 .... 11 E6
Towneley Hall Art
Gallery & Museum
BLY BB11 .... 252 A1
Towneley High School
BLY BB11 .... 11 F5
Towngate Healthcare Clinic
LEY/BBR PR5 .... 285 J3
Town Green CP School
ORM L39 .... 360 A3
Town House Gallery
LANC LA1 .... 2 C3
Townhouse Special School
NLSN BB9..................................... 199 G2
Townsmoor Retail Park
BBNW BB2 .... 8 C6
Toy & Teddy Bear Museum
LSTA FY8 .... 230 D4
Traceys Industrial Estate
LEY/BBR PR5 .... 286 B2
Trans Britannia Enterprise Estate
BLY BB11 .... 224 D8
Trawden CP School
COL BB8 .... 200 C1
Treales School
KIRK/FR/WA PR4 .... 209 J1
Trinity CP School
SKEL WN8 .... 362 E2
Trumacor CP School
HEY LA3... 52 C6
Tullyallan School
DWN BB3 .... 268 B8
Turkey Red Industrial Estate
ACC BB5 .... 272 A2
Turton Edgworth CE School
EDGW/EG BL7 .... 317 J6
Turton Tower
EDGW/EG BL7 .... 317 G8
Twin Lakes Industrial Park
LEY/BBR PR5 .... 283 G8
Two Gates Works
DWN BB3 .... 291 K1
Unity Temple
MCMB LA4..................................... 41 F7
Unity Trading Estate
BBNW BB2 .... 8 B5
University of Central Lancashire
PRES PR1.. 6 C2
University of Lancaster
HGHB LA2 .... 67 H4
Up-Brooks Industrial Estate
CLI BB7.. 166 A2
Up Holland High School
WGNW/BIL/O WN5..................... 364 E7
Vale of Lune RUFC
LANC LA1 .... 42 C8
Valley Shopping Centre
RAW/HAS BB4 .... 273 H8
Vehicle Museum
LEY/BBR PR5 .... 285 J2
Venture Caravan Park
MCMB LA4..................................... 41 H8
Vickers Industrial Estate
HEY LA3... 53 J1
Victoria Business Centre
ACC BB5 .... 248 B6
Victoria Business Park
FTWD FY7 .... 97 G8
Victoria College
LANC LA1 .... 3 D3
Victoria Hospital
BPOOLE FY3 .... 177 G6
Victoria Market Hall
BPOOLS FY4 .... 4 B6

Victoria Works
PDHM/BLYW BB12 .... **223** K3
Victoria Works Industrial Estate
BLY BB7 .... **224** D6
The Village Surgery
FMBY L37 .... **355** J1
Virgin Active Swimming Pool
LEY/BBR PR5 .... **240** A6
Visitor Centre
BLY BB11 .... **10** C4
Vulcan Works
BLY BB11 .... **224** C6
Waddington & West Bradford
CE Primary School
CLI BB7 .... **139** G6
Walker Industrial Estate
BBN BB1 .... **269** F3
Walker School Outdoor
Pursuits Centre
KKBYL LA6 .... **19** J1
Walkers Industrial Estate
HEY LA3 .... **52** D8
Walshaw High School
BRFD/BLYE BB10 .... **226** B2
Walter Street County
Primary School
NLSN BB9 .... **197** K6
Walton-le-Dale County
Primary School
LEY/BBR PR5 .... **263** G1
Walton-le-Dale County
Secondary School
LEY/BBR PR5 .... **263** J1
Walton-le-Dale School Clinic
LEY/BBR PR5 .... **263** J1
Walverden County Infant School
NLSN BB9 .... **198** D3
Walverdene Works
NLSN BB9 .... **198** C3
Walverden Secondary
Modern School
NLSN BB9 .... **198** D3
Warbreck High School
BISP FY2 .... **176** D2
War Memorial
PRES PR1 .... **7** D3
Warner Village Cinema
LEY/BBR PR5 .... **240** A6
Water CP School
RAW/HAS BB4 .... **274** D3
Waterfoot Business Centre
RAW/HAS BB4 .... **297** H1
Waterfoot County
Primary School
RAW/HAS BB4 .... **297** H3
Waterfoot Health Centre
RAW/HAS BB4 .... **297** H3
Waterfront Marine Business Park
LSTA FY8 .... **233** G8
The Waterloo Crown
Bowling Green
BPOOL FY1 .... **4** C6
Waterloo Medical Centre
BPOOLS FY4 .... **5** D6
Waterloo Primary School
BPOOLS FY4 .... **5** D6
Waterside Industrial Estate
COL BB8 .... **171** J7
Waterworks Bridge
HGHB LA2 .... **45** H3
Waterworks Cottages
ORM L39 .... **360** D7
Waterworks House
ORM L39 .... **348** E5
Watery Lane Industrial Estate
DWN BB3 .... **291** K5
Watling Street County
Primary School
FUL/RIB PR2 .... **213** J7
Waverledge Business Park
GTH/LHO BB6 .... **221** F7
Weeton County Primary School
KIRK/FR/WA PR4 .... **179** G5
Weeton St Michaels
CE Primary School
KIRK/FR/WA PR4 .... **207** G2
Wellfield Business Park
PRES PR1 .... **6** B2
Wellfield Church School
PDHM/BLYW BB12 .... **10** A1
Wellfield County
Secondary School
LEY/BBR PR5 .... **285** H2

Wennington Hall School
HGHB LA2 .... **38** C1
Wensley Business Park
BBNW BB2 .... **8** A5
Wensley Fold CE School
BBNW BB2 .... **244** D6
Wensley Gallery
RAMS BL0 .... **319** J5
Wesham CE Primary School
KIRK/FR/WA PR4 .... **208** D5
Westcliffe Infant School
BISP FY2 .... **148** C6
West Craven High School
BWCK/EAR BB18 .... **145** G2
West Craven Sports Centre &
Swimming Pool
BWCK/EAR BB18 .... **145** G2
West End Business Park
ACC BB5 .... **247** F6
West End County
Primary School
HEY LA3 .... **40** E8
West End County
Primary School
ORM L39 .... **348** C4
West End CP School
ACC BB5 .... **247** F6
Westgate County
Primary School
MCMB LA4 .... **41** H8
West Gilbrands Industrial Estate
SKEL WN8 .... **363** F4
Westholme Junior School
BBNW BB2 .... **244** C6
Westholme School
BBNW BB2 .... **244** A5
West Lancs Yacht Club
STHP PR8 .... **301** G2
West Pennine Business Park
BCUP OL13 .... **275** H6
West Street County Junior &
Infant School
COL BB8 .... **171** J7
West View Leisure Centre
PRES PR1 .... **240** A1
Westway School
PDHM/BLYW BB12 .... **10** C1
Westwood County
Primary School
LEY/BBR PR5 .... **264** A7
Whalley Abbey
CLI BB7 .... **193** G6
Whalley Banks Trading Estate
BBNW BB2 .... **8** B5
Whalley CE School
CLI BB7 .... **193** G6
Whalley Cricket Club
CLI BB7 .... **193** F5
Whalley Golf Club
CLI BB7 .... **193** K6
Whalley Industrial Park
CLI BB7 .... **193** H3
Wheatley Lane
Methodist Aided School
PDHM/BLYW BB12 .... **197** G3
White Ash School
ACC BB5 .... **247** G7
Whitechapel School
GAR/LONG PR3 .... **158** B4
White Cross Industrial Estate
LANC LA1 .... **3** E4
Whitefield County Infant School
NLSN BB9 .... **198** B3
Whitefield Road Primary School
PRES PR1 .... **238** C7
Whiteledge Centre
SKEL WN8 .... **363** H3
White Lund Trading Estate
HEY LA3 .... **41** K8
Whitewalls Industrial Estate
COL BB8 .... **170** E8
Whittingham Hospital
GAR/LONG PR3 .... **186** C7
Whittlefield Infant School
PDHM/BLYW BB12 .... **10** A2
Whittle-le-Woods CE
Primary School
CHLYE PR6 .... **287** F3
Whitworth Football &
Cricket Club
WHIT OL12 .... **323** G2
Whitworth High School
WHIT OL12 .... **323** G2

Whitworth Swimming Pool
WHIT OL12 .... **323**
Wildfowl and Wetlands
Trust Martin Mere
CHTN/BK PR9 .... **330**
Willowbank Holiday Home &
Touring Park
STHP PR8 .... **344**
Wilpshire Golf Club
BBN BB1 .... **219**
Wingate Medical Centre
NWD/KWIPK L33 .... **366**
Winmarleigh CE School
GAR/LONG PR3 .... **102**
Winstanley College
WGNW/BIL/O WN5 .... **365**
Withnell Fold Industrial Estate
CHLYE PR6 .... **265**
Withnell Fold School
CHLYE PR6 .... **265**
Withnell Junior & Infant School
CHLYE PR6 .... **289**
Witton Park Athletics track
BBNW BB2 .... **244**
Witton Park High School
BBNW BB2 .... **244**
Wolf House Gallery
CARN LA5 .... **24**
Woodclose Caravan Park
KKBYL LA6 .... **21**
Woodhey High School
RAMS BL0 .... **319**
Woodlands Primary School
FMBY L37 .... **343**
Woodlands School
BPOOLE FY3 .... **5**
Woodlands School
FUL/RIB PR2 .... **240**
Woodlands Works
NWD/KWIPK L33 .... **367**
Woodlea School Junior School
LEY/BBR PR5 .... **285**
Woodnook County School
ACC BB5 .... **248**
Woodplumpton CE School
KIRK/FR/WA PR4 .... **212**
Woodvale CP School
STHP PR8 .... **325**
Worden High School
LEY/BBR PR5 .... **285**
Worsthorne CP School
BRFD/BLYE BB10 .... **226**
Wray with Botton
Endowed School
HGHB LA2 .... **38**
Wrightington Hospital
WGNNW/ST WN6 .... **353**
Wyredale School
PLF/KEOS FY6 .... **150**
Yealand Conyers CE
Primary School
CARN LA5 .... **17**
Yorkshire Street
Medical Centre
BLY BB11 .... **11**

Notes

Notes

Notes

AA **Street by Street**   QUESTIONNAIRE

Dear Atlas User

Your comments, opinions and recommendations are very important to us. So please help us to improve our street atlases by taking a few minutes to complete this simple questionnaire.

You do NOT need a stamp (unless posted outside the UK). If you do not want to remove this page from your street atlas, then photocopy it or write your answers on a plain sheet of paper.

Send to: The Editor, AA Street by Street, FREEPOST SCE 4598, Basingstoke RG21 4GY

ABOUT THE ATLAS...

Which city/town/county did you buy?

Are there any features of the atlas or mapping that you find particularly useful?

Is there anything we could have done better?

Why did you choose an AA Street by Street atlas?

Did it meet your expectations?

Exceeded ☐   **Met all** ☐   **Met most** ☐   **Fell below** ☐

Please give your reasons

Where did you buy it?

For what purpose? (please tick all applicable)

To use in your own local area ☐   To use on business or at work ☐

Visiting a strange place ☐   In the car ☐   On foot ☐

Other (please state)

LOCAL KNOWLEDGE...

Local knowledge is invaluable. Whilst every attempt has been made to make the
information contained in this atlas as accurate as possible, should you notice any
inaccuracies, please detail them below (if necessary, use a blank piece of paper)
or e-mail us at *streetbystreet@theAA.com*

ABOUT YOU...

Name (Mr/Mrs/Ms)
Address

Postcode
Daytime tel no
E-mail address

Which age group are you in?

Under 25 ☐   25-34 ☐   35-44 ☐   45-54 ☐   55-64 ☐   65+ ☐

Are you an AA member?   YES ☐   NO ☐

Do you have Internet access?   YES ☐   NO ☐

Thank you for taking the time to complete this questionnaire. Please send it to us as soon
as possible, and remember, you do not need a stamp (unless posted outside the UK).

M